THE
CHANGING
POLITICS
OF THE
SOUTH

THE
CHANGING
POLITICS
OF THE
SOUTH

Edited by
WILLIAM C. HAVARD

LOUISIANA STATE UNIVERSITY PRESS
Baton Rouge

ISBN 0-8071-0046-3
Library of Congress Catalog Card Number 75-181357
Copyright © 1972 by Louisiana State University Press
All rights reserved
Manufactured in the United States of America
Printed by The TJM Corporation, Baton Rouge, Louisiana
Designed by A. R. Crochet

The four figures in Chapter 5 originally appeared in *The Government and Politics of Texas*, Third Edition, Clifton McCleskey, pages 84, 97, 108, 115. Copyright © 1969 by Little, Brown and Company (Inc.). Reprinted by permission.

Preface

The planning and research that went into this book extend back over more years than most of those involved care to contemplate. Shortly after the idea of doing a general survey of the contemporary politics of the southern states was originally suggested to me by Richard Wentworth, a former director of the Louisiana State University Press, I moved out of the South. But my skepticism about the project was based less on nonresidence in the region than on the fear that must be in the back of the mind of anyone who is tempted to write a general book on southern politics, a fear of having to face comparison—inevitably invidious—with V. O. Key's *Southern Politics in State and Nation*. First published in 1949, Key's study seems to me still to rank first among the books published by political scientists on the general subject of American domestic politics since World War II. The coverage was comprehensive, the author's political insights were superb, the style was clear and felicitous, the research was prodigious, and the methodology employed set an example that has still not been surpassed in redirecting the discipline of political science.

In the two decades since 1949 much speculation has taken place about the possibility of another edition of, or a successor to, *Southern Politics*. Professor Key apparently rejected the idea of further editions, perhaps for the very reasons that militate against the idea that there can be a "successor." *Southern Politics* was a unique achievement by a unique student of politics, the book set a standard

v

that other books on the subject stand little chance of reaching, and
the conditions of time, research assistance, and institutional and
personal cooperation available to the original project's director are
unlikely to be matched even with the enlarged bases of research
support for the social sciences that have been developed recently.

After I convinced myself that there could be no successor to
Southern Politics it was somewhat easier to be persuaded (and to
persuade others) that a book on southern politics which examined
the great social and political upheavals that the region has undergone in recent years could be a worthwhile pursuit. This conviction
also removed some inhibitions about relying heavily on Key as a
guidepost against which we could measure how far and how fast the
politics of the South has gone over the past twenty or twenty-five
years. Finally, the sublimation of the idea of being in competition
with Key opened the way to the planning and writing of an eclectic
book—one in which a number of contributors could participate and
no extensive effort would be made to secure a close conformity
among the participants on questions of detailed coverage or
methodology.

The contributors of the chapters on the individual states were
invited to participate on the basis of their intimate knowledge over
a long period of the politics of their respective states. Although the
time span and the broad theme of change during the period covered
were agreed upon, each author was left largely to his own devices in
the choice of methods to be used and the particular focus to be given
to the treatment of his state. We did agree that the book, which
would certainly have academic overtones because all of the authors
are academicians, should not be so esoteric as to preclude general
reader interest. We met as a group only two or three times (the most
important occasion is mentioned in the appreciatory notes below),
and a few of the participants did ask to see the outlines of other
chapters or drafts of chapters during the course of their own preparations, but for the most part the work was carried out independently by the several writers, except for general coordination by means
of correspondence between the editor and each of the contributors.
As the chapters (most of them monographic in length) came in, it

was obvious that the differences in methods and emphases subtly reflected the substantive differences in the internal politics of the various states. The focus in Florida, for example, is on the influence that that state's enormous demographic and economic change has had on its politics, while the concentration on states experiencing less rapid social change, such as Arkansas and Mississippi, is more on the way in which older bases of organization and popular support for various candidates have altered during the period covered. For the editor, at least, it was gratifying to observe the way in which the distinctiveness and, in a minority of instances, the similarities of individual states stood out as a result of the special knowledge and selective capacity each author brought into play in producing his chapter. No book on so large and diversified a subject is likely to be tightly cohesive, but we hope that the diversity of treatment here accurately reflects the substantial diversity of the component parts of the general subject.

Naturally many obligations were created in the course of preparing these materials for publication. A major debt is owed to the Department of Government of Louisiana State University in New Orleans for inviting the contributors to this book to provide the program for the third annual Symposium on Southern Politics, which was held in New Orleans on April 10–12, 1969. This symposium, the theme of which was "Politics of the New South: An Assessment of the Changing Pattern of Political Life in the Modern South," afforded us the opportunity to meet for three days, during which we were able to exchange ideas and expose our preliminary findings to our own and a general audience's critical scrutiny. Professor Werner Feld, head of the department, Professor Edward F. Renwick, the symposium director, and Mr. James Chubbuck, director of the Institute of Politics, Loyola University of New Orleans, were charming hosts and effective participants in this endeavor. We would like to express our appreciation for their courtesies on this and other occasions.

A number of individuals contributed data, ideas, constructive criticism, and, not least of all, encouragement during the course of preparation of the manuscript. Some of these persons are acknowledged in other parts of the book, but here I should like to thank the following friends, colleagues, and students for a wide variety of co-operative acts: Professor Loren P. Beth of the University of Massachusetts, to whom I am indebted for critical readings and insights, and for a friendship that has survived and even grown stronger as a result of co-authorship of earlier studies; Professors David R. Mayhew, Yale University, H. Clifton McCleskey, University of Texas, Austin, Everett C. Ladd, Jr., University of Connecticut, and Morris W. H. Collins, University of Georgia, for their repeated and always generous responses to requests for information, critical commentary, and other types of support; Brooks Hays, for his judicious counsel and for his inspiration as a southern politician whose career has exemplified the best personal qualities of his region; Professor Charles D. Hadley, now on the faculty of Louisiana State University of New Orleans and formerly a graduate student at the Universities of Massachusetts and Connecticut, Steven McClain, graduate student at the University of Massachusetts, and Mary Ball Shafer, graduate student in sociology at Virginia Polytechnic Institute and State University for collection and analysis of data; and Professor John A. Ballweg, Assistant Dean of the College of Arts and Sciences, Virginia Polytechnic Institute and State University, for his review of a mass of tabular material in an effort to improve the clarity and consistency of statistical presentations.

The Research Division of Virginia Polytechnic Institute and State University generously made resources available to enable the Technical Graphics Unit of the university to do the cartographic work necessary to make the maps and graphs uniformly presentable for the printer. The Associate Dean of the College of Arts and Sciences at this university, Thomas E. Gilmer, Jr., kindly worked out the arrangements on this institutional support and undertook a number of chores that enabled me to spend the time required to take care of many last-minute details involved in getting the manuscript off to the publisher. I am also grateful to the editors of the *Southern Review* for permitting me to incorporate into the first chapter parts of my article "The New Mind of the South," which appeared in the Autumn, 1968, issue. Parts of the concluding chapter were originally presented at a seminar for southern journalists on The South in American Politics, held at the University of Alabama on November 10–14, 1969, under the sponsorship of the Southern Newspaper Publishers Association Foundation. The same material provided the basis for a lecture at Wake Forest University in January, 1970. Parts of Chapter 14 were published under the title "Protest, Defection, and Realignment in Contemporary Southern Politics" in the Spring, 1972, issue of the *Virginia Quarterly Review*.

I should like to express my appreciation to Charles East, director, Leslie Phillabaum, assistant director, and Roberta Madden, editor, of the Louisiana State University Press for their patience and devotion throughout what must have seemed an endless (and at times hopeless) project. Having served as a member of press committees at two universities, I am fully aware of the difficult conditions under which the staffs of university presses work, mostly because of delinquent authors and inadequate resources. Finally, but by no means least, I should like to acknowledge the fine clerical work of all those persons who did typing and spot editing of various parts of the voluminous manuscript. Although their numbers and institutional dispersal are so great that they must remain anonymous, our individual and collective gratitude must not be left unstated.

WILLIAM C. HAVARD

Contents

xi

List of Tables

CHAPTER 3   *Page*

CHAPTER 4   *Page*

Page

List of Figures

Page

CHAPTER 7

CHAPTER 8

Page

THE
CHANGING
POLITICS
OF THE
SOUTH

1

THE SOUTH
A Shifting Perspective

WILLIAM C. HAVARD

The South in Retrospect

The South has long been an object of fascination for historians, social scientists, and a variety of other types of moral philosophers, southern and nonsouthern. Despite all attempts of sociologists and psychologists to subsume its distinctive traits in some Marxian or Freudian concept or in a series of deterministic assumptions, a part of the fascination has certainly arisen out of the suspicion that the South is what it is because the region has created its own mythical self-image and in some ways has made reality conform to idea rather than vice versa. This suspicion has been sharpened in recent years by the realization that the South and the southerner are far more complicated entities than they formerly were assumed to be.

An accumulating volume of first-rate historical studies suggests a subtle revision in the interpretation of the meaning of the southern experience. John Richard Alden's work on the American revolutionary and constitutional periods, especially *The First South*, reveals that the South was developing a regional distinctiveness well before either the conditions or the ideas which produced the antebellum South—or the "Old" South—had come into being.[1] In his study of *The Mind of the Old South*, Clement Eaton has demon-

---

William C. Havard is Dean of the College of Arts and Sciences, Virginia Polytechnic Institute and State University.

[1] John Richard Alden, *The First South* (Baton Rouge: Louisiana State University Press, 1961).

3

strated that, even though the southern mind had, and still has, its distinguishing characteristics, the interpretation of the region as intellectually monolithic must give way to the recognition that a complex variety of personality types and modes of perception manifested themselves even in face of socially influential factors not clearly understood and in the midst of the effort to generate a closed southern nationalism.[2] In *The Democratic South* Dewey W. Grantham argues that the imputation to southern one-partyism of a total lack of opposition and dissent ignores the titanic struggle over issues and between personalities that has continuously been waged under the singular banner of the Democratic Party.[3] And T. Harry Williams has found that the nostalgic aura of romanticism supposedly responsible for so much of southern reaction has been dispelled by economic and political realities about as often as it has lulled southern voters into gentle submission.[4] Finally, but by no means exhaustively, C. Vann Woodward has amassed an impressive array of evidence in support of the thesis that complexity rather than simplicity is the hallmark of postbellum southern history. He has ordered this evidence with such logic and stylistic grace that anyone who reads it without stereotypical response will recognize the inadequacy of the simplistic explanations that still abound.[5] In a review of Joseph L. Morrison's biography of W. J. Cash,[6] Woodward even impugned the source from which nearly all scholars continue to draw their central ideas for research on southern social and political problems: Cash's *Mind of the South*.[7] It is precisely Cash's

2 Clement Eaton, *The Mind of the Old South* (Baton Rouge: Louisiana State University Press, 1964).

3 Dewey W. Grantham, *The Democratic South* (Athens, Georgia: University of Georgia Press, 1963; New York: Norton Library, 1965).

4 T. Harry Williams, *Romance and Realism in Southern Politics* (Athens, Georgia: University of Georgia Press, 1961).

5 C. Vann Woodward, *Origins of the New South* (Baton Rouge: Louisiana State University Press, 1951).

6 C. Vann Woodward, "White Man, White Mind," a review of Joseph L. Morrison, *W. J. Cash: Southern Prophet* (New York: Knopf, 1967) in *New Republic*, CLVII (December 9, 1967), 28–30.

7 W. J. Cash, *The Mind of the South* (New York: Knopf, 1941; New York: Doubleday Anchor Books, 1954).

failure to account correctly for either the diversity within the region or the larger span of southern history that Woodward calls into question.

Penetrating beyond the stereotypes which stress the uniformity of all southerners and the South in general, the most notable feature of the southern life-style one encounters is a series of apparent contradictions; these are only superficially reconciled by what has been variously referred to as the southern mystique, the southern myth, and the schizophrenic tendency of southern moral and political attitudes. These contradictions range from purely individual characteristics to the most far-reaching aspects of the institutional arrangements of the South and of its social and political cultures. Radical individualism, amounting at times to broad tolerance of extreme personal eccentricity, is set off against a social conformity so stultifying that it has sometimes been equated with paranoia and has been described in terms ranging from "garrison psychology" [8] to totalitarianism. Personalism, with its preference for the concrete and for a traditional, direct way of handling human relations—as opposed to an abstract and legalized view of man and society—is in direct confrontation in the South with the vaguely universalized clichés of racial prejudice and an elaborate legal apparatus in support of segregation. The personalism of the southerner, manifesting itself most clearly in good manners and human solicitude in face-to-face relations, is also countermanded by the hovering omnipresence of the tendency to violence, and an apparent obliviousness to the dehumanizing effects of racial discrimination.

If in the social sense one encounters in the South a free and easy egalitarianism, one also frequently comes in contact with a subtle social stratification which is not solely the product of either economic differentiation or simple racial discrimination. The South did not talk about its self-styled, old-family aristocracy and coin phrases like "poor white trash" without the talk and the ascriptions having some effect. Similarly, one finds in the South a fierce sense of independence in conflict with a bizarre paternalism—a paternalism

8 T. Harry Williams, "Trends in Southern Politics," in Frank E. Vandiver (ed.), *The Idea of the South* (Houston: Rice University Semi-centennial Publications, 1964), 65.

which extends from purely private relations all the way to willingness to accept governmental largesse (and the obligations that go
with it) from any level of government; that is, provided the paternalism is cast in a way that avoids civil rights issues. Relatedly, much
of southern life is characterized by an innate conservatism and opposition to change in general, yet a colorful, populistic liberalism
has frequently asserted itself in the socioeconomic activities and
politics of the region. Many commentators have also noted that
despite their unremitting devotion to a sectionalism so strong that
it can only be described as a form of *regional* nationalism,[9] southerners have a nationalistic bent. This is particularly evident in the
patriotic and military traditions of the South. A final dichotomy
may be observed in the supposed unifying, consensual nature of
southern politics as opposed to actual political diversity, conflict,
opposition, and dissent, with the latter varying in intensity and
importance from time to time and from place to place in the South
throughout its history.

Most readers are likely to be aware of the extent to which the
South has been forced by circumstances to take self-conscious account of its own history in contrast to the seemingly ahistorical—or,
more accurately, the uniform historical—experience of the rest of
the country. The success of liberalism in America has continuously
provided a national sense of mission; this has made it unnecessary
for Americans to make an elaborate account of the past in order to
articulate a basis for national unity.[10] The liberal order has also
sustained a progressivist viewpoint, coupling the relative satisfac-
tions of the moment with a vast optimism about the future. It has
encouraged a positive attitude toward change for its own sake rather
than reliance on a prescriptive base in the past. The southern historical experience, on the other hand, has been discontinuous; it
was broken by defeat in war and the shattering of the South's mythi-

9 On this point see Charles Grier Sellers, Jr. (ed.), *The Southerner as American*
(Chapel Hill: University of North Carolina Press, 1960).

10 Applicable here, of course, is the theme advanced by Louis Hartz in *The Liberal
Tradition in America* (New York: Harcourt, Brace and Co., 1955).

cal self-image. Southerners, disenchanted with the notion of progress, sought to express the meaning of experience through a symbolism looking more to the past than to the future.

Examined from this perspective, one can see in southern history the emergence of most of the contradictions that have been outlined, as well as the way in which specific individuals and groups in the South have typified various aspects of these mental responses and translated them into forms of political action. Some of the contradictions result from the fact that the most ardent Confederate has always had some small stake in the Yankee camp.

If for the moment we can leave aside both the romantic mythos and the thesis that the presence of the Negro has been a singularly determinative factor in the making of the South, we can readily identify two early southern groups as counterparts of those national political groups out of which an oppositional politics was developed within the framework of the general liberal consensus. The first of these was the yeoman farmer of the frontier type, the backbone of Jeffersonian-Jacksonian democracy. From the available evidence this class seems to have been numerically dominant in the South during the antebellum period.[11] Characterized by a spirit of independence, the yeoman farmer reflected much of the simplicity of early American life, with its tendencies toward both libertarianism and egalitarianism, opposition to governmental centralization, suspicion of the entrepreneurial class, and aversion to urbanism and industrialism. Set over against this group in the Democratic-Whig dichotomy was the Whig planter and the allies he needed to operate the plantation system, i.e., factors, bankers, merchants, and others. To the extent that the plantation system may be interpreted as agrarian capitalism, the planter in the Old South may be seen to parallel the incipient Whig capitalist in the North. Significant differences existed, of course, because of the nature of the respective enterprises. Chief among these differences was the occasional variation in attitude toward the banking and credit system and interna-

[11] See Frank W. Owsley, *Plain Folk of the Old South* (Baton Rouge: Louisiana State University Press, 1949).

tional trade, the southerners generally being more favorably disposed to easy credit and, except for the sugar producers, opposed to protective tariffs.

But the differences between the yeoman farmer and the planter, and the affinity of this division with the political divisions in the North, cannot be pressed to the point of ignoring the effects on both these groups of the slave question, southern separateness, and the Civil War and its aftermath. This great break in southern history naturally made vast changes in the status of these groups, their roles in society, and their respective outlooks. But it did not entirely change the national basis of experience in which they had part of their origins, nor did it completely reorient their positions on issues. However much we may try to ignore them, history does leave its residues, and some of the characteristics discernible in the inception of these two social groupings continue to make themselves felt despite appearances to the contrary.

In the southern Redeemers of the Reconstruction and post-Reconstruction period C. Vann Woodward and other historians have identified the reemergence of the old Whig attitudes within the Democratic single-party system.[12] However, in the aftermath of redemption these attitudes were more nearly assimilated to the buccaneering spirit of the northern capitalists than had been the case in the antebellum South. The period from 1877 to the end of the century has been reviewed too completely to need much emphasis at this point. The ventures of the Redeemers in railroads and other developmental enterprises were only partly capitalized by northern finance; the great capital resource that the Whigs-turned-Democrats exploited was the labor of the southern poor white and the Negro. One of the more tragic aftermaths of the Civil War too often unnoticed was the reduction of a large proportion of the yeoman farmer class to the status of poor white; in this status the formerly independent farmer became an economic dependent in competition with the newly freed Negro, who was also left economically dependent by the settlement of 1877.[13] From this situation

12 Woodward, *Origins of the New South*, Chaps. 2–5.
13 For a detailed study of this development and its effects in one state see Roger W.

comes the continued economic frustration of the poor white; this frustration led to the radical tendencies of his sporadic political engagements, carried on largely through the medium of populism, but to some extent even by way of socialism and progressivism.

Again, the story is too well known to require extensive reiteration: the reversion to the cash crop system, the dominance of a Whig-Democratic county-seat elite in politics, and the development of the pattern of racial segregation in the late 1880's and 90's, largely as an outgrowth of the threat of alliance between poor whites and Negroes in the politics of that period. Parenthetically, it may be observed, we have only recently been made aware of the lateness of the development of both the one-party system and of segregation, again by way of the revisionists.[14] Despite the promises of the advocates of the idea of the New South in the 1880's and thereafter, the failure to diversify the prevailing form of agricultural capitalism and to develop supplemental industrial enterprises left the South in its peculiar agrarian context during most of the period of the development of the United States toward its present urban-industrial configuration. Such industries as the South was able to attract in the late nineteenth and early twentieth centuries were the more decimating kind, including the textile mills of the upper South and the exploitative lumber industries in many other parts of the region. The homogeneity of the South was in large part preserved by the enhancement of the romantic myth, what Cash effectively refers to as the Proto-Dorian bond among the whites, the retention of the spirit of individualism and independence characteristic of the early agrarian outlook, and the continued personal and familial relations which formed substitutes for and barriers to any extensive public life in the South. Mediating institutions, such as labor unions, which might have afforded a basis for collective social and political action were slow to develop in the face of attitudes growing out of these conditions and reactions.

Shugg, *Origins of Class Struggle in Louisiana* (Baton Rouge: Louisiana State University Press, 1939).

[14] C. Vann Woodward, *The Strange Career of Jim Crow* (2nd ed.; New York: Oxford University Press, 1966).

Overarching the whole structure was the romantic mythos of southern separatism, with its paternalistic overtones, its insistence on the glories of the past, and its postures of aristocracy. Even though the southern mystique[15] may have been made up out of whole cloth as a reaction against the puritan-based reformism of New England in the period between 1830 and 1860, the ideas which informed this reaction did have consequences. Anyone who has exposed himself to the limpid prose of William Alexander Percy's *Lanterns on the Levee*,[16] the finest expression of the paternalistic ideal available, can hardly fail to recognize how much effect the continuous reiteration of the ideas of *noblesse oblige*, classical education, and the importance of manners have had on the mind and behavior of southerners.

But what, one may ask, has this elaborate congeries of attitudes as reflected in varying social types to do with the politics of the contemporary South? A partial answer to this question takes us in two directions. The first is an inward one involving the effect of recent changes in the South on the subtle alteration of these ideas and the behavior of the social groups that reflect them. The second looks outward to the meaning of the South's distinctiveness in the context of the national problem.

The Winds of Change

That the South has undergone and is undergoing vast changes is undeniable. If we date the start of the second reconstruction from the school desegregation case of 1954,[17] we are already as far removed chronologically from the beginnings of that reconstruction as the South was from the beginnings of the first reconstruction at the time of the Compromise of 1877. And there is certainly no immediate indication that the second reconstruction will end as the first one did. Furthermore, the long-delayed promise of the idea of the "New South," with its implications for bringing the southern

---

15 Here and elsewhere I am borrowing the term *mystique* from the title of Howard Zinn's *The Southern Mystique* (New York: Knopf, 1964).

16 William Alexander Percy, *Lanterns on the Levee* (New York: Knopf, 1941).

17 *Brown v. Board of Education of Topeka*, 347 U.S. 483 (1954).

style of life and politics into congruence with the national pattern, seems to be far nearer fulfillment than would have seemed possible at, say, the end of World War II. Despite the fact that the civil rights movement still has a long way to go before its aspirations are realized, any middle-aged southerner can attest to the fact that changes have taken place in race relations in the South within the period of his adult experience that would have been inconceivable to his father, let alone his grandfather. Although the South as a whole is considerably behind the rest of the country in the extent of its urbanization and industrialization, its pace of movement in that direction has steadily increased over the past two decades and the gap has been closed to no small extent.

The word *change* has always been an important one in the lexicon of American political discussion, and in recent years its potency has been increased by the frequency with which the term has been preceded by the adjective *revolutionary*. Paradoxically, one might conclude that so much emphasis on the need for change reflects an inability to assimilate the increasing volume and rapidity of change that has already taken place or is currently taking place. In the case of the South, the cumulative social and political change that has been experienced over the past twenty to twenty-five years has been enormous. In addition, the capacity of the southern political culture to absorb that change has been strained by the fact that the social and economic alterations have been generated both from within and from outside the region. The self-generated change, or change from within, relates largely to economic growth, particularly in the form of the expansion of the industrial base in the South, and its concomitant social movement from a predominantly rural to a predominantly urban society. The change from without has taken the form of legally and politically induced alterations of southern practices in the field of civil rights. Although the implications of the two sources of change certainly involve interaction between internal and external influences, it seems appropriate to look briefly at them separately.

From the end of Reconstruction until the Great Depression of 1929, the southern social and political systems were in a state of semiquarantine from the remainder of the country. While the Northeast was becoming urban and industrial, and most of the rest of the United States tended to follow suit, the South remained predominantly rural and agrarian. As late as 1930 nearly half of those gainfully employed in the South were in agricultural occupations; and even in 1940, when the United States as a whole was more than two-thirds urban, the South was more than two-thirds rural. In the 1940 census Florida was the only southern state that had an urban population in excess of 50 percent. While the country as a whole was absorbing massive numbers of immigrants from all over Europe and parts of Asia and was appearing to assimilate them in the great metropolitan melting pot, the South remained fixed in its ethnic patterns (except in a few major port cities, such as New Orleans). With a caste system evolving out of the former practice of slavery, the relations between the indigenous (predominantly Anglo-Saxon) white population and the indigenous (and residentially fixed) black population were largely unchanging. In the 1870's 90 percent of the nation's black population resided in the South; and, although the out-migration of blacks to the northern cities began early in the twentieth century, the numbers remained small enough to have little effect on prevailing patterns in both the North and the South until after the 1930's. In other words, the Compromise of 1877, which ended Reconstruction and allowed the South to pursue an independent policy with respect to race relations and its regional version of Democratic politics, in exchange for a Republican victory in the disputed Hayes-Tilden election, and the subsequent triumph of the industrial order in the North, seemed to satisfy the dominant elements in the political system of both North and South for well over half a century.

From the 1940's until today the promise of the New South that had been intermittently held out since the 1880's has been in the process of realization. Each decade during this period has witnessed a substantial gain in the position of the South relative to the corresponding figures for the United States in such indices as percentage of population engaged in manufactures, personal income, proportion of population living in metropolitan areas, and numer-

ous others. Starting from a low base indeed, the South has gradually, but steadily, been catching up. And again the rate has been
different from state to state. A look at a few of these developments
and their consequences will set the stage for some of the more detailed discussions in the subsequent chapters.

Although the shift from a predominantly rural to an urban population in the South is striking, the relatively low figure established
by the census bureau to differentiate urban from rural residents
makes this classification somewhat misleading (essentially persons
living in incorporated places of 2,500 or more or in densely populated urban fringe areas or unincorporated places of 2,500 or more
are considered "urban"). The concept of the Standard Metropolitan Statistical Area[18] is probably a more accurate measure of the
extent to which the South is moving toward an urban culture.
Table 1 indicates that the South made a major leap in its metropolitan development in the decade of the 1950's, during which it
moved to the point of having half its population resident in metropolitan areas. The trend continued upward throughout the 1960's,
although at a reduced pace. But even during the latter decade the
proportionate gain was pronounced, inasmuch as the metropolitan
share of the total population of the United States increased less
than two percentage points (from slightly less than 66 percent to
slightly more than 67 percent) while the South's metropolitan proportion of its total population increased by 4 percent.

Other changes related to this sweeping demographic alteration
reflect its effect on the economy. For example, between 1945 and
1960 the South's farm population fell from over one-third to just
over 20 percent of the region's total population, and the downward
trend continued throughout the 1960's. The per capita income of
the South, as a proportion of the average per capita income of the
United States as a whole, shifted from two-thirds to three-fourths
during the twenty years from 1948 to 1968. (See Table 2.) In the

18 A Standard Metropolitan Statistical Area consists of a county or group of counties
(or towns or cities in New England) which includes a central city (or "twin cities") with
at least 50,000 population and its surrounding socially and economically interdepen-
dent "metropolitan" area.

Table 1

SMSA Southern Population Shifts, 1950–1970

State	1950 Population	1950 Total SMSA Population	1950 Proportion Metropolitan	1960 Population	1960 Total SMSA Population	1960 Proportion Metropolitan	Percentage of Change 1950–60	1970 Population	1970 Total SMSA Population	1970 Proportion Metropolitan	Percentage of Change 1960–70
Alabama	3,061,743	1,022,890	.33	3,266,740	1,557,875	.48	.15	3,373,006	1,722,825	.51	.03
Arkansas	1,909,511	196,685	.10	1,786,272	551,120	.31	.21	1,886,210	654,893	.35	.06
Florida	2,771,305	1,323,206	.48	4,951,560	3,321,051	.67	.19	6,671,162	4,497,062	.67	.00
Georgia	3,444,578	1,587,328*	.45	3,943,116	1,896,194*	.48*	.03	4,492,038	2,330,531*	.52*	.04
Louisiana	2,683,516	1,020,188	.38	3,257,022	1,750,456	.54	.16	3,564,310	1,962,871	.55	.01
Mississippi	2,178,914	142,164	.07	2,178,141	221,367	.10	.03	2,158,872	383,981	.18	.08
North Carolina	4,061,929	896,736	.22	4,556,155	1,404,318	.31	.08	4,961,832	1,857,022	.37	.06
South Carolina	2,117,027	637,586*	.30	2,382,594	987,851*	.42*	.12	2,522,881	1,145,224*	.45	.03
Tennessee	3,291,718	1,387,218	.42	3,567,089	1,789,460	.50	.08	3,838,777	1,987,990	.52	.02
Texas	7,711,194	3,643,826	.47	9,579,677	6,261,938	.65	.18	10,989,123	7,383,475	.67	.02
Virginia	3,318,680	2,371,746‡	.72‡	3,966,949	1,985,700†	.50†		4,543,249	2,628,690†	.58†	.08
TOTAL	26,398,102	14,600,520†	.41*	43,435,315	21,509,345	.50	.09	49,001,460	26,320,276	.54	.04

* These figures are inflated because the Augusta SMSA extends across the South Carolina and Georgia boundaries. The total figure has been corrected to account for this discrepancy.

† For the Washington-Maryland-Virginia SMSA, only the population in Virginia was used. Southern SMSA population percentage change, 1950–60, was 59.25%. Southern SMSA population change, 1960–70, was approximately +22%.

‡ SMSA population for Virginia is artificially high because the population in Washington and Maryland is included in the Virginia SMSA.

proportion of persons employed in manufacturing, the South has gained on the United States as a whole by a few percentage points in each of the past several decades. The hope of continued growth in the economy of the South is revealed by the fact that the 1970 census showed a slightly faster rate of increase in overall population

Table 2

PER CAPITA INCOME, UNITED STATES AND SOUTH, 1948, 1968

	1948	Percentage of U.S. Average	1968	Percentage of U.S. Average
United States	1,430		3,421	
Alabama	866	60.5	2,337	68.3
Arkansas	875	61.1	2,332	68.2
Florida	1,180	81.8	3,191	93.2
Georgia	968	67.7	2,781	81.2
Louisiana	1,032	72.2	2,634	76.9
Mississippi	789	55.2	2,081	60.8
North Carolina	973	68.0	2,664	77.9
South Carolina	891	62.3	2,380	69.6
Tennessee	944	66.0	2,579	75.4
Texas	1,199	83.8	3,029	88.5
Virginia	1,130	79.0	3,068	89.7

Source: Adapted from U.S. Department of Commerce, Office of Business Economics Reports.

in the South than in the country as a whole. Of perhaps more importance, for the first time in a century the 1970 figures indicated that the South had a net gain, rather than a loss, in population as a result of migration during the decade of the 1960's.

These favorable signs must, however, be offset by some qualifications. First, many of the gains listed are attributable to the remarkable development in a few of the southern states. Between 1960 and 1970, for example, the population growths in Florida, Texas, and Virginia accounted for the South's relative gain; all the other states of the region increased more slowly than the country at large. And the same pattern carries through the other indicators discussed

above. Some absolute gains were made in almost all the categories
by all of the states, but the peripheral southern states account for
virtually all of the moves toward overtaking the national averages
in the various indices of economic growth. Between 1950 and 1970,
for example, while Florida and Texas increased their proportions
of metropolitan population from less than 50 percent to 67 percent
(the national ratio), Mississippi moved from a 7 percent proportion
to 18 percent in this category of change.

Second, the Negro population of the South has been in a state of
migrational flux since the 1930's, both from the farms to the cities
within the South and to metropolitan areas outside the South. With
all of this movement, however, the overall black population, South
and North, has not experienced any relative gain proportionate to
the general standards of economic status in the country as a whole.
As late as 1940 approximately 69 percent of the Negro population
of the United States lived in the eleven states of the old Confederacy.
Nearly two-thirds of this population was rural, and the overwhelming number was rural farm population rather than rural nonfarm.
By 1960 the same eleven states contained only 48.6 percent of
America's black population, almost 55 percent of which was urban.
By 1970 about half of the South's Negro population lived in metropolitan areas. In most decades nearly all of the southern states
(Florida being something of a continuing exception) experienced a
large net loss through out-migration of Negroes. This migration
was, in many cases, large enough to reduce the black populations
not only proportionately but absolutely; and it accounts in large
part for the agglomeration of blacks in the central cities of northern
metropolitan areas (in both 1960 and 1970 the black populations in
the Northeast and the North Central areas of the United States were
approximately 95 percent metropolitan). Although some gains were
registered in economic terms by the blacks who moved into these
areas when compared with the Negroes remaining in the South, for
the most part they carried their poverty problems with them, so that
some of the southern economic gains during this period may be
put down to the removal of large numbers of the most disadvan-
taged segment of the population to other regions.

The political consequences of these changes have still not been realized, but some of the implications have already been observed. The flight from the cities to the suburbs by whites in the northern metropolitan areas has reached the point at which, in 1970, the suburban residents of metropolitan areas in the United States numbered almost 75 million, as compared with slightly over 62 million in the central cities (a growth of 25 percent in the suburban population, as compared to 5 percent in the central cities since 1960). Furthermore, the 1970 census indicates for the first time that the suburban metropolitan population outnumbers the nonmetropolitan population as well as the central-city metropolitan population. The problems of the central city that arise from a low tax base, welfare costs, unemployment, de facto racial segregation, and the full panoply of inadequate public services relative to needs is suggested by these cold figures. And there is some evidence to indicate that the South's metropolitan areas may be following the patterns of the North in resegregating the races residentially and in creating new local political units that are designed to accommodate the suburbs rather than the central city in both public services and the distribution of political power. Whether the new federal social policies in the areas of welfare, education, employment, housing, transportation, and other fields will make major inroads on these problems generally, and whether the South will avoid the worst effects of bad planning and execution exhibited by the North as it tries to cope with its still-developing metropolitan areas are questions that remain highly problematic.

To paraphrase a colorful description of post–World War II change in the South: cotton has moved west, cattle have moved east, the farmer has moved to town, the city resident has moved to the suburbs, the Negro has moved north, and the Yankee has moved south. The political response to these changes has been, as is usually the case, slower to develop than the conditions would seem to warrant. But we are becoming increasingly aware of the problems that are resulting, and they are no longer merely regional.

Although internally motivated change in the South has had some effect on the region's political attitudes and individual and collec-

tive political behavior, that effect has been minor compared with
the impact of the civil rights movement of the 1950's and the 1960's.
The prevailing style of politics in the South prior to that time depended on a virtual exclusion of Negroes from effective participation in politics, an exclusion which was tacitly accepted within the
national political system at large. The full story of the civil rights
movement, beginning even before the dramatic decision on school
desegregation in *Brown v. Board of Education of Topeka* in 1954,
accelerating rapidly immediately thereafter, and continuing into
the present, cannot be recited in detail here. All of the events and
personalities connected with the movement have had pronounced
effects on southern politics, from the long prehistory of litigation by
civil rights organizations such as the National Association for the
Advancement of Colored People, the American Civil Liberties
Union, and the Urban League, through the early dramatic victories
in the courts, the development of the so-called massive resistance of
the South, the increasing organized pressures against all areas of
discrimination, the emphasis on passive resistance and the countervailing actuality of violence, to the culmination of the efforts in
active political intervention by the political branches of the national government in the late 1950's and 1960's. But for purposes
of setting the background for a discussion of the politics of the individual southern states and the region as a whole, it seems appropriate to confine our attention largely to the changes in political
participation which occurred as a result of the second effort to reconstruct the pattern of race relations in the South.

Prior to the decision in *Smith v. Allwright* in 1944, which spelled
the beginning of the end of the white primary as a device for excluding Negroes from the ballot, in only two of the southern states
—Tennessee and North Carolina—were more than 10 percent of the
Negro populations of voting age registered to vote. Following the
abolition of the white primary, the proportions of Negroes registered to vote in the various states of the South increased appreciably
until the early fifties, after which they tended either to stabilize or to
increase at a much slower pace. Most of the increase during this

period occurred in the urban areas, where the popular resistance
was less pronounced and the administrative procedures in the registrars' offices were less discriminatory on grounds of race than in the
rural sectors. The passage in 1957 of the first Civil Rights Act since
1875 and the subsequent passage of the Civil Rights Acts of 1960
and 1964, all of which contained provisions aiming at preventing
the exclusion of Negro registration, had some minor effects on the
upward trend in black registration. But as late as 1964, Mississippi
still had less than 7 percent of its black voting-age population registered, and only Florida, Tennessee, and Texas had more than 50
percent of their respective black voting-age populations on the registration lists. Several of the states, particularly those in the Deep
South, adopted the practice of "legislate and litigate" in response
to the intended effect of these acts. Literacy provisions, limitations
on the number of "registration days" each month, the broad dis-
cretionary powers assigned to registrars in the counties, and the limitations on the capacity of the federal courts and the United States
attorney general to take any initiative on a sweeping scale continued
to make it possible to exclude large numbers of black aspirants from
the ballot box. The main difficulty was that the slow procedures of
litigation, earlier involving cases of individual applicants and later
extending no further than to cases involving separate counties, were
the only sources of relief. However, virtually all of these limitations
and possibilities of obstruction were swept away by the Civil Rights
Act of 1965. This act, which extended over a five-year period, and
was renewed for an additional five years in 1970, contained provisions that made the intervention of federal examiners and registrars
appointed by the Department of Justice automatic in the event certain conditions existed. In effect, if two features of local registration
procedures were present—a literacy test or "other device" of an ex-
clusionary nature, such as certification by a registered voter that the
applicant was known to him, and registration of less than 50 percent
of the population of voting age—federal administrators could liter-
ally take over the functions of the county registrars, in some cases
throughout the entire state. The provisions of the act were rapidly

applied to the states of Alabama, Georgia, Louisiana, Mississippi,
South Carolina, and Virginia, and to thirty-nine counties in North
Carolina, as well as to one county each in Arizona and Hawaii. The
results of the act are attested by the accompanying tables (3 and 4).
Today, two-thirds of the southern black population of voting age is
registered to vote, and none of the former Confederate states has
less than 50 percent of its Negro population of voting age registered.

The vote is, of course, generally conceived to be the foundation on
which all of the forms of political participation rest. But even in the
aftermath of the massive growth of Negro registration of the 1960's,

Table 3

SOUTHERN BLACK VOTER REGISTRATION, 1960–1964

State	1960	Percentage of Black Voting-Age Population	1964	Percentage of Black Voting-Age Population
Alabama	66,009	13.7	111,000	23.0
Arkansas	72,604	37.3	95,000	49.3
Florida	183,197	38.9	300,000	63.8
Georgia	180,000	29.3	270,000	44.0
Louisiana	159,033	30.9	164,700	32.0
Mississippi	22,000	05.2	28,500	06.7
North Carolina	210,450	38.1	258,000	46.8
South Carolina	58,122	15.6	144,000	38.7
Tennessee	185,000	58.9	218,000	69.6
Texas	226,818	34.9	375,000	57.7
Virginia	100,100	22.8	200,000	45.7
TOTAL	1,463,333	29.1	2,164,200	43.1

Source: Adapted from Voter Education Project *News*, IV, Nos. 1 and 2 (January–
    February, 1970).

the efficacy of the vote of the newly enfranchised black southerner
is still far from being finally determined. Measured by a simple
numerical standard, the recent success in electing blacks to public
office in the South would seem to have made the black vote most
productive. To have moved in less than a decade from a point at

Table 4

Voter Registration in the South
Spring–Summer, 1970

State	White VAP	Black VAP	Whites Registered	Blacks Registered	Percent White VAP Registered	Percent Black VAP Registered
Alabama	1,353,058	481,320	1,300,000	308,000	96.1	64.0
Arkansas	850,643	192,626	683,000	138,000	80.3	71.6
Florida	2,617,438	470,261	2,465,000	315,000	94.2	67.0
Georgia	1,797,062	612,910	1,610,000	390,000	89.6	63.6
Louisiana	1,289,216	514,589	1,137,000	318,000	88.2	61.8
Mississippi	748,266	422,256	650,000	285,000	86.9	67.5
N. Carolina	2,005,955	550,929	1,598,000	302,000	79.6	54.8
S. Carolina	895,147	371,873	656,000	213,000	73.3	57.3
Tennessee	1,779,018	313,873	1,570,000	240,000	88.3	76.5
Texas	4,884,765	649,512	3,599,000	550,000	73.7	84.7
Virginia	1,876,167	436,720	1,472,000	265,000	78.4	60.7
Totals	20,096,735	5,016,100	16,740,000	3,324,000	83.3	66.3

VAP=Voting-age population, 1960 census.

Source: Voter Education Project, Inc., Atlanta, August, 1970.

which the number of elected black officials was near zero to nearly 600 (almost 40 percent of the total number of black elected officials in the United States) is certainly a substantial achievement.

When one examines the situation in detail, however, some problems become evident. Overwhelmingly the elective offices held by blacks in the South are minor. They include positions such as seats on city councils or county commissions, memberships on school boards, justices of the peace, and mayoralties of small towns. Scattered among these officeholders are some sheriffs and other county administrative officials, a few state senators, a slightly larger number of memberships in the lower houses of some of the state legislatures, and some fairly high-level elective positions in a very few of the larger urban areas. In several smaller cities and in some counties with large proportions of black residents, black candidates have managed to make a sweep of local government offices. But as yet no black has been elected from a southern state to a seat in Congress or to any statewide elective office. Furthermore, it now appears that only in certain of the major metropolitan areas have black and white organizations managed to make any tradeoffs or coalitions designed to enhance the respective positions of the organizations or the candidates that the organizations have nominated. Particularly in the Deep South, where the proportions of Negroes in the general population are higher than in the other southern states, the tendency seems to be more toward a polarizing of the white and black voters than toward a mutual accommodation among them. In fact, if one looks at one or two side effects of the rapid increase in black voter participation, it becomes all too obvious that the conflict between blacks and whites in the southern political arena continues to be much more pronounced than their cooperation. For one thing, white voter registration has increased substantially in what can only be considered a direct response to the rise in black registration. Furthermore, participation in national elections has increased significantly over the past several presidential and congressional elections; and even though the proportion of voters participating in these national elections in the South is still substantially smaller than the average for the country at large, the increase is indicative

of more separate efforts on the part of white and black southerners
to influence the national electoral outcomes than was formerly the
case. And when one looks at the distribution of the votes for the
parties and for specific candidates among whites and blacks, as well
as the substantial defection of whites from the national Democratic
Party, the polarizing and isolating tendencies are even more apparent. Although these tendencies vary considerably among the individual states of the South, and reach their apogee in Mississippi and
Alabama, they remain present to some extent in all of them.

V. O. Key indicated that two major crises had occurred in southern politics: one was the Civil War and its aftermath, and the other
the populist movement of the 1890's. In the first instance, the South
attempted to preserve its societal form through the establishment of
independent statehood in the face of national political tendencies
which ran counter to the southern political culture. The eventual
result was physical and economic devastation, followed, ironically
enough, by the restoration of certain major features of what had
been an increasing bourbon dominance in the immediate antebellum period, a restoration which was paid for in terms of both economic deprivation and a substantial regional estrangement from
the rest of the country. The populist movement, although abortive,
was a massive effort to establish political competition along the
economic and social class lines that were loosely characteristic of
the politics of the other sections of the United States.

The civil rights movement of the 1950's and onward should be
added as a third major crisis in southern politics. If it is considered
that the movement began as a form of political action indigenous
to the black population, North and South, it managed to enlist the
direct aid of the major national institutions, first the United States
Supreme Court and later the political branches, in a cause that
struck at the very foundations of the self-interpretative myths of the
South and the social and political practices produced by this self-
interpretation. And it has, through the reapportionment decisions
of the 1950's and 1960's, further extended into the very foundations
of the restrictive representative system which maintained the dominant rural or semirural culture in political control long after it had

ceased to be the dominant social pattern. Although the southern resistance has been substantial, it has not approached the totality of either the Civil War or the countermovements against populism. But it has placed the prevailing political system in the South in considerable disarray, and has not as yet managed to reconstitute or reconstruct it substantially along the lines of the national system. The change has been sweeping, and much of it has been irreversible. In some of the states, newer forms of accommodation and newer points of stability can already be recognized. Most of these adaptations have occurred in the states or parts of states that have been most clearly affected by solid economic growth, urbanization, the movement of large numbers of persons from outside the South into the region, and the beginnings of voluntary compliance with demands, both legal and moral, for the end of racial injustice. But in other states or their subdivisions, the psychic disturbances are still quite deep, and are fully reflected in apparently deviate modes of political behavior. The South is no longer "solid," even in the old, and rather naïve, connotation of that term. Never as homogenous as it was often held to be, either in the ideology of some of its most prominent internal spokesmen or in the sweeping denunciations of its puritan detractors from outside, it is now more heterodox than ever. On the other hand, its distinctiveness remains in certain areas of its political culture that have not been eradicated by the experiences of the past quarter century. And these ingrained and subtle influences—religion, social class stratification, historical memories, family structures, and others—remain as points of individual and social self-identification that prevent the reconstitution of the southern political order generally, or of individual states in particular, in complete conformity to the pattern associated with the other broad regional divisions of the country.

Southern Reconstruction and Reaction

How well has the southern mind assimilated these changes and how do these assimilations manifest themselves in the historical context in which the change has occurred? It seems to me that many of the old ambivalences and contradictions survive and that their effect is mixed. We can still discern the basic types who embody the paradoxical features of southern thought and action, but subtle changes have occurred in both outlook and responses. The Whig mentality certainly survives among those who have most affected the growth of the new urban—or suburban—Republicanism in the South. In reading the pronouncements of many southern financiers and businessmen and of the politicians from both parties who are attempting to translate business issue-orientations into public policy, one frequently feels that he has transmigrated into the McKinley era. In its most extreme extension and under circumstances in which the change is most rapid, e.g., in the case of Florida and former Governor Claude Kirk, both the environment and the pronouncements of its most prominent public spokesman took on an air of unreality. Added to the unrelenting emphasis on the capacity of free enterprise and social Darwinism to provide a naturalistic solution to almost all the problems of a contemporary centralized society is an attitude which seems almost to deny the need for any regulative public institutions or even any concern for the *general* as opposed to the private welfare. Even the more modest apostles of the creed of industrial attraction seem to lose themselves so completely in their enthusiasm for the New South that they forget the implications that these developments will have in the area of labor organizations, social welfare, education, and the vast conglomeration of problems connected with making cities habitable and an industrial economy work. In this respect, some parts of the South have taken on an attitude of futuristic progressive optimism at the very time when, from a national perspective, we are seriously questioning whether the urban-industrial complex has not already outrun our capacity to govern it.

Over against this trend may be set the still incipient possibility that the South can develop a regional opposition to classical Whiggery which approximates the labor—small farmer—ethnic group coalition that has dominated national politics since the inception of the New Deal. This possibility is, of course, still offset by the nagging persistence of fear and frustration with respect to change that so frequently finds its outlet in racism. The outcome is the usual tension between reactionism in the social sphere and liberalism in the economic area. It should not be forgotten that the South was an enthusiastic supporter of the New Deal and that the most fervent popular support came from the same groups that dominated the national electoral coalition. The roots were in Populism and, beyond that, in Jacksonian Democracy. But as the Democratic Party moved from its concern with economic problems to the logically connected problem of civil rights, the old ambivalences of the South affected the southern small farmer and laborer. The standard demagogic uses of race as a diversionary issue were revived to assimilate all of the discrete dissatisfactions into a concentration on the single issue. The tragedy of Tom Watson has latterly been repeated in no small part by southern leaders such as Orval Faubus and George Wallace. Accustomed to expressing his opposition—economic or social—as a protest vote rather than a vote for an alternative party organization centered on issues relevant to his interests, the small farmer–laborer in the South now often finds himself in the peculiar position of voting either for Dixiecratic candidates or entering into an uneasy alliance with the new urban Republicans.

But here, too, a subtle change has been at work. The old racist clichés are no longer heard on the public platforms with the same frequency that they used to be; and even the effort to provide a plausible theory for racial separation has practically disappeared. The old postures of defiance have been seriously weakened by recent events. When the second reconstruction began, the arguments that had hung over from the era of the defense of slavery, even though faded and unrefurbished, were brought out and paraded about. In the midfifties one could still regularly encounter biblical, biological, and cultural arguments for the unalterable superiority of Caucasians to Negroes. It is somewhat ironic that the last serious attempt to provide a reasoned, persuasive argument for racial differentiation was made several years ago by Carleton Putnam, a nonsoutherner.[19] Similarly, in the aftermath of 1954, the tendency

19 Carleton Putnam, *Race and Reason* (Washington: Public Affairs Press, 1961).

to legislate and litigate was extended in many of the southern states in the passage of interposition acts. And the massive resistance promised by the politicians produced only such events as the Little Rock crisis and Governor Wallace's brief stand in the doorway at the University of Alabama.

Because we have lived so close to it, the change in tone in recent years perhaps has been more remarkable than we recognize. One might argue that even though the political rhetoric has changed in the discussions of both the inequality of the races and the legal instruments available for preservation of segregation, the new rhetoric is understood by its listeners in the South to be as implacable as, if more subtle than, the old. To the nonsoutherner the "New South" style of argument now indulged in so fulsomely by George Wallace, with its emphasis on local self-determination, law and order, and the virtues of prescriptive traditionalism, may not appear to be important. But to most southerners, who are experienced in the uses of indirection, the fact that Wallace is appealing his case to the electorate at large—assuming the issues over the nature of the legal and political systems to be national rather than exclusively sectional—cannot be considered a minor matter. Although Wallace, Lester Maddox, Strom Thurmond, and others continue to work their witch's spell on southern sentiments, the racial moderation, in both word and deed, which began in the southern periphery seems to have drifted slowly inward and affected many of the public figures even in the core areas of resistance in the lower South.

That the South was never as conservative on economic issues as it has been reputed to be has often been stressed, but a new type of cosmopolitan leadership has begun to make itself clearly visible in the South and, although small in number, such leaders are clearly having an impact on the potential liberal vote in the South. One hesitates to make a catalogue of such persons for fear of leaving out prominent examples, but Ivan Allen, Carl Sanders, Leroy Collins, Frank Smith, Terry Sanford, Albert Gore, Ralph Yarborough, Charles Weltner, and others, some of whom have even managed to hold onto their public offices, are clearly articulating

a liberal point of view and have developed a considerable following in doing so. Another catalogue, again with the same caveat
about exhaustiveness, could be made of what one might call an
older era of liberal southern leaders, some of whom are recently
deceased. These range as widely in personal type and political style
as Brooks Hays, Claude Pepper, Earl Long, Estes Kefauver, Lister
Hill, and John Sparkman, but were united in spite of their differences by their commitment to both economic and social rehabilitation of the South. In a sense such figures might be regarded
as transitional liberals, since they embody far more features of
the older southern personality and style (rural background, populistic outlook, and personalism) than most of the cosmopolites just
mentioned.

What is being suggested here is the emergence of a small core
of liberal southern leaders capable of mobilizing the reserves of
voters long rendered inactive by the diversionary tactics of Whig-
Redeemer generals and demagogic lieutenants whom the Whigs
have always managed to suborn to their cause when popular resistance has threatened.

Another formative influence on the change that has occurred
in the South has been the growth of self-criticism. Although one
should not ignore the contributions of historians and social scientists or the development of regional social science and historical
journals (including *Social Research*, the *Journal of Politics*, the
Journal of Southern History, and the *Southern Economic Journal*),
I would like to place the accent on a group of writers and public
figures which has more popular currency than these individuals
and periodicals. Southern rhetoric has recently been brought to
bear on southern problems by a host of journalists and essayists
whose views are widely disseminated. Although never wholly miss-
ing in the South, the recent tendency to self-examination began
with Cash and has broadened and deepened with experience. One
thinks immediately of the journalistic influence of Hodding Carter,
Ralph McGill, Harry Ashmore, and, though perhaps less immediately influential, of the penetrating satire of P. D. East and of the
adopted southerner Harry Golden. The last two remind us that

the rich vein of irony and humor running through the whole South has rarely been tapped for its greatest potential use—as a basic resource for social criticism. Added to this list are such public and semipublic commentators on the South as Frank Smith,[20] Charles Weltner,[21] and the important summations growing out of experience with the Southern Regional Council by James McBride Dabbs,[22] Pat Watters, and Reese Cleghorn.[23] From these and other southern writers has come an extensive literature, embracing newspaper editorials, news features, essays in leading periodicals, and books. This literature has been unremitting in its critical exposure of the faults of the South without consigning the region to the usual role of national scapegoat or projecting onto the South the entire burden of national guilt after the puritanical, or even Manichaean, fashion of so many outside critics. Both the perspectives and the sympathies of the internal critics have been southern, and their purpose has been to resolve some of the nagging contradictions by salvaging the best that is in the South and the southerner while trying to exorcise the worst. Perhaps in these writers we have gone farther than we think in meeting T. Harry Williams' suggestion that, even though the South could do with less uninformed criticism from the outside, " . . . it absolutely demands more informed criticism from the inside." [24] Even so, the process of transforming these newly and fully expressed attitudes into an effective base for political action still has a long way to go.

Noticeably absent in the foregoing remarks is any mention of the

[20] Frank Smith has written *Congressman from Mississippi* (New York: Pantheon Books, 1964) and *Look Away from Dixie* (Baton Rouge: Louisiana State University Press, 1965).

[21] See Charles Weltner, *Southerner* (Philadelphia: Lippincott, 1966).

[22] James McBride Dabbs, a former president of the Southern Regional Council, has written numerous books and articles. Two of them are most pertinent in the current context; both reflect the nonpaternalistic views of a southern gentleman in the best sense of that term: *The Southern Heritage* (New York: Knopf, 1958) and *Who Speaks for the South?* (New York: Funk and Wagnalls, 1964).

[23] Pat Watters and Reese Cleghorn have recently published a comprehensive appraisal of the Negro drive for the vote in the South in the 1960's, *Climbing Jacob's Ladder* (New York: Harcourt, Brace and World, 1967).

[24] Williams, "Trends in Southern Politics," 65.

most striking expression of the forces of change shaping the present
and future of the South—that emanating from the southern Negro.
Here indeed is a new articulation of attitudes all but denied direct
forms of expression for two centuries. Of course the white southerner had long been aware that the aspirations of the Negro were
cast in terms set for him by the general aims of a white society of
which the Negro was—and yet was not—a part. But the repression
of the Negro's opportunities to express these aspirations was also
an effective means of repressing white awareness of the Negro's
real aims and a necessary precondition for forcing on the Negro
the fictional aspirations that the white man wanted him to have.

It is not so surprising, then, to discover that the southern—and
even more, perhaps, the northern—Negro is as tortured by self-
doubts and contradictions as the white southerner. Currently most
noticeable among these ambivalences is the whole series of attitudes
toward race. Like the white southerner whose own mind-set has
been so important in defining the Negro's role in American society,
the Negro is constrained to assimilate all his frustrations and griev-
ances in the single issue of race. Having reached a certain point in
his drive for equality, the Negro is inclined to look with suspicion
on proposals for political alliance with the white man. After all,
that effort is an old and often bitter one in the memory of both
races. Even the emergence of Negro racial demagogues in the struggle over leadership of the civil rights movement is more a part of
the pattern of domestic politics than something extraneous to it.

So the Negro moves between the extremes of a quest for integration and a search for an adequate set of symbols around which
he may unite to form a racially separate community.[25] The Black
Muslim movement, the Black Panther Party, and black nationalism, each in its own way and each containing overtones of endem-
ically American tendencies, are such symbols, but none of them has
shown evidence of the expansive capacity apparent in the slogan
"Black Power." Ironically, the success of the rallying cry seems to

25 An excellent brief summary of the attitudes and the literature on the subject is
Helen B. Shaffer, "Negro Power Struggle," *Editorial Research Reports*, I (February
21, 1968), 123–40.

depend on an inability to provide any precise content for the term that is immediately relevant to a redefinition of the goals of the civil rights drive or to the realization of goals previously stressed. Is Black Power a separatist movement in the absolute sense? Or is it separatist even in the relative sense of concentrating for the moment on securing a proportionate share of political and economic power for Negroes while temporarily abandoning the quest for complete social integration? Although we have extensive statements on the subject, they are certainly contradictory enough to suggest that a reconciliation will not occur until the social action of the proximate future has indicated which, if any, of the various interpretations will prevail.

We are confronted with a related issue in the countervailing tendencies implied by the suggestions that, on the one hand, the local Negro communities have to be made over by the people who live in them and that, on the other, an enormous federal and state effort must be put into the human rehabilitation of the localities, an effort which inevitably will entail many centralized, bureaucratic actions that will not always favor local decision-making. In some respects this particular ambivalence reflects the tension between the desire firmly to reject all the apparatus of paternalism, including those paternalistic appurtenances of public authority inevitable in a technocratic, mass society. That the Negro has had enough patronizing is apparent not solely in this posture toward government; it has also been manifested in the rejection of the morally superior attitudes of white Student Nonviolent Coordinating Committee members working on the voter education and registration drives in Mississippi in 1964 and 1965.[26]

But if certain indigenous aspects of his southern background have contributed to contradictions in the expressions and actions of the Negro in his quest for equality, other southern elements in his makeup have been increasingly apparent as important supporting ideas for the whole civil rights movement. The southern Negro may be seeking separate identity as a black (or at least nonwhite), but

26 *Ibid.*, 138.

paradoxical as it may seem, he already has identity as a southerner.

Southerners have always been dimly aware that the lives of Negroes and whites of the region have been too closely bound to avoid mutual influences, although the whites have generally preferred to see the influences as working in only one direction. But we are now becoming aware that such important southern characteristics as love for elaborate rhetoric, an earthy, frontier sense of humor, the will for survival in the face of adversity (which is often expressed as sheer human endurance), the manners of the regional inhabitants, and the hedonistic propensities of the "hell-of-a-fellow" frontier type are shared traits to which neither of the races can lay exclusive claim. And we well know that in the culinary arts, in folk music, and in the creation of the colorful, metaphoric, and highly expressive language of the South, the Negro has been extraordinarily creative. His creativity has been a part of the overall culture of the region.

Like those of the white Southerner, attitudes of the southern Negro have been affected by personalism, a sense of place, attachment to family, and a strong religious commitment. I think the more perceptive observers of the South have always been aware that these traits have been important sustaining influences for the Negro in his struggle for survival within a racial caste system. As Christopher Lasch has pointed out in a penetrating evaluation of the recent literature on Black Power, the Negro was able to build a subculture in the South which was "capable of giving the Negro community the beginnings at least of cohesiveness and collective self-discipline." [27] The moral influence of the church, according to Lasch, contributed to the development of stable, patriarchal families, which provided the basis for the continuity of human relations from which Negroes began their painful struggle for self-advancement. In these developments, Lasch finds the explanation for the difference between the southern and the northern civil rights movement. The subculture the southern Negro was able to build for himself out of the adaptation of American patterns to

27 Christopher Lasch, "The Trouble with Black Power," *New York Review of Books*, X (February 29, 1968), 4.

his own needs has helped him avoid the abstractly repressive and disintegrating influences of a mass society in the ghetto, infected by its sense of alienation and *ressentiment* which can so easily be stimulated to the violence of total anarchy. The mediating influences of the institutions of this subculture, and the fact that the subculture shares many of the values of the general culture of the South and of America in general, have not only bought time during which some of the grosser injustices might be relieved, but continue to hold out promises for a reconciliation of the Negro and white cultures. These we may be able to put to use in analyzing and perhaps even resolving the national crisis.

At this point, we begin to look outward toward the possibility that some of the new attitudes and expressions in the South may be pertinent to the national experience. One phase of historical southern thought, it has already been suggested, has concentrated on the idea that the solution to southern problems was to make the region over in the image of the North. It has been further suggested that we have already gone a long way in that direction. But in the face of the national malaise over both internal and external public affairs, we may well wish to inquire whether in making ourselves over in the national image we are doomed to repeat the error of overreliance on the acquisitive elements in Lockean liberalism to the exclusion of other individual and social goods. In this respect, the South may have something to offer both by way of criticism and precept for the nation.

Although the emphasis on conservatism in the South has often been a thinly veiled guise for the defense of the status quo in economic and social relations, the experiences through which the South has passed have provided the region with a sense of history and a tendency not to sacrifice the past or even the present to an indeterminate future. These tendencies have been exemplified above all in the literature of the region; and it is in its literary preeminence during the past half-century that the South has most nearly found its place within the nation while not losing its sense of regional identity. The literature of the South has, even where it has appeared to be gothic and decadent, been concerned with the abiding realities of human existence in both the individual and social sense. And it has articulated this concern within the context of regional attributes identified with the mind of the South: a sense of place, an emphasis on familial and community relations, an awareness of the importance of the meaning of good and evil for the individual in relation to his elemental moral and religious perceptions, and a preference for dealing with the concrete and particular rather than the abstract and collective. Implicit in much of this literature—exemplified best by William Faulkner and Robert Penn Warren—is a criticism of materialism and progressivism and an expression of values that are transcendent and humanistic rather than purely utilitarian.[28] This criticism was most explicit in the writings of the southern agrarians and continues in memoirs as far apart chronologically as those of William Alexander Percy and Murry Falkner.[29] It is present in the writings of Dr. Martin Luther King as well as of the historians and essayists cited earlier.

If one wonders why *I'll Take My Stand*[30] continues to interest people after more than forty years of critical attack on it as a piece of southern reactionism and after the South has long been engaged in abandoning the agrarian life held up by it as an ideal, my advice is to read the book and then examine the subsequent careers of the contributors to it. The statement survives, not as a romantic anachronism, but because it was able to point up the problem of the two cultures some thirty years prior to the recent debate between C. P. Snow and his critics and came down solidly on the side of a religio-humanistic tradition as opposed to a metaphysic of science and a total reliance on technology to solve human problems. Although the careers of the contributors diverged widely after the book was published, and certainly some of them remained unreconstructed

28 That this type of criticism by way of literature is not altogether new is indicated by the essay on "A Southern Critique for the Gilded Age" in C. Vann Woodward, *The Burden of Southern History* (Baton Rouge: Louisiana State University Press, 1960; New York: Vintage Books Edition, 1961), Chap. 6.

29 Murry C. Falkner, *The Falkners of Mississippi* (Baton Rouge: Louisiana State University Press, 1967).

30 Twelve Southerners, *I'll Take My Stand* (New York: Harper, 1930; New York: Harper Torch Book Edition, 1962).

southerners, all of them that I know anything about continued in their various ways to inquire into the moral and social preconditions of a good life, and not simply the material ones. Southern literature in general, and the attitude reflected by the southern agrarians in particular, suggest to us the possibility that cultural conservatism can be fruitfully joined with political and economic liberalism so that we can adapt pragmatically to change without sacrificing all moral and religious values on the altar of relativism, and so that we can preserve our individuality through mediating institutions such as the family, the church, and the local community as primary associations, even in the face of a necessarily highly collectivized and centralized society.[31]

Of course all the ingredients in the personal and social makeup of the South that have been mentioned thus far have been put to both good and bad uses, so that one closes on some questions which still indicate ambiguity rather than certainty. The first of these is the question whether an urban industrial society is so inimical to the attributes of individualism, religious commitment, the extended family, and relatively decentralized social institutions that the moral and religious values of the South must inevitably disappear.[32] Or can the South preserve the distinctive qualities of its subculture and even use these qualities (as it has not always done in the past) to reconcile the races on a basis of equality rather than watch them act as a stimulus to further separation, with who knows what con-

[31] Allen Guttmann has recently presented a related position in *The Conservative Tradition in America* (New York: Oxford University Press, 1967). Guttmann's theme is that, despite the dominance of the liberal tradition in America, a strong thread of commitment to Burkean conservatism has woven its way through American literature. And he states as part of his own conclusion that "socialism with a sense of the past is the name of my desire."

[32] Howard W. Odum, a southerner whose Renaissance qualities enabled him to bridge many of the crosscurrents of southern thought and action touched upon here, has posed this dilemma well in his distinction between the universal *folk culture* and the *state civilization*. The state civilization, with its characteristic technology, industrialization, urbanization, intellectualism, cultural specialization, organization, centralization, and power, he says, "tends to assume the nature of a *technological order* rather than a *human society* or a *moral order* such as has been assumed as the universal constant in all growing societies." *Folk Region and Society* (Chapel Hill: University of North Carolina Press, 1964), 211.

sequences? Finally, can the South as a distinctive part of the nation
provide an example for the national environment, and thus aid in
the development of a sense of history and of the continuity of individual and social values that have been developed out of the
South's and the nation's experience? It seems to me that the new
mind of the South has much to say in response to these questions;
whether what it has to say can be made politically relevant will not
only help to determine what our destiny may be, but will provide an indication whether we can, in fact, use ideas to affect that
destiny.

The contemporary South, in brief, is both more heterodox and
more subject to change than it has usually been pictured. It also
continues to have identifiable social and political features that both
tie it to the nation and yet keep it distinctive in its regional identity. The extent of these complexities and their variations may be
perceived through a detailed examination of the politics of the individual states of the South.

I

The Evolving States

2

VIRGINIA
The Emergence of Two-Party Politics

RALPH EISENBERG

Virginia, described more than twenty years ago as a "political museum piece," enters the 1970's in the throes of political change. A new Virginia is emerging in the structure and dynamics of its political system. There are signs that the state is no longer part of the political South. Although the characteristics of Virginia politics remain distinctive as always, they now produce outcomes more similar to those that occur in states outside the South rather than within.

The symptoms of political change in Virginia are found in a host of recent phenomena that include election results, legislative policies, constitutional revision efforts, and the emergence of effective two-party politics. Despite the rapid pace of change over the last eight years, strong vestiges of past political values, traditions, organization, and style remain. The shape of the new political Virginia has yet to be firmly established, and the old and the new are both visible in the contemporary scene. Although with political stabilization both the traditional and the innovative may remain significant, a sharp break with the past appears probable.

The Virginia political system as it exists today has grown from seeds evident twenty years ago. Although its development did not occur in a uniform progression from that time, it can be divided cleanly into time lines that almost, but not quite, parallel those of each of the last two decades. The processes of change which were

Ralph Eisenberg is Assistant Provost and Associate Professor of Government and Foreign Affairs, University of Virginia.

clearly building in the political system after 1948 were arrested sharply in 1954, following the United States Supreme Court's school desegregation decision. But they resumed in 1961 and quickly accelerated in the years afterward. It is appropriate, therefore, to trace briefly political developments in the state in each of these decades.

Traditional Virginia Politics to 1948

As is well known, Virginia politics traditionally has been played within the arena of a small electorate, and with a small group of officeholders and political leaders.[1] The state's history emphasized the role and significance of the aristocrats, the bourbons, and the imposition upon Virginia of their values with respect to public responsibility, integrity in government, administrative efficiency, and concepts of social responsibility. While never recapturing, or even approximating, the "Golden Age" of Patrick Henry, George Washington, Thomas Jefferson, James Madison, George Mason, and James Monroe, Virginians managed to develop relatively high standards of public responsibility in honesty and integrity if not in social responsibility, welfare, and indeed democracy itself. It is best to review first the political system as it emerged in this century, since it produced the form which for so long characterized Virginia and from which the state is now evolving.

Reconstruction had a considerable political impact in Virginia. As a result of that experience, and particularly because of the participation in politics of the black man and the poor white man, the constitutional convention of 1901–1902 established the basic rules that shaped politics in the twentieth century. Most significantly, the constitution of 1902 imposed payment of a poll tax as a prerequisite to voting. The poll tax effected an immediate reduction in the size of the electorate. Whereas 264,240 Virginians had voted for the President of the United States in 1900, only 135,867 voted in the 1904 presidential election. Indeed, it was not until 1928 that

---

[1] The best exposition of Virginia politics to its date of publication was V. O. Key, Jr., *Southern Politics in State and Nation* (New York: Alfred A. Knopf, 1949).

the number of voters again reached the size of the 1900 turnout.[2]
A state law, in effect for all elections in Virginia until 1964, required payment of a poll tax at least six months prior to the date
of an election and also required that the poll tax for the three
previous years be paid before a person was permitted to vote.

The existence of a highly effective statewide political organization overshadowed almost all other characteristics of Virginia politics. The political system really functioned within the context of the
state Democratic Party organization. Credit for the formation of
the organization is ordinarily attributed to State Senator Thomas
Martin, who acted as its leader for many years in the early part of
the century, although United States Senators Claude Swanson and
Carter Glass were among its leading figures.[3] In the mid-twenties,
Harry Flood Byrd became head of the organization; and in subsequent years, the organization became popularly known as the Byrd
Organization, or the Byrd Machine. In effectiveness it rivaled the
success of the urban political machines of its day, and certainly it
endured far longer than most of the famed city political organizations. Among the states, it was unique in its durability and power.

Descriptions of the organization and how it functioned have rarely changed over the years.[4] A small electorate was undoubtedly the
key to its success. Needing few votes to secure its victories, the organization was able to mobilize more than sufficient support in almost every election to assure its continuance in office through its
local outposts in county seats across the state. At the grass-roots
level, organization power was lodged in five local constitutional officers, who were popularly elected. These officials were the commonwealth's attorney (prosecutor), the clerk of court, treasurer, com-

---

[2] Ralph Eisenberg, "Virginia Votes for President: Patterns and Prospects," *University of Virginia News Letter*, XLI (September 15, 1964), 2. Hereinafter this publication is cited as *UVa News Letter*.

[3] For an excellent history of Virginia politics in the early years of the century, see
Allen W. Moger, *Virginia: Bourbonism to Byrd, 1870–1925* (Charlottesville: University Press of Virginia, 1968).

[4] See, for example, Key, *Southern Politics*, Moger, *Virginia: Bourbonism to Byrd*,
and J. Harvie Wilkinson III, *Harry Byrd and the Changing Face of Virginia Politics*,
1945–1966 (Charlottesville: University Press of Virginia, 1968), especially Chaps. 1
and 2.

missioner of the revenue (tax collector), and the sheriff. In addition, the circuit judge (court of record judge) was often the most important of the local organization stalwarts.

The critical utility of the elected local constitutional officers to the organization lay in the political support which they developed in winning election to office and in the political organizations which they led. The significance of the circuit judge was related to his vast local appointment powers. For example, the judge appointed persons to fill vacancies for the unexpired terms of the constitutional officers and of members of the county governing body. In addition, he was empowered to appoint members of the local electoral board, welfare board, and school trustee electoral board; the latter appointed the county school board.

Potential leverage against the local agents of the organization was lodged at the state level, although it apparently seldom had to be applied. The circuit judge was elected by the General Assembly, which, dominated by the organization, insured his loyalty. The office of circuit judge was a critical position because it was not popularly elected, and its appointment powers were particularly useful in those areas that elected officials who were either independent of the organization or, worse yet, Republican.

The continuing loyalty of the locally elected constitutional officers was guaranteed by the state Compensation Board, a three-member body whose responsibilities included approving the salaries and budgets paid by the state to these local officials. Yet even this power seldom had to be exercised and the prevalent view was that the mere threat of such action preempted the need actually to invoke it. The organization's controls at the local level, therefore, were strong and were used to turn out enough loyal voters to insure the continuance of organization domination of the legislature, state officers, senators and congressmen, and key local offices. The local officials were field operatives for the organization in the election process. But they also were parts of the intelligence network by which the organization at the state level determined the reliability of potential candidates for local office and of prospective appointees. They were used to com-

municate grass-roots sentiments to the organization leadership on
state issues and candidates, albeit only from those who counted in
electoral mathematics.

The above description should not suggest that the structure of
the organization was weighted excessively at the top or that the
state leaders dictated policy. The organization's control of its local
units rested primarily upon its skill in retaining the loyalty of its
local supporters. In this sense the organization was responsive to its
grass roots. The continued political predominance of the organization was in large measure due to its shrewd ability to alter its policies and programs enough to retain its following across the state.
Although never known for sharp changes in policy direction or the
development of progressive public service programs in their time,
the organization succeeded in responding just enough to demands
for new programs or services so that it was able to retain its political
backing.

The process of selecting organization candidates for state office
dramatized best the local impact upon state organization policy-
making. In each election the identity of the organization candidate
was obvious and hence he received immediate and virtually complete support from organization leaders throughout the state. But
the period prior to the primary election date was marked by intense
competition between prospective organization candidates for the
party's nomination. The competition for the organization "nod,"
or designation, was oriented less to top leadership than to the local
organization cadres. The candidate sought to demonstrate his broad
base of support among the local party organizations, preliminary to
his endorsement by the top leadership. The consensus of local support that he amassed was then capped by concurrence of the state
leadership to his candidacy. Although the weight of the state leadership could be applied to stymie the development of a particular
candidacy, it was a high-risk course to follow. Intervention by the
state leaders could alienate local organizations committed to or
ardently backing one candidate and lead to severe political schisms
across the state. Thus, in the normal course of events, the leaders

permitted prospective candidates to survey their supporters at the local level, and then anointed the candidate who had the most backing.

The risk to the organization leadership of the candidate selection process was the possible election of candidates for whom the leaders had little enthusiasm. In such situations, the organization's leaders waited out the term of the official, or, as in the case of Governor James H. Price in the 1930's, merely blocked his effectiveness as governor through its overwhelming control of the General Assembly.

If it is an oversimplification to infer that clear hierarchical lines of authority from the top down characterized the organization, it is an equally serious error to assume that no direction at all came from the top. In the more recent years of the organization's life, there clearly existed a group of leaders who met or consulted to determine vital questions of statewide importance. These individuals were difficult to identify but included the legislative leaders, some local organization leaders, some congressmen, elected state officials, and occasionally some state department heads. The figure who stood *primus inter pares*, however, from 1926 until his retirement from office in 1965, was Harry F. Byrd, first as governor and then as United States senator. But Byrd rarely applied his vast potential power in the system. Characteristically, he did not tend to organization business on a day-to-day basis but rather was consulted as other leaders thought necessary, and intervened when he thought appropriate on matters which he deemed important. Most of these occasions involved major shifts in state policies.

The traditional base of political support for the organization lay in the rural counties, particularly those in southside Virginia and the tidewater areas. Most of these counties had sizable black populations and agricultural economies. The local leaders had conservative views toward government and public policy. The description of the organization as "a group of like-minded men" was a fair characterization of the local leaders who found Senator Byrd and other state leaders espousing views and enacting programs and policies which were generally in accord with their own attitudes. Thus, the organization clearly did not impose its will upon its supporters; rather it reflected the views of its adherents, who in turn dominated the local, and hence the state's, political process.

The organization's ability to survive with little alteration in its attitudes was also attributable to its complete domination of politics, particularly of the election process. For prospective officeholders, a political career meant climbing an organization career ladder. This route for political ambition required demonstrations of loyalty and reliability to the organization and its policies. Even the occasional maverick who managed to oust an organization figure in a primary election found it necessary to allow himself to be co-opted by the organization if his political life were to have any future. The recruitment process, therefore, insured the continued predominance of the organization.

Antiorganization sentiment was concentrated in urban areas and in traditionally Republican areas of southwestern and western Virginia. Local successes of antiorganization Democrats were almost nonexistent. Republicans were able to win some local offices in areas of traditionally Republican strength, which mirrored others of the mountain South. These local Republican successes, however, could be and were tempered by the organization's local tentacles in the offices of circuit judges. Even in Republican areas, the local Democrats characteristically backed the organization. The pervasiveness of the organization and the effectiveness of its election machinery insured the one-party character of the state and made impossible the emergence of the personal political styles and organizations found in other southern states. Factionalism became the style of political competition in one-party Virginia.

The organization's control of the Virginia political system was all-encompassing. It controlled local offices and all branches of state government. Conflict between legislative and executive branches at the state level seldom occurred because the organization controlled both branches and the socialization process inevitable in the rise of governors through the political system made later conflict unlikely. One product of this system was the continuation of the Virginia style of politics. The populistic appeals of highly personalized candidacies found elsewhere in the South could not prosper, and did not develop, in Virginia, where the small electorate and the closed organization precluded the success of the highly individual and independent politician. Instead, the style of the Virginia politician became that of the soft-spoken, calm, reserved, reasonable, attractive, and patrician-looking conservative lawyer or businessman.

The Fifties: Challenge and Survival

The organization's leadership was challenged seriously in 1949 and in the few years following. First at the polls in the Democratic gubernatorial primary election in 1949 and then in the state legislative chambers in 1954, the organization had to cope with antiorganization and moderate challenges to its string of election successes and its domination of the policy-making process. The primary election challenge was rebuffed but only after a massive and all-out effort by the organization. But the legislative challenge was more successful because it did modify organization policy. More significantly, the legislative revolt against organization leadership spawned an active and potentially effective group of young political leaders.

Adding to these successive political traumas, the state's Republican Party stirred itself to wage an intense and, for the organization, a frightening, contest for the governorship in 1953, before succumbing to an organization triumph by the smallest margin in the century. But prospects for the downfall of the organization were shattered by the 1954 *Brown v. Board of Education* decision. That decision revived race as Virginia's primary political issue. Veteran political observers credit the decision for preserving the organization, or at least for delaying its demise for another ten years.[5] Such judgments may involve serious overestimates of antiorganization political potential at the time and serious underestimates of the flexibility and hence the durability of the organization's leadership.

It is interesting to note that the challenges during this period came from within the Democratic Party in the 1949 primary elec-

[5] George M. Kelley, "The Changing Style of Virginia Politics," *UVa News Letter*, XLV (February 15, 1969), 27.

tion and from without the Democratic Party in the 1953 general election, but partially from within the organization itself in the 1954 legislative session. Thus, it can be argued that the restlessness in the state with the organization manifested itself in all significant political arenas—and logically progressed from internal factionalized primary election competition to external political party election competition and finally to internal conflict involving organization actors who earlier had played key roles in repelling the election challenges to organization predominance.

In the 1949 gubernatorial primary the organization's candidate was State Senator John S. Battle of Charlottesville. The antiorganization banner was carried by Francis Pickens Miller, who had once served as an antiorganization member of the legislature from Arlington. A third significant candidate in the primary was Horace Edwards, who had served as a state legislator and state Democratic chairman. Edwards entered the campaign because he failed to receive the organization's, and particularly Senator Byrd's, endorsement for the nomination. Miller waged a hard and vigorous campaign and, with Edwards in the race, posed a threat to Battle's nomination. Edwards was supported by some organization members to whom his call for state programs to aid local governments was appealing. The leadership perceived the possibility that the organization vote might be split between Battle and Edwards, especially since a fourth candidate, Remmie Arnold, also would siphon off some organization votes. Miller's campaign strongly attacked the organization and relied on the usual antiorganization forces for its core of support. At the time, Virginia had no runoff provision in its primary law and there was genuine concern that Miller might eke out a victory because of the splits in organization support. To forestall such a result, the organization employed its heavy artillery. Senator Byrd attacked Miller as a "labor candidate" and warned that voting for Edwards would help Miller. The chairman of the state Compensation Board, E. R. Combs, a close friend and chief lieutenant of Senator Byrd, also campaigned actively to hold organization votes for Battle. These tactics and the support that Battle received from Republicans, who had been urged by at least one of their own leaders to enter the Democratic primary, proved decisive. Battle was nominated in the primary with less than 43 percent of the total vote and a plurality of less than 24,000 votes over Francis Pickens Miller.[6]

Table 1

VOTING IN VIRGINIA DEMOCRATIC PARTY
PRIMARY ELECTION FOR GOVERNOR, 1949

Candidate	Number of Votes	Percentage
John S. Battle	135,436	42.8
Francis Pickens Miller	111,697	35.3
Horace Edwards	47,435	15.0
Remmie Arnold	22,054	7.0
TOTAL	316,622	

Source: Secretary of State Board of Elections, Official Records (Commonwealth of Virginia, Department of Purchases and Supply, Richmond).

Because the organization vote had been split by competing independent candidacies, Battle's victory had required the direct and personal participation of Senator Byrd in the campaign and the activation of the organization's resources for stimulating support from its local cadres. The Republican crossover into the primary to support Battle also was important, although it is difficult to determine exactly how decisive it was. Antiorganization forces concluded that Republicans had made the difference. What was noteworthy was the necessity for the organization to mobilize its leader, its resources, and Republicans in order to win.

The external election challenge to the organization occurred in the 1953 election for governor. The Democratic candidate was Congressman Thomas B. Stanley, who had been nominated in the primary over the opposition of State Senator Charles R. Fenwick of Arlington. Stanley's and the organization's win in the primary had been substantial with almost a two-to-one margin over Fenwick in the popular vote. Fenwick had made an earlier unsuccessful race for

[6] See Wilkinson, *Byrd and the Changing Face of Virginia Politics*, 91–98, for a somewhat more detailed discussion of the 1949 primary election.

the lieutenant governorship in 1945, but his career had largely been characterized by his support of the organization although with less reliability than the typical organization stalwart.

The Republican candidate was State Senator Ted Dalton of Roanoke, a vigorous campaigner with an attractive personality. No doubt Dalton was aided by the Republican victory in Virginia in the 1952 presidential election. He won more than 44 percent of the popular vote in 1953 and threw another scare into the organization. Dalton campaigned with a progressive platform (for Virginia). He stressed programs to raise minimum teachers' salaries, appropriate more money to state mental institutions, and launch vigorous industrial development activities. Dalton also attacked the organization, the appointive powers of judges, and election laws, and he called for repeal of the poll tax. The Republican campaign was aided by the blandness of Stanley as a candidate and the indictment of a key organization leader for federal income tax evasion. Dalton also had been supported by Francis Pickens Miller, who commended the Republican's candidacy although he would vote Democratic.

Table 2

VOTING IN VIRGINIA GENERAL ELECTION
FOR GOVERNOR, 1953

Candidate	Party	Number of Votes	Percentage
Thomas Stanley	Democratic	226,998	54.8
Ted Dalton	Republican	183,328	44.3
Howard Carwile	Independent	3,680	.9
Scattered		19	
TOTAL		414,025	

Source: Secretary of State Board of Elections, Official Records.

Observers considered Dalton's call for a $100 million highway bond issue the decisive issue of the election. Although Dalton argued that his proposal was for revenue bonds pledged by a portion of the state's gas tax revenues, his proposal seemed to threaten the state's and Harry F. Byrd's pay-as-you-go principle. It thus brought Senator Byrd actively into the campaign. The bond issue proposal

was credited with arresting the momentum of Dalton's campaign.
But the 1953 challenge was the most significant Republican performance in a statewide election in many years.[7] Together with the
Republican victory the preceding year, it spurred two-party politics
in future campaigns.

The third site of a challenge to the organization was the General
Assembly itself, and the challengers included some organization
legislators. An earlier clue to the legislative rebellion had appeared
in the 1950 legislative session, when heavy pressure from the governor's office was required to secure the agreement of the House of
Delegates to a bill sponsored by State Senator Harry F. Byrd, Jr., to
provide for tax refunds whenever a certain proportion of surplus
state funds existed. In the 1954 session, a serious revolt against organization leadership and Governor Stanley erupted from a group
of young, well-educated, new legislators who were interested in expanded state public services. Known as the Young Turks, these
legislators could hardly be styled liberals. They had worked with
the organization on many issues but acted independently on a host
of proposals to modernize the state and change public policy to meet
the needs of postwar Virginia. In 1954, they succeeded in deadlock-
ing the House of Delegates on an issue of spending surplus state
funds to improve the school system. Although the ensuing compromise did not accommodate the Young Turks' position entirely, the
organization leadership had to make a concession to resolve the
stalemate.[8]

The Young Turks' movement dramatized the generation gap at
the time between organization leaders and young rank-and-file
members. The gap arose not only from differences in policy and program outlook, but also from the monopoly of leadership positions
by the older generation. The Young Turks were viewed as portents
of future challenges to the organization. Together with the relatively close elections in 1949 and 1953, the continuation of organization dominance seemed threatened. The 1954 challenge had moved
the organization just enough to mollify the opposition. The earlier

[7] See *ibid.*, 101–105.
[8] *Ibid.*, 105–12.

election challenges too had forced the organization to respond with policy changes to meet some of the state's needs in public services. Thus, the assumption after 1954 was that the organization would have to move again, to adapt its traditionally conservative policies enough in the direction of more and better public services to offset the threats posed by its opponents. It is significant that many of the Young Turks of 1954 would later play key roles in more serious and effective challenges to the organization.[9]

In May of 1954, the ruling of the United States Supreme Court in *Brown v. Board of Education* stopped the moderating process at work in Virginia politics. The decision thrust a new, albeit very old, issue to the forefront of politics. Great effort was expended by Senator Byrd and the organization to sell "massive resistance" to Virginians. In doing so, the organization revived racial issues and fears that had plagued state politics for so long in the past. Against the specter of integration ("race-mixing"), antiorganization and moderate organization leaders could do little to rouse a popular following to their progressive causes. The organization moved the ground rules of politics into a racial context, with the lines drawn between those for and those against massive resistance, and thus defined the area of political conflict with its opponents. On such an emotional battleground, the organization's foes could not amass support to raise issues apart from the race question. It was as if the entire state had to undergo a catharsis on the issue of race before it could again face the panorama of other political issues.

Massive resistance, which cannot be discussed at length here, was an effort by the state to resist racial integration of its public schools even to the extent of closing down those schools under court order to desegregate.[10] Governor Stanley modified his initial moderate response to the *Brown* decision and affirmed his determination to re-

[9] See *ibid.*, 108–109, for a list of prominent Young Turks, some of whom later became key figures in both electoral and legislative challenges to the organization.
[10] Massive resistance in Virginia is discussed most thoroughly in Robbins L. Gates, *The Making of Massive Resistance: Virginia's Politics of Public School Desegregation, 1954–1956* (Chapel Hill: University of North Carolina Press, 1962), but also in Benjamin Muse, *Virginia's Massive Resistance* (Bloomington: Indiana University Press, 1961), and Wilkinson, *Byrd and the Changing Face of Virginia Politics*, 113–54.

sist its application in Virginia. An early study commission proposed a pupil assignment plan and a tuition grant program as tactics to evade the impact of desegregation. In order to effectuate the plan, a constitutional amendment was necessary. To secure this quickly, the organization planned to call a constitutional convention, which required a referendum. In the referendum on the use of tuition grants for private school attendance, the convention won overwhelming endorsement by a vote of 304,154 to 146,164. Opposition to the tuition grant program was led by some of the Young Turks. A special session in 1956 finally adopted the massive resistance program. It embodied the tuition grant plan and a state Pupil Placement Board, to which Negro applications to attend white schools would be referred. It also directed the governor to close public schools ordered by courts to integrate or to withhold state funds from local schools which were willing to integrate. Opposition to both the massive resistance program and the earlier tuition grant referendum was based on a defense of the public school system. Opposition forces made little attempt to defend integrated schools in principle. Instead, their arguments stressed the futility of sacrificing public schools and urged local options on desegregation. The organization carried the massive resistance program in the 1956 special legislative session by narrow margins—59 to 39 in the House of Delegates and 21 to 17 in the state Senate.

These close votes indicated the division within the organization on the massive resistance proposals. But the old leadership, spearheaded by Senator Byrd, and legislative leaders and congressmen from southside Virginia, prevailed over opposition from urban Democrats and Republicans. Massive resistance received its strongest support from southside and other rural elements of the organization, whose localities contained relatively large Negro populations. These groups were able to determine policy in this area because of their traditionally strong support of the organization and the need for organization leadership to respond to their concerns on the integration issue. It is important, however, to stress that these rural areas also were the homes of the organization leaders.

In 1957, J. Lindsay Almond was elected governor of Virginia. He had managed to secure the organization's nod for the nomination by announcing early in the pre-primary period and securing enough wide support about the state that Senator Byrd, although reluctant, endorsed his candidacy. Almond had been attorney general for eight years and had acquired an outstanding reputation as a good lawyer and skilled orator. In the general election, he easily defeated Republican Ted Dalton by polling over 63 percent of the popular vote. Dalton's attack on massive resistance and endorsement of local option made his task difficult at best in the election campaign. But he was overwhelmed after President Dwight D. Eisenhower had dispatched federal troops to Little Rock, Arkansas, early in the fall.

Almond as governor initially vowed to continue to fight desegregation. But his position became almost impossible to sustain after he closed public schools in Front Royal, Norfolk, and Charlottesville. In addition to a widespread adverse public reaction to the closing of schools, Almond encountered opposition from businessmen who feared the long-term effects of the school closings. The final test for the governor came when on the same day both a federal district court and the Virginia Supreme Court of Appeals invalidated the school-closing laws. After a final (and famous) emotional speech on television, Governor Almond went to the legislature a week later and called for an end to massive resistance. To say that other organization leaders and Senator Byrd himself were upset by Almond's sudden shift in position is an understatement. After a climactic fight during a 1957 special legislative session, Almond's program won, but by only a single vote in the state Senate. Massive resistance had collapsed. Almond had won by forging an ad hoc coalition of Republicans, moderates, antiorganization liberals, and a small group of organization legislators. The massive resistance fight left deep divisions within the organization's ranks and between the organization's leadership and outsiders. In another contest in the 1960 legislative session, Almond's efforts to obtain a state sales tax were defeated as organization opposition reflected the previous massive resistance conflict and exposed the wounds of intraorganization conflict once again.

Massive resistance was significant in Virginia political history not

only for resurrecting organization preeminence but also for crystal-
lizing opposition to the organization and its leadership. In the
confusion of issues that arose and receded in the four years of organization opposition to desegregation, coalitions were forged and
broadened. These included the usual antiorganization forces, as well
as moderates on the fringes of, or even within, the organization. The
experience, the common causes, and the technique of close cooperation in the coalitions could and would be applied in later contests.
In addition, the organization's harsh treatment of its opponents and
of those within the organization who had not remained loyal served
to bind together its victims. In part because of the organization's
unwillingness to change its politics, to accommodate even its supporters from more urban areas of the state, where organization positions could not be maintained firmly, or to recognize the changing
character of Virginia and its people, demands for changes in state
policies increased in the next few years. In a sense, then, massive resistance preserved the organization and its traditional behavior patterns but paradoxically hastened the later modifications of its
behavior and ultimately its demise as the predominant faction in
the Democratic Party.

The Sixties: Retreat and Change

The organization seemingly marched into the 1960's with its power
intact and the outlook bright. Yielding at last to the realities of
the political and economic world of Virginia at the dawn of a new
decade, the organization seemed to be willing to raise the levels of
public services in the state and finally to launch efforts for industrial development long desired by the business community. These
attitudes appeared to be embraced by the organization's 1961 candidate for governor, Albertis S. Harrison, Jr. Harrison had been
attorney general during Almond's governorship. He was well respected as a lawyer, but more importantly he seemed an ideal candidate to bind the wounds that still afflicted the organization.
Harrison had not been a strident voice of massive resistance, but
had played his legalistic role in the conflict without being identi-

fied closely with the leading school-closers. In that sense, he was a moderate whose nomination suggested that the vicious struggles of previous years were over. To assuage the organization's more conservative group, State Senator Mills E. Godwin, Jr., who had been a principal organization spokesman for massive resistance, was the candidate for lieutenant governor on the same ticket.

An antiorganization ticket was formed for the 1961 Democratic Party primary election. Its candidate for governor was Lieutenant Governor Guy Stephens. Stephens had backed Governor Almond's retreat from massive resistance and thereby earned the organization's enmity and lost his own opportunity to secure an endorsement for the governorship. The ticket included State Senator Armistead Boothe as the candidate for lieutenant governor. Boothe had traditional antiorganization support because of his leadership in the Young Turks' revolt and in the fight against massive resistance. Although the antiorganization slate polled a larger proportion of the popular vote than the Miller candidacy had polled in 1949, Harrison was nominated with a little less than 57 percent of the total vote. In the general election, he easily defeated the Republican candidate.

Harrison's was a caretaker administration. Its primary objective appeared to be to heal the wounds that had so badly split the Democratic Party in the previous four years. There was nothing new or startling in his legislative programs. Harmony was the hallmark of his legislative sessions. No significant conflicts developed in the regular sessions, although the leadership maintained tight control of the General Assembly to insure that acrimony did not develop.[11] In political terms, the Harrison administration was significant for one positive program—industrial development—and merely for holding office while events swept by—events over which the state government had no control, but which produced tremendous impact on Virginia politics. Industrial development had its own political repercussions in the economic stakes it created, the economic impact it had, the levels of public service it required, and the popu-

[11] Harrison's election and administration are discussed in Wilkinson, *Byrd and the Changing Face of Virginia Politics*, 238–47.

lation movement and growth it encouraged. What political effects economic growth and development fostered, the external events unleashed.

First, there was the impact of reapportionment.[12] Following the *Baker v. Carr* decision of the United States Supreme Court in 1962, a suit challenging the apportionment of the Virginia General Assembly was filed in the federal district court in Alexandria. The General Assembly, in accordance with state constitutional provisions, had enacted redistricting legislation in its 1962 session. This measure transferred some legislative seats from rural to urban areas of the state, but not as many as a strict population standard would have required. It is important to note that apportionment standards for both houses of Virginia's legislature seemed implicitly if not explicitly to call for population as the basis for representation. Indeed, with only minor exceptions, population seemed to have been the principal standard used for apportioning both houses in the regular legislative redistrictings that occurred in the twentieth century and even earlier. After the 1950 census, however, the General Assembly broke with past reliance on a population standard and failed to award the growing areas of the state the representation to which their populations seemed to entitle them. A similar pattern was evident in the 1962 redistricting.

The path of the Virginia reapportionment litigation was long and complex, and it is sufficient here to note that it did culminate in another redistricting. The federal district court found that the 1962 redistricting acts violated the Fourteenth Amendment; this decision was ultimately upheld by the United States Supreme Court in *Davis v. Mann,* one of the reapportionment rulings handed down with *Reynolds v. Sims* in June, 1964. These decisions required the convening of a special session of the General Assembly in the fall of 1964 to redistrict both legislative chambers. Another suit chal-

---

12 Reapportionment in Virginia is discussed in Ralph Eisenberg, "Legislative Reapportionment and Congressional Redistricting in Virginia," *Washington and Lee Law Review,* XXIII (1966), 295; and "Reapportionment: Journey Through a Judicial Thicket," in *Cases in American National Government and Politics,* ed. Rocco J. Tresolini and Richard T. Frost (New York: Prentice-Hall, 1966), 182–94.

lenging the congressional districts was initiated in state courts and a 1964 decision of the Virginia Supreme Court of Appeals, *Wilkens v. Davis,* invalidated the congressional districts, which had not been rearranged at all after the 1960 census. Both decisions and the redistricting of the legislative and congressional districts had profound effects upon the state's political system.

Yet Virginia had not been among the more noted examples of malapportionment in the nation. The 1964 redistricting of the General Assembly did not transfer a large number of seats from rural to urban areas. The reapportionment did, however, alter a considerable number of districts for both legislative houses. Most importantly, it made clear that future redistricting would have to accommodate the state's urban growth, and in that regard, it signaled the end of the rural base of the organization.

The first session of the redistricted General Assembly was held in 1966. It was a session in which Virginia's urban localities (cities and urban counties) controlled more than half of the 100 seats in the House of Delegates and almost half of the 40 seats in the Senate. While absolute distinctions between organization and nonorganization legislators cannot be drawn along urban-rural lines, urban legislators were not characteristically strong organization supporters. Although legislators from southside cities were among the organization's leaders, and some legislators from other cities and urban counties had long been identified with the organization, issues arose that affected metropolitan areas on which urban organization support could not be considered reliable. The new lineup of legislators on an urban-rural scale demonstrated that the organization could no longer count on its rural base alone to dominate all legislative policy-making.

The organization did not lose its control of leadership in the legislature after redistricting. The position of majority leader and the committee chairmanships remained firmly in organization hands. But the significance and the impact of these positions was altered by the unreliability of possible action by the full membership of each chamber. The legislative leaders now had to take account of the support they could muster on the floor before making

committee recommendations. The programs that emerged from
the 1966 and 1968 sessions suggested the leadership's awareness of
a new legislative universe.[13]

Another pair of significant external events occurring during the
Harrison administration brought about the demise of the poll tax
as a prerequisite to voting in first federal and then state elections.
The end of the poll tax as a factor conditioning the size and character of the electorate had an immediate effect upon Virginia politics in both election outcomes and in perceptions of the implications of a larger electorate, implications which all politicians in the
state seemed to grasp. The Twenty-fourth Amendment to the
United States Constitution took effect in January, 1964, and thus
poll tax payment was not required in the 1964 voting for President
and in federal elections thereafter. An indication of the significance
of the poll tax to organization strategists was the call of a special
legislative session in the fall of 1963 to enact legislation designed to
circumvent the prohibition against using the poll tax for election
objectives. To replace it, the General Assembly required that a
"certificate of residence" be filed by prospective voters at least six
months before each federal election in order to establish proof of
continuing residence in the state. The certificate-of-residence legislation was challenged in a federal district court and declared unconstitutional in May, 1964. The state's appeal to the United States
Supreme Court for a stay of that decision was rejected. In the 1964
election, more than one million Virginians cast votes, an increase
greater than 35 percent over 1960. The proportion of adults who
went to the polls jumped to 41.2 percent, compared to the 33.3
percent who had voted in 1960.[14] This one-time increase in voting,
together with the decline in turnout from 1900 to 1904, suggests the
relationship of the poll tax to voter turnout. The final blow to the

[13] The impact of reapportionment upon legislative behavior is discussed in Ralph
Eisenberg, "Reapportionment and a Legislature: Some Observations of the Virginia
Experience," State Legislatures in American Politics (Quail Roost, N.C.: Duke Univer-
sity American Assembly on State Legislatures, 1968), 7–31; and in Thomas L. Wells,
"A Pattern Emerges," National Civic Review, LVII (1968), 453.

[14] Ralph Eisenberg, "The 1964 Presidential Election in Virginia: A Political Omen?"
UVa News Letter, XLI (April 15, 1965), 29.

poll tax came from another United States Supreme Court decision in 1966, which declared that poll tax payment was unconstitutional as a prerequisite to voting in state elections. The initial impact of removing the relevance of the poll tax from state elections was felt in 1969, when 62.7 percent more votes were cast than in the preceding gubernatorial election.[15]

Virginia elections in 1964 and afterwards were affected by other developments as well. Because voting turnout was low, the state fell under the 1965 Voting Rights Act, which barred the application of literacy tests to voter registration. This act together with the demise of the poll tax enabled Negro political organizations to produce increases in both Negro voter registration and turnout, and thus in the political potency of the black vote. Negroes increasingly voted as a bloc in elections and their support became decisive in most elections from 1964 on.

In 1964, Virginia supported the Democratic presidential candidacy of Lyndon B. Johnson after backing Republican presidential candidates in the preceding three presidential elections. Negro bloc voting for Johnson in 1964 reached well over 90 percent;[16] with an estimated 160,000 Negroes voting, their support clearly was vital to the Democratic victory margin of 76,704 votes. The new importance of black votes in Virginia was dramatized again in 1965 in the gubernatorial election: Democrat Mills E. Godwin, Jr., was elected by a margin of over 57,000 when the Negro bloc vote seemed to be at least 75 percent for the Democrats.[17] In the 1966 Democratic primary elections, again black votes played a decisive role in defeating one organization candidate and threatening another.

The significance, evident in 1964, of the larger electorate, and perhaps particularly of the larger black vote, became more pronounced in later elections. The increase in voting added to the weight of the urban electorate in deciding statewide contests, and

[15] Ralph Eisenberg, "1969 Politics in Virginia: The General Election," *UVa News Letter*, XLVI (May 15, 1970), 33.

[16] Eisenberg, "The 1964 Presidential Election in Virginia," 29.

[17] Ralph Eisenberg, "Gubernatorial Politics in Virginia: The Experience of 1965," *UVa News Letter*, XLV (March 15, 1969), 25.

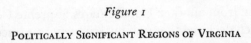

Figure 1

POLITICALLY SIGNIFICANT REGIONS OF VIRGINIA

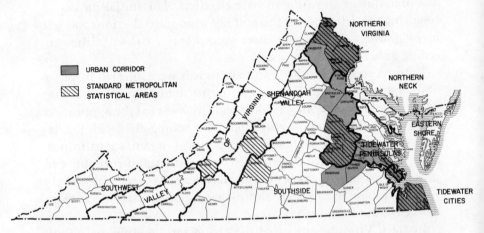

also was important in the election of legislators from urban areas, whose numbers had already increased and would undoubtedly continue to rise. From 1964 on, therefore, the symptoms of political change multiplied in Virginia. They were to be seen in elections, both general and primary and for both federal and state office; in election campaigns; in the programs of the 1966 and 1968 legislative sessions; in the 1969 special session to revise the state constitution; in the behavior of the Godwin administration; and finally in the 1969 events which produced a Republican governor for the first time in this century.

The Changed Setting

To understand recent Virginia political behavior, it is necessary to appreciate the state's urban growth and development. The 1960 census had revealed that more than half of its population was living in areas categorized as urban. The state's population had increased 23.9 percent from 1940 to 1950 and another 19.5 percent from 1950 to 1960. More importantly, most of the growth was concentrated in areas that were already urban. The tentacles of urban

Figure 2

CITIES OF VIRGINIA

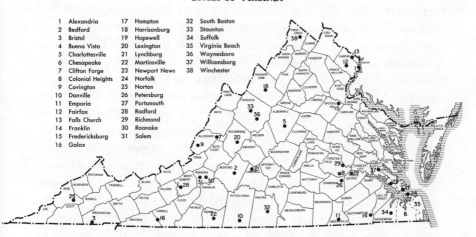

1	Alexandria	17	Hampton
2	Bedford	18	Harrisonburg
3	Bristol	19	Hopewell
4	Buena Vista	20	Lexington
5	Charlottesville	21	Lynchburg
6	Chesapeake	22	Martinsville
7	Clifton Forge	23	Newport News
8	Colonial Heights	24	Norfolk
9	Covington	25	Norton
10	Danville	26	Petersburg
11	Emporia	27	Portsmouth
12	Fairfax	28	Radford
13	Falls Church	29	Richmond
14	Franklin	30	Roanoke
15	Fredericksburg	31	Salem
16	Galax		
32	South Boston		
33	Staunton		
34	Suffolk		
35	Virginia Beach		
36	Waynesboro		
37	Williamsburg		
38	Winchester		

growth spread from the northern Virginia suburbs of Washington, D.C.; from the tidewater cities of Newport News, Hampton, Norfolk, and Portsmouth; and from Richmond. Eventually a corridor of urban growth extended from the D.C. suburbs south and west to Richmond and then south and east to the tidewater cities area. The increase in population in this corridor was far greater than the average increase for the state throughout the period. By 1960, Virginia included six Standard Metropolitan Statistical Areas (all but two of them located within the urban corridor), that contained almost half of the state's population.

Census figures indicate that the state's population growth continued during the 1960's. By 1970, the total population had increased by 17.2 percent from the 1960 total, with the increase concentrated in the urban corridor, while several rural counties in western and southside Virginia and the tidewater peninsulas actually lost population. The 1970 figures also show that 2,721,031 persons, or 58.5 percent of the state's population, now live in the six metropolitan areas. There seems little indication that these trends will be modified in the future.

Of course, with the urbanization phenomenon came a sharp

change in the pattern of economic development. Although the
idea died hard, Virginia had long since ceased to be an agricultural state. By 1960, less than one-tenth of total employment was
in agriculture, whereas 20 percent of the labor force was employed
in manufacturing in plants scattered across the state. The federal
government was another very large employer in Virginia, while
tourism, mining, and service industries and occupations became
more and more significant components of the economy. The industrial development program stimulated by Governor Harrison contributed additional increments to Virginia's technological society.
With these economic changes came increases in per capita income
and movements of needed labor forces to urban centers, where economic opportunities were to be found.[18] The movement of people
from rural to urban Virginia also marked this period. Two characteristics of this movement must be noted. First, the young were
moving from rural to urban areas, and second, Negroes moved to
the cities, particularly the larger ones, Richmond, Norfolk, Portsmouth, and Hampton.

With the concentration of Virginia's people in urban areas, never
bastions of support for the organization, the state's politics inevitably changed. Urban inhabitants seemed to favor higher levels of
public services, an attitude in sharp contrast to the organization's
penchant for a status quo level of services. Education particularly
interested urban dwellers. In the past, the rural-based organization
had been able to resist pressures for substantial betterment of educational opportunities, although from time to time, it appeased the
cities with small additional expenditures. The prospect of larger
urban populations whose local problems and concerns the organization seemed steadfastly to ignore or to make unbearable (in the
case of its use of a policy of massive resistance) could only render

18 Jean Gottman, *Virginia in Our Century* (new printing; Charlottesville: University
Press of Virginia, 1969), especially the Supplementary Chapter, 563–624; Wilkinson,
Byrd and the Changing Face of Virginia Politics, 157–69; the annual *Estimates of the
Population of Virginia Counties and Cities* (Charlottesville: Bureau of Population and
Economic Research, University of Virginia); and *Statistical Abstract of Virginia*
(Charlottesville: Thomas Jefferson Center for Political Economy, University of Vir-
ginia, 1966).

future urban organization support a risky proposition. The increasing concentration of black populations in cities also eased the task of political organization for black leaders, in an environment where retaliation for political activity could not be carried out as easily as in rural communities. In addition, the youthful move to the cities and suburbs concentrated a population not obligated to the organization, and, in the occupations of the contemporary business world, unimpressed with the traditions and loyalties of Virginia politics.

Symptoms of Political Change

The first sign that politics in Virginia was about to be altered appeared in 1964. At the Democratic state convention in the summer, the delegates, disregarding Governor Harrison and the known views of Senator Byrd himself, endorsed Lyndon B. Johnson for re-election to the presidency. The move was startling since Senator Byrd was seldom challenged in such fashion. Beginning in 1952, the senior senator had adopted what he later styled a "golden silence" approach to presidential politics in subsequent elections. Golden silence seemed to be his approach again in 1964. But the convention endorsement of Johnson, spearheaded by the usual antiorganization groups, was made possible by the support of moderates within the organization, predominantly from urban areas. Many of these delegates reflected increasing concern with the success of Republican campaigns for local offices, which they attributed to the legitimization growing out of Republican triumphs since 1952 in presidential elections under the golden silence doctrine. The convention action was clearly a sign of restlessness within the organization.[19]

In the 1964 presidential election, the Democratic campaign in the state was directed by the veteran organization leader Sidney Kellam of Virginia Beach. Kellam, a political professional, forged an effective coalition of the state's Democrats to win Virginia for the party. The 1964 coalition embraced antiorganization liberals,

[19] See Wilkinson, *Byrd and the Changing Face of Virginia Politics*, 251–55, for a discussion of the convention.

moderates, and conservatives, and included the Negro vote. The campaign demonstrated that such a coalition could win an election without relying upon the earlier rural base of organization victories. Southside Virginia, the most conservative area of the state and the core of organization support, voted for Barry Goldwater, but urban Virginia contributed the large pluralities necessary to win the state's twelve electoral votes for Johnson.[20]

The lessons of 1964, apparently well absorbed by the state's Democrats, were applied to win the governorship in 1965. Surprisingly, there was no Democratic primary election that year. The Democratic nomination was secured by Lieutenant Governor Mills E. Godwin, Jr., after he earlier had obtained endorsements from all wings of the party. His support from the liberals was attributable to assurances he reportedly had given to advance education in his administration. Disaffected conservatives bolted the Democratic Party to form the Virginia Conservative Party, which fielded a full slate for statewide office. The Republican candidate was Linwood Holton of Roanoke, a young and attractive candidate who campaigned with a moderate platform. Godwin won the election with less than a majority of the popular vote. His plurality was based upon urban areas, so that the Conservative Party's support in southside Virginia could not deny him victory. Despite his earlier support for and leadership in the cause of massive resistance, Godwin received Negro votes in large numbers. Democratic coalition politics had won again, relying on urban votes and demonstrating that victories in the state could and would be constructed upon an urban rather than a rural base.[21]

The Godwin administration was hailed almost universally as the most progressive in Virginia since Governor Byrd's in the 1920's. The regular sessions of the legislature during the Godwin years, in 1966 and 1968, and the special session in 1969, were remarkable for the shifts from traditional state policies that they produced. Godwin as governor fulfilled expectations concerning his commitment

20 Eisenberg, "The 1964 Presidential Election in Virginia," 29.
21 Eisenberg, "Gubernatorial Politics in Virginia: The Experience of 1965," 25; Wilkinson, *Byrd and the Changing Face of Virginia Politics*, 263–84.

Table 3
1965 ELECTION FOR VIRGINIA GOVERNOR

Candidate	Party	Number of Votes	Percentage
Mills E. Godwin, Jr.	Democratic	269,526	47.9
Linwood Holton	Republican	212,207	37.7
William J. Story, Jr.	Conservative	75,307	13.4
George Lincoln Rockwell		5,730	1.0
Scattered Votes		19	–
TOTALS		562,789	100.0

Source: Secretary of State Board of Elections, Official Records.

to education at all levels. The regular sessions provided significant increases in state funding of aid to elementary and secondary education and of operating costs and capital outlays for higher education. To finance the educational programs, Godwin sought and obtained in 1966 a state sales tax, which Governor Almond had failed to win eight years earlier. Permissive legislation for localities to impose a 1 percent sales tax was also enacted.[22]

Concern with education reached a high point in the 1968 legislative session, when Governor Godwin called for authorization of a bond issue to the limit of the state constitution to finance capital outlays for mental hospitals and institutions of higher education. The subsequent referendum on the bond issue of $81 million was approved in November, 1968. With its approval, the most prominent symbol of the organization fell. Pay-as-you-go had been an article of faith among organization stalwarts since Senator Byrd first enunciated the principle in the 1920's. The collapse of pay-as-you-go, more than any other event, symbolized the fall of the old organization with its traditional set of values.

These legislative sessions also laid to rest the symbols of the massive resistance period which the organization had created after 1954. The Pupil Placement Board, the tuition grant program, and the Commission on Constitutional Government (an agency created to

22 Wells, "A Pattern Emerges"; Eisenberg, "Reapportionment and a Legislature."

foster states' rights in Virginia and nationally) all died during the Godwin administration. Simultaneously, the state's commitment to a community college system, vocational education, its system of universities and colleges, and elementary and secondary education grew substantially. The urban nature of Virginia was recognized in the creation in 1966 of the Metropolitan Areas Study Commission to consider the problems that urban growth had created, and in the adoption in 1968 of most of that group's recommendations, with the governor's endorsement. The commission's work led to legislation that organized the state into regional planning districts, authorized the creation of regional districts in metropolitan areas to provide public services, strengthened the state agency responsible for planning and community affairs, and created the Urban Assistance Incentive Fund to help finance new kinds of urban governmental projects.

The spirit of change driving the state and the Godwin administration led to the creation of the Constitutional Revision Study Commission in 1968, and a special legislative session in 1969 to propose extensive constitutional revisions that had been recommended by the commission. The stringent debt limit in the existing constitution was perhaps the most important motive behind the movement for constitutional revision; and the revisions proposed a significant broadening of the state's capacity to acquire debt to finance capital projects. The revision also proposed to erase many of the 1902 constitution's anachronistic features, long since rendered inoperable by a succession of decisions of the United States Supreme Court, particularly in the area of civil rights. Another symptom of the change rampant during Godwin's administration was the adoption in 1968 of local-option liquor by the drink. The legislation was strongly urged by urban areas and its adoption dramatized the mood of change.

Governor Godwin's administration was significant as a bridge from Virginia past to Virginia future. Godwin, as an organization product and recognized leader, was able to sell his program to the continuing organization leadership of the legislature. Perceiving the changing nature of the state, particularly in political terms, the administration committed itself to programs responsive to the demands of urban Virginia and labored to have these programs adopted. The Godwin administration moved state government forward in a host of public service areas and presided over the death of many antiquated policies and postures.

Other events during Godwin's term made the changing political mood of the state obvious. The 1966 elections for the United States Senate and congressional seats produced the first defeats for the organization as the weight of the larger electorate began to assert itself. But another important event in that period both symbolically and politically triggered electoral changes that were to upset the long stability of Virginia politics. Shortly after Godwin's election in 1965, Senator Harry F. Byrd announced his resignation. To fill the vacancy until the next election, Governor Albertis S. Harrison appointed the senator's son, State Senator Harry F. Byrd, Jr. Senator Byrd, Jr., did not command the widespread personal support and devotion organization followers accorded his father. The elder Byrd's resignation and his subsequent serious illness removed from the political forum the figure most capable of diverting or arresting the movement of the Godwin administration and the succession of blows to the organization's (and Byrd's) most cherished values.

Both Senate seats were at stake in the 1966 election. In addition to Senator Byrd, Jr., who had to face election to fill the unexpired portion of his father's term, Senator A. Willis Robertson sought another term. Opposition to both candidacies developed in the Democratic primary election. Senator Byrd was opposed by former State Senator Armistead L. Boothe while Senator Robertson was opposed by State Senator William B. Spong, Jr., of Portsmouth. The candidates all ran separate campaigns. Senator Robertson's age (seventynine) was a factor in the campaign and his quest for another term produced further division within the organization. His effort to win reelection added to the restiveness of younger members of the organization already frustrated by their inability to advance their political careers because older organization leaders had refused to step aside. Presumably, efforts had been made within the organization to convince Senator Robertson not to run, but they were not successful. Senator Spong had been a Young Turk in the 1950's in the General Assembly and had also worked as chairman of a state commission to resolve moderately some of the school desegregation problems. His campaign was backed by many younger men long active in the organization.

Senator Boothe also had been a Young Turk in his early political career. His unsuccessful attempt to win the lieutenant governorship in 1961 had given him wide state exposure, and even his opponents respected his competence. Senator Byrd's appointment to the vacancy created by his father raised questions, which his opposition exploited, of a political dynasty. The younger Byrd never attracted the veneration accorded his father in the state's politics. The death of Senator Harry F. Byrd, Sr., about a month before the date of the primary election brought the campaigning to an early end.

The results of the primary election were close. Senator Robertson was beaten by only 611 votes and Senator Byrd defeated Boothe by a little more than 8,000 votes. Despite Senator Byrd's victory and the narrow margin by which Spong defeated Robertson, the 1966 primary election constituted a substantial defeat for the organization. Byrd's win did not demonstrate the wide support to which the organization had grown accustomed in primary elections. The primary demonstrated the vulnerability of the organization, even with its most illustrious name. More importantly, Spong's election and the strong showing that Boothe made in defeat were constructed upon the substantial urban support that both enjoyed. In both cases, heavy bloc voting by Negroes aided the antiorganization candidates. Indeed, black votes were essential to Spong's victory.[23]

The setbacks of 1966 for the organization were not confined to the Senate campaigns. In the Eighth District, veteran Congressman Howard W. Smith, famed nationally as chairman of the Rules Committee of the House of Representatives, was defeated in the primary. Smith was successfully challenged by George C. Rawl-

---

23 Ralph Eisenberg, "1966 Politics in Virginia: The Democratic Senatorial Primary," *UVa News Letter*, XLIII (January 15, 1967), 17; Wilkinson, *Byrd and the Changing Face of Virginia Politics*, 305–42.

Table 4
DEMOCRATIC PARTY PRIMARY
ELECTION RESULTS,
UNITED STATES SENATOR FROM VIRGINIA, 1966

Four-Year Term	Number of Votes	Percentage
Harry F. Byrd, Jr.*	221,221	50.9
Armistead L. Boothe	212,996	49.1
TOTALS	434,217	100.0
Six-Year Term		
William B. Spong, Jr.	216,885	50.1
A. Willis Robertson	216,274	49.9
TOTALS	433,159	100.0

Source: Secretary of State Board of Elections, Official Records.
* Incumbent

ings, Jr., a member of the House of Delegates from Fredericksburg. Rawlings was a political ally of State Senator Henry E. Howell, Jr., of Norfolk, the most liberal Democrat on Virginia's political spectrum. Rawlings waged a hard, aggressive, and personal campaign against Smith, forcing the congressman to take to the hustings in a somewhat unaccustomed fashion. The Rawlings organization was effective in registering new voters and delivering them to the polls; this tactic was especially significant with black voters in rural counties. Smith lost by only 645 votes. Rawlings' victory left antagonism among both organization leaders and Smith's rank-and-file supporters in the district. They were particularly resentful of the personal nature of some of Rawlings' attacks on Congressman Smith and considered Rawlings far too liberal to support in November. In the general election, many of the conservative Democrats supported the Republican candidate, William L. Scott, of Fairfax County. Scott deemphasized his Republican label in campaigning and effectively sought the support of Smith conservatives. The split in the normally Democratic vote was enough to elect Scott.[24]

[24] Wilkinson, *Byrd and the Changing Face of Virginia Politics*, 324–25; Ralph Eisenberg, "1966 Politics in Virginia: The Elections for U. S. Representatives," *UVa News Letter*, XLIII (June 15, 1967), 37.

Table 5

RESULTS OF 1966 ELECTIONS,
EIGHTH CONGRESSIONAL DISTRICT, VIRGINIA

Democratic Party Primary Election

Candidate	Number of Votes	Percentage
Howard W. Smith *	26,470	49.4
George C. Rawlings, Jr.	27,115	50.6
TOTALS	53,585	100.0

General Election

Candidate	Party	Number of Votes	Percentage
George C. Rawlings, Jr.	Democratic	37,929	42.8
William L. Scott	Republican	50,782	57.2
Write-ins		21	—
TOTALS		88,732	100.0

Source: Secretary of State Board of Elections, Official Records.
* Incumbent

It must be stressed that the outcomes of both the primary and the general election in the Eighth District were attributable to the changes made in its configuration when congressional districts were redrawn in 1965. Smith's district had changed so that about one-quarter of the population of the district was now in suburban Fairfax County, one of the fastest-growing areas of the state and one least affected by traditional organizational loyalties and fealties to the conservatism represented by Howard Smith. Smith's age, too, was a factor in the election, in which he was most vulnerable in Fairfax County.

The Republican ability to exploit Smith's defeat to win election in the Eighth District could not be duplicated in the Senate contests. Nominating by convention, and calculating that the winner of the Spong-Robertson contest was the most vulnerable, the Republicans nominated James P. Ould, Jr., to run against Spong and Lawrence M. Traylor to run against Byrd. Of the two, Ould was the better known and more effective campaigner. Traylor did not constitute a serious challenge to Senator Byrd. In the November elections, Spong and Byrd won easily, both running very well in urban areas. Significantly, Spong ran well ahead of Byrd despite Spong's more serious opposition. The Democrats conducted a unified campaign, however, which enabled Byrd to be pulled along by Spong in urban areas. In black precincts, Spong won over 90 percent of the votes while Byrd, who received no endorsement from black political organizations, won only 13.5 percent. Byrd's Republican opponent received almost 30,000 more votes than his senatorial running mate.[25]

Table 6

RESULTS OF 1966 GENERAL ELECTION IN VIRGINIA

United States Senate, Six-Year Term

Candidate	Party	Number of Votes	Percentage
William B. Spong, Jr.	Democratic	429,855	58.6
James P. Ould, Jr.	Republican	245,681	33.5
F. Lee Hawthorne	Conservative	58,251	7.9
TOTALS		733,787	100.0

United States Senate, Four-Year Unexpired Term

Candidate	Party	Number of Votes	Percentage
Harry F. Byrd, Jr.*	Democratic	389,028	53.3
Lawrence M. Traylor	Republican	272,804	37.4
John W. Carter	Conservative	57,692	7.9
J. B. Brayman	Independent	10,180	1.4
TOTALS		729,704	100.0

Source: Secretary of State Board of Elections, Official Records.
* Incumbent

Although the 1966 election was not especially successful for Republicans in the statewide contests, they won two more congressional seats. In addition to Scott's victory in the Eighth District, the Republican candidate in the Ninth District, in southwestern Vir-

[25] Ralph Eisenberg, "1966 Politics in Virginia: The Elections for U. S. Senators," *UVa News Letter*, XLIII (May 15, 1967), 33.

ginia, former Congressman William C. Wampler, ousted incumbent Democratic Congressman W. Pat Jennings. A factor in that election apparently, in addition to some local conditions, was the increased turnout that observers credited to removal of the poll tax. With these victories, the Republicans now possessed four of Virginia's ten congressional seats.

The Spong campaign gave birth to a moderate wing of the Democratic Party which had evolved about his candidacy. The moderates included younger men, some from the organization, others who had worked with the organization on certain issues, and still others who were antiorganization but unwilling to align themselves with the party's liberal wing. The liberal faction of the Democratic Party now was led by State Senator Henry E. Howell, Jr. Howell had acquired a wide reputation through his efforts in litigation to invalidate the existing legislative and congressional districts. He had emerged as a spokesman for the liberal Democrats and had forged an effective political organization in Norfolk, the state's largest city. Howell developed close ties with the black community and with labor union organizations in tidewater Virginia and throughout the state. The other third of the Democratic Party now consisted of the organization. With the death of Senator Byrd, Sr., and the narrow win of Senator Byrd, Jr., the principal leader of the organization appeared to be Governor Godwin. But Godwin's position obviously was not comparable to that which the senior Byrd had enjoyed. Godwin's efforts seemed directed to updating the organization to build support in urban Virginia for the future.

The three factions of the Democratic Party came into direct conflict at the 1968 state convention, which was to select delegates to the Democratic National Convention. But despite the national political tempest in 1968 over the selection of the party's candidate for President, and thus in selecting delegates to the national convention, the Virginia State Democratic Convention was preoccupied with its own intraparty conflict. The convention delegates were more concerned with who controlled key offices in the state party than with who went to the national convention. As for possible presidential candidates, the Virginia convention favored Vice President Hubert H. Humphrey overwhelmingly. Although the degree of enthusiasm varied, all factions preferred Humphrey.

The battles at the convention revolved around the election of the state chairman and the national committeeman, with moderates and liberals contesting the organization's continued control of these offices. State Chairman Watkins M. Abbitt, incumbent congressman from the southside Fourth District, sought reelection with the strong backing of Governor Godwin. Godwin exerted considerable pressure on behalf of Abbitt to defeat the challenge of a Howell ally for the position. But the organization won by a margin of only about 30 votes out of more than 1,300. The challenge of moderate State Senator William B. Hopkins for the national committee slot, however, was successful. The organization was spared embarrassment when its candidate withdrew before the balloting began. Hopkins' election demonstrated that when the moderates and liberals stood together, they could defeat the organization. Although the organization won the key contest, the victory seemed hollow. It had required considerable effort by the governor to defeat by a small margin a liberal candidate who lacked the broad base of support that Hopkins enjoyed. The convention fight exposed the deep divisions among the three factions of the Democratic Party and exacerbated them. An obvious factor affecting behavior at the convention was the jockeying among these groups for the 1969 gubernatorial election. Personal conflicts among leaders of the factions surfaced at the convention and their exposure made protracted conflict more evident. Governor Godwin alienated the liberals especially. By this time, he was already increasingly subjected to criticism by black leaders who believed that he should be appointing more blacks to positions of responsibility in state government. Godwin had appointed Negroes to commissions of an advisory, administrative, and study nature but in numbers black leaders considered only token.

The 1968 election dealt Virginia Democrats further defeats. Richard M. Nixon carried the state for the Republicans by a plurality of almost 150,000 votes, as Humphrey carried only 32.5 per-

cent of the popular vote.[26] The Republicans reelected all of their
incumbent congressmen by substantial margins and added a fifth
from the Second District. Once again, the Republican gain in the
Second District was due to the repercussions of intra-Democratic
strife in the primary election, which determined the nominee to
succeed incumbent Congressman Porter Hardy, who declined to
seek reelection. The liberals and moderates met head-on in the primary and the liberals won after an embittered campaign. Again
Democratic defections took place in November to elect Republican
William Whitehurst. Whitehurst's victory was important because
the Second District was Virginia's most urban, and most Democratic, district.

The presidential voting in 1968 was significant as a barometer
of political change in Virginia. The candidacy of George Wallace
under the banner of the American Independent Party won 23.6
percent of the popular vote. This percentage, however, was less
than in any other state of the old Confederacy except Texas, and
it demonstrated how far removed Virginia had become from other
southern states, where Wallace attracted more followers. Each major
party outpolled Wallace, as Virginia's voting habits reflected national voting patterns more than southern patterns. From the Democratic standpoint, however, the party had never done so poorly in
an election. More than 1,300,000 votes were cast in 1968, a record
for the state; but of the total, the Democratic share was only a little
over 442,000.

The 1969 Climax

The climax to the chronology of Virginia's political evolution occurred in 1969. The setting was the election year for the offices of
governor, lieutenant governor, and attorney general. The stages
were the Democratic Party's primary election to select its nominees
and the November general election to fill the offices. In the primary,
each faction of the Democratic Party put forth its candidate for

26 Ralph Eisenberg, "The 1968 Election in Virginia: Voting Patterns and Party Competition," *UVa News Letter*, XLV (June 15, 1969), 37.

governor. The resulting campaign and its aftermath left deep scars upon the party that contributed to the election of a Republican governor. By winning the governorship, the Republicans took control of the strong executive branch of state government, and they acquired major party status in state elections to add to their string of successes in presidential elections. The Republican victory effectively ended one-party politics in Virginia.

The 1969 election campaign and its outcome are best remembered for the chaotic developments which followed one upon the other. The internal Democratic conflict seemingly tore the party apart, producing defections in the general election by both conservative and liberal voters. In the primary, all three factions collided only in the race for governor. But only the organization presented candidates for all of the offices at stake. The organization's gubernatorial candidate was the incumbent lieutenant governor, Fred G. Pollard, who previously had served as a delegate and state senator from Richmond. The moderate candidate was William C. Battle of Charlottesville, whose father had been the organization's successful candidate for governor twenty years earlier against the challenge of Francis Pickens Miller. William Battle had held no previous elective office, but he had been the Virginia campaign manager for Kennedy in 1960 and chairman of Spong's successful primary campaign in 1966. In the interim, Battle had served the Kennedy administration as ambassador to Australia. The liberal candidate was State Senator Henry E. Howell, Jr. Howell had gradually expanded his following across Virginia, after his initial state exposure in reapportionment litigation, by challenging public utilities and insurance companies in the courts and before the state's regulatory agency. His support had continued to grow among labor and black voter groups.

The primary campaign was vigorously fought. Howell stood as the liberal champion of the people. He ran a "people's campaign" with a slogan pledging to "keep the big boys honest." His antiestablishment campaign made effective use of billboards and television, which portrayed him as defender of the "little man." The Howell campaign admittedly was a populist one that sought to win the nomination on a base of blacks, labor, white small farmers, and blue-collar workers. Battle steered a middle course, arguing for modernization of the state and its policies and replacement of the old leadership. Pollard, as the organization's candidate, did not run a conservative campaign. He sought to exploit his own urban background to demonstrate his awareness of contemporary state problems. But Pollard could not escape the organization label and thus was forced to run against the swell of antiorganization sentiment in the party.

Table 7

RESULTS OF 1969 DEMOCRATIC PARTY
PRIMARY ELECTION FOR VIRGINIA GOVERNOR

July 15, 1969, Election

Candidate	Number of Votes	Percentage
William C. Battle	158,956	38.9
Henry E. Howell, Jr.	154,617	37.8
Fred G. Pollard	95,057	23.3
TOTALS	408,630	100.0

August 19, 1969, Election

Candidate	Number of Votes	Percentage
William C. Battle	226,108	52.1
Henry E. Howell, Jr.	207,505	47.9
TOTALS	433,613	100.0

Source: Secretary of State Board of Elections, Official Records.

The organization's candidate for lieutenant governor was W. Carrington Thompson, an incumbent delegate from Pittsylvania County. His principal opponent was J. Sargeant Reynolds, state senator from Richmond and member of the Reynolds Metals Company family. Reynolds was a formidable candidate. He was young and wealthy, had great personal appeal, and drew strong support among black voters in Richmond. The other two candidates for the office were never serious contenders. For attorney general, the organization ran incumbent Delegate Guy O. Farley, Jr., of Fairfax County.

His principal challenger was Andrew P. Miller of Abingdon, the son of Francis Pickens Miller. Miller had long been active in politics and had first received wide notice as president of the state's Young Democrats. He was known as a liberal but was not associated with the Howell faction. The two other contenders for attorney general did not materialize as serious possibilities for nomination.

Nomination under Virginia law required a majority of the popular vote in the primary. In the July 15 primary this requirement was fulfilled for only one office. No organization candidate finished first in the contest for any office. More significantly, two of the three organization candidates were eliminated. Pollard ran third among the gubernatorial candidates, receiving only 23.3 percent of the popular vote. Battle led the balloting with 38.9 percent to Howell's 37.8 percent, for a plurality of less than 5,000 votes. The Democratic nomination for lieutenant governor was settled in the July primary, as Reynolds gathered almost 64 percent of the popular vote. Thompson finished second but received only 23.7 percent. For attorney general, Miller ran first with 41.2 percent of the vote; Farley was second with 35 percent. The remaining two candidates almost evenly divided the remaining votes.

The runoff primary was held on August 19. Miller polled over 63 percent of the vote to trounce soundly the last remaining organization candidate in the election for attorney general. Battle won the nomination for governor, receiving 52.1 percent of the vote, for a majority of less than 19,000 over the liberal Howell. In the runoff campaign for the governorship, a long-time precedent was upset as incumbent Governor Godwin intervened in the primary to endorse Battle's candidacy, incurring the enduring wrath of the Howell forces.

The significance of the 1969 primary lay in the rout of the organization's candidates. Organization candidates received less than one-fourth of the votes cast in July; in the contest for attorney general, the more than 35 percent of the vote won by the organization's candidate seemed attributable to the voters in his home area in populous Fairfax County. The primary elections demonstrated that the moderate and liberal factions of the Democratic Party together could produce about two-thirds of the vote. The scope of the victories by Miller and Reynolds, who were supported by both anti-organization factions, emphasized this fact. Obviously the organization was no longer in control of the Democratic Party.

More important to the eventual outcome of the general election for governor and to the future of the Democratic Party was the turnout in the primaries. More people voted in August than in July; but only 434,000 votes were cast in August. That total was smaller than the number of votes cast in the 1966 Senate primary, when there had been fewer registered voters and a less frantic and heated campaign. Following the record turnout of more than 1,300,000 voters in 1968, the turnout was small and suggested that many voters were sitting out the primary election in anticipation of making their choice in the general election.[27]

Virginia Republicans nominated their candidates for state offices in convention. Linwood Holton was selected to run for governor again. Holton had no serious competition for the nomination because as the party's candidate four years earlier he was known throughout the state and seemed to be the candidate most likely to be able to win the governorship. This consideration overcame some delegates' doubts about his moderate rather than conservative posture. As Holton's running mates, the Republicans nominated H. D. "Buz" Dawbarn, a state senator from Staunton and a successful businessman, for lieutenant governor; and Richard D. Obenshain of Richmond, a former candidate for Congress, for attorney general. Obenshain on the Republican ticket was the conservative to balance Holton's moderate image, while Dawbarn stood somewhere between the other two candidates.

To add to the confusion of the election, the conservatives fought over whether to unite in presenting candidates. Even they reached no accommodation. Thus, the Virginia Conservative Party ran candidates for all three offices, while the American Independent Party contested the top two offices. The votes for both parties in Novem-

[27] Ralph Eisenberg, "1969 Politics in Virginia: The Democratic Party Primary," *UVa News Letter*, XLVI (February 15, 1970), 21.

ber were negligible and reinforced the conclusion that the conservative parties would have no lasting effects upon state politics.

Battle's Democratic campaign was fatally affected by the wounds produced in the primaries. His liberal support was lukewarm at best and many liberals argued for his defeat to "nail the coffin shut" on the defeat of the organization. Labor unions and black political groups endorsed Holton while they simultaneously endorsed the Democratic candidacies of Reynolds and Miller. Conservatives long associated with the Byrd organization, including many who had contributed heavily to it in the past, now announced themselves to be Republicans and pledged their support to the Republican ticket. Many of the new Republicans made considerable financial contributions to the party's campaign.

The Republican campaign was marked by good organization throughout the state and skillful use of virtually all media. Holton pushed the theme "time for a change" very hard and concentrated upon securing support in urban areas. In contrast, Battle's campaign seemed lackluster and almost lethargic. The Battle forces may have been fatigued from their efforts in the two primary elections. The high cost of the primaries for all factions of the Democratic Party created real financing problems in the fall.

In November the voters elected the Republican candidate Holton governor and Democrats Reynolds and Miller lieutenant governor and attorney general respectively. The split-ticket voting that produced this outcome was especially apparent in urban areas. Holton eliminated normal Democratic majorities in the major cities and ran extremely well, even for a Republican, in suburban areas. Reynolds and Miller both retained heavy Democratic majorities in cities and drew good support in suburbs. Holton's margins in the cities were attributable to his support among black and labor union voters. These same groups backed Reynolds and Miller with even more substantial majorities than those by which Holton won. In the state's metropolitan areas alone, Holton received a majority of over 58,900 votes, a large portion of his final statewide plurality of 65,000 votes. Holton's election must be traced to his urban success,

Table 8
1969 ELECTION FOR VIRGINIA GOVERNOR

Candidate	Party	Number of Votes	Percentage
Linwood Holton	Republican	480,869	52.5
William C. Battle	Democratic	415,695	45.4
Beverly B. McDowell	Conservative	10,596	1.2
William A. Pennington	American Independent	7,382	.8
George R. Walker	Independent	1,182	.1
Others		40	—
TOTALS		915,764	100.0

Source: Secretary of State Board of Elections, Official Records.

part of which at the very least resulted from defections of normally Democratic liberal voters.[28]

A vital factor in the outcome of this election was the size of the turnout. A record number of votes for state elections was cast in 1969. More than 915,000 votes were recorded in the gubernatorial contest, over 62 percent higher than in 1965 and over 24 percent higher than in 1966. The 1969 total reached 67.3 percent of the record 1968 turnout.[29] The impact of the record totals was felt in urban areas; and importantly for the future, in metropolitan areas most of the votes were suburban. The Republican performances in Virginia's suburbs had steadily improved over the years. The suburban vote had been an important ingredient in President Nixon's triumph in Virginia in 1968, and it was very adeptly exploited by Virginia Republicans in 1969. Adding to the impact of their success statewide, the Republicans also nearly doubled their previous representation in the House of Delegates.

The Components of Change

It is impossible to provide a simple answer to the question of why Virginia politics changed so rapidly over the twenty-year period.

[28] Ralph Eisenberg, "1969 Politics in Virginia: The General Election," *UVa News Letter*, XLVI (May 15, 1970), 33.
[29] *Ibid.*

The web of personalities, economic developments, new social attitudes, constitutional evolution and amendment, legislative policies, and psychological sets interwoven across the state was so complex that a single strand cannot be isolated to explain the dimensions of political change. Although even the purely political factors cannot be neatly partitioned into cause-effect channels, enough political data exist to analyze most of the emerging conditions that made a new Virginia politics inevitable. Tracing the political developments chronologically has highlighted the key elements affecting the political environment. The urbanization process, the irrelevance of the poll tax, the Voting Rights Act, and legislative and congressional redistricting all directly affected state voting patterns. Changing voting patterns were vital to the pace and thrust of political developments.

The most startling and most important characteristic of voting in Virginia over the past twenty years was the tremendous increase in the size of the electorate. Using presidential elections as a barometer of the potential effective electorate in the state (because presidential turnouts are uniformly larger than others), we find in 1968 more than three times as many votes cast as in 1948, more than twice as many as in 1952, and nearly twice as many as in 1956. Following the poll tax amendment, the number of votes cast for President in 1964 was more than 35 percent greater than in 1960; the increase in 1968 over 1964 exceeded another 30 percent. These proportionate increases reflect presidential voting totals from just over 419,000 in 1948 to more than 1,361,000 in 1968. Similar increases in vote totals appeared in gubernatorial elections. Voting in gubernatorial general elections increased almost three and a half times from 1949 to 1969. The 1969 general election total was nearly three times greater than the primary vote in 1949 (when the primary outcome was still tantamount to election). In each election for governor after 1949, however, more votes were cast in the general than in the primary election, although in most of those years the Republican challenge was hardly serious. The increase of more than 62 percent in the 1969 turnout over that in 1965 followed poll tax removal from state elections.

Table 9

MAJOR PARTY VOTING FOR PRESIDENT IN VIRGINIA, 1948–1968

Year	Total Votes Cast	Democratic Number of Votes	Democratic Percentage of Votes	Republican Number of Votes	Republican Percentage of Votes	Other Number of Votes	Other Percentage of Votes
1948	419,256	200,786	47.9	172,070	41.0	46,400	11.1
1952	619,689	268,677	43.4	349,037	56.3	1,975	.3
1956	697,978	267,760	38.3	386,459	55.4	43,759	6.3
1960	771,449	362,327	47.0	404,521	52.4	4,601	.6
1964	1,042,267	558,038	53.5	481,334	46.2	2,895	.3
1968	1,361,491	442,387	32.5	590,319	43.4	328,785	24.1

Source: Secretary of State Board of Elections, Official Records.

Table 10

Major Party Voting in General Elections for Governor and United States Senator in Virginia, 1948-1969

Year	Election	Total Votes Cast	Democratic		Republican		Other	
			Number of Votes	Percentage	Number of Votes	Percentage	Number of Votes	Percentage
1948	Senator	387,015	253,865	65.6	119,366	30.8	13,784	3.6
1949	Governor	262,350	184,772	70.4	71,991	27.4	5,569	2.1
1952	Senator	543,516	398,677	73.4	—	—	144,839	26.6
1953	Governor	414,025	226,998	54.8	183,328	44.3	3,699	0.9
1954	Senator	306,510	244,844	79.9	—	—	61,666	20.1
1957	Governor	517,655	326,921	63.2	188,628	36.4	2,106	0.4
1958	Senator	457,640	317,221	69.3	—	—	140,419	30.7
1960	Senator	622,820	506,169	81.3	—	—	116,651	18.7
1961	Governor	394,490	251,861	63.8	142,567	36.1	62	—
1964	Senator	928,362	592,260	63.8	176,624	19.0	159,478	17.2
1965	Governor	562,789	269,526	47.9	212,207	37.7	81,056	14.4
1966	Senator	729,839	389,028	53.3	272,804	37.4	68,007	9.3
1966	Senator	733,879	429,855	58.6	245,681	33.5	58,343	7.9
1969	Governor	915,764	415,695	45.4	480,869	52.5	19,200	2.1

Source: Secretary of State Board of Elections, Official Records.

Table 11

Voting in Democratic Party Primary Elections in Virginia, 1948–1969

Year	Election	Organization Number of Votes	Organization Percentage	Antiorganization Number of Votes	Antiorganization Percentage	Other Number of Votes	Other Percentage	Total
1948	Senator	80,340	70.3	33,928	29.7	—	—	114,272
1949	Governor	135,436	42.8	111,697	35.3	69,489	22.0	316,622
1952	Senator	216,438	62.7	128,869	37.3	2	—	345,309
1953	Governor	150,459	65.9	77,715	34.1	14	—	228,188
1957	Governor	119,307	79.5	30,794	20.5	8	—	150,109
1961	Governor	199,519	56.7	152,639	43.3	6	—	352,164
1966	Senator	216,274	49.9	216,885	50.1	—	—	433,160
1966	Senator	221,221	50.9	212,996	49.1	—	—	434,217
1969	Governor	95,057	23.3	313,573	76.7	—	—	408,630

Source: Secretary of State Board of Elections, Official Records.

The increasing size of the electorate made it more and more difficult for the organization, and later for the Democratic Party, to
win elections, as the growing proportions of urban votes caused
fundamental changes in the political balance. By 1966, more than
half the state's votes were cast in its urban corridor in the general
election, and nearly 60 percent in the primary. In 1968 and 1969
the urban corridor areas provided more than 54 percent of the
state vote in the general elections, and in the 1969 primary election, the corridor again provided over 59 percent of the total vote.
The proportion of urban voting in each election increases even
more when the votes in the two metropolitan areas lying outside
the corridor are added to the corridor's totals. Such concentrations
of urban voting obviously hurt the organization. The base of organization votes was reduced even more because increases in the votes
of rural areas were often provided by newly registered black voters,
who did not back the organization.

The increase in black voters contributed directly to the new politics. In some forty predominantly black precincts in Virginia cities,
for example, voting totals climbed from 15,000 in 1964 to more
than 44,000 in 1968, with comparable increases evident also in state
elections.[30] Voting among black populations in rural areas probably rose more substantially. An estimate of black registered voters
noted that the total had increased two and a half times from 1960
to 1968, leaping from 100,100 to 255,000. The addition of substantial numbers of black voters to the electorate had a profound political impact. Through political organizations that were particularly
active in the larger cities and increasingly active in smaller cities
and rural areas, the weight of the black votes was successfully mag-
nified by effective bloc voting far beyond its proportion of the total
potential state vote. In 1968, it was estimated that black registered
voters constituted only about 10 percent of the total number of
registered voters. But black voters, gauged by performances in predominantly black precincts, voted in blocs that gave some candidates majorities higher than 95 percent. Even Godwin won over 75

30 See *UVa News Letter* articles by Ralph Eisenberg analyzing elections in 1964, 1965,
1966, 1968, and 1969 for the data on voting patterns in Virginia over the period.

percent of the votes in these precincts. The capacity to deliver a large bloc of votes could and did mean the difference in the outcome of elections. Lyndon Johnson's victory in 1964, Spong's and Rawlings' primary triumphs in 1966, and Howell's strong showing in the 1969 primaries could all be attributed, as far as one can attribute electoral outcomes, to black votes.

Moreover, arguments could be made that black votes were key ingredients in the gubernatorial elections of Godwin in 1965 and Holton in 1969. The increasing participation of black voters in Virginia elections became important in rural counties with large black populations. In these areas, registration efforts and the votes cast eroded conservative organization majorities, and, in the context of Democratic primaries by 1969, eliminated some of them completely to deprive the organization of its previous foundation for statewide campaigns. The election impact and the policy impact of black voting thus became very significant components of Virginia politics.

These patterns of voting inevitably could only be destructive to the organization. With urban voting on the rise, assisted by Negro bloc voting in cities, and with enormous rural majorities for the organization a phenomenon of the past, continued organization hegemony became almost impossible without accommodating the new voting groups. As related earlier, such efforts were undertaken at least within the Democratic Party but could not overcome the hostility of these voters toward the organization and what it had stood for in the past. The base left to the organization in the Democratic Party was exposed in the 1969 primary to constitute less than 35 percent of the total vote, and its predominance within the party ended.

The increased number of participants in Virginia politics had constructive as well as destructive effects. The latter were evident in the almost inevitable fall of the organization. The constructive product of the enlarged electorate was the rapid development of the Republican Party. It must be concluded that there was more than a coincidence between the large turnouts and Republican successes. After President Harry S. Truman had carried Virginia in

1948 by a plurality, Republican candidates won victories in the state in every subsequent election with the sole exception of 1964 in Goldwater's ill-fated campaign. Undoubtedly spurred by Senator Byrd's "golden silence" and conservative Democratic defections to Republican candidacies, the early Republican presidential victories legitimatized Republican voting habits for many Virginians and aided the development of Republican Party organizations. In-state migrations, a product of Virginia's economic development, and the suburbanization of metropolitan areas, a by-product of the broader urbanization movement, produced heavier Republican voting in those areas than appeared in the rest of the state, with the exception of the Valley of Virginia, the traditional Republican stronghold. With the overall increase in voting, rising proportions of the total metropolitan vote were suburban, until over half of the metropolitan vote was cast in the suburbs in general elections.

As the state continues to grow, the prospects for future Republican political growth lie in the suburbanization movement. One of the more interesting aspects of the 1969 election year, for example, was the central city predominance in metropolitan areas in the Democratic primaries and the suburban predominance in the same areas in the general election. Although more conservative in political outlook than the central city voter, the suburban voter nevertheless was not strongly attracted to the conservatism characteristic of the Byrd organization in earlier years. Generally, in recent elections, most suburban areas exhibited relatively moderate voting tendencies. In 1964, for example, Goldwater, while he won rural bastions of normally conservative Democratic voting habits, ran very poorly in what had become Republican suburbs in presidential voting. Where third-party efforts by conservative candidates were attempted in state elections, they failed to generate much support in the suburbs.

Holton's election as governor signified that the Republican Party in gaining the responsibility of conducting state government for four years had come of age. There were, however, other signs of Republican permanence, such as the party's hold on half the state's congressional seats. A legislative delegation that included almost one-fourth of the membership of each chamber in 1970 represented a notable increase for the Republicans and gave them the potential to make an impact upon legislative policy-making. The most recent effort to determine Republican success at the local level indicated that at least one-fourth of elected local officials were Republicans. The string of Republican successes at all levels of government is too impressive to dismiss. The Republican Party now is and will continue to be competitive in the Old Dominion.

Although many of these Republican victories were the result of defections from the Democratic Party in national, state, and local elections, they are no less permanent. Republicans benefited in various elections from defections of diverse kinds of Democrats. Conservative Democratic defections undoubtedly were instrumental in Republican presidential victories and in some of their congressional triumphs. But in many local contests and in the Holton victory of 1969, Republicans benefited from liberal Democratic defections. In Holton's election, Republicans had the best of all worlds, reaping defectors from both conservative and liberal Democrats. This seeming paradox arises from the present Republican posture, which is more conservative than the liberal faction of the Virginia Democratic Party and the image of the national Democratic Party, but less conservative than the Byrd organization. To this extent, Republicans in Virginia now occupy a middle ground in Virginia politics. Democrats who became Republicans permanently were conservatives, but not those who had occupied the extreme right wing of the organization. Although the conservative Democratic movement into the party will make it difficult for Republicans to continue their moderate position, they must retain urban support in order to win elections. In suburban areas especially, Republicans must avoid swinging to the conservative policies of the old organization. The lessons provided by the presidential victories throughout this period illustrated the importance of urban support to statewide triumphs.

The formation of conservative third parties contributed to the present form of the two major parties and resulted from Democratic and Republican perceptions of the changed political map.

The Virginia Conservative Party was organized just prior to the 1965 election. Its founders included very conservative former organization members who disagreed with the evolving organization response to urban Virginia and who concluded that the Republican Party offered no haven. The Conservative Party reached its zenith in state elections in that year, when it polled between 13 and 15 percent of the votes for state offices. The party has persisted although it received less than 8 percent of the vote in the 1966 senatorial elections. It did not field a presidential candidate in 1968 but supported George Wallace, candidate of the American Independent Party. However, in 1969, the Conservative Party and the Virginia branch of the American Independent Party each refused to step aside to support the other's candidate. The result was that both parties ran candidates for state office, and in their best joint performance polled less than 4 percent of the total vote. If the conservative parties retain any centers of strength, they are in southside Virginia rural areas, long the bastion of the most conservative political elements in Virginia.

George Wallace polled almost 24 percent of the vote in Virginia in 1968, but that effort did not have much impact upon state politics. The charisma of Wallace, the concern with national issues that he addressed, and his populist appeal all suggested that his 1968 success in Virginia could not be transferred to state issues and state politics. Certainly the performances of both conservative parties in 1969 indicated that Wallace's intrusion in Virginia politics was not meaningful. The establishment of third parties weeded out of the Democratic Party its most ultraconservative followers. In that sense, it was another setback to the organization, which increasingly needed all the support it could get within the party. Realistically, however, the retention of such supporters would not have made a difference in the survival possibilities for the organization.

Much of the foregoing discussion bears upon the contemporary condition of the Democratic Party. The moderate and liberal factions now dominate the state Democratic Party in selecting candidates for statewide office and in controlling the 1972 state convention. What organization power remains in the party lies in the hands of organization figures who are still members of the state legislature, where, because of seniority practices, they hold virtually all the leadership positions, including chairmanships of the most important committees. Although the conservative defections weakened the organization in the Democratic Party, they also reduced the probability of continued three-way internal conflict. Struggles for control of the party now will take place between the moderate and liberal factions. The only effective input which organization old-timers can make will be to back one of these two factions, either overtly or covertly. The remnants of the organization can decide which faction will become dominant, but the organization cannot regain that position for itself.

The attrition of organization leadership in recent years, which has not been directly discussed here, must be considered as another ingredient of the process changing the Democratic Party. Old age decimated the leadership in one way or another. Senator Byrd's death was the central event in this process, in both the actual and symbolic sense. The advanced ages of Senator Robertson and Congressman Smith when they sought renomination in 1966 made both a little more vulnerable in those campaigns, and their setbacks demonstrated the possibilities open to challenging liberals and moderates. Death or advancing years also claimed many organization leaders in the legislature. Some concluded that the prospect of competition in newly altered legislative districts after redistricting made it wiser to step down from office than to be exposed to the rigors of meaningful competition. Others found themselves in districts where their reelection prospects were doubtful. And still others merely confronted the realities of age or health and voluntarily stepped aside. These factors contributed in a variety of ways to political events. They were manifest in Godwin's emergence as organization spokesman, in the 1966 primary and general election results, and in the progressive legislative policies that were permitted to emerge from an organization-dominated General Assembly. These are the factors most difficult to measure but most important not to omit.

As a result of the decline of the organization, the Virginia Demo-

cratic Party now relies on a foundation of support that includes labor union members, black voters, and white liberals in cities; loyal
Democrats in rural areas, particularly in southwestern Virginia;
and moderate Democrats distributed throughout the state. It is still
unclear where conservative Democrats will ultimately align themselves. Forced to choose between major parties with which they
share little ideologically, the conservatives have not yet charted a
course. They probably will continue to behave erratically in the
years ahead. The attraction that conservative votes hold for both
Democrats and Republicans is tempered by the obvious need to
court urban Virginia to win state elections. Leaders in both major
parties appear aware that departing from the middle ground of
Virginia politics can cost them future political success.

Indeed, paradoxically, both the successful independent campaigns by Harry F. Byrd, Jr., for the United States Senate in 1970
and Henry E. Howell, Jr., for lieutenant governor in 1971, in three-
way contests against little-known major party opponents, eroded
traditional sources of major party strength in urban Virginia to
fashion victory and demonstrate the erratic outcomes produced by
the continued intraparty conflicts.

3

FLORIDA
The Different State

MANNING J. DAUER

Florida is different, both from the rest of the southern and south-eastern states and from the nine other most populous states. One of the factors of difference is Florida's rapid growth rate. In 1940 the population was two million, in 1950 three million, in 1960 five million, and in 1970 over six and two-thirds million; for 1980 the projection is just over nine million. The growth rate from 1950 to 1960 showed an increase of 79 percent in the decade, the highest rate of increase of any state in the nation. From 1960 to 1970 preliminary figures show a growth rate of 34.7 percent, exceeded only by that of Nevada. The consequence is a rapidly changing politics, with voters having little background in local politics and few local ties.

In one respect Florida is typical. Its urban population is, at 80.5 percent, just over the national average. Another index of urbanism is that there are fifteen Florida counties each with a population of over 100,000 and with a total population of 5,387,904. Together, they include over 79 percent of the state's total population of 6,789,443. These urban counties are listed in Table 1 and are assigned to the appropriate region of the state—north, central, or south.

A major political consequence of this population concentration is a change, over the last twenty years, of the method of campaigning in statewide races and even in local urban races. The popula-

Manning J. Dauer is Chairman, Department of Political Science, University of Florida.

92

Table 1

FLORIDA COUNTIES WITH OVER 100,000 POPULATION, 1970 CENSUS

State Region	City or Cities	County	Population
North Florida	Pensacola	Escambia	205,334
	Tallahassee	Leon	103,047
	Gainesville	Alachua	104,764
	Jacksonville	Duval	528,865
Central Florida	Orlando	Orange	344,311
One Standard	⎰ Tampa	Hillsborough	490,265
Metropolitan	⎱ St. Petersburg	Pinellas	522,329
Statistical Area	Melbourne-Titusville	Brevard	230,006
	Lakeland	Polk	227,222
	Sarasota	Sarasota	120,413
	Daytona Beach–Ormond Beach	Volusia	169,487
South Florida	West Palm Beach	Palm Beach	348,753
	Ft. Lauderdale	Broward	620,100
	Miami	Dade	1,267,792
	Ft. Myers	Lee	105,216
All Regions			5,387,904

Source: U.S. Department of Commerce, Bureau of the Census, *1970 Census of Population, Advance Report, Final Population Counts, Florida.*

tion of Florida is now too large to reach through the old style of personal campaigning. Campaigning must now be through the mass media—television, the press, and radio. Moreover the importance of television is greater than that of the other media. Campaign and public relations staffs emphasize television most. But a bland saturation TV campaign is not the way to win elections. There must be some content, as Reubin Askew demonstrated in his successful campaign for governor in 1970 and Lawton Chiles showed in his Senate campaign.

With reapportionment accomplished, the fifteen metropolitan counties easily dominate Florida's politics. The election of the governor and other statewide officers, the choice of three-fourths of the legislature, and the control of nearly the entire congressional delegation are in their hands. While other aspects of the state will be discussed, including regional political differences, what is important for understanding the present politics of Florida is an understanding of the characteristics of these fifteen counties. Who are the people that live in these counties? Where did they migrate from? What are their attitudes?

The first important factor to be considered is that the population of Florida is divided among a number of metropolitan areas rather than being concentrated in one main metropolis. Further, if it seems an oversimplification to concentrate almost entirely on these areas, it should be noted that their characteristics, different as they may be in various parts of the state, spill over their defined areas into the other urban counties adjacent to them.

Social and Economic Patterns

To consider these elements, it is necessary to depict the economic, social, and demographic characteristics of Florida. In the broadest sense, Florida might be described as a giant suburbia, with internal modifications in different regions of the state, and with true metropolitan diversity in a few of the largest cities. "A giant suburbia" means that the conservative and preponderantly Republican voting patterns of certain types of suburbia[1] characterize much of the political behavior of Florida. In the United States as a whole the term *suburbia* is not equivalent to a Republican monolith; there are several varieties, including the prototypical conservative suburbs, the industrial suburbs, and even some suburbs controlled by minorities. However, in Florida the conservative suburbias are dominant, as will be demonstrated by focusing on specific economic and social factors and the voting results in recent elections.

Daniel Elazar has stressed that one characteristic of the new urbanism is a population based on mobility. This trend is especially true of Florida, with its rapid growth. But the new urbanism also

[1] Robert Wood, *Suburbia: Its People and Their Politics* (Boston, 1959); W. A. Dobriner (ed.), *The Suburban Community* (New York, 1958); Frederick M. Wirt, "The Political Sociology of American Suburbia: A Reinterpretation," *Journal of Politics,* XXVII (1965), 647–66; Daniel Elazar, "Are We a Nation of Cities?" *Public Interest,* Summer, 1966, pp. 47–58.

lacks a tradition, a sense of identification, a relationship to the past. In 1949, V. O. Key stressed the importance of earlier voting patterns in explaining some aspects of the immediate post–World War II voting patterns in Florida. The present writer prepared certain materials on past voting behavior with the idea of including them as a section of this article. But they did not explain current voting trends (except, to a degree, for north Florida). Therefore the section has been eliminated. Present voting patterns are rather explained by a current socioeconomic analysis of the state. In this respect Florida is again different from other southern states, where the cultural tradition explains many voting patterns.

The mobility of Florida's suburban population is accentuated by the climate. Every Florida city has a number of mobile home or trailer parks. Some of these, as on the west coast of the state, are havens for elderly migrants; in other areas, such as Cape Kennedy, there are trailer villages for workers. Some people work in the state only part of the year. Only a small percent of all the suburban residences are trailers or mobile homes; most of the dwellings are typical houses. But these ubiquitous trailer parks serve to point up the mobility of the new suburbia in Florida and elsewhere.

Another aspect of the pattern of suburbia is urban sprawl. Elazar has noted that the pattern of urban growth is not in the central city. This observation is especially true in Florida. Subdivisions blossom across the countryside. Many of these in the metropolitan areas become incorporated municipalities. In Dade County alone some twenty-five of these satellites cluster around Miami and Miami Beach. As citizens seek identification with smaller communities, a loose conglomeration of cities and towns grows up, constituting a metropolitan area. Often there is little identification with the total urban area or with the state. In extreme circumstances this condition can lead to alienation by the voter or even to anomie. The so-called tax revolt may well be related to this lack of identification.

So that other socioeconomic factors can be analyzed, Florida may be divided into three geographic areas—north, central, and south. Figure 1 shows these three areas and the fifteen counties in each with populations greater than 100,000 dark-shaded. Three metro-

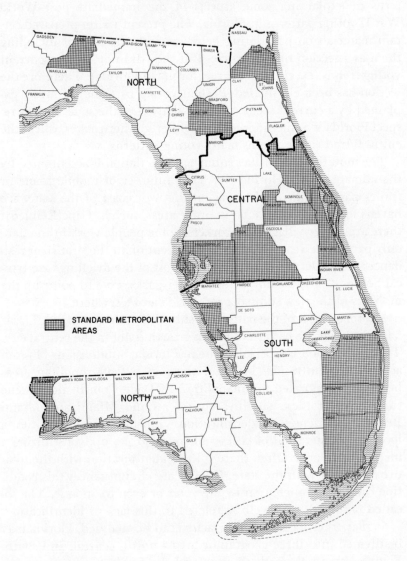

Figure 1

POLITICAL SECTIONS OF FLORIDA

politan areas of northern Florida—Jacksonville, Tallahassee, and Pensacola—share many characteristics of other growing cities in the South such as Charlotte, North Carolina, and Savannah, Georgia. Gainesville, another metropolitan area in the north, has displayed a somewhat different voting pattern recently, as the educational and research complex of the University of Florida has increasingly influenced the politics of the city. The change here has been dramatic. In the 1948 presidential election, Alachua County (in which Gainesville is located) went for Strom Thurmond, and in 1952 and 1956 for Dwight D. Eisenhower. But in 1960 the county went for John F. Kennedy, in 1964 for Lyndon B. Johnson, and in 1968 was one of only four counties in the state for Hubert H. Humphrey.

Central Florida contains the cities of Daytona Beach, Orlando (with the missile complex), Tampa, and St. Petersburg. Except for Tampa, which has an industrial and labor complex, these cities predominantly resemble conservative midwestern suburbs. They were carried by Thomas E. Dewey in 1948, Eisenhower in 1952 and 1956, and Richard M. Nixon in 1960 and 1968.

In south Florida are the cities of Miami, West Palm Beach, Fort Lauderdale, and Sarasota. The last three of these duplicate the political behavior of the central Florida cities, but Miami is a piece of Manhattan Island which floated off one thousand miles to the south and is warmed by the waters of the Gulf Stream. It is a genuine metropolitan complex with ethnic minorities and a substantial percentage of organized labor. Miami is strongly Democratic in presidential elections and liberal in Democratic nominating primaries.

The number of employees in manufacturing in Florida is small, for the state ranks low among manufacturing states. See Table 2. Among the thirteen states listed in the table, the population rank of Florida is second; the rank in manufacturing is eighth.

Compared with the nine other most populous states, Florida ranks at the bottom in employees in manufacturing. See Table 3.

Other distinctive characteristics of Florida's employment picture may also be discerned. Much of the state's manufacturing is of new types, especially the missile complex area from Cape Kennedy

Table 2

EMPLOYEES IN MANUFACTURING, SELECTED SOUTHERN STATES, 1967

(in thousands)

Rank in U.S. Population	State	Total 1967 State Population	Number of Employees in Manufacturing
18	Maryland	3,682	282.5
14	Virginia	4,536	344.7
33	West Virginia	1,798	132.7
11	North Carolina	5,029	656.9
26	South Carolina	2,599	319.4
15	Georgia	4,509	437.2
9	Florida	5,995	292.6
22	Kentucky	3,189	230.2
17	Tennessee	3,892	435.2
21	Alabama	3,540	298.4
28	Mississippi	2,348	167.1
19	Louisiana	3,662	173.4
5	Texas	10,869	663.7

Sources: U.S. Department of Labor, *Handbook of Labor Statistics, 1968.* U.S. Department of Commerce, *Statistical Abstract of the United States, 1968.*

through Orlando and over to the St. Petersburg area on the state's west coast. Central and west central Florida are sites of sizable electronics industries, which make heavy demands for skilled labor; the unions are often defeated in their attempts to organize this labor force. Thus, from the political standpoint, these areas have a low union component. In addition, there are three other types of basically non-union employment: the large numbers of service trades enterprises scattered widely throughout the state, the insurance industry (Florida is the headquarters of the southeastern branches of many insurance companies employing white-collar and clerical workers), and the smaller-scale hotels and motels in many areas of the state, with service employees whom it is difficult to unionize.

The strength of organized labor is shown in AFL-CIO gross figures. According to the federation, Florida in 1964 had 201,000

Table 3
TEN LARGEST STATES IN POPULATION, 1967,
WITH NUMBER OF EMPLOYEES IN MANUFACTURING
(in thousands)

Population Rank	State	Total State Population Estimated	Employees in Manufacturing
1	California	19,153	1,591.7
2	New York	18,336	1,891.2
3	Pennsylvania	11,629	1,557.6
4	Illinois	10,893	1,392.8
5	Texas	10,869	663.7
6	Ohio	10,458	1,398.6
7	Michigan	8,584	1,104.6
8	New Jersey	7,003	876.4
9	Florida	5,995	292.6
10	Massachusetts	5,421	696.8

Sources: U.S. Department of Commerce, *Statistical Abstract of the United States, 1968.*
U.S. Department of Labor, *Handbook of Labor Statistics, 1968.*

union members.[2] Although it ranked seventeenth among the fifty states in union membership, among heavily urban states this membership figure is quite low. Other states which are comparable in population include Indiana with 522,000 union members, New Jersey with 814,000, and Massachusetts with 572,000. In the percentage of its nonagricultural employees that belong to unions, Florida ranked forty-fifth among the states.

Those types of enterprise with large union memberships include the transportation industry, with rail complexes in Tampa, Jacksonville, and Miami; the paper industry in some areas of Florida; and the construction industry generally throughout the state. But except in Miami, Tampa, and Jacksonville, the total labor component is not great enough to affect politics as it does in metropolitan areas elsewhere among the ten largest states. In Miami, other factors reinforce the rail and construction unions. There are large

[2] AFL-CIO, *Directory of Industrial Labor Unions in the United States, 1965*, Bulletin No. 1493, p. 58. See also Table 9, Structure of the Labor Movement.

airline shops, as this city is the United States terminus for airplane overhaul on the national North-South air routes and is also the overhaul center for lines to and from Latin America. In Miami, moreover, the hotels and motels are so large that their employees are relatively easy to organize, and most of them are union members. This labor factor added to the comparatively large proportion of minorities in the population (as yet most of the newly arrived Cubans are not naturalized) makes Dade County the only Florida area with a liberal voting pattern. One final factor should be added. The metropolitan character of Miami and the differences in its culture and outlook again tend to reinforce this trend of distinctive voting patterns. The interaction of the minorities, the unions, and the communications media creates in that area a voting pattern unlike those in the remainder of the state.

Next highest in unionization is Hillsborough County (Tampa), with older heavy industries such as cement manufacturing, phosphate processing, shipping and stevedoring, railroads, and construction. As in Miami, there are in Tampa substantial minorities of older-generation Latin migrants. The cigar industry centered in Ybor City and West Tampa (originally separate towns but now parts of Tampa) drew Cuban, Italian, and Spanish immigrants as early as the turn of the century.

Some of the north Florida areas, such as Jacksonville and Pensacola, are developing manufacturing complexes, but the union component is small and the culture of these cities is more typically southern than in the other urban areas. Some of the differing employment characteristics of the fourteen largest counties are shown in Table 4.

The agricultural vote of Florida is also distinctive. Approximately forty-four of the sixty-seven counties have large rural population components, and these, too, may be considered from a standpoint of the three general regions of the state. But farming in Florida, even in the northern part of the state, is not cotton-based. The one crop in north Florida which also is common to much of the rest of the South is tobacco, but even in this section vegetable and fruit farming are important. In central Florida, citrus and

Table 4
EMPLOYED PERSONS BY INDUSTRY— SELECTED FLORIDA COUNTIES, 1960

County	Total Employed	Construction	Manufacturing	Communications	Railroad	Trucking and Warehouse	Utilities	Eating and Drinking Establishments
Alachua	26,515	1,841	2,420	390	222	121	247	746
Brevard	39,822	4,223	9,782	447	102	191	515	1,397
Broward	117,542	15,537	12,544	1,629	204	1,078	1,515	6,105
Dade	360,097	24,297	41,623	5,506	2,187	3,215	4,982	14,448
Duval	160,594	13,430	21,236	2,799	4,623	3,023	1,733	4,246
Escambia	54,163	4,817	11,054	754	566	614	832	1,589
Hillsborough	140,568	12,973	25,677	2,048	2,125	2,269	2,427	4,197
Leon	28,464	2,441	1,913	470	148	140	240	883
Orange	93,288	9,669	15,701	1,576	180	1,118	1,231	2,622
Palm Beach	87,859	7,949	6,267	1,122	264	666	1,112	3,351
Pinellas	115,381	12,931	13,754	1,425	379	595	2,493	4,970
Polk	69,572	5,769	10,945	647	1,005	1,092	728	1,776
Sarasota	26,162	3,348	2,354	305	28	127	438	1,089
Volusia	41,662	4,502	3,860	609	603	261	764	2,121

Source: *U.S. Census of Population, 1960.*

truck crops, many of them on a large scale, predominate. Also in central Florida, cattle ranching is extensive, and the ranches are sizable. In the rich Everglades soils and in other areas of south Florida, truck farming is extensive and, again, is characterized by large farms.

Florida farming is lucrative. In 1965 the total value of the state's agricultural production amounted to just over $1 billion. The gross value of farm production was about the same in Georgia, but the rural farm population of Florida in 1960 was only 2.1 percent of the state population—109,419 individuals on 40,541 farms (a 1961 figure)—while Georgia's rural farm residents constituted 10 percent of the state population, or 407,208 individuals on 83,366 farms. Mississippi, with $800 million of farm income, had in the comparable years 25 percent of its population, or 542,839 individuals, on 109,000 farms.[3]

Other characteristics of Florida offer further bases for socioeconomic comparison with other states. Total personal income in the state for 1965 came to $10 billion. Agriculture produced 5 percent of this total, manufacturing 16 percent, construction 9 percent, and service trades 19 percent. When compared with other large industrial states, Florida's low percentage in manufacturing and high percentages in service trades and professions are significant. In 1962 Florida was ninth or tenth in population, but only twenty-fifth in manufacturing, although it was eighth in construction and third in hotel and motel receipts. Thus the economy is peculiar: high per-farm income, few farms; low manufacturing income; high proportion of wage-earners in service trades; and high earnings in hotels and motels.[4]

However, Florida's per capita income in 1966 was $2,614, a figure somewhat below the national average of $2,963. Among the ten largest states this average is the lowest of all, except for Texas; but among southeastern states it is the highest, the others ranging from $1,777 per capita in Mississippi to $2,605 in Virginia.

3 Data from Bureau of Business and Economic Research, *Florida Statistical Atlas* (Gainesville, 1971).
4 Erwin Raisz and John R. Dunkle, *Atlas of Florida* (Gainesville, 1964), 1.

Another notable factor in these per capita income figures is that income varies extensively among the counties. Only eleven counties exceed the Florida average. In the main these are the counties with populations higher than 100,000 (see Table 1). Furthermore, Florida income is skewed in another way. The distribution of income is parallel to that of the southeastern states except that Florida bulges in the top 15 percent of the income category. In other words, all but 15 percent of the state's population has a rather low income. Florida is above the southeastern average because of concentration at the top levels of income.

A comparison of internal revenue figures is also useful. In 1958 the United States, the South, and Florida all had large percentages of the population with incomes below $3,000. The figure for Florida was 15.2 percent as compared with 16.9 for the South; the national average was 12 percent. Florida figures on income distribution parallel the southern average until $10,000 is reached. Then the Florida figures move up to the national average until incomes over $20,000 are reached; at this point the figures show the national average to be 10.2 percent, that of the South 9 percent, and Florida 12.1 percent. The state has 1,264 returns on incomes from $100,000 to $500,000, 45 from $500,000 to $1 million; 17 over $1 million annually. For North Carolina the comparable figures are 632, 18, and 8; for Virginia 537, 6, and 7; for Mississippi 152, 6, and 4; for Louisiana 573, 10, and 3.[5]

Another characteristic of Florida is that the median age of its population is 31.2, compared with a national average of 29.5 in 1960. Moreover a high proportion of the Florida population is over 65—as of 1968, 14 percent of the state population. This part of the population is concentrated in certain counties. (See Table 5 and Figure 2.)

As a comparison of Tables 10 and 11 and Figures 16 and 17 shows, there is a high correspondence between the counties listed in Table 5 and heavy Republican registration and voting in the state. Seven-

[5] Bureau of Business and Economic Research, *Florida Statistical Abstract, 1968* (Gainesville, 1968). U.S. Department of Treasury, *Federal Income Tax Figures* (Washington, 1965).

Table 5

FLORIDA COUNTIES WITH HIGH MEDIAN AGE POPULATION
AND HIGH PERCENTAGE OF POPULATION OVER SIXTY-FIVE, IN ORDER OF RANK

County	1960 Median Age	1960 Percentage over 65	1968 Percentage over 65
1. Pinellas	44.9	24.9	32.3
2. Charlotte	44.8	20.8	36.0
3. Manatee	44.1	22.0	28.9
4. Sarasota	40.5	18.4	28.7
5. Volusia	39.5	19.7	27.0
6. Osceola	38.8	22.8	22.8
7. Pasco	38.5	16.0	31.0
8. Citrus	37.5	14.8	24.3
9. DeSoto	36.5	15.7	14.7
10. Martin	35.8	16.0	23.0
11. Lake	34.3	12.7	19.1
12. Lee	34.1	12.7	23.5
13. Palm Beach	34.0	11.4	15.4
14. Broward	33.9	11.6	18.0

Sources: Ronald E. Beller, *Estimates of the Population of Florida Counties by Age: July 1, 1968*, Population Series, Bulletin No. 19, January, 1969, Bureau of Business and Economic Research, Gainesville. *Florida Statistical Abstract, 1968*.

teen of the sixty-seven Florida counties have Republican registrations exceeding 30 percent of the total Democratic county registrations. Twelve of these counties appear in both the high age table and in the high Republican registration table: Broward, Palm Beach, Pinellas, Sarasota, Volusia, Charlotte, Lake, Lee, Martin, Manatee, Osceola, and Pasco.

High per capita income counties in Florida are presented in Table 6. Nine of the top twenty-two counties in per capita income are included in the seventeen Florida counties with the highest Republican registration.

Before analyzing the Republican strength, however, it is important to examine the Negro vote. In 1960 the black population constituted 15.2 percent of Florida's voting-age population, a decline from 20.1 percent in 1950. Although more whites than blacks were

Figure 2

Percentage of Florida Population 65 Years Old and Older, 1960

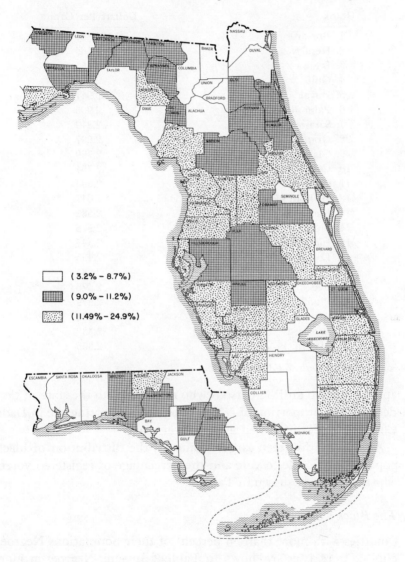

Table 6

PER CAPITA INCOME, HIGHEST FLORIDA COUNTIES, 1966

Rank	Dollars Per Capita
1. Brevard	4,206
2. Hendry	3,164
3. Dade	3,055
4. Gulf	2,971
5. Duval	2,947
6. Palm Beach	2,906
7. Sarasota	2,849
8. Orange	2,807
9. Glades	2,799
10. Collier	2,764
11. Okaloosa	2,695
12. Hillsborough	2,647
13. Escambia	2,582
14. Monroe	2,575
15. Indian River	2,545
16. Leon	2,496
17. Polk	2,484
18. Lee	2,426
19. Pinellas	2,379
20. Alachua	2,342
21. Broward	2,332
22. Martin	2,306

Source: *Florida Statistical Abstract, 1968.*

among the two million persons who migrated into the state in that decade,[6] the proportion of Negro population of voting age in Dade County actually increased in 1960 over 1950.

Among the fourteen largest counties, the distribution of black population eligible to vote and the percentage of registered voters who are black are shown in Table 7.

The Black Voter

Counties with more than 20 percent of their populations Negroes eligible to register are shown in Table 8. In sum, Negroes in Flor-

[6] Annie Hartsfield and Elston Roady, *Florida Votes, 1920–62* (Tallahassee, 1963), 10.

Table 7

ELIGIBLE NEGRO VOTERS, 1960, AND PROPORTION OF NEGROES
REGISTERED IN FLORIDA'S LARGEST COUNTIES IN 1968

County	Percentage of Blacks Eligible, 1960	Percentage of Registration That Is Black, 1968
Alachua	24.5	15.4
Brevard	10.0	4.2
Broward	12.5	8.8
Dade	12.3	12.9
Duval	22.3	20.7
Escambia	19.0	16.8
Hillsborough	12.7	11.0
Leon	30.4	18.9
Orange	13.6	6.0
Palm Beach	19.8	13.1
Pinellas	6.5	4.5
Polk	16.5	10.8
Sarasota	7.7	3.5
Volusia	13.5	9.4

Source: Hartsfield and Roady, *Florida Votes*, 10.

ida constitute just over 15 percent of the state population that is eligible to vote and 11.4 percent of those actually registered to vote.

Florida's system of closed primaries limits eligibility to voters who are registered members of the party conducting the primary. In general elections all candidates, of course, appear on the same ballot and voters may cross party lines. In 1968, of the 308,092 Negroes registered in Florida, 294,649 were listed as Democrats (14.1 percent of the Democratic total). Only 13,443 Negroes were registered as Republicans (2.2 percent of the Republican registration).

As late as 1964 two of the sixty-seven Florida counties, Lafayette and Liberty, had no Negroes registered to vote. Earlier, some counties had exerted intense pressures against Negro registration. In 1951 the state chairman of the National Association for the Advancement of Colored People, Harry T. Moore, was killed in a dynamite explosion which destroyed his house.[7] Even then Negroes could

[7] New York *Times*, December 27, 1951, p. 1.

Table 8

FLORIDA COUNTIES WITH OVER 20 PERCENT OF ELIGIBLE VOTERS THAT
ARE NEGROES, AND PERCENTAGE OF REGISTERED VOTERS THAT ARE NEGROES

County	Percentage of Eligible Negroes of Total Population Over 21—1960	Percentage of Registered Voters That Are Negroes, 1968
Alachua	24.5	15.4
Baker	20.1	14.2
Columbia	27.8	20.9
Duval	22.3	20.7
Flagler	32.1	16.4
Gadsden	51.1	40.7
Glades	41.1	16.0
Gulf	21.3	15.2
Hamilton	39.5	28.3
Hendry	25.6	17.8
Jackson	37.7	21.3
Jefferson	52.2	38.1
Leon	30.4	18.9
Levy	25.9	11.7
Madison	41.2	31.1
Marion	30.7	19.9
Nassau	22.7	18.7
Putnam	28.0	15.7
St. Johns	23.9	15.3
St. Lucie	27.5	17.9
Seminole	22.4	12.8
Sumter	25.1	16.4
Suwannee	24.0	15.7
Union	27.3	24.8
Wakulla	26.2	18.8
STATE AVERAGE	15.2	11.4

Sources: Hartsfield and Roady, *Florida Votes*, 11. Voter Registration Figures, 1968,
    Secretary of State of Florida.

register and vote in many Florida counties; they are now, of course,
free to do so in all of them. Actual registration is currently about
4 percent below the percentage of voting-age population which is
Negro. This gap is no longer due either to legal restrictions or to

white pressures against Negro voting or registration; it is now a product of such cultural factors as limited relevance to the Negro of campaign issues, insufficient registration drives, and deficient organization in some areas. Negro registration has gone up under the impact of particular drives in special contests where both organization and interest in issues have been present. For example, in the senatorial primary contest between George A. Smathers and Claude Pepper in the spring of 1950, Hillsborough County Negro registration rose to 7,387; by 1954, however, the figure was down to 3,630.[8] Studies of Florida elections show the same phenomena— low Negro registration and turnout in many local elections when the relevance of issues is not apparent to the black population or when no black candidate is running.[9]

As to styles of local politics in the early 1960's, a survey of Florida communities by a University of Florida research team offers a typology relative to Negro participation: (1) the nonvoting town; (2) the unorganized town (a few Negroes voting but no organization); (3) the manipulative town (with organization white-controlled); (4) the independent bargaining town (with Negro organization and strong control); and (5) the officeholding town, with Negroes as elected and appointed officeholders.[10] By 1968, the most restrictive category, the nonvoting town, had become obsolete in Florida.

Many of the background factors affecting the comparison of white and Negro political participation are treated in the monumental work *Negroes and the New Southern Politics* by Donald R. Matthews and James W. Prothro.[11] Table 9 shows the variations

8 Charles J. Parrish, "Minority Parties in Tampa" (M.A. thesis, University of Florida, 1960).

9 O. R. McQuown, William R. Hamilton, and Michael P. Schneider, *The Political Restructuring of a Community*, University of Florida Public Administration Clearing Service Study No. 27 (Gainesville, 1964).

10 Alfred B. Clubok, John M. DeGrove, and Charles D. Farris, "The Manipulated Negro Vote," *Journal of Politics*, XXVI (1964), 112–29.

11 Donald R. Matthews and James W. Prothro, *Negroes and the New Southern Politics* (New York, 1966). Earlier studies, confined to Florida Negroes, are reported in Hugh Douglas Price, *The Negro and Southern Politics* (New York, 1952).

between southern whites and blacks in the number of school years completed. As the number of years of schooling increases, the southern white and the southern Negro tend to move closer together in the extent of their respective participation in politics. Matthews

Table 9

WHITE AND NEGRO EDUCATION IN THE SOUTHERN STATES

	Negro	White
0–3 grades	21%	2%
4–6 grades	21	11
7–8 grades	17	16
Some high school	13	14
High-school graduate	20	31
Some college	4	16
College graduate	4	10
	100%	100%

Source: From *Negroes and the New Southern Politics* by Donald R. Matthews and James W. Prothro, © 1966 by Harcourt Brace Jovanovich, Inc., and reprinted with their permission.

Figure 3

EDUCATION AND POLITICAL PARTICIPATION IN THE SOUTH, BY RACE

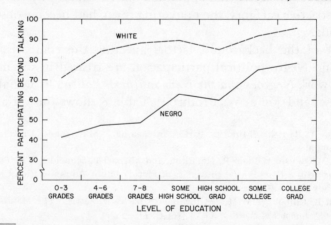

Source: From *Negroes and the New Southern Politics* by Donald R. Matthews and James W. Prothro, © 1966 by Harcourt Brace Jovanovich, Inc., and reprinted with their permission.

and Prothro also examined other factors in participation. Sharp discrepancies appear between Negro and white rates of participation at the low levels of the income scale. White participation beyond talking remains at the 90 percent level regardless of income, whereas Negro participation starts with only 40 percent at the lower incomes and rises to the levels of white participation at income over $4,000. On the other hand, the proportionate number of Negroes at the higher income levels of the Matthews-Prothro sample is much smaller than the number of whites:

Number	Under $1,000	1,000– 1,999	2,000– 2,999	3,000– 3,999	4,000– 4,999	5,000– 5,999	6,000– 7,499	7,500+
Negro	205	147	83	75	31	39	16	11
White	60	58	73	75	86	82	78	158

Source: From *Negroes and the New Southern Politics* by Donald R. Matthews and James W. Prothro, © 1966 by Harcourt Brace Jovanovich, Inc., and reprinted with their permission.

Table 10

FLORIDA REPUBLICAN VOTER REGISTRATION, 1938–1970

Year	State Total Republicans	State Total Independent and No Party	State Total Democratic	Total Registered Voters	Republican Registration as Percentage of Democratic Registration
1938	35,377	—	593,048	628,425	6.0
1944	53,935	29,033	673,514	756,482	8.0
1950	60,665	—	1,006,580	1,067,245	6.0
1952	116,794	7,659	1,215,085	1,339,538	9.6
1956	210,797	11,506	1,384,447	1,606,750	15.2
1960	338,390	22,223	1,656,023	2,016,586	20.43
1964	458,156	33,548	2,009,842	2,501,546	22.8
1966	465,605	33,694	1,964,533	2,463,832	23.7
1967	472,966	33,892	1,966,371	2,473,179	24.1
1968	619,062	55,467	2,090,787	2,765,316	29.6
1970	711,090	61,523	2,024,387	2,797,000	35.1

Table 11

DEMOCRATIC AND REPUBLICAN REGISTRATION IN SELECTED
FLORIDA COUNTIES, 1970

County	Total Republican	Total Democratic	Total Other	Grand Total	Republican Registration as Percentage of Democratic Registration
Counties with over 100,000 Population					
1. Alachua	4,212	31,177	898	36,287	13.5
2. Brevard	28,718	55,546	2,543	87,961	52.0
3. Broward	91,515	144,952	8,402	244,869	63.5
4. Dade	69,843	389,070	7,060	465,973	18.0
5. Duval	20,484	182,980	4,214	207,678	12.0
6. Escambia	6,517	73,867	1,209	81,593	9.0
7. Hillsborough	26,736	179,381	2,700	208,817	15.0
8. Leon	3,462	34,865	525	38,852	10.0
9. Orange	36,535	86,031	2,902	125,468	42.0
10. Palm Beach	50,466	96,748	4,818	152,032	52.5
11. Pinellas	118,928	129,390	6,436	254,754	93.0
12. Polk	14,248	79,791	1,015	95,054	18.0
13. Sarasota	29,719	23,578	1,682	54,979	120.0
14. Volusia	19,849	59,877	1,809	81,535	33.0
15. Lee	12,313	29,984	621	42,918	41.1
Smaller Counties with Republican Registration Higher than 30 Percent of Democratic Registration					
A. Charlotte	5,234	8,424	379	14,037	62.1
B. Collier	3,834	8,290	348	12,472	46.0
C. Indian River	4,045	10,608	425	15,105	39.8
D. Lake	2,451	7,312	601	30,364	32.5
E. Lee	12,313	29,984	621	42,918	41.0
F. Manatee	14,407	26,453	1,277	42,137	55.0
G. Martin	3,283	9,101	167	12,551	36.0
H. Osceola	3,086	9,323	141	12,550	33.0
I. Pasco	9,575	22,148	665	32,388	43.4
J. Seminole	7,047	20,817	620	28,534	34.0

Contributing to Florida's rapid population growth has been
much in-migration, with many of the newcomers moving from
northern Republican states. An analysis of Florida's version of con-

servatism reveals that it is orthodox conservatism as to national politics, but heterodox as to aspects of local and state government. On local and state issues, even conservatives must provide for growth and expansion. So again Florida's conservatism is different. What this means will be apparent in explaining Florida's politics.

Republicans and Democrats: A Changing Ratio

Republican growth statewide and in the fifteen largest counties is shown in Tables 10 and 11, which were compiled from official registration figures supplied by the secretary of state. The last column of each table shows Republican statewide registration as a percentage of total Democratic registration.

In the fifteen largest counties the distribution of vote between Republicans and Democrats is shown in the first part of Table 11. The second part of this table shows the other counties with Republican registrations amounting to 30 percent or more of the Democratic registration.

The counties with Republican registration higher than 30 percent of Democratic registration in the county totaled seventeen, including seven of the fifteen counties with 1970 populations over 100,000, and ten others. These seventeen counties are located as shown in Table 12.

Table 12

FLORIDA REPUBLICAN REGISTRATION
COMPARED WITH DEMOCRATIC REGISTRATION, BY SECTIONS OF STATE
(Number of Registered Republicans Expressed as Percentage of the Number of Registered Democrats)

	Counties Over 100,000		Smaller Counties	
	Over 30 Percent	Under 30 Percent	Over 30 Percent	Under 30 Percent
Region				
North	0	4	0	31
Central	3	2	6	4
South	5	1	4	7

Source: Secretary of State of Florida.

New Programs, New Faces

Having discussed the socioeconomic and demographic features of Florida, we may next examine the structures of political machinery and parties. Before Claude Kirk became governor in 1967, the last Republican to serve as the state's chief executive went out of office on January 7, 1877. In the general election of 1876 the Democratic candidate for governor won. At this point party machinery was of importance. But the Republican strength soon declined, and Florida became a one-party state by the 1880's.

Florida's closed primary system dates from the early 1900's, when it was established by the Democratic state committee,[12] which in turn was influenced by a rather strong populist tradition. Subsequently state law extended the primary system to both political parties. To participate in these elections voters must register in one party or another and only those registered in that party may participate. Voters who declare no party preference may vote only in the general election. Thus the choice of nominees for the party falls, at the county, congressional district, and state levels, to the primary. In many city elections nonpartisan primaries and nonpartisan elections are used.

The primary machinery provides for county committeemen and committeewomen to be chosen by the party voters in the primary. Then the party voters of each county choose one committeeman and one committeewoman to serve on the state party executive committee. Until 1969 the state party structure had never been reapportioned. Each of the sixty-seven counties was equally represented on the committee—Liberty County with a population of 3,000 and Dade (Miami) with more than 1 million inhabitants. During the long period without Republican opposition in the general election, this malapportionment was relatively unimportant. But since Florida has become a two-party state, the Democratic party structure has been unable to adapt. By 1970 partial reapportionment of the state and congressional district Democratic com-

12 Manning J. Dauer, "Toward a Model State Presidential Primary Law," *American Political Science Review*, L (1956), 140–53.

mittees has been achieved, in an effort to modernize the party structure.

On the Republican side, at the start of the period covered by this study, the party leadership was principally concerned with presidential patronage. Throughout the 1940's and early 1950's, the leaders campaigned only in presidential campaigns and encouraged neither local candidates nor registration drives. No funds were contributed to Republican local, congressional district, or statewide campaigns. In fact, active Republicans were regarded as a nuisance, threatening control of the party machinery and of patronage coming through presidential appointments.

But this situation was not permitted to continue. Starting in Pinellas County (St. Petersburg) in 1950, the party machinery was taken over by William C. Cramer. Only two years out of Harvard Law School, he directed a campaign which succeeded in electing a majority of Republicans to local offices in Pinellas County, as well as a Republican delegation to the Florida Legislature from Pinellas. He became the minority leader in the legislature and in 1952 was narrowly defeated in a race for the United States House of Representatives.

Cramer was elected to Congress in 1954 and served in the House of Representatives for seven terms. He is also Republican national committeeman from Florida, and has gradually forged a strong position for himself in the party's state committee. Under Cramer and William Murfin, a Florida east coast Republican leader, the state committee has been built into an effective organization which now encourages local and statewide candidates. With the retirement of the veteran Democratic United States Senator Spessard Holland in 1970, Cramer ran for the Senate but was defeated by his Democratic opponent, Lawton Chiles.

Unfortunately for the Republicans, the four years of Republican rule under Governor Claude Kirk left the party badly split at the end of his term between the governor's faction, also supported by Republican Senator Edward Gurney, and the Cramer faction. Since the defeat of Kirk for reelection as governor in 1970 and the defeat of Cramer for the United States Senate, the party has remained deeply divided. After the state chairman in 1968, William Murfin, accepted a Nixon appointment, the Kirk-Gurney faction placed their man, Duke Crittenden, in the state party chairmanship. Crittenden then supported his faction's candidate, G. Harrold Carswell, for the Republican Senate nomination. Cramer defeated Carswell soundly in the primary. Crittenden was then voted out of the chairmanship by the Cramer faction, and L. E. "Tommy" Thomas of Panama City replaced him. This internecine warfare has disrupted the state organization, which has lost elections heavily at all levels in 1970.

The Democratic party structure, on the other hand, was relatively ineffective until a revival in 1970. Democratic leadership in Florida came from the governor, members of the state cabinet, legislative leaders, the congressional delegation, and the senators, who often operated outside the party machinery. After the disastrous 1966 and 1968 defeats the Democratic Party has reorganized. While still not a strong party organization, in 1970 it waged a united campaign behind new faces. With this leadership the Democrats have increased their strength in both houses of the state legislature and have recovered the governorship and kept one United States Senate seat. Much of this success is due to the new faces. The winning statewide candidates, Reubin Askew for governor and Lawton Chiles for senator, are probably more responsible for the new look than is the party organization.

One other point needs to be made about the impact of party organization. It is lessening in Florida, not only because the type of party organization has changed, but also because of the impact of the strong primary system which is important today in both parties. Finally, while the Democratic registration is much greater than the Republican, polls show that 40 percent of the voters in Florida actually consider themselves independents. When these persons are asked why they register as party voters they indicate that in heavily Democratic counties they do so in order to vote in city and county elections (under Florida's closed primary system, only those may vote in a primary who register as party members, and those who register as independents can vote only in the general election).

Similarly, 40 percent of the registered Republicans indicate that they are tied to no party but are concerned with local elections.

It is important, therefore, not to stress too much the effect on parties of the Democratic comeback in winning the governorship and the United States Senate seat in 1970. This outcome was much more dependent on the failure of the Republican Governor Kirk to have a program, and on his spending, his arrogance, his unpopularity. On the other hand, the Democrats presented new programs, new faces, and in the case of the senatorial candidate Chiles, new campaign techniques. Thus the Democratic victory is more personal and programmatic than party. It is probably confined to state politics. Nixon still wins majority support in polls partly because the economic recession had not as yet affected Florida so severely as of 1971, and because of a favorable view of his program.

A Collegial Executive

Florida's cabinet organization of the state executive branch is a distinctive feature that affects the larger structure of politics. The cabinet consists of six constitutional statewide elective officials in addition to the governor: the secretary of state, attorney general, comptroller, state treasurer, superintendent of public instruction, and commissioner of agriculture. So far this system is not peculiar to Florida. Many states also have such elected officials, whose duties are primarily related to the titles of their offices. In Florida, however, while these officials have similar duties, the unique feature is that they also sit ex officio on many boards or commissions. Some of these agencies contain all the cabinet members plus the governor, whereas others contain only part of the cabinet. It may be observed at this point that the executive branch was reorganized by the reapportioned 1969 Florida Legislature in the first general restructuring since 1885. Before this reorganization there were some 150 executive agencies, boards, or commissions. Now these are reduced to 22. The governor has increased power and heads half of these departments. Others fall under individual cabinet members or under a collegium of the governor and the cabinet; hence for many functions Florida has a collegial executive. It is true that the governor usually has more influence than the individual cabinet members, but many employees in the state bureaucracy are under the cabinet.

Executive responsibility in Florida is very hard to pin down. Furthermore, under the 1885 constitution the members of the cabinet were eligible for reelection—but the governor was not eligible to succeed himself until the new constitution was adopted in 1968. Moreover, incumbent cabinet members were rarely defeated. Since 1901 (counting out two brief cabinet appointments for short terms where members did not seek reelection) the six members of the Florida cabinet averaged terms of 11.94 years. One secretary of state served for thirty years.

The consequence is that these cabinet members developed a general influence apart from the governor. They interacted with the legislative leaders, who until reapportionment showed a similar continuity, and with many members of the permanent state bureaucracy. Rarely did cabinet members move up to the governorship or the United States Senate. They served. Many died in office and the governor appointed their successors. This pattern changed somewhat in 1970, when three new cabinet officers, in addition to a new governor, were elected.

An additional factor which contributes to the continuity and persistent influence of the cabinet is the fact that most members have developed special constituencies around the particular duties of their offices. The state treasurer is assigned by statute responsibility for regulating insurance companies; the insurance companies in turn contribute to his election campaign (although in 1970 this practice led to the defeat of the incumbent state treasurer). The superintendent of schools is tied in closely to county education officials and the Florida Education Association, the state comptroller to state banks, the attorney general to the bar and to public attorneys, the commissioner of agriculture to the farming interests. These relationships were evident in campaign contributions and in campaign supporters. But with reapportionment, the legislature has assumed a new composition. Thus a new state constitution was proposed in 1967 and was approved by the voters in 1968. This document forced reorganization of the Florida executive into a maximum of 25 departments. These may be still placed under the cabinet or under the governor, but the new concentration of the 150 old agencies should make some difference in the management of this branch.

These, then, are some of the leading factors in Florida party and government structure: a strong primary system, a governor whose powers are quite limited, a unique cabinet system, a weak Democratic party organization. One final element needs to be considered —the long battle over reapportionment.

Reapportionment

Reapportionment in Florida has been an important issue ever since World War II. The problem is created by the fact that Article VII of the 1885 Florida constitution created an impossible apportionment system. The constitution provided for equal apportionment on a population basis in the state Senate, but accompanying this provision was a limitation of each county to no more than one senator. In the 1960 census Dade County contained 18.9 percent of the state population, but the constitution limited it to 2.6 percent of the membership of the Senate, or one of thirty-eight members. Moreover, the five largest counties had over 50 percent of the state population but only 14 percent of the Senate membership. Calculated under the 1960 census, 12.3 percent of the Florida population controlled a majority of the Senate seats.

The constitutional provisions for the state House of Representatives were also quite faulty. The House contained ninety-five members, and each of the sixty-seven counties in the state was guaranteed one representative, with a maximum of three members for any county. Consequently, 14.7 percent of the Florida population (under the 1960 census) elected a majority of the House and thus controlled it. Efforts to improve this situation required not merely a majority vote, which is needed to pass a law, but a three-fifths vote, needed to propose a constitutional amendment. This provision meant that members from the smaller districts would have to vote for a formula which would eliminate themselves from the legislature.[13]

The 1885 constitution also provided for reapportionment every tenth year. Originally, the constitution contained a provision for a state census at ten-year intervals, midway between federal censuses, on which reapportionment was to be based. The state census system was subsequently abolished by constitutional amendment, but no change was made as to the required reapportionment year. Thus Florida was required to reapportion on the basis of the federal census, but five years after the count had been taken.

Under these circumstances the first effort at reapportionment after the close of World War II came in 1955. Governor LeRoy Collins convened the legislature in special session and urged that a new formula be adopted in the state constitution. The extraordinary session convened on June 6, 1955, and adjourned on September 29. A constitutional amendment was finally proposed by the legislature, but was rejected by a majority of more than 100,000 votes in the general election of November 6, 1956. The proposed amendment would actually have made little improvement had it been adopted. Since 1955, nine special sessions of the Florida Legislature have been devoted primarily to reapportionment. In addition, there have been attempts at reapportionment during the regular sessions. Three constitutional amendments have emerged, the last of which went to the voters on November 3, 1964, and was defeated by a majority of almost 300,000 votes.

This battle of reapportionment relates to certain larger governmental questions. As has been noted, Florida has become increasingly urbanized, following the national trend. Yet the ability of the states to enact legislation which would permit counties and cities

13 Manning J. Dauer, "Florida Reapportionment," *Business and Economic Dimensions*, III (March, 1967), 8–14; Manning J. Dauer and William C. Havard, *The Florida Constitution of 1885—A Critique*, Studies in Public Administration, XII (Gainesville, 1955); W. C. Havard and L. P. Beth, *The Politics of Mis-Representation* (Baton Rouge, 1962); and Malcolm Parsons, "Tension and Conflict in a One Party Legislative System: The Florida Senate, 1947–1961," *American Political Science Review*, LVI (1962), 605–14.

to grapple with urban problems has decreased. For that reason metropolitan centers and urban communities have increasingly gone to the federal government for relief. Congress has proved much more responsive than state legislatures to the problems of city planning, urban sprawl, and many other matters affecting metropolitan living. The states have lagged behind. Not all of their inadequacy can be attributed to legislative malapportionment, but it is significant that under malapportionment the legislatures have not acted.

Ultimately, after hearings that were appealed to the United States Supreme Court, a three-judge federal court, in the case of *Swann v. Adams* (February 8, 1967), ordered new elections under a reapportionment plan (proposed by the author of this chapter). The plan provided for a House of 119 members and a Senate of 48 members with a variation of no more than 5 percent from district to district.

While this conflict was progressing, a polarization occurred in legislative politics that lasted from 1955 to 1966. The cleavage in each chamber was between the small-county dominant bloc, which was known as the "pork choppers," and the minority urban bloc, called the "lamb choppers." Before this polarization developed, some Speakers and Senate presidents had been selected from urban areas. It should be noted that in Florida the presiding officers of the two legislative houses are designated by the party caucus of the majority party, and the officers rotate every two years. After 1957, under the influence of the reapportionment issue, the rural bloc coalesced and voted solidly against the urban candidates. Legislative policies favoring rural areas also tended to predominate during the period. These included (1) the distribution of some appropriations on a per-county basis, e.g., the racetrack pari-mutuel tax, which was divided equally among the sixty-seven counties; (2) the distribution of road funds to favor the small counties; (3) the location of more state institutions in the small counties than in the urban ones; (4) the blockage of legislation for urban renewal; (5) prevention of a general state law enabling urban renewal programs to be adopted (some were adopted on a local basis); (6) the failure

Table 13

CONTINUED REAPPORTIONMENT OF THE
FLORIDA HOUSE AND SENATE, 1955–1967

	Total	Dade County	Percentage of Population Electing a Majority
1955 Florida House	95	3	17.7%
1955 Florida Senate	38	1	17.2
1961 Florida House	95	3	14.7
1961 Florida Senate	38	1	12.3
1963 Florida House*	112	14	26.9
Florida Senate*	43	2	14.2
Legislative Bill 19xx 1965 Florida House*	109	18	41.6
Legislative Bill 19xx 1965 Florida Senate	58†	10	44.7
Legislative Bill 17xx 1966 1967 Florida House*	117	22	47.8
Legislative Bill 17xx 1966 1967 Florida Senate*	48	9‡	48.4
Reapportionment, 1967 (court-ordered) Florida House	119	22	49.6
Florida Senate	48	9	50.9

Source: Secretary of State of Florida.
* Declared unconstitutional.
† It should be noted that the presence of seven holdover senators gave duplicate membership to certain districts for 1967. Actually there were as many as sixty-five senators for that year. Five small counties were guaranteed senators although grouped with larger counties. The measure was declared unconstitutional by the United States Supreme Court.
‡ Includes Monroe County.

to enact enabling legislation for comprehensive planning and zoning (again, some acts were passed on a local basis); (7) the avoidance of most legislation authorizing governmental reorganization; (8) the setting of the level of welfare payments and of state salaries for executive and legislative posts at the rural rather than urban pay levels. Following reapportionment, legislative control shifted, presiding officers changed, and some legislation patterns in these areas have begun to change. Also, as will presently appear, the legislative voting pattern has changed from a factional one-party arrangement to a two-party system. Politics is no longer the conflict of "pork chopper" versus "lamb chopper." The presiding officers for the period 1967–71 (all having been designated by the Democratic caucus) have been: 1967, Speaker Ralph Turlington, Gainesville; 1969, Speaker Fred Schultz of Jacksonville; 1971, Speaker Richard Pettigrew of Miami, the first ever from that county. In the Senate, presidents serving or designated are: 1967, Verle Pope, St. Augustine; 1969, John Matthews, Jacksonville; 1971, Jerry Thomas, lower east coast.

Legislative politics has now become two-party politics: Republican versus Democratic. Table 14 shows the gradual rise in Republican representation in the legislature. Table 15 uses the 1967 election returns to show the party distribution if the apportionment had been on the basis of earlier districts.

Table 14

REPUBLICANS AND DEMOCRATS IN THE FLORIDA LEGISLATURE

Year		Actual Districts		Republican Percentage
		Democrat	Republican	
1961	Senate	37	1	.03
1961	House	88	7	.07
1963	Senate	43	2	.04
1963	House	109	16	.03
1965	Senate	42	2	.05
1965	House	102	10	.09
1967	Senate	28	20	.42
1967	House	80	39	.33
1969	Senate	32	16	.30
1969	House	78	41	.35
1971	Senate	32	16	.30
1971	House	79	38	.32

Source: Data from Manning J. Dauer and Elston Roady, study for National Municipal
League (manuscript, Gainesville, Fla.).

Table 15

1967 ELECTION RETURNS FOR LEGISLATURE APPLIED TO FLORIDA
LEGISLATIVE DISTRICTS FOR EARLIER YEARS

| | Constructed District | | Republican Percentage |
	Democrat	Republican	
1961 Districts			
Senate	27	11	.29
House	71	24	.25
1963 Districts			
Senate	30	15	.33
House	90	35	.28
1965 Districts			
Senate	29	15	.34
House	81	31	.28
Actual 1967 Districts			
Senate	28	20	.42
House	80	39	.33
Actual 1969 Districts			
Senate	32	16	.30
House	78	41	.35

Presidential Politics and the Urban Horseshoe

With this background on the state's demographic, economic, governmental, and party structure at hand, we may now examine its
political composition during the years from 1948 through 1968.
At the start of this period Florida was, except for presidential politics, an overwhelmingly Democratic state. Table 16 shows that
of the eight presidential elections since 1940 the Democrats have
carried four and the Republicans four. But except for the loss by
Barry M. Goldwater in 1964, the Republicans have carried every
election beginning with that of 1952. Eisenhower defeated Adlai E.
Stevenson in 1952 and 1956. Nixon has carried Florida twice, in
1960 and in 1968. Overall, recent presidential politics has been Republican. In 1948 there were foreshadowings of the future. In the
race for the presidency Harry S. Truman ran against Thomas E.
Dewey, with Henry A. Wallace (Progressive Party) and J. Strom

Thurmond (States' Rights Party) also on the ballot. The results in Florida may be summarized as follows:

Thomas E. Dewey	194,280	
J. Strom Thurmond	89,755	
	284,035	Combined Dewey, Thurmond
Harry S. Truman	281,988	
Henry A. Wallace	11,620	
	293,608	Combined Truman, Wallace

Truman carried the state and the Wallace incursion was minor, but the combined Dewey-Thurmond vote exceeded the Truman vote and was only 9,600 less than the combined Truman-Wallace vote. This election result marks the inception of Florida's change in the direction of urban conservatism, and begins to show the extent to which changes in the state differentiate it from the rest of the South.

Table 16

FLORIDA PRESIDENTIAL VOTE,
GENERAL ELECTIONS, 1940–1968

Year	Republican Candidate	Vote	Democratic Candidate	Vote
1940	Wendell Willkie	126,158	Franklin D. Roosevelt	359,081
1944	Thomas E. Dewey	143,215	Franklin D. Roosevelt	339,377
1948*	Thomas E. Dewey	194,280	Harry S. Truman	281,988
1952	Dwight D. Eisenhower	544,036	Adlai E. Stevenson	444,950
1956	Dwight D. Eisenhower	643,849	Adlai E. Stevenson	480,371
1960	Richard M. Nixon	795,476	John F. Kennedy	748,700
1964	Barry M. Goldwater	905,941	Lyndon B. Johnson	948,540
1968†	Richard M. Nixon	886,804	Hubert H. Humphrey	676,794

Source: All election figures, Florida Secretary of State.
* J. Strom Thurmond, candidate of the States' Rights Party, won 89,755 votes. Henry A. Wallace, under the banner of the Progressive Party, won 11,620 votes.
† George C. Wallace, nominee of the American Independent Party, won 624,207 votes.

By the time of the Republican victories in 1952–68, a conservative pattern in the urban growth areas of central and south Florida had developed. Dade and Monroe counties remain Democratic, but on the east coast, a conservative urban geographical pattern appeared, resembling a horseshoe on the map. The horseshoe starts at Fort Lauderdale and Palm Beach, goes up the east coast to Daytona Beach, then across to Orlando, then to the west coast at St. Petersburg, and down the west coast to Fort Myers and Naples. This election pattern has predominated in presidential politics, and is clearly seen in the maps for the elections of 1952, 1956, and 1960 (see Figures 4, 5, and 6) and also holds for the 1968 presidential election (see Figure 7). Republican strength is greatest in the new growth areas of this horseshoe.

Florida has had a presidential preferential primary since 1904.[14] In 1948 the state's delegation at the Philadelphia convention voted for Richard Russell, and in 1952 the majority of the delegates was pledged to Russell. Four years later, delegates pledged to Adlai Stevenson carried most of the state. Since then, except in 1964, the delegation has been pledged to favorite-son candidates.

In the 1968 Democratic presidential primary, a favorite-son slate appeared for Senator George Smathers. A majority of the state's party leadership apparently favored this arrangement. In the convention the Florida delegation helped to nominate Hubert Humphrey. However, most of the state leaders were inactive in the general election. Holland campaigned for Humphrey, as did the Speaker of the House and some of the congressmen, but the rest of the Democratic leaders remained aloof from the campaign.

In the presidential primary a delegate slate for Senator Eugene McCarthy was nominated to oppose the slate for Senator Smathers. In the statewide delegate races and in ten of the twelve congressional contests, the Smathers slate won. The two congressional districts in which McCarthy delegates won were in Dade County.

The 1971 Florida Legislature has changed the presidential primary law. In the first place the general shift of the party primary

14 Dauer, "Toward a Model State Presidential Primary Law," 138–53.

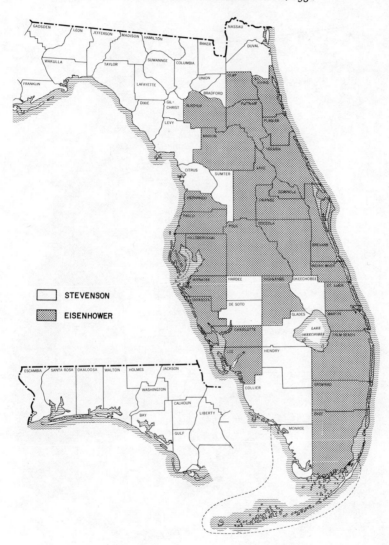

Figure 4
FLORIDA IN PRESIDENTIAL GENERAL ELECTION, 1952

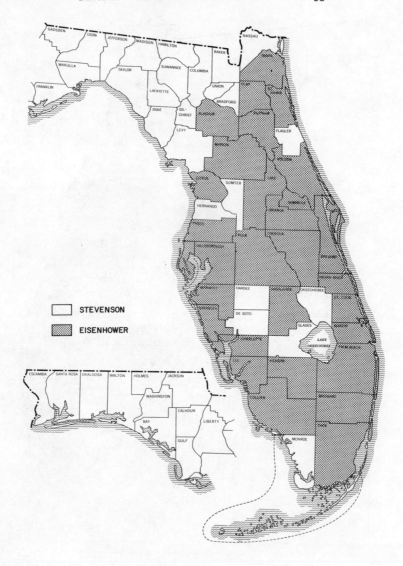

Figure 5
FLORIDA IN PRESIDENTIAL GENERAL ELECTION, 1956

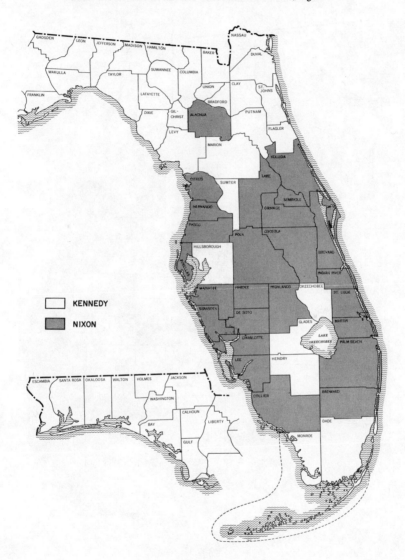

Figure 6
FLORIDA IN PRESIDENTIAL GENERAL ELECTION, 1960

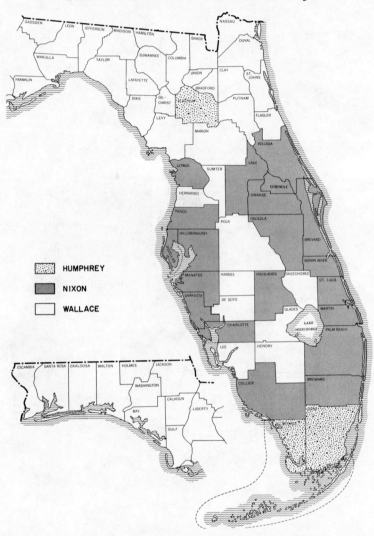

Figure 7
FLORIDA IN PRESIDENTIAL GENERAL ELECTION, 1968

HUMPHREY

NIXON

WALLACE

to September made it necessary to change the date. At the same time the legislature was attracted by moving the date early enough in the year to compete with the New Hampshire primary. At the time of writing the primary was scheduled to be held Tuesday, March 14, 1972. Furthermore, the new primary law sets up a bipartisan commission to place on the ballot the names of presidential candidates who are seriously considered nationally. To stay off the ballot any candidate must declare by affidavit that he is not seriously entertaining the possibility of accepting the presidential nomination. Also, instead of the convention delegates filing on the ballot under the name of the candidate, they will be chosen by the respective party committees through a procedure of county, congressional district, and state conventions. In these conventions a national presidential candidate, in addition to having his name entered on the primary ballot, may also enter delegate slates in the party convention races. Great interest was shown in the primary by those who were major figures in the parties.

Florida Senators: Moderate, Conservative, or Republican

Florida elections for the United States Senate since 1940 reveal the same trend. Either a Democratic moderate or conservative has been elected or, as in 1968, a Republican has won, as shown in Table 17.

Table 17

FLORIDA UNITED STATES SENATE VOTE, 1940–1970

Year	Republican Candidate	Vote	Democratic Candidate	Vote
1940	No candidate		Charles A. Andrews	323,216
1946	J. Harry Schad	42,408	Spessard L. Holland	156,232
1950	J. Booth	64,226	George A. Smathers	238,987
1952	No candidate		Spessard L. Holland	616,665
1956	No candidate		George A. Smathers	655,418
1958	Leland Hyzer	155,956	Spessard L. Holland	386,113
1962	Emerson Rupert	281,381	George A. Smathers	697,663
1964	Claude R. Kirk	562,212	Spessard L. Holland	997,585
1968	Edward J. Gurney	1,131,499	LeRoy Collins	892,637
1970	William Cramer	772,817	Lawton Chiles	902,438

Source: Election figures, Florida Secretary of State.

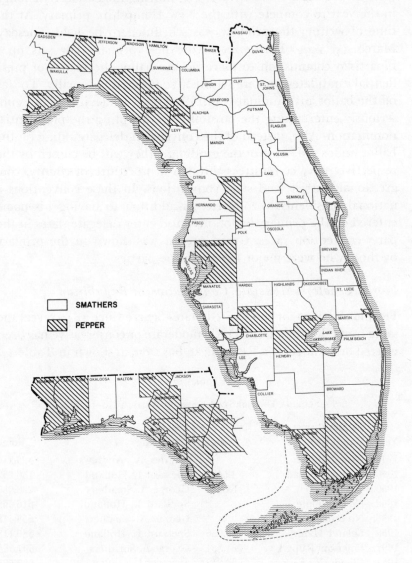

Figure 8
FLORIDA U.S. SENATE DEMOCRATIC PRIMARY, 1950

On the Democratic side, Senators Holland and Smathers dominate
the picture in the 1950's and 1960's. Holland, a former governor,
was elected to the Senate for four terms. When he first went to
Washington he was junior to Senator Claude Pepper, one of the
outstanding liberal Democratic leaders of the United States Senate.
Originally elected in 1936 for the two-year remainder of a senatorial
term, Pepper was reelected in 1938 and 1944. In 1950 he was opposed for the Democratic nomination by Smathers, then a congressman. Pepper campaigned on a liberal platform, calling for health
insurance, while Smathers took a conservative position. He criticized Pepper's labor union ties, his votes in favor of governmental
expenditures, and his moderate stance with regard to the Soviet
Union in foreign policy. The primary came just as Senator Joseph
McCarthy was waging his national campaign against communism
and alleged Communist influences. The result was a Democratic
primary victory for Smathers by a vote of 387,215 to 319,754. Pepper still had sufficient ties with the agrarian panhandle of old
Florida to divide the vote in that area (see Figure 8). He carried
Key West, Miami, Tampa, and Pensacola, but lost heavily in other
urban areas—Fort Lauderdale, Palm Beach, Daytona, Jacksonville;
and the rapidly growing areas of Orlando, St. Petersburg, and
Sarasota. He lost the wealthy agricultural counties of the orange
belt and of truck farming in central Florida. The new geographical
pattern of the urban conservative horseshoe was beginning to
emerge, this time in the Democratic primary. In the late fifties, as
the missile complex developed, Brevard County (Cape Kennedy)
and adjacent areas were also characterized by new growth areas
with conservative voting patterns.

Gubernatorial Politics: Moderate Conservatism

At the start of the period, in 1948, local and state government were
controlled by the Democrats (see Table 18). The dominant faction
was the one headed during 1944–48 by Governor Millard F. Caldwell. Caldwell threw his support in the 1948 election to the former
Speaker of the House, Dan McCarty of Fort Pierce. A more liberal

candidate, Fuller Warren of Jacksonville, defeated McCarty for
the Democratic nomination. Warren came from a populist and pro-
Roosevelt tradition, and had the covert support of Senator Pepper.
Warren appealed to both rural and urban liberals. More colorful
than McCarty, he had a program for developing tourism and the
citrus industry. As an administrator Warren was not adept, but had
he been a skilled administrator, it is still doubtful that he could
have developed the liberal position into a more lasting influence in
the state. In 1952 Dan McCarty won the governorship. He died
after only a few months in office.

Table 18

FLORIDA GUBERNATORIAL VOTE,
GENERAL ELECTIONS, 1940–1970

Year	Republican Candidate	Vote	Democratic Candidate	Vote
1940	No candidate	—	Spessard L. Holland	334,152
1944	Bert L. Acker	96,321	Millard Caldwell	361,007
1948	Bert L. Acker	76,153	Fuller Warren	381,459
1952	Harry S. Swan	210,009	Dan McCarty	624,463
1954	J. Tom Watson	69,852	LeRoy Collins	287,769
1956	William A. Washburne	269,980	LeRoy Collins	747,753
1960	George C. Petersen	569,936	Farris Bryant	849,407
1964	Charles R. Holley	686,297	Haydon Burns	933,554
1966	Claude R. Kirk	821,190	Robert K. High	668,233
1970	Claude R. Kirk	746,243	Reubin Askew	984,305

Under Florida constitutional provisions an election was held in
1954 to fill the remainder of McCarty's unexpired term. A Tallahassee state senator, LeRoy Collins, won this contest over the former
state Senate president, Charley E. Johns of Starke, who had succeeded McCarty in the governorship for a year and a half. This
1954 election probably was dominated by expectations of what
the candidates would do on the race question and on issues affecting
urban areas such as reapportionment, state constitutional revision,
and the building of more roads for rapidly growing areas. Collins
won, as Figure 9 shows, by handily carrying the urban counties. He

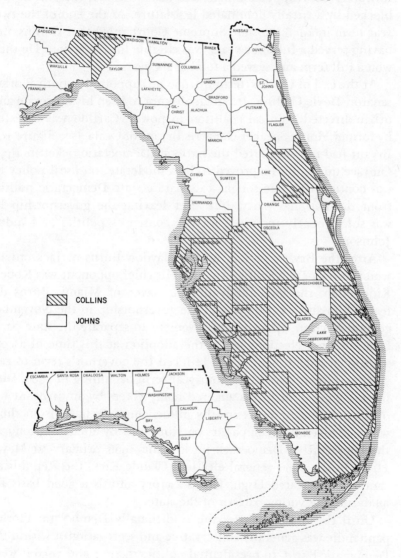

Figure 9
FLORIDA DEMOCRATIC GUBERNATORIAL PRIMARY, 1954

tried to press forward his policies and did start work on the Florida turnpike. On reapportionment and constitutional revision he was blocked by a rurally dominated legislature. At the end of the two-year term in 1956 the state Supreme Court ruled that Collins, not having served a full four years, was eligible for reelection. He then won a full term and served a total of six years.

At the end of Collins' term in 1960 he supported a south Florida senator, Doyle Carlton, Jr., in an attempt to keep his moderate and urban-directed political coalition in power. Carlton was defeated by former House Speaker C. Farris Bryant of Ocala (see Figure 10). Bryant had not supported the national Democratic ticket in 1952. On race questions, he proved to be a moderate; on fiscal policy he was conservative. He sought to separate state Democratic politics from the national party, but after leaving the governorship he was subsequently recruited for the consensus politics of Lyndon Johnson.

After the Bryant period, Mayor Haydon Burns of Jacksonville won the 1964 Democratic primary. His chief opponent was Robert King High, the moderately liberal mayor of Miami. Burns defeated him and went on to win the governorship in the November general election. However, a movement to separate the state party from national elections led to the adoption at this time of a constitutional amendment which reduced the governor's term to two years and then restored the four-year term beginning in 1966. During his short term Burns angered many voters by an arrogant use of his patronage powers and by influencing purchases from those who had given him campaign contributions. By alienating some of the conservative Democrats, he lost the 1966 primary to Mayor High. In the 1966 general election, Claude Kirk, the Republican candidate, defeated High. Kirk's victory affords a good basis for analyzing the voting pattern of the state.

Until the middle sixties the traditionally Democratic Florida panhandle was generally conservative and segregationist within the Democratic Party. In presidential politics in 1952 and 1956 it went for Stevenson. In 1948 and 1968 it favored Thurmond and Wallace, respectively (Figures 4, 5, 6, 7 for 1952, 1956, 1960, 1968). In

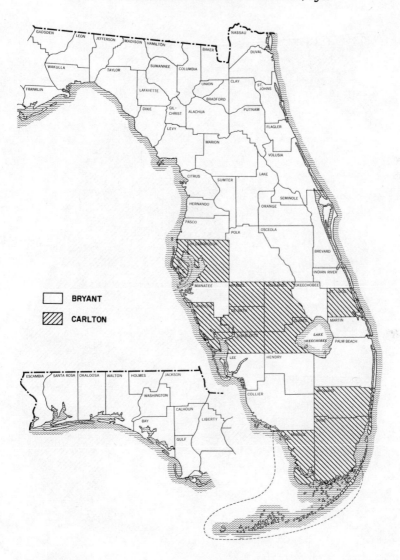

Figure 10
Florida Democratic Gubernatorial Primary, 1960

BRYANT

CARLTON

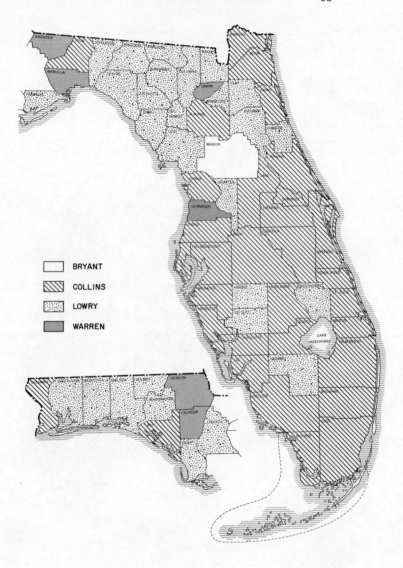

Figure 11
FLORIDA DEMOCRATIC GUBERNATORIAL PRIMARY, 1956

BRYANT
COLLINS
LOWRY
WARREN

Democratic primaries the panhandle supported conservative guber-natorial nominees. On this point let us consider the moderately liberal Collins versus the segregationist Sumter L. Lowry in 1956 (Figure 11). Lowry carried the panhandle areas of north and west Florida (although not the urban counties of Duval [Jacksonville]; Alachua [Gainesville]; Leon [Tallahassee]; Bay [Panama City]; and Escambia [Pensacola]). This candidate was too extreme a segrega-tionist for the urban areas, even in north Florida. Moreover, Collins was a moderate.

As time moved on, Republican registration increased during the sixties, as has already been shown. At the same time Negro registra-tion rose. In many of the urban areas there is now an overall ma-jority which favors moderate conservatism. But what does this term mean in Florida? It means, in addition to economic conserva-tism, some resistance to integration, but not to the point of support for a Eugene "Bull" Connor, a Lowry, or a Wallace. But the con-servative vote is now divided as to actual political party affiliation. Part of it is registered in the Democratic Party and part in the Republican. Almost all the Republican vote is conservative. In the Democratic Party, on the other hand, the major share of the urban vote is liberal. Sarasota and Pinellas counties may be taken as examples. In the 1966 Democratic gubernatorial primary the liberal candidate, Robert King High, carried Sarasota against Haydon Burns. But in the general election the party's conservatives left the Democratic candidate and voted Republican, so Kirk carried the general election. (See Figures 12 and 13.) Basic Republican strength was shown in the general election for attorney general, Earl Faircloth (Democrat) versus Ellis Rubin (Republican). The same thing happened in the Democratic primary race in 1968 for the Senate. The moderately liberal Collins narrowly defeated his opponent, Earl Faircloth, in the second Democratic primary. Col-lins' strength, however, was concentrated in Dade and the strongly Republican urban counties of the horseshoe configuration. (See Figure 14.) In the general election in November, Collins faced Edward J. Gurney, the Republican candidate, who carried sixty-three of the counties, the exceptions being the liberal counties of

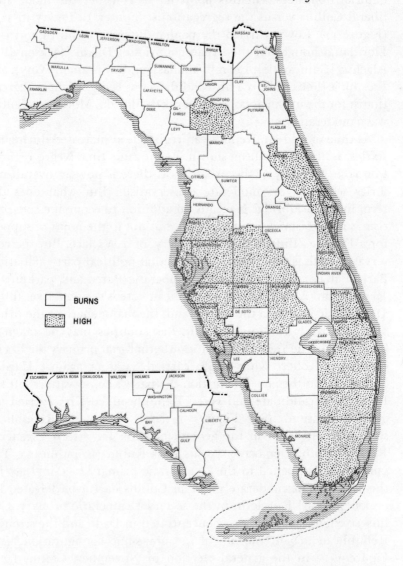

Figure 12
FLORIDA DEMOCRATIC GUBERNATORIAL PRIMARY, 1966

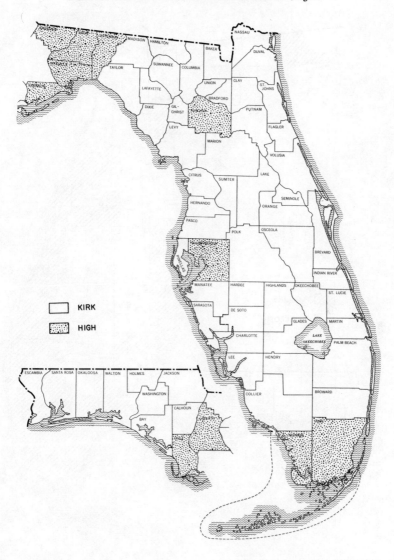

Figure 13
FLORIDA GUBERNATORIAL GENERAL ELECTION, 1966

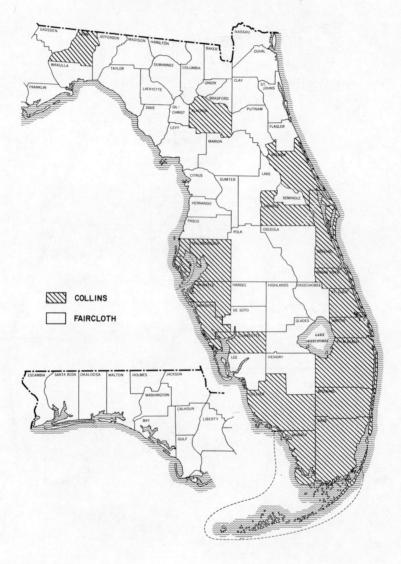

Figure 14
FLORIDA U.S. SENATE DEMOCRATIC PRIMARY, 1968

COLLINS

FAIRCLOTH

Figure 15
FLORIDA U.S. SENATORIAL GENERAL ELECTION, 1968

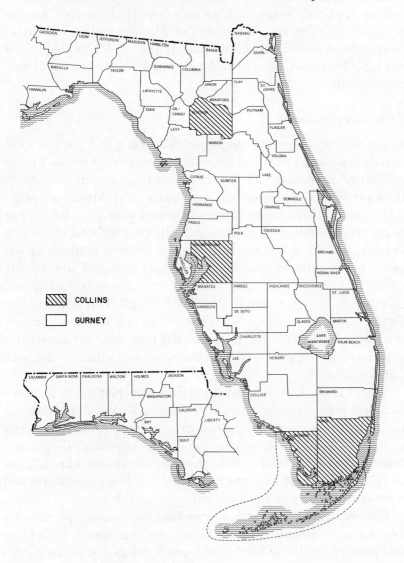

COLLINS

GURNEY

Dade (Miami), Monroe (Key West), Hillsborough (Tampa), and Alachua (Gainesville). (See Figure 15.) This is virtually the same pattern displayed in the Kirk victory over High in 1966 for the governorship. The Old South area of Florida, which is the panhandle and northern part of the state, is (except for local elections and most legislative races) breaking away from traditional Democratic voting.

Republican Outreach

At the start of the period, the Republican Party did not run local or state candidates with any organization support. The state party committee campaigned for the presidency only; then if the Republican candidate was elected the committee distributed patronage. This state of affairs began to be challenged after 1950 by the rise of county Republican organizations, following the lead of the one headed by William C. Cramer in Pinellas County. Before long Republicans established county organizations and then won county offices including virtually all county commission, school board, sheriff, and other positions in Pinellas, Broward (Fort Lauderdale), Orange (Orlando), and Sarasota counties, among others. Ultimately the leadership of this group of counties took over the state party machinery and began to build a statewide participatory Republican organization.

Next, Claude Kirk entered the Republican picture. A businessman and promoter who turned to politics, Kirk did not come to the fore through work in the county or state machinery. In 1964 he won the Republican nomination to oppose veteran Democratic Senator Spessard L. Holland. In that race he was unsuccessful, but in 1966 he benefited from the nomination of High over Burns and went on to victory in the 1966 gubernatorial election.

Kirk immediately sought to move into the national picture. He began a campaign for the Republican vice presidency. To achieve this goal, he needed to control the state's delegation to the party's national convention in 1968. In addition to efforts in that direction, the governor began a frantic campaign to become known in other states, spending from half to two-thirds of his time away from the state capital. The result was a factional split among Republicans and a disaster for Kirk. The state party organization liked Nixon and was pledged to him, but Kirk was unacceptable as a Vice President to Nixon. Then Kirk began to support Nelson Rockefeller and sought to deliver the Florida delegation for a Rockefeller-Kirk slate. The governor failed in efforts to wrest control of the delegate slate from the Murfin-Cramer leadership. He also lost the New Hampshire primary to another candidate for the vice presidency, Chief Burning Tree. During this period he collected funds at dinners for the Republican Party but, along with state moneys, they were then used in his own vice-presidential campaign. Subsequently, he established a Governor's Club to accept contributions separate from those made to the party. When Kirk sought renomination for a second term a tight primary race against a Republican opponent resulted and then led to his defeat for reelection in the general election of November, 1970.

By 1970 the split in Republican ranks was acute. On the one hand the Kirk-Gurney machine controlled the governorship and one United States Senate seat. Kirk himself sought reelection and first persuaded his lieutenant governor, Ray Osborne, to seek the Republican Senate nomination. Then, when Federal Circuit Judge G. Harrold Carswell of Tallahassee was defeated by the United States Senate for nomination to the Supreme Court, Kirk and Gurney persuaded Carswell to resign his circuit judgeship and run for the Senate. They then sought (unsuccessfully) to pressure Florida's senior Republican congressman, William C. Cramer, to withdraw. A bitter battle developed in the September Republican primary with Cramer defeating Carswell by two to one but then losing the general election.

At the same time the Cramer faction supported the campaign of Jack Eckerd, a multimillionaire chain drugstore owner, against Kirk in the Republican primary. Thus the campaign for the September primaries witnessed a strong division in Republican ranks. Eckerd forced Kirk into a second primary and Kirk then lost his reelection bid by 238,000 votes to his Democratic opponent.

This organizational (or personal) split has somewhat decreased Republican power in the state and contributed to the loss of a seat in the Florida Senate between 1966 and 1968 and three House seats in 1970. But the basis for the general rise in Republican strength can be understood if we analyze the relationship between voting patterns and the socioeconomic data considered earlier.

A Closeup of Ten Elections

What socioeconomic factors account most effectively for the way the electorate votes? To help answer this question the voting behavior of Florida's sixty-seven counties was studied for ten elections covering the period 1960–68. The election returns were secured for major statewide races, by counties. For the same counties certain socioeconomic data were secured, including the following: (1) income level by counties; (2) education level by counties; (3) percentage of county population over age sixty-five; (4) percentage of county population in manufacturing; (5) percentage in agriculture; (6) in-migration into county since last census. Then two types of correlation were calculated. First, single correlations were figured between the ranking of each county on such a factor as income and ranking in each county's vote percentage for Collins, the liberal Senate candidate. The details will not be presented here, but the best correlation may be summarized. In most elections high-income counties vote Republican, and low-income counties vote Democratic (or, in 1968, for Wallace). Counties with heavy urbanism, a low labor union vote, a large proportion of population over sixty-five years of age, high college attendance, and high expenditure per pupil on education vote Republican in most elections. Democrats led in counties with low urbanism (not true of Dade with its large labor union vote), low per capita income, low levels of education, and low proportion of population over sixty-five.

When George C. Wallace is added to the picture, his strength shows up in most rural counties in any part of the state, north or south. He also encroaches on the Democrats in some counties with low per capita income, without regard to the extent of their ruralness. All of these points may be clearly perceived in Figures 2, 16,

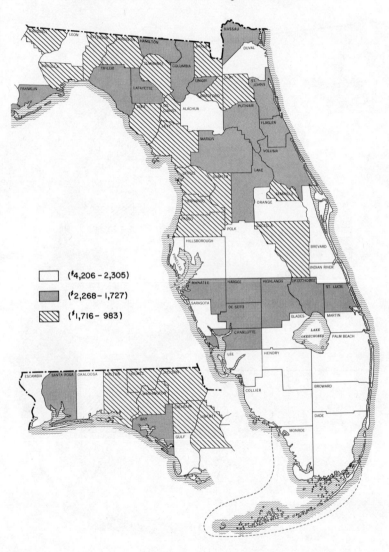

Figure 16
PERSONAL INCOME PER CAPITA, 1966, IN FLORIDA

($4,206 – 2,305)
($2,268 – 1,727)
($1,716 – 983)

Figure 17
FLORIDA REPUBLICAN REGISTRATION IN OCTOBER, 1968

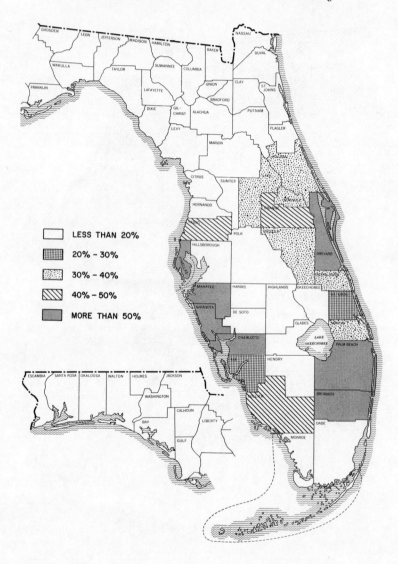

and 17. Counties with heavy in-migration of those born in other states tend to be Republican. Counties with the highest proportion of foreign-born populations tend to be Democratic. In employment by categories, counties with the heaviest manufacturing tend toward the Democrats, or the liberal candidate in primaries. Counties with high proportions of government workers tend to be Democratic. On the other hand, counties with large numbers of people employed in service trades correlate positively with Republicanism.

Another type of correlation was also calculated and is presented in Table 19. This is a stepwise multiple correlation analysis. In this table all the socioeconomic variables are run at the same time against the rank order of the counties for Wallace. Then the factor named in Step 1 emerges as explaining why voters in these counties favored Wallace. In this case it is the percentage of county population with income over $15,000, and the correlation is negative. So low per capita income in a county matches a vote for Wallace; the next factor is death rate among whites; then education; and so on through other factors listed in the value column of the table.

Voter turnout has sharply increased in Florida. At the start of this period in presidential elections it hovered around 39 percent. It rose to 52.9 percent of the eligible voters in 1964 and to 55.8 percent in 1968. The 1964 turnout is about 10 percent below that of other large urban states but is the highest in the southeastern states. Off-year elections for state and federal offices now bring a high turnout, contrasted with a vote as low as 20 percent of eligible voters in the 1940's and early 1950's. This upswing is due to more competitive politics and to increased Negro registration.

Candidates normally must carry Florida's counties of over 100,000 population to win. In ninety-two general elections and primary nominations between 1956 and 1968 for Florida statewide races, candidates carrying a majority of the vote in the fifteen such counties won the nomination or election in eighty-seven instances. Only five candidates lost the populous counties but won the nomination or election. All constitutional amendments adopted since 1956 carried majorities in the populous counties. Clearly emphasis on the urban areas is significant in statewide campaigns.

Table 19

WALLACE VOTE IN 1968, FLORIDA COUNTIES
IN MULTIPLE CORRELATION STEPWISE REGRESSION ANALYSIS

Multiple R Value	Positive or Negative on Single Correlation	Step I	Value of F*
.7635	−	% Income over $15,000	90.848
		Step II	
.8408	−	Deaths per 1000 White	77.174
		Step III	
.9059	−	% Completing High School	96.137
		Step IV	
.9171	+	% Employed by Government	90.848
		Step V	
.9234	−	% In-migrated	70.619
		Step VI	
.9300	−	Mean High School	64.050
		Step VII	
.9354	−	% Urban	58.970

* Value of F is significant in all cases.

A Changing Conservatism

How have these changes in Florida politics affected state and national policy? We may start with congressional voting.

Congressional redistricting was forced in Florida by a United States Supreme Court decision in 1968. As a result one congressional seat has been moved from north Florida, which had been overrepresented, to south Florida, which had been underrepresented. The outcome is a Republican gain of one seat in the Fort Lauderdale district, the most rapidly growing area in the South. As in the state legislature, a rural conservative has been replaced by an urban conservative. There is a change in party affiliation, but the rural conservative who voted about one-third of the time for liberally oriented legislation has been replaced by one who has voted almost unanimously for conservative legislation. The voting pattern of the

Florida congressmen is shown in Table 20. These 1968 AFL-CIO congressional ratings are based on a liberal-conservative division, as organized labor perceives it.

Table 20

AFL-CIO RATING, FLORIDA CONGRESSIONAL DELEGATION, 1967–1968

	Right*	Wrong*
Senate		
Holland	17	79
Smathers	30	46
House		
Sikes (D)	33	55
Fuqua (D)	6	30
Bennett (D)	38	51
Herlong (D)	20	69
Gurney (R)	1	36
Gibbons (D)	28	9
Haley (D)	6	73
Cramer (R)	3	70
Rogers (D)	22	54
Burke (R)	1	12
Pepper (D)	39	0
Fascell (D)	57	19

* AFL-CIO terminology.

The voting patterns of half the Democrats are close to those of the Republicans on the measures in this index. The same voting configuration appears in indexes of the Americans for Democratic Action and the Americans for Constitutional Action. Thus cohesion among Democrats is also breaking down. V. O. Key found that through 1945 the Democrats of the South were voting with each other and with the northern Democrats. This pattern was no longer true in the 1960's in Florida. Except in the Miami and Tampa districts congressmen who opposed federal spending policies were popularly supported throughout Florida. During 1971, newly elected United States Senator Lawton Chiles established a moderate-liberal voting record.

At the state and local levels also there is a pronounced emphasis on economy. The provisions of the 1885 Florida constitution and of its 1968 counterpart assure a regressive tax system. Both documents exempt homesteads from real property taxation on the first $5,000 of assessed value. The 1968 constitution extends this exemption to condominiums and cooperatives and authorizes the legislature to increase it to more than $10,000 for those over sixty-five years of age. The Florida constitution also prohibits a state income tax unless in the future there is federal sharing of this tax. The state supreme court has extended this provision to include a prohibition against the corporate income tax. Although the constitution does not prohibit a state severance tax, none has been levied. The effect of this regressive tax system is a fiscal policy dependent on consumer taxes. Another conservative provision in the Florida constitution is the "right-to-work" amendment, restricting the union shop for labor organizations.

Spending policies at the state level may next be examined. The construction of roads proceeds at a high level of efficiency, and appropriations are substantial since modern highways are recognized as necessary in a tourist state. Welfare expenditures, on the other hand, are kept at a comparatively low level. Florida ranked thirty-seventh among the states in 1964 in per capita expenditures for public welfare.[15] In expenditures per pupil in public schools during 1964–65, the state ranked thirty-sixth.[16] Yet, as has been noted, Florida stands just below the national average in per capita income level; the ability to pay is here.

In the case of public institutions, there is again inadequate fiscal support, especially for a rapidly growing state. For example, a wooden barracks from World War II at a state prison camp in Jay caught fire and burned thirty-eight prisoners to death in 1967. Again, the inadequacy of the Delinquent Boys Training Center in Marianna led to investigations in 1969, but the subsequent reorganization made few fundamental changes. A state hospital in DeSoto

15 Bureau of the Census, *Compendium of State Finance, 1964,* cited in *Book of the States, 1966–67* (Chicago, 1966).
16 National Education Association, *Research Report 1965–R17* (Washington, 1965).

County, also in worn-out World War II buildings, was the object of an investigation, but in 1969 the legislature refused to make further appropriations for this facility. The state university system is not supported at a high level of expenditure. However, in other areas of education, urbanism has produced more adequate support. Florida has a system of about twenty-five two-year colleges providing college and vocational education to nearly 140,000 enrolled students. This is the best record in the southeast. Though earlier administrations had shown little concern for significant prison or welfare reform, Reubin Askew, the new governor, has proposed a substantial program of prison reform and other social measures.

An example of the incidence of taxation is given in a recent study on costs of higher education in Florida. This study shows the costs to families at various income levels, what the families paid in taxes, and what they received. It reveals that fewer poor families send their children to college, but they pay more of the taxes going to higher education. The results are shown in Table 21.

Table 21

COSTS PER INCOME GROUP AND
STATE APPROPRIATIONS RECEIVED PER INCOME GROUP,
FLORIDA HIGHER EDUCATION, 1967–1968

Income Group	Taxes Paid for Higher Education	Benefits Received from Higher Education
Under $3,000	$10.3 million	$ 6.4 million
$5,000–10,000	$45.9 million	$41.2 million
Over $10,000	$25.7 million	$41.5 million

Source: Douglas M. Windham, "State Finance of Higher Education and Distribution of Income in Florida" (Ph.D. dissertation, Florida State University, 1969). See also Miami *Herald*, July 6, 1969, p. B1.

The regressive tax structure of Florida has finally caused a revolt by Florida's voters. In the 1970 Florida Democratic primary, State Senator Reubin Askew was almost a one-issue candidate. He came out flatly for a corporate income tax, pointing out that the Florida tax burden was inequitable as to its exemption for business and its heavy incidence on the consumer. Until he stressed this issue he was probably the least known among four candidates in the primary. But on this issue he won a place in the second primary, also won it easily, and then confronted the Republican incumbent, Claude Kirk. Kirk's arrogance had made him quite unpopular and Askew then won the general election handily. Once in office, Askew sought a reinterpretation of the Florida Supreme Court's decision ruling the corporate tax unconstitutional. When the court handed down its decision, he called a special session of the state legislature to submit an emergency constitutional amendment to the voters. This amendment was approved by 70 percent of the voters and the legislature subsequently enacted the tax.

The consequence of the low levels of provision for welfare, education, and public institutions naturally is a rather low level of public services. This problem has led to such developments as the statewide teachers' strike in 1968. Only after the strike did the governor agree to add a fourth cent to the state sales tax and to increase public school spending.

Welfare expenditures in Florida may be considered for a few specifics. Among agricultural counties with high per capita incomes are Lee and Collier counties. In March, 1969, Senator George S. McGovern of South Dakota led an investigation by the Select Committee on Nutrition and Human Needs of food requirements and welfare needs of migrant workers in these and other agricultural areas. The committee found no program for meeting the costs of distribution of federal food by the Collier County officials; in Lee County some provisions for food distribution had been made.[17] In still another welfare area, Florida had no provision for participation in Medicaid, until the 1969 legislature appropriated funds for minimum participation. In general the welfare picture shows a low level of state effort and minimal state programs.

Florida has been slow to introduce regulatory legislation or regulatory agencies in many areas of the economy affecting the public

[17] St. Petersburg *Times*, March 19–21, 1969; Senator George S. McGovern, press release, March 23, 1969 (clipping in possession of author).

interest. Public power regulation by the Florida Public Service Commission is hampered by lack of funds for investigating rates. For a long time there was inadequate water and air pollution control and unrestrained sale of riparian lands to private investors. Now the problem of water and air pollution is bringing a changed attitude toward regulation; also much greater concern is being shown for the preservation of public access to waterways and beaches. Pollution is bad for business, and the growing shortage of natural resource areas for public use is causing the state to assume greater responsibility in this field. For a long time, Florida lagged in planning and zoning in urban renewal. Finally, however, legislation was adopted in 1969 authorizing urban renewal by local government units and providing authority for planning and zoning. Previously, only local bills had authorized such programs.

In 1970 and 1971 the politics of ecology became greatly intensified in Florida. Interestingly, support for ecological legislation is strongest in the heavily populated areas of the state and in higher-income Republican areas such as Broward County (Fort Lauderdale), Orange County (Orlando), and Pinellas County (St. Petersburg). Among the pressing problems is the fact that raw sewage is being poured into rivers, streams, the Gulf of Mexico, and the Atlantic Ocean. Moreover the water supply of south Florida has raised critical questions about the drainage of the Everglades, the lowering of the fresh water table, and resulting salt water intrusion. In another, more critical issue, a jetport for transatlantic air transport planes was proposed for a location west of Miami in the Everglades. Construction of this was stopped by the Nixon administration. Although some individuals with adjacent investments have objected, the action has been widely popular. Further, the Nixon administration moved to stop construction of the Cross Florida Barge Canal, which was projected to connect the port of Jacksonville by way of the St. Johns River with an outlet near Crystal River on the Gulf coast. This canal promised severely to diminish central Florida's water supply; at the same time the plan was uneconomical in that the size of the barges would be below that of standard ocean-going barges, and there is no waterway connection between the Gulf terminus except by ferrying open barges across part of the Gulf. In the problems of the Florida ecology generally, Democratic officials have taken some measures, but the Republican national administration has taken a strong lead.

In the field of governmental structural change, Florida has progressed more than in labor, welfare, and regulatory areas. Efficiency in local government has long been popular among both conservatives and liberals. City-manager government is popular, and in 1962 there were 107 city-manager communities in Florida, the largest number for any state in the southeast.[18] Another structural change, consolidation of government at the local level, took place as early as 1955 in Dade County and Miami under a new home rule amendment to the Florida constitution. The Miami-Dade plan provides a federal system of coordination between local county and city governments.[19] An amendment authorizing consolidation of local governments in Jacksonville and Duval County was added to the state constitution in the 1930's, but at that time a local referendum defeated any such change. Then a new plan for complete consolidation in Jacksonville and Duval County, introduced in the 1967 legislature, was approved by the voters. In other parts of Florida plans for consolidating city and county governments are under consideration. Furthermore, the new constitution authorizes consolidation of local governments in any county. The adoption of such programs requires that local legislators introduce measures to effect the change and that these measures be approved by the voters of the area affected. Two or more counties may also, under the constitution, consolidate their school systems. Election of county officials may be changed to appointment by the county commission in a small county, and a county-manager system may be adopted. Innovation and experimentation at the local level has even meant authorization of a special government charter for Disneyworld (the eastern version of Disneyland), which has opened in the Orlando area.

18 Gladys M. Kammerer, Charles D. Farris, John M. DeGrove, and Alfred B. Clubok, *City Managers in Politics: An Analysis of Manager Tenure and Termination*, University of Florida Monograph, Social Sciences, No. 13 (Gainesville, 1962), 4.
19 Edward Sofen, *Miami's Metropolitan Experiment* (Bloomington, Ind., 1963).

This special charter provides for an entire planned community, including recreation, business, and housing areas. In contrast to such innovative governmental provisions, fiscal stipulations of the 1968 constitution affecting localities require very strict millage limitations on real property taxes and also increase homestead exemptions. Any expansion of local facilities may require bond issues, which only postpone the date of ultimate fiscal reckoning. Thus, in aid to local government the new constitution giveth but it also taketh away.

Racial politics in Florida is, on the other hand, moderate. At the height of southern racial tension in 1956, the segregationist Sumter L. Lowry was defeated by LeRoy Collins. Thurmond ran far behind Dewey in 1948. Wallace was third, behind Nixon and Humphrey, in 1968. Former Governor Kirk is a fiscal conservative and initially was a moderate on race questions. With the advent of school busing under federal court orders in 1970 Kirk believed defiance of courts to be good politics. He has expressed sharp opposition to decrees for busing in a number of counties and has for a time won wide publicity by defying one court order. He sought legislation to cut off the use of state or local funds for busing to bring about integration. He moved to the position of claiming state sovereignty. On the other hand other legislation affecting race relations has not been extreme, and school integration proceeded rather well until school busing rekindled controversy in 1970. Business programs for employment of Negroes and some vocational training programs for blacks and whites are moderately successful.

On foreign policy, Florida's Republicans and conservative Democrats in Congress are close together. They are skeptical of foreign aid or they oppose it outright. They supported construction of the Anti-Ballistic Missile System. Originally they were hawkish on Vietnam; later, as is the case with Senator Edward J. Gurney, they have begun to advocate an either-or policy—either go all out and win or get out. This position evidently reflects that of the majority of Florida voters.

The voters' approval of the new state constitution showed their willingness to modernize the structure of government. On labor, on welfare, and in the areas of public finance this is a conservative document, but fiscal conservatism does not mean opposition to structural change. The 1969 legislature reorganized the executive branch of the state government and submitted a constitutional amendment for judicial reorganization to the voters in 1970, but this met with defeat at the polls. The new constitution provides for annual sessions and adequate staff for the legislature. Another provision places the state auditor's department under legislative control. The structure of local government may be drastically modified through new constitutional provisions in this area, and many such modifications are in process.

Some effective steps have been taken to regulate pollution and to preserve natural resources (although a cross-state barge canal threatened interference with many wildlife areas). But welfare, health, and institutional problems have been swept under the rug. A proposed constitutional amendment to enfranchise eighteen-year-olds was defeated by the voters in 1970.

Campaigns and Lobbies

The style of Florida politics has changed in twenty years. At the time of V. O. Key's study, Florida politicians relied heavily in statewide elections on county campaign organizations, put together by a particular candidate, who campaigned at local rallies and through radio and newspaper advertising. Now, with the state population doubled and concentrated in fifteen urban centers, the picture has changed. The campaign depends on what happens in these centers containing 80 percent of the population. Local and neighborhood meetings cannot reach enough voters. The emphasis is on television coverage and on the candidate who "projects" through the TV tube. Kirk and Gurney, the successful candidates in the 1968 major statewide races, are such candidates. Kirk, although lacking a comprehensive program, is an effective promoter. Gurney has an excellent television personality. LeRoy Collins had both a program and a fairly effective TV manner, but his program was not attractive to many of the newer voters, and he did not match Gurney in skill of presentation. Even the local races in metropolitan areas are increasingly dependent on television.

To campaign in this fashion requires money; recent successful statewide campaigns have cost as much as one million dollars. Thus big political contributors become more influential. After an investigation of campaign spending in 1949, Florida enacted a law requiring that contributions be reported. This law places no ceiling on the amount that a candidate may spend. Observers feel that even the reporting requirement is ineffective.[20]

With the advent of large-scale TV campaigning has come the professional manager. Claude Kirk's successful 1966 campaign for the governorship was managed by Robert E. Lee, who had directed effective Republican campaigns in Colorado. Lee's specialties include the packaging of issues, development of central themes to be stressed, and skillful use of TV. He specializes in mass-media presentation rather than political organization. After Kirk was elected, Lee pursued the goal of further publicizing the governor. Kirk had the state Development Commission award Florida's annual advertising contract to the firm of William A. Safire of New York. Safire then provided publicity materials known as the politics of confrontation, as the basis of Kirk's national campaign for the Republican vice-presidential nomination in 1968. The adverse effects of this effort have been described.

On the Democratic side, no effective campaign manager connected with the official party committees has emerged. Professional public relations personnel are employed, but not at the level at which major strategy is determined. In primary campaigns one professional manager, Elmer Rounds, has appeared. The weakness of the Democratic state committee, factionalism among political leaders, and dissidence from the national party have prevented effective state party coordination.

Racial politics has changed in Florida. It is no longer possible to hold segregated campaign meetings for voters. Also the increased Negro vote causes candidates to be somewhat moderate on racial

[20] E. F. Roady, "Florida's New Campaign Expense Law and the 1952 Democratic Gubernatorial Primaries," *American Political Science Review,* XLVIII (1954), 465.

issues. Not only do white extremists not win statewide elections, but Negroes sometimes win local elections, as in city council or school board contests in Miami, Gainesville, and Jacksonville. One black member of the legislature has also been elected from Dade County. When the Negro vote helps to nominate a liberal, however, that candidate is likely to lose the general election. In Florida, as in most states outside the South, the concentration of the Negro vote in certain localities, rather than its mere presence, is the most important factor in its effect on politics.

With the 1970 campaign there was a change away from the emphasis on TV spending. Two new Democratic candidates emerged on the state scene—Reubin Askew in the gubernatorial race and Lawton Chiles in the United States Senate contest. Both lacked money for heavy TV expenditures. Askew solved the problem by probing the state tax structure and promising to solve the state fiscal crisis by supporting a corporate income tax. With this issue he transcended the bland TV presentations by other candidates and won both nomination and election contests. Chiles chose another avenue to make himself known. Having a pleasant personality, he conducted his campaign by walking the length of the state, over 1,000 miles from Pensacola to Key West. Meeting people as he walked, he impressed the voters with his ability to talk to the general citizen and to discuss matters in lay terms. Gradually he received more and more attention and full TV and news coverage. He easily won the primary contest against a former governor, C. Farris Bryant, and then won the general election against Florida's "Mr. Republican," the seven-term congressman William C. Cramer. Cramer had also the support of President Richard Nixon, who vainly made three campaign stops in Florida seeking to aid him.

Lobbying in Florida has undergone change since reapportionment. In the old legislature, dominated by the rural counties, the proportion of lobbying conducted in the state capitol was heavy. Lobbyists entertained legislators while the sessions were held, and there was much direct contact with the legislators. Lobbying at the capitol continues but with much less entertaining of legislators and less expenditure at the capitol. On the other hand there is extensive contact with the urban legislators through lobbying in the towns and cities. There are more contributions to campaign costs there, and more direct interaction between local business, labor, and ethnic groups with legislators in their localities. Many of the older lobbyists have retired and a new lower-key lobbying has developed.

Among the chief conservative lobbying groups in Florida are Associated Industries, whose lobby is headed by Jack Lee, an effective individual in the legislative halls. The Florida Power Corporation, Florida Power and Light, the racetracks, the Phosphate Council, and the state Farm Bureau are also prominent in lobbying and in campaign contributions to legislators and to statewide races. Other powerful forces are chain stores, the liquor industry, and two groups of bankers. In 1969 and in 1970 Ed Ball, heading the Florida Dupont interests, tried to have a bill enacted to authorize branch banking. He is affected by federal legislation requiring sale of either the manufacturing and railroad interests or the more than twenty banks of the Florida Bank chain. To date he has been defeated by the independent bankers. The Dupont interests headed by Ball have been important in enacting laws and electing governors. Before the election of the present governor, Ball had backed the last two victorious Democratic governors, Farris Bryant and Haydon Burns, and the victorious Republican Claude Kirk. He likewise backed Edward Gurney, who won the contest for the United States Senate seat over the Democrat LeRoy Collins.

These conservative groups are opposed by the Florida Education Association, the AFL-CIO, and representatives of retired people. This combination is much less effective in legislative impact. Florida is one of the states with a "right-to-work" provision in its state constitution. The level of school support is somewhat higher than in most other southern states, but below that of other highly urbanized states. In common with many other states, by 1970–71, a critical attitude had developed toward higher education, particularly in the Florida Senate. The same low level of support applies to welfare payments and assistance for the aged. The 1971 legislature reflected urban areas, but it reflected the conservative dominance of suburbia, not the core-city liberal groups, which in Florida are in the minority on a statewide basis.

The dominant conservative mood of Florida includes a marked

strain of antigovernmentalism. This conservatism is especially critical of the federal government, federal power, and federal spending.
In the heavy growth areas of central and south Florida, some of the
newspapers are not stridently antigovernmental, but organizations
of business leaders and civic clubs in this area strongly reflect this
attitude, as do the voting patterns. This antigovernment attitude is
especially strong in the growing "missile country" around Cape
Kennedy. This is the home of Edward Gurney, formerly a congressman, now a senator.

In north Florida, antigovernmentalism includes strong criticism
of the federal guidelines for school integration, although even here
opposition on the basis of race has not reached the level of defiance.
But most of the north Florida press is even more critical of the
federal government than is the press of central and south Florida.
This dominant conservatism has produced a politics that began
with the presidential Republicanism of 1952 and 1956, and by 1968
had led to a Republican governor, a legislature in which one-third
of the members of each house are Republican, a Republican in the
United States Senate, and three Republican congressmen. This
pattern is the response to the urban growth of Florida and to the
economic and social trends noted earlier. On the other hand, although liberal Democrats (as the voters conceive them) like Robert
King High in 1966 and LeRoy Collins in 1968 cannot win, moderate Democrats like Reubin Askew and Lawton Chiles can win.

Florida's Peculiar Urbanism

What conclusions may be drawn from this analysis? The point has
been made that the socioeconomic and demographic composition
of Florida have much to do with its politics. To a considerable extent the voters react in terms of their outlook, which reflects the
social and economic environment and the new suburbia. This political outlook is related to the growth of the state, to Florida's peculiar variety of urbanism. But at the same time there is a boom psychology. Roads must be built. New government structures must be
created. The economic recession of the Nixon administration has

not yet seriously affected the Florida economy except for cutbacks in the space industry area around Brevard County. The population is still rapidly increasing. In this sense, Florida conservatism differs from that of states with smaller growth in their populations and economies. There is a reluctance to increase either real property or consumer taxes and a growing tendency to borrow on the future by floating bonds. Florida has not realized her tax potential as some other states have done. But even so, there is growing evidence of the need to restudy federal-state relations in the realm of taxation. A case for tax sharing in the future can well be argued, and the case for a corporate income tax has proved popular.

In its support for public institutions and welfare services, Florida maintains the low level of expectations carried over from a rural society. In the long run this situation will probably produce a crisis, which will lead to a changed policy—as has probably begun with the 1970 state elections. An example can be drawn from the local level. The public schools in Jacksonville became so bad as the result of neglect in the 1950's and 1960's that disaccreditation of all Jacksonville high schools followed in the mid-sixties. At the same time local assessment of property for tax purposes was in the range of only 20 percent of market value. At that time, also, corruption of local officials and failure to provide local services were widespread. The effects eventually led to some changes in assessment policies, to reorganization of the schools, and to city-county consolidation. Ultimately, it is suggested, pent-up demands will force similar changes at the state level. Under the new governor, as indicated earlier, much legislation of this type has already been introduced, and some of it enacted.

The rapid growth of the state provides a whole series of problems as to governmental structure and as to the level of other public services. At the structural level the 1970 census provides Florida with three new congressional seats. At least two of these must go to counties which vote heavily Republican. So the Republican congressional representation is likely to increase. With one proposal for judicial reorganization rejected by the voters, court dockets are becoming ever more crowded. Further reorganization is desperately

needed. The 1970 census also requires a further reapportionment
of the Florida Legislature in both houses.

At the national and state levels the politics of ecology has moved
to the forefront. There are serious problems of standards for industrial pollution, of city sewerage systems, of pollution of rivers
and harbors, of access to beaches. Two of the problems in this area
have already received national attention. President Nixon has
stopped construction of an intercontinental jetport west of Miami
and bordering the Everglades. More recently he has called for a
halt in the construction of the Florida Cross State Barge Canal in
north Florida as damaging to the ecology. Both of these measures
receive support from most of populous south Florida, and seem to
be favored by the Democratic state administration.

All of these changes take place in a state which is rapidly becoming a two-party one. Republican registration continues to increase.
A Republican governor has left office after only one term, but Nixon
continues to lead in state polls. An increase in the Republican congressional delegation is to be expected after 1972 unless there should
be international or further domestic crises. If Republicans can pull
themselves together they can increase their strength in local and in
legislative offices. Florida, in political characteristics, has come to
resemble most of the other rapid growth states—such as Nevada,
Arizona, and California—rather than to resemble the rest of the
South. Florida may be expected to continue to grow, to continue in
a moderate conservative direction, and to continue to develop as
a two-party state.

4

TENNESSEE
A Politics of Peaceful Change

LEE S. GREENE AND JACK E. HOLMES

Contemplating sequences of political events in the southern states since V. O. Key depicted them in 1949, the analyst inevitably tends to think in terms of dependent variables—the things moved or moving in response to changes on the national scene. Yet each state is actor as well as reactor and moves at its own characteristic pace and style in response to broad events. Each represents a historic residual which poorly accommodates to otherwise powerful modes of comparative statistical analysis. So it was here, but in triplicate, that the tourist, warmly welcomed by an area avid for his expenditures, was advised by billboard upon his entry that he was now in the "three states" of Tennessee—a reference to the three "grand divisions" officially recognized in the state's government structure and in political practice.

The politician surveyors who set the long northern and southern boundaries by extending North Carolina from the Appalachian crest to the Mississippi River produced a state with distinct physical subregions which were to set agricultural, settlement, and transportation patterns. The differentials ensuing were then so firmly imprinted culturally and politically by the great trauma of the Civil

Lee S. Greene is Distinguished Professor of Political Science, University of Tennessee. Jack E. Holmes is Professor of Political Science, University of Tennessee. The authors wish to take this occasion to thank their former and present students and colleagues, Dr. Leonard Ritt, Jerome Diamond, and Dr. William McCoy, for their studies and help.

War that even now they are part of the framework—the intervening variables—for the practice or study of Tennessee politics.

It is certainly possible to overemphasize the differences between East, Middle, and West Tennessee. But whether these differences are, in fact, profound, they are a daily part of Tennessee political consciousness. At least they have been; it is possible that communication and a changing political climate may shortly render these differences more a matter for antiquarians than for campaign managers.

East Tennessee differs rather more sharply from the central and western sections than the middle and west differ from each other. The east is Appalachia—with its beauty and its problems. This was the small farm area; slavery could not take a firm hold here—a fact that stamped the area as it did other less well recognized mountain areas of the South. This is also an area of abundant water and considerable mineral resources, particularly coal. Its scenic resources surpass the quiet interest of Middle Tennessee, and certainly the monotony of the landscape toward the Mississippi. East Tennessee has never been particularly hospitable to Negroes. They have little place in rural life there, and they are a smaller minority in the urban areas of the east than they are in Nashville or Memphis. Certain mountain areas were supposed to be actively hostile to their presence, in the manner often associated with poor whites. East Tennessee has been poor. Some observers have suggested that the poverty and the backwardness have stemmed not exclusively from lack of natural resources but from a lack in the people themselves. In any event, the area has long been high on the list of economic problem areas.[1]

Political writers and the public have long spoken of the South as a region separate from the remainder of the country, enforcing a degree of separatism that some of the states once sought to make complete. It is true, of course, that other sections have also been lumped together in similarly arbitrary fashion. So, if there is southern cooking, there is also a western breakfast. There are eastern

[1] Louis Brownlow pays his disrespects to East Tennessee political attitudes in *A Passion for Anonymity* (Chicago: University of Chicago Press, 1958), Chap. 15.

bankers and western cowboys. The Bible belt wobbles between the Midwest and the South, depending upon the target of one's animosities. But it is the South that has seemed most permanently distinctive.

In truth, of course, the South is by no means homogeneous. Tennessee is not, by any means, Alabama, Mississippi, or South Carolina. Florida is not Georgia or North Carolina. Tennessee is a border state, and the character of its population reflects this geographical position.

The population of Tennessee is slowly growing but at a rate considerably below that of the country as a whole. Its growth is the largest among the four states classed by the census as East South Central (Kentucky, Tennessee, Alabama, Mississippi). A further, but unspectacular, growth is projected for the seventies. A net out-migration of substantial proportions from 1950 to 1960 has been succeeded by a net in-migration from 1960 to 1966. The stability of Tennessee's position is reflected in its continuing range in rank among the states from fifteenth to nineteenth. In 1970 it was the seventeenth state in size. A border state, seventeenth among the entire fifty, is not calculated to land many of its favorite sons near 1600 Pennsylvania Avenue; national prominence must be sought by other means.

Tennessee is a state of native-born Americans. In 1960, only fifteen thousand of its people were foreign-born whites. Tennessee's Negroes accounted in 1960 for 16.5 percent of its population, a figure exceeded by Alabama, Mississippi, Virginia, North Carolina, South Carolina, and Georgia. Only Kentucky among its neighbors had a smaller percentage of black citizens. This population makeup also tells much about Tennessee politics.

In the state as a whole, the black man has always held a minority position. (See Figure 1.) The white man gradually squeezed the Indian out; in some sections the enslaved black was introduced into the state's population, but in very few areas has he ever equaled the white man numerically. The black in Tennessee has constituted a depressed minority, but a minority with political uses at times. Such use demanded that the Negro vote, and he has voted in Tennessee.

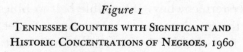

Figure 1

TENNESSEE COUNTIES WITH SIGNIFICANT AND
HISTORIC CONCENTRATIONS OF NEGROES, 1960

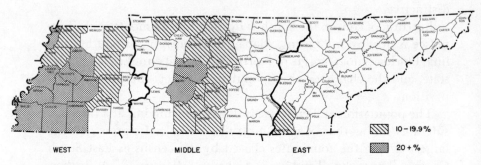

WEST   MIDDLE   EAST

⬚ 10 – 19.9 %

⬚ 20 + %

He was a component in the Crump machine (Edward H. Crump
was not without a sincere although patronizing sympathy for the
Negro's welfare) and he has been cautiously courted in other Tennessee cities. He has even held local office (two black men were long
members of Nashville's city council), but he had no hope of pre-
ferment or even significant employment in state political or high
administrative office.

Negroes in Tennessee were, of course, segregated—in schooling,
housing, recreation, transportation, and certainly in marriage relations, although localized breakdowns in this pattern were developing before federal pressure made the great break in tradition in the
1960's. But without that pressure, the black position would have
remained, at best, that of a subordinate group.

Tennessee has had its history of political leaders, state and local,
determined and powerful enough to be called bosses. Andrew Jackson was such a man, intolerant of any opposition. In the last twenty
years no local or state boss has become sufficiently significant or
colorful enough to capture the loyalty or hate of voters as Crump
did in the second quarter of the century. Crump left marks on
Memphis and Tennessee that are still discernible, although the
process of popular forgetfulness is, in his case, now well advanced.
Starting as a reformer in the business-efficiency style, Crump exercised great power for a time, but his authority was never complete

in the state and was subject to some challenge even in Memphis. He was powerful in state affairs, and yet opposition was possible and ultimately successful. Since his day, no single visible person has dominated state politics; individuals must fight their own battles and build their own factions.

Local satrapies have existed in the rural areas and some still do. But they arouse little interest. A generation ago certain vicious East Tennessee local dictatorships, attempting to control vote counting, ran into the opposition of returning GIs, who crushed them. Those regimes have not returned and local affairs in the livelier counties begin to take on the character of the more open struggles of urban politics.

The political traditions of Tennessee were, of course, shaped in a rural environment. Until the case of *Baker v. Carr*, the legislature was thoroughly dominated by rural and small-town forces; escape hatches for urban growth, particularly in the four larger cities, were provided by the system of special legislation. The governorship was usually held by a small-town resident, although big-city candidates occasionally were offered. Some of these patterns still remain. Big-city politics is not yet an avenue to the governor's chair; candidates prominently figuring in the Democratic or Republican primaries of 1969–70 have not made careers in urban politics. The legislature of Tennessee, however, has been recast, partly along suburban rather than urban lines. In any event, the small town's passionate concern for payrolls is slowly eroding rural life in Tennessee as elsewhere, and the rurality of political life is headed toward alteration.

Before World War II, Tennessee was with justice regarded as a rural state. It had an urban population, rather oddly distributed among four large cities (above 100,000), one city in the range 25,000 to 100,000, and a host of small towns. The urban population was dominated by the rural; the cities were subject to special legislation passed by a malapportioned General Assembly, a system which did in fact give a sort of rough home rule if the local legislative delegation and the local governing body were not at odds. Ripper legislation was an ever-present threat to the large cities. An early attempt to organize a municipal league failed; apparently the league became involved in politics of a purely personal sort.

A generation later the urban environment and urban political power are both greatly altered. The four large cities have continued to grow; all of them suffer from "metropolitan problems." The middle bracket of population has been reached by a number of places, and in certain areas, particularly upper East Tennessee, several bustling medium-sized towns are close enough to each other to give the impression that another metropolitan conurbation is forming. The state as a whole in 1960 was 52.3 percent urban.

The cities have begun to claim political power, openly, sometimes almost too openly, and at least sometimes successfully. The principal instrument of this power is the Tennessee Municipal League, re-formed with a modest claim on a share of the gasoline tax at first, but since then pressing successfully for chunks of sales tax, increased state grants, constitutional home rule, and limits on special legislation, with side achievements in technical assistance and training activities. Tennessee may still give the impression of rurality to the passing traveler, but its politics are far more urban than the sweeping forests indicate.

The Vote: Unused, Used, and Misused

The South has a distinctive record of low voter participation in the general elections, a record not significantly changed by participation in the primaries.[2] The history of Shelby County offers some indication of this aspect of Tennessee politics.

Scholarly judgment differs on the weight and intent of the several changes wrought in the suffrage by the Tennessee Constitution of 1870 and the subsequent statutory changes of 1889 and 1890. An early poll tax imposed pursuant to the new constitution was never enforced and was repealed within three years,[3] but the other changes

[2] See Lester W. Milbrath, "Political Participation in the States," in Herbert Jacob and Kenneth N. Vines (eds.), *Politics in the American States: A Comparative Analysis* (Boston: Little, Brown and Company, 1965).

[3] Frank B. Williams, Jr., "The Poll Tax as a Suffrage Requirement in the South, 1870–1901," *Journal of Southern History*, XVIII (1952), 471–77.

achieved a broad restoration of the franchise to ex-Confederates with the result that the state and Shelby County electorates participated in presidential elections of the two decades at a healthy 70 to 80 percent rate. A second wave of restrictions required the use of printed ballots (in a manner resulting in a literacy qualification), established registration of voters in cities, and reimposed a poll tax. Frank B. Williams, Jr., maintains, in effect, that the charge that the poll tax was designed to disfranchise the poor and the blacks of Tennessee must be dismissed with the Scottish verdict "not proven";[4] Stanley J. Folmsbee sees the changes as "facilitating" the suffrage;[5] and V. O. Key refers to "exaggerated estimates" of the effects of the poll tax.[6]

Reliance upon single-factor explanations of broad changes in social phenomena is risky, but the suffrage legislation must be considered a critical component in events and forces which led to an immediate and very sharp change in voting behavior in Shelby County (an event with parallels in several similar but much less urban counties in Middle and West Tennessee). As Figure 2 indicates, turnout in Shelby County in dropping from 70 percent in 1888 to 23 percent in 1892 opened a sixty-year period in which only 15 to 30 percent of the potential electorate voted in any election. The downward slalom of turnout in the state at large, although present, was much more gentle and prolonged.

Voting levels in the elections of 1872–88—when the population of Memphis and Shelby County was largely former small farm owners, tenants, and contract farmers, half white and half black, and nearly all poor[7]—could only have been sustained by a very broad franchise, a venture into democracy brought to an abrupt halt by the laws of 1889 and 1890. Yet that broad democracy had long been more apparent than real.

[4] *Ibid.*, 481–82.

[5] Stanley J. Folmsbee, Robert E. Corlew, and Enoch L. Mitchell, *Tennessee: A Short History* (Knoxville: University of Tennessee Press, 1969), 397.

[6] V. O. Key, Jr., *Southern Politics in State and Nation* (New York: Alfred A. Knopf, 1949), 608–609.

[7] Gerald M. Capers, Jr., *The Biography of a River Town: Memphis—Its Heroic Age* (Chapel Hill: University of North Carolina Press, 1939), 162–74, Chaps. 8 and 9.

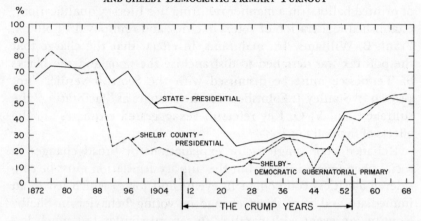

Figure 2
APATHY OR DISFRANCHISEMENT?
DIFFERENCES IN PRESIDENTIAL ELECTION TURNOUT,
TENNESSEE AND SHELBY COUNTY;
AND SHELBY DEMOCRATIC PRIMARY TURNOUT

Although the new laws were probably the precipitating factor in the change in the electoral pattern, the city had earlier slipped into bankruptcy, its charter had been revoked, and by 1879 it was a ward of the state, which enacted its budgets and shared in their administration. All these matters limited the local effects of the then broad franchise and permitted their weight to be felt only in statewide electoral results and in the makeup of the local legislative delegation. The battle of the ballots in Shelby was thus a game that engaged attention while the way was being prepared for the political *modus vivendi* of 1892–1952. What was to become the efficient paternalism of the Crump regime of 1910–52 (off and on) was firmly rooted in and made possible by the ancient and highly prized localism of Tennessee politics and government. The cloak of general law in the state is rent with exceptions in the form of private or local acts that have the effect of permitting each county or municipality to determine many of the attributes and processes of government, to define the level and tenor of debate, and to structure and guide the acculturative impact of the schools. This localism has permitted a McMinn County for years to suborn its relatively broad franchise with electoral fraud and violence, a Coffee County to settle upon a static gentility incorporating a clean courthouse and a firm consensus about what is "right," a Sevier County to dedicate itself to the proposition that the budget should be no higher than needed to sustain its public jobholders, and a Montgomery County (like the Shelby of old) to equate good government with managerial competence and low levels of popular participation.[8] Tennessee's tradition of local autonomy grants an enormous latitude to those locally dominant and it can be highly plebiscitarian; it can also be repressive of those who are deviant or who make up its minority elements. It permits a broad range of practices, both good and bad. It is, in short, local democracy in its broadest form.

Regionalism, Republicanism, and Democratic Dominance

Tennessee has been classified as a modified one-party state; in some ways it could more felicitously be dubbed a double one-party state because the Republicans have maintained a long preeminence in the east, with the Democrats holding a similar lordship in the middle and west. But the Republicans have been significant enough, with the help of dissident Democrats, to deliver the state to Republican presidential electors from time to time (increasingly in recent years), and they have always managed to survive as a political force. The Democrats, normally in power at the state level, have been rent for decades by factionalism and a kind of *personalismo* in which every important candidate must build his own following. Discontent in the Democratic ranks, with some help from Republicans, has produced a succession of third-party movements after the Civil War—Greenback, Prohibition, Agricultural Wheel, Farmers' Alliance, and Populists.[9] Twenty years ago the Dixiecrats occasioned a momentary spasm in the body politic; and George C. Wallace made a third-rank candidate out of Hubert Humphrey in the 1968

[8] For data analogous to these observations, see Jack E. Holmes, Walter N. Lambert, and Nelson M. Robinson, *The Structure of County Government in Tennessee* (Knoxville: University of Tennessee Bureau of Public Administration, 1966).

[9] Folmsbee and others, *Tennessee: A Short History*, 397–401.

election, which made Tennessee something of a key element in the "southern strategy" of the Nixon administration.

To observers outside the state and to those concerned with questions of party strategies and tactics on the national scene, the unit of analysis is the state as a whole with its complement of electoral votes. From this point of view, politics is presidential politics and the fate of congressmen and governors tends to be seen as effects of broader causes than those arising within the several states. The movement of populations within the state, emergence and decline of centers of party strength, and the like, are of moment only insofar as they affect the outcome of the election in question and movements which may culminate only after x more years tend to be overlooked. From this angle of vision, Tennessee is and was a Democratic state with a tendency, never completely fulfilled, to move to a two-party and highly competitive equilibrium. However, it is a state which is rather highly susceptible to third-party movements with differing impacts upon the standing strength of the two major parties.

The sequence of elections may be examined starting in 1892 (a year immediately following legislation designed to define and perhaps limit the electorate when electoral turnout was still at its zenith) and ending with 1928, the year presumed to mark the end of the generation-long period of Republican dominance in the nation. The second sequence of ten elections spans the period from Franklin D. Roosevelt to Richard Nixon.

The points on Figure 3 representing the Republican percentage of the 1892–1928 total statewide vote typically ranged close to the mid-40 percent mark, with a tendency to increase after 1916. Republicans won a majority of the statewide vote only in 1920 and in 1928, but the generalized two-party division of the vote as estimated in the heavy regression line went from 39.7 percent to 47.5 percent Republican. By 1928 the state could be regarded as two-party competitive but more likely than not to return a Democratic majority. (If we were to apply the calculus developed by Donald Stokes the odds as of 1928—and hence of 1932 as well—were about

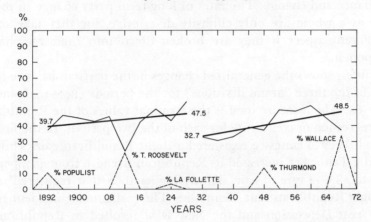

Figure 3
TOWARD A COMPETITIVE EQUILIBRIUM?
THE REPUBLICAN TREND IN TWO SEQUENCES OF
THE STATEWIDE TENNESSEE VOTE FOR PRESIDENT,
AND RELATIVE RESISTANCE TO THIRD-PARTY INCURSIONS,
1892–1928 AND 1932–1968

seven to three in favor of a Democratic victory.)[10] Fate (or economics) intervened, however, with a depression that produced in Tennessee, as elsewhere, a profound realignment[11] (in Tennessee's case probably a reversion to an earlier pattern) of the partisan affiliations of numerous voters so that the regression line generalizing the results of the 1932–68 sequence of elections starts at 32.7 percent —a break or loss in the Republican Party percentage of nearly fifteen points. Nevertheless, in the second series of elections, 1932 to 1968, the tendency to a two-party equilibrium again reasserted itself. As a result the elections of 1944 and 1948 produced Republican percentages six to eight points higher than in the strongly Democratic elections of 1932–40. Republican percentages (and turnout) went

10 Donald E. Stokes, "Spatial Models of Party Competition," and Donald E. Stokes and Gudmund R. Iversen, "On the Existence of Forces Restoring Party Competition," in Angus Campbell and others, *Elections and the Political Order* (New York: John Wiley and Sons, 1966), Chaps. 9 and 10.
11 Campbell and others, *Elections and the Political Order*, Chaps. 2–8.

up sharply with the elections of 1952–60 and were apparently less affected by third-party voting than the Democratic percentages in 1948 and 1968.

But any calculus of party change in Tennessee must eventually deal with the stubborn realities of regional differentials in party allegiance and change. The rates of long-term party change in the state as a whole are only clumsily descriptive, for they take on a different aspect if they are broken down into their regional components.

Table 1 shows the generalized changes in the partisan balance of each of the three "grand divisions" for the periods 1892–1928 and 1932–68. The measure used is the terminal values of the Republican regression or trend vote for each of the two periods. In the first period, West Tennessee registered a slight Republican gain while Middle Tennessee increased its Republican strength from 30.8 percent to 38.3—a rate of gain slightly higher than that registered in strongly Republican East Tennessee. The realignment incident to the Great Depression and the New Deal resulted in Republican losses far higher in Middle and in West Tennessee than in the eastern division. East Tennessee recouped only part of its Republican losses in the second period and Middle Tennessee also wound up in 1968 as less Republican than it had been in 1928 (see Table 1), but West Tennessee—which experienced a very large break in the face of the New Deal—climbed by 31 percentage points from its 1932 Republican nadir so that it was 13 points more Republican (at 46.8 percent) in 1968 than it had been in 1928.

The change in the western division may be one of the most pronounced instances of party change in the South. What is perhaps more problematic for West Tennessee and the state's political leaders is whether this remarkable change in the area is becoming well enough institutionalized to afford Republicans a new and reasonably secure party base. The permanence of Republican power is still open to question even after the election of a Republican governor and a second Republican senator in 1970.

The scope of the Republican problem, if not its probable outcome, may be seen more clearly in Table 2. The two segments of

Table 1

LONG-TERM REPUBLICAN GAINS AND LOSSES IN TENNESSEE: THE CHANGING REGIONAL BASES OF PARTY STRENGTH, 1892–1928 AND 1932–1968

Grand Divisions and Total	"Percentage Republican" (at terminal regression values)		Period Gain	The Great Depression Break: GOP "Losses" 1928 to 1932	"Percentage Republican" (at terminal regression values)		Period Gain	Net Republican Loss or Gain: Terminal Value of 1928 to Terminal Value of 1968
	1892	1928			1932	1968		
East	57.8	63.3	5.5	−11.8	51.5	59.1	7.6	− 4.2
Middle	30.8	38.3	7.5	−15.5	22.8	36.5	13.7	− 1.8
West	32.5	34.1	1.6	−18.5	15.6	46.8	31.2	12.7
STATE	39.7	47.5	7.8	−14.8	32.7	48.5	15.8	1.0

Source: Regression values were calculated from electoral data tapes supplied by the Inter-university Consortium for Political Research, Survey Research Center, University of Michigan.

Table 2

CONVERGENCE OF TENNESSEE COUNTIES UPON A TWO-PARTY PRESIDENTIAL
COMPETITION
(Arrayed by 1932 Starting Point and by Region)

By Percent GOP, 1932 (The "a" value)	Counties by Size of Quadrennial GOP Percentage Increment (The "b" value of Y= a+bX for 1932–1968)						
	−0.99 to 0	0 to 0.99	1 to 1.99	2 to 2.99	3 to 3.99	4 to 4.99	Totals
0 to 19.9		5	10	9	7	3	34
20 to 29.9		6	5	3			14
30 to 39.9		3	4	1			8
40 to 49.9	1	4	5	2			12
50 to 59.9	3	9					12
60 to 69.9	5	4	1				10
70 to 79.9	1	2					3
80 to 89.9	2						2
TOTALS	12	33	25	15	7	3	95
By Grand Division							
West		5	4	4	6	3	22
Middle	3	16	14	7	1		41
East	9	12	7	4			32
TOTALS	12	33	25	15	7	3	95

the first column show the incidence of long-term Republican losses
in the ten elections of 1932–68. These were largely confined to
highly Republican counties of East Tennessee. The other counties
of that region have generally shown very limited rates of gain. In
other words, the modal Republican county of East Tennessee registered a cumulative election-to-election gain of less than 1 percentage point in the ten elections. Conversely, the modal set of West
Tennessee counties was accumulating quadrennial gains of 3 to 4
percentage points, and thirteen of the twenty-two counties fell into
the range of 2 to 5 points accumulated per election over the series.

Middle Tennessee's counties have been much more prone to

move slowly. Three showed a Republican loss in the period bridging 1932 and 1968, thirty gained less than two points per election,
and only eight exceeded that rate. Table 2 shows that for the state
as a whole a modal set of thirty-three counties has shown a rate of
Republican gain that is glacially slow, but Republicans can take
considerable comfort from the fact that fifty of the ninety-five counties have gained at least ten percentage points over the series. The
gains of half of that Republican-moving set have been at the rate
of an impressive two points or more per election. But these accum-
ulations are probably not firmly based on an avowed Republican
Party identification for many voters, and, as we remark elsewhere,
the party majorities of these fast-moving counties are highly
variable.

A casual glance at the current balance of party strength in the
state as measured by the 1968 value of the 1932–68 regression line
of Figure 2 indicates that Republicans are nearly breaking even—
certainly they are in a competitive position by this measure—in
party strength and the 50–50 possibility of party success at, say,
the 1972 election. Yet Republican chances are not that close to the
break-even point if one considers the long-standing peculiarities of
the several counties and "grand divisions" of the state.

Table 3 groups the counties by grand division and by percent
Republican as estimated by the 1968 terminus of the 1932–68 trend
line of the county. Half of the twenty-two counties of West Tennessee are still heavily Democratic (over 60 percent) by this measure
and thirty, or three-fourths, of the counties of Middle Tennessee
are still strongly Democratic. In short, in forty-one counties of the
state, which contain 23.4 percent of the population, the Republican
voters are outnumbered by ratios in excess of six to four. These
counties are also, by and large, those whose party margins are least
variable from election to election. More than half of the counties
of Middle Tennessee will produce party margins that typically will
vary through less than 6 percentage points on either side of the
generalized or regression line value, and eighteen of the forty-one
counties have shown a variance one way or the other of 6 to 9 percentage points.

Table 3

REGIONAL DISTRIBUTION OF TENNESSEE COUNTIES BY 1968
REPUBLICAN STRENGTH, PRESIDENTIAL ELECTIONS

Percentage Republican by 1968*	Number of Counties by Grand Division			1966 Population as Percentage of State Total
	West	Middle	East	
0–39.9	11	30	0	23.4
40–44.9	2	5	0	14.3
45–54.9	7	2	8	33.6
55–59.9	1	0	6	13.6
60 or more	1	4	18	15.1
	22	41	32	100.0

Sources: Electoral data tapes of the Inter-university Consortium Survey Research Center, University of Michigan; "Estimates of the Population of Counties, July 1, 1966," Series P-25, September, 1968, Bureau of the Census.
* The 1968 value of the 1932–68 regression curves of the several counties.

In West Tennessee, conversely, nine of the twenty-two counties (and these typically have been making large secular gains in their Republican vote) have been varying their party margins by more than 9 percentage points from election to election. Since the party vote can be either more or less than the norm expressed by the regression line for each county, this means that it is quite normal for these nine Republican-tending counties to be highly erratic in their party vote, with a likely range of some 18 percentage points. By this measure, the party votes in East Tennessee are considerably more flexible than those of Middle Tennessee, for twenty of its thirty-two counties will now typically range above and below the regression values by more than 6 percentage points.

As Table 3 shows, thirty-one of the state's ninety-five counties are competitive as between the two parties in that their 1968 regression line terminal values fall between 40 to 60 percent Republican. (Figure 4 shows the location of the competitive counties by grand division.) These counties contain 61.5 percent of the state's total potential vote and include all of the metropolitan counties and nearly all of the counties of more than 40,000 inhabitants. But as a

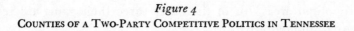

Figure 4
COUNTIES OF A TWO-PARTY COMPETITIVE POLITICS IN TENNESSEE

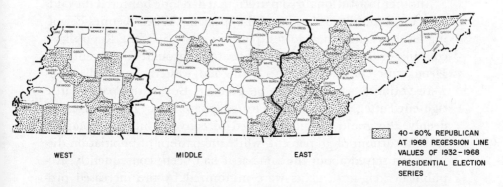

WEST   MIDDLE   EAST

> 40 – 60% REPUBLICAN
> AT 1968 REGESSION LINE
> VALUES OF 1932 – 1968
> PRESIDENTIAL ELECTION
> SERIES

group they are characterized by relatively flexible party margins, and they have been relatively prone to reflect national partisan tides and candidate preferences. Fourteen of the competitive and variable counties are in East Tennessee and tend to be Republican; Middle Tennessee contributes only seven counties to the competitive group and Davidson County, the largest of this aggregation, is only marginally two-party, for its Democratic margin is still close to 60 percent; the remaining ten competitive counties are in West Tennessee, but about half of these have been reacting very strongly in opposition to welfare and racial reform policies of recent national administrations and it may not be certain that the party divisions shown in recent votes are firm indicators of permanent shifts in party allegiance of most voters.[12]

Table 3 also indicates that the cluster of Republican counties with consistent party margins musters only 15 percent of the state's vote; the Democratic counties with similar characteristics produce 23 percent of the vote. The thirty-one competitive counties typically produce highly variable majorities; they are about evenly divided between the two parties, but Republicans can rely upon a historic party preponderance or preference in only one of the four

[12] See Angus Campbell and others, *The American Voter* (New York: Wiley and Sons, 1960), 120–67.

metropolitan areas, for in the other three their gains are recent, marginal, and tentative.

Another institutionalized pattern that had long bolstered the odds a bit for Republicans has been disappearing. When Tennessee voting levels reached their lowest point in the 1920's, the Republican counties of the east were voting at rates of around 30 percent; the Democratic counties of the middle and western grand divisions were voting at rates close to 20 percent. But as the party battle tightened after 1948, when the issues apparently began to cut more deeply, the grand divisions tended to converge upon a common level of turnout of 50 percent, while the pattern of population distribution stayed about the same as it had been; consequently, Republican long-term gains were minimized by the increased propensity of marginal and strongly Democratic counties to cast a larger share of the state's total vote.

The Negro: A Latent Force

Negroes are not complete strangers to Tennessee politics. Negroes formed a significant factor in the brief and bitter politics of Reconstruction, but they never became the force which temporarily they were in some other southern states of that period. The first Negro to serve in the legislature was elected in 1872, and the last one to serve there before 1965 was elected in 1885 and reelected in 1887. During the 1880's several Negroes were delegates to the General Assembly, largely from West Tennessee counties.

The Negro has voted in Tennessee, although not in all places and not at all times; in any case his exclusion from the ballot has not been complete. He has since Reconstruction held local offices, but he had no hope of attaining the more important posts. Often he was a tool of machines which could furnish him some benefits in return for support. In Shelby County, for example, the Negro played a political role, subordinate but significant. In Crump's view, which reflected accurately enough the opinion of white Mississippi and West Tennessee, the Negro was an inferior being. However, he could vote and his vote could be weighed in white disputes. And in

Crump's view, the Negro had the right to expect a modicum of governmental care and service. The practice under Crump honored this expectation, but in an atmosphere of paternalism in which the black man had his "proper place."

The civil rights movement of the 1960's has greatly changed Negro tactics and Negro expectations. The top offices are still closed to the black man, as a practical matter, for the Negro vote is by no means a majority in the important constituencies. A. W. Willis, Jr., who had been in the General Assembly, made a bid for the Memphis mayoralty in 1967, after the city adopted the mayor-council plan. His campaign was pitched on a frankly racist appeal to the Negroes, but he was unsuccessful. In Memphis, as elsewhere in the state, the black vote cannot be delivered as a bloc, and the Negro vote was not united behind the Willis candidacy. The split among Shelby County black votes was present also in 1966, when some Negro leaders backed John J. Hooker and others supported Buford Ellington for governor. Nevertheless, in the state as a whole, considerable bloc voting by blacks has occurred. In 1964, the Tennessee Voters Council attempted to unite the black voters, and in the 1966 primary battle for the United States Senate between Frank Clement and Ross Bass, the incumbent, Bass was clearly the Negroes' favorite. In Memphis, Bass received 60 percent or more of the total Democratic vote in the Negro precincts. In Chattanooga, Bass won 75 percent of the vote in the all-Negro precincts, and analogous data indicate that his level of support was 79 percent in Knoxville and 87 percent in Nashville.

The division of the state's urban Negro vote in the 1968 presidential contest is about what we would expect in view of the results of numerous national surveys, so Table 4 may be of interest here chiefly for what it reveals of the city-to-city variations of the vote among whites. Conversely, the high and uniform levels of Negro support for the incumbent senator (Bass) and the gubernatorial challenger (Hooker)—both liberals in Tennessee's perspective—in the state's largest cities are a little surprising in view of the well-known inattention of most voters to abstract political information.

Bass, a former congressman, had been elected two years earlier

Table 4

NEGRO BLOC VOTING AND THE 1968 PRESIDENTIAL ELECTION
IN TENNESSEE'S URBAN CENTERS

City	Number of Precincts	Percentage of Vote for		
		Humphrey	Nixon	Wallace
Chattanooga				
Negro (25–100%)	11	86.4	7.3	6.3
Others		23.6	35.8	40.6
All Precincts		42.3	27.3	30.4
Knoxville				
Negro (25–100%)	7	86.5	9.2	4.3
Others		25.9	53.5	20.6
All Precincts		31.3	49.5	19.2
Nashville-Davidson				
Negro (60–100%)	11	90.9	4.5	4.6
Others		28.0	34.7	37.3
All Precincts		32.8	32.4	34.8
Memphis				
Negro (40–100%)	74	90.7	4.2	5.1
Others		23.8	37.4	38.8
All Precincts		39.8	29.4	30.8

Sources: Unofficial returns from the Chattanooga *Times*, Knoxville *News-Sentinel*,
and Nashville *Tennessean*, November 6, 1968, and the Memphis *Commercial
Appeal*, November 7, 1968. Precincts are those in the groupings developed by
M. Jerome Diamond, "The Negro and Organized Labor as Voting Blocs in
Tennessee, 1960–64" (unpublished M.A. thesis, University of Tennessee, 1965),
and tabulations have been made by Dr. William McCoy.

to fill out an unexpired term, but his name was hardly a household
word across the state. Hooker had been active in Democratic politics
but he was running against the better-known Buford Ellington, a
former governor and long-time associate of Governor Clement. The
results (based on rather crudely aggregated data) imply a high
level of cohesion and information. Black voters could simply have
been voting *against* Clement and Ellington, but their spokesmen
and leaders across the state are now highly practiced politician-

watchers and, in this case, they had ample time to appraise the candidates and to communicate that appraisal to the voters.

The Populist Strand—From Weaver to Wallace

Those addicted to musing on the vagaries of American politics may find a mild or wry satisfaction in the fact that a skilled analyst wrote on the eve of the 1968 campaign, "Not in the last fifty years has the United States seen a movement of mass political protest." [13] The book in point was probably still in press when George C. Wallace was well on the way to getting his name on the ballot in each of the fifty states.

Those similarly addicted to discovering the relatedness of all things political might also take a bit of satisfaction from the correlation matrix of Table 5, which shows a strong (0.62) correlation between the 1892 Populist candidacy of General James B. Weaver and the American Party candidacy of Governor Wallace more than seventy years later. The table also reveals that J. Strom Thurmond in 1948 shared some common ground with Weaver (0.27) and still more with Wallace (0.54). Conversely, the column for Barry Gold-

Table 5

CORRELATIONS OF THE TENNESSEE COUNTY VOTE FOR THIRD
PARTIES AND GOLDWATER

Candidate, Party, and Year

Year	Weaver Populist 1892	Roosevelt Progressive 1912	LaFollette Progressive 1924	Thurmond Dixiecrat 1948	Goldwater Republican 1964	Wallace American 1968
1892	1.00	−0.49	−0.20	0.27	−0.53	0.62
1912	−0.49	1.00	0.21	−0.40	0.68	−0.68
1924	−0.20	0.21	1.00	−0.02	−0.09	−0.04
1948	0.27	−0.40	−0.02	1.00	−0.19	0.54
1964	−0.53	0.68	−0.09	−0.19	1.00	−0.69
1968	0.62	−0.68	−0.04	0.54	−0.69	1.00

Source: Electoral data tapes, Inter-university Consortium, Survey Research Center, University of Michigan.

[13] Frank J. Sorauf, *Party Politics in America* (Boston: Little, Brown and Company, 1968), 195.

water indicates that the only positive correlation with the 1964 election occurred in 1912, when Theodore Roosevelt's Bull Moose candidacy cut away half of the Republican vote of the eastern counties. A powerful limit in the 1892 and 1968 results was, of course, simply a shortage of Republicans in the counties of the west and middle grand divisions.[14]

Protest or independent candidates have appeared on Tennessee's presidential ballots in nineteen of the last twenty elections. Only five have drawn more than 3 percent of the total vote:

1892,	Populist	10.8
1912,	Progressive	23.2
1924,	Progressive	3.6
1948,	Dixiecrat	14.0
1968,	American	34.0[15]

All the elections listed have been marked by strong regional differences in the proportion of the vote attracted by the third-party challengers—differences which show up sharply in the relatively large losses in the vote of the party dominant in the counties or grand divisions most affected. Wallace's candidacy was the only one of the lot which had a significant appeal to adherents of both major parties. Although strong regional differentials persisted, only one county in six failed to give Wallace at least 20 percent of its total vote. (The nature of the "ecological correlation" involved in this exposition of what appears to be the relatively strong resistance of the long-time Republican counties[16] to grass-roots populism is evident in Figure 5.)

14 Cf. Philip E. Converse and others, "Continuity and Change in American Politics: Parties and Issues in the 1968 Election," American Political Science Review, LXIII (1969), 1101–1105.

15 The American Party fielded inexperienced candidates for governor and senator in 1970, but they did very poorly. So far the party exists primarily for presidential purposes.

16 Converse and others, "Continuity and Change in American Politics." These authors remark that "for the South, 68% of Wallace voters considered themselves Democrats, and 20% Republicans . . . . these partisan proportions among Wallace voters do not differ very markedly from those which characterize the regional electorates taken as a whole."

Figure 5

TENNESSEE POPULISM, BACKLASH, AND NEOPOPULISM, 1892 AND 1968

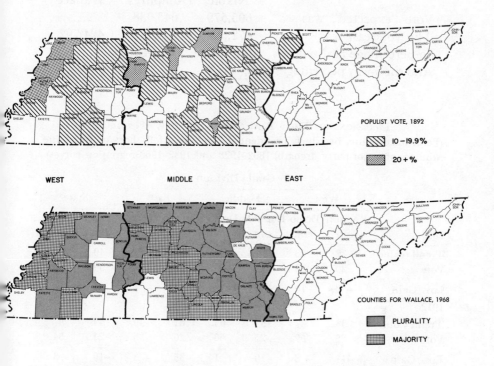

The characteristic features of the five elections mentioned above and the results of 1968 sample surveys encourage us to make some crude but reasonable estimates (granting certain heroic assumptions) of relative voter losses of the two major parties in 1968 and in the earlier elections. The "losses" are the differences between the actual vote received by the major parties and the "normalized" expected vote, that is, the party trend line percentage value at the election involved. For example, the 1932–68 Republican trend line shown in Figure 2 had a value in 1968 of 48.5 percent. If everything else in 1968 had been equal and had not Wallace appeared, the vote "should" have divided between Nixon and Humphrey as shown. But Wallace was definitely *there*, so the example works out as follows:

	Nixon	Humphrey	Wallace
Vote "expected" was	605,579	643,038	....
The vote cast was	472,592	351,223	424,792
So percentage realized was	78.0	54.6	....
And the 3-way percentages were	37.8	28.1	34.0

Table 6

INCURSIONS OF THIRD PARTIES IN TENNESSEE, 1892–1968
(Percentage points by which presidential candidates fell short of trend-line estimates of major-party strength, 1892–1928 and 1932–1968 regression curves)

By Grand Division							State	
	West		Middle		East			
1892	Republican	Democrat	Republican	Democrat	Republican	Democrat	Republican	Democrat
Trend value	32	68	31	69	58	42	40	60
Vote	29	58	29	60	58	38	39	52
Loss/Gain	– 3	–10	– 2	– 9	0	– 4	– 1	– 8
1912								
Trend value	33	67	35	65	61	39	43	57
Vote	22	59	25	66	26	36	24	54
Loss/Gain	–11	– 8	–10	1	–35	– 3	–19	– 3
1924								
Trend value	34	66	37	63	63	37	46	54
Vote	30	66	30	67	62	35	44	53
Loss/Gain	– 4	0	– 7	4	– 1	– 2	– 2	– 1
1948								
Trend value	29	71	29	71	55	45	40	60
Vote	24	48	24	62	55	41	37	49
Loss/Gain	– 5	–23	– 5	– 9	0	– 4	– 3	–11
1968								
Trend value	47	53	38	62	59	41	48	52
Vote	31	31	29	30	51	25	38	28
Loss/Gain	–16	–22	– 9	–32	– 8	–16	–10	–24

Nixon apparently suffered nearly as many defections in the western division as did Humphrey, but the systematic west-to-east differentials by grand division worked heavily in his favor. Our arithmetic shows that Humphrey's losses among the not-so-faithful legions of his party were about four out of ten in the west and east and well over half in the Democratic stronghold of Middle Tennessee. The regional patterns of relative major party losses in the whole series of elections (Table 6) show similar features although they reverse in 1912 and 1924, when the Republicans suffered most. Nowhere were the partisan alignments so starkly revealed as in 1912 in the Republican highlands of East Tennessee.

Figure 6

WEST TENNESSEE CLOSES THE GAP:
GROWTH AND SHIFT BY GRAND DIVISION IN
PERCENTAGE VOTING IN RECENT PRESIDENTIAL ELECTIONS

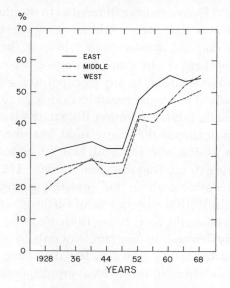

The Displacement Effects of Urban Politics

The changing character of Tennessee politics is evidenced in the growing importance of the cities. A generation ago, the essentially rural character of Tennessee politics was partially obscured by the prominence of "Boss" Crump of Memphis. Crump, in fact, was primarily interested in Memphis. Under the system prevailing at that time, some control of the legislature and of the governor was necessary to Crump if he was to retain authority in his home city. Not only could special legislation be used against him, but general acts could also threaten. He had once been ousted from office following the establishment of a procedure generalized for the whole state. There is considerable reason for believing that Crump's interest in state affairs would have been different if home rule for cities had been in the constitution before 1953. But these matters aside, the state's policy outlook was essentially rural, both in the legislature and in the governor's office.

No longer is this the case. Breaches in the rural fortress were made when the cities organized a municipal league for the second time. Somewhat timidly the league began to campaign for a share of the state's gasoline tax. Opinions have differed as to whether Tennessee can be classified as a state where lobbies are powerful or as one where they are weak, and opinions may vary as to the effectiveness of the Municipal League. In some legislative sessions, it would seem more feared than loved. In any case, political aspirants listen to league proposals. The league began its campaign for a more substantial share of state funds in Gordon Browning's last term as governor; the governor turned the league aside, but when he ran for a succeeding term against the youthful Frank Clement, he took a position acceptable to the league's point of view. He was too late; Clement took the same position and probably gained the trust of municipal officials. With the beginning of Clement's lengthy tenure in the governor's office, the cities began to secure important portions of an increasingly demanding program. Not only have the cities obtained a share of the state's sales tax, but they have obtained the authority (since widely used) to levy local supplementary sales taxes, thus cutting into a revenue source of paramount importance to state finance. Substantial structural gains for localities generally were made in the constitutional changes of 1953, for a sharp brake was put on special legislation, making it heavily dependent on local approval, and cities obtained constitutional home rule. The league was particularly influential in the drafting of the home rule amendment. This amendment contained a clause, little noticed at the time, which provided for annexation by general law, rather than special acts, as had formerly been the rule. In 1955 the legislature, again under league pressure, passed a very strong annexation law, never since then substantially weakened, that has enabled the central cities to expand significantly, in spite of suburban opposition.

The sharp, persistent, sometimes belligerent, and surely single-minded pressure exerted by the league's principal spokesman, the long-time executive secretary, Herbert Bingham, has aroused some opposition, as might be expected. Wiseacres are heard who think Bingham's welcome is often withdrawn in the state capitol, but his legislative record remains impressive, whether from his own efforts or from the justice of his cause (or causes, because the achievement of one objective is promptly superseded by the announcement of another).

It should surprise no one that the league apparatus is unfriendly to undue extension of federal authority (federal dollars are naturally welcome) and to centralized state power, especially if exercised by a clearly designated state cabinet post for urban affairs. The threat of the latter was foreseen and hampered by the creation in the University of Tennessee of the Municipal Technical Advisory Service, which has for twenty years produced high-grade technical assistance without any threat of compulsion or substitute administration. It has not been possible, however, for the league to turn aside the need for state coordination of federal activities concerning urban affairs, and the Office of Urban and Federal Affairs has been created in Governor Ellington's cabinet, and the Office of Local Government as a subordinate to the comptroller of the treasury.

Tennessee contributed a major chapter in the history of American federalism in *Baker v. Carr*, a decision that forced open a way to reapportionment of state legislatures, of the national House of Representatives, and now of local governments. The litigants in this case, who eventually persuaded the judiciary to enter this "political thicket," signal the changes in Tennessee politics—they included both Democrats and Republicans from metropolitan areas, east, middle, and west. Charles Baker is a Democrat, currently a member of the Shelby County Court (and its chairman), from one of the smaller communities outside Memphis. Another complainant was the late Walter Chandler, once mayor of Memphis during the Crump period. At the opposite end of the state, a third complainant was a conservative Republican figure, the late State Senator Hobart Atkins of Knoxville.

Senator Atkins, in building his case for reapportionment, had attempted to pinpoint the policy disadvantages of malapportionment without too much success, and it is still not easy to prove that urban areas have gained sharply in terms of legislative policy. Nevertheless, shifts in climate are clearly taking place. For example, the educational agencies in the state are aware that agricultural interests and groups (notably the Farm Bureau Federation) are less significant than they once were and they are seeking to build political fences (or should one say *sidewalks?*) in urban areas.[17]

As a result of the November, 1965, reapportionment, the four metropolitan counties had the following numbers of seats:

	Senate	House
Knox	2	8
Davidson	4	11
Hamilton	2	7
Shelby	6	16
	14	42

In the Senate, 17 make a majority; in the House, 50. If the metropolitan counties acted together (certainly in many cases they will not), control could be secured with only a little aid from other heavily urbanized areas, such as Sullivan County in East Tennessee or Madison County in the West. The metropolitan areas are split between the two major parties and the seats in both houses are now apportioned among single-member constituencies.[18] The party

17 A detailed study of the political and constitutional background of *Baker v. Carr* has been made by Richard C. Cortner, *The Apportionment Cases* (Knoxville: University of Tennessee Press, 1970).

18 The changes made by reapportionment in Kentucky and Tennessee have been compared in Malcolm E. Jewell and Lee S. Greene, *The Kentucky and Tennessee Legislatures* (Lexington: University of Kentucky Department of Political Science, 1967).

alignment of the 1969 General Assembly in the metropolitan counties was:

| | Senate | | House | |
	Rep.	Dem.	Rep.	Dem.
Knox	2	0	7	1
Davidson	0	4	2	9
Hamilton	2	0	4	3
Shelby	1	5	8	8

In 1971 the line-up was as follows:

| | Senate | | House | |
	Rep.	Dem.	Rep.	Dem.
Knox	2	0	7	1
Davidson	0	4	1	10
Hamilton	2	0	4	3
Shelby	2	4	8	8

The single-member district has already had the effect of weakening the position of the central cities in the metropolitan areas. So far the crucial statute, the annexation law, has not been touched, but its use has been hampered.

The rising power of the urban and suburban voter is also fostered by the reapportionment of Tennessee seats in the national House of Representatives, a process that altered to some degree the traditional relationship of Democrats and Republicans.

Tennessee's congressional districts were redrawn before 1952, and the number of its representatives reduced from ten to nine. The nine districts had the following populations in 1960:

District	Population
1	460,583
2	497,121
3	412,664
4	389,563
5	399,743
6	324,357
7	232,652
8	223,387
9	627,019

The scheme was arranged to the disadvantage of Republicans and the big-city voters; the two did not always coincide. The Ninth District was Shelby County, including Memphis, formally a Democratic fief, but one with an increasingly hopeful Republican minority. Chattanooga and Knoxville were included in large districts, both with respect to population and area. Davidson County (Nashville) formed the Fifth District, with a medium-sized population. The First and Second Districts, long-time Republican strongholds, were large districts, as was the Third, sometimes Democratic, lately Republican. The two smallest districts, in population, were rural Democratic areas in West Tennessee.

With the national judiciary now insisting on a fundamentally decent respect for equality in apportionment, it was clear that this wildly unbalanced scheme could not persist. The 1965 General Assembly had redistricted the state as follows:

District	1960 Population
1	441,516
2	453,298
3	436,421
4	411,585
5	399,743
6	341,468
7	343,843
8	380,636
9	358,579

This was certainly an improvement on the old scheme, but it failed to satisfy a federal three-judge panel, which declared the plan unconstitutional and substituted its own scheme:

District	1960 Population
1	395,918
2	404,968
3	401,152
4	395,594

5	399,743
6	388,240
7	400,916
8	390,836
9	389,722

Numerically, this was much better. The new arrangement split Shelby County into three parts, and in the process strengthened the Republican hold on Memphis. Democratic Congressman Ray Blanton was also strengthened. The Sixth and Fourth Districts were burdened with very large territories, and the Fourth District was given some mountain counties with Republican voters, but it seems doubtful that these can override the general Democratic tradition of the Fourth District. The First, Second, and Third Districts remain fairly safely Republican. The 1966 vote for congressional representatives was as follows:

District	Percentage	
	Democratic	Republican
1	13.2	86.8
2	20.7	79.3
3	35.6	64.4
4	65.4	34.6
5	63.0	37.0
6	85.6	14.4
7	56.8	43.2
8	76.3	23.7
9	47.0	53.0

(In some cases the minority vote is an independent vote, rather than a party vote for either Republican or Democratic candidate.)[19] Tennessee will lose a representative after the 1970 census, and further painful readjustment will be necessary; the legislature elected in 1970 has a Democratic working majority in both houses.

[19] *Congressional Quarterly*, July 19, 1968, p. 1824.

Republican Gains and Republican Hopes

The long impact of FDR, Truman, Kennedy, and Johnson has produced a partially triumphant, sometimes persistent, and still hopeful Republican Party in Tennessee (Republican politicians, like
Democrats, are not always familiar with statistical theory). Republicans could always count on some seats in the Tennessee legislature. The party alignments in the Eighty-third and Eighty-fourth
General Assemblies were as follows:

83rd (1963–65)	Rep.	Dem.
Senate	6	27
House	21	78
84th (1965–67)		
Senate	8	25
House	24	75

In the 1966 election, however, dramatic changes began; the alignment changed:

	Rep.	Dem.
Senate	8	25
House	41	58

And in the 1968 election, the Republicans made further gains:

	Rep.	Dem.	Ind.
Senate	13	20	
House	49	49	1

(Later, the Senate line-up became 12 Republicans, 21 Democrats.)
But, in 1970, the General Assembly was again Democratic:

	Rep.	Dem.	American
Senate	13	19	1
House	43	56	

Republicans have always had more than a shadow existence even outside East Tennessee. They showed some strength in state contests throughout the last third of the nineteenth century, by taking advantage of the frequent splits among the Democrats. Their strength was increased by Negro enfranchisement. The Republican candidates for governor in the late nineteenth century and in the twentieth were often found in Middle and West Tennessee. But only occasionally could Republicans capture the executive branch of the state. For a time, in fact, they gave up really trying. Recent failures of the Republican Party to contest for the governorship are probably understandable, in view of the party's history since 1932. In the preceding decade the party had made a significant, if not threatening, series of challenges to Democratic dominance. Even during the dispiriting times of heavy odds during the Rooseveltian and later Crump years, the party typically had a candidate in the field who would campaign with as much energy as his resources permitted. With the disappearance from the scene of Congressmen B. Carroll Reece and Howard Baker, Sr., the party was bereft for a time of some of its most experienced and astute (albeit highly cautious) leadership. The implications of data such as those represented by Figure 7 and Table 7 were doubtless painfully obvious to money-short potential candidates. Much more than in more competitive two-party states, the gap between the presidential and gubernatorial party votes has long been both large and extremely variable. And, as William Goodman has pointed out,[20] the quality of the local organizations available to Republican candidates in half or so of the counties was simply not conducive to strong campaigns whether conducted by outstanding volunteer candidates or by the party on behalf of candidates it might enlist. On three occasions after 1950 Republicans failed to field a candidate for governor.

Senator Howard Baker, Jr., has demonstrated on two occasions, however (once successfully and once not), that some local organizations can be rejuvenated or refurbished and that others can be

[20] William Goodman, *Inherited Domain: Political Parties in Tennessee* (Knoxville: University of Tennessee Bureau of Public Administration, 1954), 40, 82–84.

Table 7

FROM DEFEATISM TO RESURGENCE:
TENNESSEE REPUBLICANS TRY AGAIN FOR THE GOVERNORSHIP

Elections	Elections Contested	Mean of Republican Percentages
1920–28	5 of 5	43.1
1930–38*	5 of 5	30.3
1940–48	5 of 5	31.7
1950–66†	3 of 6	15.0
1970	1 of 1	52.0

* In 1934 the Republican candidate backed Independent Lewis Pope in a fusion ticket.
† Since 1954 governors have been elected for four-year terms and are barred from consecutive terms.

Figure 7

SEPARATE AND UNEQUAL: THE DISCRETE ARENAS OF
PRESIDENTIAL AND GUBERNATORIAL VOTING IN TENNESSEE

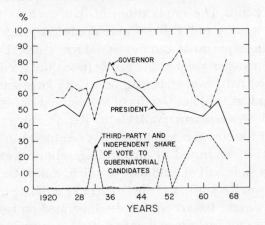

supplemented by local ad hoc campaign organizations. Moreover, the old-line Republican organizations are finding new and middle-class organizations building up in some of the major counties and municipalities of Middle and West Tennessee. A successful mating of the county-oriented old organizations of East Tennessee and the new and relatively ideological sets of activists in the west will not be easy, but it could result in some profound changes if it should occur.

Overview

If Tennessee is a fair example, then its politics must reflect as well as contribute to the "incredibly complex" southern politics Key outlined in 1949. And it does—from its black-belt counties of the west to its Appalachian and Republican counties of the east. Its western and midstate counties were rocked by Populism; developed a highly ingrown but vigorous courthouse-centered local politics; and, after decades of low voting rates, turned much of their recently enlarged vote to Wallace in a curious blending of neopopulist, white-backlash sentiment.

The urban areas of the state, which now contain most of the Negro population, have not only become centers for a black politics striving for leverage in Nashville and Washington, but they have possibly developed the financial and organizational bases for a "new Republicanism." The old Republican strongholds of East Tennessee seem now to be less buttressed by tradition, if not by topography, for fourteen counties in the valley troughs of the Tennessee and Sequatchie rivers and the southern Cumberlands increasingly become two-party competitive. The half-dozen or so newly competitive counties emerging in West Tennessee have merely moved from a Democratic attachment in presidential elections, for they are much less competitive in local affairs and both their electoral turnout and party margins are apt to be highly variable from election to election. The more durably Democratic counties of Middle Tennessee are far less subject to short-term variations in their party vote. These homogenous and stable counties are also rather more likely than those elsewhere in the state to turn their residents to a favorable vote to support the civic weal in the form of a clean courthouse, new school buildings, or even a library, despite the attendant necessity of new taxation.

Recent Republican victories in Tennessee, capped by the taking of a senatorial seat and the governor's chair in 1970, may seem to put Tennessee into the ranks of the two-party states. Four of the nine Tennessee members of the national House are still Republican, after the settling of the dust of November, 1970, and one of these districts is in the former Democratic citadel of Memphis. Tennessee now has a Republican governor and two Republican United States senators. On the other hand, the Democrats now control both houses of the state legislature, a position they temporarily lost in 1968 in the lower house. And since there is so much *personalismo* in Tennessee politics one cannot be certain whether animosities toward Senator Gore and gubernatorial candidate John J. Hooker are more responsible for the Republican victories than basic new Republican strength. Nevertheless, given the rather even division of the votes, the presence of four Republicans in the national House, the frequency with which Tennessee picks Republican presidential electors, and the growth in the number of Republican voters in the West, one might cautiously consider that the Republicans are not "just visitin'." Tennessee ought now to be dropped (if it ever belonged there) from the list of one-party states.

5

TEXAS
Land of Conservative Expansiveness

O. DOUGLAS WEEKS

Meeting Place of South and West

Texas is the largest state in the South and in many ways the least
southern. In fact, it is the meeting place of South and West. The
first Anglo-Saxon settlers, however, were from the South and they
were responsible for making East Texas distinctively southern and
for extending a southern veneer more or less over the entire state.
They introduced slavery and the plantation system, led Texas into
secession and the Civil War, experienced Reconstruction along with
the rest of the South, and fixed upon Texas much of the southern
tradition in her social and political institutions. Although the
southern stamp was thus being impressed upon the state, the Anglo-
Saxon settlements scarcely extended farther west than Austin. Far
to the South and West were Mexican settlements, but except for
the San Antonio region they were sparse and of little significance in
the activities of the state. On the eve of the Civil War scattered
German settlements were made in the south-central and west-central
areas among Anglo and Mexican populations, but they were of little
significance until later. Slavery scarcely penetrated the Latin and
German areas, since Negroes were largely confined to Anglo-Saxon
East Texas and Central Texas, where they are still found to a large
extent.

O. Douglas Weeks was Professor Emeritus of Government, The University of Texas
at Austin. He died in 1970.

201

Today Negroes constitute around 12 percent of the state's population. They have tended in recent times to concentrate in cities;
in 1960 eight urban counties contained 60 percent of the Negro
population.[1] One-third of the Negroes are to be found in the two
largest counties—Harris and Dallas. Latin Americans make up
around 15 percent of the state's people and have also tended to go
to the cities, concentrating in some seven urban counties.[2] Some
rural counties, however, along the Mexican border, are largely
Latin; for example, Starr County is 90 percent so. The presence of
these principal minorities gives rise to many of the social and political problems associated with ethnic conflict in some of the other
states, although in Texas this conflict is limited mainly to the cir-
cumscribed areas in which the various groups settled, rather than
being a continuing problem of statewide politics. Other national
groups tended to settle in certain counties. Thus many people of
German origin continue to live in the so-called German counties
of south-central and west-central Texas, where their ancestors were
pioneers. The German settlers of the 1840's and 1850's were largely
liberal refugees who left the home country after the failure there of
the democratic movements of the mid–nineteenth century. Opposed
to slavery, they settled in the new country beyond the Anglo-Saxon
areas. They were sympathetic with the purposes of the newly
formed Republican Party and as a matter of tradition they still
support that party, at least in presidential elections. Other scattered
counties in various parts of the state attracted various other peoples
of Europe.

In the newer portions of the state, mainly in west-central and
western Texas, which became populated only after the Civil War,
many of the settlers came from the northern and western areas of
the United States and introduced Republicanism and northern
ways into the newer counties. Thus scattered counties in West Texas

---

[1] Harris (Houston), Dallas (Dallas), Galveston (Galveston), Bexar (San Antonio),
Jefferson (Beaumont), McLennon (Waco), Tarrant (Fort Worth), and Travis
(Austin).

[2] Bexar (San Antonio), Hidalgo (Edinburg), El Paso (El Paso), Cameron (Brownsville), Nueces (Corpus Christi), Harris (Houston), Webb (Laredo).

and the Panhandle have strong Republican tendencies and resemble states such as Kansas more than they do the neighboring southern state of Louisiana.

Thus Texas has a mixture of tradition that is reflected strongly in her politics and party voting. The state is a world in itself, a fact poorly understood throughout the United States and even in most southern states. False stereotypes of Texas and Texans are no doubt responsible for widespread mistaken attitudes and erroneous impressions of this great commonwealth and its people, and thus its politics is also poorly understood. The social and political picture of Texas is as varied as its topography and climate, which include almost as much variety as the United States itself. Texas is also a land of change. This is particularly true in the rural-urban picture of the present century. In 1900 the state was 82.9 percent rural. By 1960 it had become 75 percent urban, with 63.7 percent of its people located in twenty-one Standard Metropolitan Statistical Areas.

Texas, like her currently most notable citizen, Lyndon B. Johnson, is grossly misunderstood unless one takes the complexity of its history and cultural characteristics into account.

Politics in the Southern Mold

Whatever may be the sectional and ethnic variations of the state, the political system of Texas has been more distinctively southern than many other aspects of its life. This phenomenon is explained by the early dominance of the southern element in its population, which fixed a southern pattern on its political life. Only recently has this influence begun to show any signs of disintegration.

The one-party system, long typical of the South, developed early in Texas and is still a strong tradition. Under the Texas Republic personal followings of leaders largely took the place of political parties. At the time Texas was admitted into the Union in 1845, the existing two-party system of the United States was beginning to weaken and the Whig Party to go to pieces. Opposition to the annexation of Texas had been stronger in the Whig Party than among the Democrats, since the Democratic efforts to organize in the state were more successful than those of the Whigs. The Democrats were not fully organized until 1856. The Whig Party, never fully developed, was in the process of disintegration all over the United States after 1854. The Democrats were thus dominant from the start. In the first three presidential elections under the United States, Texas counted considerable numbers of Whig votes, but Whig strength in the state never approached that of the Democrats. The Know-Nothings gained some strength but not enough to threaten the Democrats. As the Civil War approached, the Democrats divided into states'-righters and Unionists. When the secessionists prevailed, war brought normal politics to an end. In the postwar period the Democratic Party was revived and became the chief bulwark of the whites. "Carpetbag" and "scalawag" Republicans organized the Negroes into the Republican Party, which enjoyed a brief control. By 1874, however, Reconstruction was over in Texas and the Democratic Party entered a new period of supremacy, but with continued opposition by minor parties and a Republican Party that was of some consequence until the turn of the century.

During the last quarter of the nineteenth century, the minor parties which made considerable trouble for the Democrats were, successively, the Greenbackers and the Populists, both products of the depressions of the 1870's and 1890's. The western half of the state was being settled, and agricultural discontent and the advent of industrialism, with its problems of railroads and trusts, produced a turbulent politics. To this confusion the Republican Party made significant contributions by coalescing with minor parties.

The Greenback Party from 1878 to 1884 and the Populist Party during the late 1880's and all through the 1890's strenuously defended the cause of the depressed farmers and new settlers and advocated "cheap money," tax reforms, and railroad regulation. The Greenbackers reached the crest of their strength in the state election of 1882, when a Greenback-Republican coalition polled 102,501 votes for its candidate for governor as opposed to 150,891 for the Democratic candidate. The Greenbackers declined after 1884, but agricultural discontent persisted and produced the larger Populist Party of the 1890's. The Republican Party, partly supported by

Negroes, continued to poll formidable presidential votes up to 1900, but had little effect in state elections except to tip the scales to the benefit of Greenbackers or Populists.

In the period of Greenback decline and the rise of the Populists, the Democrats fell under the liberal power of James Stephen Hogg, who served as attorney general and governor and accomplished some notable reforms between 1887 and 1895. Hogg steered clear of the more radical ideas of the Populists, but fought for trust and railroad regulation and against reactionary Democrats and Republicans and helped to establish the middle-of-the-road tradition that became firmly entrenched in the Texas Democratic Party in later years. Governor Hogg was succeeded by Charles A. Culbertson, who was equally progressive. In 1896 with William Jennings Bryan's nomination to the presidency by the Democrats and their adoption of many of the Populist ideas, populism as a movement became absorbed by the later progressivism in both major parties, symbolized in the leadership of Theodore Roosevelt and Woodrow Wilson.[3]

One Party and Its Primary

A new era of politics began in Texas near the turn of the century. Rather suddenly the Democratic Party found itself without rivals. The minor parties were gone. The minority Republican Party became less and less a factor in state politics, and its presidential vote declined after 1900. Diminishing Negro support for the Republicans was a factor. The adoption of a poll tax as a voting requirement early in the new century, which was designed to discourage the voting of both Populists and Negroes, had a considerable effect. The growth of white control within the Republican Party by the 1920's virtually eliminated Negroes from its leadership.

The complete dominance of the Democratic Party and the full development of a one-party system were greatly aided by the enactment in 1905 of the Terrell Election Law. This law made the direct primary mandatory for parties polling as many as 100,000 votes for

[3] See Stuart A. MacCorkle and Dick Smith, *Texas Government* (6th ed.; New York: McGraw-Hill Book Co., 1968), Chap. 4.

their candidates for governor in the last general election, a figure
which the Republicans did not attain until many years later (and
then they were able to have the number changed to 200,000). Thus
the primary was virtually required only for the Democrats as the
method of nominating candidates for state, district, and county elective offices. Displacing the convention system of nominating, the
primary handed over the naming of party candidates to rank-and-
file party members. Nominations by popularly elected delegates to
party conventions had constituted only indirect nomination by the
people, but the direct primary meant direct nomination.

Texas was not peculiar at this time in adopting the direct primary. Its adoption was a principal tenet of the progressive movement, which was sweeping the United States in the opening years
of the twentieth century and which resulted in laws requiring this
method of nomination in both parties in a great many states. The
party conventions, which had been largely unregulated by law,
were now stripped of their nominating functions or abolished outright in many states for all parties. They had been largely unregulated by law and had frequently been manipulated and corrupted
by politicians and political machines. With the party voters nominating their candidates directly, it was thought politics would be rid
of corruption and democratic control restored. Indeed, in the South
the direct primary was popular for another reason: it allowed voters
in a one-party situation a real chance to elect public officials and
took this important function out of the hands of convention
delegates.

Thus in the South and in Texas, the Democratic primary became the real election and voters flocked into it and neglected the
general election. Many voters no doubt forgot about the general
election and came to look upon the Democratic primary as the only
election, which in effect it was. While southern primaries were
usually closed to members of other parties, the barrier was inten-
tionally not very effective. In Texas a pledge supposedly kept non–
party members out of the primary. The law required this pledge to
be printed at the top of the primary ballot: "I am a ―― [Demo-
crat] and pledge myself to support the nominee of this primary."

This pledge, adopted in 1907, is still required. Its interpretation did not become a matter of controversy until 1924. During the next eight years its binding character received considerable attention and was subject to extended litigation as the result of party bolting in the elections of 1924 and 1928, when many Democrats refused to vote in the general elections for Miriam A. Ferguson for governor and Alfred E. Smith for President. The court interpretations were liberal; for instance, the voter's promise to support the party's candidate was construed to be a moral and not a legal obligation. Thus the Texas primary is virtually an open primary in which nonmembers of the party are free to vote.[4]

The Texas primary law for many years, like other southern primary laws, made it possible to bar Negroes from participation in the primary and thus virtually to disqualify them. There was prolonged litigation over the so-called white primary and Texas figured in several prominent United States Supreme Court decisions. Finally in 1944 the Court wiped out the white primary; subsequently Negroes gradually have taken an increasingly greater part in Democratic primaries.[5] It should be added that the large Latin American population[6] has also increased in importance, taking a larger part in the politics of South Texas and in some cities. Thus more active Negro and Mexican minorities have increased the liberal element in the state and particularly in the Democratic Party. The Mexican vote is still largely a controlled, or machine, vote, and to some extent the Negro vote is also controlled.

A factor which helped make the Democratic primary the real election was the adoption early in its history of the runoff, or second primary, which insured majority nomination and thus lessened the need of vitalizing the general election as a means of insuring majorities.

[4] O. Douglas Weeks, "The Texas Direct Primary System," *Southwestern Social Science Quarterly*, XIII (1932), 95–120.

[5] O. Douglas Weeks, "The White Primary: 1944–1948," *American Political Science Review*, XLII (1948), 500–10.

[6] O. Douglas Weeks, "The Texas-Mexican and the Politics of South Texas," *American Political Science Review*, XXXIX (1945), 606–27.

The All-Embracing Democrats

With the perfection of the primary system vital elections tended to
become something that took place within the shell of a single party,
with factionalism within the party becoming something of a substitute for a two-party system. This pattern has never become so pronounced in Texas as in some other one-party states. For example,
the Democratic Party in Louisiana and the Republican Party in
North Dakota were long divided into two well-organized and distinctive factions which nominated complete tickets and opposed
each other as if they were parties. Texas has never gone this far in
developing cohesive factions; its candidates in primary contests
limit their organizational and campaign efforts largely to the office
sought by each individual, and general voter interest is confined to
a few important offices. Thus races for governor and United States
senator usually attract the principal attention, and have little connection with each other in a factional sense.

Until comparatively recently the all-embracing Democratic Party
has provided a sufficient stage for Texas politics. This has been definitely true of state, district, and county politics and only slightly
less so in presidential politics. Progressivism played its part in the
first twenty years of the twentieth century in dividing Texas Democrats, but not to the extent that they were later split by the more
serious issues of the Great Depression, the New Deal, the Fair Deal,
and later events and movements. Certain early governors of the
present century, securing inspiration from such state leaders as Governor Hogg or such national leaders as Woodrow Wilson, were described as progressive Democrats. Thomas M. Campbell, governor
from 1907 to 1911, was responsible for a considerable program of
progressive legislation. Oddly enough, Governor James E. Ferguson
helped push through additional progressive laws. His wife as governor was responsible for much support given by Texas to the
launching of the New Deal in the 1930's. Unlike the primary systems
of some other southern states, the Texas primary has not produced
many eccentric characters among the party's candidates and leaders.

For Patronage Only: Texas Republicans

For many years after 1900 the Republican Party in Texas ceased to have much significance. From 1923 to 1950 the organization of the party was under the control of its long-time national committeeman, R. B. Creager of Brownsville, who looked upon the party in Texas as mainly a national patronage dispenser for Republican Presidents. He allowed incomplete state Republican tickets to be nominated, but he took little or no interest in working for their election. During the Creager period of control, a single Texas seat in the national House of Representatives was held by a Republican and another in the state lower house. In 1924 opposition to the candidacy of Miriam Ferguson for the governorship produced a large but minority vote for the Republican candidate for governor. In 1928, the Republican presidential candidate, Herbert Hoover, won the vote of Texas against Alfred E. Smith. In neither case did the Creager organization, however, offer much help. Dissenting factions within the Democratic Party of Texas—"Anti-Ferguson" and "Hoovercrat"—produced the results. Few, if any, permanent conversions of Democrats to Republicanism took place. Creager did not expect more than occasional Republican victories, under very exceptional circumstances. This remained the Republican attitude until after Creager's death in 1950.

Much to the party's discomfiture, the Republican gubernatorial vote in 1924, 1928, and 1932 exceeded 100,000; these results necessitated Republican primaries in 1926, 1930, and 1934. When the 100,000 figure was passed in 1944 the Republicans persuaded the legislature to increase the number to 200,000. In 1952 the Republican candidate for governor received 468,319 votes under a temporary provision that allowed one party to cross-file candidates of another party. Republican growth in later years required the party to hold primaries not only in 1954, but in 1958, 1962, 1964, 1966, 1968, and 1970.

Republican reluctance to hold party primaries was broader-based than the opposition of Creager. It should be noted that primaries

Figure 1

COUNTIES OF TEXAS IN WHICH THE REPUBLICAN PARTY
MAKES ITS BEST SHOWING

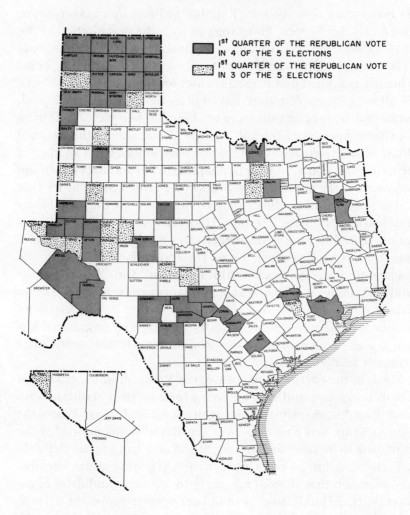

1ST QUARTER OF THE REPUBLICAN VOTE
IN 4 OF THE 5 ELECTIONS

1ST QUARTER OF THE REPUBLICAN VOTE
IN 3 OF THE 5 ELECTIONS

in Texas have always been regarded as purely private affairs to be conducted and financed by parties and not by public election officials. They are thus financed by assessing candidates in primaries, and the management of these elections is strictly in the hands of party agencies and officers. The bulk of the assessments obviously has to come from candidates for local and minor offices; consequently if little interest is taken in such offices and no nominations made to them, there is no way to finance primaries. In fact, the Texas Supreme Court has twice held that public money may not be appropriated for holding primaries because they are not for a public purpose.[7] This peculiar legal holding is found in only four states other than Texas, all of which are southern. The Democratic Party has always had a near-monopoly on local offices and its primaries are in fact the local elections. Hence if Republicans cannot be induced to run for local office, there is no source of funds for holding Republican primaries even when a large vote in the previous general election of a Republican candidate for governor makes it mandatory. Thus the law severely handicaps the growth of the Republican Party by placing this impossible financial hurdle in its way.

Democratic Family Affairs

The one-party political system of Texas had been under a growing strain since the advent of the New Deal in the early 1930's. The Democratic Party in the South had long tended to be conservative or to the right of center, but with its capture nationally by the more liberal elements of the nation, a much more definite liberal-versus-conservative factionalism tended to develop within the party in the South and in Texas which could less adequately be contained within the shell of a single party. Thus splits in the party became more frequent and more vital in presidential, congressional, and statewide elections.[8]

In the presidential election year of 1936 occurred the first of a

[7] *Waples v. Marrast*, 184 S.W. (1916); *Bell v. Hill*, 74 S.W. (2d) 113 (1935).

[8] See James R. Soukup, Clifton McCleskey, and Harry Holloway, *Party and Factional Division in Texas* (Austin: University of Texas Press, 1964).

series of divisions in the Democratic Party that became chronic. In that year the "Jeffersonian Democrats" emerged, but these anti-Roosevelt Democrats were restrained from producing a real split partly because of the presence of John N. Garner of Texas on the ticket as vice-presidential candidate. In 1940 with the absence of Garner, with Roosevelt more to the left, and with the presence of "Democrats for Willkie," the opposition to Roosevelt increased— although it was not as yet sufficiently strong to cause a real break. In 1944, however, the split came with the formation of the Texas Regulars, who were economically conservative and opposed to a fourth term for Roosevelt. In 1948 opposition throughout the South to President Truman's civil rights program produced the States' Rights, or Dixiecrat, Party which in some states captured the organization of the Democratic Party, but which took the form of a minor party in Texas. Support for this group came largely from East Texas and was predominantly racist, whereas the earlier Texas Regulars based their opposition mainly on economic conservatism, which was more widespread over the state. So far, the Republican Party had not figured much and the divisions were mainly Democratic family affairs.

Drift Toward Two Parties

Throughout the 1950's a real effort was made to develop a two-party system. In the interval between Creager's death and the rise of new leadership in 1952, the Republican organization was led by Henry Zweifel of Fort Worth, who attempted to carry on in Creager's fashion. There were those, however, who sought to gain control of the party with a view to winning converts and elections. In 1947, Captain J. F. Lucey of Dallas organized the Republican Club of Texas for the purpose of attracting into the party anti–Fair Deal Democrats and thus creating a two-party system. Although apparently well financed, this organization soon collapsed. In 1948, Jack Porter of Houston, later state campaign manager for Eisenhower, opposed Lyndon B. Johnson for the United States Senate and received 349,655 votes to Johnson's 702,985. In 1950, Ben Guill of

Pampa in a special election won a seat in the national House of Representatives, to become the first Republican congressman from Texas in twenty years. In the same year Edward T. Dicker of Dallas was elected to a seat in the Texas House, the first in twenty-five years to be held by a Republican.

Aside from these Republican stirrings on the state and local level, many Texans had long been in the habit of voting Republican in presidential elections. Such voters had been called presidential Republicans. It had also been true that the Republican vote for governor increased greatly in presidential election years. The great growth of population in Texas in the previous forty years had been due largely to the influx of people from other states, many of whom were Republicans. These, combined with many Democrats, it was felt, constituted a large potential following for the Republicans. The first great effort to organize these elements took place in 1952 behind the popular presidential candidacy of General Dwight D. Eisenhower.[9] In that year a shift of control from the Old Guard was accomplished with the aid of a strong combination of conservative and moderate Democrats under the leadership of Democratic Governor Allan Shivers and known as the Shivercrats. Thus Shivercrats and Republicans carried Texas for Eisenhower and the Republican Party by a 53.13 percent vote. Figuring largely in the result were conservative and moderate Democrats who under Shivers retained control of the state Democratic organization, driving out the party's liberals, or "loyalists," as they called themselves.[10] As a matter of fact the Democratic element was the chief factor in the strength of the newly revived Republican organization, although the Republican element made a heroic effort to swell itself into a major party.

Since that time the Republican Party has continued to grow at a moderate rate. What was the Shivercrat faction has remained the majority element of the Democratic Party and is now spoken of as

[9] See O. Douglas Weeks, *Texas Presidential Politics in 1952*, Public Affairs Series No. 16 (Austin: Institute of Public Affairs, University of Texas, 1953), 116.

[10] The Shivercrats took the strongest stand against Adlai E. Stevenson on the latter's position on the tidelands. In August, 1952, Shivers completely broke with Stevenson and the national party.

the conservative faction. Thus conservatives in Texas have had really two organizations—the Republicans being the more conservative of the two, and the majority faction among the Democrats consisting of a coalition of conservatives and moderates. These majority Democrats were the backbone of support of the Eisenhower regime and have controlled the state since that time.

The Cities Like Ike

The large urban counties were the most important element in the Republican victory in 1952. The total Eisenhower vote in the thirteen most populous counties[11] amounted to 555,443. Adlai Stevenson, the Democratic candidate for President, however, in the same counties won a vote of 421,285, but received majorities in only four of them. Seven of these thirteen populous counties contained cities over 100,000.

Only where there was a strong labor vote, a traditional Democratic vote, or a Latin American population of some size was Stevenson given a majority. Other areas of Eisenhower strength were the counties of the Gulf Plain, the lower Rio Grande Valley, the agricultural Panhandle, and the ranching areas of western and southwestern Texas. The Democrats also won a number of the oil-producing counties and some counties of northern and west-central Texas.

The Republican presidential majorities in Texas in 1952 did not go much farther. In other elections there were few opposing Republican candidates. Thus it can be said that no two-party system got started in Texas as a result of the Eisenhower success in 1952.

Groups, Factions, and Cliques

In 1956 Texas again went for Eisenhower, with an even larger majority than in 1952.[12] The two major factions of the Democratic

11 Harris, Dallas, Bexar, Tarrant, El Paso, Nueces, Travis, Jefferson, Hidalgo, Mc-Lennan, Cameron, Galveston, and Lubbock.

12 O. Douglas Weeks, *Texas One-Party Politics in 1956*, Public Affairs Series No. 16 (Austin: Institute of Public Affairs, University of Texas, 1957), 50.

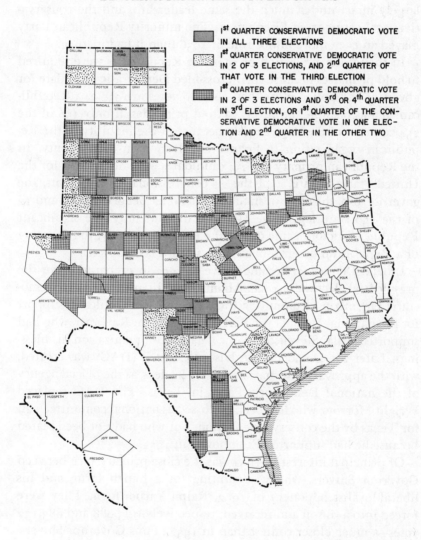

Figure 2

COUNTIES OF TEXAS IN WHICH THE CONSERVATIVE
DEMOCRATIC FACTION MAKES ITS BEST SHOWING

1st QUARTER CONSERVATIVE DEMOCRATIC VOTE IN ALL THREE ELECTIONS

1st QUARTER CONSERVATIVE DEMOCRATIC VOTE IN 2 OF 3 ELECTIONS, AND 2nd QUARTER OF THAT VOTE IN THE THIRD ELECTION

1st QUARTER CONSERVATIVE DEMOCRATIC VOTE IN 2 OF 3 ELECTIONS AND 3rd OR 4th QUARTER IN 3rd ELECTION, OR 1st QUARTER OF THE CONSERVATIVE DEMOCRATIC VOTE IN ONE ELECTION AND 2nd QUARTER IN THE OTHER TWO

Party, now referred to as conservatives and liberals, remained largely intact under much the same leadership, and the conservatives again supported Eisenhower. The minority Republican Party played an even more minor role in 1956 than it had in 1952.

In the midterm election of 1954 the Republicans were required to hold primaries because their cross-filed Democratic candidate for governor had polled more than 200,000 votes in 1952 as a Republican. It was possible, however, to hold primaries in only 150 of the 254 counties of the state, largely because of the inability of the Republican organization to finance an election in each county. In the Republican primary of 1954 candidates were nominated for the United States Senate, 5 of the 21 congressional district seats, the governorship, the office of state commissioner of agriculture, and 12 of the 150 state legislative House seats. But only one significant Republican victory came out of the election, namely, the choosing of a Republican congressman from the Dallas district.

Liberal Democrats became active in 1953 in preparation for the presidential election of 1956. About 300 of them created the Democratic Organizing Committee for the purpose of building support for the national Democratic Party. Speaker Sam Rayburn, who had supported Adlai Stevenson in 1952, gave this organization his blessings. Later the Democratic Advisory Council (DAC) was created, with the approval of the national party leaders, as the official agency of the national Democratic Party in Texas. The DAC replaced Wright Morrow, who had been endorsed as national committeeman for Texas by the conservative faction, but who had not been seated because he had supported Eisenhower in 1952.

Of principal interest in 1954 was the close primary race between Governor Shivers, who was running for a fourth term, and his liberal-loyalist opponent of 1952, Ralph Yarborough. They were forced into a runoff and received, respectively, 775,088 and 683,132 votes—a much closer contest than in 1952. Thus Governor Shivers' strong coalition of conservatives and moderate Democrats of 1952 went to pieces, as many of the moderates joined the liberal Democrats. The votes showed that the Republican Party, standing alone and without benefit of cross-filing[13] and of Eisenhower's name on the ticket, had sunk back to its normal insignificance in state politics. Cross-filing, effectively used only in the election of 1952, was repealed in 1955.[14]

As the year 1955 wore on, it became clear that the Democratic Party of Texas was seriously divided and that trouble was in store for 1956. A more even balance had developed between conservatives and liberals, as was indicated by the close contest of Shivers and Yarborough. Even Senator Johnson and Speaker Rayburn, who were trying to patch up party difficulties in Texas, were not in complete harmony. Democratic gubernatorial candidates of every shade of political belief were emerging. The still-small Republican organization was deriving what pleasure it could from the Democratic confusion. Conservative and liberal factions both showed cracks in their organizations. Douglass Cater, at the end of 1955, pointed out that Democratic division in Texas was not a simple struggle between two factions but resembled more the multiparty system of France.[15]

On April 10, 1956, both Johnson and Shivers made bids for the delegation chairmanship to the Democratic National Convention. Johnson announced also for the place of favorite son; Shivers indicated that he was not interested. Johnson was aloof to both the Rayburn and Shivers organizations in Texas, stating that he did not represent "any group, any faction, or any clique." The Texas delegation, he advised, "should abide by the decision of the majority of the convention and return to Texas to work for the election of the nominees." [16] Thereafter, Shivers attempted to win control of the Texas delegation. The precinct and county conventions leaned heavily toward Johnson. He won 1,149 convention votes to Shivers' 66 votes; 224 votes were in dispute and the remainder uninstructed.

13 The Democratic Party in 1954 had refused to allow the cross-filing of its candidates. *Ibid.*, 4.
14 H.B. 45, *House Journal*, 54th Legislature, Regular Session, March 15, 1955, p. 919.
15 Douglass Cater, "The Trouble in Lyndon Johnson's Back Yard," *Reporter*, December 1, 1955, p. 32.
16 *Texas Observer*, April 11, 1956.

The state convention approved Johnson as favorite son and delegation chairman.

In the campaign of 1956 the national Democratic ticket, consisting of Adlai Stevenson and Estes Kefauver, was energetically supported by Johnson and Rayburn. Shivers was equally busy furthering the cause of the Democrats for Eisenhower with aid from the Republicans. Eisenhower's victory was even more sweeping than in 1952: over 55 percent of the total presidential vote, as against slightly over 53 percent in 1952. The Republicans continued to hold most of the counties won for Eisenhower in 1952. In East Texas, eleven counties with large Negro populations shifted to Eisenhower. In West Texas, twenty-two counties, mostly in the drought-stricken and High Plains regions, shifted to Stevenson. Elsewhere shifts were few. Six metropolitan counties remained loyal to Eisenhower. In the congressional races, Republican candidates appeared in only five; and in all except the Dallas district, the Democratic candidates won by huge majorities. There Bruce Alger, the incumbent Republican, was reelected. In the governor's race, Price Daniel won overwhelmingly against his Republican opponent. The same was true in the two other races for statewide office in which Republicans were nominated. Only two state Senate seats were contested by Republicans, who likewise lost. Thus the much boasted two-party system which was supposed to come into being in 1952 was not much in evidence.

A Little Solidarity

In the later 1950's the three outstanding leaders in Texas politics were Price Daniel, Lyndon Johnson, and Sam Rayburn. This triumvirate dominated the Democratic Party organization in the state in 1956 and prevented party convention bolts like those of 1944, 1948, and 1952. It had not been able to break the power of Shivers and to prevent the Eisenhower victories of 1952 and 1956, but after 1956 Shivers would no longer be governor and Eisenhower no longer eligible for the presidency. Could Texas now be restored to her old one-party status? Would the rising stock of Johnson as a presidential possibility be able to push the right and left factions aside and to enlarge and solidify the moderate Democrats? As it turned out, this did happen, and Texas once again gave its electoral vote to the Democratic ticket, but by the very narrow margin of only 46,000 popular votes. Not very encouraging to the Democrats was the fact that the Republican presidential ticket of 1960 received the highest vote on record, polling 41,080 more votes than in 1956, when President Eisenhower had carried the state.

Another fly in the majority Democratic ointment was the special election for United States senator in 1957. This election was called to fill the vacancy created when Price Daniel resigned in order to run for the governorship, which he won in a runoff race against Ralph Yarborough, a leading Democratic liberal, in August, 1956. On the eve of his own retirement from the governorship Shivers appointed an ultraconservative Dallas millionaire, William A. Blakley, as temporary occupant of the Senate seat and left the calling of a special election to the incoming governor, who set it for April 2, 1957. Ralph Yarborough won this election by a plurality after a bill in the legislature to provide for a runoff and majority election failed to pass in time. Later, however, the measure passed; it was first used in 1961 in the special election to fill the vacancy left by the resignation of Senator Lyndon Johnson.

Encouraged by the victory of Yarborough, the liberal Democrats kept the pot boiling for 1957. In December of 1956 their leaders organized in Austin the Democrats of Texas, which soon came to be known as DOT and was bent on capturing the state organization of the party in 1958. In the July, 1958, Democratic primary most interest was taken in the contest for a full six-year nomination to the United States Senate seat to which Ralph Yarborough had been elected in 1957 and for which he announced his candidacy. William A. Blakley, the arch-conservative, was his only opponent, and Yarborough won the nomination by a vote of 760,856 to 536,073.

In 1959 Johnson's presidential possibilities began to shape up. The legislature enacted a law moving the primaries up to May and dispensing with the second series of precinct and county conventions, which had been previously held in the summer of even-numbered years to choose delegates to the September state convention.

Beginning in 1960 one set of precinct and county conventions elected delegates to serve in both the presidential and gubernatorial state conventions, with the precinct conventions to be held on the moved-up day of the first primary. The earlier dates for the primaries allowed Johnson to be nominated for reelection to the United States Senate and simultaneously to have his name on the ballot as presidential candidate.[17] One set of delegates would also eliminate any possible shift in party control, as sometimes had happened in presidential election years in the summer precinct and county conventions. Another new law was more to the liking of the liberals. This provision, requiring the voter to have his poll tax receipt or exemption certificate stamped with the name of the party in whose activity he participated, prevented his taking part later in the year in the affairs of any other party.[18]

Kennedy and Johnson Court Texas

Throughout the early months of 1960 Johnson's candidacy received many endorsements from various leaders in Texas and across the country. The liberal Democrats in the state held back. Because of loud objections that their name too closely resembled the name of the party, they changed it from Democrats of Texas to Democrats of Texas Clubs and henceforth were referred to as DOTC. Senator Yarborough refused to follow the opposition of DOTC to Johnson's candidacy.

This opposition to Johnson eventually brought about the liquidation of DOTC at the time of the 1960 Democratic state convention, which instructed the Texas delegation to support Johnson. In the Democratic National Convention the Texas delegation made every effort to block Senator John F. Kennedy, the leading presidential aspirant, and to win delegate votes for Johnson. In the subsequent balloting, Kennedy won 806 votes; Johnson, with 409 votes, was second, however, with all other aspirants far behind.

17 *General and Special Laws of Texas*, 56th Legislature, Regular Session, 1959, Chaps. 161, 165.
18 *Ibid.*, Chap. 480.

Kennedy's choice of Johnson for vice-presidential candidate and Johnson's acceptance have been explained in various ways. No doubt a desire to carry the South was important. In any event, the election would be close in Texas. Many Democrats displeased with Kennedy and the liberal Democratic platform would no doubt again support the Republican presidential slate in spite of Johnson's presence on the Democratic ticket. Texans had no particular objection to Richard Nixon, the running mate of Eisenhower in the two previous presidential elections, in which Texas had gone Republican.

Both Democratic extremes were highly organized, as were Texas Republicans and Democrats for Nixon. Early polls indicated a close vote. Kennedy and Johnson made extensive tours of the state. In Houston, Kennedy staged his telling confrontation with the Greater Houston Ministerial Association, which was one of the turning points in Kennedy's partially successful campaign efforts to allay public fears about a Catholic in the White House. The September state Democratic convention was successfully controlled by Governor Price Daniel, who pushed through a conservative platform and postponed the seating of the troublesome Houston delegation until the convention was nearly over. In the subsequent campaign the most strenuous efforts were staged by all groups in both town and country. In October, Allan Shivers went on the stump for Nixon, and many national Democratic and Republican leaders visited Texas.[19]

Return to Democratic Fold

The election of 1960 produced the closest vote for the presidency across the country since 1884. In the South the increase in voter participation was the highest of any section of the country. Texas had a record turnout of voters and the presidential vote was the closest ever. The Democrats polled 1,167,932 votes and the Republicans 1,121,699, with very few votes going to minor tickets.

[19] O. Douglas Weeks, *Texas in the 1960 Presidential Election*, Public Affairs Series No. 48 (Austin: Institute of Public Affairs, University of Texas, 1961), 80.

The reasons for Texas' return to the Democratic column in 1960 deserve some attention. First, it must be noted that the Democratic margin was very slender. Small though the margin was, Johnson's name on the ticket no doubt contributed significantly to the Democratic victory. Pride in his prominence and the honor he reflected on the state temporarily silenced many of his old enemies. Johnson's candidacy and his heroic efforts, as well as those of many other Democratic leaders, had the effect of producing within the party organization in Texas a temporary suppression of the usual divisiveness and an unusual spirit of harmony. Other factors were the absence of Eisenhower in the campaign of 1960 and the waning influence of Shivers, whose prominence had greatly declined since 1952 and 1956. Still another factor was the great decline of the importance of the religious issue since 1928, when Alfred E. Smith's Catholicism had lost Texas to the Democrats. While Catholic bloc voting in Texas augmented the strength of Kennedy, the possible countereffect of uniting Protestants against him on the basis of an anti-Catholic bias did not materialize to any appreciable extent.

The most important result of the election of 1960 in Texas was the encouragement it gave the Republicans. It proved beyond all doubt that the party did not need Eisenhower to augment its support, for Nixon, even though defeated, received a larger vote than the victorious Eisenhower had in 1956. This result encouraged the Republicans in 1962 to nominate a more complete ticket, which included candidates for 8 statewide elective offices, 18 congressional seats, 13 state Senate seats, 84 state House seats, and about 150 local offices. They made some notable gains and piled up large votes against several Democratic nominees for important offices.

Most encouraging for the Republicans was the sizable vote polled for John G. Tower, their candidate to fill Johnson's United States Senate seat. Johnson's dual candidacies in 1960 for Vice President and for reelection to his Senate seat had not pleased a good many voters. Hence Tower secured a large vote, not too far behind Johnson's (926,653 to 1,306,625). After Johnson resigned from the Senate before assuming the vice-presidency, a special runoff

election was held May 27, 1961, to fill the seat. Tower won over interim Democratic Senator William A. Blakley by 448,217 to 437,-
874. In this race a conservative Republican proved more palatable
to the voters than a reactionary Democrat. The effect of this phenomenal Republican voting was to cause the party to do its utmost
in the general election of 1962 to win as many places as it could. It
nominated candidates for an unusual number of elective places
with some encouraging results.

An important outcome of the election of 1962 was the choice of
John B. Connally as Democratic candidate for governor. Connally
was a close friend of Vice President Johnson and could be expected
to pour oil on Texas Democratic factionalism for the election of
1964 and help prevent a Republican victory. President Kennedy's
trip to Texas at the time of his assassination was supposedly inspired by the state's political possibilities for 1964.

The liberalism of the Kennedy administration and the growing
influence of Senator Barry Goldwater in Republican councils after
1960 caused the moderate approach of the Eisenhower-Nixon period
to give way to a reactionary mood among Republicans in Texas and
elsewhere. Voters who despaired of maintaining a large conservative
Democratic faction turned more to the Republicans. Goldwater's
economic conservatism and his opposition to national intervention
in racial conflicts influenced many to join the Republican Party.
As the election of 1964 approached, Texas Republicans became
more and more enamored of Goldwater.

The assassination of President Kennedy had a profound effect on
the politics of Texas. Just before, the conservative-liberal pattern
was shaping up again for 1964 with Vice President Johnson and
Senator Yarborough moving forward as opposing leaders. The sudden elevation of Johnson to the presidency made him remote from
the Texas scene and pushed him into closer identification with
Kennedy liberalism. To Texans, this liberal role was unconvincing.
Johnson to them had always been the temporizer and the com-
promiser, never moving too far from center. Essentially he was a
legislative and not an executive leader. Nevertheless, President

Johnson with the aid of Governor Connally exercised a restraining influence on the usual factionalism of the Democratic Party in Texas, as was quite evident in the primary of 1964.

Harmony and Control

Similar restraint was shown in the party conventions held before the national convention of 1964. The Democratic state convention, displaying unusual harmony, under Connally's control chose a delegation pledged to President Johnson and headed by Connally. The Republicans, equally harmonious, adopted a unit rule pledging Texas to Senator Goldwater. Many Republicans, however, disliked Goldwater, and organized a Republicans for Johnson group. The Republicans had no hope of winning Texas for Goldwater, but they campaigned strenuously for their other candidates, of whom they had a fairly full slate. The landslide for Johnson and the Democrats, however, was overwhelming; Johnson polled 63.3 percent of the popular vote and carried Texas with a majority of more than 700,000 ballots.

More Continuity than Change

Although the Republican Party in Texas received considerable encouragement as a result of Senator Tower's decisive victory for reelection to his Senate seat in 1966, the 1968 elections indicated more continuity than change in the general tenor of Texas politics. In the presidential nominating process, control by dominant leaders in the respective parties was manifest. Although some of the conservative Republicans supported Ronald Reagan's candidacy at the state convention in June, the general desire for Republican success made for rather more harmony than conflict in the ranks. The GOP delegation from Texas to the national convention was pledged to Tower as a favorite son; most of those responsible for this decision were aware that Tower was a Nixon supporter. Prior to the national convention, Tower released his delegates and most of them, as expected, supported Nixon.

The conservative faction under Connally's leadership was in substantial command of the Democratic state convention, which also met in June, 1968. The liberal element was even more divided than usual. Vice President Hubert Humphrey received the support of most of the delegates from organized labor. Robert F. Kennedy made some substantial inroads with minority groups and younger activists of the liberal persuasion, and Eugene McCarthy received some scattered support from among those whose chief concern was Vietnam. The delegation to the national convention was safely conservative and the unit rule was imposed. To appease the liberals a few of their number were included in the delegation, but they were chosen from those who were also of the Humphrey persuasion. Although the state convention was generally conceded to be one of the fairest in terms of management in a good many years, the McCarthy forces objected to the way it was conducted, and in the national convention they succeeded in obtaining the elimination of the unit rule and reform of the party's system of representation.

The Republicans entered the 1968 presidential campaign in Texas with great optimism. The early stages of the Humphrey campaign in this state, as in most others, were heavily in the shadow of the withdrawal of Lyndon Johnson, the turmoil of the national convention in Chicago, and a general organizational debility. The conservative Democrats were expected to sit out the election, and some of the more vocal liberals, particularly McCarthy supporters, not only indicated that they would seek revenge for Chicago by refusing to support Humphrey, but would actively work for Nixon as a punitive action against the Democrats.

In late September and early October, however, the Democrats began to exhibit signs of life. Although not very effectively coordinated, both the liberal and conservative elements of the party mounted considerable campaigns among their respective constituents. The liberal wing was headed by Ralph Yarborough, previously a McCarthy supporter; he was joined by a number of other liberal-loyalists. The outgoing chairman of the State Democratic Executive Committee, Will Davis, was primarily responsible for managing the effort of the moderate and conservative Democrats. This uneasy coalition between the two factions, and Humphrey's second swing through Texas late in October, gave the impetus necessary to lift the morale of Democratic supporters in the state to the point of producing the slim plurality which was eventually delivered for the party. Texas thus became the only former Confederate state to remain in the Democratic Party column in the 1968 presidential election.

As in most of the rest of the peripheral South, and in the country at large, the presidential candidacy of George Wallace in Texas was something of an enigma. Some polls in the summer and early fall gave him as much as 29 percent of the vote in the state. He actually received 19 percent of the Texas vote. Since his support came largely from the extreme right wing, which in itself includes many cross-currents of racial and economic interests, it is still not entirely clear which of the major parties was done the most damage by Wallace. As might have been expected, a great deal of Wallace's support came from the southern-oriented section of East Texas, but he also made some inroads into other normally Democratic areas, such as the industrial suburbs of Houston, Beaumont, and Port Arthur. However, these are also areas into which the Republicans have made some presidential incursions in recent elections, and the Republican vote actually fell off in some of the West Texas and Panhandle areas in which Wallace ran quite well. Since the fringe areas between the Texas Republicans and the conservative Democrats are not always clear, it is difficult to attribute any precise effect on the major parties to the Wallace effort.

The 1968 gubernatorial election indicated a tendency to perpetuate the internal divisions and factionalism in the Democratic Party. In the Democratic primary, the liberal candidate, Don Yarborough, made a strong bid for the nomination by leading in the first primary, only to lose the runoff to a rather colorless rural West Texas conservative, Preston Smith. In the general election in November, Smith won over a vigorous Republican opponent, Paul Eggers, by some 400,000 votes.

The 1970 elections considerably dimmed the prospects of the liberal faction in the Democratic party in Texas and perhaps slightly raised the hopes of the Republicans. Ralph Yarborough, the incumbent liberal senator, lost the primary to his conservative opponent,

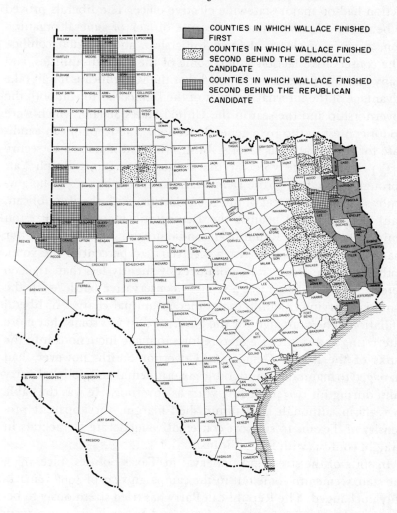

Figure 3

COUNTIES OF TEXAS IN WHICH GEORGE WALLACE MADE
HIS BEST SHOWING IN THE 1968 PRESIDENTIAL ELECTION

COUNTIES IN WHICH WALLACE FINISHED
FIRST

COUNTIES IN WHICH WALLACE FINISHED
SECOND BEHIND THE DEMOCRATIC
CANDIDATE

COUNTIES IN WHICH WALLACE FINISHED
SECOND BEHIND THE REPUBLICAN
CANDIDATE

Lloyd M. Bentsen, Jr., and thus loosened the last hold that the faction had on major statewide elective office. The liberals proved to be in considerable disarray because of lack of general organization, absence of clearly defined leadership, and internal conflict. The conservative faction suffers some of the same disabilities, and many political pundits anticipated that the Republicans might take advantage of the internal disorder of the Democrats to win both the governorship and the seat in the United States Senate, which were up for contest in the 1970 general election. The Republican candidate for the Senate was George Bush, who had managed to secure 43.6 percent of the vote for the Senate seat against Ralph Yarborough in the face of the Democratic landslide in 1964. The governor's race was a repeat of the 1968 election, with the Republican, Paul Eggers, pitted against the Democratic incumbent, Preston Smith. Although the Republican candidates did substantially better than they had previously (each received 46.6 percent of the vote), both lost to the Democratic nominees by slightly less than 150,000 votes. The Senate race was a straight conservative battle, with the candidates trying to outdo each other in mutual charges of liberal affiliation. The campaign for the governorship was somewhat more interesting as a result of Eggers' efforts to make incursions into the ranks of the liberal Democrats. Governor Smith, however, had managed to maintain considerable governmental and political party calm during his two preceding years as governor. He was thus able to reaffirm, although by a diminished margin, the apparent propensity of Texans to support conservative-moderate Democrats in straight contests with Republicans.

In spite of the stress and upheaval in Texas politics since 1952, the state seemed to come out in the campaign year of 1968 remarkably unchanged. The Republican Party has tried strenuously to become a second major party in Texas and to establish a two-party system, but still the Democrats hold the center of the political stage. Eisenhower's carrying Texas in 1952 and 1956 has receded into the past. Adlai Stevenson has passed from the scene. Allan Shivers is no longer visibly active in politics. Lyndon Johnson has made himself a has-been. Texas in the elections of 1966, 1968, and 1970 went

Figure 4

COUNTIES OF TEXAS IN WHICH THE LIBERAL DEMOCRATIC FACTION MAKES ITS BEST SHOWING

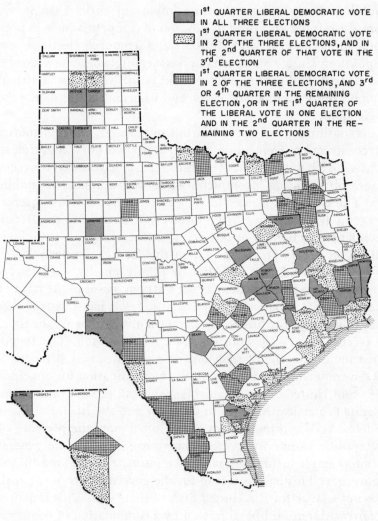

largely back to normal—a one-party state with its politics mainly confined to the factionalism of the Democratic Party. And yet the Republican Party is a much more important entity than it was before 1952. It has improved its position of competitiveness in presidential, gubernatorial, and United States senatorial elections, and a Republican United States senator has seemingly become a fixture. State, district, and county elective officers still remain as a virtual monopoly of the Democratic Party, and its primaries constitute the real elections.

This continuity does not stem from any overpowering memories of Reconstruction. Depending upon one party is not a tradition so much as it is a habit, and the Republican Party has seemed to accept the idea of providing incomplete tickets of candidates for public office. The Republicans are chiefly a reactionary or very conservative group, but they have by no means won away from the Democrats a large reactionary or conservative faction, which still clings to the latter party. To a large extent this faction, formerly led so ably by Lyndon Johnson and later by John Connally, has been responsible for keeping the Democratic Party in Texas to the right of center or in the moderate center. Thus Texas has a system that successfully blocks the success of liberalism most, if not all, the time. The recent primary elections illustrate that very well. The Democratic runoff primaries of 1968 and 1970 provided real alternatives between conservatives and liberals in the nomination for governor (1968) and United States senator (1970). Both times, as usual, the moderate center leaned more to the right and the liberal element was defeated. If a primary does go the other way, the presence of the Republicans offering a conservative candidate in the general election is ample insurance against the ultimate choice of a liberal for governor. This has been true for the governorship; until 1970 it was not so true for the United States Senate seat. This isolation of a fairly substantial liberal faction by a combination of conservative-moderate Democrats and a highly conservative Republican organization maintains conservative Democratic control in the face of a potential dichotomy that might otherwise resemble the divisions manifested in national politics.

II

The Wavering States

6

ARKANSAS
Independent and Unpredictable

RICHARD E. YATES

Sectionalism, Urbanism, and Social Change

The politics and government of this southern-southwestern state are still influenced by sectional divisions, although not so significantly as in the nineteenth century. A diagonal line, drawn from the northeastern to the southwestern corner and running through Little Rock, divides the state into two sections which possess distinctive geographical, demographic, economic, and social characteristics. This sectional division has persisted in strength for more than a hundred years, and despite the accelerating changes of the mid-twentieth century it is still relevant to any consideration of Arkansas politics.

Southeast of this diagonal line lies the old plantation area through which the White, Arkansas, and Ouachita rivers flow sluggishly to the Mississippi. The land is low in elevation, high in fertility, and relatively unbroken by hills and other obstacles to cultivation. As nineteenth-century settlers moved in from Kentucky, Tennessee, and Mississippi, these rich soils were converted into cotton plantations with mules and Negroes as the chief laboring force, small towns to provide centers of county government, and a white population dominated socially, economically, and politically by the larger landowners.

Time and technology have made their changes. Many acres once

Richard E. Yates is Professor of History, Hendrix College.

devoted solely to cotton now yield rice, soybeans, and cattle. Some of the towns have grown into cities, still chiefly serving, however, an agricultural hinterland. Mules have been replaced by tractors. Combines and mechanical cotton pickers have filled the void left by many emigrating Negroes. But the area retains, in great measure, its distinctive plantation qualities. Large landholdings, some running into thousands of acres, continue to dominate the economy. Negroes, though reduced in numbers, still heavily populate this part of the state. In five counties bordering the Mississippi, they constitute more than 50 percent of the population.[1] And the conservative, states' rights political philosophy appears to retain its greatest strength in the southeastern section.

West and northwest of the diagonal dividing line lies a region less favorable to large-scale agriculture, though even here along the river bottoms the plantation economy of the east has thrust long but narrow fingers into the interior. The great bulk of the western section, however, is hilly and mountainous. The farms are smaller, and the economy is more varied. Milk, poultry, fruit, and cattle are the chief agricultural products. Into this section, especially since the mid-1940's, many light industries have moved. Economic change has been especially pronounced in the northwestern corner of the state.

Two great national forests, separated by the Arkansas River, are in the western section, and large parts of the entire area are still covered with pines and hardwoods. The timber industry has long been important; and in recent years, the growing of pulpwood and the manufacture of paper products have become significant elements of the economy, especially in the south-central and southwestern counties. Living conditions throughout much of this hill country, most notably in the Ozark region of the northwest, still bear some resemblance to those of the frontier. Log cabins have fallen into decay and disuse, but a few are still occupied. A student of Arkansas politics has described the region as largely rural, fundamentalist in

---

[1] Unless otherwise indicated, all census data are drawn from the 1960 census.

religion, individualist, loyal to family and soil, and characterized by "puritanic protestantism." [2]

This small-farmer, timbering, and factory-employee population is largely white and native-born. In the nineteenth century, its forebears moved in from Missouri and, to a significant extent, from the Appalachian area of the eastern South. Natural conditions which excluded the slaveholding, plantation economy of eastern Arkansas have had the effect of excluding Negroes. In a few southern counties adjacent to the Red and Ouachita rivers, there is a large Negro population (running from 26 to 37 percent in four of these counties); but as one moves north in this western region into the hills and mountains, the nonwhite population quickly thins to the vanishing point. In thirteen of these counties, according to the 1960 census, Negroes numbered .1 percent or less of the population; in six counties no Negroes were listed; and in the remainder of the mountain counties the Negro population did not reach 4 percent of the total population.

Between this hill country and the flatlands to the east, suspicion and hostility once flared. The hill country was antisecessionist and Unionist and blamed the plantation east—and, indeed, the whole plantation South—for the calamities of the Civil War. The considerable Republican strength in the mountain counties is an enduring monument to this hostility. Late in the nineteenth century, when Populism disordered the politics of some southern states, the western area of Arkansas was more affected by this mild radicalism. Jeff Davis, three-term governor and United States senator, was an early twentieth-century manifestation of populism among the hill people. In Orval Faubus we find at least a strong suggestion of this ideology, caught perhaps from a liberal and independent-minded father.

The vital interests of the two sections with which governments can deal are not in serious conflict, although some differences still

[2] Boyce A. Drummond, Jr., "Arkansas Politics: A Study of a One-Party System" (Ph.D. dissertation, University of Chicago, 1957), 2–3. A microfilm copy of this excellent study is in the Arkansas History Commission, Little Rock.

exist. The agricultural policies of the New Deal and its successors, which sought to aid small farmers and tenants, aroused the anger of dominant elements in the east, but the rugged, small-farmer country of the west found these policies helpful to its interests. This was especially true of the rural electrification program. To this difference between the two sections can be attributed some of the conservatism of the east and the liberalism of the west. Certainly Arkansas's most liberal congressmen of the mid-twentieth century have been James W. Trimble, Brooks Hays, and Clyde Ellis, all elected by western districts. In the United States Senate, the liberal J. William Fulbright and the conservative John L. McClellan afford further evidence of this sectional cleavage in politics.

Since Negroes are an important element in the eastern area, the dominant whites there have thought they had a strong interest in the political suppression and the economic exploitation of the black race. Political leadership of the east, therefore, has moved vigorously to use the power of state government and party organizations to achieve desired ends in this field of activity. The hill people have not liked or desired to protect the Negroes; but since so few are in their midst, the whites of the west and northwest look upon these enterprises in racial discrimination with only a mild interest.

Curiously, there have been few hard and fixed customs in regard to sharing the offices among representatives of the two sections. Perhaps this is a result of one-party politics and nominations made by the direct primary. Balanced tickets would be more essential if the voters had a choice between two slates of candidates. As it is, Arkansans do not look upon the governor as a sectional representative. A Ben Laney of the south can be followed by a Sidney S. McMath of the southwest and by a Francis Cherry of the east, and the people of the northwest do not feel especially aggrieved. In turn an Orval Faubus of the northwest can serve for six terms without arousing the hostility of voters or political leaders in the east. There appears to be a half-expressed feeling that the two United States senators should represent the two sections, and since 1944 the east and west have shared the offices. But in the preceding era Joseph T.

Robinson and T. H. and Hattie Caraway, all from the east, held the two Senate seats for a number of years.

Near the center of the state, Little Rock and North Little Rock, with adjacent areas of Pulaski County, lie on the boundary between the two sections, possessing some of the characteristics of each. An appreciation of the economic and political power of this rapidly growing central region is crucial to an understanding of Arkansas politics. The region is a great distribution center for most of the state. From it radiate the interstate and secondary highways. As the center of government, it produces the bulk of political news and a considerable portion of the political activity that has agitated the state during the last twenty years. In Little Rock are published two newspapers of statewide circulation, and from this center the state's most powerful TV and radio stations attract the eyes and ears of a wide voting audience. In wealth and population, Pulaski dwarfs the other Arkansas counties, with an estimated population in 1965 of 281,521, the next largest county having only 88,091.[3]

Although in voting strength Little Rock and Pulaski County have grown enormously in recent decades, this very growth has somewhat disqualified its politicians from running for the chief offices in the state government. In other parts of Arkansas, a belief seems to exist that Little Rock, like Washington, is a capital city and not a constituency. Anyway, since Little Rock has the capitol and all the economic gain that flows from the salary checks of state employees, the rest of the state ought to have the offices. The capital city, it is thought, should be pacified by the reflection that its voters have great power in statewide elections. Consequently, in recent years no candidate with a Little Rock address has been elected governor, and only one serious candidate from that city has run for the office.

A generation ago the *Arkansas Gazette*, Little Rock's morning newspaper, seemed disposed to play the quiet and unobtrusive role that state politicians have marked out for the capital city's residents.

[3] *State and County Economic Data for Arkansas, 1960 and 1965* (Industrial Research and Extension Center, College of Business Administration, University of Arkansas, n.d.), 4.

In the late 1940's, however, when Harry Ashmore began his editor-
ship, the *Gazette* became vibrant in its interest in politics at all
levels, comprehensive in its coverage of political news from all parts
of the state, and hard-hitting in its editorials and cartoons against
political chicanery and demagoguery. As a bastion of liberalism,
this newspaper contrasts sharply with a great deal of the state's press,
and its distribution over the entire state has inspirited and unified
many groups of geographically separated liberals.

Although other Arkansas newspapers, such as the North Little
Rock *Times* and the Pine Bluff *Commercial*, are outspoken on
political matters, an important part of the state press remains aloof
from the hurly-burly of politics. Many county weeklies and small
city dailies apparently have no desire to investigate and publicize
derelictions in city and county governments. In such communities
misgovernment and illegal election practices get no public exposure,
and reformers find it impossible to arouse and energize public opinion. As urbanization continues and makes shoddy government a
more serious evil, this detached attitude of many newspapers im-
pedes the state's political progress.

The rapid growth since World War II of the Little Rock–North
Little Rock area has been shared by the larger towns and cities of
the state. This shift of population from rural areas to urban centers,
so notable in most of the country, has changed even rural and agricultural Arkansas into a state in which most of the gainfully employed probably earn their livelihood in towns and cities, even
though a large but unknown number commute to urban jobs from
homes in the country. In addition to enlarged economic opportunities offered by the city, this change has been produced by a post–
World War II revolution in agriculture. The increase in the number of large farms through the absorption of smaller ones has sent
many small farmers to town; the increasing mechanization of agriculture has swollen this number at what appears to be an accelerating pace.[4]

---

[4] There has been an uninterrupted decrease in the number of farms since 1935. In
that year, there were 253,000. By 1949, the number had dropped to 182,000. Ten
years later, the number fell to 95,000; and in 1968, there were only 80,000 farms in

While many rural Arkansans were moving to town, a great number were leaving the state. The 1950 census, for the first time in the state's history, showed a decline in total population, fixing the number of Arkansans at 1,909,511, as compared with 1,949,387 in 1940. With the decline continuing in the 1950's, the population fell to 1,786,272 in 1960, a figure 6.5 percent lower than in 1950 and 9 percent lower than in 1940. Indeed, Arkansas's population in 1960 was only about 35,000 higher than in 1920.[5] An important part of this population loss was caused by the migration of Negroes. Most counties declined in Negro population; a few with large towns and cities gained. In Arkansas, as in the nation, the Negro is rapidly becoming an urban dweller. A significant emigration of young people of both races, especially college graduates, has also occurred.

These population changes have produced important effects on Arkansas politics. The loss of population reduced the state's congressional seats from seven in 1940 to four after the 1960 census. Perhaps of greater importance, population shifts within the state have created a situation leading to belated but drastic reapportionment of congressional and legislative districts in accordance with the doctrine of Baker v. Carr and related cases. Following the 1960 census, the state legislature established boundaries of the four congressional districts, but a federal court set aside the act as an insufficient reapportionment. A second effort paid more heed to population shifts and has not been successfully attacked. In this drastic redistricting, very large districts were established in the southeast and in the western-northwestern sections, to the political advantage of the more heavily populated northeastern and the central area.

In making legislative districts conform to population changes,

---

operation. The average size of farms increased from 103 acres in 1949 to 173 acres in 1959. In the meantime farm tenancy fell from 63 percent in 1930 to 45 percent in 1944, and to 24 percent in 1959. John L. Ferguson and J. H. Atkinson, *Historic Arkansas* (Little Rock, 1966), 303; *Arkansas Gazette* (Little Rock), January 13, 1968.

[5] Estimates by the Census Bureau and the University of Arkansas Industrial Research and Extension Center indicate that this decline in population has been replaced by a gain of 8.5 percent since the 1960 census. The counties showing the greatest increases are in the northwest and in the central area. *Arkansas Gazette* (Little Rock), June 21, 1967.

the state encountered greater obstacles. In 1956, when it became evident that the rural population decline could be expected to continue, the Farm Bureau Federation and some urban business groups led a successful campaign to "freeze" the state senatorial districts by a constitutional amendment. The state House of Representatives, as then apportioned, reflected the distribution of population somewhat more accurately, but not accurately enough. Each of the seventy-five counties was allowed one representative, and twenty-five additional seats were divided among the more populous counties. The effect was to overrepresent the small, rural counties and to underrepresent the urban counties. The inevitability of fairer reapportionment, after a series of United States Supreme Court decisions and a federal district court order, led the state Board of Apportionment in 1965 to apportion seats in both houses on the basis of population.[6] The use of multimember districts, however, led to a legal attack on behalf of rural dwellers and urban Negroes. The Pulaski County circuit court declared the apportionment unconstitutional, but the state Supreme Court reversed the decision. Strong efforts to persuade the state Board of Apportionment to create single-member districts were underway in the summer of 1969.

There has been too little experience with the reapportioned legislature to determine the effects produced by the infusion of more urban members. Some actions of the 1967 and 1969 legislatures suggest that voting alliances and other sympathetic associations of rural with urban legislators will be difficult to break.

In the long run, the increase in urban and the reduction in rural legislators probably will effect an important change in the state's government. There are conflicts of interest between city and country far more significant than differences between the eastern and western sections of the state. The rural areas need improved secondary roads; urban areas are more interested in the main highways. Consolidation of school districts is more favored by the city than by the country. Rural legislators resist more fiercely than do their urban

6 *Ibid.*, July 15, 1965.

colleagues any relaxation in the laws governing alcoholic beverages and gambling. The bill was never brought to a vote, but it is probable that a recent proposal to repeal the anti-evolution law would have been defeated by the votes of rural legislators.

Behavioral patterns of the Arkansas House and Senate may be altered by urbanization and reapportionment. For a long period, Paul Van Dalsem of Perry County was a dominant and domineering figure in the House. Possessed of a bullhorn voice, an irascible temper, and a disposition to start unseemly legislative brawls, he contributed generously to the disrepute into which the legislature fell. In the summer of 1963, he addressed a Little Rock civic club, and in the course of his remarks his mind fell upon a subject which promised amusement to a male audience—women in politics, especially some Little Rock women who had lobbied during the recent session of the legislature. "They're frustrated," he said. "We don't have any of these university women in Perry County, but I'll tell you what we do up there when one of our women starts poking around in something she doesn't know anything about: We get her an extra milk cow. If that don't work, we give her a little more garden to tend to. And then if that's not enough, we get her pregnant and keep her barefoot." [7]

This bucolic witticism received adequate coverage in the press; and Little Rock women, who are well organized and active in politics, were somewhat vocal in their responses. Van Dalsem, safe in his rural Perry County constituency, chuckled and dismissed the matter from his mind. His safety was short-lived. In 1965 reapportionment of the House threw Pulaski and Perry counties into the same legislative district. The Democratic primary of 1966, in which Little Rock women enthusiastically participated—some thoughtfully removed their shoes before entering the polling places—returned Van Dalsem to private life, where he remains. Reapportionment, in this instance, brought peace and quiet to the Arkansas House.

[7] *Ibid.*, August 28, 1963.

Structural Change and the Persistence of Electoral Problems

Other changes in the ground rules of Arkansas politics have occurred in the period since 1948. Beginning in 1908, payment of an annual poll tax of one dollar was required as a prerequisite to voting in any primary or election (proceeds of the tax were spent on public schools). An unsuccessful effort in the 1890's to establish this tax-paying qualification for voting was an important part of a program of Negro disfranchisement;[8] and it is evident that the successful effort in 1908 was produced, in part, by the same motivation. But the chronic weakness of the Republican Party and the exclusion of Negroes from the Democratic primary made the poll tax a superfluous instrument of racial discrimination. When Negro voting became significant in the late 1940's, after the repeal of the white primary rules, it grew clear that the tax had only a limited effect in disfranchising Negroes. The adoption in 1964 of the Twenty-fourth Amendment to the Constitution, banning a tax-paying requirement as a prerequisite to voting in federal elections, ended this restriction on voting.

The change was accompanied by some embarrassment, for payment of the poll tax was the only act a citizen performed to establish his right to vote. It operated crudely as a registration system, although the tax receipt noted only the taxpayer's name and race, his voting precinct, and the fact that he had paid the tax. The presence of other voter qualifications and the absence of disqualifications were generally taken for granted by election officials. It was a grossly imperfect registration system, but it was the only one the state had.

As national efforts to abolish poll taxes gathered strength, Arkansas political leaders took steps to prepare for the future. The 1874 constitution, reflecting fears generated during Reconstruction, forbade the requirement of any "previous registration" as a qualification to vote. In 1948, a constitutional amendment was adopted, authorizing the legislature to enact a registration system. This authority remained unused. In 1956, a proposed amendment to abol-

---

8 John William Graves, "Negro Disfranchisement in Arkansas," *Arkansas Historical Quarterly*, XXVI (1967), 216–20.

ish the poll tax was decisively defeated by a popular vote of 210,237 to 161,403. Early in the next decade, as the anti–poll tax amendment to the national Constitution began to receive the ratification of state legislatures, it became clear that time was running out. In the 1961 and 1963 sessions, the Arkansas legislature demonstrated an unwillingness or an inability to assume leadership in an effective movement to abolish the poll tax and establish a registration system. A private citizens' group, headed by a public-spirited physician, Dr. H. D. Luck, stepped into this breach and pushed through an initiated constitutional amendment which abolished the poll tax as a voter qualification and established a model permanent-registration system. In obtaining popular ratification of this amendment in 1964, Dr. Luck's group coordinated the efforts of the League of Women Voters, the American Association of University Women, labor unions, and other statewide organizations.

One purpose of the new registration system is to reduce the incidence of fraudulent voting, which has been a significant factor in Arkansas politics over the years. Under the loose administration of the poll tax laws, political leaders purchased numerous poll tax receipts in the names of economic and political dependents, many of whom were not otherwise qualified to vote. Even when these dependents had the qualifications of voters, the payment of their poll taxes by superiors placed them under obligations and indicated the extent of their dependence. It is expected that the present requirement of personal registration will lessen this evil.

Much more than a new registration system, however, is required to clean up the conduct of Arkansas primaries and elections. Little fault can be found with the laws that deal with corrupt practices. Over the years, they have kept pace with the fertile imaginations and the luxuriant versatility of dishonest politicians. Nearly every species of electoral chicanery is matched by a statute which seeks to prevent or punish such derelictions. It is well known, however, that many of these laws can be disobeyed with nearly complete impunity; it is equally well known that in a number of counties they are disobeyed whenever disobedience promises to produce an electoral victory. There appears to be insufficient disposition, either among the people or among the officials charged with the interpretation and enforcement of laws, to enforce those which govern elections. Revelations of lawbreaking in this field provoke more public amusement than public indignation. Prosecuting attorneys rarely file bills of information; grand juries return no bills of indictment. Even the state Supreme Court has rendered a gentle and benign interpretation of some election laws.[9]

Under these circumstances, negligence and fraud are not unusual in the conduct of Arkansas elections. Voting booths, required by statute, have not been provided. Accordingly, voters sometimes find it difficult to mark their ballots free from the glances of the curious or interested.[10] Ballot boxes widely used do not meet legal requirements. Tin tobacco cans, candy boxes, and many other types of cardboard receptacles have been observed all over the state. Ballots are frequently not counted in the manner prescribed by law, and unauthorized persons often aid in making the count. Electioneering closer to the polls than permitted by law is a frequent, unpunished offense; and at times the election officials themselves, seated at their desks, engage in this illegal practice. The cruder forms of vote-buying, false tallying, ballot box stuffing, and destruction of ballots are not so uncommon as to provoke astonishment, especially in "machine counties." Conversations with politicians who perform arduous tasks at grass-roots levels have produced interesting stories of ballot destruction. On one occasion, it was reported, ballots were dropped through a crack in the floor; another

[9] "All evidence suggests that many of the election laws in this state are flagrantly violated year after year. The courts may be responsible for the general lack of public concern. The supreme court, for example, has held that election laws are mandatory if enforcement is sought before an election in direct proceeding, but that after an election they should be held directory only, with certain exceptions." Drummond, "Arkansas Politics," 130–31.

[10] The Election Research Council, financed by private funds, has sought since 1964 to study election irregularities and to improve election practices. It has made available at less than cost several thousand cardboard voting booths. Many of these, however, were not used by the election officials, and "some in Conway county were deliberately burned," the council reported. *Arkansas Gazette* (Little Rock), February 21, 1965.

story, not lightly to be believed, relates that an election clerk disposed of some unwanted ballots by eating them.

In recent years the most serious widespread illegality has centered upon the absentee ballot box and the procedures associated with its misuse. Until 1964 the general public had only vague impressions of the nature and extent of this irregularity. In that year, however, the Election Research Council[11] was established to investigate and publicize the violation of election laws, with particular emphasis upon absentee voting. A study of the records related to absentee voting in the 1964 general election convinced the council's director that of the 30,930 absentee ballots counted, not more than 10,000 were valid. Nursing homes having a close connection with the state Welfare Department appear to have been responsible for many fraudulent absentee ballots, forgery of the signatures and even of the X marks having been discovered. Some county clerks, to whom applications for absentee ballots are sent, have not obeyed the law governing this portion of their duties. In Phillips County 835 names appeared on the absentee voters' list. Of these, 209 names were either illegible or not in the poll books. The county clerk had on file only 301 applications; the remaining 534 persons were allowed to vote absentee without applications. An examination of the voters' statements disclosed that in one ward more than 100 of them bore signatures forged by the same person.

Absentee voting has been a useful device for the nonresident voter and for political managers who obtain his vote. Madison, Perry, and Conway counties have made the greatest use of the absentee ballot box and have been most hospitable to nonresident voters, many of whom have not visited these counties for years and some of whom have never lived in them. In the 1964 general election, Madison's absentee box held more than 10 percent of the

---

11 The council describes itself as a nonpartisan, nonprofit corporation. By February, 1965, it had spent more than $40,000 in its investigations from funds contributed by more than 100 firms and individuals, "including a 'substantial' contribution from Winthrop Rockefeller." The director stated, however, that Rockefeller's gift was "not substantial enough to be considered the principal support." *Ibid.*

county's vote. Governor Faubus received 91 percent of the votes in the absentee box, but only 64 percent of the county's total vote was cast for him. Disappearance of the voting records precluded a more thorough investigation.[12]

Violation of the election laws, until quite recently, had its greatest usefulness in Democratic primaries, since Republican candidates could easily be defeated in general elections without extraordinary exertions. After the disfranchisement of the Negro during the period 1890–1910, the Republican Party became a hopeless and despairing minority. It retained considerable strength in a few mountain counties, occasionally electing county officials and from time to time electing a legislator or two. But in statewide elections it had been overwhelmingly defeated so many times that by the 1940's it had almost ceased to fight. It maintained state, district, and county organizations, and it routinely nominated candidates for governor and lieutenant governor, thus retaining its status as a political party and its minority-party representation on state and county election boards. The party organizations could be useful in dividing federal patronage whenever the Republicans elected a President. By the late 1940's, however, the loaves and fishes of the 1920's were more a happy memory than a spur to action. As a viable element in Arkansas politics, the Republican Party had only a nominal existence.

Factions and Parties: The Limits of Loyalty

Most of the political activity in Arkansas up to the 1960's was produced by factional fights within the Democratic Party. Factions are formed to win primary elections, not to advance principles or policies of government. A faction in state politics consists of a leading gubernatorial candidate and his most influential supporters. In its appeal for votes, it stresses the personal qualities of the candidate and usually avoids issues, if there are any, for issues might divide the voters. Each candidate announces his determination to improve

[12] Election Research Council Report, February 21, 1965 (mimeographed copy in possession of author).

schools, highways, and welfare payments; each declares his firm opposition to any tax increase. Since all candidates run on substantially the same attractive platform, the exposed portion of each primary campaign generally resolves itself into an effort by each candidate to establish his own capability and to point out the defects of character, personality, and ability of his more menacing opponents.

Considering the nearly uniform ideology of the chief candidates and the electorate's apparent lack of interest in issues, this campaign strategy seems inevitable. Most of the candidates probably would assume a conservative position on issues that divide conservatives and liberals, but the voters appear to prefer a campaign in which personalities clash and the air is filled with charges, countercharges, and mutual recriminations. "In primary elections," one scholar asserts, "candidates seldom can be characterized on the basis of their platforms as either conservative or liberal. In any case, it is doubtful if such distinctions are clearly defined in the minds of the voters." McMath, who was considered a liberal, received a vote in 1948 that "was not consistently lower" in the counties which voted for the "right-to-work" amendment in 1944.[13]

No faction at the state level down to 1954 has been able to perpetuate itself in office. Within four to six years, these groups have split up and re-formed as new candidates emerge. The two-term tradition in the governor's office has had some influence in making factions short-lived. In a number of counties, however, factions led by sheriffs, county judges, and state senators have endured for years. Perhaps their longevity may be attributed in part to their close relations with the voters and the election machinery. County factions have the ability, also, to intimidate and punish their political enemies. Apparently responding to vigorous and persistent criticisms, the Conway County faction has prosecuted a series of civil and criminal suits against a Morrilton newspaperman. Successful appeals to the state Supreme Court, made possible by wealthy sympathizers, have prevented his ruin.

[13] Drummond, "Arkansas Politics," 68–73.

The Democratic primaries, which have been the culmination of most political activity in Arkansas, are regulated by statute and party rules, but they are run and financed by party officials. Substantial filing fees are exacted from candidates for the higher offices: $2,500 for United States senator, $1,500 for governor and justice of the Supreme Court, and $600 for attorney general. On the county level, filing fees are appreciably lower, although party organizations in a few counties charge rather high fees to finance primaries in these areas.[14]

Party rules regulate participation of voters and candidates in primaries. Officially, the primary is closed; that is, voting for candidates of another party technically disqualifies a Democrat. Actually, however, Arkansas has open primaries, for no machinery to exclude defecting Democrats and Republicans has been placed in operation.[15] Candidates must pledge their loyalty to the party and promise to support its nominees. Usually these pledges are fulfilled, but there appears to be no disposition or method to punish the occasional bolter. In 1958 a write-in candidate for the United States House of Representatives, running as an independent, received enough support from Democratic voters and nominees to win the election. Instead of punishing the defectors, party officials amended the rules to excuse and forgive the bolters in this district. Loyalty of the state party to the national party has been officially weak for nearly a quarter of a century. In 1944 the Democratic state convention adopted a new rule which carefully omitted any declaration of allegiance to the national party. As the new rule was popularly interpreted, one could vote against a Democratic presidential nominee without losing one's standing as an Arkansas Democrat. The permissiveness of the rule was amply demonstrated when an associate justice of the state Supreme Court, elected as a Democrat, supported Goldwater in 1964, and became the Democratic nominee

14 Henry M. Alexander, *Government in Arkansas* (Little Rock, 1962), 21.

15 The constitutional amendment establishing the registration system in 1964 did not require the voter to list his party affiliation. In 1967, the legislature enacted a statute to require the listing of party affiliation, but the act was defeated by the voters in a referendum in November, 1968.

for governor in 1966. A new party loyalty rule was enacted by the Democratic state convention in 1968, which, in ambiguous language, squinted in the general direction of loyalty to the national party, but late in 1969 the state central committee interpreted the rule so as to invite all supporters of George Wallace's presidential candidacy to participate in the 1970 Democratic primaries as candidates and voters.

Since 1940, the "double primary" to assure majority nominations has been in effect. If no candidate gets a majority in the first primary, the two highest candidates wage a marathon fourteen-day campaign before a second primary. This schedule has had the effect of exhausting candidates and increasing campaign expenses. The inflationary spiral after World War II and the increased availability of money in recent years have added considerably to the sums spent in winning nominations and elections. Since there is no effective regulation or public recording of total expenditures and contributions, this important information remains dark and obscure to all except candidates and managers.[16] Circumstances and an occasional revelation, however, enable one to draw a few inferences with a measure of confidence.

There can be no doubt that very large sums have been spent on senatorial and gubernatorial campaigns during the past quarter-century. An investigation of the senatorial race of 1944 indicated that total expenditures could not have been less than $321,000 and might have been as high as $500,000. It has been estimated that in the three-candidate gubernatorial primary campaigns of 1952, total spending exceeded $450,000, with nearly $200,000 spent on behalf of one candidate.[17] During the long period of Governor Faubus' tenure (1955–67), the scarcity of strong opponents apparently re-

16 There are statutory limits on the amounts which *candidates* may spend and they are required to report their campaign expenditures. Candidate expenditures are so small compared with total campaign expenses that these reports, while fulfilling legal requirements, produce more cynical laughter than public enlightenment.

17 For a detailed discussion of campaign expenditures, contributions, and related matters during the 1940's and early 1950's, see Drummond, "Arkansas Politics," 145–68. See also John L. Fletcher, "Costly Political Campaigns," *Arkansas Gazette* (Little Rock), May 28, 1950.

duced campaign spending to more moderate levels. It is probable, however, that the efforts of two strong candidates to force Governor Faubus into a runoff primary in 1962 were accompanied by expenditures even higher than those estimated for the early 1950's. The resurgence of Republican strength after 1960, followed by a vigorous general election campaign in 1964 and by the expensive primary and general election campaigns of 1966, led to an outburst of spending which probably broke all previous records. According to figures compiled by the Federal Communications Commission, a total of $1,079,943 was spent on political radio and television broadcasts in Arkansas during 1966. Of this sum, $302,118 was spent by the Republicans, $757,934 by the Democrats, and $19,891 by independent candidates and on behalf of ballot measures.[18] These figures do not include, of course, other legitimate expenditures such as those for office rent, salaries of campaign personnel, postage, newspaper and billboard advertising, printing, and travel. Unless the campaigns of 1966 were highly unusual, additional amounts of money were entrusted to local leaders, a part of which was used to buy votes, the remainder being retained as "payments for influence."

There is reason to believe, although proof is lacking, that a discrepancy sometimes occurs between the amount raised and that spent for campaign purposes, the former being larger than the latter. No candidate has to give any accounting of the two sums; this interesting financial data is locked in the breast of the candidate and, perhaps, his chief campaign managers. Minor politicians have been known to express, privately, a willingness to run for some office if they could be assured that campaign contributions would be generous enough to leave them a comfortable surplus. Perhaps an occasional major politician succumbs to this temptation. Some candidates have emerged from campaigns with at least the appear-

18 *Arkansas Gazette* (Little Rock), September 7, 1967. It should be noted that Democratic candidates waged two expensive primary campaigns in 1966, while Republican candidates spent very little in primaries. It is probable that Republican expenditures in the general election campaign of 1966 considerably exceeded those of the Democrats.

ance of affluence. Others find a deficit on the day after the election. If the candidate has been elected, such a deficit poses no serious problem. A surge of generosity, sometimes from unexpected sources, will relieve all financial anxiety. But if the deficit-harried candidate has been defeated, little aid can be expected from any except the most devoted and disinterested friends.

The spending of campaign funds, including total amounts spent, is covered by a hazy obscurity. The raising of these funds is an even darker subject. Two well-established facts, however, provide some illumination: (1) Large sums are needed to wage statewide campaigns. (2) Rank-and-file voters are rarely solicited for small contributions. It is not illogical to conclude that funds come from a relatively small number of contributors and that these contributors have an interest in the outcome of the election that is not shared by the general voting public. Some reports from reliable sources tend to support this conclusion and to suggest the identity of economic and occupational groups that provide the bulk of campaign funds. When a governor runs for reelection, appointed officials and employees of the state government are expected to make contributions. Methods of realizing these expectations may be as mild as a simple statement inviting contributions or as rigorous as a direct assessment exacting a percentage of the employee's salary. Either method produces a considerable sum for the campaign chest. Economic groups whose interests are affected in many ways by the state government yield, perhaps, the largest part of campaign funds. Hearings of the Highway Audit Commission in 1951 revealed that contractors and vendors of supplies and equipment made large contributions. Individual businessmen, from a variety of motives, find it expedient to contribute to the funds of one or more gubernatorial candidates in every primary. It is plausibly reported that one prominent Arkansas businessman, tiring of these biennial importunities in the 1960's, decided that he could become a candidate for governor more cheaply than he could support the efforts of others. Accordingly, he announced his candidacy in the hopeful accents with which he had become so familiar, paid the filing fee, ran a campaign of such Spartan austerity that it would have mortified a candidate for sheriff in one of the smaller counties, and accepted the inevitable defeat with philosophical resignation and a virtually intact bank account.

Some campaign contributions come from relatively disinterested sources. Every candidate has friends and relatives who wish him well and who are willing to provide financial support for these wishes. There are a number of individual contributors who have no immediate ax to grind, nor any prospect of one, but who would like to have access to an important officeholder as a matter of pride or in the contingency of some undefined future need. A number of contributions, it is probable, come from men who know that a governor can fill several hundred seats on boards and commissions and hope for the honor of serving in one of these unpaid positions. Some campaign funds are received from obscure individuals, scattered over the state, who simply believe the candidate can fill the office he seeks with credit to himself and advantage to the public. The slight efforts made to tap this source, however, suggest that politicians do not look upon it as a promising one.[19]

In appealing for votes, candidates for major offices find they must make increasing use of radio and television, but that they dare not relinquish the old standbys of newspaper advertising, personal appearances, and close contacts with local political leaders. Thus radio and television have added to the labor and expense of campaigns. This fact became evident in 1952, when the late Francis Cherry launched a radio "talkathon" as a major part of his gubernatorial campaign. For a protracted number of hours, he sat in a radio station and responded to questions telephoned in from all over the state. But this did not spare him from traveling and speaking in the midsummer Arkansas sun.

With other types of amusement and instruction so readily available, it is becoming increasingly difficult to assemble and hold

---

[19] There has been at least one notable exception to this general rule. An important part of Brooks Hays's campaign fund, in his gubernatorial race of 1966, was provided by small contributions of $5 to $100 which came in response to a solicitation by mail.

crowds to hear a candidate describe his platform, praise himself, and berate his opponents—but it must be done. These campaign speeches on the hustings make news; and although only a small crowd may be present to hear the perspiring candidate speak on the courthouse lawn, thousands of newspaper readers may be influenced by the highlights of his speech. Local leaders and voters would no doubt feel slighted if the candidate did not consider them important enough to come to their town. Various techniques have been adopted to make this necessary chore produce a greater return. If great numbers of people are going to assemble for some celebration or observance, then candidates will flock to this ready-made audience. For many years, it has been traditional for major candidates to appear and speak at the Fourth of July picnic at Portia and at the Johnson County Peach Festival. In assembling their own audiences, candidates have outriders enter a town in sound trucks which alert the populace to the imminent appearance of the candidate and whatever troupe of entertainers he might bring with him—a hillbilly band, folk singers, and other crowd-catchers. If the town is the site of an important state agency and if the candidate is a governor or one who appears to be headed for the governorship, there are ways of inducing employees of this state agency to attend in satisfying numbers. Food is a traditional and effective catcher of campaign crowds, with the speaking shrewdly preceding the eating. An unfeeling history has kept no account of the number of barbecued hogs and fried chickens that have made their contributions to Arkansas politics.

Newer ways of spreading the campaign message force the weary candidates to hasten back to Little Rock at frequent intervals, where they make tape recordings, video tapes, and "live" appearances on radio and television. The latter medium has great and obvious advantages, but it is not an unmixed blessing. Some candidates are ill at ease and ineffective when operating under the bright lights and remorseless cameras of television, and any candidate is likely to incur the wrath of numerous voters when he knocks out a favorite television program. Both of these disadvantages are being increasingly bypassed by the use of video-taped spot announcements, which are flashed on the screen at the end of programs.[20]

Campaign literature, delivered by mail or by canvassers, reaches the voters in huge volume. Three types may be identified: (1) the usual leaflets, booklets, and handbills which sketch the good qualities of the candidate and his program, (2) the cartoon-illustrated story of the candidate's life and of his determination to place whatever remains of it at the disposal of the people, and (3) the scurrilous and libelous attack upon the public character and private life of an opposing candidate. This last class of literature frequently receives a furtive distribution and circulation, but the mails have carried some extraordinary examples of character assassination. Candidates in whose interest this literature is circulated always disavow it and express their regrets, and in some instances the disavowals are quite honest. Overzealous supporters and hate-peddlers sometimes work independently.

In elections to the governor's office, the state's political life ran through customary channels from 1948 to 1954, with only a few examples of aberrant behavior. It had long been a tradition that Arkansas governors would serve two terms and then withdraw with whatever grace they could muster. Accordingly, Governor Ben Laney announced his retirement in 1948, and the track was thrown open to a stable of hopefuls. Nine men paid their filing fees and entered the race, but only four of them could be considered serious candidates: James "Uncle Mac" MacKrell, a radio evangelist; Jack Holt, a former attorney general; Horace Thompson, recently a United States collector of Internal Revenue; and Sid McMath, prosecuting attorney of a district which included Hot Springs. In 1946 McMath had led a "GI movement" in this district and had broken the power of a corrupt political machine in Hot Springs. A favorite in the gubernatorial race, he was viewed by many as a liberal and a reformer who would make needed changes in the state government. In the first primary, McMath led with 87,829 votes;

20 See Karr Shannon, "Today's Teevee Type of Political Campaigning," *Arkansas Democrat* (Little Rock), July 22, 1956.

Holt was second with 60,313. Because neither candidate obtained a majority, a runoff was held two weeks later, with McMath winning 157,135 to 146,880.[21] The victor's greatest strength was in the southwestern quarter of the state and in eight counties of the northeast. He was weakest in the central counties, except for Pulaski, and in the plantation counties of the east. It would be impossible to draw from this distribution of the vote any sectional attitudes on governmental policies. The campaign itself did not stress issues which would have enabled the voters to distinguish between the ideologies of the two candidates, except for Holt's efforts to associate McMath with President Truman's civil rights program.

Instead of gaining the customary second term with slight opposition, in 1950 McMath was confronted with the candidacy of former Governor Laney, whose friends sought to conceal the untraditional third-term attempt by using the slogan "Reelect Ben Laney a Second Time." This campaign pitted a conservative businessman against a liberal reformer, who had done little reforming during his first term. McMath won an overwhelming victory, carrying sixty-six of the seventy-five counties and amassing a total vote of 209,559 to Laney's 112,651. The campaign did not clearly present contrasting policies of the two men, but the election returns disclosed that McMath's greatest strength was in the area north and west of a line drawn between the northeast and southwest corners. He was weakest south and east of this line, an area which enclosed all the counties Laney carried, except one. (See Figure 1.) In this election, one section of the state voted in great numbers for a liberal; the other section gave the conservative most of the few votes he received.

The magnitude of this victory may have induced McMath to fasten his attention upon the Senate seat held by John L. McClellan, but the calendar posed an embarrassing problem. McMath's second term would end in 1952; McClellan would not come up for reelection until 1954. How could the governor hold an organization

---

[21] All election figures used in this study were obtained, unless otherwise noted, from official election returns in the office of the secretary of state in Little Rock.

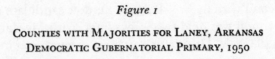

Figure 1

COUNTIES WITH MAJORITIES FOR LANEY, ARKANSAS
DEMOCRATIC GUBERNATORIAL PRIMARY, 1950

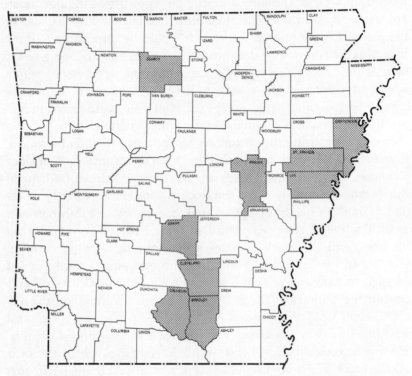

together and keep himself politically alive for two years? This
would be difficult, if not impossible, if he withdrew from the governorship at the end of his second term. But if he should be defeated in a campaign for a third term, he would be under an even
graver disadvantage in running against McClellan. He decided,
however, to take that risk.

In the meantime, McClellan and his supporters were aware of
McMath's ambition, and they began to take appropriate measures.
It is not improbable that Laney's ill-fated third-term candidacy was
encouraged by the McClellan forces in order to nip the McMath

menace in the bud. When the state legislature established the Highway Audit Commission in 1951, the move was widely looked upon as an effort to discredit and weaken the governor. The work of the commission had that effect. It revealed an unwholesome collusion among the Highway Department, contractors, and politicians. No proof could be found that McMath had profited financially, but the scandal besmirched his administration. Carrying this burden into a third-term campaign in 1952, he was forced into a runoff by Francis Cherry, a chancery judge from eastern Arkansas, and was beaten, 237,448 to 139,052. It was a stunning and overwhelming defeat for the governor. He attained majorities in only nine counties, all but two of which were in the north and northwest. Cherry gained a huge majority in all sections of the state, but he had somewhat more strength in the east. He carried ten counties in the west, however, with majorities of 70 percent or more. It appears that widespread dissatisfaction with McMath's administration and the effective work of county machines were largely responsible for the outcome.[22]

Governor Cherry entered office with a great reservoir of goodwill. Within eighteen months, most of it was dissipated. He had won the governorship on a platform of progress and economy in government, but he was unable to convert these generalities into specific performance, thus disappointing the high expectations of many voters. He showed poor leadership and indecision in dealing with the legislature, and he was sometimes tactless in his relations with individuals and influential groups.

Near the end of his first year in office, the signs were growing that he would not win a second term with merely token opposition. In the spring of 1954, three opponents announced their candidacy, only one of whom demonstrated the ability of an effective campaigner: Orval Faubus, highway director in McMath's administra-

[22] Cherry received 70 percent or more of the votes of the following counties: Arkansas, Boone, Bradley, Clay, Cleburne, Craighead, Crittenden, Faulkner, Grant, Hot Spring, Perry, Polk, Prairie, Sebastian, Sevier, Union, and Washington. McMath received 70 percent or more of the votes of Madison and Newton counties. By this date, political organizations in these two counties, it appears, were able to deliver almost any desired percentage of the counties' votes. In the ensuing years, this reputation became so well established that only the most naïve commented upon it with wonder.

tion and publisher of a country newspaper in Madison County. Emphasizing the weakness and ineptness of Cherry's administration and probably getting help from the McMath organization, the three challengers forced the governor into a runoff, although he led the poll by what appeared to be a comfortable margin. Faubus, with the next-highest vote, entered the second primary. During the ensuing two-week campaign, Cherry hurled a Joe McCarthy–like bombshell: Orval Faubus, he charged, had once attended Commonwealth College at Mena and had taken a prominent part in student affairs. (This little college, with labor-movement affiliations, had been established in the early 1930's near a small town in western Arkansas. It was suspected of being a Communist institution and was closed by local law enforcement officials in proceedings not marked by a punctilious adherence to legal technicalities.) Faubus, obviously shaken by the charge, responded with a statement that seemed not altogether candid, particularly in regard to the brevity of his student days at Commonwealth. After recovering his composure, he explained that he was a poor boy in the 1930's and was unable to attend any other college. As soon as he discovered the nature of the institution, he left. Some observers of this crucial campaign believe Cherry's charge backfired and created widespread sympathy for Faubus, who won the election with a vote of 191,328, to Cherry's 184,509.

A study of the vote distribution by counties reveals some interesting features of this election. The counties which Cherry carried were confined to the eastern and southeastern section of the state, except for five counties in the central and southwestern area. In the plantation counties of the east, his majorities were greatest, reaching 74 percent in Crittenden and Prairie. Faubus' strength can be noted in all parts of the state, reaching its highest point in the north and northwest. Newton County gave him 88 percent of its vote, and Madison, the candidate's home county, lavished 98 percent of its vote on him. In twelve other counties of that area, his majorities ran 70 percent or higher. (See Figure 2.) His vote in the east and southeast was astonishingly high; here he carried fourteen counties—all, however, with majorities of 61 percent or less.

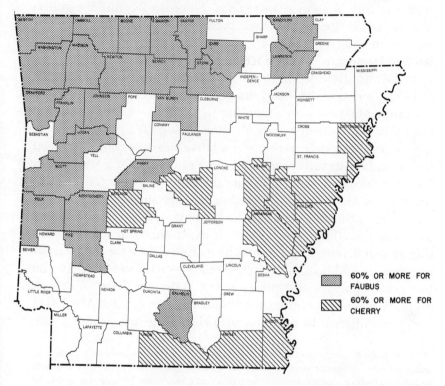

Figure 2

SECOND ARKANSAS DEMOCRATIC GUBERNATORIAL PRIMARY, 1954

To some extent, therefore, the election represents a discernible division between the conservative east and the more liberal west.

The victor had waged two primary campaigns, but not enough enemies had been subdued to make the general election a certainty. Disappointed and somewhat embittered supporters of Governor Cherry so clearly indicated their distaste for Faubus that the lethargic Republicans were galvanized into action. Nominating Pratt Remmel, who had twice been elected mayor of Little Rock, they launched a spirited campaign to hold the faithful in line and to gather in disaffected Democrats. Numerous Cherry supporters flocked to the Republican standard; and the governor, though never publicly endorsing Remmel, appears to have given no aid to Faubus. The threat was a formidable one, but the Democrats turned it back with a victory of 208,121 to 127,004. Since no Republican gubernatorial candidate in the three preceding elections had received more than 51,000 votes, it appears certain that thousands of dissatisfied Democrats voted for Remmel.

In the meantime, while Governor Cherry was struggling with his three opponents in the first primary, Senator McClellan and former Governor McMath were grappling in the long-awaited senatorial campaign.[23] For the first and only time during the past two decades, the voters of the state were given a fairly clear-cut choice between liberal and conservative candidates in a campaign for a Senate seat. McMath appeared eager to debate the issues with the conservative senator, but McClellan declined the challenge and ran his campaign according to the pattern which has proved useful to congressional incumbents, calling attention to his experience and seniority, declaring that his challenger would be unable to care for the interests of Arkansas, and maintaining close relations with local leaders who had great influence and power at the ballot-box level. Although McMath waged his campaign with great vigor, Senator McClellan won renomination by a narrow majority in the first primary, with

[23] In this study congressional politics receives little attention, except in those rare instances when a senator or a representative found himself confronted by a serious and determined challenger. During the past twenty years, the Arkansas congressional delegation has been remarkably successful in retaining office, accumulating seniority, and obtaining committee chairmanships. Normally, an incumbent has no significant opposition either in the primaries or in the general election. Running for reelection usually involves the simple sequence of announcing candidacy, paying the filing fee, making a few speeches to civic clubs, and, after the election, expressing gratitude for the continued faith of the electorate. Of the eleven representatives who served during the twenty-two-year period ending in 1970, only two have been defeated for reelection, six held their seats for a protracted period, three were squeezed out through redistricting, one died in office, and two retired undefeated.

Senator McClellan was first elected in 1942. In 1954 he met the only dangerous opponent he has encountered throughout his long tenure. Senator Fulbright, first elected in 1944, had no serious opposition until 1968.

A seat in Congress appears to arm the incumbent with such a degree of political power in his state or district that few opposing candidates can get the resources with which to wage campaigns that give reasonable promise of success.

Figure 3

ARKANSAS DEMOCRATIC SENATORIAL PRIMARY, 1954

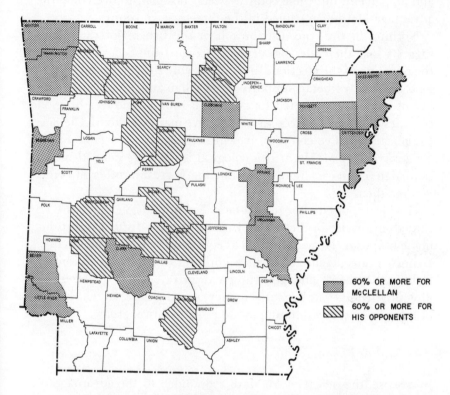

60% OR MORE FOR McCLELLAN

60% OR MORE FOR HIS OPPONENTS

a vote of 164,905 to McMath's 127,941. Two minor candidates polled a total of 31,068 votes. McClellan's overall majority, which spared him from a runoff primary, was less than 6,000.

When the results of this election are plotted on a map of the state, no sectional pattern of voting emerges. (See Figure 3.) Of the thirty-seven counties (of the state's seventy-five) which gave McClellan a majority against his three opponents, twenty are in the southeast and seventeen in the northwest. The victor appears to have had an advantage in counties where a lopsided vote suggested the operation of effective local machines. Mississippi, Crittenden, and Clark counties, all in the east and south, gave McClellan majorities of 76 percent, 81 percent, and 73 percent. In the northwest, McMath carried Madison and Newton counties with majorities of 77 percent and 85 percent, but these counties were too small to overcome the advantage McClellan gained in the three eastern counties.

Nothing in the vote distribution of the two major candidates suggests that their ideological disagreements importantly affected the outcome of the election. Indeed, the vote in some counties suggests that many liberals supported McClellan and an unusual number of conservatives voted for McMath. Pulaski and Washington counties, not noted for conservatism, gave majorities to McClellan; Craighead and Lee counties, in which liberalism is a faint spark, were carried by McMath. If ideological issues were defined in the campaign, it appears highly probable that a great number of voters ignored them.

Having repulsed this 1954 attack, Senator McClellan has continued his service in the Senate without further disturbance in his home bailiwick. He has acquired a reputation as a powerful senator, staunch in his defense of states' rights and in his investigations of "labor racketeers" and governmental extravagance, generous in directing federal public works money into the state, so that he appears to be virtually immune to successful political attack.

The Faubus Phenomenon

In a sense, the defeat of McMath redounded to the advantage of Faubus. Although the two had been close political associates, the new governor did not owe his victory to the McMath organization. A close examination of the election returns in the senatorial and gubernatorial primaries discloses that Faubus had built an organization of his own. With McMath defeated, the new governor could take over the shattered fragments of the old organization, weld it to his own, and build a machine which was to control the state for twelve years.

Near the beginning of his long tenure, the governor displayed a skill in administrative and political management which has rarely been equaled in Arkansas. In his selection of department heads and other key personnel, he was careful to choose men who added to his own political strength and who could discharge their official duties at an acceptable level of competence. He came into office with a fair working knowledge of the ramshackle governmental structure that had grown up over the years. His experience in the Highway Department, and the still-fresh memory of the political grief its loose administration had brought to McMath, admonished him to keep a sharp eye on every department that might succumb to temptation. Whatever happened, he was determined not to allow any underlings to hang the millstone of a major scandal around his neck.

He respected power wherever it existed. Legislators, a few weeks after his inauguration, discovered that mutually agreeable relations could be established and maintained with him. Political organizations in the counties, mostly concerned with local offices and emoluments, found that the governor would support them if they supported him. Special-interest groups learned that if this new governor was a liberal, he was a very reasonable and a very practical liberal. If they acted with discretion and the appearance of restraint, they had nothing to fear from him. At the beginning of the Faubus era, a large number of these well-organized groups had been operating successfully for many years. The most active and effective represented interests in transport, agriculture, utilities, public school education, natural resources (especially oil, timber, and bauxite), insurance, local government (the County Judges Association and the Arkansas Municipal League), and labor. In addition, the state Chamber of Commerce and the Arkansas Free Enterprise Association sought to advance and protect the common interests of industry, finance, and business. The conservative climate of opinion prevailing in Arkansas has been a strong ally of most of these groups, enabling them to get amendments to the state constitution, to elect friendly legislators, and to influence the actions of administrative departments and independent agencies which regulate economic affairs.

The new governor never demonstrated any desire to interfere with the great power exercised by these special-interest groups. He apparently viewed them as centers of power which he must accommodate and which, perhaps, he could manipulate to strengthen his own power. His appointments of directors, commissioners, and board members of regulatory agencies included personnel drawn from the economic interests they were charged with regulating; other appointments brought into the state service political supporters of the governor who would not be too unreasonable in interpretation and enforcement of regulatory statutes. In these respects, Faubus' actions did not mark any break from the past. His predecessors had used their appointive power in the same manner. But his long tenure enabled him to get complete control of all the regulatory agencies and to use this control, if he chose, to provide more protection for the people of the state.

He chose, however, to aid them in other ways. He had sprung from poor and hardscrabble origins, and he often reminded the voters of his identification with them. Just as Andrew Johnson never tired of sharing the memories of his years as a tailor, Governor Faubus spoke often of hard work on the farm, of following the harvests as a berrypicker, of the ring of his ax as it bit into the trees of the Pacific Northwest in his days as a lumberjack. It was not all talk. As his administration demonstrated, he took a deep interest in education, welfare assistance to the aged, and good roads for rural areas. His first term, in these respects, was successful. So far as the general public could see, moreover, he had been an able administrator and had provided effective leadership for the legislature.

But the preceding years had nourished the hope that a governor could be turned out after only one term, and in 1956 a field of four candidates bet their filing fees, their time, and their supporters' money on that hope. Two of these candidates may be disregarded, following the example set by the voters. The other two were serious: Jim Snoddy, a businessman from western Arkansas, and Jim Johnson, a former state senator from south Arkansas. Snoddy waged a determined campaign, but Johnson was able to attract greater attention. Shortly after the May, 1954, Supreme Court decision in the school segregation cases, he had become active in organizing Citizens' Councils to resist integration. Further, he had involved himself in an effort to prevent the integration of a school in eastern Arkansas, until a federal court decree rendered the attempt hopeless. In these activities he had achieved a degree of prominence as a young and vigorous politician whose vituperative vocabulary ranged beyond the boundaries which normally confine political debate in Arkansas.

Governor Faubus, after the manner of governors running for a second term, informed the voters of his accomplishments, spoke of the additional progress a second term would provide, and warned against entrusting the affairs of the state to untested and untried hands. Johnson, in the meantime, moved over the state charging that the governor was supinely submitting to the integration of schools while other southern states were manfully resisting this Supreme Court assault upon states' rights. Arkansas's leading newspaper characterized Johnson's campaign as a "mish-mash of distortions, half-truths and deliberate lies served up to the voters against a background of string music and pious exhortations on behalf of the bedraggled, revenue-producing crusade of the white Citizens Council." It was, the paper said, "demagogy, with the addition of racial overtones." [24]

The primary election apparently demonstrated that the Johnson type of campaign had insufficient appeal to Arkansans in 1956. The governor easily won renomination, receiving 180,760 votes (58 percent of the total vote) to 83,856 for Johnson and 43,630 for Snoddy. In sixty counties Faubus won majorities ranging from 51 to 98 percent of the vote.[25] Johnson carried only two counties (Ashley and Bradley in the southeast) and led the governor in five other counties, all in the east or southeast. In the general election, Republican strength fell to 77,215 from the high mark of 127,004 of two years before.

[24] *Arkansas Gazette* (Little Rock), August 2, 1956. During the campaign, Governor Faubus declared that "a handful of little, vicious men" were stirring up "strife and racial hatreds and tensions . . . to the detriment of the state as a whole. They have found a willing mouthpiece in one of my opponents who has made a living for the past year as a purveyor of hate."

[25] Madison, the governor's home county, gave him 96 percent of the vote, while adjoining Newton returned for him 98 percent. In votes for Johnson, it was a dead heat between the two counties. Each returned nine for him.

When Governor Faubus began his second term in January, 1957, few changes in state government had been produced in the preceding ten years. None of the three governors had achieved any reorganization or coordination of the numerous departments, boards, and commissions. As a legacy of the McMath administration, a constitutional amendment had lessened the power of the executive by placing the Highway Department under a commission whose members served overlapping terms. The archaic constitution of 1874, with its augmenting tail of amendments, continued to restrict changes in governmental organization, tax rates, salaries of officials, the judicial system, and even methods of voting. No old functions of state government had been dropped and few significant new ones had been added. Tax rates during this period were not raised, but the growing prosperity of the state and the increasing federal aid produced a steady upward climb in revenues. These funds made possible a considerable expansion and improvement in old governmental functions and services, especially in education, highways, and welfare assistance. To a great extent, however, the state's governors were doing business at the same old stand and in the same old way, and the political forces with which they contended remained essentially unchanged.

In the last half of the 1950's new forces began to emerge. These gathered strength as the old decade ended and a new one began, and they produced changes which made the years from 1957 to 1970 a period of storm and stress and political upheaval.

The Currents of Change: Racial Politics Emerges

Negro voting, an almost negligible factor in the late 1940's, became an important political force in the 1960's. Although the ending of the white primary had removed the chief impediment to Negro voting, long years of political deprivation had inured the race to passive submission. According to the Southern Regional Council, approximately 65,000 Negroes were paying poll taxes in 1950 and were qualified to vote in Arkansas. Although this estimate is perhaps a little high for that year, during subsequent years of the 1950's there was a slow but steady growth as state leaders of the National

Association for the Advancement of Colored People urged Negroes to pay their poll taxes. By 1958, it is estimated, 63,000 Negroes were qualified to vote. This number had increased to 73,000 in 1960, to 77,000 in 1964, and to approximately 100,000 by 1966. In that year, the total number of white and Negro registrants was 740,609.[26] It is probable that as issues of special interest to Negroes emerged, there was an increase in the percentage of qualified Negroes who actually voted.[27]

In the late 1950's another political development promised changes in the future—the resurgence of the Republican Party. Since the election of 1928, there have been two overlapping groups of Republicans in Arkansas, which may be labeled "presidential Republicans" and "state Republicans." The former group has been much the larger, for it has included the state Republicans and a considerable number of Democrats who opposed the candidacy of Alfred E. Smith and all subsequent Democratic presidential candidates. In 1928, Herbert Hoover received nearly 40 percent of the state's popular vote, and in subsequent elections Republican presidential candidates have won percentages ranging up to 46 percent for Dwight D. Eisenhower in 1956. In recent presidential elections, fourteen counties have returned majorities for the Republican candidates. The GOP carried three counties in the four elections during the period 1952–64, and it carried eleven counties in three of these elections. As Figure 4 indicates, all except one of these counties are in the northern and western section.

26 *Arkansas Gazette* (Little Rock), December 12, 1966; Donald R. Matthews and James W. Prothro, *Negroes and the New Southern Politics* (New York, 1966), 148.

The estimated percentage of qualified Negroes who paid poll taxes or, in 1964 and 1966, were registered, was in 1940, 3 percent; 1947, 21 percent; 1952, 27 percent; 1956, 36 percent; 1958, 33 percent; 1960, 38 percent; 1964, 40 percent; 1966, 54 percent. Percentages and total Negro registrations for 1964 and 1966 are merely approximations, since the registration records (unlike the poll tax receipts) do not list the race of the registrant.

27 The increase in Negro voting does not produce an equivalent increase in Negro political power. There is reason to believe that, especially in the plantation area of the east and south, the votes of Negro laborers and tenants add to the power of white landowners. Urban Negroes, however, are able to vote far more independently, and election returns indicate that they do.

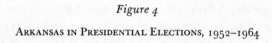

Figure 4

ARKANSAS IN PRESIDENTIAL ELECTIONS, 1952–1964

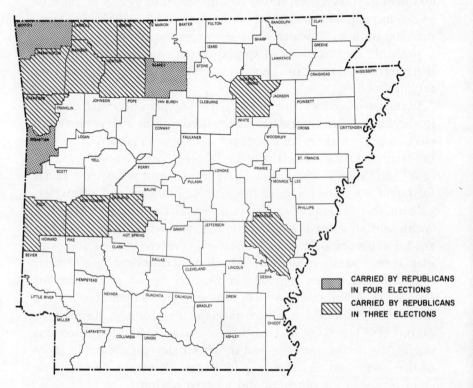

Until the 1960's, the Republicans who voted for candidates of their party in state elections have been a much smaller group, as shown by Table 1.

During Eisenhower's administration the state Republicans were inspirited by a modest amount of federal patronage and by the infusion, at all levels of organization, of new and younger leadership, drawn in part from executives and businessmen who managed the growing industries of Arkansas. Perhaps of greater importance was the arrival and permanent residence of Winthrop Rockefeller, who moved to Arkansas in 1953 and soon established his home and a large cattle farm on Petit Jean Mountain in Conway County. Al-

Table 1

REPUBLICAN VOTE IN ARKANSAS IN PRESIDENTIAL AND
GUBERNATORIAL ELECTIONS, 1932–1960

	Republican Vote for President	Percentage of Total Vote	Republican Vote for Governor	Percentage of Total Vote
1932	28,467	13	19,713	9
1934			13,121	10
1936	32,039	18	16,875	14
1938			11,974	9
1940	42,121	21	16,600	8
1942			No candidate	—
1944	63,555	30	30,442	14
1946			24,133	15
1948	50,959	21	26,500	10
1950			50,309	16
1952	177,155	44	49,292	13
1954			127,004	38
1956	186,287	46	77,215	19
1958			50,287	18
1960	184,508	43	129,921	30

though busy with expanding agricultural and real estate developments, he quickly acquired an interest in state government and Republican politics. In 1955 Governor Faubus appointed him chairman of the recently established Arkansas Industrial Commission, which sought with increasing success to attract industry to the state. For nine years Rockefeller devoted an important segment of his time to the work of the commission and to rebuilding the Republican Party in Arkansas, giving to the latter task generous financial support.[28]

By 1957 the Democratic legislature began to view the revival of the Republican Party with a vague uneasiness and in that year enacted a statute apparently intended to embarrass its growth. The

[28] In May, 1969, the state chairman of the Republican Party said that in the preceding four or five years Rockefeller's contribution to party activities had been "close" to $1,000,000. In 1969, he contributed approximately one-third of the total budget. *Arkansas Gazette* (Little Rock), May 11, 1969.

statute required all political parties to nominate state, district, and county candidates in primary elections, which must be financed by party funds. In hampering Republican expansion the act had little effect, for primaries were unnecessary if only one candidate filed for a party nomination. When primary elections were held, as in 1958, the expense appears to have been moderate. The growth and invigoration of the party continued, with Rockefeller exerting leadership in state and local organizations. In 1961 he won commanding influence over the state central committee and was named national Republican committeeman for Arkansas. Some Democratic lawmakers sought to enact legislation which would make holding such a party post incompatible with membership on the Arkansas Industrial Commission. This maladroit and unsuccessful effort aroused a storm of disapproval all over the state, giving publicity and increased strength to Rockefeller and his party. By the early 1960's the Democrats were discovering that the opposition party had become something more than a nuisance in state politics, although it still remained weak and poorly organized at the local level.

Neither increased Negro voting nor Republican growth promised immediate change in 1957, but a third development exerted a sud-

Table 2

TOTAL VOTES FOR GOVERNOR IN ARKANSAS DEMOCRATIC PRIMARIES
AND GENERAL ELECTIONS, 1948–1968

	First Primary	Second Primary	General Election
1948	257,776	305,015	249,301
1950	327,559	—	317,087
1952	329,050	376,500	391,584
1954	324,599	375,837	335,125
1956	311,227	—	399,012
1958	383,904	—	286,885
1960	406,817	—	421,985
1962	405,112	—	308,092
1964	365,037	—	592,050
1966	420,065	405,985	563,527
1968	414,873	339,967	615,595

den and wrenching effect upon state politics before the year ended. Even prior to the Supreme Court's decisions of 1954 and 1955 declaring racial discrimination in public education to be unconstitutional, a few Negroes had been admitted to the University of Arkansas. In the fall of 1954, two school districts began programs of gradual desegregation, and in 1955 eight additional districts announced similar plans. Five of the six state-supported white colleges, in the same year, admitted Negroes; and a school district in Lawrence County, in the northeastern part of the state, began desegregation with the enrollment of twenty Negroes. The last instance was accompanied by threats and intimidations, allegedly inspired by a white Citizens' Council, which led the school board to obtain a federal court order to restrain "troublemakers."

White public opinion was overwhelmingly opposed to integrated schools, but there seemed to be a widespread though reluctant willingness to continue and extend the court-imposed policy. "Arkansas will obey the law," Governor Cherry had quietly announced in 1954; and Governor Faubus never indicated during his first term nor in the campaign to win a second term that he would use his power against local school boards and federal court decrees. When the Little Rock school board announced a plan, approved by the federal district court, to begin a limited integration of Central High School by enrolling nine Negro children, no significant opposition was anticipated. But in the days preceding the September, 1957, school opening, rumors of resistance by unruly elements and rumors of action by Faubus began to spread. Late in the evening, a few hours before the opening of school, the governor announced that he had called out National Guard units to preserve the peace. In the ensuing days the world discovered that peace was being preserved by preventing the Negro children from entering the school, while a white mob heckled the children and applauded the soldiers.

The governor's action produced a direct confrontation between state and federal authority which many believed would be ruinous to the state. Congressman Brooks Hays, in whose district these events were occurring, arranged a meeting between the governor and President Eisenhower on September 13. After the meeting the governor issued a statement in which he said, "I have never expressed any personal opinion regarding the Supreme Court decision. That decision is the law of the land and must be obeyed." [29] Upon his return to Little Rock, however, he took no steps to remove the obstructions he had erected to prevent the execution of court decrees. Later events suggest that he felt no gratitude for Hays's efforts to help; instead he seems to have harbored a deep resentment.

On September 20 the federal district court ordered Governor Faubus to end his resistance to the entry of the Negro children. The National Guard was withdrawn, the children were admitted, and for two days the mob rioted near the entrances to the school and overpowered the local police. For their own safety the Negro students were withdrawn. President Eisenhower issued a proclamation commanding the mob to disperse; one day later, federal troops were flown in to scatter the mob and, with the assistance of federalized National Guard units of the state, to protect the nine Negro children during the remainder of the school year. A special session of the legislature in 1958 authorized the governor to close public schools which had been integrated "by force." By this authority all Little Rock high schools were closed during the 1958–59 school year. In June, 1959, the federal district court declared the school-closing law to be unconstitutional, and a reorganized school board reopened the high schools in September.

Before these difficulties had run their course, Faubus announced his candidacy for a third term in the spring of 1958. A Little Rock meat-packer and a chancery judge from eastern Arkansas, both newcomers to state politics, entered the field and fought a futile campaign which netted them a total vote of less than 120,000 to the governor's 264,346. In a nearly clean sweep, the victor received a majority of the votes in seventy-three counties and led his opponents in the remaining two counties. County majorities of 80 percent and higher were scattered in all sections of the state. Madison and New-

29 Hays later recalled, "I tried desperately to help the Governor work out a course of action that would be both morally impregnable and politically viable. I was tragically disappointed in the final results." Brooks Hays, "Little Rock—Ten Years Later" (typescript, 1967, in author's possession).

ton, as usual, were nearest to unanimity, each giving Faubus 95 percent of its vote. Of the state's total vote, he received 69 percent.

Another segregationist, with a greater claim to being old in the faith, won a Democratic nomination in a statewide race. Jim Johnson waged a successful campaign against Associate Justice Minor Millwee of the state Supreme Court, in which Johnson made it clear that states' rights segregationists should man this high judicial bastion.

Still another effect of the governor's intervention at Central High School was felt in the 1958 general election. Although Congressman Brooks Hays had served since 1943 with only token opposition and had easily won his party's renomination in the summer primaries of 1958, he encountered the governor's implacable hostility in the fall. A week before the general election, Faubus threw the support of his organization to Dr. Dale Alford, a former member of the Little Rock school board, who suddenly launched a vigorous "paste-in" campaign as an independent. Hays and his supporters were caught off guard, and Alford won by a narrow margin, in an election marked by more than the usual number of irregularities.

The 1958 elections inaugurated a period in which the governor appeared to be invincible, despite the sustained opposition of a great number of individuals, hastily organized groups, and a few newspapers led by the *Arkansas Gazette,* whose courageous editorials in an atmosphere of crisis won it a decline in circulation and in advertising and Pulitzer prizes for its editor and publisher. The Women's Emergency Committee of Little Rock was most effective and hard-hitting in opposition to the governor's school policies. Under the leadership of Mrs. David D. Terry, wife of a former congressman, it aroused public opinion and exerted a significant power in several school board elections. In stimulating and leading opposition to the governor, this group extended its influence far beyond the Little Rock area and helped to create a climate of opinion which affected the elections of the 1960's.

Individual businessmen, lawyers, ministers, farmers, and teachers raised their voices against the governor, but none of their organizations or associations pitted their strength against public opinion and the growing political power of Faubus.[30] As the years and the gubernatorial terms passed, he tapped each source of power which he could influence and extracted whatever additional political strength it could yield. The legislature became a pliant instrument in his hands and rarely withheld the statutes and constitutional amendments he requested. Boards and commissions, organized with overlapping terms for their members on the assumption that no governor would serve for more than two terms, fell steadily under his complete control. Local political organizations more and more became his hands and fingers all over the state.

The next two elections revealed, however, a decline in the governor's power over the voters. In 1960, against four opponents, he won a fourth-term renomination with 238,997 votes—59 percent of the total vote, a 10 percent drop from the preceding election. He won majorities in sixty-eight counties and led his opponents in all except one of the remaining seven counties. Two years later he gained a fifth-term renomination, polling 208,996 against 196,116 for five opponents, among whom were former Governor McMath and former Congressman Alford, who had lost his seat through redistricting. Faubus' vote was only a little more than 51 percent of the total. Thus he narrowly escaped a runoff primary. He was saved, in part, through exertions in counties which had long been his favorites. Crittenden County gave him 84 percent, Newton slipped down to 83 percent, but Madison gave him 97 percent. Even this figure does not do justice to the prodigious labors performed in this little county. It really gave its native son a vote equal to approximately 104 percent of the qualified voters listed in the poll tax book.

The governor announced his candidacy for a sixth term in the spring of 1964, but no seasoned campaigners took the field against him as they had in 1962. Three obscure and inexperienced candi-

[30] The AFL-CIO state president, Odell Smith, sought to throw the strength of his organization against the Faubus school policies. "The public schools must be maintained," he declared, "and the law must be obeyed." But this statement, appearing in the *Arkansas Labor Bulletin*, produced a schism in Arkansas labor which persists. Victor K. Ray, "Arkansas—the Role of the Labor Unions," *Arkansas Gazette* (Little Rock), May 25, 1969.

dates, who could offer scarcely more than token resistance to the Faubus organization, met an inglorious defeat. The governor received 239,890 votes—66 percent of the total vote; his three opponents got 125,147. The customary top-heavy majorities were returned by the three most faithful counties: Crittenden, 93 percent; Newton, 96 percent; and Madison, ever striving for perfection, 99 percent.

Republicanism Emerges: Reform Over Reaction?

As in his first campaign ten years before, Faubus confronted a formidable Republican opponent in the general election. Winthrop Rockefeller had spent nearly a decade in organizing, nourishing, and strengthening the Republican Party. He was now ready to give it a trial run, with himself at the helm. Nominated without those difficulties that sometimes beset a Democratic candidate, he launched a hardworking campaign in the summer and sustained the grueling pace until November. His chief issues were the long tenure of the governor and the advantages the state would derive from new leaders with fresh ideas. Faubus emphasized the progress made during his administration and occasionally touched upon the business iniquities of Standard Oil and Rockefeller's grandfather. The outcome was not close. Faubus won by a vote of 337,489 to 254,561, receiving 57 percent of the votes. Although he carried sixty-four of the seventy-five counties, he won narrowly in many of them, and he lost the large, urban counties of Jefferson, Pulaski, Sebastian, and Washington. All but one of the counties Rockefeller carried were in the west and north, but in the eastern area, where Negroes were most numerous, he received a strikingly heavy vote.

Although Rockefeller was running for the governorship in the year of Barry Goldwater's candidacy for the presidency, the two campaigns in Arkansas were somewhat disconnected. Rockfeller's views on race relations and civil rights were considerably more liberal than those reputedly entertained by the presidential candidate, and in other respects the Arkansan appeared to be less conservative than Goldwater. Since Rockefeller was making his chief appeal to anti-Faubus Democrats, he carefully avoided any connec-

Governor Faubus Addresses a Friendly Legislature

tion with the Republican presidential campaign that would have disturbed his liberal allies. This precaution may not have been necessary. A county-by-county examination of the votes cast for the Republican gubernatorial and presidential candidates in 1964 reveals that they polled a strikingly similar number of votes in most of the counties, as shown in the scattergram in Figure 5. The elec-

Figure 5

ARKANSAS VOTE FOR GUBERNATORIAL AND PRESIDENTIAL CANDIDATES, 1964, BY COUNTIES

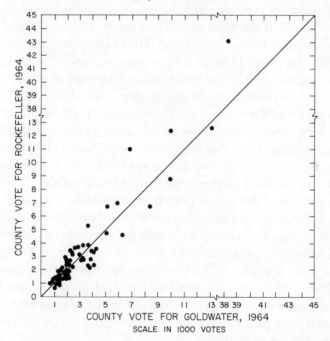

tion returns suggest, though they do not prove, that Arkansans paid little attention to the ideological differences between Rockefeller and Goldwater.

Midway through his sixth term Faubus declared that he would not be a candidate in 1966. Even earlier, Jim Johnson announced his candidacy for the governorship. He was followed by Dale Alford,

Brooks Hays, Frank Holt (who, like Johnson, was an associate justice of the state Supreme Court), and three others who were making
their first statewide races. It was widely believed, and with adequate
cause, that Faubus was supporting Holt in an effort to defeat Johnson and Alford, both of whom had opposed the governor in earlier
campaigns. Hays and Alford were serious contenders, but the chief
attention centered upon Holt as the favorite of the Faubus organization and upon Johnson as a colorful campaigner who mixed into
a curious medley religious sentiments, racism, and personal attacks
upon his opponents. In the first primary these two candidates led
the poll, Johnson receiving 105,607 votes and Holt 92,711. As the
pace quickened in the brief runoff campaign, Johnson lashed with
fine impartiality both Faubus and Holt. Referring to the composed and dignified Holt as a "pleasant vegetable," he charged
that his rival was merely a puppet who would perpetuate the Faubus
regime. Holt avoided any open alignment with the governor's organization, for many voters were determined to end its power, and
sought to fix the attention of the people upon a program of progress
and improvement in the state's government. Faubus maintained a
neutral silence in public, but it is obvious that he tugged on the
strings that tied many county organizations to his office.

The outcome of the second primary demonstrated that this secret
aid was not enough. Johnson carried fifty-two counties and won by
a vote of 210,543 to 195,442. Although his strength was greatest in
the east and south, nearly half of his counties were in the north and
west. Eight of Holt's twenty-three counties were in the east and
south, had large Negro populations, and had given Faubus great
majorities in preceding elections. Most of the remaining Holt counties carried were in the northwest, where Madison and Newton returned majorities of 86 percent.

While the Democratic primaries stormed over the state, the Republicans were making their nominations in comparative quiet.
Rockefeller was compelled to go through the motions of waging a
primary campaign, for an obscure lifelong Democrat suddenly discovered he was a Republican and filed for the party's gubernatorial
nomination. Easily winning the mild and sedate primary, Rocke-

feller entered the general election campaign of 1966 in company
with Republican nominees for lieutenant governor, attorney general, and more than a hundred nominees for district and county
offices.

This well-staffed and generously financed campaign had been
planned for two years. In some respects preparations for it had been
made even earlier. For five years or more, Rockefeller and his associates had emphasized the advantages a two-party system would
bring to Arkansas. For two years the Election Research Council had
been investigating and publicizing the irregularities and illegalities
that marked elections in some counties. Public opinion had been
aroused against these practices, and some measure of fear may have
entered the minds of election officials. Certain that he would be the
nominee in 1966, Rockefeller and his staff had adequate time to
gather needed information and to make detailed plans for the campaign which, if successful, must detach thousands of Democrats
from the nominee of their party.

The nomination of Jim Johnson was an unexpected bonus for
the Republicans. His personality and attitudes drove liberal Democrats promptly, and without nagging self-doubts, to the Rockefeller
standard. "Women Democrats for Rockefeller," many of whose
members had developed political motivations and skills as members of the Women's Emergency Committee, organized an effective
statewide campaign against the Democratic nominee. To them,
Johnson was a dangerous and detested example of the segregationist politicians they had been fighting since 1957. Their effect upon
the election was great, and it may have been decisive. Johnson's
bitter tongue-lashing of Faubus during the primary campaigns im-
pelled many of the governor's supporters to sulk in silence or to
work quietly for Rockefeller. The governor remained aloof until
late in the campaign, and then made only perfunctory gestures in
support of the Democratic nominee. The Johnson campaign alienated increasing numbers of Democrats, especially the liberals.
Rockefeller was attacked as an outsider, a phony cowboy, a "prissy-
sissy," a rich man who was trying to buy the governorship and add
it to his other valuable properties. Under the best of circumstances,

Johnson would have found it difficult to attract Negro voters. During the primary campaigns, he had worsened the circumstances by asserting that he would not seek Negro support and by refusing, it was convincingly charged, to shake hands with a man of that race. In the general election campaign, he refrained from anti-Negro actions and expressions, but Republican campaign literature frequently refreshed the memories of Negroes on Johnson's long career as an intemperate segregationist.

Rockefeller waged an energetic campaign in all parts of the state, avoiding personalities and elaborating a program of industrialization, improved education, and higher living standards for all the people. An enthusiastic staff organized the disaffected Democrats and strengthened their grim determination to defeat Jim Johnson. Discreet emissaries moved quietly among the Negroes, holding meetings in their homes and urging them to register and vote.

The election gave the Republicans their first governor since 1874, and their candidate for lieutenant governor, Maurice "Footsie" Britt, was also elected, by a small majority. John Paul Hammerschmidt, the Republican opponent of the ailing and aged Congressman Trimble, won the House seat in the northwestern district. In county and district races Republican candidates fared poorly. Three were elected to the state legislature, and less than a half-dozen won county offices. These successes were concentrated in the northwestern counties, where Republican strength had been formidable in local politics ever since the Civil War.

Carrying thirty-five counties and 54 percent of the total vote, Rockefeller received 306,324 votes to Johnson's 257,203. Of the 740,609 registered voters, 76 percent participated in the governor's election, casting a total vote of 563,527, a total exceeded only by the 1964 gubernatorial election, when 592,050 voted.[31]

---

[31] The percentage of qualified voters participating in general elections has been highest during presidential election years. In six of the last eleven elections the vote in the general election has exceeded the vote in the Democratic primary. (See Table 2.) The percentage of qualified voters participating in Democratic primaries between 1932 and 1968 has ranged from a low of 47 percent to a high of 85 percent. In recent years, because of the increase in Republican strength, the percentage has been

When the vote for the two gubernatorial candidates is examined county by county, little division on the basis of section or of race can be discerned in the gross figures. Both candidates carried counties in all the identifiable sections of the state; and the counties in the east and south having large Negro populations were shared by both, though it is significant that Rockefeller had majorities in four of the five counties which have a Negro population of more than 50 percent. Rockefeller had a marked advantage, also, in the more heavily urbanized counties, carrying Chicot, Craighead, Garland, Jefferson, Miller, Phillips, Pulaski, Ouachita, Sebastian, Union, and Washington. As Table 3 shows, there is a positive relationship between urbanization and the percentage of the total vote received by anti-Faubus and anti-Johnson candidates in the elections of 1962, 1964, and 1966.

An examination of the election returns on subcounty levels reveals voting patterns that determined the outcome of the election. Cities and large towns in all parts of the state generally favored the Republican candidate, while the Democratic candidate received the bulk of his votes in rural areas. Negro wards in cities voted with a marked enthusiasm for Rockefeller, returning top-heavy majorities such as 445 to 39; 564 to 32; 245 to 2; 536 to 15; 409 to 9; 770 to 44; 366 to 4; 185 to 1.[32]

When counties are grouped according to median family income, as in Table 4, it appears that another factor might be added to urbanization and Negro voting in identifying the type of voter who has opposed Faubus and Johnson in recent elections. In the elections of the period 1962–66, the anti-Faubus and anti-Johnson candidates received an increasing percentage of votes in the middle- and higher-income counties. Only the second Democratic primary in 1966 reveals an interruption in this progression.

Thus Rockefeller's victory was produced by three identifiable groups which are somewhat overlapping: urban residents, Negroes,

---

decreasing. Only 54 percent of the qualified voters participated in the Democratic primaries in 1968.

32 *Arkansas Gazette* (Little Rock), December 11, 1966.

Table 3

Relation Between Urbanism and Voting in Recent Gubernatorial Elections in Arkansas

Number of Counties	Counties Grouped According to Percentage of Urban Population	Percentage of Total Vote Received				
		Faubus' Opponents, Democratic Primary, 1962	Rockefeller, General Election, 1964	Holt, 2nd Democratic Primary, 1966	Rockefeller, General Election, 1966
26	0–14%	41	39	48	46
12	15–29%	41	36	48	44
24	30–44%	47	40	45	51
10	45–59%	52	47	48	56
3	Over 59%	59	51	56	64

and voters with higher-than-average incomes. Most of the voters in these groups had another characteristic: they were disaffected Democrats. This circumstance raises a question about the nature and consequences of the election. Was it a Republican victory, or was it the triumph of a temporary fusion of anti-Johnson Democrats and regular Republicans? Could the Democrats who helped to elect Rockefeller be persuaded to remain, at least in gubernatorial elections, within the Republican Party?

The new Republican governor assumed office in January, 1967, and an overwhelmingly Democratic legislature convened in the same month. In a sense these events marked the beginning of the 1968 campaign, for the regular session of the legislature and subsequent extra sessions produced a series of angry clashes in which a large part of the governor's program was blocked, legislative measures were vetoed, and mutual recriminations rang through the capitol. Accustomed to following a Democratic governor's leadership, the legislature refused to be led by a Republican governor and appeared incapable of providing its own leadership. Out of this disorderly situation, however, two significant pieces of legislation did emerge, both initiated by the governor. A Department of Administration was established to coordinate and render more efficient the activities of several executive departments, and a Constitutional Revision Study Commission was authorized to examine the 1874 constitution and to make recommendations to a constitutional convention, if the voters in the 1968 general elections should approve the convening of such a body.

Between sessions of the legislature, Governor Rockefeller concentrated his attention upon reform. New department heads, fully supported by the governor, revealed and corrected a number of serious abuses which had characterized several areas of state government for decades. The director of the Insurance Department, to the pained surprise of some segments of the business, began a methodical and unrelenting enforcement of insurance laws and regulations. As a result, many unscrupulous insurance agents were forced to seek other employment, and a significant number of insurance companies ended their operations in Arkansas. The state Securities De-

Table 4

Relation Between Income and Voting in Recent Gubernatorial Elections in Arkansas

Number of Counties	Counties Grouped According to Median Income of Families	Percentage of Total Vote Received			
		Faubus' Opponents, Democratic Primary, 1964	Rockefeller, General Election, 1964	Holt, 2nd Democratic Primary, 1966	Rockefeller, General Election, 1966
28	$1500–2500	40	37	48	49
38	$2501–3500	46	40	64	50
9	Over $3500	57	49	48	67

partment, under the leadership of a former law school professor, discovered that Arkansans had lost millions of dollars in the purchase of worthless and near-worthless securities during the preceding ten years. The department's strict regulation of the sale of securities struck Arkansas from the list of states in which the pickings were easy. For a number of years, the open and large-scale violation of anti-gambling laws in Hot Springs had converted that resort city into a little Las Vegas. A new director of the state police led a number of successful raids which resulted in the destruction of gambling equipment, angry outcries from Hot Springs legislators, and the end of casino gambling. An investigation of the state's prisons revealed scandalous administration and callous mistreatment of prisoners. A new prison director gave adequate, and even flamboyant, publicity to the misdeeds which were uncovered; and a program of reform, hampered by insufficient appropriations, was begun.

As Governor Rockefeller's first year in office ended, aspirants for the 1968 Democratic gubernatorial nomination began to come forward. Some days before the deadline, five candidates had filed: Bruce Bennett, former attorney general; Ted Boswell, a youthful newcomer to Arkansas politics; Clyde Byrd, a former state senator; Marion Crank, former Speaker of the Arkansas House and a veteran legislator; and Frank Whitbeck, an insurance company executive. Just before the filing deadline, a husband-and-wife team made a dramatic appearance: Virginia Johnson filed for the governorship, and Jim Johnson declared his candidacy for the Democratic senatorial nomination in opposition to Senator Fulbright. Two relatively obscure candidates also filed, thus completing the ballot for a four-man race.

From the beginning of the senatorial primary campaign, the attention of the voters centered upon the struggle between Fulbright and Johnson. Fulbright's conservative position on civil rights deprived Johnson of the "race issue," except for a few references to "the burning and looting of our cities." Johnson relied chiefly, therefore, upon charges that Fulbright was an arrogant intellectual, out of touch with the common people, and was tainted with socialism and a sympathy for Communist countries. References to "Chairman Fulbright" were probably intended to produce associations with Chairman Kosygin and Chairman Mao. Labeling Fulbright "the pin-up boy of Hanoi," Johnson charged that his opposition to the Vietnam war had given aid and comfort to North Vietnam.

In a thorough but low-key campaign, Fulbright paid little attention to the challenger, except to dismiss his "ridiculous" charges as "utter trash and hogwash" and to denounce his "irresponsible tactics." Fulbright moved methodically over the state, clad in slacks and an open-collared sport shirt, attending picnics and outdoor rallies, and walking the main streets of towns and villages. Calling attention to the advantages which the state derived from his seniority, he reminded voters of the federal funds received for the Arkansas River development and of his part in enlarging foreign markets for Arkansas farm products.[33]

With 53 percent of the total vote, Fulbright defeated his three opponents and won renomination in the first primary. He carried forty-one counties by majorities and twenty-eight by pluralities. Jim Johnson won a majority of the votes in one county and a plurality in four counties.[34]

In the meantime, the six-sided race for the Democratic gubernatorial nomination was demanding the attention of the voters. It soon became evident that the six candidates fell into three groups. Bennett, Crank, and Byrd had long been prominent in Arkansas politics, were identified to some extent with the Faubus regime, and bore an Old Guard label which they vainly tried to shed. Boswell and Whitbeck ran as progressive candidates who would reform abuses and unify a party that had been ruinously divided by Jim Johnson's 1966 candidacy. Mrs. Johnson had no difficulty in asserting her independence of the Faubus organization, for her husband's character sketches of Orval Faubus during the preceding two years had delighted all admirers of vituperative language, but her cam-

[33] *Ibid.*, July 28, 1968.
[34] Out of a total vote of 417,023, Fulbright received 220,684, Jim Johnson 132,038, with the two minor candidates dividing the remaining 64,301.

paign of reform and party unification did not elicit a sufficient response at the polls.

Out of a total vote of 414,873, Crank led the ticket with 106,092; and Mrs. Johnson, in a nip-and-tuck race with Boswell, won the number two position with 86,038 votes. The runoff primary was brief and unexciting, and Crank won it overwhelmingly. Out of a total vote of 339,967 (down nearly 75,000 from the first primary), Crank received 215,087 and carried every county in the state except two. Counties which have acquired the reputation of possessing smoothly operating machines delivered especially handsome majorities to the victor.[35]

After a brief respite at the end of the summer, the state gathered its energies for the climactic political battles of the fall. Three pairs of armies occupied the field and waged campaigns marked by vigor, a profusion of money, and a firm determination not to get mixed up in anybody else's fight.

The Rockefeller Republican organization entered an imposing number of candidates for state offices, seeking the posts of governor, lieutenant governor, secretary of state, attorney general, land commissioner, treasurer, and auditor; in addition thirty-seven Republican candidates campaigned for seats in the state legislature (a slight reduction; forty had run in 1966). The Republican campaigns for the state offices were especially well organized and lavishly supported with money. Governor Rockefeller's headquarters, employing data processing and computers, deluged every promising group of voters with campaign materials.[36] Although lacking the more sophisticated techniques of the Rockefeller campaigners, Crank's organization waged a vigorous battle all over the state, and in newspaper and television advertising the Democrats rivaled the Republicans in extremely heavy campaign expenditures.

Two other campaigns attracted statewide interest. Charles Ber-

[35] Conway, Crittenden, Garland, Madison, and Newton.

[36] Notably successful efforts were made by both parties to encourage registration. Between the summer primaries and the cutoff date for registration prior to the November election, there were more than 75,000 new registrations, producing a total of nearly 850,000 qualified voters, the highest in the state's history.

nard, a wealthy farmer-businessman from eastern Arkansas, easily received the little-valued Republican nomination for the Senate and waged an energetic campaign against Fulbright. Employing substantially the same tactics and charges that had characterized Jim Johnson's primary campaign, Bernard aroused the anxiety and hostility of numerous Fulbright Democrats who supported Rockefeller but wondered aloud if the governor was encouraging Bernard's candidacy. Repeated assurances were given that Bernard was running his own race, with only the most nominal support from Rockefeller.

A similar delicacy on the part of state candidates characterized the 1968 presidential campaign in Arkansas. It had been evident ever since spring that the George Wallace candidacy would be formidable and that it would draw strong support from voters of both parties. With Jim Johnson and Orval Faubus (each keeping a wary eye on the other) working for the victory of Wallace electors, it became increasingly probable that the former Alabama governor would carry the state. Neither the gubernatorial nor senatorial candidates cared to menace their own elections by working actively for the presidential candidates of their parties. Late in the campaign, however, special organizations became active in the presidential race, with Congressmen Wilbur D. Mills and David Pryor leading the Democratic effort.

Wallace, Fulbright, and Rockefeller: Realignment or Reversion?

The Arkansas vote in the presidential election confirmed the fears of both old parties. Wallace received 39 percent of the popular vote, carried thirteen counties by majorities, and had pluralities in thirty-six counties. All his majority counties were in the south and east, but his plurality counties were scattered over the state. Only in the northwestern corner was his strength low. Richard Nixon received 31 percent of the vote and led the poll in nineteen counties, three of which he carried by majorities. Hubert Humphrey won 30 percent of the vote and led in only seven counties. (See Figure 6.) For

Figure 6

ARKANSAS IN PRESIDENTIAL ELECTION, 1968

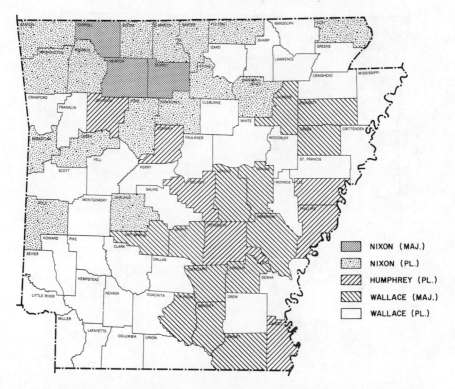

NIXON (MAJ.)
NIXON (PL.)
HUMPHREY (PL.)
WALLACE (MAJ.)
WALLACE (PL.)

the first time since Reconstruction, Arkansas had failed to give its electoral votes to the Democratic nominee.

The returns in the senatorial election were almost an anticlimax. Fulbright won a decisive victory, 349,965 to 241,731, receiving 59 percent of the vote and carrying sixty-seven counties. Bernard's strength was greatest in the northwestern counties where, even in normal years, Republicans compete on better than even terms with their Democratic opponents. In this northwestern congressional district Hammerschmidt, the Republican incumbent, won easily against a hard-campaigning Democratic challenger.

Figure 7

ARKANSAS GUBERNATORIAL ELECTION, 1968

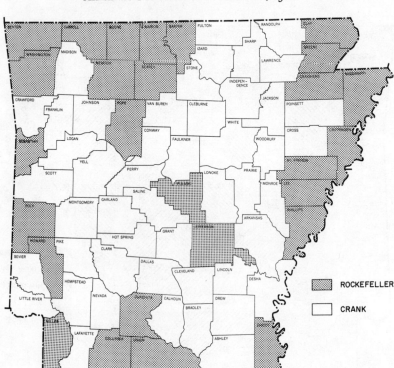

In the elections for state offices, including the legislature, Republicans won at the top, but the usual defeats rewarded their efforts elsewhere. Governor Rockefeller was reelected, 322,782 to 292,813, winning 52.4 percent of the votes and carrying twenty-seven counties, compared with the thirty-five he had won in 1966. (See Figure 7.)

As in his first election, Rockefeller owed his victory to the Republican counties of the northwest, the heavily urbanized areas of the state, and a few counties in the east with very large Negro populations. Lieutenant Governor Maurice "Footsie" Britt gained a narrow victory, with a lead of only 4,200 over his Democratic opponent.[37] All other Republican candidates for state constitutional offices were easily defeated by Democratic incumbents; and of the thirty-seven Republicans who sought election to the legislature, only five succeeded—one in the Senate and four in the House. A ballot measure, endorsed by both parties, to call a convention for the drafting of a new state constitution won by a slender margin.[38]

After a decade of hard work, the Republican Party in Arkansas still had significant strength only at the top; but organizational efforts begun at the county and precinct levels to win and hold these positions may ultimately give the party a broader base. A people who will give their presidential vote to George Wallace, their senatorial vote to William Fulbright, and their gubernatorial vote to Winthrop Rockefeller show a cross-grained independence that could redound to the advantage of the minority party.

If this willingness of Arkansans to depart from former voting patterns raised Republican hopes in 1968, the elections of 1970 dashed them. Governor Rockefeller announced his candidacy for a third term and easily won the Republican nomination in a mild contest with three other candidates, one of whom, James "Uncle Mac" MacKrell, raised nostalgic memories of the 1940's. Sterling Cockrill, former Speaker of the Arkansas House of Representatives, withdrew from the Democratic Party and became the Republican nominee for lieutenant governor.

The Democratic primaries were more exciting and unpredictable, with a large number of hopeful candidates and forlorn hopes seeking the gubernatorial nomination. Orval Faubus, divorced from a middle-aged wife and promptly married to a considerably younger one, left his post as manager of Dogpatch, U.S.A., and sought a

[37] The discrepancies in the total vote cast in the major statewide elections of 1968 give some indication of the extent and nature of voter apathy:

Number of qualified voters	845,759
Vote for presidential electors	609,590
Vote for United States senator	591,696
Vote for governor	615,595
Vote for lieutenant governor	595,226

[38] The delegates to this convention met for their first session during the summer of 1969 and began drafting a document to be presented to the voters in 1970.

seventh term as governor of Arkansas. He was joined in the race by Attorney General Joe Purcell; Speaker of the House Hayes McClerkin; Bill Wells, who had been narrowly defeated for the lieutenant governorship in 1968; Dale Bumpers, who had no previous political experience and was well known only in the small west Arkansas town in which he practiced law; and by a few other candidates who apparently could hope only for that exhilaration invariably imparted to the participants in Arkansas politics. Faubus rapidly became a front-runner and a target for attacks in a campaign which concentrated attention on personality and character. The relatively unknown Bumpers avoided these attacks and devoted his time and funds to painting a self-portrait of a young, honest, and vigorous advocate of improvement in state government. In the preferential primary of August 25, 1970, Faubus had a commanding lead over his rivals, but he lacked the overall majority required for nomination; and Bumpers, to the astonishment of the experts, won second place on the runoff ballot.

The ensuing two-week campaign pitted the old master of Arkansas politics against the attractive and unflappable newcomer who had no record to assault and who carefully refrained from laying out the specifics of his program. Faubus sought in vain some chink in his rival's armor into which he could plunge the usual Faubus attack, but Bumpers blandly continued his work of self-portraiture. He thought it unnecessary, he said, to call attention to the Faubus record, for everyone was familiar with it.

The more thoughtful observers of Arkansas politics were prepared for a Bumpers victory, but the size of his vote and its distribution over the state produced gasps of astonishment. By a vote of 258,848 to 182,008 he defeated the former governor and carried fifty-five of the seventy-five counties. Most of the Faubus counties lay in the east, where his anti–civil rights image continued to evoke a favorable response, but in the west the ever-faithful Madison and Newton counties returned top-heavy majorities for their favorite.[39]

In the general election campaign, Governor Rockefeller swamped the readers of newspapers and billboards and the listeners to radio

39 *Arkansas Gazette* (Little Rock), September 10, 1970.

and television with the most generously financed effort in Arkansas history. He sought to present the accomplishments of his two administrations and to drive Bumpers from his fortress of generalities into the open field of combat over specific programs. But the Democratic candidate smilingly refused the increasingly urgent invitations and continued his efforts to make himself well and favorably known to the voters of the state.

Bumpers' overwhelming victory in the November election apparently proved the astuteness of his campaign style. He won the governorship by a vote of 375,648 to 197,418 and carried seventy-three counties. Only in Lee and Phillips, both with heavy Negro populations, did Rockefeller win majorities. In a number of other eastern counties he approached the Bumpers vote, but the Democratic landslide defeated him in even the few usually Republican counties of the northwest.

For nearly all the Republican candidates, state and local, the election was a debacle which left the party in the shambles of widespread defeat. Sterling Cockrill, Republican candidate for lieutenant governor, lost to Bob Riley, a college professor of political science, and all other Republican aspirants for statewide offices were defeated. The party ran ten candidates for seats in the state Senate and 36 for the House. Of these, only two candidates for the House won election. In the western congressional district, however, Congressman Hammerschmidt easily retained Republican control of that seat.[40] It appears that tens of thousands of Democrats who left the party during the gubernatorial candidacies of Jim Johnson and Marion Crank came back home under the banners of Dale Bumpers.

While restoring the Democrats to executive power, the electorate staunchly resisted further innovations. Two initiated acts were rejected; and the proposed state constitution, offered as a replacement for the 1874 document, was defeated by a margin of more than 75,000 votes. The Arkansas voters, it appears, yearned for the good old days.

40 *Ibid.*, November 5, 15, 1970.

7

GEORGIA
Static and Dynamic

JOSEPH L. BERND

The trademark of Eugene Talmadge was the red galluses which he revealed to his audience when he shucked his coat at the climactic moment of a speech from the hustings. Herman Talmadge inherited this symbol from his father, who died in 1946. Herman Talmadge won the governorship in 1948 and again in 1950. Ineligible to succeed himself under the Georgia Constitution, Herman briefly held no office at the expiration of his term in January, 1955. But in 1956 his candidacy for the United States Senate forced the retirement of the septuagenarian incumbent, Senator Walter F. George, and Talmadge easily won the seat vacated by George. Talmadge's six years as governor were followed by eight years in which the office was held by men closely identified with the Talmadge faction and the Talmadge political organization: Samuel Marvin Griffin, 1955–59, and Ernest Vandiver, 1959–63.

The truculent, irascible public personality of Eugene Talmadge, whether in or out of office, had dominated Georgia political life from 1932 to 1946. His more affable and no less puissant son dominated the state for about a decade, 1947–56. Senator Herman Talmadge remained *the* major political force on the Georgia scene for several years in the late fifties and the early sixties. Thereafter, new

Joseph L. Bernd is Professor of Political Science, Virginia Polytechnic Institute and State University. Grateful acknowledgment is made for the assistance of Ben W. Fortson, Jr., Georgia Secretary of State; Gus Bernd, editor of the *Georgia Journal*; and James E. Hilley.

political figures gradually emerged on the domestic scene, while in Washington the more important role belonged to the senior United States senator, Richard Brevard Russell. The younger Talmadge had sought successfully, as his career and the years progressed, to communicate a more genteel and less flamboyant image in order to appeal to all major elements of the electorate. In 1968 he was elected to his third Senate term, as usual without formidable opposition.

About the time that Herman Talmadge began his career in the United States Senate, Lester G. Maddox, a once-poor boy from the Atlanta metropolis, began to become politically visible. Although he received only a rudimentary education as a youth and in spite of the fact that his political antics often appeared uncouth to decorous persons, Maddox was a shrewd strategist. Apparently without benefit of Madison Avenue assistance, Maddox dramatized himself and his Atlanta restaurant, the Pickrick, as a symbol of resistance to racial integration. The ax handles which he has sold or given away as souvenirs throughout his recent career may be repugnant to some in their representation of violence, but they graphically convey the notion of a vigorous defense of white supremacy and they win votes in Georgia.

In 1957 and 1961 Maddox ran unsuccessfully as a candidate for mayor of Atlanta and in 1962 he was defeated for lieutenant governor, although he ran strongly on each occasion among relatively poor white voters and forced runoffs in 1961 and 1962. In 1966 Maddox sought the office of governor of Georgia. He won and many Georgians felt more comfortable to have a puritan version of W. J. Cash's "hell-of-a-fellow" in the governorship again.

Old South Genteelism

But there is another side to the coin of personality.

The genteelism of many southerners, particularly of those who belong to or identify with the old families, is as much as part of the culture of the region as the hell-of-a-fellow type. An attitude of *noblesse oblige* toward the Negro often characterizes the genteel southerner, whose hero is Robert E. Lee or Thomas Jefferson rather than Tom Watson or other fire-eaters. Eugene Talmadge was too cantankerous for this type of southerner. (Talmadge could be decorous when he wanted to but he seldom wanted to be when newspaper reporters were around him—and besides, under the county-unit system there were a lot more votes to be won by rabble-rousing.)

The enemy of the genteel southerner is the "white trash," who is usually referred to in Georgia with the prefix "pore." The genteel southerner has demonstrated his superiority to the pore white trash by holding a tolerant, paternalistic view of the Negro. In 1953 when Dr. Rufus E. Clement, a Negro educator and president of Atlanta University, was elected to the Atlanta Board of Education, a knowledgeable publicist and ghostwriter who had a hand in the affair said, "We elected the doctor with the votes of the good colored people of Atlanta and white persons of good will." The combination of Negroes and genteel whites formed the moderate coalition which supported anti-Talmadgeism from 1946 to its collapse in 1954. They supported Carl Sanders successfully in 1962. Businessmen, particularly in the cities and larger towns, have often been identified with the moderate view of the genteel people, or "better element," as they have often been called.

Tom Watson is associated with four traditions which have exerted a major impact on Georgia politics in the middle decades of the twentieth century. Three of these traditions may be identified: (1) rabble-rousing versus genteelism, (2) the cleavage of farmers and city folks, and (3) the ever-recurrent question of race. Watson is also associated with the revival of the county-unit system—that unique institution which exerted so powerful an influence on Georgia primary elections during the Talmadge era (1926–54) and until its demise as a result of decisions of the federal courts in 1962 and 1963.

The Compartmentalized Electorate

In the 1908 gubernatorial primary the influence of Thomas E. Watson was decisive in bringing about the victory of Joseph M. Brown over Hoke Smith. Brown promptly restored the Democratic Party rule, recently abolished by Smith, which required that the primary election be decided on a county-unit basis. In 1917 the General Assembly enacted the county-unit system into law.[1]

Used exclusively in party primary elections, the system apportioned unit votes among the counties according to the following formula: the 8 most populous counties each received 6 unit votes; the 30 next most populous counties each received 4; and the remaining 121 counties each received 2 unit votes. A majority of 206 unit votes out of the total of 410 was needed to win a statewide contest for the Senate or for the governorship. Otherwise a runoff was required. In statewide races to fill lesser offices a plurality was sufficient for victory. The distribution of county-unit votes among the counties, 1942–52, is illustrated by Figure 1.

The county-unit system, it should be noted, allocated electoral power in proportion to legislative power (two unit votes for each representative in the state House of Representatives). In the nineteenth century, when Georgia was largely rural, the apportionment was reasonably related to population except in rare cases. However, with the growth of large metropolitan areas in the twentieth century, the system became an increasingly grotesque caricature of a democratic representational system. But as long as the courts refused to rule on it and as long as the populace accepted it, the power to alter or abolish the unit rule remained the exclusive preserve of the General Assembly, dominated by the representatives from the small counties, the principal beneficiaries of the system. Discrepancies in population became enormous. The most extreme, based on the 1960 census, shows Echols County, population 1,876, with two unit votes compared to Fulton County (Atlanta), population 556,326, with six unit votes.[2] The ratio is 98.9 to 1.

One of the most venal influences of the system was its impact on

[1] C. Vann Woodward, *Tom Watson: Agrarian Rebel* (New York: Macmillan Company, 1938), 392–93. See also Joseph L. Bernd and Lynwood M. Holland, "Recent Restrictions Upon Negro Suffrage: The Case of Georgia," *Journal of Politics*, XXI (1959), 507–508.

[2] Unless otherwise indicated, all census data are taken from *1960 Census of Population* (Washington, D.C.: U.S. Department of Commerce, 1961).

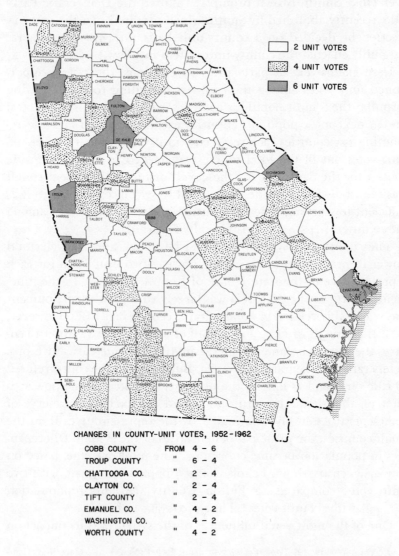

Figure 1

DISTRIBUTION OF GEORGIA COUNTY-UNIT VOTES, 1942–1952

☐ 2 UNIT VOTES

▨ 4 UNIT VOTES

■ 6 UNIT VOTES

CHANGES IN COUNTY-UNIT VOTES, 1952–1962

COBB COUNTY	FROM	4 – 6
TROUP COUNTY	"	6 – 4
CHATTOOGA CO.	"	2 – 4
CLAYTON CO.	"	2 – 4
TIFT COUNTY	"	2 – 4
EMANUEL CO.	"	4 – 2
WASHINGTON CO.	"	4 – 2
WORTH COUNTY	"	4 – 2

the way primary elections were conducted. Ralph McGill of the Atlanta *Constitution* said once that in a statewide primary 60 of Georgia's 159 counties were for sale to the highest bidder. The figure is exaggerated but there is little question that many small counties were controlled by bosses or "courthouse crowds." Elsewhere, manipulation of the voting rolls or simply falsification of the vote totals would swing unit votes from one candidate to another.

Under a popular vote system, except in rare cases where a contest is extremely close, large-scale fraud affecting thousands of ballots is necessary to affect the decision and fraud on such a scale will seldom remain undetected. Under county-unit rule, however, the vital plurality in a given county often depended upon the manipulation of a handful of ballots or a simple change of totals. The purchase of local influences able to produce victory in a county was a common occurrence in the often bitter bifactional elections of the thirties, forties, and early fifties. One can appreciate the appeal of money used to buy support of leaders or individual votes in areas oppressed by the poverty which was common to Georgia in the late nineteenth century and much of the first half of the twentieth century. After the death of the Georgia white primary at the hands of a federal court,[3] more than 135,000 Negroes qualified to vote in the Georgia primaries. In the late forties and early fifties the partisans of white supremacy used intimidation, violence and the threat of violence, and purges of the voting rolls and other legalistic tactics to try to bar blacks from the polls. Under these conditions the winner-take-all compartmentalization of the electorate via the county-unit rule contributed to the effectiveness of a variety of anti-Negro measures as well as to simple malapportionment.[4]

The integrity of Georgia's electoral processes began to improve significantly, however, some years before the demise of the county-unit system. During Herman Talmadge's first term as governor

[3] *Chapman v. King,* 154 F. (2d) 460 (1946).
[4] See Bernd and Holland, "Recent Restrictions Upon Negro Suffrage," 487–513. For an earlier analysis see V. O. Key, Jr., *Southern Politics in State and Nation* (New York: Alfred A. Knopf, 1949), 117–24.

(1948–50), a mandatory secret ballot law was enacted.[5] Improving standards of living and improving levels of education also contributed to the trend. Men on the margin of economic distress, after the failure of a cotton crop, would sell their votes or political influence for a few dollars, but once they attained some measure of economic security, middle-class morality began to assert itself.

The first efforts to attack the county-unit system through resort to the federal courts came in 1946 after a gubernatorial candidate (Eugene Talmadge) and a congressional candidate (James C. Davis) had won in the primary elections, although each had a minority of popular votes. The federal courts refused to accept jurisdiction. The reasoning of the judges was in accordance with that of Justice Felix Frankfurter in the leading case of *Colegrove v. Green*: "Courts ought not to enter this political thicket. The remedy for unfairness in districting is to secure State legislatures that will apportion properly, or to invoke the ample powers of Congress." [6] In 1950 the United States Supreme Court refused jurisdiction in *South v. Peters*.[7] The *per curiam* opinion, relying on the *Colegrove* case, said: "Federal Courts consistently refuse to exercise their equity powers in cases posing political issues arising from a state's geographical distribution of electoral strength among its political subdivisions." In a strong dissent, Justice William O. Douglas, joined by Justice Hugo L. Black, called the county-unit system "the last loophole around our decisions holding that there must be no discrimination because of race in primary as well as in general elections." [8]

In 1951 two young Atlanta attorneys, Morris B. Abram and C. Baxter Jones, Jr., challenged the county-unit rule in both state and federal courts. Abram had been the counsel for the unsuccessful plaintiff in *South v. Peters*. The new challenges were defeated. The successful defense was led by Charles J. Bloch and B. D. Murphy.

---

[5] *Georgia Laws, 1949*, pp. 1291–93.

[6] *Colegrove v. Green*, 328 U.S. 549, 556 (1946).

[7] *South v. Peters*, 89 F. Supp. 672, 339 U.S. 276.

[8] *South v. Peters*, 339 U.S. 276, 277–78 (1950). See Louis T. Rigdon, *Georgia's County Unit System* (Decatur, Georgia: Selective Books, 1961), *passim*.

In 1958, Mayor William B. Hartsfield of Atlanta filed another suit attacking county-unit rule. Hartsfield, after an adverse ruling in the federal district court, asked leave to file a petition for a writ of mandamus to convene a three-judge court to hear his complaint. The petition, if granted, would have in effect evinced a willingness on the part of the Supreme Court to have the case heard on its merits. The motion was rejected by a single vote, with Justices Hugo Black, William J. Brennan, William O. Douglas, and Earl Warren dissenting. The time for a new idea had almost come.

In 1962 in early spring the Supreme Court handed down its momentous decision in *Baker v. Carr*,[9] which overruled the stand taken in *Colegrove* that apportionment was a "political issue" and that courts ought not to enter the "political thicket." If the federal judiciary was now willing to intervene actively to insure that a state legislature was based at least roughly on population, could the county-unit system long survive? Its invalidation would require only a popular vote system. No periodic policing of representational schemes would be required of federal courts as a consequence of such a decision.

On the same day that the *Baker v. Carr* decision was announced, attorney Morris B. Abram, evidently apprised in advance of the Court's ruling, filed suit attacking the constitutionality of the county-unit rule. Abram relied heavily on two provisions of the United States Constitution in addition to the equal protection clause of the Fourteenth Amendment. These were (1) the provision of Article I, Section 2, "The House of Representatives shall be composed of members chosen every second year by the people of the several States," and (2) the Seventeenth Amendment, which says, "The Senate of the United States shall be composed of two Senators from each State, elected by the people thereof." These two provisions, said the plaintiff, required choice "by the people" and not by county-unit votes.[10]

9 *Baker v. Carr*, 369 U.S. 186 (1962).
10 Abram also made use of a heavy volume of statistical evidence and cited the works of a number of social scientists regarding the detrimental effects of the county-unit rule on political process and political behavior. According to an unpublished M.A.

Abram on behalf of plaintiff James O'Hear Sanders won a two-to-one victory from a three-judge panel in the federal district court. Georgia officials unsuccessfully sought a delay in the implementation of the decision. These defeats meant that in 1962 Georgia primary elections were held on a popular vote basis for the first time since 1908. In the following year the United States Supreme Court ruled the county-unit system unconstitutional.[11] United States Attorney General Robert F. Kennedy entered an oral argument and brief against the county-unit system as *amicus curiae*. It was Kennedy's first appearance before the high court.

Gentility and the Fourth Estate

A significantly vocal group among genteel Georgians has been the press. The Atlanta *Journal* and the Atlanta *Constitution* were usually anti-Talmadge during the period of bifactional politics. They supported Negro voting and later desegregation. Most prominent of Georgia newsmen during the period was Ralph McGill, editor and later publisher of the *Constitution* and for many years a nationally syndicated columnist. For a time McGill supported the

---

thesis (Emory University) written by Mrs. Merle Lefkoff, wife of a young attorney who assisted Abram in the case, "a pamphlet entitled 'Recent Restrictions Upon Negro Suffrage: The Case of Georgia' . . . had excited Mr. Abram's curiosity with its possibilities for use in the case." The pamphlet was a reprint of an article which appeared in the *Journal of Politics*, XXI (1959), 487–513. The article was written by Joseph L. Bernd with the research collaboration of Lynwood M. Holland of Emory University.

11 *Gray v. Sanders*, 372 U.S. 368 (1963). For the decision in the district court see 203 F. Supp. 158 (1962). Just prior to the hearing, the Georgia legislature radically revised the unit system in a last-ditch attempt to save it. Under the revision the following formula would have applied:

Population	Unit Votes	Population	Unit Votes
0–15,000	2	15,000 additional	5
5,000 additional	3	15,000 additional	6
10,000 additional	4	30,000 additional	8

For each additional 30,000, two unit votes would be added. All candidates would be required to have both a popular and unit majority. Otherwise a runoff primary would be required.

county-unit system, although most metropolitan daily papers opposed the system. In 1947–48 McGill argued that the unit rule protected the state against corrupt city political machines.

In spite of their initial dislike of Talmadgeism the Atlanta papers publicized the irregularities of the second administration (1939–41) of Governor E. D. Rivers, the first successful leader of the anti-Talmadge faction. Rivers and a number of associates were indicted; several, not including Rivers, were convicted. One conviction was obtained against Hiram Evans, the Imperial Wizard of the Ku Klux Klan. McGill and the Atlanta *Constitution* later turned their wrath against another anti-Talmadge leader, M. E. Thompson.

In the forties and early fifties the Talmadges engaged in bitter exchanges with the liberal press. "Those lying Atlanta newspapers" became a favorite phrase. Subsequently Herman Talmadge and these papers were reconciled. In the middle fifties Marvin Griffin and later Lester Maddox fought with the newspapers after being attacked by them for racial extremism and other sins.

Other dailies in metropolitan areas tended to be anti-Talmadge and racially liberal: the Macon *Telegraph* and *News*, the Columbus *Ledger* and *Inquirer*, the Augusta *Chronicle* and *Herald*. Later, when desegregation rather than Talmadge and Negro voting became the issue, the Augusta *Chronicle* grew more conservative. In general a majority of the papers, even of the weeklies in rural Georgia, tended to oppose Talmadge and some favored moderation on the racial issue. Herman Talmadge outlived this animosity and became very popular during the last year of his final term as governor in 1954–55.

An exception among the city dailies was the conservative Savannah *Morning News*, whose publisher, the aged Herschel Jenkins, favored both Talmadges consistently. This paper relegated political news to the back page. It was very popular among whites in southeastern Georgia, where the liberalism of the Atlanta papers was not well received.

Several newspapers owned by Negroes and designed for a black readership were published during this period. One of them, the Atlanta *World*, has prospered.

Static and Dynamic Georgia

The total population of the state in 1960 was 3,943,116, an increase of about one-half million since 1950. Figure 2 reveals the contours of the black belt of heaviest black population. The dimensions of the black belt fall clearly between a North Georgia area of sparse

Figure 2

NEGROES AS A PERCENTAGE OF GEORGIA POPULATION AND
COUNTY POPULATION BY THOUSANDS, 1960

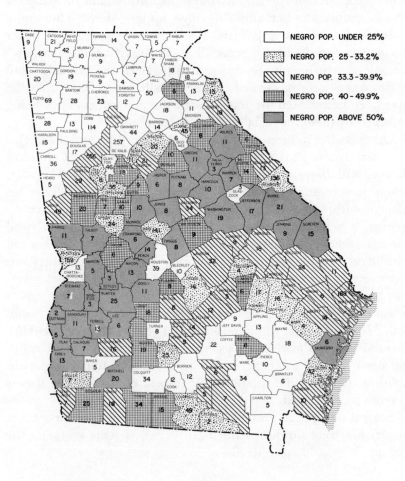

Negro population which spans the area from east (South Carolina) to west (Alabama) and from Tennessee and North Carolina to Fulton County (Atlanta) and dips below Atlanta on the east. Some counties of North Georgia, such as Fannin and Dawson, had no blacks at all. Another contiguous area which is composed of counties in which Negro population was under 25 percent is found in the southeast. This group includes eleven counties, not so large as the area of North Georgia, which numbers thirty-eight counties.

The black belt includes most of what was once plantation country, cotton acreage tilled by slaves and ruled by the slavocracy. Above the fall line it is an area full of red clay hills; below the fall line it has multicolored soils, increasingly sandy as it approaches the sea coast. Wiregrass abounds here. Both south and middle Georgia are covered with long-leaf pine trees. The area west of the Flint River has been characterized in the modern period by the most determined opposition to Negro voting (see Figure 3). This hostility is in sharp contrast to attitudes in the group of counties stretching from Savannah along the coast to the Florida line, an area where Negro voting began on a large scale in 1946 immediately after the federal courts ended the white primary. In these latter counties Negro blocs have been strongly linked with white officialdom in the courthouses. West of the Flint River this pattern was not tolerated by white opinion and Negro voting was viciously and vigorously suppressed for a number of years.

Figure 4 shows the pattern of population shifts from 1950 to 1970. Of 159 Georgia counties, 83, or slightly more than half, mostly the smaller agricultural counties, lost population in spite of the state increase of over one million (or about 28 percent) during the period. Georgia, like many states, has a declining agricultural population, less emphasis on cotton, more on beef cattle, and a flourishing industry of chickens and turkeys (in the northern part of the state). Another 22 counties showed very small gains, less than 10 percent. The figure shows that with the exception of Dougherty County and Albany, a commercial town and distribution center in southwestern Georgia, the other 10 counties showing gains of more than 100 percent during these two decades were in suburban areas

Figure 3

NEGROES AS A PERCENTAGE OF GEORGIA REGISTERED VOTERS, 1952,
AND POPULATION BY COUNTIES, 1950

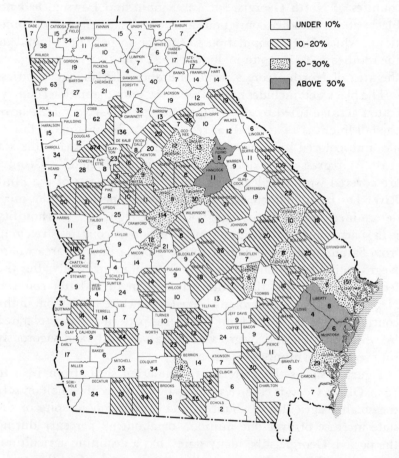

adjacent to the major cities. Cobb (home of Lockheed aircraft),
Douglas, Clayton, DeKalb, Rockdale, and Gwinnett counties are
participating in the burgeoning of Atlanta, the premier city of the
southeastern United States. Chattahoochee County near Columbus,
Houston County near Macon, and Liberty County near Savannah
are the sites of major military installations: Fort Benning in Chat-

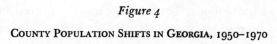

Figure 4

COUNTY POPULATION SHIFTS IN GEORGIA, 1950–1970

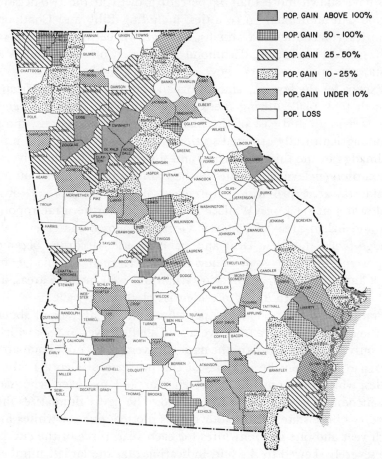

tahoochee, Warner Robins Air Force Base in Houston, and Camp Stewart in Liberty. Columbia County is close to Augusta, Camp Gordon, the Savannah River, and the Clark Hill Reservoir on the river which separates Georgia and South Carolina.

The middle section of the state, comprising part of the black belt, is a major area of declining population. Northwest Georgia, adjacent to Chattanooga, Tennessee, contains a bloc of counties of significant population growth. In all Georgia only 34 of 159 counties have shown more than 25 percent growth in the two-decade period. An additional 20 counties, including Bibb and Chatham counties (Macon and Savannah), have grown between 10 and 25 percent. Muscogee and Richmond counties (Columbus and Augusta) are in the category above 25 percent growth.

Except for the few city and suburban counties where significant growth took place during these two decades, the black belt and the area south and east of the black belt were the poorest, most rural, agriculturally oriented sections. This is *static* Georgia, pro-Talmadge in the thirties, forties, and fifties except for the Rivers-Thompson enclave of counties in the Lanier and Lowndes County (Valdosta) area, pro–white supremacy, pro-Griffin in 1954, pro-Goldwater in 1964, pro-Wallace in 1968. The northern metropolitan and urban areas of *dynamic* Georgia opposed the elder Talmadge when the New Deal and gubernatorial decorum became important issues in 1936. They opposed Herman Talmadge in 1948 and 1950. In 1954, Marvin Griffin did well in these areas, as did George Wallace in the presidential election of 1968.

Static Georgia in 1960 had a per capita income average of about $1,100 compared with a state average of slightly over $1,600, which was only about two-thirds of the national average. Figure 5 compares for 1950 and 1960 the incomes of the universe of Georgia adult males, white and nonwhite, fourteen years old and over, who had net income or loss for the year specified. The figure dramatizes the poverty of the state. Of the four curves plotted, one for whites for each year and one for nonwhites for each year, three of the curves are severely skewed to the left, indicating that the largest number of persons in the three categories had incomes at the lower end of the scale. Those are whites for 1950 and nonwhites for 1950 and for 1960. Only in the case of whites for 1960 is there evidence of a higher peak to the right center ($4,000 to $4,999) and of a consistency to the right which shows that almost as many white males received above $4,000 income as received less than $4,000. Of the

Figure 5

INCOME LEVELS OF MALES 14 YEARS OLD AND OVER
IN GEORGIA, 1950 AND 1960

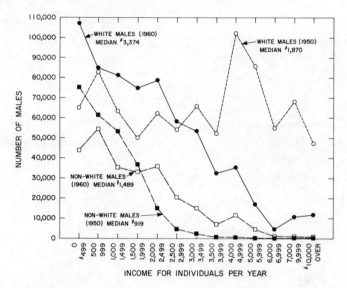

860,000 white males in Georgia fourteen and older who had income or loss, 48.2 percent had an income in 1960 above $4,000.[12]

The figure reveals the growth of income in the decade but even more starkly does it portray the poverty of the nonwhites, who in 1960 made significantly less than did the whites even ten years earlier. The curves and the recorded figures for median incomes for the four categories depict the increasing disparity of whites and nonwhites in the economic sphere. The disparity is national in scope, and in Georgia, where the level of income has been only about 65 percent of the national average for all population elements, the plight of the blacks is exceptionally painful. The median income for nonwhites shows an increase of $570 for the decade, approxi-

[12] *1960 Census of Population: Georgia* (Washington, D.C.: U.S. Department of Commerce, 1961), Table 67, pp. 12–209.

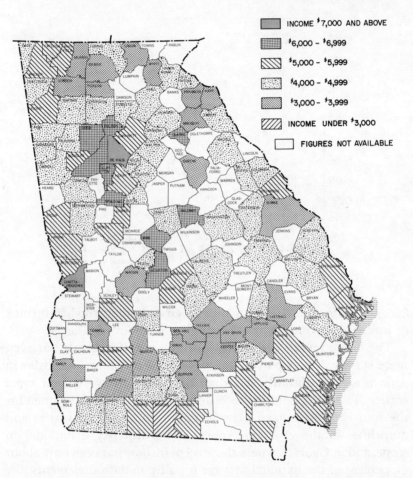

mating the increase in the cost of living during the period. For
whites, on the other hand, the increase was $1,504. Thus the in-
crease among nonwhite males was only 37.9 percent of the increase
among white males.

Figure 6 depicts the regional aspect of family income in Georgia for 1959. As might be expected, the two areas with family income in excess of $7,000 are suburban DeKalb County in the Atlanta area and Chattahoochee County, the site of Fort Benning. Fulton, Cobb, and Clayton counties in the Atlanta area have family incomes between $6,000 and $7,000, as do Bibb County (Macon), Baldwin County (Milledgeville), Houston County (Warner Robins), Spalding County (Griffin), and Clarke County (Athens, home of the University of Georgia).

Elsewhere there is relatively greater prosperity in the smaller cities of Floyd County (Rome) and Dougherty County (Albany), as in other counties in the greater Atlanta area (Gwinnett, Douglas), in Muscogee (Columbus), in Richmond (Augusta), along the coast in Chatham County (Savannah) as well as in Glynn and Camden counties, and in Catoosa County, near Chattanooga, Tennessee. Southern Georgia appears poorer, perhaps because it is more rural and also because its city counties (Dougherty, Lowndes, Thomas, Ware, and Chatham) are less prosperous than the cities and suburbs in middle and northern Georgia.

How can these economic patterns be related to voting behavior? In the period of bifactionalism when the major political battles were contested in the Democratic primary, the coalition of high- and middle-income dwellers in the cities and the larger towns and of the blacks wherever found tended to align against the poor whites.[13] This pattern reemerged in 1962 and thereafter. But the higher-income white suburbanites, less extreme on the racial issue than low-income whites, tended to be Republican. In 1964 they voted for Goldwater, in 1966 for Callaway, in 1968 for Nixon (when George Wallace won the lower-income white voters). In 1970, these progressive whites voted for Hal Suit in the Republican primary and were sorely missed by Carl Sanders in the Democratic primary.

---

[13] Probably a majority of high-income whites voted against the Talmadges before 1956 but leaders in the textile manufacturing, electric power, and other major industries often supported them. See Key, *Southern Politics*, 116–17. See also Joseph L. Bernd, "The Role of Campaign Funds in Georgia Primary Elections," *Georgia Journal*, XVII (1958), 1–15. Talmadge favored low taxes, a balanced budget, and businessmen's views in general.

Bifactionalism at White Heat: 1947 and 1948

In the 1946 gubernatorial primary the county-unit rule gave victory to Eugene Talmadge, although he actually received over 16,000 fewer popular votes than his chief foe, James V. Carmichael. Talmadge carried 105 counties with 242 unit votes, Carmichael obtained 44 counties with 146 unit votes, and former Governor E. D. Rivers carried 10 counties with 22 unit votes. But Eugene Talmadge became ill not long after his primary election victory. On December 21, 1946, he died.

Fearful that the loss of their champion would rob them of victory's fruits, the Talmadgeites, in the general election of November, 1946, cast a number of write-in votes for Herman Talmadge, the son of "Ole Gene." The constitution provided that if no person received a majority of votes in the general election, the General Assembly could elect a governor from the three persons having the highest number of votes.[14] Talmadge leaders reasoned that the General Assembly could elect the son to replace his dead father, if Herman received enough write-in ballots to become one of the three persons with the highest total of votes in the general election.

The constitution provided that the lieutenant governor should perform the duties of the governor in case of the death or disability of the latter, but it was silent as to the role of the lieutenant governor–elect in case of the death of the governor-elect.[15] Another constitutional provision stated that the governor should continue in office until his successor was chosen and qualified.[16] Governor Ellis Arnall interpreted this provision to mean that he was required to remain in office until the next general election in 1948, or until a legally qualified successor could be sworn in. He reasoned that death had removed his only legally qualified successor and he did not believe the General Assembly could properly choose a governor, since Eugene Talmadge had been "elected." An official opinion of the state attorney general, Eugene Cook, agreed with Arnall. Arnall

14 *Georgia Laws, 1945,* p. 31.
15 *Ibid.*, 32.
16 *Ibid.*, 31.

did, however, make it clear that he would resign in favor of the lieutenant governor, M. E. Thompson, as soon as that official had taken the oath of office. This procedure, Arnall thought, was conformable to the intent of the lawmakers, who had only recently created the office of lieutenant governor.

Pro-Talmadge forces in the General Assembly, masterminded by former Speaker of the House Roy V. Harris,[17] "elected" Herman Talmadge governor early in 1947 and they seized the executive offices by force. Talmadge thus held de facto control of the state executive for sixty-seven days while the legal question of his title to the governorship was decided in the state courts.

The Georgia Supreme Court, on March 17, 1947, rendered a decision in favor of Lieutenant Governor M. E. Thompson, in whose favor Arnall had resigned after Thompson had been sworn in. The reasoning of the court's majority closely followed the line of argument which had been advanced by Governor Arnall and Attorney General Cook. Five members of the court supported the majority ruling and two dissented.

Under the impetus of the Talmadge-Harris leadership, the General Assembly, prior to the court's decision, sought to restore the white Democratic primary by repealing all laws (including the county-unit provisions) which regulated the primary. Their hope was to restore the white primary by divorcing it from any color of "state action," but in doing so they found it necessary to repeal the laws protecting the primary against fraud. Another measure passed by the General Assembly under Talmadge-Harris leadership outlawed the closed shop. When Thompson succeeded Talmadge as acting governor, following the ruling by the state Supreme Court, he vetoed the white primary legislation and signed the closed shop bill. Some analysts have argued that Thompson might have fared better if he had signed the white primary legislation into law and vetoed the anti–labor union measure. He would, they say, have won more labor support in his 1948 bid for reelection and the fed-

17 Harris, following his break with Governor Ellis Arnall, had been defeated for reelection to the General Assembly. Harris had led the fight against the legal measures which would have permitted Arnall to run for reelection to the governorship in 1946.

eral courts would have nullified the effort to bar Negroes from the primary wherein they would have supported Thompson against Talmadge. This reasoning is probably false. The altered policy would have meant less Negro and liberal support for Thompson and probably not much more from organized labor, whose white rank and file were captivated by Talmadge's fervor on the race issue. Emotionalism ruled the day. One significant advantage did accrue to Thompson. After the Supreme Court ruled in his favor, the General Assembly failed to pass an appropriations bill. Thompson, as governor, was able to spend money by executive order and to enjoy increasing revenues and flexibility in their expenditure.

The legal dispute over the governorship was followed by court action over control of the state Democratic Party machinery. Here Talmadge won.[18] Party control for the Talmadgeites meant control of the delegation to the July, 1948, Democratic National Convention. On the convention floor they were active in the bitter fight against a strong civil rights statement in the platform. This was the controversy which preceded the walkout of Alabama and Mississippi delegates and led to the formation of the States' Rights Democrats, or "Dixiecrat" Party. Georgia delegates, facing an intense fight for the governorship in the September primary, did not bolt the convention, but there was little doubt that the sentiments of the pro-Talmadge delegation lay with the insurgents. The pro-Talmadge Georgia delegation supported Senator Richard B. Russell for the presidential nomination, which ultimately went to President Truman. Charles J. Bloch placed Russell's name in nomination and he received almost solid backing from the southern delegates in the convention. (In 1952 Russell was again a candidate for the presidential nomination, which went ultimately to Adlai Stevenson.)

In the primary two months later Talmadge appealed for states' rights and white supremacy in opposition to "Yankee meddling and a federal civil rights program." [19] Important support came from friends of Senator Russell. Under Thompson's administration the

18 *Morris v. Peters,* 203 Ga. 350 (1948). Charles J. Bloch, a Macon attorney, achieved this brilliant victory for Talmadge.

19 Atlanta *Constitution,* July 4, 11, 18, 1948.

state purchased Jekyll Island for $675,000. Talmadge attacked the purchase as a waste of state funds. Jekyll is one of the "Golden Isles" near Brunswick, Georgia. Twenty years after the purchase, Jekyll is a vacation land of unique charm with relatively inexpensive motels, restaurants, and shops on land leased from Georgia. The isle may be the most enduring memorial to the Thompson administration.

Thompson also stated his opposition to a federal civil rights program, but he had received many Negro votes in his race for lieutenant governor in 1946, and he had vetoed the white primary bill. The principal appeal of Thompson was based on his record in office. Heavy emphasis was placed on road-building and other state services, but these lures, which had won many a county for anti-Talmadge candidacies in the past, could not compete with the appeal of Talmadge. In 1948 racial feeling far outweighed economic considerations among the majority of voters.

The gubernatorial primary was held September 8, 1948. Herman Talmadge received 357,865 popular votes (51.8 percent). He carried 130 counties with 312 county-unit votes. Thompson received 312,035 popular votes (45.1 percent) and carried only 29 counties with 98 county-unit votes. Three minor candidates polled slightly more than 21,000 votes and did not affect the outcome. Talmadge carried all congressional districts except two, the Fifth (primarily Atlanta) and the Seventh in the northwest corner of the state.

The magnitude of the Talmadge victory was due first to the powerful appeal of the white supremacy issue among white voters, particularly those in the lower-income categories, both rural and urban. But the Talmadge campaign was well organized and well financed. The candidate had an attractive personality and was an effective speaker. His staunch supporters were highly motivated because of their feeling that the decision by the Georgia Supreme Court, denying Talmadge the office of governor in the previous year, had thwarted the popular will. Talmadge also enjoyed the organizational skills of prominent leaders formerly identified with the opposition—Roy Harris, Jim L. Gillis, Marvin Griffin, and a majority of local bosses and courthouse crowds. In comparison with the campaigns of Eugene Talmadge, Herman Talmadge in 1948 had very little in the way of a public record and few personal enemies. These were major advantages.

Thompson too was well financed and enjoyed support from traditional anti-Talmadge sources: Negroes; the so-called better element of bourgeois voters, chiefly in the cities and towns; pockets of traditional anti-Talmadgeism in many counties; the mountain labor vote in the textile industry of northwest Georgia. In addition he was able to spend state funds with emphasis and effect in a few counties where leadership and voters were receptive to his largess and willing to reciprocate for favors received: Gilmer, Screven, McIntosh, and Long counties, which had rather consistently supported Eugene Talmadge in the past.

In the 1948 presidential race, Georgians, unlike Alabamians, Louisianians, Mississippians, and South Carolinians, had a chance to vote for President Harry S. Truman under the Democratic Party label in his bid for reelection. This occurred only because Acting Governor M. E. Thompson called a special session of the General Assembly to insure that Truman electors were on the ballot. In other Deep South states the States' Rights Democratic electors supporting J. Strom Thurmond were placed on the ballot under the Democratic Party label.

The results of the election in Georgia were as follows:

Harry S. Truman (Democrat):	254,646
Thomas E. Dewey (Republican):	76,691
J. Strom Thurmond (States' Rights Democrat):	85,055
Henry A. Wallace (Progressive):	1,636[20]

The showing for Thurmond was disappointing to his backers. A number of prominent political leaders, including Roy Harris and Charles Bloch, had supported the Dixiecrats. The mood of the state as evident in the September primary, in which Herman had swept to victory on the issue of white supremacy, seemed to augur ill for Truman in Georgia. But the election returns showed that the mystique of the party was still powerful among rural Georgians.

20 The National Prohibition Party received 732 votes.

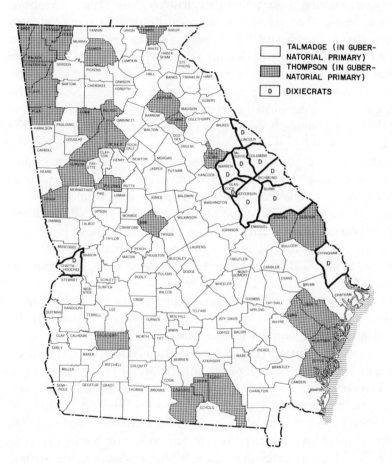

Figure 7

TALMADGEITES AND DIXIECRATS: GUBERNATORIAL PRIMARY AND
PRESIDENTIAL ELECTION IN GEORGIA, 1948

Thurmond carried only ten counties. His voting percentage was
20.3 percent. (See Figure 7.) True, former Governor Ellis Arnall
had campaigned actively for the Truman ticket and had predicted
its victory, but in light of the polls showing Dewey far ahead, few
took Arnall seriously. Almost no one imagined the extent of the
Truman sweep in the state. Except for a bloc of eight counties near

the Savannah River (adjacent to Governor Thurmond's home area in Aiken, South Carolina, and also in the home area of Augustan Roy Harris, whose political reputation was at a peak following the Talmadge victory in the September primary), the Thurmond showing was feeble. The result illustrated a phrase someone coined to describe rural Georgians: "They are 1,420-day anti-Democrats and 1-day Democrats. They holler for white supremacy and damn the national Democratic Party every day for four years. On the one day of leap year—the Tuesday after the first Monday in November—they go to the polls, and vote for the Democratic national ticket or else they stay at home because they cannot bring themselves to vote against *the party.*"

A comparative analysis of the 1948 gubernatorial primary and the presidential election of that year reveals a fairly strong correlation between Talmadgeism in the primary and support for the States' Rights Democrats in the presidential election. All ten of the counties carried for Thurmond were Talmadge counties in the primary. In eight of them young Talmadge won majorities of more than two to one. Talmadge carried thirty-eight of the forty counties in the highest quartile of Dixiecrat support.

There is less correlation between anti-Talmadgeism and anti-Dixiecratism. Thompson carried ten of the forty counties in the lowest quartile of support for the States' Rights ticket. Several of Thompson's mountain counties showed considerable Republican strength, indicating that all of the anti-Dixiecrat sentiment was not pro-Truman. The division in the presidential election, however, has a clearly regional weighting. Thirty-five of the forty counties in Thurmond's lowest quartile were above the fall line. The fact that thirty of them were in the Fourth, Seventh, and Ninth Congressional Districts indicates that the sectional opposition was strongest both southwest (the Fourth) and north of Atlanta.

County-Unit Rule Saves Another Talmadge

The tide of popularity which in 1948 swept young Talmadge into office began to recede soon after he became governor. Among other difficult problems, the governor faced a financial impasse. Either increased revenue must be secured or state services would have to be curtailed. Promising not to increase taxes without a referendum, Talmadge asked the legislature to permit a vote on taxes. In April, 1949, the voters opposed a tax increase by a margin of three to one. By summer the fiscal problem had become acute, and Talmadge called a special session of the General Assembly to ask for increased taxes on cigarettes, gasoline, and hunting and fishing licenses.[21] Although the levies were moderate, the implied promise to abide by the popular referendum had been broken by the son of the man who had, with pride, borne the name "the promise-keeper."

Another source of unpopularity with his backers was Talmadge's failure to find a workable means of preventing or restricting Negro voting. Federal courts had invalidated the attempt by South Carolina to bar blacks from the polls by making the Democratic primary a "private club" affair.[22] In Alabama a vague literacy test had been voided.[23] In Georgia the General Assembly tried to solve the problems by requiring a complete reregistration of all voters and by testing them on reading and writing or answering a set of objective questions.[24] But these tests hit white persons as well as Negroes. Many voters resented the necessity of reregistration, and the heavy expenses of the procedures caused hardship in the counties.[25]

But in early 1950 several events strengthened the position of Talmadge. Most importantly, his foes failed to center upon a strong candidate to oppose him. M. E. Thompson appeared determined to run, but Thompson had been decisively defeated in 1948, and an investigation by the Talmadge administration of illegal liquor operations which had occurred during the Thompson administration upset his drive for support during a crucial stage of the pre-

[21] *Georgia Laws, 1949*, pp. 2132–34; *Georgia Laws, 1949*, Special Session, Sec. 5–23.
[22] *Elmore v. Rice*, 72 F. Supp. 516 (1947).
[23] *Davis v. Schnell*, 81 F. Supp. 872 (1949).
[24] *Georgia Laws, 1949*, pp. 1204–27.
[25] According to Roy V. Harris, who no longer dominated the Talmadge councils, the governor suffered most from his failure to keep engagements in his office and elsewhere. It was rumored that Talmadge had been drinking heavily. Apparently Talmadge quickly reformed because such claims have not been continued.

primary maneuvering.[26] Talmadge influence in the legislature secured postponement of the new voter registration act.[27] An early date was set for the primary election so that it might be held before the monetary problem of the administration became really severe.[28]

After the formal campaign began, Thompson developed surprising strength among the voters. Talmadge spoke for increased road-building, teacher salaries, and other expanded services, but he did not explain how these measures would be financed. Thompson, by contrast, spoke for a 2 percent sales tax and attacked the Talmadge record vigorously. In a popular vote contest he probably would have won, but under the unit system he faced virtually insurmountable odds. His financial support was meager, while that of Talmadge was more than ample. Most of the influential local leaders were supporting Talmadge. Former Governor E. D. Rivers and many of the men who had followed Rivers in their support of Thompson in 1948 were now in the Talmadge camp. On June 28, 1950, Talmadge won with 287,637 popular votes (49.4 percent), carrying 124½ counties (Atkinson was a tie) with 295 county-unit votes. Thompson received 279,137 popular votes (47.9 percent) and carried 34½ counties worth 115 county-unit votes. Three minor candidates received 16,000 votes and carried no counties.

In terms of counties carried and unit votes won, Thompson's showing was only slightly better than it had been in 1948. However, Talmadge lacked a popular majority. Thompson had led for a long time on election night in popular totals and until what Jack Tarver of the Atlanta *Constitution* called "the morning after scramble on the part of the State's 'kept counties' to get right." [29] The contests in a large number of counties had been extremely close.

Organizational factors appear to have been decisive in 1950.

26 Atlanta *Constitution*, October 19, 1949. The results of the investigation were legally barren: no indictment.

27 *Georgia Laws, 1950*, pp. 126–31.

28 *Ibid.*, 79–84. The Georgia Constitution bars a governor from succeeding himself after a full four-year term. Talmadge was declared eligible by the attorney general on the grounds that he had served only an interim term of two years.

29 Atlanta *Constitution*, June 30, 1950.

Thompson lacked the funds and the personal support of major leaders which he had enjoyed in 1948. Although the crusading zeal had gone out of the Talmadge forces and their candidate was vulnerable, the Thompson candidacy probably lost largely because it was expected to lose. The powerful lure of the bandwagon is exceptionally effective when each county outcome is determined on a winner-take-all basis and a governor is able, willing, and determined to reward loyal supporters with material advantages. (The Georgia governor is exceptionally powerful in controlling patronage and state purchases because he appoints key officials such as the purchasing agent and the revenue commissioner. The governor is ex-officio director of the budget.) In county after county E. D. Rivers persuaded local leaders to back Talmadge. "You know I would be with M. E. if he had a chance," Rivers was quoted as saying. Thus for almost every county which Thompson won over by his vigorous and forthright campaign against a vulnerable opponent, Rivers' influence caused a switch in the other direction in each county where he enjoyed powerful connections. As a former governor, a sponsor of Thompson, and his principal campaign director in 1948, Rivers was in an ideal position to maximize his influence.

Atlanta on the Winning Side for Once

In 1949 the General Assembly passed a constitutional amendment which provided for the application and use of the county-unit system in general elections.[30] The proposal applied to the election of the governor, United States senators, and statehouse officials. The Talmadge administration devoted its energies to securing ratification of the amendment by the voters in the general election of 1950. Opposition came from a committee formed to fight the measure and from DeWitt H. Roberts and other leaders who had backed Thompson in the 1950 primary. On November 7, 1950, the amendment was defeated by a margin of about thirty thousand popular votes.[31]

Talmadge forces explained away the defeat. The campaign in

30 *Georgia Laws, 1949*, pp. 528–32.
31 *Georgia Official and Statistical Register, 1951–1952*, p. 474.

favor of the proposal had not been well organized. Administration
influence was generally weak at this time because of the scarcity of
state funds. Inclement weather had discouraged voting in rural
areas. The legal provisions of the amendment plan had not been
well understood. Talmadge's newspaper confidently predicted passage of a new proposal to strengthen the unit system, and it called for
a campaign to educate the public as to the need for the measure.[32]

In 1951 the General Assembly passed an amendment somewhat
similar to the earlier one.[33] It provided that aspirants for state offices must be nominated in a county-unit primary in order to become
eligible for the general election ballot. The Talmadge administration, now fortified with the revenues derived from a newly enacted
3 percent sales tax, conducted an intensive campaign to secure ratification. They were supported by the same political groups which
had backed the renomination of Talmadge in 1950. Ed Rivers and
most of his South Georgia following again joined Roy Harris, Jim
Gillis, and Marvin Griffin in the administration camp.[34]

The Committee Against the County Unit Amendment, headed
by former United States District Judge Neill Andrews, included
M. E. Thompson, John W. Greer, and Osgood Williams, who were
leaders in Thompson's 1950 campaign, and others. A number of
newspapers, some of which had failed to back Thompson in 1950,
opposed the amendment. A large number of civic groups, which
were usually nonpartisan in purely factional competition involving
personalities, contributed important support to the opposition.
Among these associations were the Junior Chamber of Commerce
and the League of Women Voters. Leaders of organized labor were
active in opposition to the amendment.[35]

Supporters of the amendment argued that the county-unit system protected the state against political machines because it divided

---

32 Atlanta *Statesman*, November 16, 1950.

33 *Georgia Laws, 1951,* pp. 101–107.

34 Atlanta *Constitution*, November 2, 3, 1952.

35 *Georgia Journal*, October 28, 1952. Andrews had been a victim of senatorial courtesy. Appointed a federal judge by Truman as a favor to his Georgia supporters,
Andrews was rejected for the nomination by the United States Senate because he was
not favored by Senators Richard B. Russell and Walter F. George.

them up at the county lines. Some spokesmen suggested that city voters include sinister and subversive elements: Negroes, Yankee influences, labor unions, agents of the Soviet Union, Catholics, and Jews. They stressed the protection which the amendment would afford by giving the county-unit system constitutional status and by requiring county-unit nomination as a prerequisite to candidacy in the general election.[36] The abusive rhetoric provoked the ire of several Protestant ministers, including the president of the Southern Baptist Convention.[37]

The amendment was defeated only because the decision was based on popular rather than county-unit votes. Altogether, 121 counties, including most of those in the two-unit-vote class, supported the amendment. Opposing it were 38 counties, including all of the city counties. Despite large pro-amendment majorities in South Georgia areas which had formerly backed anti-Talmadge candidacies, the amendment failed to carry in many rural precincts in middle and upper Georgia, where Talmadge had usually won. Although the turnout of voters was much heavier than in 1950, the proposal was defeated by almost the same margin—thirty thousand votes.

A major factor in the defeat of the amendment was the legalistic nature of the controversy. Talmadge noted that it was easier to sell his candidacy to the voters than it was to sell law. Foes of the amendment realized that many voters were still confused as to the exact legal significance of the proposal. "If you are in favor of the county unit system as it now stands, but you don't want it changed," they counseled, "vote against the amendment." This advice, when offered by polling officials, was very effective.

More than one hundred thousand dollars was spent in support of the amendment; probably not more than twenty thousand dollars was spent in opposition to its passage.[38] Under the unit rule, where

---

[36] See the Atlanta *Statesman*, September 11, October 16, 23, 30, 1952.

[37] Atlanta *Constitution*, October 23, 26, 1952.

[38] *Ibid.*, November 3, 1952. Anti-amendment publicity efforts received aid of incalculable value from the daily newspapers, many of which were opposed to ratification. Here was support which helped to counterbalance the financial disadvantage. It was, moreover, support which money could not buy.

a heavy premium is placed upon the purchase of influential support in small counties, a candidate with only one dollar to spend for his opponent's five dollars is wasting his time.

In 1952 under the popular system the majority cast against the amendment in Fulton County almost tripled the vote cast for the amendment in fifty small counties. Under the unit rule the vote of Fulton would have been overmatched 106 unit votes to 6. Figure 8 illustrates the discrepancy in a spatial sense. This figure also includes the even more dramatic contrast offered by 1950 returns.

Figure 8
THE POWER OF POPULAR VOTES COMPARED
WITH THE POWER OF COUNTY-UNIT VOTES
IN GEORGIA, 1950 AND 1952

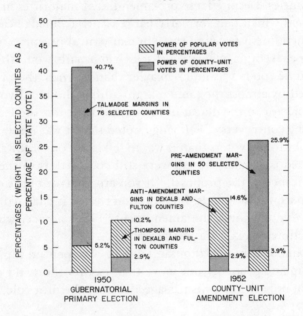

Coup de Grace to Bifactionalism

Herman Talmadge was constitutionally prohibited from running in the 1954 Democratic primary for governor, but his record and personality nevertheless dominated the contest. State revenue had more than doubled as a result of the sales tax, and Talmadge was proving to be a capable administrator in applying the funds. Public schools made great progress with financing of the Minimum Foundation Program for Education, and road-building and other state services received conspicuous benefits. Talmadge's championing of southern rights at the 1952 Democratic National Convention brought him increased support among the home folks.

In 1954, for the first time in a quarter of a century, the Talmadge name was not on the ballot in a major Georgia primary. Under these circumstances, it was not surprising that a quarrel over the gubernatorial succession should occur within the Talmadge faction. Ironically, most of the principals in this dispute were men who had joined the faction in 1946. It did not include the old-timers who had been consistently loyal to "Ole Gene." Marvin Griffin had announced as a candidate for governor in 1946. When his chances appeared unfavorable, he ran for lieutenant governor and was defeated in a close contest. Running again for lieutenant governor in 1948, he was nominated and elected. Griffin was well known and popular throughout the state, but he was regarded with disfavor by other important Talmadge lieutenants. Roy Harris, Highway Department Chairman Jim Gillis, Speaker of the House of Representatives Fred Hand, Speaker Pro Tem George Smith II, and Commissioner of Agriculture Tom Linder were active leaders in the anti-Griffin movement.[39]

In 1953 these leaders, joined by Rivers, Arnall, and Thompson, united behind Jim Gillis. In early 1954 the alignment was broken when Hand announced his own candidacy. Within a week Thompson entered the race. Three months later Linder entered the lists. Marvin Griffin remained determined to be a candidate; Roy Harris offered his managerial talents to the candidacy of Hand; and Gillis was effectively active in behalf of Linder. With the Talmadge faction split three ways, Thompson, who had shown surprising

---

[39] Linder, a long-time Talmadge man, had not been consistently loyal, for he had supported Ellis Arnall in 1942.

strength on shoestring financing in 1950, appeared likely to win. Arnall and Rivers backed Thompson, who also claimed many "Talmadge men who are supporting me for the first time."

But weaknesses of a fundamental nature were inherent in the anti-Talmadge faction, and the pressure of events weakened the Thompson candidacy decisively at the very moment it appeared headed for victory. The Atlanta daily newspapers had exposed the scandals of the second Rivers administration and had vigorously combated the influence of the former governor. When it became known that a major backer of Thompson was John Horace Bowen, the papers reprinted all of the charges concerning his sales of liquor in dry counties during the previous Thompson administration. The papers made clear their lack of confidence in any candidate who accepted major support from Rivers and Bowen.[40] Since Griffin, an alleged participant in the "pardoning racket" of the Rivers administration, was ill-regarded by the Atlanta dailies, they offered their support to Speaker of the House of Representatives Fred Hand. Linder, a long-time state commissioner of agriculture, was not seriously considered by these newspapers. The press attacks on Thompson and Griffin were of substantially equal intensity, but the damage to the former was greater. The urban and "better-element" centers of his support were subject much more to the influence of the newspapers than were the white supremacy–minded backers of Griffin.

The Thompson dilemma contained facets of even more fundamental difficulty. To win he must regain the support of the county courthouse crowds, which had not backed an anti-Talmadge candidate in anything like full force since the campaign of 1942. These men and their followings were essentially conservative. For a decade they had been conditioned to support the Talmadges and white supremacy. Thompson had been the candidate of the Negroes, the urbanites, and the "better element." To win conservative support, he found it necessary to turn away from his traditional posture. In 1951 and 1952 he had denounced the county-unit system in unequivocal language. Now in order to win conservative financial and

40 Atlanta *Journal*, July 4, August 17, 1954.

ballot support he promised not to disturb the unit plan either by abolition or revision; he would leave it just as he found it.[41]

The problem of the Negro rose once more to plague the anti-Talmadgeites. In 1953 the General Assembly had passed the so-called private school amendment, authorizing the state to make tuition payments in fulfillment of its educational obligations.[42] The amendment was sponsored by Governor Talmadge and was offered in anticipation of the invalidation of the "equal and separate" principle of education. When racial segregation in public school education was invalidated by the United States Supreme Court on May 17, 1954 (*Brown v. Board of Education of Topeka*), the racial question, never far from the center of the stage, became once more the dominant theme of Georgia political life. Although the private school amendment was unpopular with many of the traditional elements of anti-Talmadgeism, Thompson declined to take a vigorous stand against it. He believed that Herman Talmadge would like to remain aloof from a campaign which featured an important division among his friends. If Thompson made an issue of the amendment, however, Talmadge might be compelled to defend his principles and to use his considerable influence in behalf of Griffin, who was supporting the amendment and who was regarded as the strongest candidate in the Talmadge faction. All of the major candidates, meanwhile, stated their preference for segregated schools.

For a time the anti-Griffin strategy appeared to succeed. The Linder candidacy caused consternation in the Griffin camp. Linder's strength was greatest among traditional Talmadge supporters. As commissioner of agriculture, he had maintained close ties with rural white voters. He was able to muster financial and organizational support by virtue of his state office. Thompson, meanwhile, subordinated all differences of opinion with the traditional foe and capitalized on the three-way division of the Talmadge faction. The bandwagon psychology brought him ample campaign funds and major support from many dominant local leaders.

[41] Macon *Telegraph*, February 10, 26, 1954.
[42] *Georgia Laws, 1953*, pp. 241–42.

But the disadvantages of the Thompson situation were too pronounced to remain permanently obscured. Charles Gowen had been
the first aspirant to announce for the gubernatorial nomination.
Gowen was a veteran legislator, identified with the anti-Talmadge
group, but he had never been a candidate for a state office and was
little known among the voters. Thompson backers sought to persuade Gowen to withdraw and support Thompson. When these efforts failed, the directors of the Thompson campaign still hoped that
the Gowen campaign would remain a minor irritant, rather than
the cause of a major division in factional strength. Their worst
fears were realized during the final weeks of the campaign. Gowen
conducted a series of around-the-clock radio programs (with some
TV) called "talkathons," in which he talked with the public and
answered questions.[43] The talkathons were effective, not merely because of the advantages offered by the vehicle of communication, but
also because of the appeal of the candidate. Gowen said things which
many urban voters wanted to hear. He vigorously attacked the suggestion that the public schools must be closed to protect segregation,
and he offered as an alternative a plan for pupil placement under
administrative discretion. Gowen made a direct appeal for Negro
votes. His appeal was primarily directed toward counties and groups
of voters, Negroes and the "better element," who had been anti-
Talmadge with regularity. As a result, the Gowen effort was directly
injurious to the Thompson campaign.

Griffin, meanwhile, praised Talmadge as "Georgia's greatest governor," and he alone of the major candidates gave unqualified support to the governor's private school amendment. He stood for
"Georgia's two greatest traditions—segregation and the county unit
system." He drew the support of labor with promises of specific

---

[43] Thompsonites had anticipated the talkathons, and they tried to beat Gowen to
the punch with a series of radio parties, featuring the candidate's reply to questions
from the radio audience. But the "radio parties" were conducted early in the year,
when political interest was low. The Gowen effort featured a fresh personality, un-
tarnished by the scars of incessant attack, and it was timed for the climax of a long,
and often dull, campaign.

benefits. Griffin won the heaviest urban support in spite of the opposition of the Atlanta press, his alleged involvement in the "pardoning racket" under Rivers, and his alleged unsavory support by certain liquor interests.

Some professional political leaders thought that Hand and Linder, despite their identification with Talmadgeism, were taking as many votes from Thompson as from Griffin. Apparently encouraged by this appraisal during the final weeks of the campaign, Talmadge entered actively into the behind-the-scenes drive to line up support for Griffin. Talmadge was convinced that the lieutenant governor was the only candidate with a chance to defeat Thompson.

The outcome was victory for Griffin with a popular plurality of 36 percent and more than three hundred county-unit votes. Thompson won less than 25 percent of the popular vote and he received fifty-six county-unit votes. Gowen, Hand, and Linder each polled between 10.5 percent and 13.5 percent of the popular vote. Linder and Hand each won a handful of county-unit votes. Gowen carried only his home county. Minor candidates Ed Barfield, Ben Garland, Arthur Neeson, and Grace Thomas polled few popular votes and no county-unit votes.[44]

In 1956 the aged and venerable Senator Walter F. George announced his retirement. The action was made necessary when important financial backers withdrew their support of him. George, it was felt, was too old to withstand the challenge of the youthfully vigorous and enormously popular Herman Talmadge. Conservative leaders were confident that Talmadge would provide effective representation in the United States Senate. When his habitual foe, M. E. Thompson, made a belated entrance into the primary, Talmadge carried every county and won more than 80 percent of the popular vote. Senior Senator Richard B. Russell continued to be a figure of high prestige and importance in the upper branch of Congress. But for Georgians, Herman Talmadge remained the dominant figure in

[44] Popular totals: Griffin—234,690; Thompson—162,007; Linder—87,240; Hand—78,125; Gowen—73,809; others—10,364. See Joseph L. Bernd, *Grass Roots Politics in Georgia* (Atlanta: Emory University Research Committee, 1960), 139.

the politics of the state.[45] His faction had reached a low level of prestige and popularity after his father's defeat in 1942. Yet within a short time there had come a metamorphosis. What had occasioned this striking change in the fortunes of Talmadgeism? Most important perhaps had been the influence of the racial issue, but scarcely less significant were the personal qualities of Herman Talmadge himself and that weird institution, the salvation of some and the despair of others, the county-unit system. The era of bifactionalism, whose merit as a mechanism for genuine competition offering voters viable alternatives V. O. Key had discerned, was effectively dead.[46]

An Era of Good Feeling

In the 1958 campaign for the gubernatorial primary nomination Ernest Vandiver, then the lieutenant governor, opposed William T. Bodenhamer, a last-ditch white supremacist from Tift County in South Georgia. Vandiver was the establishment candidate, close personal and political friend of Senator Herman Talmadge and nephew of Senator Russell, choice of the Atlanta and Georgia establishments. Bodenhamer was the candidate of retiring Governor Marvin Griffin, but Griffin, like other governors before him, was not fully able to control the political sentiments of some parts of his administration. By the time of the contest the prestige of the Griffin administration had fallen quite low, partly because of the usual reaction toward a lame-duck governor, and partly because of exposés regarding alleged corruption among some of the governor's close associates. The Bodenhamer campaign was characterized by a rather foul-mouthed racism. Vandiver was a credible advocate of segregation partly because of his association with the Talmadge faction and with Russell. By default he also secured much of the moderate vote. A third candidate, Lee Roy Abernathy, was also named on the ballot.

45 A Talmadge was a candidate for either governor or United States senator ten times during the period 1932–56. About these races swirled the great controversies. By contrast Russell was a distant figure seldom seen on the hustings. After he defeated Eugene Talmadge in 1936, he had only negligible opposition until his death in 1971.
46 Key, *Southern Politics,* 106–12, 128–29.

Vandiver won easily with 499,477 popular votes (80.5 percent) and 400 county-unit votes to Bodenhamer's 87,830 popular votes (14.2 percent) and 10 county-unit votes. Bodenhamer carried only his home county (Tift), the home county of Griffin (Decatur), and Worth County. Abernathy received 33,099 popular votes (5.3 percent) and carried no counties.[47]

The eight-year period from 1954 to 1962 has been termed "the era of good feeling" in Georgia politics, for electoral competition was at a low ebb. The 1954 gubernatorial primary was immediately recognized as the death blow of the anti-Talmadge faction. In the presidential elections of 1952 and 1956 Adlai E. Stevenson carried Georgia by substantial margins over Dwight D. Eisenhower, although the latter polled a substantial vote in the cities and carried several of them. The New Republicanism of the urban South was evident. Eisenhower carried Savannah and Chatham County and Augusta and Richmond County in 1952. In 1956 he carried these two by increased margins and also carried Columbus and Muscogee County. His proportion of the vote in the eleven city counties was 40.5 percent in each year. In 1952 his statewide vote was 30 percent; in 1956 it was 34 percent. Although Eisenhower's name was not on the ballot in 1960, the returns in the presidential election demonstrated the durability of urban southern Republicanism. Nixon lost Georgia to John F. Kennedy by a substantial margin (62.6 percent to 37.4 percent) but Nixon with 48.5 percent almost equaled Kennedy in the eleven city counties of the state. He won the three counties which Eisenhower had carried in 1956, and he lost by a very narrow margin in Atlanta (Fulton and DeKalb counties).[48]

Victory for Moderation

To many observers and participants the Democratic gubernatorial primary of September 12, 1962, seemed to be the beginning of a new political age. The county-unit system was dead. City votes now counted equally with any other votes. One candidate (Marvin Grif-

47 Richard M. Scammon (ed.), *Southern Primaries, 58* (Washington, D.C.: Governmental Affairs Institute, 1959), 17–22.
48 Cities are defined as places with population above 25,000.

fin) seemed to represent the past, the old rural traditions including the preference for the unit rule and white supremacy. His opponent (Carl Sanders) was a racial moderate, a city resident.

Sanders had served in both the state House of Representatives and the Senate. In 1959 he functioned as floor leader and in 1960–62 was president pro tem of the Senate. In 1959 he was named young man of the year by the Augusta Chamber of Commerce.

Griffin's great advantage at the beginning of the 1962 campaign was that he had served as governor from 1955 to 1959 and had held office in state government for most of the previous decade and therefore was *known*. Griffin's public image as a former governor was known to the rank and file of voters, and Griffin himself was widely known personally. He had traveled the social circuit interminably—dinners, barbecues, fish fries in all parts of the state. Griffin's great handicap derived from the investigations of alleged irregularities and exposés arising out of his administration. Various grand juries had named several members of his administration, including his brother, Chaney Griffin. The major daily newspapers of the state fought his candidacy, reprinting everything useful to injure his chances.

Carl Sanders by contrast, although he had been a member of the state Senate, had virtually no public image and was not extremely well known among local political leaders in many parts of the state. The effects of the demise of the county-unit system,[49] however, were immediately evident in Sanders' headquarters. Personal connections in small counties were still important but not nearly so decisive as formerly. Professional public relations people, the image-builders, were in the saddle. They knew that now a vote anywhere counted as much as any other vote, and their candidate, new to the political scene, did not have to remain consistent with an image already established. In Sanders' Atlanta campaign headquarters there was a notable absence of the kind of old political war-horses whom one

---

[49] The decision against the constitutionality of the unit rule had come in the spring of 1962.

was accustomed to find in county-unit election contests.[50] Undoubtedly Sanders' aides devoted some attention to delicate negotiations
with individual local leaders, but the emphasis to an unprecedented
degree was on reaching the mass of voters through the media.

Not so with Griffin. The old-style emphasis on individuals, as well
as the media, remained evident. Griffin continued to emphasize the
old conservative values, opposition to desegregation, support for
"the southern way of life." Sanders was the progressive candidate,
the businessman's candidate. He too favored segregation, but he did
not spend a great deal of time talking about it. The University of
Georgia had already been integrated during the Vandiver administration. Close associates of Senator Herman Talmadge, such as
James S. Peters, chairman of the state Board of Education, had already accepted the inevitability of integration. The leaders of the
Georgia business community accepted the basic premise that violence and racial strife were bad for business. Hardly a single new
industry had moved into Arkansas since Governor Orval Faubus
had confronted the Eisenhower administration in the Little Rock
crisis of 1957.

In the Democratic gubernatorial primary of September 12, 1962,
Sanders received 494,978 votes (58.1 percent) to Griffin's 332,746
(39.0 percent). Three minor candidates split slightly over 24,000
votes. The counties in which principal candidates polled more than
60 percent of the votes are shown in Figure 9. It is evident that the
Griffin strength was confined essentially to the more rural counties,
and his strength was most pronounced in southwestern Georgia,
which is his home area and also the area in which measures to bar
Negro voting have been most successful. Sanders' strongest areas
were the city counties (see Table 1) and North Georgia. He also
won a few rural counties in which Negro voting was heavy (Greene
and McIntosh) or in which local politics revolves around a major

---

50 For a more complete discussion of the "purchase of influence" arrangement to
which the realities of county-unit campaigning contributed so heavily, see Bernd,
Grass Roots Politics in Georgia, 36–56. See also, by the same author, "The Role of
Campaign Funds in Georgia Primary Elections," 1–15.

Figure 9
GUBERNATORIAL PRIMARY IN GEORGIA, 1962

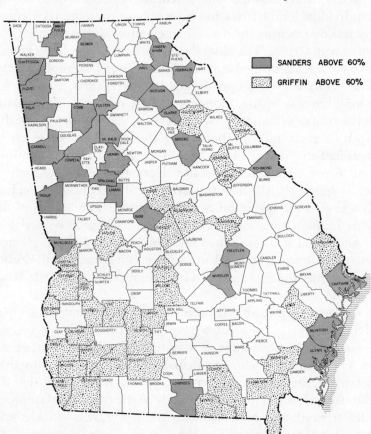

political figure: Henry County (Herman Talmadge), Coweta County (Arnall), Treutlen County (Gillis), and Gilmer County (Cicero Logan).

Table 1 demonstrates that the lion's share of Sanders' strength was located in the eleven city counties. These areas contain 45.4 percent of the population of Georgia (1960 census). In them Sanders garnered 50.4 percent of his statewide vote, while in the same city counties Griffin received only 30.5 percent of his total. Alto-

Table 1
CITY COUNTIES IN THE 1962 GEORGIA GUBERNATORIAL DEMOCRATIC PRIMARY

County	Griffin	Sanders	1960 Population
Bibb (Macon)	12,953	19,882	141,249
Chatham (Savannah)	11,649	21,179	188,299
Clarke (Athens)	1,989	6,442	45,363
Cobb (Marietta)	7,819	16,107	114,174
DeKalb (Atlanta)	13,249	44,536	256,782
Dougherty (Albany)	5,865	6,174	75,680
Floyd (Rome)	4,359	8,995	69,130
Fulton (Atlanta)	27,107	91,773	556,326
Lowndes (Valdosta)	2,665	4,523	49,270
Muscogee (Columbus)	7,297	13,014	158,623
Richmond (Augusta)	6,463	17,003	135,601
	101,415	249,628	1,790,497
Percentage of state total	30.5	50.4	45.4

Sanders' margin in the city counties as a proportion of his state margin:
91.4 percent.

Eleven city counties: 42.4 percent of the total vote.

A city county is defined as a county containing a city with population of 25,000 or more (1960 census).

gether the city counties accounted for 91.4 percent of Sanders' margin. Sanders actually carried more counties than Griffin, 86 to 73. If the votes had gone exactly as they did and with the county-unit rule prevailing, Sanders would have won, 256 county-unit votes to 154 county-unit votes.[51] Of course under the unit rule, campaign techniques, expenditures, and participant psychology would have been significantly altered.

There is a strong likelihood that knowledge of the fact that the decision would be based on the popular vote rather than on county-unit votes produced a self-fulfilling prophecy in the sense that the

[51] Returns are from the *Georgia Official and Statistical Register, 1961–1962*, pp. 1439–44, which reported the returns in both popular vote and county-unit vote terms. Although the primary election was held on a popular vote basis in compliance with an order of a federal court, an appeal to the United States Supreme Court was pending.

knowledge that ballots of city-dwellers would count at full value in
this contest encouraged city voters and discouraged their country
cousins from casting ballots. The expectation that Griffin, the rural
candidate, no longer enjoyed the advantage of county-unit weighting of small-county votes was a strong psychological factor in a state
in which the unit system had been an issue for many years. The
county-unit system had been declared unconstitutional by a federal
district court only six months before the September primary.

The Bottom Rail Is on Top

In the 1964 election a Republican presidential candidate carried the
state for the first time. In Georgia, Goldwater electors won approximately 54.0 percent of the two-party vote. The popular totals were
616,600 to 522,557.[52] The division in terms of popular percentages
was close to that of the 1948 gubernatorial primary, in which Herman Talmadge had defeated M. E. Thompson. In 1964, however,
it is evident that Negro votes in absolute numbers (estimated 200,-
000) and in proportion were much greater. White support for Goldwater was even more pronounced (estimated 65.6 percent) than it
had been for the white-supremacy champion Herman Talmadge in
1948 (59 percent). This fact is even more significant when one considers the traditional infatuation which Georgia voters have had
with presidential candidates wearing the label of the Democratic
Party. The vote is understandable in view of reaction to the 1964
Civil Rights Act with its public accommodations provisions. The
social structure of a racial caste system seemed threatened as it had
never been since the Reconstruction era.

Figure 10 reveals the sharply sectional division of the electorate
in 1964. This figure should be compared with Figure 2, which
demonstrates the counties of high Negro population. A clearer division is along the fall line which divides the Piedmont plateau and
the coastal plain, an imaginary line connecting Augusta (Richmond
County), Macon (Bibb County), and Columbus (Muscogee County).
Except for a handful of counties, 7 in all, most of the 68 counties of

52 *Georgia Official and Statistical Register, 1963–1964,* pp. 1368–73.

Figure 10
PRESIDENTIAL ELECTION IN GEORGIA, 1964

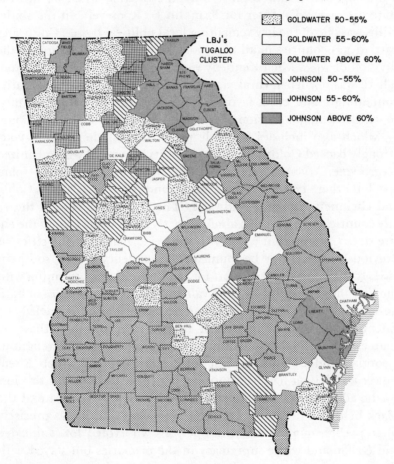

LBJ's
TUGALOO
CLUSTER

GOLDWATER 50-55%

GOLDWATER 55-60%

GOLDWATER ABOVE 60%

JOHNSON 50-55%

JOHNSON 55-60%

JOHNSON ABOVE 60%

high Goldwater strength (above 60 percent) are south of the line in the black belt and below it. Of the 22 counties showing strength of 60 percent or better for Lyndon Johnson, 18 counties are above the line. All of the strong Johnson counties are devoid of heavy Negro population except Greene, Taliaferro, Liberty, Long, and McIntosh. Each county of the latter group has been characterized by a strong black vote allied with white courthouse officialdom.

Treutlen County, which favored Johnson, is the home of Jim Gillis, a lifelong Democratic loyalist since the thirties, when he was the state patronage dispenser for Franklin D. Roosevelt. In the sixties Gillis was one of the few remaining local political bosses. Goldwater carried 114 counties in all to 45 for Johnson, in comparison to the division of 1960, when Kennedy won 149 to 10 for Richard Nixon. There was no urban-rural cleavage in 1964.[53] All of the counties containing major cities favored Goldwater except Fulton County, in which the major portion of Atlanta is located. But DeKalb County, which also includes a sizable proportion of the Atlanta vote, strongly backed Goldwater. Because of its heavy and well-organized Negro vote, Atlanta alone among the Georgia cities favored Johnson, but other "bedroom" counties around Atlanta—Clayton, Cobb, and Gwinnett—favored Goldwater. The Goldwater vote in the 11 city counties (53.7 percent) almost exactly mirrors his vote in the entire state (54.0 percent). A key to the performance of the cities, as previously noted, may be found in the tendency among southern cities to show increased support for the Republicans beginning with the Eisenhower candidacy. The values and money and votes of businessmen and of the higher-income classes in the cities fueled the Eisenhower-Nixon campaigns of 1952, 1956, 1960, and these resources were available to Goldwater as a nucleus for his strength in Georgia. Undoubtedly, he lost some black support which Eisenhower and Nixon had had but he more than made up for this loss by the addition of lower-income whites in South Georgia and the black belt. As Numan V. Bartley has pointed out, it was precisely these poorer, more rural, white persons who voted for Talmadge and Griffin and white supremacy in the primaries but stayed with the national Democratic Party in presidential elections.[54] The party's spell for them was finally broken in 1964, when Goldwater presented an attractive "choice, not an echo."

The 1964 general election was undoubtedly the most fiercely

---

53 Key, *Southern Politics*, 115, had called the rural-urban cleavage the most persuasive basis for analyzing Talmadgeism.

54 See Numan V. Bartley, *From Thurmond to Wallace: Political Tendencies in Georgia, 1948–1968* (Baltimore: Johns Hopkins Press, 1970), 57–65.

fought and expensive contest on the presidential level in twentieth-century Georgia. Under the impetus of an intensely politically conscious, knowledgeable, and vigorous President, Georgia's Democratic leaders, led by Governor Carl Sanders, pulled out all the stops. The Democrats, with John W. Greer as campaign manager, were well financed and fought fiercely to defeat Goldwater, but were handicapped because the racial-social structure erected by the white South had been under ceaseless attack for two decades in federal court decisions and more recently from acts of Congress. When this attack was intensified by enactment of the public accommodations provisions of the Civil Rights Act of 1964 and when the Republicans nominated a clear-cut foe of this legislation, the wonder is that Georgia, which had never before supported a Republican for President, did so in 1964 by only 54 percent.

The pattern of the returns (see Figure 10) shows the sharpest south-north division since the 1946 gubernatorial primary, when Eugene Talmadge and James V. Carmichael had divided the bulk of the votes along these sectional lines. But Carmichael's support and the traditional anti-Talmadge strength were located largely in the industrial and progressive areas of the northwest. The Johnson strength against Goldwater, on the other hand, was among the more rural "Tugaloo Democrats" of the northeast. Twelve of these are contiguous counties with not-very-high Negro population. One suspects strong organizational factors with Governor Sanders particularly effective in the Tugaloo area; still these organizational considerations must have fallen on highly receptive voters. Traditional Democratic Party loyalty and an emphasis on economics rather than race may be suggested as other root causes for Tugaloo loyalty.[55] In South Georgia and the black belt, on the other hand, most white voters reacted to the candidates and issues very much as did the majority of the whites in South Carolina, Alabama, Mississippi, and Louisiana—Goldwater and southern racial tradition all the way.

55 A chance factor helps to explain the deviant behavior in the Tugaloo area. The Johnson candidacy received optimal media coverage in the region; Goldwater media coverage was weak.

Fundamentalism and Ax Handles

The 1966 Democratic gubernatorial primary attracted six candidates, including one former governor, one former lieutenant governor, a former Georgia Democratic chairman, two often-defeated candidates, and one newcomer. For almost the first time in the twentieth century, the party primary was only an elimination tournament because the Republicans appeared to have a very strong candidate for governor in the person of Congressman Howard H. "Bo" Callaway to face the Democratic nominee in the general election.

The candidates in the Democratic gubernatorial primary were Ellis Arnall, Garland T. Byrd, James H. Gray, Jimmy Carter, Hoke O'Kelley, and Lester Maddox. Arnall was a former governor (1943–47), perhaps the most progressive of all Georgia's governors, with a national reputation as a fighting liberal. In 1942 he became the only man ever to defeat the late Eugene Talmadge in a race for the governorship. Arnall gained renown for this feat in an election in which the major issue was his opponent's alleged political interference with the state university system, which Talmadge said he was trying to save from a small group of "race-mixing" professors. Arnall's books and lectures; his support of Negro voting, the eighteen-year-old vote, and poll tax repeal; his efforts to secure equal freight rates for the South; his support for national Democratic candidates (Henry Wallace for Vice President in 1944 and Harry S. Truman for President in 1948) earned him an image somewhat more liberal than most white Georgians find politically compatible. Yet Arnall as governor had run a tight ship characterized by economy (without raising taxes he had paid off the state's debt, a task begun by Eugene Talmadge). Arnall also ran a scandal-free administration, achieved a number of reforms designed to limit the governor's opportunities for political abuses, and led the successful fight for a new state constitution. After leaving office Arnall served as president of an insurance company and of a group of independent motion picture producers. He also practiced law and briefly held appointive political offices (including, in 1952, director of price controls). In spite of his liberal image Arnall began the campaign as the favored candidate. He was known, heavily financed, and had a reputation as a vigorous and effective speaker.

Former Lieutenant Governor Garland T. Byrd was a conservative candidate for governor. A lawyer from rural middle Georgia (Taylor County), Byrd had been a leader among the younger supporters of Herman Talmadge. He won the office of lieutenant governor and served during the Vandiver administration (1959–63). In 1962 Byrd appeared headed for a strong showing in the gubernatorial sweepstakes. He had numerous pledges of support but was compelled to withdraw because of a heart ailment. He later ran for Congress in the Third District (southwestern Georgia) but was defeated by Howard W. Callaway, an ultraconservative Republican.

James H. Gray, publisher of the *Albany Herald* and a former state Democratic Party official, was a conservative gubernatorial candidate who carried the banner for much of the organization which had been associated with Herman Talmadge. The fourth candidate was State Senator Jimmy Carter, a well-to-do peanut farmer of Sumter County. Carter pitched his campaign on a progressive note and cut into the Arnall support, particularly in urban and suburban areas. The other major candidate was Lester G. Maddox, who had little money and less organization. His background was in real estate and in the grocery, restaurant, and furniture businesses. Maddox had sold his restaurant, the Pickrick, rather than integrate it after turning away Negroes, defying the civil rights law, and brandishing ax handles.

The Arnall candidacy appears to have suffered from a generation gap. Numan Bartley, quoting a press reporter, says the former governor did not dazzle the voters with his speeches as he had in 1942.[56] He made the mistake of being too much the loyal national Democrat at a time when the role had gone out of style, even in Georgia. In the first primary Arnall polled only 29.4 percent. He had been expected to win 40 to 45 percent. Although he led the field, he suffered a severe loss of prestige. He carried forty counties, winning a

---

56 Bartley, *From Thurmond to Wallace*, 72.

majority only in his home county, Coweta, and four others. (See
Figure 11.)

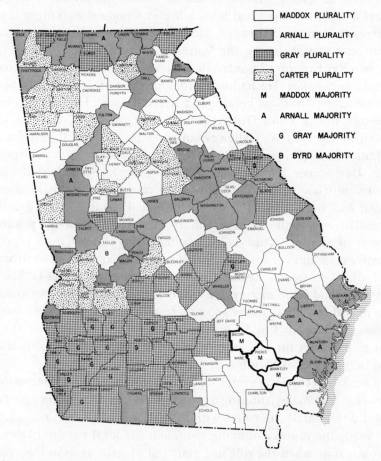

Figure 11
FIRST GUBERNATORIAL PRIMARY IN GEORGIA, 1966

☐   MADDOX PLURALITY

▨   ARNALL PLURALITY

▦   GRAY PLURALITY

▨   CARTER PLURALITY

M   MADDOX MAJORITY

A   ARNALL MAJORITY

G   GRAY MAJORITY

B   BYRD MAJORITY

Gray carried thirty-seven counties and won a majority in eleven
of them, mostly in his home area of southwestern Georgia. Elsewhere he won a scattering of counties where his organizational
strength was able to deliver. His popular percentage was 19.4. Gray,
in fourth place, trailed Carter, who had a majority in no counties

but carried twenty-one, mostly north of his home in Sumter County. Carter ran well in dynamic Georgia. Byrd won only his home county and secured but 5.1 percent. Hoke O'Kelley, running his fifth gubernatorial race since 1932, received 1.7 percent.[57]

In spite of Gray's solid standing with the organization conservatives it was Maddox who captured the allegiance of rural white Georgians with his outspoken opposition to integration, civil rights, and the United States Supreme Court and by his homespun fundamentalism on morals and religion. Although Maddox won only three counties with a majority, he led in sixty counties and was strong in all sections of the state, with twenty-nine counties above the fall line and thirty-one below it. Gray carried only five counties above the fall line and Arnall carried only three in South Georgia below the black belt. Arnall carried most of the coastal counties. Maddox secured 23.5 percent and earned a berth against Arnall in the runoff primary held two weeks after the September 14 primary. In the city counties Maddox (17.7 percent) trailed not only Arnall (36.7 percent) but also Carter (23.7 percent). In the three Atlanta counties Maddox had 18.1 percent, Arnall had 35.4 percent, and Carter had 26.1 percent.

First Gubernatorial Primary, 1966

Popular Totals and Percentages

Arnall	231,480 (29.4)	Gray	152,973 (19.4)
Byrd	39,994 (5.1)	Maddox	185,672 (23.5)
Carter	164,562 (20.9)	O'Kelley	13,271 (1.7)

In several respects the 1966 primary resembles the 1932 gubernatorial primary. In both elections a multitude of candidates participated. In each the winner was a flamboyant and colorful champion of the rural white people. Eugene Talmadge in 1932 ran his first race for governor. Like Maddox in 1966, he was strong in all sections of the state and carried a majority of the rural counties against seven opponents who enjoyed the support of friends and neighbors or

---

[57] Official Returns, Secretary of State Ben W. Fortson, Jr. (Atlanta, 1966).

special classes but lacked statewide appeal. Abit Nix was the 1932 counterpart of Arnall. Nix carried the cities and ran second. Significant differences may also be identified: in 1932 Talmadge, with 42.5 percent of the popular votes, carried a majority of counties against seven opponents. Maddox had only five opponents and he carried only sixty counties with 23.5 percent of the popular vote. Talmadge won under the county-unit system without a runoff. Maddox barely made it into the runoff. He had only 2.6 percent more support than Carter and only 4.1 percent more than Gray. Under the county-unit system, Maddox, the city resident, might not have survived at all and Arnall would probably not have been a candidate. Twice defeated in races for the mayoralty of Atlanta (1957, 1961) and once for lieutenant governor (1962), Maddox emerged in 1966 as a newly powerful political force, the symbol of poor white protest in the tradition of Tom Watson and the Talmadges.

In the runoff primary two weeks later Maddox defeated Arnall handily.[58] The cleavages were rural-urban and white-black. Arnall carried 6 small counties in which blacks balloted in heavy numbers. Maddox carried 109 counties by more than 60 percent and 28 additional counties by smaller majorities. As usual the white man's champion swept the southern part of the state and was strongest in southwestern Georgia. Maddox won only 42.7 percent of the city vote. He secured just over one-third of the votes in Atlanta's Fulton County, where 15.1 percent of the state vote was cast. The division of total voters is quite similar to the Goldwater-Johnson contest of 1964. Goldwater won 54.0 percent and Maddox 54.3.

But Arnall's support was far more urban-metropolitan than that of Johnson, who had lost the cities to Goldwater. There is no significant positive correlation of Arnall and Johnson counties. Johnson was strong in the Tugaloo area, but Maddox took all ten of the rural counties in the Tugaloo country—eight of them by better than 60 percent. Johnson had carried forty-five counties, more than twice the number that Arnall won. Evidently, Johnson enjoyed more

---

[58] Maddox—443,055; Arnall—373,004. Official Returns, Secretary of State Ben W. Fortson, Jr. (Atlanta, 1966).

rural partisans and more supporters among white industrial workers than did Arnall. On the other hand, Arnall attracted much more support in the high-income areas of the cities, where Republican strength has been greatly in evidence in recent years. A prime example of this support is found in DeKalb County, Atlanta's upper-class bedroom area. Arnall won the county with a margin of nearly 7,000 votes. Goldwater had secured a margin of over 12,000 votes in DeKalb.

In the 1966 general election for governor the final official vote showed Republican Howard H. "Bo" Callaway with a vote total of 453,665, a narrow plurality. Democrat Lester Maddox had 450,626. An organized write-in campaign for Ellis Arnall resulted in the following official totals: for Arnall (with the name spelled correctly), 45,603; apparently for Arnall (with name spelled incorrectly), 5,-894.[59] In addition 1,333 miscellaneous write-in votes were cast for other persons. The absence of a majority for any gubernatorial candidate in the general election resulted in litigation in the federal courts to determine whether the General Assembly might constitutionally elect a governor. The details of this controversy are discussed in the next section of this chapter.

The 1966 general election is remarkable for sharp urban-rural cleavage even though both candidates were ultraconservative on any spectrum of political belief relevant to opinions held across the United States. Maddox was the earthy champion of white rule as well as a man identified with Christian Protestant fundamental-

---

[59] A photocopy of the work sheet used for tabulation, furnished by the Georgia secretary of state, shows Arnall votes in two columns: (1) tallies with the official total of 45,603, shown above; (2) totals 176 votes. The figures used by the General Assembly to achieve the 5,894 votes (the "name misspelled" votes, shown above) do not appear on the work sheet. In twenty-six counties, including Fulton, no write-in votes for Arnall are shown on the work sheet. It is hard to believe that write-in votes were not cast for Arnall in these counties, when he was receiving thousands elsewhere. Hence the discrepancy may be due to the failure of officials to report them. The alternate hypothesis, that all of the Arnall write-ins in Fulton County were misspelled, is not believable. The problem (in Fulton County) may well be traceable to the problem of casting write-in votes when punched card ballots are used. The problem in the other twenty-five counties for which no write-in votes are shown on the work sheet is unexplained.

ism.[60] Apparently he possessed considerable charisma for poor white Georgians. "Bo" Callaway was a member of Congress from the Third District and the representative of a wealthy West Georgia textile-owning family. Callaway's genteel ultraconservatism, coupled with the Republican Party identification, earned him the support of higher-income and "better element" whites, particularly in city and suburb. Unquestionably blacks, whose votes were not diverted by the write-in campaign for the liberal Arnall, cast the bulk of their ballots for Callaway, in the cities at least. One black said he would vote for the "devil himself" in opposition to Maddox. Politically speaking, he almost did. The event illustrates in dramatic fashion the principle of countervailing force—that some voting blocs, city blacks and genteel middle- and upper-income whites, are repelled by the very qualities which endear a candidate to other voters—poorer whites in the cities and rural whites in the countryside. Maddox carried 130 counties, 96 of them by better than 60 percent. Table 2 shows that the city proportion for Callaway was even larger than that for Arnall in the runoff primary, in spite of the siphoning off of thousands of anti-Maddox votes via the write-in campaign.

It would be a mistake, however, to conclude that Maddox did not receive substantial black support anywhere. The image of an ultraconservative Republican candidate provoked ire in country counties where Negroes aligned with strong Democratic courthouse crowds. In Hancock, Greene, Long, Liberty, Taliaferro, and elsewhere the black vote was for Maddox. Perhaps the most dramatic delivery of a black voting bloc to Maddox was in Long County, where a strong political machine produced a margin for Maddox of 1,443 to 156.[61]

Equally impressive was Hancock County in the black belt. In this predominantly Negro county Maddox won 2,242 votes to 446 votes.

[60] According to Reuben Smith, Callaway said he stood for "God, the individual, and free enterprise." Could Maddox have said it more clearly? See Atlanta *Constitution*, September 19, 1966.

[61] Ironically, Governor Maddox later broke with Ralph Dawson, the Long County boss, not only because of bossism but because of alleged gambling and vice in the county.

Table 2
CITY COUNTIES IN THE GEORGIA DEMOCRATIC RUNOFF PRIMARY AND IN
THE GENERAL ELECTION FOR GOVERNOR, 1966

County	Runoff Primary		General Election	
	Arnall	Maddox	Callaway	Maddox
Bibb	13,268	13,025	22,329	13,235
Chatham	21,390	13,452	24,811	11,212
Clarke	6,113	3,583	5,934	3,477
Cobb	11,094	14,700	15,700	14,919
DeKalb	33,816	26,873	56,143	24,880
Dougherty	4,526	6,893	7,930	5,719
Floyd	6,219	7,218	7,843	6,976
Fulton	80,278	43,295	78,293	37,761
Lowndes	2,826	3,559	4,490	3,855
Muscogee	11,272	8,429	21,344	7,646
Richmond	12,255	10,290	12,405	7,284
	203,057	151,317	257,222	136,964
	(57.3%)	(42.7%)	(65.2%)	(34.8%)

(11 city counties=43.4 percent of state total)   (43.6 percent of state total)

Arnall's margin in the city counties = 51,740
Maddox's margin statewide   = 70,051

Callaway's margin in the city counties = 120,258
Callaway's margin statewide   = 3,039

Statewide, Maddox enjoyed strong support from the Democratic organization, including Senator Herman Talmadge, quietly active behind the scenes.[62] Most of the state leaders, including Jim Gillis and Roy Harris, who had backed James Gray in the first September primary, moved into the Maddox camp against Arnall in the runoff and against Callaway in the general election.

Bartley says that Maddox's financial resources were meager compared with those of Callaway.[63] Undoubtedly, much big money from Atlanta and elsewhere rode with Callaway for a long time, but the organizational support which Maddox enjoyed in local court-

[62] Arlie Schardt, "Georgia: Lester Maddox and the Mad Democrats," *Reporter*, XXXV (October 20, 1966), 29–30.
[63] Bartley, *From Thurmond to Wallace*, 76.

houses was perhaps equally valuable, even without the county-unit system. Maddox's financial position took a sharp turn for the better the moment it became known that he would be in the runoff against Arnall. By the time of the general election Maddox did not suffer for funds. For a time Maddox was hurt by the suspicion that he might live up to his image and stir up turmoil—which would hurt business and injure the kind of image businessmen wanted for Georgia. For this reason Maddox was not as well favored by big industry as Callaway, who was one of their own people.

In 1966 occurred two unusual, if not unique, political events which soon found their way to the federal courts. The first was the Julian Bond case; the second was the failure of any candidate in the general election to receive a majority in the contest for governor and the subsequent resort to the constitutional provision which requires the General Assembly to choose a governor.

Julian Bond, a young Atlanta Negro, was elected to the Georgia House of Representatives in 1965 from a predominantly black district, after court-ordered legislative redistricting. After his election but before he assumed office, he issued a public statement critical of American military operations in Southeast Asia. Bond was affiliated with the Student Nonviolent Coordinating Committee (SNCC), for which he served as spokesman, denouncing United States military policy for "crimes" at home and in South Vietnam. In a press interview, Bond agreed with the SNCC statement and supported it with these two principal points: (1) as a "second class citizen" he was not required to support the war, and (2) as a pacifist, he was opposed to all wars. Members of the Georgia House of Representatives, their ire and their constituents provoked, challenged Bond's right to be seated in that body on the grounds that Bond's statement (1) aided enemies of the United States; (2) violated selective service laws; (3) discredited the Georgia House of Representatives; and (4) was inconsistent with the mandatory oath of the legislator to support the Constitution.[64]

In answer to an investigation by a committee of the House, Bond

64 New York *Times*, January 8–16, 19–25, 1966. See also *Bond et al. v. Floyd et al.*, 251 F. Supp. 333 (1966).

denied these charges and asserted his rights to free speech under the First Amendment. The committee, nevertheless, recommended against seating Bond. The Georgia House supported the committee recommendation by a vote of 184 to 12, and the doorkeeper of the House refused to admit Bond to the chamber.[65]

Bond then sought to have the federal district court order his seating by the Georgia House. In a two-to-one decision the district court refused Bond's plea. This court said that (1) it had jurisdiction to decide the constitutional issue; (2) Bond had been granted due process of law; and (3) Bond could not in good faith, after his statement, take the required oath of office to support the Georgia and United States constitutions and meet the requirements of legislative membership.[66] While Bond's appeal from this adverse opinion was pending before the United States Supreme Court, he was once more elected to the Georgia House. He refused to recant his previous statement and was once more refused a seat in the legislature.[67]

The denouement of the bizarre controversy came when, to the surprise of almost no one, the high court voted unanimously to support Bond's right to his seat in the Georgia House. The Court said Bond's statement showed no intent to violate the Selective Service Act. Although states may require an oath of office, said the opinion of the nine justices, a state may not use the oath or any other device to limit the capacity of a legislator to express views on local or national policy. The decision found the action of the Georgia House in denying Bond his seat to be in violation of the First Amendment, which is made applicable to the states by the Fourteenth Amendment. In January, 1967, Bond was seated without protest in the Georgia House of Representatives.

The other court decision followed in the wake of the 1966 general election. As noted, more than 50,000 write-in votes had been

65 New York *Times*, January 11, 1966.

66 *Bond et al. v. Floyd et al.*, 251 F. Supp. 333 (1966). Voting to reject Bond's plea were Judges Griffin Bell and Lewis R. Morgan. Voting to uphold Bond was Chief Judge Elbert P. Tuttle.

67 New York *Times*, September 16, December 13, 1966.

cast for Ellis Arnall. Consequently, neither Callaway nor Maddox received a majority. Callaway received about 3,000 more votes than Maddox, and each received about 47 percent.

The case was brought into court by a number of interested citizens affiliated with the American Civil Liberties Union. Their argument centered on the claim that the election of a governor by the legislature, as provided by the Georgia Constitution when no candidate had a majority in the general election, violated the equal protection and due process guarantees of the Fourteenth Amendment. In particular, they emphasized that the decision invalidating the county-unit system had relied heavily upon the concept of election by the people to afford constitutionally required equal protection. In *Morris et al. v. Fortson*, a three-judge federal district court unanimously ruled in favor of the plaintiffs, saying that election by the General Assembly would violate equal protection. As in the Bond case, the judges were Lewis R. Morgan, Griffin Bell, and Chief Judge Elbert P. Tuttle.[68] The decision was reversed by the United States Supreme Court. By a five-to-four ruling, with Justice Hugo Black speaking for the narrowest of majorities, the Court said that the federal Constitution does not provide the method a state must use to choose its governor. Said Black: "Not a word in the Court's opinion [in *Gray v. Sanders*] indicated that it was intended to compel a State to elect its governors or any other state officers or agents through election of the people rather than through selections by appointment or elections by the State Assembly."

Joining in support of this opinion were Justices Tom Clark, John M. Harlan, Potter Stewart, and Byron White. Justice William O. Douglas wrote a dissenting opinion which was concurred in by Chief Justice Earl Warren and by Justices William Brennan and Abe Fortas. Fortas wrote a separate opinion in which Douglas and Warren concurred.[69] One additional aspect of the case which added a fillip of added equal-protection concern was the fact that the Georgia General Assembly was already under a court order to re-

68 *Morris et al. v. Fortson*, 265 F. Supp. 93 (1966).
69 See *Fortson v. Morris et al.*, 385 U.S. 231 (1966).

apportion before the elections of 1968.[70] The Court's majority evidently gave weight to the fact that the 1965 order in the *Toombs* case did not require immediate reapportionment.

The decision by the United States Supreme Court paved the way for the General Assembly to elect Maddox as governor in early 1967. Obviously, Maddox owed his election to the Democratic Party label.[71] Within four years as governor, he broadened his political base to the point where in 1970, barred from succeeding himself as chief executive of the state, he ran for the office of lieutenant governor and won an absolute majority over a well-liked incumbent, George T. Smith, and several other candidates.

Wallace, a Southern Neighbor

In 1964 the Goldwater candidacy achieved the first Georgia victory for a Republican in a presidential election. Four years later George C. Wallace, the American Independent candidate, eclipsed both national party candidates. In the 1968 Democratic National Convention in Chicago, while police battled longhaired youths in the streets outside, a black delegation led by Julian Bond had been given half of the convention votes of Georgia. The reaction in Georgia is not difficult to imagine. The results:

Candidate	Popular Votes
Wallace	535,550 (42.8 percent)
Nixon	380,111 (30.4 percent)
Humphrey	334,440 (26.8 percent)[72]

With Senator Strom Thurmond, former Democrat and former Dixiecrat, campaigning for the Republican ticket throughout the Deep South, it is logical to classify both Wallace votes and Nixon votes as conservative. On this basis a measure of Georgia voting in

[70] *Toombs v. Fortson*, 384 U.S. 210 (1965).

[71] The closeness of the Callaway-Maddox vote (the difference was only 3,000 of almost a million cast) undoubtedly helped Maddox. If Maddox had trailed Callaway by 50,000, many legislators and their constituents would have felt some ethical obligation to Callaway.

[72] Official Returns, Office of Secretary of State Ben W. Fortson, Jr.

1968 reveals few liberals. The highest quartile of Humphrey support, county by county, shows a range from 59.7 percent (Hancock County) to 29 percent (Dooly County). Thirty-six of these forty counties are in the black belt. Only three counties of Humphrey's highest quartile (Fulton, Richmond, and Clarke) are city counties. The 1968 returns show that the Humphrey support was less than 20 percent in sixty counties in the state, of which forty-five counties were outside the black-belt area. It seems probable that over half of the Humphrey support came from black voters. Humphrey's white vote, perhaps 10 percent, is a great reduction in the level of support for Georgia's traditional political home, the national Democratic Party. But George Wallace was a southern neighbor, a symbol of the fight against desegregation and for "law and order."

A significant correlation of racial politics in the national election is seen in a comparison of Wallace strength in 1968 and Goldwater strength in 1964 with the Thurmond–States' Right Democratic vote of 1948. Of the forty counties in the highest quartile of support for Thurmond in 1948, twenty-eight cast over 60 percent of their votes for Goldwater in 1964. On the other hand, in Wallace's sweep of Georgia in 1968, the correlation of Wallace's strongest counties (forty-eight carried by better than 60 percent) with the highest quartile of Thurmond strength in 1948 is not statistically significant. The correlation between the 1964 Goldwater vote and the 1968 Wallace vote is better. Thirty-one of the forty-eight counties in which Wallace won more than 60 percent were also carried by Goldwater among the sixty-eight counties he carried with a vote of 60 percent or higher. Of the twelve counties in Johnson's 1964 Tugaloo bloc, on the other hand, five cast 60 percent or better for Wallace in 1968 and one cast above 60 percent for Nixon. Of the other six, four were for Wallace by a majority and two by a plurality. Hubert Humphrey carried not one. Nixon received 38.3 percent of the vote in the city counties and Wallace received 29.8 percent. He carried Bibb, Dougherty, Floyd, Lowndes, and Muscogee counties. Humphrey carried Chatham and Fulton. Nixon carried the other four city counties. Nixon carried Atlanta (41 percent); here the Wallace vote was only 23 percent.

A Kennedy Type for Wallaceites?

In 1970, a very busy political year in Georgia, the favorite to win the governorship was the former incumbent, Carl Sanders. But Sanders was challenged by a wealthy peanut-grower from Plains, Georgia, State Senator Jimmy Carter. Carter was a strong vote-getter in 1966, when without previous statewide campaigning experience, he narrowly failed to beat out Maddox for a spot in the gubernatorial runoff primary opposite Arnall. Carter had been ranked as a moderate in 1966. Apparently he was well financed and he ran best in "dynamic Georgia" areas, the cities and the northern part of the state. A young man, he ran a campaign which projected an image of vigor and "let's keep Georgia moving" which was somewhat reminiscent of John F. Kennedy.[73] He ran poorly in the small rural counties of static Georgia, where Goldwater and Wallace were strongest.

In 1970 Sanders seemed to have enjoyed the backing of the political establishment, including Jim Gillis; Mills B. Lane, an Atlanta banker; and generally the elements of the winning coalition which had swept Sanders into office in 1962. Carter, on the other hand, did not have the political liabilities which marked Sanders' opponent, Marvin Griffin, in 1962. Sanders as governor had made enemies, and he had incurred the wrath of the Wallaceites. He seemed a little too distant from the people. Without actually saying so directly, Carter implied that he would protect white supremacy. He did not wage a reactionary campaign and he was an attractive candidate, a fresh political image to the voters. It was a dull campaign almost to the end. Then the Carter camp charged that Sanders had become rich while serving as governor and Sanders people said that Carter was a cruel landlord.

Three aspects of the primary election for governor colored the picture and two of them probably contributed heavily to Carter's impressive victory in the first primary, in which he led Sanders with 388,280 votes (48.6 percent) to 301,659 (32.8 percent). The first of these three aspects was the candidacy of a Negro from Albany, C. B.

[73] Bartley, *From Thurmond to Wallace*, 71.

King, who polled 70,424 votes (8.8 percent). The second factor not present in Sanders' earlier campaign for governor was the Republican primary, held the same day as the Democratic primary and won by an Atlanta moderate, Hal Suit. King and Suit both received the bulk of their support from voters who would probably have supported Sanders in a single two-candidate primary. Yet it is by no means clear that divisive elements were significant in bringing about Sanders' defeat. James L. "Jimmy" Bentley polled 40,251 votes to Suit's 62,868 votes and many Bentley voters would doubtlessly have favored Carter over Sanders. Further there is no assurance that these Republicans on either side would have wished to participate in the Democratic gubernatorial primary if the Republicans had not held their own primary on the same day, September 9, 1970. A third factor favored Sanders. This was the candidacy of J. B. Stoner, a Savannah attorney who had at one time represented James Earl Ray, the convicted slayer of Martin Luther King, Jr. Stoner's campaign consisted of denunciations of Jews, Negroes, Communists, and liberals. Governor Maddox, campaigning for lieutenant governor, walked off the platform and refused to appear on the same program with him after Stoner made anti-Semitic remarks.[74] Once more Maddox revealed his flair for the dramatic gesture, and he no doubt won some moderate votes thereby. Carter backers accused Stoner during the campaign of being a vote-splitter put into the contest by friends of Sanders to divert support from Carter. He polled only 17,663 votes (2.2 percent), far fewer than C. B. King no doubt took from Sanders. Other first primary candidates were Jan Cox, McKee Hargrett, Thomas J. Irwin, Adam B. Matthews, and Charles F. Swint, Jr., all little known politically. Collectively, they polled 20,634 votes (2.5 percent).[75] As noted above, Carter polled 48.6 percent. He was, therefore, only 1.4 percent short of a first-primary majority. In the runoff two weeks later he submerged Sanders. Carter won 506,462 votes (59.42 percent) to Sanders' 345,-906 (40.58 percent).

In the first primary Sanders carried only twenty-three counties.

---

74 Macon *Telegraph*, August 8, 1970.
75 Official Returns, Office of Secretary of State Ben W. Fortson, Jr.

His support—even its nature and location—is reminiscent of the last bleak years of the old anti-Talmadge faction. Nineteen of the twenty-three counties had supported M. E. Thompson one or more times in his losing campaigns of 1948, 1950, or 1954. The correlation is a significant one. It is attributable to a coalition of black voters with moderate whites in a few cities and coastal counties, to voters in mountain counties who were more interested in economic issues than in racial protest. In most small counties the pro-Sanders vote is also evidence of strong local organizations. In the second primary Sanders carried only eight counties. It is significant that the voter turnout in the second Democratic primary exceeded that in the first primary by over 50,000. Persons who voted in the Republican primary on September 9 were permitted to participate in the Democratic runoff primary on September 23. On the latter date there was no statewide Republican contest. The increase is evidence of the high interest in the contest. By September 23, the Carter victory appeared assured and additional thousands—118,000 to be precise—joined the bandwagon.

The Sanders strength in the city counties (a margin of 12,600 over Carter) in the first primary contrasts with his weakness in the countryside. The vote of these city counties as a proportion of the total state vote is surprisingly low, due no doubt to the fact that the Republican primary that day attracted far heavier support in the cities than in the smaller counties. Compare the proportion of votes in the city counties for the first Democratic primary, 40.7 percent of the state total, with the proportion for the November 3 general election, 48.2 percent of the state total. The eleven city counties cast 70.8 percent of the statewide vote in the Republican primary—an eloquent statistical measure of urban Republicanism in Georgia.

James L. Bentley is an old friend and supporter of United States Senator Herman Talmadge. In 1962 he ousted a long-time incumbent, Zack D. Cravey, from the office of comptroller general. Later Bentley switched to the Republican Party. He was undoubtedly hurt politically by the revelation that he had sold land which was to be used for atomic waste materials. Hal Suit was an Atlanta television performer. His 1970 candidacy was his first state political venture. He carried only 50 counties to Bentley's 108 and 1 for a third candidate, J. C. "Jep" Tanksley. But the popular totals tell a different story:

> Bentley—40,251 (37.4 percent)
> Suit—62,868 (58.5 percent)
> Tanksley—4,438 (4.1 percent)

In the eleven city counties, Suit's margin was 22,395 votes, close to his statewide margin of 22,617 votes.

The county-by-county fluctuation of Republican participation in the 1970 primary is an interesting clue to the problem of building the second party in what had been a one-party state. The Republicans exceeded 1,000 votes in only 13 of the 159 counties. In each of 99 counties, almost all carried by Bentley, fewer than 100 Republicans voted in the primary. In each of 8 counties fewer than 10 votes were cast in the Republican primary. In each of 10 others fewer than 25 votes were cast. In Quitman County 1 Republican vote was recorded.

Carter won the general election with 620,419 votes to Suit's 424,983 votes.[76] Superficially, there is a considerable parallel between the division of votes in the general election and in the first Democratic primary for governor in 1970. South and middle Georgia were Carter country against Suit just as they had been against Sanders. To be sure, Suit carried only six counties while Sanders won twenty-three. But the rural–city county division is grossly similar. Sanders had a margin over Carter of 12,617 in the cities; Suit's margin in them was 18,360. Yet there are striking differences: Sanders carried Richmond (his home) and lost Cobb; Suit carried Cobb and lost Richmond; both carried Fulton by about 20,000. The big difference: Sanders carried DeKalb County over Carter by 4,000 votes; Suit carried it by 43,000. DeKalb is, of course, heavily white and upper-class Republican. Its Negro population is small and its income average for a family of four in 1959 was the highest in Georgia.

---

76 A total of 1,261 write-in votes was officially tabulated for various candidates.

Ironically Carter's strongest areas in 1970 had been his weakest in 1966, and vice versa. It is evident that the basic elements of anti-Carter strength were (1) Negroes and (2) upper-income whites. But at no time did they maximize and unite their strength. In the first primary many Negroes voted for C. B. King and many upper-income urban and suburban whites flocked to the Republican primary. In the Democratic runoff primary to nominate for governor, many Negroes and many upper-income whites voted for Sanders, but by then the Carter bandwagon was rolling ahead and many former Sanders supporters and potential future supporters had been lost. In the general election when the DeKalb County "silk-stocking vote" gave Hal Suit an unprecedented margin—over two to one, an advantage of 43,000 votes—he had lost much of the anti-Carter Negro strength, particularly in the rural counties.[77] Suit, the Atlantan, was more attractive to DeKalb Countians and less attractive to blacks than Sanders. The Carter who ran against Suit in November projected an image more attractive to Negro voters than the Carter of September.

City Candidates with Rural Values

Supporters of the county-unit system held that the system broke up political machines at the county line and prevented the domination of the state by the corrupt bloc votes in the cities (particularly Atlanta). Yet it is clear from an analysis of the election returns of the major contested races for governor in 1962, 1966, and 1970 and for presidential electoral voters in 1964 and 1968 that the cities have not dominated Georgia. Indeed, during the period following the federal decision in 1962 barring application of the county-unit system, the state trend has been in a conservative direction and the voters in the city counties, excepting their support of Sanders in 1962, have usually cast a majority or plurality of their ballots for the loser in gubernatorial primaries. Often the city vote has been sharply divided. The city counties of South and middle Georgia—

77 In the Democratic runoff Carter had carried DeKalb by 1,600 votes. Among the cities Sanders carried only Fulton by 28,000 and Richmond by 10,000. In the eleven city counties Sanders had a margin of about 3,000.

Lowndes, Chatham, Dougherty, Muscogee, Bibb, and Richmond—
have voted more conservatively than Fulton, DeKalb, and Clarke.

Obviously, the cities have not dominated Georgia politics since
the demise of the county-unit system nor has the state become more
liberal in its choice of public officials. Figure 12 summarizes the per-

Figure 12

THE VOTES IN THE ELEVEN CITY COUNTIES IN GEORGIA
AS PERCENTAGES OF (A) STATEWIDE TOTALS,
(B) STATEWIDE TOTALS FOR WINNERS, AND
(C) THE VOTE OF THE THREE ATLANTA
AREA COUNTIES AS PERCENTAGES OF (A) AND (B)

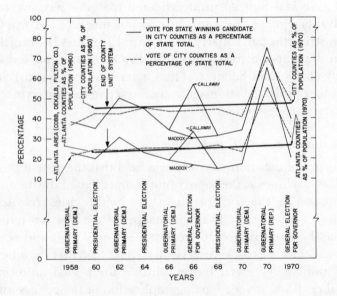

formance of the eleven city counties in comparison with the balance
of the state since 1958, when Vandiver was elected governor. In this
figure the broken lines represent the city vote as a percentage of the
total state vote in the principal elections from 1958 to 1970. The
unbroken lines show the city vote of the winning candidates as a
percentage of their individual statewide votes. Thus when the

unbroken line is above the broken line, the winning candidate received stronger support in the cities than elsewhere.

This figure shows that Vandiver, the winner in 1958, did slightly better in the city counties than elsewhere in the state and that John F. Kennedy in 1960 did considerably worse in the city counties than elsewhere in Georgia. This is consistent with what we should have expected because the new southern Republicanism of the Eisenhower years and in 1960 was largely urban and suburban. Traditional Republicanism continues to exist in the Appalachian Mountains, as it has since 1861.

After the end of county-unit rule in 1962, Carl Sanders, the establishment moderate, did extremely well in the cities. The vote of the city counties in the 1962 contest was only 42.4 percent of the state total but Sanders received 50.4 percent of his vote in these eleven counties. In 1964 the Goldwater proportion in the city counties almost exactly mirrored the statewide picture. The figure shows graphically that the city vote for Maddox in 1966 (in both the run-off primary and in the general election) was significantly low. The same was true of Wallace in 1968 and of Carter in 1970. The message in these returns for 1966, 1968, and 1970 is that the cities have been voting for the losers: Arnall, Callaway (a loser only because the General Assembly voted to choose a Democrat for governor in preference to a Republican), and Suit. In 1968 the city vote divided, but both Nixon and Humphrey did better in the cities than Wallace, who swept the countryside and won the state by a margin of 155,000 votes over Nixon, his nearest competitor. Figure 12 dramatically illustrates the fact that the Republican primary vote in 1970 was predominantly a vote of the city counties and even more dramatically illustrates the metropolitan source of Hal Suit's support in the Republican primary.

The heavy black lines on Figure 12 show the population of city counties as a percentage of Georgia's total population. The population of the eleven city counties in 1960 was 45.4 percent of the state population and the city county population of 1970 was 47.4 percent of the total for Georgia. Except in the 1964 presidential race and in the truly aberrant Republican primary[78] of 1970 the city county vote in ratio to state vote is slightly lower in percentage terms than the ratio of city population to state population.

If the figure fairly clearly demonstrates the failure of city-dwellers to identify themselves with the recent winning candidates or effectively to shape the major trends of the state, it even more clearly reveals the limited power of Atlanta voting strength. Atlanta has plainly not dominated, and given the conservative, antidynamic, traditionalistic tendencies of Georgia taken as a whole, Atlanta voters are unlikely to dominate unless startling changes occur. The three Atlanta-area city counties, Cobb, DeKalb, and Fulton, contained in 1960 only 23.5 percent of Georgia population and in 1970 only 26.8 percent, slightly over one-fourth. The Atlanta voters, as Figure 12 reveals, tend to parallel the performance of voters in the city county group except that Atlanta gave proportionately greater support to Kennedy and slightly less to Goldwater. Since 1960, the Atlanta area has tended to vote slightly more heavily in proportion to population than the rest of Georgia.

The end of the county-unit system has not meant more liberal politics in Georgia, but the centripetal forces at work in the nation as a whole and in the state must be appraised to give a true perspective. If Georgia voted for an ultraconservative racist in *candidate* Lester Maddox, it did not get one in *Governor* Lester Maddox. Maddox has not tried by force to block court-ordered desegregation; he has appointed blacks to government positions and treated blacks with personal respect.[79] If Carter appeared more conservative than Sanders or Suit, there was no evidence of racism—indeed the reverse—in Carter's eloquent plea for tolerance and justice in

78 The Republican primary is not necessarily aberrant in terms of primaries since apparently most Republicans live in these counties, but it is aberrant when one measures voter turnout, assuming it will bear a close proportionate relationship to population.

79 In a perceptive paragraph Donald S. Strong suggests that Deep South conservatism is distinguished by its "style." He calls George Wallace and Lester Maddox "poor man's segregationist[s]." See "Further Reflections on Southern Politics," *Journal of Politics*, XXXIII (1970), 253.

his nationally televised remarks on the occasion of his inauguration. Indeed, Carter in these remarks may have gone beyond anything in the public utterances of Carl Sanders or even Ellis Arnall.

Only an analyst with remarkable temerity and an ignorance of
history would suggest that racism is dead in Georgia politics, but
there is considerable evidence that political folkways are changing.
Virtually all serious candidates now treat Negroes with outward
respect and political gatherings are thoroughly desegregated. Although the mainspring of Georgia's 1964 abandonment of the
Democratic presidential ticket was racial, it is not clear that the
1968 negation of Humphrey was of the same quality. The law-and-
order issue, as well as the national convention seating of Julian
Bond's group with half of the delegation votes, was involved in
the presidential election picture. George Wallace symbolized a reaction against hippies, youthful protest, violence in the streets and
ghettos, and rising crime. Georgians, like a majority of American
voters elsewhere, were sensitive to these concerns. Voters, thus an-
noyed, tend to blame the incumbents. Besides, the Democratic
Party image was tarnished by the behavior of violent blacks and
rowdy, hairy youths.[80]

Granted, then, the end of county-unit rule has not made Georgia
a city-dominated or liberal state. Yet it has opened the highest offices to persons with official city residences. Of the last three governors, two (Sanders and Maddox) have been city residents. Of the
seven principal candidates in the last three gubernatorial years,
four (Sanders twice, Maddox, and Suit) have been city residents.
Ironically, the favorite city candidacies of 1966 (Arnall and Callaway) were from small towns, one a liberal, and the other perhaps
the most basically conservative (after Eugene Talmadge) of modern
major gubernatorial contenders in Georgia. Maddox, who won by
virtue of his ability to sweep the countryside (and the legislature),
probably would not have received serious attention from the rural

---

[80] See Richard M. Scammon and Ben J. Wattenberg, *The Real Majority: An Extraordinary Examination of the American Electorate* (New York: Coward-McCann,
1970), *passim.*

voters under the county-unit system.[81] The demise of the county-unit system has meant change also in electioneering techniques: the purpose for which campaign money is spent to seek votes and where the money is spent. Political pragmatists like Roy Harris and Ed Rivers and scholars like V. O. Key, Jr., and Alexander Heard have agreed that under county-unit rule, campaign managers forgot the voters in "sure" or "lost" counties and concentrated on "doubtful" counties.[82] Under a popular vote system one vote anywhere is as good as another. Campaign efforts have reflected these contrasting facts. In a popular vote election, moreover, $25,000 used in building an attractive television image is likely to be a better investment than the same amount used to insure the delivery of Fannin, Long, or Chatham County.

The advent of more prosperous times, the mandatory secret ballot, and a public more fully educated in and imbued with the democratic ethic are factors which have contributed to the sharp decline in political bossism in Georgia as well as elsewhere in the United States. The end of the county-unit system has diminished the economic utility of local county political machines and bosses. In Georgia few of them remain. Even Jim Gillis has not always prevailed in Treutlen County. The late Ralph Dawson of Long County remained politically dominant in spite of the efforts by Maddox, as governor, to strip him of his power, at least by means of public denunciation. In the 1970 primary Long County voted against Maddox's candidacy for lieutenant governor by two to one, but in the general election Maddox won there with over 1,100 votes against 94 for Suit.

Ironically, the decline of the bosses and courthouse crowds means increased potency for the popular passions of voters. In the thirties

[81] Georgia voters have long enjoyed a reputation for articulating vigorous protest in their political actions. Perhaps the most persuasive interpretation of recent elections is the voters' hostility to incumbents and former major officeholders. From 1962 onward the winners have been new and fresh. Former Governors Griffin, Arnall, and Sanders have fallen before men who had no record in major office. President Johnson, Vice President Humphrey, and former Vice President Nixon have each been defeated in the state by holders of less exalted offices.

[82] See, for instance, Key, *Southern Politics*, 122.

and forties a major element of political balance derived from the tendency of cantankerous Eugene Talmadge to antagonize the bosses and courthouse crowds as well as significant economic voting blocs such as textile workers. Today there are few local bosses and courthouse crowds able to command important blocs of votes. Under a popular vote system these votes are less potent because they cannot be translated into winner-take-all unit votes. Unlike Eugene Talmadge, where race is concerned Maddox, Carter, and Herman Talmadge appear quite pragmatic or ideologically moderate. The result is that the sharp and viable alternatives of the bifactional era have no counterpart in today's politics.

The impact of Republicanism and the growth of a substantial two-party system are matters for the future to determine. Atlanta has two Republican congressmen. Macon has a Republican mayor who wants to arm firemen for law enforcement, who orders police to shoot to kill rioters, and who wants to give Lieutenant William Calley the Congressional Medal of Honor. Elsewhere there is a scattering of Republican officeholders.[83]

One measure of a growing perception by voters of a two-party politics is evident in Figure 13. The principal contest, at least in terms of voter turnout, is no longer the Democratic Party primary. In the fifties the numbers of voters in presidential elections began to rival the major gubernatorial primaries. In 1964 and 1968 more Georgians voted than ever before in choosing Goldwater and Wallace. In 1970 the general election turnout exceeded that of the Democratic and Republican primaries combined. Of course popula-

[83] In Atlanta the coalition of Negroes and upper-income racial moderates has remained durable. The late William B. Hartsfield, long-time mayor, depended on the coalition for periodic election, at least from 1947 until his retirement in 1961. In that year Ivan Allen, Jr., inherited the coalition support. In 1969 when Allen retired, Atlantans elected a Jewish mayor, Sam Massell, Jr., and a Negro vice mayor, Maynard Jackson. In Atlanta municipal politics Republicanism has seemed irrelevant. The city has enjoyed a national reputation for efficiency, racial and economic progress, and harmonious desegregation, at least until recent disputes with labor and some blacks have troubled Massell's administration. According to 1970 census figures, Atlanta's population is 51 percent Negro. In this study, the county rather than the city has been used as the unit of measurement. Hence suburban voters as well as those within Atlanta proper are included in the Fulton and DeKalb County figures.

Figure 13
A Measure of Voter Participation in Georgia for
Gubernatorial and Presidential Contests Only, 1948–1970

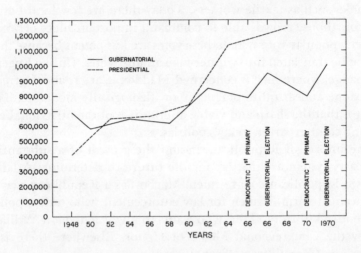

tion has been increasing, and an increase in voter participation is expected. The important variables are the comparative figures for general elections and major primaries.

From the Hustings to the Tube

Undoubtedly, television has enabled political candidates to communicate with more potential voters than did the old-style personal campaigning from the hustings. In 1950 M. E. Thompson campaigned for two months, day after day, in town after town, county after county, several stops a day, giving the same basic speech for days at a time with local variations. Saturday speeches were climactic and a special effort was made to get out big crowds. Special speeches for special locales were featured along the way. For instance, a major effort was made in Unadilla, where a young newspaperwoman had used her column to attack the local Ku Klux Klan and its anti-Negro activities. She in turn received threats. Thompson went to Unadilla for an evening speech. "When I am your governor, no one will have to shutter their windows and pin their curtains back because they are afraid. People of Georgia, do not be afraid. Do not be afraid!"

In 1948 a crowd tried to walk out on former Governor E. D. Rivers in a Talmadge stronghold, but the oratorically gifted and quick-witted Rivers shamed them into coming back to hear him. In 1954 Marvin Griffin announced that in his opening speech he would "skin some skunks and nail their carcasses to the smoke house door." He dutifully nailed to the door skins which he named for each of his opponents after characterizing them in colorful language.

Campaign openings often began with a major speech, featuring motorcades from various cities and counties with banners waving, horns tooting, and cowbells ringing. Refreshments were barbecue or fried fish or chicken dinners. Nowadays, political rallies have been largely eliminated except for very special occasions. Television is far more important and the public seems generally uninterested in traveling any distance to see a political candidate. Perhaps public tastes in entertainment have become too jaded to include homespun politicians. But a few old-timers may yearn to see a Talmadge shuck his coat, snap his red suspenders, and listen to the tree-climbing Haggards of Franklin County yell, "Pore it on, Gene!" or "Tell us about them lying newspapers, Herman!" Is political nostalgia so *passé* that there are none today who would like to eat fried fish after a political rally in which Jack Brophy of Rhine, Georgia, yelled ten times, "It's Thompson's time"?

8

NORTH CAROLINA
Bipartisan Paradox

PRESTON W. EDSALL AND J. OLIVER WILLIAMS

"Good government is a habit in North Carolina—and the Democratic party has made it so." [1] These oft-repeated words state an article of faith among North Carolina Democrats. Certainly the Democratic Party has dominated the state government—legislative, executive, and judicial—and most partisan local governments during the entire twentieth century. Only in 1928 and 1968 have Republican presidential candidates won the state's electoral votes; the last Republican United States senator, Jeter C. Pritchard, was replaced by Democrat Lee S. Overman in 1903. Between 1911 and 1929 and again between 1931 and 1953, no Republican congressmen were included in the state's Washington delegation, though four are currently serving. So if it is agreed that North Carolina has experienced seven decades of good government, the Democratic Party has a just claim to responsibility for them, *provided*, of course, that it is also ready to accept a fair share of blame for the state's shortcomings. To these shortcomings the Republican state platforms regularly point as evidence of the failure of decade after decade of Democratic dominance and call impiously for a change.[2]

Preston W. Edsall is Professor Emeritus and J. Oliver Williams is Assistant Professor, Department of Politics, North Carolina State University at Raleigh.

[1] "North Carolina Democratic Platform for 1964," *North Carolina Manual, 1965* (Raleigh: Secretary of State, 1965), 146. Manuals appear biennially and are cited hereinafter as *N.C. Manual*.

[2] Major state party platforms regularly appear in the *N.C. Manual*, as do primary and election figures.

Key's Progressive Plutocracy

Southern Politics characterized North Carolina in the twentieth century as a "progressive plutocracy" wherein at least one northern Negro reporter thought he found "a living answer to the riddle of race." [3] North Carolinians were "determined and confident." The state's economy was in balance and its government free from corruption and demagoguery. It had experienced "a political and educational renaissance" in the early years of the century, with the result that, as it "began to educate," it also "began to produce, and there were set in motion the progressive, productive forces" that in 1948 distinguished the state. Key conceded that by many economic indices North Carolina ranked "far down the ladder, even among southern states," but none of them, he said, had recorded more sustained progress. Indeed the progressive vogue, Key reported, meant a sense of community responsibility toward the Negro and a willingness to accept new ideas.

"The financial and business elite," as Key called the economic-political combination that dominated the state under the label of the Democratic Party, demonstrated both a "sympathetic respect for the problems [interests?] of corporate capital and of large employers" and "a sense of responsibility in community matters." As evidence Key cited a bond-supported highway construction program, ambitious health programs, improved compensation for teachers and state employees, and substantial outlays for higher education. Among the many specifics that Key did not mention were the assumption by the state of responsibility for secondary roads and for the base salary of public school teachers (both formerly charges of local government), and the enactment of a state retirement system, a workmen's compensation law, and a law to safeguard local governments against excessive debt. This record added up in the minds of the oligarchy to "the capitalistic system liberally and fairly interpreted," as former Governor Oliver Max Gardner put it in 1946. Key does add two skeptical sentences: "The

3 The quotations in this section are from V. O. Key, Jr., *Southern Politics in State and Nation* (New York: Alfred A. Knopf, 1949), 205–11.

effectiveness of the oligarchy's control has been achieved through the elevation to office of persons (chiefly lawyers) fundamentally in harmony with its viewpoint. Its interests, which are often the interests of the state, are [thus] served without prompting."

Although the conventional portrait of North Carolina in the late 1940's was thus a comfortable one of "progress, tolerance, and enlightenment," many Tar Heels, as Key points out, saw things somewhat differently. While the latter citizens did indeed take pride in actual accomplishments, they "seldom indulge[d] in complacency that ignores work yet undone." Some of them surely saw ominous challenges in the facts that the state stood forty-fifth in per capita income; that its thriving textile, tobacco, and furniture industries paid notoriously low wages; that labor organizations were anathema in most major industries; that increasing farm mechanization was driving farm laborers from the land; that illiteracy remained a serious problem; and that opportunities for the black minority were decidedly inferior. But little evidence exists to show that even these uncomplacent Tar Heels had any sense of impending crisis.

Key's analysis of the roles played by the black-belt counties in the politics of his period, his appraisal of sectionalism's impact on both major political parties, and his recognition of the influence of the Republican Party on its dominant Democratic rival cannot be gainsaid. That these factors have undergone change since he wrote is not surprising. One cannot now be so confident when speaking of the black belt; sectionalism has changed in character and the party images based upon it have largely disappeared. Certainly no responsible observer today thinks that the Republicans are "unable to make a serious bid for the governorship" or to "endanger Democratic control of the state." Nor could the previously mentioned reporter look "with a critical eye" at the North Carolina of the post–Key decades and conclude the state "bid[s] fair to be a model community in its race relations, 'something of a living answer to the riddle of race.' "

When Key published his monumental study, the shape of things to come was indistinct. That an activist federal judiciary would press inexorably forward from an already widening base to upset even

North Carolina's answer to the racial riddle, that it would force
upon the state a "reapportionment revolution," that the Congress
would legislate persistently in the civil rights field—these things
were certainly not apparent in 1949. Neither could it be foreseen
that militant blacks would press relentlessly for an end of discrimination and for equality of opportunity. And what seer in the 1940's,
judging the future by the past, could have prophesied that the
state's relatively affluent college students would in the late sixties
begin to demand the reshaping of higher education and a reorder-
ing of national and state priorities, especially with regard to a war
which they and many of their elders regarded as both illegal and
immoral?

Between 1949, when W. Kerr Scott became governor, and 1971,
when his son Robert W. Scott held the office, the politics of the
state underwent extensive and unforeseen change. No enduring
organizations developed in the dominant party to replace the
machine of Furnifold Simmons, which controlled North Carolina
politics from 1901 to 1928, or the Shelby dynasty, which ruled for
the next twelve years. There was factionalism, but no dominant
authority. The historic bisectionalism of east and west declined in
importance and was replaced by a tri-area politics in which the central Piedmont became increasingly dominant. Nonlawyers brought
a different expertise and perspective to the governorship and to one
United States senatorship during much of the period. A resurgent
Republican Party increasingly threatened Democratic control as
more and more disgruntled Democrats broke party lines to support
not only Republican presidential nominees but also Republican
candidates for Congress, for governor, and for other state and local
offices. Actual defection occurred with greater frequency and as
Republican "respectability" increased so did Republican registration. Issues changed or evolved new forms: rural improvement, industrial expansion, educational growth and reorganization at all
levels, judicial and administrative restructuring, taxation of tobacco
and soft drinks—hitherto untouchable sources, legislative reapportionment, general constitutional revision, and, most difficult of all,
search for new and valid answers to the riddle of race.

The Agrarian-Liberal Interlude

The accession of agriculturist W. Kerr Scott to the governorship on January 6, 1949, interrupted the long dominance of the "progressive plutocracy." The gubernatorial campaign of 1948 had begun as a contest between the organization candidate, State Treasurer Charles M. Johnson, who had the support of most of the business and financial interests, and R. Mayne Albright, a young Raleigh lawyer, who sought to make himself and his antimachine program familiar to voters by touring the state in a trailer appropriately named "The Challenger." Until mid-February, 1948, a Johnson primary victory seemed inevitable. Then, almost without warning, Scott resigned as commissioner of agriculture and filed for the gubernatorial nomination. His campaign stressed the needs of rural people and criticized the long-standing practice of the state treasurer of keeping large balances of state funds in non–interest-bearing acccounts with favored banks. Participants in the May primary gave Johnson, Scott, and Albright respectively 40.1 percent, 38.1 percent, and 17.1 percent of their 423,125 votes. Such an indecisive result made Scott's call for a second primary inevitable. In it, his vote increased by 56,327, for a total of 217,620, or 54.3 percent of the 400,304 ballots cast. Scott appears to have won most of the first primary support given Albright. Although Johnson's vote was 12,543 higher than in the first primary, he salvaged only ten eastern counties, seven of them in the southeast (where his home was located), and suffered some reduction of his earlier lead in the western Piedmont and the mountains, where, according to Key, the organization could expect regular support. Scott's victory in the black-belt counties of the east likewise conformed to Key's generalization that these counties were the center of political insurgency against the organization dominated by the "economic oligarchy."

Scott's principal opponent in November, George M. Pritchard, who had served in the Seventy-first Congress (1929–31), carried only six counties in the mountains and western Piedmont, winning 206,166 votes while Scott got 570,995, or 73.2 percent of the total. There can be little doubt that Scott's long-standing concern for rural problems, which he again expounded in an aggressive and colorful campaign, served to cut into Republican strength in its mountain strongholds as well as in marginal areas elsewhere.

"The Squire of Haw River" was an atypical governor. Scott was the first nonlawyer to occupy the governor's chair in the twentieth century, and his entire career, public and private, had produced a deep understanding of rural problems and the perspective to see these in the context of the total economy. The "Go Forward" program outlined in Scott's inaugural address and in a series of special legislative messages in 1949 urged a $200 million bond issue for secondary roads and $50 million to assist counties in public school construction. Dirt roads and inadequate school facilities penalized rural people, who had to endure seasonal isolation and yet helped pay for primary highways—who had, as Scott put it, to pay a "mud tax." The same isolation, he argued, slowed industrial development in rural areas, where the mud roads frequently made labor mobility unpredictable. Both road and school construction proposals required bond issues. The road bonds were to be retired with the aid of a one-cent increase in the gasoline tax, and both issues were subject to popular approval. The new governor also promoted the extension of electrical power and telephone service to rural areas. By the time of his second legislature (1951), he was recommending state government reorganization, a state minimum wage law, and the voting privilege for eighteen-year-olds.[4]

Key's observation, contained in a footnote to *Southern Politics*, that Scott's "inauguration may have marked the beginning of a new phase in the state's politics" and that the new governor "showed signs of a more aggressive liberalism" than the state had heretofore experienced thus proved accurate.[5] Scott encountered a phalanx of stand-patters in the General Assembly, which agreed grudgingly to the $200 million in secondary road bonds but reduced the school construction bonds to $25 million. During the contest, the gover-

[4] David Leroy Corbitt (ed.), *Public Addresses, Letters, and Papers of William Kerr Scott, Governor of North Carolina, 1949–1953* (Raleigh: North Carolina Council of State, 1957), cited hereinafter as *Kerr Scott Papers*.

[5] Key, *Southern Politics*, 215 n.

nor resorted to public appeals utilizing radio to rally his supporters. One Wednesday night, he summoned supporters to Raleigh
the following day for a public hearing on the school program. "I
am standing by the people. I need your help now. Be here tomor-
row." He packed the Memorial Auditorium, and many of the visi-
tors took his advice to contact their legislators in behalf of the
entire "Go Forward" program and thus offset "some of the insidi-
ous propaganda you hear around the Capitol." The bond issues
referendum occurred on June 4, and both won by wide margins.

Scott's personal popularity remained high; his supporters included many younger political leaders such as Terry Sanford.
Though a Scott faction developed within the party, it was frequently
unable to control the party organization and lost several crucial tests
at the polls. In 1951, the General Assembly refused confirmation
of two appointees to the state Board of Education.

The greatest disappointments Scott suffered probably were the
defeat of Dr. Frank Porter Graham for the United States senatorship in 1950 and of Hubert E. Olive in the 1952 Democratic gubernatorial primary. Overlapping the Olive defeat chronologically was
Scott's break with Democratic State Chairman B. Everett Jordan
over the selection of delegates-at-large to the 1952 Democratic National Convention. The governor dramatized this break by publicly
declining a seat on the platform during the 1952 state convention;
he preferred instead, he anounced from the floor, to "stay back
here with the Branch Head Boys." This controversy expanded in
subsequent weeks, and Scott saw the chairmanship of the state's
national convention delegation, which goes traditionally to the incumbent governor, awarded to his predecessor by thirty years, the
aging Cameron Morrison.[6]

Smith-Graham Campaign

Governor Scott, who faced serious difficulties with his legislative
program, allowed sixteen days to elapse before filling the Senate

[6] Paul T. David, Malcolm Moos, and Ralph M. Goldman (eds.), *Presidential
Nominating Politics in 1952*, Vol. III of *The South* (Baltimore: Johns Hopkins
University Press, 1954), 44–46, 49.

seat which had become vacant with the death of J. Melville Broughton in 1949. During this time he considered lists containing the names of fifty-four available Democrats. The political consequences of selecting any one of the three leading candidates would, he felt sure, mean loss of support at a moment when he could ill afford it. Furthermore, he felt strongly that the new senator should not be a corporation lawyer.[7]

Scott's gift for the dramatic never more clearly revealed itself than when, at the first O. Max Gardner Award dinner, in the presence of the faculties of the three major institutions then constituting the consolidated University of North Carolina, he announced in an almost casual manner that he had selected the university's president, Dr. Frank Porter Graham, to be the state's junior senator. The appointment stirred the enthusiasm of the new senator's academic colleagues and of liberals in and out of the South, for as V. O. Key put it, Graham was "by all odds the South's most prominent educator and versatile public servant" and stood in the "forefront of American progressivism."[8] To conservatives and many ambitious Democratic politicians the appointment came as a shock, but in the enthusiasm of the day, their voices were little heard.

In 1950, Graham was opposed by Willis Smith, Speaker of the state House of Representatives in 1931 and later president of the American Bar Association; former Senator Reynolds; and the perennial office-seeker Ola Ray Boyd. The campaign occurred when much of the nation was in a mood to reject the national policies of the Truman Fair Deal and was beginning to listen open-mouthed to the charges of Communist infiltration made freely by Senator Joseph McCarthy. The report of the President's Commission on Civil Rights, of which Dr. Graham had been a member, and the debates over the federal Fair Employment Practices Commission, the Brannan plan for agriculture, Truman's proposal to extend social security legislation to cover national health insurance, and the effort to modify or repeal the Taft-Hartley Labor-Management Relations Act were all matters of nationwide concern. Upon them a

7 *Kerr Scott Papers*, 172.
8 Key, *Southern Politics*, 206 n.

large fraction of North Carolinians already had taken or could be led to take strong negative stands. Most of these matters were passed over in silence by the 1950 Democratic state platform, which confined itself to praise for President Truman's foreign policy and concentrated its attention on balancing the budget without increased taxes. The state's congressional delegation was enjoined to let nothing but "National Disaster or National Defense deter them from these two worthy peacetime objectives." The Republican platform, as one would expect, expressed sharp criticism of the conduct of Truman's administration in foreign and domestic affairs and, unlike its adversary, touched the racial issue by declaring, "We believe in equal rights of all under our laws. We condemn unreservedly the injection into American life of appeals to racial, religious, or other prejudices, such, for example, as are embodied in so-called Fair Employment Practices legislation." [9]

The Smith-Graham contest between two honorable and able men soon became a bitter fight involving every one of the issues mentioned above. The Scott administration, supporters of the national administration, and the liberal Democrats lined up solidly behind Senator Graham. In the face of the charges brought by the Smith camp, in which Smith himself joined, Graham tried to make clear his relatively moderate position on racial matters by declaring his opposition to compulsory FEPC legislation and to compulsory integration of schools. To charges that his softness on communism was evinced by his affiliation with alleged Communist front groups, Graham cited his opposition to communism and his support of policies designed to contain Communist countries. His successes as a negotiator in Indonesia were already a matter of record. He declared that he preferred the existing parity program for agriculture to the Brannan plan and stood on his record as an experienced statesman.

In the first primary, Graham received 49.1 percent of the vote to Smith's 40.4 percent; the senator's plurality over Smith was 53,585 and, in a total vote of 618,479, he lacked 5,635 votes of a clear

[9] *N.C. Manual, 1951,* 132–33, 181–82.

majority. So substantial was Graham's lead that a runoff seemed futile to many Smith supporters. Therefore it is not surprising that Smith hesitated to call for a second primary and did so only a few hours before the legal limit was reached.

How Graham's defeat was accomplished has been described with essential accuracy by Samuel Lubell.[10] The emphasis on the race issue was enormously important. Desegregation all along the line was prophesied. Negro bloc voting for Graham in Piedmont cities and the false charge that he had appointed a Negro to West Point were played up. White wage-earners were threatened with desegregation and possible loss of employment to blacks. But not all the pressure was on race. Graham's support of New Deal–Fair Deal policies was used to appeal to the economic interests of those to whom the race issue was not controlling. Added to these tactics was a serious effort to get to the polls voters known to be anti-Graham but who had not voted in May. In Wake County, for example, which switched to Smith in June, the total second primary vote was up 1,961 votes.

Umstead's Brief Tenure

In light of Scott's difficulties in controlling the state Democratic Party, there was little surprise when Hubert Olive, who had Scott's open support, lost the gubernatorial nomination to William Umstead of Durham. Umstead, a former congressman and senator who had foregone a race against Graham in 1950, received 52.1 percent of the vote to Olive's 47 percent. Olive carried only one metropolitan county, Forsyth, and the other six counties having the largest cities provided 17,032 of Umstead's 28,495 lead over Olive.

The Umstead governorship began on January 8, 1953, and ended on November 7, 1954. Long in fragile health, the governor had been incapacitated by a heart attack after forty-eight hours in office. Fortunately he had already set forth his program for the state in his inaugural address; now he had to work almost wholly through his

10 Samuel Lubell, *The Future of American Politics* (New York: Harper and Brothers, 1952), 100–108.

legislative counsel, former Speaker Frank W. Taylor; his youthful
secretary, Edward L. Rankin, Jr.; and his brother John W. Umstead, Jr., one of the most influential legislators of the century and
already a veteran of eight terms. After several weeks, the governor
was able to receive small groups of legislators and is said to have
argued for his legislative program effectively, but the state had experienced a near-paralysis of executive leadership.[11] Although the
state constitution provided for the devolution of the gubernatorial
powers and duties upon the lieutenant governor during the disability of the governor, no move in this direction occurred and
nearly a decade was to pass before a revision in the constitution
provided clear coverage for cases like Umstead's illness.

Following his recovery, Governor Umstead devoted himself without stint to the duties of his office. He faced the crisis created by
Brown v. Board of Education of Topeka with restraint. On May 27,
ten days after the *Brown* decision, he issued a carefully worded statement concerning the case; a few days later he attended the Conference of Southern Governors, but refrained from committing the
state to any specific action. Then in August, he appointed the racially mixed Governor's Special Advisory Committee on Education,
under the chairmanship of Thomas J. Pearsall, a former speaker of
the state House of Representatives, "to study the problems resulting from the decision." [12]

As is usual in North Carolina, Governor Umstead devoted much
time to preparations for the 1955 legislative session and especially
to the hearings and conferences of the Advisory Budget Commission, which faced, for the first time since the depression, a probable
deficit. For three weeks in October, and again in early November,
he was hospitalized and died on November 7.

During his brief administration, Umstead filled both United
States Senate seats by appointment. Willis Smith had not complet-

11 Edward L. Rankin, Jr., "William Bradley Umstead," in David Leroy Corbitt (ed.),
*Public Addresses, Letters, and Papers of William Bradley Umstead, Governor of North
Carolina, 1953–1954* (Raleigh: North Carolina Council of State, 1957), ix–xii, herein-
after cited as *Umstead Papers.*

12 *Umstead Papers,* xix–xx, 199, 208–209, 211–13.

ed four years of service when he died in 1953 and was replaced by State Senator Alton A. Lennon from coastal New Hanover County. Senator Hoey died eleven months later and was replaced by Sam J. Ervin, Jr., then an associate justice of the state Supreme Court. Ervin continued to serve in 1972, but Lennon's career as a senator was cut short by W. Kerr Scott, who defeated him in the 1954 primary involving seven candidates. Scott's margin of victory was less than 10,000, but it demonstrated his basic strength with the voters, and it likewise provided a chance for his campaign manager, State Senator Terry Sanford, to become a major figure in the Scott wing of the party. Lennon carried forty-two counties—eleven in the mountains, eighteen in the Piedmont, and thirteen in the east, including those surrounding his Wilmington home. Metropolitan counties were equally divided, Buncombe, Mecklenburg, and Guilford going to Lennon; and Forsyth, Durham, and Wake to Scott. Most of the black-belt counties turned up in the Scott camp.

Businessman in Politics

Luther Hartwell Hodges, Umstead's successor, possessed striking and unusual qualifications. After a rapid rise in the textile industry, he had retired as vice president of Marshall Field and Company in 1950. His political and official experience in North Carolina had been confined principally to the Gardner and Ehringhaus administration, during which he served first on the Vocational Education Board and then on the state Highway and Public Works Commission. In 1940 he moved to New York. He served briefly as head of OPA's textile division, as consultant to Secretary of Agriculture Clinton Anderson, as textile consultant for the army in Germany, as industry division chief for the Economic Cooperation Administration in West Germany, and as a State Department consultant for the International Management Conference. An active leader in Rotary International, he was that organization's consultant and observer at the United Nations Conference on International Organization in San Francisco and later at the UN Security Council. This varied career had not provided the usual political experience from precinct to governor, but it had enabled him "to learn a lot about government."

Clearly, Hodges had belonged to the progressive plutocracy in the Gardner period. He had become convinced that businessmen should not leave politics to lawyers and politicians; so when associates suggested he practice what he preached, he soon decided to run for lieutenant governor.[13] Once in the field, he found himself in a contest with three experienced politicians. He campaigned the state, traveling 11,000 miles and making the most of his political inexperience: "My name is Luther Hodges. I'm running for lieutenant governor. I'm not a politician, and I've never run for office before. I'd appreciate your vote." Many an old pro watched the Hodges campaign with amusement, and William Umstead expressed displeasure at Hodges' suggestion that they stood for the same ideas, for it is regarded as a risky thing for primary candidates for governor and lieutenant governor to run as a team. When the primary votes were counted, the neophyte Hodges held a 75,000-vote plurality over State Senator Roy Rowe, but lacked 16,441 votes of a majority. Rowe's decision not to call for a runoff opened for the "businessman in politics" the road to the governorship and national prominence.

Thrust suddenly into the governorship by Umstead's death, Hodges faced a highly controversial legislative session in 1955 and a special session in late July, 1956, to deal with the problems created by the 1954 and 1955 United States Supreme Court decisions in the *Brown* case. During the early part of this period, the new governor had made himself master of administrative matters to the limited extent possible under the state's weak-governor constitution. Seek-

---

13 Luther H. Hodges, *Businessman in the Statehouse: Six Years as Governor of North Carolina* (Chapel Hill: University of North Carolina Press, 1962), hereinafter cited as Hodges, *Businessman.* See also A. G. (Pete) Ivey, *Luther H. Hodges, Practical Idealist,* Men of Achievement Series (Minneapolis: T. S. Denison and Co., 1968), cited hereinafter as Ivey, *Hodges,* for a laudatory but illuminating biographical sketch. A brief sketch describing Hodges' career to 1961 appears in Vol. I of James W. Patton (ed.), *Messages, Addresses, and Public Papers of Luther Hartwell Hodges, Governor of North Carolina, 1954–1961* (3 vols.; Raleigh: North Carolina Council of State, 1960, 1962, 1963), cited hereinafter as *Hodges Papers.*

ing a full term in 1956, he found the Democratic primary but a minor obstacle; three opponents garnered only 65,572 votes to Hodges' 401,082, and then, in a year when Adlai Stevenson carried the state by only 15,468, Hodges defeated Republican Kyle Hayes, 760,480 to 375,379.

In retrospect, the achievements of the Hodges administration loom large. The governor met only one serious defeat, namely, the legislature's refusal to pass a tax on tobacco products and soft drinks, a measure which he sought in early 1955, with the support of the Advisory Budget Commission, to meet about three-fifths of an anticipated biennial revenue deficit of $52 million. In the end the deficit turned out to be less than half the projected figure. Other major tax proposals, however, produced different results. The first, made in 1957, bore directly on the governor's drive to attract new industry to the state and involved an "allocation formula" that restricted the 6 percent corporate income tax to that portion of a company's income "reasonably attributable to the operations performed on the property owned in North Carolina." The second major tax change, urged upon him by State Senator David M. Hall in 1955, involved application of the withholding principle to personal income taxes. Adopted in 1959, after Hall had gone to Congress, the device presented the state with a $27½ million windfall in the 1959–61 biennium and, contrary to the prophecy of its opponents, did not compel the governor and the Advisory Budget Commission to recommend new taxes for the 1961–63 biennium.

Ever since the administration of Cameron Morrison (1921–25), highway construction had occupied a central place in state development. Supported by taxes restricted to highway purposes and by bond issues, the primary road system steadily moved North Carolina forward among the states. Secondary roads long left underdeveloped had been a major concern of the Scott administration and had helped Scott to strengthen his position with rural people throughout the state. The whole system was under the jurisdiction of a fourteen-member Highway and Public Works Commission appointed by the governor from each of fourteen districts. The chair-

man functioned as the political head of the system and each commissioner determined road-building policy in his own district. The
commission was accustomed to having its development programs
supported by most governors, who had left it general freedom in
preparing its own recommendations for the General Assembly.[14]

Hodges secured authorization for an interim study commission,
which recommended a total reorganization. The result was the reduction of the Highway Commission to seven members, none of
whom was responsible for a particular district. The new highway
commissioners were to concern themselves with statewide policy
rather than district matters. The new administration devised a point
system for the choice of secondary roads for hard surfacing.

The most enduring management accomplishment of the Hodges
years came with the establishment of the state Department of Administration. "The chief executive of our state government," the
governor told the 1957 General Assembly, "needs to be as free from
the details of direct day-to-day administration as is reasonably possible. Yet he must have a practical means of keeping himself informed as to how the fiscal and other agencies are functioning." This
major department, which the Reorganization Commission had
proposed and which the governor now endorsed and the legislature
authorized, brought together under one director the budgetary,
purchasing, and property control functions.

Governor Hodges, who had been deeply involved in North Carolina's low-paying textile industry for many years, rather surprisingly
confessed to shock that North Carolina ranked forty-fourth in per
capita income. The shock, however, moved him quickly to analysis
and action. He discovered that, low though they were, industrial
wages placed North Carolina fifteenth in that particular category
and kept the state from dropping lower than forty-fourth in overall
standing. Several major efforts to change the total picture followed.

Hodges' immediate predecessors had been aware of the state's
position and, as previously noted, one of Scott's objectives in his

14 Hodges, *Businessman*, Chap. 6, "Pushing Politics Off the Highways," 126–49.
Many regarded the governor's objective, as suggested in the chapter title, as evidence
of his political naïveté.

secondary road program had been to establish dependable access of rural people to nonfarm employment. Hodges grasped firmly the beginning his predecessors had made. Working through the industry-oriented Department of Conservation and Development and his wide contacts among the business leaders in the state, he sought to develop in all parts of the state a welcoming attitude toward industry. Likewise he supported educational legislation designed to give the state industrial schools. Industry-hunting, domestic industry expansion, and geographical distribution of plants were to remain features of state leadership in subsequent administrations, but in the late 1960's more emphasis was put on the quality of industry attracted and the environmental hazards created.

Recruiting new industry from beyond the state's borders and providing credit for small business ventures within those borders would, it was correctly expected, increase payrolls and many new employees would come under the national minimum wage law. Thousands of workers, however, did not share in these benefits. Three commissioners of labor and Governors Scott and Umstead had urged the adoption of a state minimum wage law. A 75-cent-an-hour bill, from which farm labor and concerns employing less than six were excluded, was enacted in 1959. Some 55,000 workers were covered and, in spite of the dire predictions of many opponents, the new minimum wage proved to be "something that employers can afford, employees deserve and need, and . . . North Carolina's economic progress demands." [15]

Certainly Hodges' performance in office justified his self-description as a "businessman in politics"; but the main crisis in his administration concerned the future of public education in light of the racial segregation cases usually identified as *Brown v. Board of Education*. His attitude in this controversy has been called moderate. His support for the first Pearsall Commission report and share in developing and securing the enactment of the recommendations of the second Pearsall Commission did not so impress many of his

[15] *Ibid.,* 161–68. *Hodges Papers,* II, 35, 103, 136, 481, 561; III, 14, 156, 200–201. Hodges, *Businessman,* 224–50.

critics at the time. Neither did his appeal for voluntary segregation nor his attitude toward the National Association for the Advancement of Colored People and other black organizations. But his record in these matters must be judged both in the context of the times and in the perspective of subsequent years.

During the course of his governorship Hodges became acquainted with the principal Democratic candidates for the presidency. His support of Lyndon Johnson in 1960 contrasted with his successor's activity in behalf of John F. Kennedy, but it was given with the assurance to Kennedy that, were he nominated, Hodges would work vigorously for the ticket. This he did, often at considerable inconvenience to himself, both locally and nationally. As a result of this activity, plus his evident qualifications, and on the basis of endorsement by his successor, President-elect Kennedy named Hodges secretary of commerce, a position which he assumed shortly after the expiration of his term as governor.

After serving in the Kennedy and Johnson cabinets, Hodges returned to the state to serve as chairman of the Research Triangle Institute, helping to promote the research triangle that he helped initiate as governor. The triangle, one of the more successful planned industrial areas in the country, is a 5,000-acre center for research and development in the Raleigh–Durham–Chapel Hill area. Eighteen large corporations and governmental agencies, including the new Environmental Protection Agency, have located research facilities in the triangle, providing $150 million in laboratories and jobs for 8,000, many of whom are highly trained scientists.[16]

Sanford and "the New Day"

As the Hodges administration entered its last year, the certain Democratic contenders for the governorship were John Larkins of Trenton in tidewater Jones County and Terry Sanford of Fayetteville in Cumberland County. Because he had been state Young Demo-

---

16 Hodges, *Businessman*, Chap. 9; Ivey, *Hodges*, Chap. 13; W. B. Hamilton, "The Research Triangle of North Carolina: A Study in Leadership for the Common Weal," *South Atlantic Quarterly*, XLV (Spring, 1966), 254–78.

cratic Club chairman in 1948–49 and then manager of W. Kerr Scott's senatorial campaign in 1954, Sanford had many connections throughout the state and could activate much of the Scott following. In addition, he was young and attractive in a year when the presidential aspirations of John Kennedy, who was the same age, put an obvious emphasis on youth. Larkins, on the other hand, had the advantage of close connections with the established politicians and had contacts in every county. Both men were from the east, and both presumably held moderate racial views. Larkins, who had served several terms in the state Senate to Sanford's one, had been Democratic state chairman and was at the moment a member of the Democratic National Committee. He had some claim on Hodges, whose legislative counsel he had been during 1955 and 1956. Disagreements between the two had made the incumbent governor less than enthusiastic about Larkins, and the business support the latter might have expected Hodges to corral was not forthcoming. Instead the Sanford candidacy attracted numerous prominent leaders in the business world, among them Charles A. Cannon, the textile baron, whose attitude toward union labor was less than enthusiastic. Simultaneously, Sanford picked up the support of the president of the AFL-CIO, civil rights advocates, and states' righters. Circumstances were to ensure his endorsement by academicians and by blacks. His support, says his former press secretary, was a composite of the populace, and included Kerr Scott's principal primary opponent, Charles M. Johnson, and O. Max Gardner, Jr. Such a coalition, early put together, made him the front-runner.

Sanford and Larkins were not alone in the field. A coterie of Hodges backers in the business community, though not with the governor's active initiative, decided to throw their support, which otherwise might have gone to Larkins, to Malcolm B. Seawell, who was then serving by appointment as attorney general. Seawell, who had previously been disinclined to enter the race, now did so. His candidacy, which many attributed to political naïveté, strengthened Sanford's position against Larkins.

The major threat to all three conventional candidates came, however, from Dr. I. Beverly Lake, a former law professor at Wake

Forest College, who as assistant attorney general had represented North Carolina in an *amicus curiae* appearance before the United States Supreme Court in the second phase of the *Brown* case. Dr. Lake had shared in designing the 1955 pupil assignment plan, but subsequently had developed an approach which was presented as an alternative to the 1956 Pearsall Commission proposals. He believed strongly that compulsory integration was not only unconstitutional but also opened sure roads to violence. In a campaign based largely on constitutional issues and particularly on the race question, he quickly became the most dramatic of the candidates.

The primary attracted 653,060 voters, with Sanford, Lake, Seawell, and Larkins getting respectively 41.3 percent, 27.8 percent, 15.5 percent, and 15.4 percent of the total. Lake promptly called for a second primary and, following a heated campaign in which he pressed his anti-Court, anti-NAACP, and prosegregation position against Sanford's insistence that the state needed, not massive resistance but massive education, Lake won 44 percent of the vote to Sanford's 56 percent. The voting performance of the so-called blackbelt counties demonstrated the accuracy of Key's judgment that they did not entertain "a radically atypical attitude on race relations." County-by-county, Sanford ran well in each region; Lake's strength was slight in the mountains and strikingly below his rival's in the Piedmont and the east, including most of the black belt.

Sanford's first major political decision subsequent to his nomination concerned national politics. Most North Carolina delegates to the Los Angeles convention favored Lyndon Johnson; Sanford, who had conferred with Robert Kennedy several weeks earlier, declined to commit himself at a press conference just before leaving for the convention. Once there, however, he announced his support of John F. Kennedy and subsequently made a seconding speech in his behalf, but the delegation gave only 6 votes to Kennedy, whereas Johnson received 27½. The Kennedy votes came from 12 half-vote delegates, who were promptly dubbed "the Dirty Dozen." Anti-Catholicism reminiscent of 1928 made itself felt, thus demonstrating that religion might play a part in the November election comparable to that of race in the May and June primaries.

Sanford's continuing forthright support of Kennedy, as well as the prominence of Hodges in the campaign and the appearance of the candidate himself, proved sufficient to overcome Richard M. Nixon, whose popularity in the state could not match that of Eisenhower in 1952 and 1956. The effect of Sanford's deep involvement in Kennedy's campaign and the quality of his Republican adversary probably served to reduce Sanford's margin of victory. Kennedy's majority was 57,716 to Sanford's 120,236. Kennedy's percentage was 52.1 and Sanford's was 54.4, of a total vote exceeding 1,350,000.

Sanford in his campaign and throughout his administration concentrated his major effort on providing a quality of public education second to none. The budget, which he had watched the outgoing administration prepare, was in balance for the goals set by that administration, but it did not provide for the large additional costs envisioned by Sanford. In nominating and electing him, the voters had been fairly warned that he would call for additional taxes if necessary. For a year he had been called "High Tax Terry," and to the accusation that he offered "pie in the sky," he replied: "If it's pie in the sky, let's put it in the oven and start cooking." [17]

The governor considered two possible tax sources: higher taxes on income and / or changes in the general sales tax law. The former alternative Sanford rejected because the existing income tax was already a major source of state revenue and because the federal government taxed income "almost to the breaking point." The sales tax, however, reached all who shared in the services provided by government and, Sanford said, taken together with the income tax, "is about as fair a method as possible for distributing the costs because the more a man spends, the more he pays in sales tax." Since the sales tax was to be the source, a choice had to be made between in-

[17] Memory F. Mitchell (ed.), *Messages, Addresses, and Public Papers of Terry Sanford, Governor of North Carolina, 1961–1965* (Raleigh: North Carolina Council of State, 1966), contains an essay on Sanford by Graham Jones, his press secretary, xxi-xxxvii. Cited hereinafter as *Sanford Papers*. Other sources of information are Terry Sanford, *But What About the People?* (New York: Harper and Row, 1966), which deals with the role of the author's administration in education; Sam Ragan (ed.), *The New Day* (Zebulon, N.C.: Record Publishing Co., 1964).

creasing the rate to 3½ or 4 cents or to remove the existing exemptions. In recommending the elimination of exemptions, Sanford suggested some special benefits for farmers and motor vehicles but on other hitherto exempt categories the standard 3 percent rate would apply.

The principal and most widely applicable exemption that the governor would eliminate was the tax on food. Originally a part of the sales tax coverage, it had been taken off during the Broughton administration, and the proposal to restore it brought an avalanche of protest from many sources. In the end, the Sanford program passed the General Assembly with minor changes as did also ten multipurpose, capital improvement bond issues. "Food Tax Terry," as his opponents and a resentful part of the public labeled him, had his way at the grocery store cash register, but not at the November ballot box, where the bond issues involving over $61 million went down to stunning defeat by two to one margins in a total vote averaging about 360,000. The largest of the ten, calling for $31 million for the state's educational institutions, carried, usually by small margins, in seven mountain, four Piedmont, and seventeen eastern, or coastal plain, counties. No urban county except New Hanover supported this issue. Among the numerous reasons assigned for defeat were the lack of a vigorous campaign, the inclusion of some seemingly low-priority issues, the impact of the food tax, and the fact that, in many counties, sharply increased property tax bills had just reached voters.[18]

Closely allied with Sanford's multifront efforts to raise the level of public education were his programs regarding gifted children at one extreme and school dropouts and the mentally retarded at the other extreme. Several specialized institutions, including the North Carolina School of the Arts (described by its legislative opponents as a toe-dancing academy) and a Learning Institute designed "to seek, to test and to evaluate all that is known . . . about learning and education," were created. Education beyond high school likewise

18 *Sanford Papers*, xxvi, 26–33; *N. C. Manual, 1963*, 295–302.

presented serious problems, and resulted in a creation of a study commission.

The Sanford administration, like its predecessors, revealed a deep concern about low per capita income. Efforts to attack poverty by raising the minimum wage and attracting industry to poorer portions of the state were partially successful, although the governor had to settle for an 85-cent minimum wage instead of the $1 he had recommended.[19] Sanford demonstrated his talent at involving private foundations in a war on poverty through the North Carolina Fund, as he had in some of his specialized school ventures. The fund became a major source of support for community projects to break the cycle of poverty, and was a precursor of the national antipoverty program.

Next to education roads were the state's most heavily supported enterprise. Sanford recommended and the legislature authorized some sweeping changes. The Highway Commission itself was more than doubled in size. While its professional staff continued to exist, the role of the chairman was enhanced, and the secondary road program was released from the strictures of the impersonal point system and made more amenable to local wishes, largely as expressed by county commissioners.

Dan K. Moore and the Middle Way

A governor constitutionally unable to succeed himself may behave in office differently from one seeking reelection, but, at the very least, he can hardly lack interest in the choice of his successor. Nevertheless a posture of neutrality between aspirants within his own party is often preserved as long as possible. Scott, Hodges, and Sanford remained publicly silent as long as feasible, and their preferences, when at last they were declared, probably helped defeat their choices–Olive, Seawell, and Preyer.

Attention centered on the recently appointed United States district judge, L. Richardson Preyer, whose consent to seek the nomina-

19 *Sanford Papers*, xxxi, 43, 140, 236, 350, 545, 594–95.

tion was won after some 16,000 of his fellow Guilford County citizens had signed petitions urging him to do so and after a September meeting with an influential group of Sanford leaders.

Meanwhile middle-of-the-road conservatives had conducted careful soundings under the guidance of Joseph M. Hunt, Jr., Speaker of the 1961 state House of Representatives and himself a potential candidate. Two caucuses were held in which known aspirants to the governorship participated. While no one committed himself to the race, all but Dr. Lake agreed to support the member of the group who would become a candidate. After this meeting and shortly before Preyer's candidacy became official, former Superior Court Judge Daniel K. Moore, chief counsel for the Carolinas Division of the Champion Paper Company, resident in Canton, declared his candidacy and very soon received the support of all but one of the caucus members.[20]

That one was Dr. Lake, who thought circumstances were more favorable to his own candidacy than to that of the less well known "mountain man," as Moore was sometimes called. Confident of better financial support and county organization than in 1960 and aware of mistakes made in that campaign, Dr. Lake formally declared his candidacy in November, 1963. Unlike his adversaries, for whom he was indeed a formidable rival, he did not have to fumble for a major issue or even make it the main topic of discussion. Instead he could attack or improve upon the policy proposals put forth by Moore and Preyer and make several of his own. All candidates asserted opposition to the civil rights legislation then pending in Congress, but Moore and Preyer were more moderate. Preyer's critics continually pictured him as pro-Negro and took care to emphasize the point as the primary returns came in on May 30 by showing Negro precincts to have bloc-voted for Preyer.

As expected, Preyer led in the May primary with 281,430 votes to Moore's 257,872 and Lake's 217,172. Had Lake placed second, Preyer's second primary chances would have been improved, but

20 For a backward look at the 1960 gubernatorial campaign and a full examination of the 1964 campaign, see James R. Spence, *The Making of a Governor: The Moore-Preyer-Lake Primaries of 1964* (Winston-Salem, N.C.: John F. Blair, 1968).

his elimination, as a few of Preyer's key people had ascertained, would result in seven-tenths of the Lake voters going to Moore. Preyer made a futile attempt to gain either endorsement or neutrality from Dr. Lake, hoping thus to reduce the pro-Moore trend. His failure was less due to Lake's lack of receptivity than to the latter's knowledge that he would be unable to lead his supporters into the Preyer camp had he wished to do so.[21]

The second primary, on June 27, showed only a 12,433-vote increase in Preyer's support compared to a 222,559-vote increase for Moore. Preyer led in only seven Piedmont counties whereas he had carried twenty-eight in all three areas in May, including ten in the east. In the relatively uneventful Republican primary in May, Robert A. Gavin had won renomination by a five-to-one margin over Don Badgely and Charles W. Strong.

During the fall campaign Moore remained relatively aloof from the national ticket, leaving support for Lyndon Johnson chiefly to the candidate for lieutenant governor, Robert W. Scott. Moore's margin of victory over Gavin exceeded that of Sanford four years earlier. However, then as in 1960, an even division of the black vote might have reversed the outcome.

Repeatedly Governor Moore spoke of his goal as the total development of the state, and of partnership with local government, community leadership, and private enterprise.[22] His ideological closeness to the Hodges regime was suggested not only by his policies but also by his appointments to key positions. For example, Ed Rankin became the director of the Department of Administration and Joseph Branch, who had been legislative counsel to Hodges in 1957, returned to the same task in 1965. Moore faced the evolving racial problem by continuing and strengthening the biracial Good Neighbor Council, which Sanford had established and which David S. Coltrane headed until his death in 1968.

Regionalism revealed itself as an important concept in Moore's

21 *Ibid.*, 90–91.
22 Memory F. Mitchell (ed.), *Messages, Addresses, and Public Papers of Daniel Killian Moore, Governor of North Carolina, 1965–1969* (Raleigh: State Department of Archives and History, 1971), hereinafter cited as *Moore Papers.*

total development program. Through regional conservation and development offices industry-hunting received a localized emphasis. He gave support to the Appalachian Regional Development Program and established a Governor's Committee on the Piedmont Crescent to promote orderly growth in this populous, industrialized area. The Coastal Plains Regional Commission, involving North Carolina, South Carolina, and Georgia, was designed to bring to the eastern counties benefits similar to those incorporated in the Appalachian program. Like his predecessor, Hodges, he engaged in one overseas industry-hunting mission.

Governor Moore took a special interest in improving and upgrading law enforcement. With the aid of federal funds, the Governor's Committee on Law and Order was established. The most trying period of disorder came immediately after the assassination of Martin Luther King, Jr., and it became necessary to supplement local law officers with the National Guard.

As his administration drew to a close, Moore remained publicly aloof from the primary contest, supported the national party ticket quietly, and, in the end, took steps to make his successor's transition smooth, efficient, and pleasant.

Bob Scott Moves Up

Robert Walter Scott some years ago described the governorship as representing "the might and majesty of the people of North Carolina," and asserted that "the man who holds it has unequalled opportunity to lead his state . . . and make his contribution to its progress." He gave serious consideration to running in 1964. Although he had held some local party posts and had served two years as master of the state Grange, he offered no such long record of public service as his father had claimed in 1948. To have entered the gubernatorial race against Preyer, Moore, and Lake would have involved grave political risk since he could scarcely have expected Sanford's support. He therefore decided to try for lieutenant governor, winning over primary and general election opposition.

Scott devoted his years as lieutenant governor to upgrading the office and utilizing it to the fullest in forwarding his gubernatorial ambitions. As 1968 approached, it became apparent that his principal gubernatorial opponent would be J. Melville Broughton, Jr., a prominent figure in the Hodges regime, and son of the World War II governor. Scott and Broughton were joined in the first primary by Dr. Reginald Hawkins, a dentist, the first black ever to seek the governorship. Hawkins made an effort to demonstrate that white wage-earners and blacks had common interests and that he deserved their support. Many racially liberal whites, dissatisfied with both the other candidates, gave him support, but in the end he received only 129,808 votes (18.5 percent) compared to Scott's 337,368 (48.1 percent) and Broughton's 233,924 (33.4 percent). Broughton carried only his home county of Wake and six others including Durham. Hawkins ran second in six counties, including Durham and Orange, and his vote was numerically highest in Mecklenburg, his home county, and in the largely urban counties in which he ran third, namely Forsyth, Guilford, Wake, and Cumberland. He showed real strength in the black-belt counties.

Broughton was strongly urged by his conservative supporters to call for a second primary. However, after some deliberation and certain alleged patronage agreements with the Scott organization, he appeared with Governor Moore and Scott to announce his support of the ticket in the interest of party harmony. The decision, for which he received high praise, avoided intraparty carnage in a year of major interparty strife. Scott refrained from active support of the Humphrey-Muskie national ticket, but only announced that he would vote Democratic. Confident that liberal Democrats would not support his Republican adversary, Fourth District Congressman James C. Gardner, Scott and his managers worked hard to hold the east, where George Wallace was strong and where Gardner was conducting a vigorous drive. The result in November was a Scott victory with 52.7 percent of a total vote of 1,558,307.

Scott had repeatedly warned during his campaign that if new taxes were needed to meet the needs of the state, he would recommend them. His comprehensive program in numerous areas made this necessary. Since he was asking over $118 million additional taxes to meet expenditures beyond those included in the budget handed him by the outgoing Moore administration and since these taxes were to fall on sources protected heretofore by inside and outside lobbies, the governor faced a major fight. Efforts to cut the tobacco taxes by levying a tax on soft drinks and increasing the sales tax were made in each house. Ultimately the soft-drink tax and a reduced cigarette tax won out and to meet the need of the state Highway Commission, a penny was added to the gasoline tax. Politically these new taxes provided the groundwork for battles in the 1971 General Assembly and lessened the rapport between the administration and the party chairman, James V. Johnson, who was a large-scale soft drink bottler and lobbied against this particular tax.[23]

Other major legislation passed in 1969 created a state housing corporation and expanded the authority of local governments to do by ordinance various things that had hitherto been handled by local legislation at the state level. Looking to the improvement of state government itself, the governor was authorized to have a reorganization study made, and a constitutional amendment directing that by 1975 the number of administrative agencies (which by some counts numbered over 300) be reduced to not more than 25 was submitted to the people and later ratified by them. A new Department of Local Affairs was created to provide general assistance to local governments, and the Governor's Committee on Law and Order was transferred to it.[24]

During the interim between the 1969 and 1971 legislatures, a special biracial committee recommended major reforms in the Democratic organization. The proposed reorganization limited the tenure of county chairmen, made room on executive committees

---

[23] For Scott's messages to the 1969 legislature and the history of his proposals, see the *Journal of the Senate of the General Assembly of the State of North Carolina, Session 1969*, and a similarly entitled House journal.

[24] A state government reorganization study has been carried on since September, 1969; its recommendations were worked over by a citizens' committee that reported to the governor, who made recommendations based thereon in 1971.

for racial minorities and youth, lessened the centralized control over the choice of delegates and alternates to national conventions, and urged that the legislature establish a presidential primary.

Meanwhile Governor Scott began to play an increasingly important role in national politics as chairman of a Democratic Governors' Committee looking toward 1972. He himself endorsed the candidacy of Senator Edmund Muskie and aided in bringing him to North Carolina to address the inaugural meeting of the state Young Democratic Clubs. This endorsement illustrates how much easier it is for a lame-duck governor to involve himself in a presidential race than for a gubernatorial candidate when support for the national candidate may cost him votes. Sanford resolved this problem in one way, Scott in another. Not all of Scott's political actions were anti-Nixon however, as his support of the Cambodian invasion, in spite of sharp student protest, and his endorsement of revenue-sharing showed.

When the 1971 biennial legislative session met, Scott confronted a concerted effort to repeal the soft-drink tax, to reduce the tobacco tax, and to make available to local governments a half-cent of the recently added penny of the gasoline tax. Only a few million dollars were available to meet the demands of state agencies and institutions above the sums provided in the state budget. Legislation concerning administrative reorganization and major reorganization in higher education divided the legislature on both rational and emotional grounds.

In mid-April the presidential primary law was enacted. This measure alone of those in use in the country provides that the state's delegation to a national party convention shall divide itself proportionately on the first ballot between the top four candidates or as many thereof as receive a minimum of 15 percent of the primary vote. Nationally recognized candidates go on the primary ballot automatically upon payment of $1,000 filing fee; other candidates may use the petition route; 10,000 voters must sign such a petition and 10 cents a name must be paid to local election authorities for a name check. Though this measure arose originally from a Democratic source, its final drafting and enactment were distinctly bi-partisan.[25]

Higher education had been a central area of controversy through-out the late 1950's and 1960's and came to its latest crisis in 1971. The 1959 General Assembly had sharply trimmed the authority of the Board of Higher Education. The 1963 legislature accepted the recommendations of the report of the Study Commission on Educa-tion Beyond the High School, which had been chaired by Irving E. Carlyle. The Carlyle Commission insisted that the state could sup-port only one major university. Doctoral programs, the commission held, should be the exclusive responsibility of the consolidated University of North Carolina, which should be authorized to estab-lish campuses in addition to those at Chapel Hill, Raleigh, and Greensboro. All new programs should receive the prior approval of the Board of Higher Education. In addition, the 1963 legislature hastily enacted a law barring speeches on state-supported campuses by known Communists or persons who had taken the Fifth Amend-ment rather than reveal their ideological position. In the ensuing furor, Governor Moore in 1965 recommended that a special com-mission study the speaker ban law. This commission recommended that authority over speakers be restored to the trustees of the vari-ous institutions. Over vigorous but numerically weak opposition, this recommendation was adopted in a special session in the fall of 1965. Subsequently the law was held unconstitutional by a three-judge United States district court.

The expansion of the consolidated University and the contro-versy over the structure of higher education began anew in 1965 when Charlotte College was renamed the University of North Caro-lina at Charlotte. Two years later, colleges at Wilmington and Ashe-ville became the fifth and sixth campuses. Meanwhile, the state moved to make its independent four-year colleges into regional uni-versities. Over the opposition of Governor Moore and the Board of Higher Education, the 1967 legislature designated four regional universities and two years later, the remaining five state-supported

25 *North Carolina Session Laws, 1971*, Chap. 225, ratified April 22, 1971.

colleges were made universities by legislative decree. So North Carolina found itself in the summer of 1969 with a six-campus consolidated university and twelve regional universities. Adding to the problem was a long fight over the establishment of a medical school at East Carolina University.

The continuing difficulties with higher education led to the reorganization of the Board of Higher Education in 1969, adding to the board as ex officio members the governor, the chairmen of the Senate and House committees on appropriations, finance, and higher education, and designating the governor as chairman. Governor Scott's experience in his role as chairman was responsible, in part, for his appointment of a study committee headed by former Senator Lindsay Warren, Jr. The regular session of the legislature was unable to deal with the controversy surrounding the committee's recommendations; however, a special session in the fall established a single university system under a board of governors which includes representatives of minority races, women, and the minority party. All of the state's institutions of higher learning are now units of the new University of North Carolina. Each member institution has a board of trustees with delegated powers.

Decline of One-Party Dominance

One-party dominance persists, but the minority party never wholly abandoned the field and in recent years has experienced an impressive resurgence. Republicans have maintained their mountain county strength and have developed elsewhere to produce wide interparty rivalry at all levels of government. Increasing urbanization and the concentration of greater proportions of state voters in an urban crescent from Raleigh to Charlotte, a noticeable change in race relations following the 1954 school desegregation decision, and increased school integration of the 1960's have affected traditional sectional voting patterns and the political ideology of both the Democratic and Republican parties.

Although urbanization has increased the size of the Republican vote, particularly for presidential and gubernatorial candidates, the

Republican Party is far from an urban party in the state. Its failure to attract any measurable support from the state's urban black electorate, nearly all of which has gone to Democratic candidates, has produced spirited party competition in urban and metropolitan regions, but no predominantly Republican vote. The success of Republican candidates in state assembly and local elections is still concentrated in areas of sectional strength of the party.

The rise of presidential and gubernatorial Republicanism can be attributed largely to the ability of the party's candidates to attract the support of urban, middle-class voters with issues and campaign styles that cut across traditional, regional voting patterns. The development of competition for executive and congressional offices has increased gradually in the state since 1940. However, the development of competition has differed in time and degree in presidential, gubernatorial, and congressional politics. Presidential and congressional competition developed early in the post–World War II period, but gubernatorial rivalry has been vigorous only in the decade of the 1960's. Congressional competition has been affected by factors other than urbanization–notably reapportionment and sectional strength of the Republican Party–and requires separate analysis.

In North Carolina, as in the rest of the South, the principal question raised in connection with the growth of interparty competition in what was once a solid one-party region has to do with the impact of urbanization. North Carolina remains one of the more rural states, with 55 percent of its population still living in places of less than 2,500 population. Yet urbanization has affected the state economically and politically, primarily through the growth of the Piedmont crescent. This band of twelve counties, extending from Raleigh in the east to Charlotte and Gastonia in the southwest, has experienced dramatic change during the past two decades. One in three North Carolinians lives in the crescent, and by 1980 it is predicted that one in two will live there. During the decade from 1960 to 1970, these counties grew at almost double the state's population growth rate, while other counties in the east and mountain region

Table 1

POPULATION CHARACTERISTICS OF GEOGRAPHIC REGIONS
IN NORTH CAROLINA

Region	Percentage of State Population 1970	Percentage of State Population Increase from 1960	Percentage Urban 1970	Percentage of State's Urban Population 1970	Percentage Black in Population 1970	Percentage Black in Population Increase/Decrease from 1960
East	31.0	.5	29.7	25.7	37.4	−1.9
Piedmont	24.1	7.2	21.4	17.7	22.2	− .5
Piedmont Crescent	36.6	19.0	57.5	52.6	19.0	− .3
Mountain	8.3	5.6	10.1	4.9	4.9	+2.6
STATE	100.0	11.5	45.0	100.0	23.4	−1.1

were losing population. (See Table 1 for a comparison of population characteristics of the crescent and other regions.)

The importance of the crescent in state politics (Table 2) is nearly as dramatic as its economic importance. Over a third of the state's presidential popular vote was cast there in 1968—a 16 percent increase from the 1960 election. Four of the governors and seven of ten United States senators have claimed residence there between 1946 and 1971. While black voter registration is low, the concentration of blacks in this urbanized region and the greater tendency of urban blacks to vote have added to the impact of the urban black electorate, which nearly equals the impact of black voting in traditional black-belt counties.

Regionalism, or sectionalism, has long been an important factor in the politics of North Carolina. V. O. Key thought the state's sectional rivalries more tender than elsewhere in the South. Examining state politics by regions—separating the urbanized Piedmont crescent from the coastal plain, rural Piedmont, and mountains—highlights the continuing importance of regionalism as well as urbanism.

At the beginning of the postwar period, Republican presidential

Table 2

Electoral Characteristics of Geographic Regions in North Carolina

Region	Percentage of State Vote Cast in 1968	Change from 1960	Black Percentage of Registered Vote	Percentage of State's Black Voter Registration	Percentage of State Registration	Voter Registration			
						Democrat	Republican	American Independent	Other
East	30.3	12.6	24.5	45.7	27.7	87.6	10.7	.3	1.3
Piedmont	25.9	7.9	14.5	19.1	26.8	71.0	25.7	.4	2.9
Piedmont Crescent	35.6	16.6	13.3	33.4	36.2	73.6	23.2	.4	2.8
Mountain	8.2	− 5.9	1.5	1.8	9.3	62.2	35.3	.1	2.4
STATE	100.00		15.3	100.0	100.0	75.7	21.5	.3	2.4

candidates fared no better in the Piedmont crescent counties than
elsewhere outside of the traditionally Republican mountain counties. Increasing Republicanism in the crescent was concomitant
with growing urbanization. Support for Eisenhower was particularly strong in the crescent, approaching the Republican vote in the
traditional mountain counties in 1952 and exceeding it in 1956.
The importance of the Piedmont crescent vote for Republican
presidential candidates is indicated in Figure 1. Not only has the

Figure 1
REPUBLICAN PERCENT OF NORTH CAROLINA PRESIDENTIAL VOTE,
BY REGION, 1948–1968

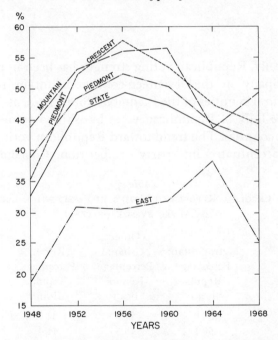

Republican vote in this region exceeded the traditional mountain
vote in three of the six elections since 1952, but the vote for the
party's presidential candidates in metropolitan Piedmont counties
has consistently exceeded the Republican vote in nonmetropolitan
Piedmont counties since 1952.

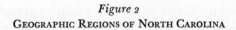

Figure 2
GEOGRAPHIC REGIONS OF NORTH CAROLINA

Historically, Republican voting strength has been in rural counties—principally in the seventeen-county mountain region and
scattered rural counties of the Piedmont. Since 1948, as Table 3 indicates, the bulk of Republican votes has shifted to metropolitan
and urban counties. The trend toward Republican voting in urban
areas has accentuated interparty competition. Concomitant with

Table 3
NORTH CAROLINA REPUBLICAN VOTING IN PRESIDENTIAL ELECTIONS,
1948–1968, BY SIZE OF PLACE

Year	Metropolitan: Percentage Repub- lican	Other Urban: Percentage Repub- lican	Rural: Percentage Repub- lican	State: Percentage Repub- lican
1948	33.0	24.8	34.7	32.6
1952	50.1	45.3	41.4	46.0
1956	55.5	48.0	41.5	49.3
1960	51.8	46.9	45.0	47.8
1964	44.9	43.6	42.7	43.8
1968	58.4	37.9	37.3	39.5

Source: *North Carolina State Government Statistical Abstract* (Raleigh: Department
of Administration, 1971).

the growth of urban Republican voting is a marked shift of population growth and voter turnout in metropolitan and urban counties. Since 1948, metropolitan counties have increased from just under one-fourth to around one-third of the state's population (Tables 1 and 2). Likewise, the percentage of the vote cast in metropolitan counties has grown during the past three decades from 22 percent to 37.6 percent.

Table 3 analyzes the trend in Republican voting in the past six presidential elections. The eight metropolitan counties are those which had an urban area of 50,000 or more population in 1970. The other urban counties include those with at least one-fourth of the population living in towns of 2,500 or more (excluding metropolitan counties). Fifty of the state's one hundred counties do not meet this classification of urbanism and are considered rural.

Although the data support the hypothesis that rising Republicanism in the South is tied to increasing urban and metropolitan growth,[26] it would be misleading to characterize the Republican Party in North Carolina as an urban party. The strength of Republican presidential candidates among urban and metropolitan voters is mostly based on candidates and issues rather than party identification. Much of the Piedmont crescent remains Democratic in orientation in state, congressional, and local voting, and not all presidential candidates have fared equally well. The setback for the Republican Party in the state in the 1964 presidential election and 1966 state voting resulted from two factors—the appeal of Johnson in traditional Republican areas, particularly in mountain counties, where the Appalachian programs were a Democratic asset; and the failure of Barry Goldwater to capture the support of urban Democrats. However, it is noteworthy that Goldwater was able to maintain more support in the Piedmont crescent than in the traditionally Republican mountain counties.

[26] Donald S. Strong, *Urban Republicanism in the South* (University, Ala.: University of Alabama Press, 1960); Bernard Cosman, *Five States for Goldwater* (University, Ala.: University of Alabama Press, 1966); and Douglas Gatlin, "Socio-Economic Bases of Party Competition: A Case Study of North Carolina" (Ph.D. dissertation, University of North Carolina, 1963).

The 1968 election in the state was interesting in several respects. Not only was it the first time in forty years that a Republican received the state's electoral vote, but the irony is that Nixon won with 39.5 percent of the popular vote after having lost to Kennedy in 1960 with 47.9 percent. In 1968, Nixon gained non-Republicans at a greater-than-anticipated rate in metropolitan areas, but fared worse than recent Republican candidates in the other urban areas. Wallace's gain at the expense of both Humphrey and Nixon in rural areas raises the question of which of the major party candidates was hurt most by the third party. One preelection opinion poll found that 64 percent of Wallace voters would be drawn from Democratic voters, on the basis of votes cast in three preceding gubernatorial elections.[27] A comparison of presidential and gubernatorial voting in 1968 tends to confirm the speculation that most of Wallace's support came from previously Democratic voters. Nixon's loss to Wallace can be calculated on the basis of the difference between the Republican presidential and gubernatorial votes. Heretofore, the Republican presidential vote had exceeded the Republican gubernatorial vote by 18,000 to 200,000 votes. In 1968, however, Nixon received 109,833 votes less than the Republican gubernatorial candidate. Assuming those persons who favored the Republican gubernatorial candidate would have preferred Nixon if Wallace had not been on the ticket, Nixon would have received 737,025 votes rather than 627,192. This estimate assumes that the rest of Wallace's votes —or roughly 65 percent who voted Democratic in the gubernatorial election—were lost by the Democratic presidential candidate. On the basis of this distribution, Humphrey would have had 850,418, or 53.5 percent of the vote, and North Carolina would have remained Democratic.

The Governorship—Democratic Preserve?

Gubernatorial competition in the state has developed not only at a more deliberate pace but also has been less intense, until the decade

27 A. W. White, "The Wallace Voter in North Carolina in 1968" (M.A. thesis, University of North Carolina, 1969).

of the sixties. From 1940 until 1956, Democratic gubernatorial candidates received in the neighborhood of two-thirds of the vote, but
starting in the 1960's, Democratic nominees have won with relatively fewer votes. The competitiveness of gubernatorial politics
is pointed up by the sizable vote (45.5 percent) received by a relatively unknown Republican, Robert Gavin, against a popular
Democrat, Terry Sanford, in 1960. Gavin did not run quite as well
against Dan K. Moore in 1964, but James Gardner, in 1968, came
within 3 percent of becoming the first Republican governor in the
twentieth century, despite the fact that his Democratic opponent,
Robert W. Scott, was also a well-known Democrat and the son of the
governor who realigned Democratic Party control in 1948.

In gubernatorial elections, Republican success in attracting a
large number of votes followed intensely fought Democratic primaries. Undoubtedly the two are related. Democratic officials, at
least, have felt that the party can afford the luxury of primary competition only if party factions are willing to make a special effort to
reunite for the Republican challenge in the fall. But factors other
than Democratic factionalism have contributed to Republican voting. The politics of the state has changed. While regional voting
patterns are still identifiable, the margin of victory for Democratic
candidates has dropped appreciably across the state. Party registration remains three-fourths Democratic, but more and more Democrats are willing to vote for Republican candidates whose issues
and campaigns are more appealing than those of the Democratic
candidate. The same factors that have helped Republican presidential candidates have worked to the advantage of gubernatorial
candidates. In the three elections of the 1960's, Republican gubernatorial candidates received over half of the popular vote in the
urbanized Piedmont crescent counties, running considerably better
there than in the traditional mountain region. Republican candidates also have cut into the traditional Democratic support in the
east, rising from a low of less than 10 percent of the gubernatorial
vote in 1948 to an average of 30 to 40 percent of the vote in the
1960's. (See Figure 3.)

One factor which has enabled the Democratic Party to maintain

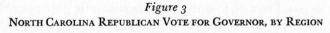

Figure 3
NORTH CAROLINA REPUBLICAN VOTE FOR GOVERNOR, BY REGION

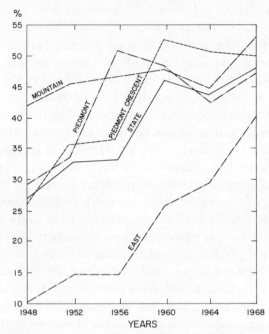

the governorship as a Democratic preserve is the absence of widely known Republican candidates. It was not until 1960 that the Republican Party was able to put up a candidate with a program and campaign resources to make a statewide appeal.

The first Republican to give any serious challenge to Democrats was Robert Gavin in 1960 and 1964. A moderate with definite ideas about the state's needs, he held Terry Sanford to a 120,000-vote margin. Gavin's campaign was progressive, pushing for a $1-an-hour minimum wage, bond issues for highway construction, civil service for all state employees, and advances in education, industrialization, and per capita income. He noted repeatedly that North Carolina ranked thirty-eighth to fiftieth among the states in various economic and educational indicators.

Gavin ran well in the Piedmont, particularly in the crescent, where his vote exceeded Sanford's. In 1964, he hoped to maintain the urban vote and, with the help of Barry Goldwater, to make inroads into the Democratic stronghold of the rural east, which continued to hold the balance of power in gubernatorial elections. However, the Goldwater coattail effect did not materialize, and Gavin did little better in the east than he had in 1960. Johnson ran better than Goldwater in the east, winning some 60 percent of the vote, and Gavin's Democratic opponent, Dan K. Moore, greatly reduced the Republican vote in the west. The first modern-day Democratic governor from the mountains, Moore carried Buncombe County, the area's only SMSA, by a margin of 9,000 votes.

More important was Gavin's failure to get his party to broaden its appeal beyond sectional and urban middle-class voters. Despite a vigorous, issue-oriented campaign, Gavin never addressed civil rights questions, and by his own estimation, received no more than 3 percent of the 200,000 votes cast by blacks. With Moore's winning margin only 184,000 votes, a broader voter appeal might have helped the Republican Party considerably.

In 1968, former Congressman James W. Gardner not only came closest of any twentieth-century Republican to capturing the governorship but also by most prognostications might have succeeded had it not been for several strategic decisions which alienated the more moderate and Old Guard Republicans in the state. Gardner, a thirty-two-year-old businessman from the east, two years previously had made a successful second attempt to defeat sixteen-term Congressman Harold D. Cooley, chairman of the House Committee on Agriculture. A former party chairman, Gardner had already developed statewide contacts, and he used his congressional offices as the base for making himself the apparent party leader. Gardner waged a vigorous campaign, but like Gavin earlier, appealed to the more conservative Democratic voters in the east. In what was regarded by political strategists as a more serious mistake, Gardner, after defeating John L. Stickly in a party primary, switched from his pledged support of Nixon at the Republican National Convention and became a fervent backer of Ronald Reagan. Though he managed to swing a majority of the North Carolina convention delegates to Reagan, Gardner suffered thereafter from lukewarm support of some key party regulars in his own campaign. Nixon's philosophy was closer than Reagan's to that of the GOP Old Guard in the state.

The Regional Republicans

Unlike executive politics, where the regional strength of Republicanism has been a hindrance to the party in broadening its base into Democratic strongholds, the sectional strength of the party as well as its ability to attract urban voters has helped in congressional races. The state's Republicans have gained a slow but steadily increasing foothold in the House of Representatives.

However, in the United States Senate, the Republicans have not been able to mount a serious challenge. Both Senate seats are held by Democrats who have received wide margins of support. Until the 1960's Democratic majorities in United States Senate races averaged two-thirds of the vote. The margin has narrowed, but still the most recent elections were not competitive. B. Everett Jordan received 61 percent of the vote in 1960 and 55.5 percent in 1966. Sam J. Ervin was reelected with 60 percent of the vote in 1964.

The solid Democratic hold on the state's House seats was broken in 1952, when Charles R. Jonas was elected from the then Tenth District (Charlotte). Jonas was the first Republican congressman from the state since 1931, when his father and George M. Pritchard were defeated after serving one term each.

In 1961, the Democratic state legislature, faced with the necessity of eliminating one of the state's twelve seats in Congress, redistricted in a manner that they hoped would eliminate Jonas. But Jonas once again defeated an incumbent Democrat, and a second Republican, James Broyhill, was elected in the neighboring Ninth District, defeating Hugh Q. Alexander, a five-term incumbent. One of the most spectacular recent Republican victories was Gardner's defeat of Cooley in 1966 in the Fourth District. Facing a serious Republican challenge, Cooley banked on his seniority and chairmanship of the important House Agriculture Committee. However,

Gardner's heavily financed campaign appealed to urban voters of the district who were not as concerned with the state's voice in national agricultural policy as other voters of the district. Gardner polled a 10,000-vote margin in Raleigh and Wake County, and Cooley suffered a loss of support in other areas because of what has generally been described as a lack of contact with his constituents. In 1968, the Republicans gained two more congressional seats with the election of Wilmer D. Mizell in the Fifth District and Earl B. Ruth in the Eighth. Both defeated Democrats well-known in state politics. Simultaneously, however, the Fourth was won back by Nick Galifianakis.

Several factors have contributed to Republican success in congressional politics in the state. As Donald Strong has pointed out, the most logical place for southern Republicans to make inroads in a Democratic area is the House of Representatives.[28] House victories are of much greater value than victories at the local level and the possibility of success is much greater than at the statewide level. The three types of southern Republicanism which Strong identifies—mountain, immigrant, and metropolitan—have all worked to Republican advantage in North Carolina. The Jonas and Gardner victories are largely the result of metropolitan voting, with Jonas benefiting from both metropolitan and traditional Republican voting (which in North Carolina has not been limited to the mountain region). Gardner's urban vote, in the congressional race with Cooley, had a strong element of immigrant Republicanism. North Carolina's Fourth Congressional District, which subsequently reverted to the Democrats when Gardner dropped out to run for governor, contains one of the fastest-growing urban areas of the state, with a heavy influx of voters from outside the region. Three other Republican seats are largely the result of sectional strength of the party. Mizell and Ruth were both local Republican officeholders, and Broyhill was elected in a district which traditionally votes heavily Republican in state and local elections.

From 1941 to 1952, Democratic gerrymandering of congressional

28 Strong, *Urban Republicanism in the South.*

districts sufficed to ensure the unanimous control of the congressional delegation, and of all but the Tenth District for another decade. Districts drawn in 1941 gave Democrats a considerable advantage, if in no other way, by keeping in office three rural Democratic congressmen who lived in adjoining eastern counties. When the loss of a seat in Congress forced the General Assembly to redistrict in 1961, the new reapportionment plan still reflected some partisan imbalance as well as considerable population inequity. In 1965 a suit was instituted in a United States district court challenging the state's congressional districts as well as the House and Senate plans of the General Assembly. In *Drum v. Seawell* both the state and congressional reapportionment and redistricting plans were invalidated and the legislature was given a deadline to enact valid plans. The new districts, drawn in January, 1966, in a special legislative session, came considerably closer than previous districts to the court's one-man, one-vote requirement. The court approved the state legislative districts, but disallowed the congressional district pattern and gave the General Assembly until July 1, 1967, to redraw the lines. The legislature ran past this date, but in the end provided its third congressional map of the decade.[29]

Redistricting according to the court's standards has forced upon the Democratic legislature congressional districts with considerable Republican advantage. In fact, it would be extremely difficult now to draw districts that would put Republicans at a disadvantage. This the legislature at least tacitly recognized when districts were redrawn in 1971 with considerably greater ease than most political observers had expected. Yet, the effect of the 1971 reapportionment was to increase the Republican advantage in seven of the eleven districts. In most cases the net advantage was small, but it is possible

[29] Preston W. Edsall, "North Carolina: 'This Bill or Nothing'" in *The Politics of Reapportionment*, ed. Malcolm E. Jewell (New York: Atherton Press, 1962); *Reapportionment and Redistricting in North Carolina, 1961–1965* (Chapel Hill: Institute of Government, 1965); John Sanders, *Legislative Representation in North Carolina: A Chapter Ends* (Chapel Hill: Institute of Government, 1966), reprinted from *Popular Government*, February-March, 1966.

that a fifth Republican district was created when the Fourth District, represented by Democratic Congressman Nick Galifianakis, lost Orange County, the home of the University of North Carolina, which gave Galifianakis a 2,000-vote edge in a close race in 1970. The influx of immigrant Republicans to the Raleigh-Durham metropolitan area has already made this a "swing" district, and the loss of the most consistently Democratic county creates a considerable advantage for Republican candidates.

After the 1971 redistricting, six of the state's eleven congressional districts include urban concentrations, a considerable shift in the balance of urban-rural control even from 1960. Three of the six urban districts are already represented by Republican congressmen. Should the Republican national record look good in 1972 and in subsequent national elections in the 1970's, further Republican congressional gains are not inconceivable in North Carolina.

Difficult as congressional redistricting has proven, legislative reapportionment has been even more complicated. Prior to *Baker v. Carr*, the General Assembly had been complete master in the field. Each of the hundred counties had one representative in the House; twenty seats were left to be distributed among the more populous counties in accordance with a constitutionally established mathematical rule. Senators, each of whom was supposed to represent an equal number of inhabitants, numbered fifty. All efforts to reapportion and redistrict failed in the 1930's and 1950's, but the 1961 legislature succeeded in meeting state constitutional requirements regarding the House. Senate redistricting went unresolved until a 1963 special session. Then, in 1965, the entire geography of congressional and legislative representation was held unconstitutional in *Drum v. Seawell*. A special legislative session in January, 1966, established a system of House and Senate districts electing from one to seven House members and from one to three senators. This plan enabled all voters in Mecklenburg County to vote for 1/17 of the total membership of the legislature, while in some counties voters could choose only 1/85. There were various gradations in between, but federal courts allowed this combination of multimember and single-member districts to stand.[30] Indications as of July 1, 1971, were that this type of legislative districting would again prevail, but a strong probability exists that constitutional tests are forthcoming. Solving the problem either with equal multimember districts or with single-member districts is rendered more difficult by a recently adopted constitutional provision forbidding the division of any county in the formation of a state legislative district.

Further to complicate matters, some districts follow the "numbered-seat" plan, which requires that a candidate designate the particular seat for which he runs. This device necessarily makes bloc voting ineffective. Bloc voting itself is forbidden by law in some counties, and efforts to repeal these laws failed in 1971 as did a statewide measure requiring that, when there are three or more of the same types of offices to be filled, a voter must vote for at least a majority of them.

The GOP in Town and Country

The level of electoral support used in judging the growth of interparty competition in executive and congressional elections is less useful than the number of contested seats, the frequency of party success, and the geographical spread of Republican competition in local politics.[31] These variables are used in determining the base of the Republican Party in state legislative and local elections. Of the three, the geographic concentration of Republicanism is the best indicator of the strength of the party in the early 1970's.

Republicanism at the local level is basically much as it has been throughout the entire era of one-party dominance. The frequency of party success in local elections is concentrated in the mountain region, with only scattered officeholding in the east. However, as

30 Preston W. Edsall, "North Carolina: People or Pine Trees," in Jewell (ed.), *The Politics of Reapportionment*; Preston W. Edsall, "State Legislatures and Legislative Representation," *Journal of Politics*, XXX (1968), 281–90; and Sanders, *Legislative Representation in North Carolina*.

31 In this section, we have used a mode of analysis similar to that employed in Jack D. Fleer, *North Carolina Politics: An Introduction* (Chapel Hill: University of North Carolina Press, 1968).

Malcolm Jewell has pointed out, success for the Republican Party in state legislative politics, outside of traditionally Republican counties, is likely to come from metropolitan counties.[32] This has been the case as the Republican Party in North Carolina has spread out from its traditional mountain base. Of the thirty-one House and Senate seats which Republicans held in the 1971 General As-

Figure 4
REPUBLICAN REPRESENTATION IN NORTH CAROLINA GENERAL ASSEMBLY

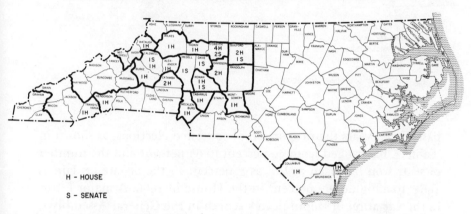

H - HOUSE

S - SENATE

sembly, sixteen were in the Piedmont crescent, nine others were in counties adjoining the crescent, and only six were in traditional Republican counties. Only three were east of Guilford County, in the geographic center of the state. The same geographic concentration holds among the twenty-two county boards of commission controlled by Republican officeholders. In the 1970 election, Republicans elected 22.4 percent of county commissioners, and among the county governments dominated by Republicans, six were in the Piedmont crescent, including the metropolitan counties of Mecklenburg, Forsyth, and Guilford.

The success of the party in winning legislative elections and the ability to contest General Assembly seats has been erratic. In the

---

32 Malcolm E. Jewell, *Legislative Representation in the Contemporary South* (Durham: Duke University Press, 1967), 105–21.

Figure 5
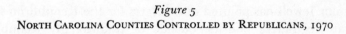
NORTH CAROLINA COUNTIES CONTROLLED BY REPUBLICANS, 1970

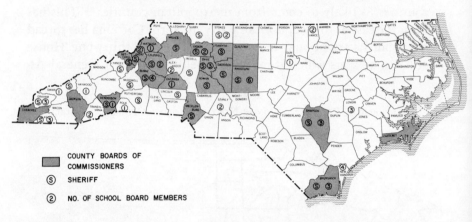

◼ COUNTY BOARDS OF
   COMMISSIONERS

Ⓢ SHERIFF

② NO. OF SCHOOL BOARD MEMBERS

past fifteen years the proportion of contested elections, as shown in Table 4, has ranged from 32 percent to 67 percent and the number of seats won has been as low as 2 percent in the Senate, as late as 1964, to a high of 22 percent in the House in 1966. A major factor in the variation of Republican strength in the General Assembly is the availability of Republican candidates. Even the metropolitan counties, the source of recent southern Republicanism, have not provided as many Republican legislative candidates and legislators as might be expected. In the seven SMSA's, where the Republican Party is frequently better organized and which have a larger pool of potential candidates, the party has had problems in recruiting and rarely has a full slate of candidates for legislative seats. Recruitment has improved recently in these counties. In 1970, Democrats were unchallenged in only nine out of forty-seven legislative races in the seven metropolitan counties, although the Republicans had a full slate only in Guilford, Forsyth, and Buncombe counties.

Based on local officeholding, Republicans control local, county, and state legislative government in only 10 of the 100 counties. Although 266 Republicans were elected to various local offices in the state in 1970, including 24 sheriffs, 90 county commissioners,

Table 4
PROPORTION OF LEGISLATIVE SEATS CONTESTED AND
WON BY REPUBLICAN PARTY IN NORTH CAROLINA

	House		Senate	
	Percentage Contested	Percentage Won	Percentage Contested	Percentage Won
1952	53%	12%	46%	4%
1954	53	8	50	2
1956	33	11	32	6
1958	49	3	42	2
1960	49	12	44	4
1962	61	16	58	4
1964	67	12	58	2
1966	50	22	52	14
1968	39	23	48	18
1970	60	20	64	14

Source: Adapted from Malcolm Jewell, *Legislative Representation in the Contemporary South* (Durham, N.C.: Duke University Press, 1967), Chap. 4.

64 school board members, and 31 state legislators, these were mostly scattered victories. Republicans dominate local government only in the mountain counties of Avery, Clay, and Mitchell; one metropolitan county, Forsyth; five Piedmont counties, namely, Burke, Caldwell, Davidson, Davie, and Randolph; and one eastern county, Sampson. Sampson, located in the coastal plain with a population of over 30 percent black, is interesting for its deviant political behavior, which dates back to the days of the Populist revolt before the turn of the century. As an indication of the strength of political tradition on the southern voter, Sampson County in the heart of Democratic country has given the Republican Party the majority in ten of the last seventeen presidential elections.

Bipartisan Paradox

There is no doubt that North Carolina has become an area of serious bipartisan conflict at both the state and national levels and in metropolitan regions at the local level. Yet, somewhat paradoxically, the state has found itself virtually unmatched even among some of the former one-party states of the South in an allegiance to Democratic presidential candidates and Democrats in statewide races for governor, offices of the Council of State, and the United States Senate.

The Republican Party structure in the state is bolstered by Old Guard moderates and some bright young leaders, including James E. Holshouser, Jr., the present chairman. The party platform is not much different from the state Democratic platform, but Republicans, unlike the Democrats, have suffered from a shortage of candidates who will champion progressive programs. The party has had few candidates like Gavin; more often it has been susceptible to opportunists whose ill-fated campaigns have left the party in disarray. As a result, Republicans have entered recent elections at a considerable disadvantage against Democrats.

The great excess of Republican votes on election day over Republican registration is explained at least in part by the fact that Democratic victories have been by wide margins until recently. This has meant that many thousands of ideological Republicans have remained registered Democrats so as to participate in the actual choice of the ultimate winners. Perhaps the increasing closeness of key elections, the consequent greater attractiveness of Republican nominations, and such new ventures as the Presidential Primary Act will encourage these pseudo-Democrats to change their registration.

It seems necessary for the party's healthy development that it increase its voter registration substantially and recruit more candidates of sufficient statewide stature to overcome the relative prominence of Democratic candidates, most of whom are either incumbents or have considerable public records. Of even greater importance is the need to broaden the party's base of voter appeal, particularly among young voters, organized labor, and blacks.

Candidate recruitment appears to be less difficult, but the supply of widely known names is still not great. Republican congressmen, the highest-ranking officeholders, are frequently mentioned as possible gubernatorial candidates; however, with the exception of Gardner, congressmen have not yielded to the temptation to run for governor. Recently the party has been able to develop potential candidates of statewide stature in the legislature. In addition to Holshouser, Representative Charles Taylor and Senator Harry Bagnal have demonstrated an interest in state-level problems and have swung Republican Party support to issues of legislative ethics, the gubernatorial veto, and a presidential preference primary, as well as state budgeting and spending. The party has the choice of candidates who are becoming involved in issues and problems of the state or continuing to turn to candidates like James C. Gardner, who can mount an aggressive "new politics" campaign without building a base for continued two-party competition.

As long as Democrats are willing to continue voting for Republican candidates, Republican leaders have been relatively unconcerned about the status of the party's voter registration, which stands now at barely one-fourth of the registered voters. However, the party cannot be unconcerned about the potential of the black and young vote. This concern was stated most aptly by gubernatorial candidate Robert Gavin shortly after his defeat by Dan K. Moore, a conservative whom blacks refused to endorse in 1964. In a speech to the Republican Governors Association, Gavin said, "The Negro vote is increasingly rapidly. From 200,000 in North Carolina this time, it will be 250,000 in 1966 and possibly 300,000 in 1968. I do not believe we can ignore this vote."

The problem of the Republican Party in appealing to black support in state politics is less one of enticing an immovable black voting bloc than of deciding if a better strategy is to appeal to this vote at the risk of losing some support that the party already has— other philosophical questions aside. North Carolina historians agree that prior to their disfranchisement in 1900, blacks constituted a majority of the Republican Party. The few blacks who voted between 1900 and the advent of the New Deal probably voted Republican. Since that time, they have become a fairly solid Democratic bloc. However, blacks currently are not entrenched in the Democratic Party. In the last two gubernatorial elections, they have demonstrated their political independence, first by refusing to endorse either candidate in 1964, and then by casting 129,000 votes for Dr. Hawkins in the 1968 Democratic primary. With 300,000 blacks registered to vote, blacks are aware that no Democratic candidate for governor in the 1960's would have won without solid support in black precincts. Yet, the black leaders have been relatively unsuccessful in impressing this political fact on the Democratic Party; as a result the problem of maintaining black support is almost as precarious for the Democrats as swinging black support is for Republicans.[33]

The Democratic Party has, in the past year, revised the party organization to reward minority group registration with local and state party posts. Provisions were made for blacks and young voters to obtain vice-chairmanships in precinct and county party organizations; and Howard Lee, the black mayor of Chapel Hill, was named first vice-chairman of the state Democratic Party. In addition, Democrats in their last state convention attempted to move into a more liberal posture without incurring the wrath of traditionalists. The 1971 platform commits the party to support guaranteed health care and public housing, to end various forms of discrimination, and to liberalize state laws and attitudes toward labor relations. At the same time it takes a firm stand against campus disruptions.

How firmly both blacks and young voters are committed to the Democratic Party is problematical. Despite recent organizational and platform gestures, blacks still remember recent Democratic actions such as the appointment of Dr. Lake, the conservative gubernatorial candidate, to the state Supreme Court. And blacks have formed the Committee for More Representative Participation, headed by Dr. Hawkins, to determine basic political strategies.

Young voters are another important bloc and will become more important as eighteen-year-olds begin voting in state elections. Democrats probably have an edge with the young voter group and probably will gain the most with the eighteen-year-old vote—which

---

[33] For a critical discussion of the attitude of the Republican party toward blacks, blue-collar workers, and youth see Michael S. Lottman, "The GOP and the South," *Ripon Forum*, VI (July–August, 1970), particularly Chap. 6, "North Carolina: The Politics of Paradox."

by some estimates could add 300,000 new voters. Yet, the youthful leadership of the Republican Party can be expected to attract some of this young vote away from the Democrats. The role of Governor Scott in campus disturbances at the University of North Carolina at Chapel Hill—which has been criticized as interference neither necessary nor wise—could also cause Democrats some problem with the young vote. The stance of the present governor on law and order and war issues has made him unpopular on college campuses.[34]

With the problems facing both parties, the future of bipartisan conflict is difficult to predict in North Carolina. Some Republicans believe that a gubernatorial victory was thrown away in 1970, when Gardner switched from Nixon to Reagan at Miami and so damaged his standing at home. These same Republicans believe that, given a successful national administration, they can win the governorship in 1972 and possibly gain one or two additional congressional seats. Even if no dramatic Republican sweeps bring the era of one-party dominance to an end in the seventies, North Carolina is likely to move closer toward vigorous two-party competition.

It is apparent that the Republican leadership, including both Gardner and Holshouser, is ready to mount an appeal both to blacks and to the newly enfranchised eighteen- to twenty-year-old voters. If the Republican Party really offers an alternative on a statewide basis and its primaries become major contests, a strong possibility exists that registered Democrats, who regularly constitute more than half of the Republican general election vote, will switch their registration. The newly enacted presidential primary may stimulate this transfer.

The Riddle of Race Remains

North Carolina for decades has been pointed to as the inspiring exception to southern racism. The state had gone further than most of the South in narrowing the gap in expenditures for white and

[34] North Carolina was the thirty-seventh state to ratify the Twenty-sixth Amendment to the United States Constitution. *North Carolina Session Laws, 1971,* Chap. 725 (July 1, 1971).

Negro schools; the poll tax as a prerequisite for voting was lifted in 1920; and white supremacy was not a predominant issue in state campaigns for fifty years. All of this relative freedom from racial fixations was attributed to the state's atypical origins in the Old South (characterized by fewer slaves and less landed aristocracy) and to a political and educational renaissance that took place at the turn of the century. For years, North Carolinians took quite a pride, and sometimes displayed a touch of smugness, in the belief that they were somehow different from other southerners.

Yet, when the "living answer to the riddle of race" was put to a test in the 1950's and 1960's, it failed. The racial peace was breached in the senatorial campaign of 1950 when Dr. Frank Porter Graham's record in this matter was made a major though often *sub rosa* issue. It came to the front again when the opening of the University of North Carolina Law School to blacks was decreed judicially in 1951. The Supreme Court's action in *Brown v. Board of Education* led to the establishment of a commission to study the problems created in 1954. Legislation concerning pupil assignment went on the statute books during 1955, but after the second decision in *Brown* the main problem was diverted to the so-called Pearsall Commission. Pupil assignment was to be locally controlled; if a child was assigned to a school with members of another race, his parents might take him out. Schools might even be shut down by local vote of the people in a school district. Students not attending public schools for racial reasons might receive tuition grants to go elsewhere. In retrospect, the Pearsall plan may have served a useful purpose in preventing more extreme action. No public school was ever closed under it, and when the first tuition grants were requested, legal action resulted in the expected judgment of unconstitutionality.

Although North Carolinians can still take pride in the fact that, by southern standards, they have not reacted to the race question with hysteria, much of the smugness about racial harmony has evaporated in the fifties and sixties. School desegregation and black activism resulted in a noticeable change in the posture and reputation the state had maintained in race relations and political ideology. The state continues in the 1970's under a conservative reaction that set in soon after V. O. Key wrote. This reaction, which has made North Carolina more conservative politically on race and other aspects of public philosophy, has manifested itself in several ways. In school desegregation, North Carolina has lagged behind border states which took some initiative at compliance, as well as resisting states which have been forced into compliance.

In the eastern part of the state, where Negro enrollment is highest, school boards adopted "freedom-of-choice" plans and blithely went their way, apparently content in the feeling that a handful of Negroes attending predominantly white schools would satisfy the national government. In some respects, North Carolina was treated gently in its tokenism. It was nearly four years after the passage of the 1964 Civil Rights Act before administrative proceedings, as the preliminary step to cut off federal funds, were initiated against a North Carolina school district. When the Department of Health, Education, and Welfare did act, twelve districts were found guilty of noncompliance. Eleven of these were in the east, but Raleigh and Charlotte, among the state's metropolitan areas, also avoided massive integration until Charlotte became the test case in the busing issue to desegregate neighborhood schools.

The crackdown of the national government on North Carolina tokenism came in the aftermath of racial unrest which followed the assassination of Martin Luther King. North Carolina had as much civil disorder as any state, with most of the strife occurring in eastern Carolina towns. A congressional probe into the activities of the Ku Klux Klan revealed that North Carolina had more dues-paying members than any state and most of the Klan's activities were concentrated in the area that had resisted school integration and reacted violently to the upheaval of the King assassination. The Klan's membership by 1970 was down to a hard core of a few hundred members and billboards proclaiming North Carolina as "Klansville, USA" have begun to deteriorate. Indicative of the prospects of racial harmony, the 1971 legislature enacted one of the first statewide equal employment laws in the South which applies to both state and local governments.

The political anger stirred among eastern North Carolinians has affected both political parties. The Republican Party first attempted to win by default much of the dissident Democratic vote in the gubernatorial campaigns of 1960 and 1964 and after failing to do so, Gardner in 1968 openly courted conservative Democrats of the east. Neither strategy was successful in putting together a winning coalition. Democratic Party officials responded by backing away from national Democratic candidates. Robert Scott, although he supported the national Democratic ticket in 1964, avoided it in 1968, and the state delegation to the 1968 national convention employed a strategy infrequently used by North Carolina—offering Dan K. Moore as a presidential favorite son after imposing the unit rule on the first ballot. Earlier, party leaders had rebuffed a sizable and well-organized bloc of liberals supporting Eugene McCarthy at county and state conventions.

Although blacks cast a sizable bloc of votes in state elections and have probably been responsible for keeping North Carolina in the Democratic column in recent presidential and gubernatorial elections, blacks remain virtually powerless politically. Only two blacks have served in the General Assembly since 1900, when five were serving. Both have been elected in the 1960's. Representative Henry Frye, of Forsyth County, has served two terms in the House, and Representative J. J. Johnson was elected to the 1971 session from multiracial Robeson County, where blacks and Indians outnumber whites. Blacks have made some gains in municipal elections, but compared to other southern states, local officeholding among blacks is not great. The predominantly white university community of Chapel Hill has twice elected a black mayor, and blacks hold single seats on municipal and school boards across the state. Thirteen blacks were elected to municipal boards in eastern counties in 1971. But it is mostly through the device of single-shot voting that blacks have been able to obtain even token representation, and in no place in the state are they represented on decision-making boards proportionately to their number in the population.[35]

35 Indians constitute considerably less than 1 percent of the state's population. In 1970 Indians were registered in twenty-six counties, but only in the Cherokee area of mountainous Jackson and Swain and in eastern Robeson are they sufficiently concentrated to have appreciable political influence. In Robeson, the Lumbees have long had their own schools and a state-supported college, now integrated and named

The low ratio of blacks in the General Assembly is partially the result of measures taken by the legislature which are aimed at the defeat of Negroes or their white supporters. Negroes have bloc-voted and still do, but the single-shot device to advance their favored candidates has been effective on occasion. It can be used, of course, only where there are multiple offices, such as several legislative seats to be filled at large. Several counties have secured local legislation invalidating any ballot on which fewer than the full number of candidates has been voted for, thus effectively canceling the single-shot as a device. A numbered-seat system in multimember districts, which some counties employ, probably has the effect of defeating blacks. This arrangement was believed to have resulted in the defeat of one black candidate in Forsyth County, while another was elected in adjoining Guilford, where the numbered-seat plan did not apply.[36]

Blacks, although they have become increasingly active politically, are both underregistered, and if registered, are likely to be non-participatory. The election laws left precinct registrars responsible for deciding literacy, and there are many examples of the arbitrary use of this authority to refuse to register blacks. North Carolina's literacy test was upheld by the United States Supreme Court in the *Northampton Board of Elections* case, but, with the passage by Congress of the Voting Rights Act in 1965, the use of the test was forbidden in forty-one counties. A state constitutional amendment barring literacy tests on a statewide basis proposed by the 1969 legislature was, however, defeated at the polls in 1970.

The One-Party Era Ends

The most important fact about North Carolina politics is that the era of one-party dominance is nearing an end. No longer is intra-

---

Pembroke State University. No Indian serves in the General Assembly, though Robeson sent a black there in 1971.

[36] In 1968, the state Board of Elections ruled that single-shot voting legislation did not apply to legislative elections, and in January, 1972, a three-judge federal district court held such laws and numbered-seat legislation in multiple-member legislative districts unconstitutional. *S. G. Dunstan et al. v. J. Bryan Scott et al.*, Case No. 2666, U.S. District Court, Raleigh Division. Opinion filed January 10, 1972.

party competition of Tar Heel Democrats the most distinguishing characteristic; more important in understanding the politics of the state is the growing interparty competition and the factors that have produced a change in the dominant political culture of the past sixty years.

In a political system that had achieved the equilibrium of racial harmony, progressive economic development, and stable one-party government, which V. O. Key ascribed to the "progressive plutocracy," it is not surprising that the political change that has occurred in the post–World War II period has been more continuous than dramatic. The era of one-party dominance is not yet history and Republicans face real difficulty in winning statewide races. Yet a new political culture has emerged. Based less on traditional geographic voting patterns, it now reflects the interest and ideology of a growing urban electorate, of a potentially more volatile black vote as well as that of younger, less traditional political participants, many of whom are middle-class immigrants from other states. Little partisan realignment has occurred. The urban, middle-class voter retains a Democratic Party identification while voting Republican. The American Independent Party, whose 496,188 votes enabled Nixon to carry the state with 39 percent of the vote, had only 6,429 registered members in 1970.

The spread of blacks from rural areas and the eastern coastal plain, so that they now form a significant portion of the electorate of the Piedmont, contributes to the strategic importance of the black vote. Urban blacks maintain a higher level of voting turnout than do blacks residing in the traditional home of slavery and to some extent counter Republican gains among white urban voters.

Elements of the old political culture remain. The economic oligarchy that has dominated the ruling Democratic Party maintains control of candidate recruitment for statewide offices, and the candidates are often second- and third-generation politicians. And few doubt that textiles and tobacco interests or banking and insurance are able to obtain most of the favorable legislation they seek. Yet, the economic interests that have ruled the state no longer count on traditional regional support and an unquestioning electorate—two factors that have favored Democratic control. The interests of the economic oligarchy, long considered coterminous with the public interest, are more often tempered now with concerns for higher minimum wages, the environmental impact of industry, equal opportunities for blacks, and urban problems.

Though much remains of the "progressive plutocracy," a persistent effort on the part of organized labor, women, newly enfranchised voters, and blacks may produce major changes in the state's political future. Organized labor, predominantly Democratic in affiliation, has made very limited progress in organizing the industry of the state, which has one of the earliest "right-to-work" laws. It has central organizations in only fifteen counties and is relatively though not numerically strongest in mountainous Haywood County. Recently the state AFL-CIO has taken the lead in drawing together the groups listed above into a North Carolina coalition whose potential is as yet untested.

III

The Protest States

9

ALABAMA
Transition and Alienation

DONALD S. STRONG

Alabama and the Nation: The Gap Narrows

A common image of Alabama is that of a huge cotton field filled
with Negroes picking the cotton and singing mournful songs. This
image errs in a number of important respects. "In 1959 only . . . 1.5
per cent of the income of the people of Alabama came from growing cotton." [1] Insofar as Alabama is an agricultural state at all, it
is more of a livestock than a cotton state. In 1960 cotton provided
less than one-fourth of the cash receipts from farm marketing in
Alabama, whereas livestock and its products made up over half the
sales of agricultural products. The flight from agriculture is indicated by the fact that between one-fourth and one-third of all
Alabama farmers quit the soil between the years 1954 and 1959.
Those who left included nearly half of the tenant farmers in the
state. In fact, it is doubtful that Alabama can fairly be called an
agricultural state, since only 5.8 percent of the income of its people
came from agriculture.

After this description of the decline of farming, it is almost
redundant to note the changing urban-rural distribution of the

Donald S. Strong is Professor of Political Science, University of Alabama. The research for this chapter was made possible by a grant from the University of Alabama
Research Committee.

[1] Alabama Business Research Council, *Transition in Alabama* (University, Ala.:
University of Alabama Press, 1962), 1. A large part of the economic data presented
here leans heavily on this excellent study.

population. Noting the population losses in forty-six of the state's sixty-seven counties between 1940 and 1960, one would suspect rural decline. Actually, the state showed a 14.3 percent drop in rural population between 1950 and 1960, a figure substantially above the national figure, −0.8 percent. The rural decline was very nearly statewide. "Sixty-two counties had fewer rural inhabitants in 1960 than in 1950." [2] Although many rural dwellers left the state, many others must have moved to its cities, for there was a 33 percent gain in urban population between 1950 and 1960, leaving Alabama with 54.8 percent of its population urban. However, it should be recalled that almost 70 percent of Americans are urban dwellers, and Alabama ranks thirty-fourth among the states in percentage of urban population. Almost three-eighths (36.2 percent) of the state's inhabitants live in the six urbanized areas.[3] Three cities had populations of over 100,000, according to the 1960 census—Birmingham, Mobile, and Montgomery.

The Negro population in the state has registered a long-run decline from a high of 47.5 percent in 1870. By 1940 the percentage was down to 34.7, by 1950 to 32, and by 1960 to an even 30 percent. Between 1950 and 1960 there was the absurdly low net gain in Negro population of 654. This should be compared with the net gain in white population of 204,018. Alabama's ratio of Negroes to whites is the fourth highest in the nation, ranking after Mississippi, South Carolina, and Louisiana, in that order. It might be noted, however, that other states exceed Alabama in the *number* of Negro inhabitants. The 1960 census takers counted 980,271 Negroes in Alabama. Yet six states have more than one million Negro inhabitants: Georgia, Illinois, Louisiana, New York, North Carolina, and Texas.

Most other data on income and education suggest a slow convergence with the national average. Thus, in 1940 the per capita

2 *Ibid.*, 24.

3 The figure would be 45 percent if one used the Standard Metropolitan Statistical Area, which includes an entire county if it has a city of 50,000 or over. When applied to Alabama this definition could be misleading since some of these counties are large in area and contain substantial rural populations.

personal income of Alabamians was 47 percent of the national average; by 1960 it had risen to 66 percent. In most indexes of educational achievement or expenditures on education, Alabama ranks somewhere between forty-first and fiftieth among the states. Yet when one ignores the rankings and concentrates on median school years completed or expenditures per student, the convergence reappears in that the gap between Alabama and the national average is narrower than it was twenty years ago.

The Alabama Electorate Expands

A low rate of participation in elections has historically been characteristic of Alabama. V. O. Key found that during the years 1920 through 1946 only 19.2 percent of the adult population voted in the Democratic primaries for governor. Key chose these primaries because the turnout was much greater than for presidential elections in those years—a pattern which is, of course, contrary to the American norm. The evolution in subsequent years is set forth in Table 1. Note that the percentages are based on the potential electorate, that is, all residents twenty-one and over, *not* on the number of registered voters. In the 1950 Democratic primary for governor the turnout was only slightly above the earlier twenty-seven-year average. A large increase came in the gubernatorial primary of 1954. The participation rate hovered at almost the same figure for the next two gubernatorial primaries before making a big jump in 1966. The impressive increase between 1950 and 1954 is accounted for by the repeal of the cumulative feature of the Alabama poll tax. Prior to its repeal in December, 1953, voters had to pay $1.50 a year poll tax from age twenty-one through forty-five. If one failed to pay the tax any one year, he had to pay this delinquent tax as well as the current year's tax if he wished to vote in the second year. The tax was fully cumulative so that one might run up a bill of $36.00 by the age of forty-five. While no tax was levied on the forty-sixth and subsequent years, a person owing $36.00 would have to pay that bill before he would be entitled to a free vote in his middle and later years. The 1953 amendment

Table 1

PERCENTAGE OF THE POPULATION 21 AND
OVER VOTING IN ALABAMA ELECTIONS

Year	Presiden-tial Elections	Democratic Primary for Governor	General Election for Governor	General Election for U.S. Senator
Average 1920–46		19.2		
1940	18.9			
1944	15.2			
1948	12.8			
1950		23.1		
1952	24.8			
1954		34.0		
1956	28.5			
1958		34.4		
1960	30.9			
1962		34.4		21.5
1964	36.0			
1966		44.8	44.3	40.5
1968	51.0			44.6

permitted a person delinquent in his poll tax to vote if he paid the tax for the current year and the one immediately preceding it. This measure enabled a citizen to become enfranchised for $3.00 regardless of what his poll tax–paying record had been, and the amendment was construed to mean that all persons forty-six and over were to be forgiven any past poll tax indebtedness they might have incurred. In the gubernatorial primary of 1954 some 200,000 more persons participated than had four years earlier. Skeptics attributed the increase to the candidacy of colorful James E. "Jim" Folsom, but this theory was exploded by the continuing high rate of participation in 1958 and 1962. This increase in the electorate by nearly 50 percent was accounted for largely by white voters. Although we have no firm figures, a good estimate is that not more than 10 percent of the new voters were Negroes.[4] The impact of increased Negro registration stemming from the Voting Rights Act

[4] The state maintains no official registration records broken down by race.

of 1965 is more nearly reflected in the impressive increase in participation in the gubernatorial primary of 1966, over that of 1962.

While turnout in presidential elections has not been wholly uninfluenced by the above consideration, the real explanation here seems to be an increase in party competition. Note that the sharpest rise in participation occurred between 1948 and 1952. V. O. Key wrote with levity about the "so-called Republican party in the South." Beginning in 1952, presidential elections in Alabama became somewhat more significant. In that year Dwight D. Eisenhower spent a few hours in Alabama and addressed a large throng in front of the Jefferson County courthouse. A live presidential candidate addressing voters in Alabama was a sign that times were changing. From then on the trend was steadily upward. In 1964, for the first time in the years covered by these figures, participation in the presidential election exceeded that of the preceding gubernatorial primary. The 36 percent turnout in 1964 was substantially below the national average (63 percent) and left Alabama still in fortyninth place in a ranking of states by voting participation. However, the 44+ percent turnout in 1966 for both the Democratic primary and the general election for governor was not far from the rate in other states in nonpresidential years. Participation in the primary for United States senator is always less than that for governor. Figures on general elections for governor and senator are given only for 1962, 1966, and 1968 because these were the only years in which serious races were made.

Every student of southern politics knows that the real political action in Alabama takes place in the Democratic primary. Here, for a long time, white men, and whites only, have been electing other whites to all public offices in the state. The two great changes of the last twenty years have been the increasing support for candidates running on the Republican ticket and the reentry of Negroes into politics. Let us first consider the rise of Republican voting.

The Rise of the Republicans

Although most officeholders in Alabama are still Democrats, a dramatic change has taken place in the number of Alabamians willing to support Republican presidential nominees. How many voters have changed their party identification and whether Alabama has by some definition become a two-party state are questions less readily answered.

There has never been a complete absence of support for Republican presidential nominees in Alabama. Table 2 indicates the fortunes of the party in the elections from 1920 to 1964. The party won more than one-quarter of the votes in 1920 and 1924, then profited handsomely by the Hoovercrat defections of 1928. In the years 1932–48 the party's fortunes followed the downward trend of the GOP nationally, but at a much lower level. The watershed year was 1952, as we noticed earlier in connection with participation. Here the Republican share of the state's vote rose to 35 percent. In the two succeeding elections it remained on this plateau with a gently upward movement.

A closer inspection of the 1952 election may give some insight into what happened in Alabama. First, the state's sixty-seven counties are ranked in the order of their percentages of Republicans. Now we examine the top quartile of seventeen counties. Not surprisingly, this quartile contains a number of counties where earlier

Table 2
REPUBLICAN PERCENTAGE OF THE
TOTAL PRESIDENTIAL VOTE
IN ALABAMA, 1920–1964

Year	Percentage
1920	31.9
1924	26.0
1928	48.5
1932	14.3
1936	12.8
1940	14.4
1944	18.2
1948	19.0
1952	35.0
1956	39.4
1960	41.7
1964	69.5

Republican candidates have done well. Alabama lacks the large number of mountain Republican counties one finds in eastern Tennessee or western North Carolina, but it has a handful of counties that belong in this category although the Appalachians do not extend very far into Alabama. "Traditionally Republican" counties may be defined operationally as those counties in which Republican presidential candidates received a minimum of 35 percent of the vote in three-fourths of the presidential elections from 1900 to 1948 (excluding the election of 1912). Seven Alabama counties fit this definition—namely, Chilton, Cullman, De Kalb, Fayette, Franklin, St. Clair, and Winston. Five of the seven traditional counties are in the top quartile of seventeen counties, and the other two rank eighteenth and nineteenth.

Also ranking high in Republican strength are the counties containing the state's three largest cities. Mobile, Montgomery, and Jefferson (Birmingham) counties rank fourth, seventh, and eighth respectively. Residents of metropolitan Alabama were more willing to support a Republican nominee than were residents of other parts of the state. One rather unusual feature is the presence in the top quartile of five black-belt counties, that is, those counties where Negroes make up more than 50 percent of the population, according to the 1950 census.[5] Black-belt counties traditionally have been the bulwark of white-supremacist Democracy and the least Republican counties of the state.

The behavior of traditional, metropolitan, and black-belt counties will be analyzed in another way in order to facilitate comparison among election years. Let us consider first the traditionally Republican counties. The total number of votes received by Eisen-

[5] This is an arbitrary, operational definition of the term *black belt*. A bloc of counties running across the southern half of the state is characterized by fertile, black earth. Although the term comes from the color of the soil, these counties also have the highest percentages of black residents, either because the original planters prospered with this fine soil and were able to buy slaves or because they started out with large amounts of capital with which they were able to buy both slaves and the best agricultural land in the state. So defined, the counties are Barbour, Bullock, Choctaw, Dallas, Greene, Hale, Lowndes, Macon, Marengo, Monroe, Perry, Russell, Sumter, and Wilcox.

Figure 1

METROPOLITAN, TRADITIONAL REPUBLICAN, AND BLACK-BELT AREAS
OF ALABAMA

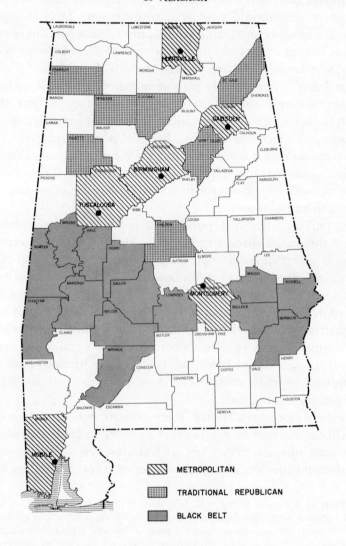

METROPOLITAN

TRADITIONAL REPUBLICAN

BLACK BELT

hower in these seven counties is divided by the total vote cast in the same seven counties. It turns out that he secured 43.9 percent of this traditional vote. He polled 34.8 percent of the vote in the state's fourteen black-belt counties. In discussing metropolitan counties we include Etowah County, to conform to the census definition of a metropolitan county as one with a city of at least 55,000 population, in this case Gadsden. The total vote of Etowah, Jefferson, Mobile, and Montgomery counties was 44.6 percent Republican in 1952.

The results of the 1956 and 1960 presidential elections in this three-way analysis were quite similar to those of 1952. Table 3 compares the several divisions of the state in the three elections. Note that the GOP's statewide percentage moved steadily upward.

Table 3
REPUBLICAN PERCENTAGE OF TOTAL
PRESIDENTIAL VOTE IN ALABAMA, 1952–1960

	1952	1956	1960
Statewide	35.0	39.4	41.7
Traditional	43.9	51.3	50.4
Metropolitan	44.6	48.4	48.3
Black belt	34.8	32.1	36.7

In 1956 the party registered gains over its 1952 showing in the traditional and the metropolitan counties, and the vote remaind at substantially this level in 1960. By contrast, Republican strength in the black belt was substantially below that of the other two areas as well as appreciably below the statewide percentage in both 1956 and 1960. The 1960 census adds to the list of metropolitan counties Madison (Huntsville) and Tuscaloosa counties. All fourteen black-belt counties have been retained in the computation for 1960 and subsequent years although the nonwhite population of both Choctaw and Russell counties dropped to 49.6 percent.

The reader must bear in mind that these three divisions have been chosen because of their demographic characteristics; they are not of equal size. (For example, the total vote of Jefferson County alone exceeds that of all traditional counties plus all black-belt counties.) Moreover, the three divisions include only twenty-seven counties, not the entire state.

Eisenhower did well in the metropolitan areas, but not all city dwellers liked Ike. A classic finding of investigators of political behavior throughout the 1930's and 1940's was the Republican leaning of the more prosperous. This behavior was now appearing in Alabama. Consider the city of Mountain Brook, an exclusive suburb of Birmingham, with by far the highest median income of any city in the state. In 1952 it went for Eisenhower by 79.5 percent, and in 1956 by 77 percent. The countywide averages for those years were 46 and 55 percent, respectively. Bernard Cosman demonstrated a similar class differential in Mobile in both 1952 and 1956.[6] He identified eleven of the city's nineteen wards as substantially white residential areas, that is, none of them having as much as 4 percent Negro population. Then, on the basis of average rental level and average home value he classified the eleven as upper-income, middle-income, and lower-income. In both years the Republican vote varied directly with income. In 1952 the range extended from 42.5 percent in the lower-income wards to 70.6 percent in the four upper-income wards. In 1956 it was from 45.2 percent of 64.1 percent. While the range is impressive and clearly underlines the notion of a class-based politics, it is noteworthy that the Republican nominee picked up more than 40 percent of the vote in the lower-income white wards in both elections. The more prosperous were much more enthusiastic for Eisenhower, yet his support was by no means confined to the upper-income levels.

The class aspects of voting preferences in the election of 1960 may be observed in the cities of Birmingham, Mobile, and Montgomery. Voting units that were at least 90 percent white were divided into five classifications on the basis of the median value of owner-occupied dwellings. Rental values were also computed in

---

[6] In the analysis of election results on the level of city precincts the author leans heavily on two studies by the late Bernard Cosman. The one referred to here was his doctor's dissertation, "Republicanism in the Metropolitan South" (University of Alabama, 1960). Similar analyses for the elections of 1960 and 1964 appear in his *Five States for Goldwater* (University, Ala.: University of Alabama Press, 1966).

order to identify and discard precincts or wards where these two characteristics did not coincide. The five categories were upper, upper-middle, middle, lower-middle, and lower. The range in Birmingham went from 76.3 percent Republican in the three upper-income voting units to 58.2 percent Republican in the lower-income white voting areas. The scale had one imperfection: the three middle-income units were more Republican than the upper-middle ones. In Mobile the ratings moved nicely from an upper-middle-income percentage of 64.9 to one of 40.2 for the lower-income units. In Montgomery the range was from 60.7 percent in the middle-income areas to 41 percent in the lower-income areas. Richard M. Nixon evoked greatest enthusiasm from prosperous whites, but he polled a very respectable vote among lower-income whites.

Nixon's demonstrated appeal for upper-income urban areas, like that of Eisenhower before him, challenges the interpretation of Republican strength as merely a vote-for-the-man (Eisenhower). This interpretation is hard to defend if both men derive their support from the same areas—as was substantially true for the elections of 1956 and 1960. A rank order correlation of the Republican percentages of the state's sixty-seven counties for the years 1956 and 1960 produces a coefficient of .88. The vote-for-the-man concept is an elusive one. Had the Republican ticket been headed in 1952 by a less well known figure than Eisenhower, the party presumably would have not done so well. However, if this vote-for-the-man interpretation is carried to its logical extreme, the support for the general should have been virtually uniform throughout the state. His winning personality should have projected uniformly in both rich and poor neighborhoods. All sixty-seven counties should have produced approximately the same percent of support. The willingness of the more prosperous to support both Eisenhower and Nixon is significant because it parallels the behavior of prosperous voters outside the South and suggests a perception of class interest.

After the 1960 election, considerable time and effort were given to the task of perfecting a Republican organization in the state. It must not be thought that there was no GOP organization before this time. There had long been a state committee, and probably the majority of counties had county committees. Alabama Republicans operate on a convention basis save for a very few traditional counties which have primaries for county offices. The law provides that on primary day precinct conventions or mass meetings may be held to nominate candidates for public office and to select party officials. Any county resident of Republican persuasion can attend a meeting and help elect his county committee. In presidential years he can vote for delegates to the congressional district convention, who usually go on to the state convention. Each district elects a delegate to the national convention, and the state convention chooses additional delegates. The county convention is empowered to decide whether or not to nominate candidates for local office. If they decide affirmatively, nominations are made forthwith.

Before 1952 these Republican gatherings were not well attended, and it is scarcely necessary to note that such feeble organizations contributed little toward mobilizing the impressive vote polled by Eisenhower and later by Nixon. These conventions did get into the news when large numbers of Democrats flocked into the erstwhile exclusive meetings in order to help nominate Eisenhower. Yet it was only in 1963 that a permanent professional staff was established at state headquarters and a serious effort made to develop an active committee in every county. A youthful and dynamic leadership from the headquarters toured the state and organized hitherto unorganized counties and supplanted inactive county committees with more zealous ones. In the city of Birmingham and in Jefferson County steps were taken to develop a full-blown precinct organization. The press began quoting Republican leaders as saying that they were the only organized political party in the state.

The growth of party organization probably contributed to Republican James Martin's near-victory for the United States Senate in the general election of 1962. Heretofore, Republicans had de-emphasized contests below the presidential election; of this, more later. Martin, an ardent admirer of Barry Goldwater, was running at an appropriate time. As will be indicated, the impact of *Brown v. Board of Education* had already manifested itself on Democratic politics. The use of federal troops to suppress the riot on the campus of the University of Mississippi in the early fall of 1962 whipped segregationist sentiment to a fever heat. Large numbers of Alabamians were furious with their national government—"that government in Washington." Venerable Senator Lister Hill had been around Washington for a long time and was made the scapegoat. Martin was not a demagogic segregationist; he did not yell "nigger" at every crossroads. He held forth earnestly on "states' rights" and "constitutional government." Both expressions had become code words for segregation. The use of federal troops in Oxford to uphold the supreme law of the land was somehow a violation of "constitutional government."

Martin almost made it, with 49.1 percent of the vote. The real surprise of the election was his strength in the black belt, where he polled 54.8 percent of the vote. This is a gain of 18.1 percentage points over Nixon's showing in the area two years earlier. More impressionistically, Martin swept the entire southern half of the state, whether black belt or otherwise. This is not, of course, to overlook his impressive 52.6 percent in the metropolitan areas, but here his percentage-point gain over Nixon in 1960 was only 4.3. In the traditional counties he received 47.3 percent, a figure slightly below both his state average and Nixon's vote in this area in 1960. This relative weakness in areas of traditional Republican strength calls attention to the fact that Martin had found a basis of support not available to earlier GOP nominees. Democrat Hill carried the northern half of the state; twelve of his seventeen top-quartile counties were in this area. Republican Martin's top seventeen included fourteen in the southern half of the state. Yet south Alabama has been the historic home of white-supremacist Democracy. With race the salient issue, the GOP now attracted the support of the white voters most deeply concerned about segregation.

Martin's strong showing should not obscure another interesting fact about the 1962 general election. No less than eighteen Republicans contested seats in the state legislature—an unheard-of number for Alabama—and two candidates were successful. This contesting of local offices was probably associated with the growth of party organization. Both developments suggested a new breed of party leader and a desire to introduce serious two-party competition at all levels. We should recall that the presidential Republicanism of 1952–60 was unearned increment. The national party offered little or no help, and the vote polled in these years was all out of proportion to the limited exertions of the local Republican leaders. The lack of interest in converting presidential Republicanism into the grass-roots variety had a certain logic. One voted for a GOP presidential nominee to "stop this socialistic nonsense in Washington," but there was no comparable menace on the state and local level. And why endanger friendly relations with Democratic city and county officials by running Republicans against them? By 1962 the increased number of candidates for local office suggested that this reasoning was no longer so persuasive. Here was a flicker of interest in serious two-partyism.

The election of 1964 turned the political world upside down. Republicans were strongest in those areas where they had previously been weak—stronger than in their areas of traditional strength. To be sure, Goldwater's Alabama support was not really weak anywhere. He polled 69.5 percent of the state's total vote. Yet attention is called to Table 4. In the traditional Republican

Table 4
REPUBLICAN VOTE FOR PRESIDENT IN
1960 AND 1964 IN ALABAMA

	Percentage Republican, 1960	Percentage Republican, 1964	Percentage-Point Gain, 1960–64
Statewide	41.7	69.5	+27.8
Traditional	50.4	63.9	+13.5
Metropolitan	48.3	69.4	+21.1
Black belt	36.7	76.1	+39.4

counties Goldwater secured almost 64 percent of the vote, but in the black belt he polled 76.1 percent. Here is the first time that a Republican presidential nominee has done better in the black belt than in either the traditional or the metropolitan counties. The change from customary behavior is possibly revealed more vividly

in the right-hand column of the table. Here a computation of the
percentage-point gain between 1960 and 1964 shows an increase
of 39.4 percentage points in the black belt, whereas the comparable
figure in the traditionally Republican counties was only 13.6. A
rank order correlation between the Republican percentages in
Alabama counties in 1960 and in 1964 produces a coefficient of .06,
clearly indicating a virtual absence of any relationship between
the behavior of voters in these two presidential elections. A correlation of the vote won by Goldwater and that secured by J. Strom
Thurmond, the States' Rights Party candidate in 1948, produces a
coefficient of .52. This moderately high positive relationship suggests that both Thurmond and Goldwater were perceived as segregationist candidates.

Another effect of the Goldwater candidacy was a de-emphasis on
class differences in voting and the creation of something of a white
man's front regardless of economic status. In Birmingham Republican support increased over the four-year period in every income category, but the greatest increase was in the five lower-
income white voting districts. Their vote for Nixon had been 58.2
percent, but they gave Goldwater a tremendous 85.7 percent support. The three upper-income white voting units increased their
Republican sentiment by only five percentage points. The result
was that the Republican percentage in the lowest-income white
voting units differed from that of the upper-income boxes (precincts) by only a few percentage points. Here was a white man's
front rather than a class politics. In Mobile, although the 1960–64
gain was impressive in all four income categories, the same brush-
ing aside of class politics appeared. All four income categories were
in the range of 76 to 81 percent Republican. Montgomery produced
great Republican gains in lower-income boxes, but the class differential remained.

Nineteen sixty-four was in another respect a banner year for Alabama Republicans. Five United States congressmen rode in on the
Goldwater coattails. A sixth Republican congressional nominee
narrowly lost in the Fifth District, receiving 47 percent of the vote.
In addition, the party picked up a county treasurer in Jefferson

County, probate judges in five counties, members of county commissions in three counties, three members of the Montgomery
County Board of Education, and assorted lesser offices. Apparently
the only interpretation of the party's gains is the Goldwater-
coattail phenomenon. The Republican elected Jefferson County
treasurer, when asked over television to explain his victory, replied,
"They all just pulled that one big lever." It is difficult to offer a
better explanation. Alabama voters were not accustomed to ticket-
splitting. Surely no one in particular was dissatisfied with the work
of the various local officials who lost their offices. The head of the
Republican ticket was perceived as standing for segregation, and
that was all the average Alabamian wanted. We will return to the
Alabama Republicans after examining another element in the mix
of recent political developments.

The Negro Goes to the Polls

Estimating the number of Negroes qualified to vote in Alabama is
a familiar problem. Alabama is one of the majority of southern
states that does not maintain official statewide registration statistics
by race. Hence, the story of the increasing Negro electorate is a
statement of a general trend rather than a set of precise statistics.
For 1947, three years after *Smith v. Allwright*, the late Luther Jackson estimated that there were 6,000 qualified Negro voters in the
state. By 1952 the number had probably risen to around 25,000; by
1954, to 50,000. The repeal of the cumulative feature of the Alabama poll tax in 1953 resulted in an increase of 200,000 voters, and
to assume that one-eighth of these were Negroes does not seem unreasonable. The rate of increase was slow for the next few years.
Voting, the 1961 report of the Civil Rights Commission, put the
1960 Alabama figure at 66,000. Registration drives in the succeeding four or five years nearly doubled the figure; it is rather generally
agreed that when the Voting Rights Act went into effect in August,
1966, there were somewhat over 113,000 qualified Negro voters.
Two years later the figure had shot up to 250,000. This was clearly
the period of the most dramatic and largest increase in registration

in the state's history. In the succeeding two years the rate of increase tapered off so that prior to the 1968 elections the figure was 273,000.

The general pattern of permissiveness and resistance seems pretty much to parallel the well-documented conclusion of Donald R. Matthews and James W. Prothro, namely, that there is a rather general inverse relationship between the Negro percentage of a county's population and the percentage of the adult black population registered to vote.[7] Two counties had no Negro registrants. One noteworthy Alabama feature was the intense resistance to Negro registration in Birmingham, the state's largest city. As late as September, 1960, there were only 11,900 Negro registrants in Jefferson County, or about 10 percent of the voting-age population. No other southern city of comparable size was so resistant to Negro registration.

The state's immediate reaction to the *Allwright* decision was the enactment of the Boswell Amendment to the state constitution. This amendment revived a turn-of-the-century practice of requiring that all registrants be able not only to read and write any article of the United States Constitution but also to "understand and explain" any part of that document to the satisfaction of a board of registrars. Three whites in each county made up the board of registrars. None of them were trained in constitutional law, and few of them approved of Negro voting. The federal courts were not impressed with this obvious fraud and tossed it out in *Davis v. Schnell*.[8] For most of the remaining period up to 1965 the chief legal disfranchising device was the requirement that a lengthy and complex application form be filled out by the applicant in his own handwriting without any assistance. This provision was applied so strictly to Negroes that even the best educated were denied registration for trifling and inconsequential errors or omissions. By contrast, the vast majority of county boards of registrars applied the law indulgently to whites. Assistance was given freely, and only a few counties enforced the law in a manner that prevented a poorly educated white person from becoming a voter. The effect of the ques-

---

[7] Donald R. Matthews and James W. Prothro, *Negroes and the New Southern Politics* (New York: Harcourt, Brace and World, 1966), Chap. 5.

[8] *Davis v. Schnell*, 81 F. Supp. 872 (1949).

tionnaire was to disfranchise Negroes, not illiterates. To refer to the form as a "literacy test" is absurd. The emphasis here on this double standard is not meant to suggest the absence of violence, threats of violence, and economic reprisal. Alabama was one of three states producing most of the litigation arising from the Civil Rights Acts of 1957 and 1960—legislation that dealt almost entirely with voting. It was, of course, the intransigent attitude of the Dallas County (Selma) registrars which made that county an inviting target for the demonstration led by Martin Luther King; and the inept and brutal response to the demonstration supplied the impetus necessary for enactment of the Voting Rights Act of 1965.

As soon as Negroes began to vote in appreciable numbers, they gave thought to local organizations that would enable them to maximize their effectiveness by identifying and endorsing the candidate most favorably disposed toward Negro interests. Organizations formed early in the state's larger cities, although Negro political activity was not in direct proportion to the size of the city, nor was it absent in less urban areas. It was not long before two statewide organizations formed. The Alabama State Committee on Registration and Voting emphasized the importance of political participation, but it was strictly nonpartisan. The other statewide group was the Alabama Democratic Conference, a group of Negro Democrats.

Each local group developed some procedure for evaluating candidates. This screening committee was usually able to recommend a preferred candidate. The word of an endorsement was conveyed to voters in the form of a printed sample ballot or occasionally a mimeographed sheet. It was important to distribute the sample ballot at the last minute lest the news of Negro endorsement be used by his rivals to brand him the "niggers' candidate." The approved procedure was to pass out the word of endorsement the night before an election, when it was too late for the opposition to do anything.

The effectiveness of Negro participation in this period is hard to assess. Jim Folsom was elected governor in the Democratic primary of 1954. He won the first primary narrowly, and it can be argued that Negro voters gave him the necessary margin. Also it is probable that the Negro vote was crucial in the 1962 election in Birmingham when the form of city government was changed from a commission to a mayor-council type. This was really no mere technical change in the form of city government. It was part of a scheme to change both the personnel and policies. The proponents of change were victorious, and probably the Negro votes supplied the winning margin. In the following year, the Negro vote may again have been crucial in defeating the candidate for mayor under the new plan, arch-segregationist Eugene "Bull" Connor. The effectiveness of Negro participation in one county is easier to assess. By 1964 Macon County, home of Tuskegee Institute, and the city of Tuskegee each had Negroes in public office. The county is 83 percent black, and able leadership was available both from the faculty of Tuskegee and from Negroes on the staff of the Veterans' Hospital in the community. The stories of the struggle for the ballot and of early political activities in this area have been recounted in several studies.[9] Yet, with these exceptions, the real emphasis of the Negro's position was the struggle not to be excluded from politics altogether. The question of effectiveness was more a problem for the future.

Among the Democrats

Despite occasional Republican victories and increased Negro effort, almost all officeholders in Alabama are white Democrats. They are elected in the Democratic primary, which is still the chief political contest. The organization of the party which conducts this primary can be easily described, but it should not be assumed that the party organization is either active or particularly important. Each county has an executive committee chosen by the voters at the primary, usually on the basis of one member per precinct. Since there are great variations in population among precincts, the committees do not represent a one-man, one-vote situation. Each committee is responsible for some aspects of the conduct of the primary: receiving

9 Charles V. Hamilton, *Minority Politics in Black Belt Alabama* (New York: McGraw-Hill, 1960); Bernard Taper, *Gomillion versus Lightfoot* (New York: McGraw-Hill, 1962); Harry Holloway, *The Politics of the Southern Negro* (New York: Random House, 1969), Chap. 5.

qualifying papers and fees, certifying the returns, paying expenses. These committees are not active in interparty warfare; they are not busy in October and November marshaling the faithful. Long unaccustomed to carrying the battle against the Republican foe, they lack the ability and will to do so when the occasion arises. Most of these remarks apply to the state executive committee, a seventy-two-member body with eight delegates elected from each of the nine congressional districts as they stood prior to the reapportionment of the early 1960's. The committee elects a chairman, usually a lawyer, and his law office becomes the state headquarters. The chairman devotes as much time to party business as he can spare from his law practice. Generally he has no staff, although for a period in 1967–68 the chairman had a salaried assistant. The committee's one important role will be discussed in another context.

Recent Alabama political history can be divided into the periods before and after *Brown v. Board of Education*. So much of Alabama political history has consisted of contests over who can be the toughest segregationist candidate for governor that it is sometimes forgotten that there was an earlier era of blander race relations. The outstanding figure of this period was two-time governor Jim Folsom. Folsom made his first race for governor in 1942—the standard get-acquainted race. In 1946 he won in the runoff. Unable to succeed himself, he ran again in 1954 and won without a runoff.

Folsom, a latter-day populist, preached a doctrine of what might be called *rural liberalism*. The term *liberalism* refers here to his belief in the free spending of state funds to help lower-income groups. The rural character of the man came out largely in his campaign style. His vocabulary was earthy, and some of the anecdotes he told from the stump were of the robust, barroom variety. His campaign style contrasted with that of Senators Lister Hill and John Sparkman. Both men shared Folsom's economic orientation, and both were repeatedly reelected against opponents who worked the racial angle much harder than they. Hill was capable of occasional flights of camp meeting–style oratory, but usually his campaign behavior, like Sparkman's, was restrained. Folsom, on the other hand, never let his audiences forget that he was "an old country boy." Folsom's appeal, however, was not chiefly that of a clown. His stress on being "the little man's big friend" was convincing. He persuaded his hearers that unlike most of his predecessors he was genuinely concerned about the welfare of low-income people in Alabama. His style both attracted and repelled. To the well-washed and prosperous urban dwellers, "old Jim" was simply not respectable. The state's larger newspapers were unanimously against him. Yet the very qualities that repelled the country-club set convinced those lower on the economic pyramid that "old Jim" was indeed one of their own.

His support was rural. Until recently, it would not have been a great oversimplification to describe Alabama politics as a clash between poor farmers and black-belt planters allied with business leaders. By the time Folsom appeared on the political scene the population had shifted so that the rural black belt enjoyed representation in the legislature far out of proportion to its population in the middle of the twentieth century. In the 1946 runoff the high points of Folsom strength were rural north Alabama and the southeast corner of the state, a not very prosperous agricultural area popularly designated the wiregrass section. Generally his support came from the counties where the Populists had been strongest half a century earlier. His area of greatest weakness was the black belt. Of the fourteen counties with Negro populations of 50 percent or more, ten were in his lowest quartile. Parts of urban Alabama were distinctly cool to him; both Mobile and Montgomery counties were in the lowest quartile. However, Jefferson County was only five percentage points below the state average of 58.7 percent, and Etowah (Gadsden) and Calhoun counties (Anniston) were in his top quartile.

In 1954 Folsom won the nomination in the first primary with 51.3 percent of the total vote, against what had been considered formidable opposition. He won a clear majority in forty-two counties; of these, twenty-four gave him a vote of 60 percent or better. In several of the remaining twenty-five counties, he had a plurality. Yet only two of the state's fifteen counties with towns of 10,000 or more gave Folsom a plurality. In the state's two largest counties,

Jefferson and Mobile, his percentages were 34 and 39 respectively. Seven of the fourteen black-belt counties were in his lowest quartile.

Folsom's program called for increased state expenditures for highways, welfare, and education. Seemingly of top priority was the highway system. At that time many secondary roads in rural Alabama were by no means all-weather roads. The program called for an increase in payments to old-age–assistance recipients. Although Folsom may not go down in history as Alabama's "education governor," he was more than receptive to the idea of increased educational expenditures. In his first administration his finance director put forth great effort to have the property tax assessment on the Southern Railway raised. In many circles this was regarded as conduct unbecoming a gubernatorial appointee. Whereas many Alabama politicians viewed the national government with suspicion, Folsom called attention to the many advantages of federal grants-in-aid. He stated repeatedly that the basic plank in his platform was the calling of a new constitutional convention to bring about a fair apportionment of the legislature. That body never gave the idea any serious consideration. Why should the overrepresented areas of the state surrender their advantage? He bought support in the legislature by his ability to give or withhold highway money or other items that individual legislators needed for their home counties. Historians will not classify him as a distinguished administrator. He was plagued by alcoholism, and his skill on the stump was not matched by an ability to preside over the state's large administrative machine.[10] Moreover, he had difficulty in recruiting skilled administrators to be his chief subordinates. Folsom's followers included few people with these qualifications.

Folsom was a "liberal" not only on economics but also on race. This language must be understood to mean that he was liberal measured by a yardstick calibrated for his state and his time. Although Folsom was governor in a period of relatively placid race relations, one or more candidates opposing him always took a tough

10 See Marshall Frady, *Wallace* (Cleveland: World, 1968), 103–108 for some jarring descriptions of the impact of Folsom's alcoholism.

line on segregation. He ignored race in his own campaigning. Coming from Cullman County with a Negro population of 1 percent, he did not believe that the state was about to be engulfed by a rising black tide. In the whole northern half of the state the Negro population is comparatively small, and Folsom regarded the economic issues as the really fundamental ones. His response to a question put to him by a newspaperman in 1955 is probably a forthright statement of his racial attitude. "I could never get excited about our colored brothers. They've been here 300 years and I estimate they'll be here another 300 years or more. I'm not going to get my ulcers in an uproar. I find them to be good citizens. If they had been making a living for me like they have for the Black Belt, I'd be proud of them instead of kicking them and cussing them all of the time."[11] This is not to suggest that Folsom was a crusading integrationist; presumably he felt that the interests of poor whites and poor blacks were similar. Moreover, he showed a remarkable ability to work with individuals whose names were to become household words as symbols of segregationist leadership. His 1954 campaign manager for south Alabama was George Wallace, and his appointee to a vacancy in the post of Dallas County sheriff was James Clark.

In fact, it was Folsom's mildness on the race issue that ultimately put him out of touch with the temper of the times. The *Brown* decision did not have a sudden impact on Alabama opinion. The white citizenry did not rise up in spontaneous outrage on that day in May, 1954, when the decision was handed down. Some time in the ensuing year the intensity of segregationist sentiment began to rise. Consider the story of the visit of Congressman Adam Clayton Powell in November, 1955. Powell was scheduled to speak at Alabama State College, a Negro institution in Montgomery. Folsom extended the standard courtesy to the visiting congressman, sending the official limousine to meet him at the airport. Later the governor invited Powell over to the executive mansion where the two officials consumed a little Scotch and soda and engaged in friendly conver-

[11] Birmingham *Post-Herald*, June 29, 1955.

sation. Southern etiquette provides that a governor may drink his Scotch with either branch water or soda but never with Negroes. This conduct unbecoming a southern governor did not escape the attention of the news media; adverse comments about it in and out of the media were numerous.

The inhospitality of the times to integrated drinking was emphasized by the nullification resolution passed by the Alabama Legislature in January, 1956. The language had a certain unreal quality about it—prose that might have been written by an Alabama legislator in 1856. It began: "Whereas the Constitution . . . was formed by the sanction of the several states, given by each in its sovereign capacity . . ." The resolution continued with this remarkable language: "The Legislature of Alabama declares the decision and orders of the Supreme Court of the United States relating to separation of the races in the public schools are as a matter of right, null, void and of no effect; and the Legislature of Alabama declares to all men that, as a matter of right, this State is not bound to abide thereby . . ."[12] The House passed the resolution with only five dissenting votes. The Senate concurred. The resolution, a newspaper reported, "thundered through the state Senate by voice vote on the birthday of Robert E. Lee." Folsom proved himself a first-rate constitutional lawyer when he said of the resolution, "It's just a bunch of hogwash."

So Folsom occupied the governor's mansion for another two years and watched his populist-like supporters conclude that race was the really vital issue after all.

The first man to win the governorship on the basis of a racist appeal was John Patterson. To be sure, considerations of race permeated all aspects of Alabama politics, but the toughest segregationists had not been elected. Alabama had no Eugene Talmadge or Theodore Bilbo. Possibly by the spring of 1958 the significance of the *Brown* decision had dawned on the Alabama electorate. Patterson, then attorney general, played segregation to the hilt. Cor-

---

12 *Journals of the House of Representatives of the State of Alabama, Extraordinary Sessions of 1956*, I, 255.

rectly sensing the climate of opinion, he made race his central theme, and in speeches at every crossroads he played on racial fears. Eventually he faced George Wallace in the runoff. Patterson hit the racial theme so heavily that Wallace unwittingly became the candidate of moderation and received heavy support from Negro voting boxes in Birmingham. Wallace drew the correct inference from his 64,902-vote defeat, asserting, "John Patterson out-segged me. And boys, I am not going to be out-segged again." [13] Once elected to office, Patterson played the role of a tough segregationist but avoided any direct clashes with the federal government, on the very rational ground that he did not believe he could win. As governor he interested himself in a variety of matters other than segregation, for instance property tax revision and educational financing. He was not alienated from the national party, and he worked for the election of the Kennedy-Johnson ticket in 1960.

In June, 1962, George Wallace won the runoff and became the Democratic nominee for governor. He had spent nearly all of his adult life in politics, having served earlier as a state legislator and then as a circuit judge. Inasmuch as Wallace has come to symbolize segregation and Negrophobia, it is worth noting that on nonracial matters he is clearly in the liberal tradition. (The word *liberal* is used here to designate a belief in using the powers of government to aid lower-income people.) Wallace was a poor boy from a poor county in a poor state. After his return from military duty in World War II, he served in the state legislature during Folsom's first term. Like Folsom, whom he admired greatly, he was very much in the populist tradition. As a legislator he had a definitely liberal record, both in the bills he supported and those he introduced. In fact, at this early period he was a little "soft" on segregation. At the 1948 Democratic National Convention, half of the Alabama delegation walked out rather than be identified with the civil rights plank in the party platform; Wallace was among the half that remained at

[13] There are slightly differing versions of this famous remark. Frady has the location of the statement in the Jefferson Davis Hotel, Montgomery, and the language, "John Patterson out-nigguhed me. And boys, I'm not going to be out-nigguhed again." Frady, *Wallace*, 127.

the convention. As governor, Wallace pushed a free-spending program. Large sums were appropriated for highways, and an ambitious program for the creation of state trade schools and junior colleges was inaugurated. Here was no champion of frugality in government; here was not the governor to delight the hearts of those championing "fiscal responsibility."

However, his economic views were not the ones that made national news. It was his several dramatic confrontations with the federal government that catapulted him onto the national scene. Unlike Governor Patterson, who avoided direct confrontations with the national government, Wallace sought them out. The most-publicized instance was his "stand in the schoolhouse door" at the University of Alabama. Viewed from an entirely rational standpoint, this episode, which culminated in the entrance of the first two Negro students to the university, was an absurdity. The governor delayed integration for perhaps two hours; then he lost. But this rational explanation is probably too simple. The stand obtained for the governor excellent coverage on every television newscast for the next twenty-four hours, and it made him a national figure. One writer sees in the incident an example of Wallace's magnificent grasp of southern psychology. The argument is that there is nothing more "Confederate" than going down to foreseeable defeat before overwhelming odds.[14] Most references to "southern psychology" are complete nonsense. Possibly this one is entitled to a little more respect.

Probably some consideration of this same southern psychology is needed to understand Wallace's entry into three presidential primaries in the spring of 1964. Here was a boy from the Deep South who was going up to play ball in the major leagues. Probably this gesture brought emotional gratification to large numbers of Alabamians. It certainly kept the governor very much in the public eye. But now there loomed an obstacle to his political future in the form of a provision of the Alabama constitution which prohibits a governor from succeeding himself. In September, 1965, Wallace

14 *Ibid.*, 149–50.

called a special session of the legislature and asked them to remove
this prohibition. A long struggle ensued; ultimately the Senate
killed the proposed constitutional amendment.

Sometime thereafter Wallace began toying with the idea of
running his wife Lurleen. This would be in the great tradition of
Texas Governor James Ferguson, whose impeachment rendered
him ineligible for public office, but who had his wife, "Ma" Ferguson, elected governor in the 1920's. The most promising candidate
already in the field was State Senator Ryan deGraffenried, whom
Wallace had defeated in the runoff of 1962. DeGraffenried was
personable and energetic, and seemed to have ample financial backing and a wide popular following throughout the state. At this
point, fate intervened on behalf of Wallace. The light plane in
which deGraffenried was barnstorming the state crashed on a moun-
tainside, killing him and his pilot. Not long thereafter the name
of Lurleen Wallace was entered as a candidate for governor.

White Reaction and Counterreaction

Nineteen sixty-six was an unusually lively election year for the
state, with other developments besides the candidacy of the wife of
the incumbent governor. Other interesting features included unprecedented political activity by Negroes and Republicans. The
increased Negro activity resulted from passage of the Voting Rights
Act of 1965. Its effect in the state had been to double the Negro
electorate, bringing it to about 250,000. It will be recalled that the
act suspended literacy tests and other devices that had been used to
bar Negroes from the polls. Some 60,000 Negroes presented themselves to their respective county boards of registrars and were registered. The act also authorized the United States attorney general
to appoint examiners, who in practice were specially trained employees of the Civil Service Commission. Although the attorney
general had considerable discretion over when to appoint examiners, they were usually assigned to a county on one of two grounds—
that the local registrars were still imposing literacy qualifications or
that registrars did not expand their facilities and working hours to

accommodate the masses of new Negro applicants, as they had in
the past, to meet high registration demands by whites and as they
would need to do to correct the effects of past discrimination.
Examiners were assigned to thirteen counties in Alabama; they
registered approximately 60,000 persons, most of whom were
Negroes.[15] The general law governing registration in most rural
counties provides that the board of registrars shall meet only two
days a month. Even in the absence of an intentional slowdown, the
number of persons who could be registered in any month was severely limited. One noteworthy feature was that examiners were
named for two of the state's largest counties—Jefferson and
Montgomery.

The increased number of Negro voters was associated with an
increased number of Negro candidates. At least seventeen counties
produced Negro candidates in the Democratic primary. Eleven
Negroes filed for the Alabama House of Representatives, one for
the state Senate, and at least four for the office of sheriff. In Governor Wallace's home county, Barbour, an even dozen Negroes sought
public offices, ranging from sheriff to member of the county Democratic committee.[16] Elsewhere Negroes were running for tax assessor, member of the board of revenue, tax collector, and member
of the county board of education.

Another effect of doubling the Negro electorate was to decrease
the manageability of the black vote by established Negro political
organizations. Newly enfranchised Negroes were disposed to create
their own local parties. Black Panthers organized in Lowndes
County. The idea of statewide organization, leadership, and the
bloc vote were not readily accepted. "Freedom" meant the right to
do as one pleased, not to follow the urgings of Negro leaders. Enfranchisement certainly did not produce instant sophistication.
More important, the Alabama Democratic Conference was seriously
split over who was to get the endorsement for governor. The ma-

15 These counties were Jefferson, Montgomery, Dallas, Marengo, Wilcox, Hale,
Perry, Lowndes, Greene, Elmore, Autauga. In April, 1967, Choctaw and Sumter
were added to the list.

16 Birmingham *News*, March 2, 1966.

jority favored former Congressman Carl Elliott. However, a minority of the leaders, disagreeing both on this endorsement and on general policy, followed the defeated candidate for the conference's presidency out of the organization and began working for Attorney General Richmond Flowers.

This was the year of Republican optimism. Its leaders had been greatly heartened by James Martin's near-victory in 1962 and the election of five congressmen (including Martin) in 1964. The party now had a state headquarters with a salaried director, several other full-time employees, and better organization on the county level than ever before. Morale was high. Six of the eight seats in the United States House of Representatives were contested. So were the statewide offices of public service commissioner, auditor, treasurer, and attorney general. John Grenier challenged veteran Senator John Sparkman. In the state House of Representatives 85 of the 106 seats were contested, as were 26 of the 35 state Senate seats. Nearly 100 candidates ran for local office. Congressman James Martin decided to try for the governorship, despite the strenuous objections of many Republican leaders who thought it a serious mistake to challenge Wallace.

Ten persons sought the Democratic nomination for governor. Surprisingly, the idea of a man running his wife for governor to evade a constitutional limitation provoked no mirth. There was no widespread feeling that Wallace's ploy was ridiculous. Mrs. Wallace's campaign appearances were brief. She would talk for less than five minutes while the audiences listened impatiently for her husband to take the microphone. His speeches were pretty much standard fare, with appeals to barbers, beauticians, and steelworkers. He had less to say about segregation than four years earlier, possibly because he had already established his reputation as the number one racist. Noting that Wallace now tended to attack Communists rather than Negroes, one opposing candidate related this change to the fact that there were now 250,000 Negro voters in the state whereas Communists constituted a rather small percentage of the electorate. The most unusual candidate was Attorney General Richmond Flowers, who made a direct and unambiguous appeal to the recently expanded Negro electorate. He did not work quietly through their leaders as had been the standard practice. Instead he toured the county seats of the black belt and talked openly to crowds of Negroes, shook hands with them, and appealed for their support. Negro leaders felt that such tactics indicated a lack of integrity. Open solicitation of black votes might put him into a second primary, but would virtually guarantee him a defeat there by the white majority. Former Governor Patterson, who did not run a strong race, said on the stump that if elected, he would be governor "of all the people." Even the use of this cautious code word was in sharp contrast to the tone of his 1958 campaign. None of these appeals worked. Mrs. Wallace was nominated in the first primary with 54 percent of the vote. Flowers took 19 percent, and veteran Congressman Carl Elliott mustered only 8 percent. Most Negro candidates fared badly, although the Reverend Peter Kirksey won a place on the Greene County Board of Education.

During the autumn campaign of 1966 the Republican onslaught compelled the Democrats to act somewhat like a party. The degree of teamwork was limited, but even a slight suggestion of Alabama Democrats behaving as a party is newsworthy. Jefferson County officeholders, threatened by a nearly complete slate of Republican challengers, set up a Democratic county campaign headquarters. The state executive committee mailed publicity material to county committees, urging voters to support the Democratic ticket. But this was about the extent of the unprecedented teamwork. Wallace would not appear on the same platform with Senator Sparkman, and he attempted to stop the use of the state committee's newspaper advertisement with Mrs. Wallace's picture in the center, surrounded by smaller pictures of Sparkman and the Democratic congressional nominees. The senator hired his own opinion polling organization and tailored his campaigning faithfully to their findings and recommendations—an interesting example of an older political figure adapting himself to newer campaign methods.

Wallace could rely on his own organization. The term *organization* when used in the context of Alabama politics is a slippery one. When a person with any considerable political appeal announces for governor, persons throughout the state volunteer their support. They may do so because of personal enthusiasm for the candidate, or because they pick him as a winner and foresee personal advantage if their prediction is correct. The candidate—win or lose— if he expects to run again, can keep a neat card file of his chief supporters in each county. The zeal of these supporters is directly related to their candidate's apparent chance of victory. The Wallace organization is a more sophisticated development along this line. The term *Wallace coordinator* is often used to refer to the chief Wallace leader of a county. Top Wallace aides in Montgomery may call a meeting of all the county coordinators in the northern half of the state, not only during a campaign but during the governor's tenure of office.

Mrs. Wallace might well have won even without a sophisticated organization. No one doubted that Congressman Martin was an Alabama segregationist, but it is hard for a rich man's segregationist to beat a poor man's segregationist. Mrs. Wallace won 63.4 percent of the vote; James Martin got 31 percent; and an independent candidate, Carl Robinson, picked up the remaining 5.6 percent. She carried everything: the metropolitan areas, the traditionally Republican counties, and the black belt. Candidate Martin had a majority in Winston County and a plurality in Greene and Madison counties. The general pattern of the Republican vote suggested a return to the pre-1962 era. The GOP's greatest strength (42.8 percent) was in the traditional counties. Six of the seven traditionally Republican counties were in Martin's top quartile. The metropolitan counties gave him approximately 37 percent and the black-belt counties, 24 percent. Martin in 1962 and Goldwater in 1964 had been able to capitalize on the resentments of the strongly segregationist black belt. Since no one could "out-seg" a Wallace, it is not surprising that Martin did poorly in these counties. Of course, the black-belt electorate had undergone a dramatic change in composition. In 1960 it was less than 6 percent Negro; in 1966 it was over 41 percent Negro. In the black belt and elsewhere, Negroes faced the dilemma of choosing between two segregationists or supporting the independent, Carl Robinson. As a result, the turnout in Negro boxes that fall was considerably lower than in the May primaries. Returns from predominately black precincts throughout the state indicated that there was no consensus on a favored candidate. In some of them Mrs. Wallace was the front-runner, a fact George Wallace was to cite frequently to counter assertions that he was in any respect anti-Negro. In the election for the United States Senate, blacks voted heavily for John Sparkman. Five Negroes won contests in black-belt counties. The most important office was won by Lucius Amerson, who turned back a write-in effort to be elected sheriff of Macon County. In Lowndes County, an outnumbered but unified white vote prevailed over the independent Black Panther slate. A low Negro turnout and the fact that some Negroes voted for white candidates contributed to the defeat of the Black Panthers.

The real curiosity of the 1966 election was the outcome of the congressional races. Most of the politically sophisticated opined that "the five Republican congressmen got in on Goldwater's coattails, and they'll go out on Wallace's." A national polling organization advised its client that "because of straight-ticket voting, . . . it seems pretty likely that four out of five, if not all five, Republican congressmen will go." The prophecy held true for Glenn Andrews; he lost his Fourth District to Democrat Bill Nichols. James Martin had to abandon his seat in the Seventh District to run for governor, and the GOP nominee who sought to succeed him was defeated. But the three Republican incumbents representing the cities of Mobile, Montgomery, and Birmingham won reelection easily. The Mobile and the Birmingham incumbents each polled nearly two-thirds of the vote. Montgomery's William Dickinson had a somewhat tighter race but still won almost 55 percent of the vote.

The year 1966 was in all other respects a disastrous one for the party. The GOP elected a state senator from Jefferson County, but all other nominees, from United States senator to constable, went down to defeat. The party's brave organizational and financial efforts availed them nothing. More precisely, it availed them three seats in the national House of Representatives and a heavy burden of debt.

Alabama Provides a Presidential Candidate: Politics in 1968

The first major political event of 1968 was a sorrowful one. Governor Lurleen Wallace died of cancer after an extended illness. She was succeeded by Lieutenant Governor Albert Brewer, long a Wallace lieutenant.

The primary to name a successor to retiring Senator Hill was an exercise in expressing alienation from the national government. James Allen won in the runoff after a campaign consisting almost entirely of assaults on "that Washington crowd." He defeated Congressman Armisted Selden, who had indeed served in Washington for sixteen years. It is ironic that Selden, a segregationist and a man with a top ranking by Americans for Constitutional Action, should have been stuck with the "Washington crowd" label. His congressional seat was won by Walter Flowers, whose chief campaign theme was the service he had rendered George Wallace. Flowers had been among a group of lawyers who had gone to other states to remove legal obstacles to placing Wallace's name on the presidential ballot.

There were three Democratic parties on the November ballot. Under the traditional rooster emblem of the Democratic Party was a slate of electors pledged to George Wallace. Then the Alabama Independent Democrats and the National Democratic Party of Alabama each ran separate slates of electors, both pledged to Hubert Humphrey. This unusual arrangement stemmed from Alabama's leadership of an effort to breathe life into the electoral college. Here the review of a little history may be useful. Let us note, first, that Alabama Democratic electors are chosen by popular vote in the primary. In 1948, just before the deadline for filing names in the primary, the segregationist leaders of the Democratic State Executive Committee, outraged by Truman's civil rights proposals, had publicly urged all nominees for Democratic elector to pledge themselves not to vote for Truman. An anti-Truman slate of electors won. Later, these Democratic electors pledged their votes to Strom Thurmond, then governor of South Carolina and presidential nominee of the States' Rights Party. In a final ingenious ploy, the committee issued a warning that all candidates and persons planning to run in future years would be well-advised to support the presidential nominees of the Democratic Party of Alabama. Those supporting some other candidate, such as President Truman, would be considered disloyal to the party and would be barred from entering the 1950 Democratic primary. In that year and again in 1954 party "loyalists" captured control of the state executive committee. They exacted a loyalty oath of all persons entering the primary in a presidential year to support the nominees of the national convention. The oath was chiefly significant for persons running for elector. In 1958 and again in 1962 the committee was captured by "states' righters"—persons alienated from the national party and generally ardent segregationists. They required no oath for the primary of 1960. The absurd result was the victory of six states' rights electors and five loyalists. In December, 1960, five electors cast their ballots for John F. Kennedy; the other six voted for Harry F. Byrd.

In 1966, oddly enough, the executive committee turned up with a loyalist majority and elected a loyalist chairman. Yet as the presidential election approached, the loyalist (now meaning anti-Wallace) majority did not feel strong enough to require a pledge of loyalty to the nominees of the Democratic National Convention from all persons entering the primary. At their January, 1968, meeting the committee voted to require no loyalty oath for the primary that year.

Since it was foreseen that the electors chosen in the primary would be pledged to support George Wallace, a group of party loyalists, working with the covert cooperation of the chairman of the executive committee, used a petition procedure to create a new party, the Alabama Independent Democrats, which put on the November ballot a slate of electors pledged to support the nominees of the Democratic National Convention. This group ran no candidates other than presidential electors since they regarded themselves as faithful Democrats merely seeking to assure loyalty on the national level. The Alabama Independent Democrats hoped to bring together all anti-Wallace Democrats. This was not to be the case. The Negro leaders who in 1966 had broken away from the Alabama Democratic

Conference had organized the National Democratic Party of Alabama, a group committed to running candidates for state and local offices in November. Its leader, Dr. John L. Cashin, Jr., believed that since the winners of most state and local offices in the Democratic primary would be Wallace people, it was absurd for Negroes and white racial liberals to support an overwhelmingly segregationist party. The NDPA then proceeded to name a goodly number of candidates for county offices and for Congress, most of them Negroes. Leaders of the Alabama Independent Democrats replied, in effect, that in local races Wallace people who were vulnerable could be beaten just as well in the Democratic primary. Also this group looked to a time in the future when Wallace's fortunes might decline, and they assumed that the party could be "saved" under their leadership.

The nonpartisan municipal elections in August produced some interesting results. Six Negroes won places on the twelve-man city council of Fairfield, an industrial suburb of Birmingham. Likewise, a Negro member was elected to each of the city councils of Homewood, Jacksonville, and Uniontown. These were not strictly firsts because blacks had in 1964 been elected to the city council of Tuskegee and before that to the governing body of all-Negro Hobson City.

The presidential election of 1968 produced Alabama's all-time-high turnout. To nobody's surprise Wallace swept the state with 65.9 percent of the vote. The Republicans came in second with 14 percent. The Alabama Independent Democrats polled 13.6 percent, and the National Democratic Party of Alabama 5.2 percent. Two smaller parties together managed to get some 15,000 votes. The three-part analysis of Republican strength used earlier appears almost ludicrous applied to this election. The sources of relative strength were again back to the pre-1964 pattern. The traditional counties were 26.7 percent Republican; the metropolitan counties 17.4, and the black-belt counties a mere 6.1 percent. The GOP's weakness in the metropolitan counties, as in 1966, may be partly attributed to the increased Negro electorate. Before 1965 the kinds of persons who had been voting Republican constituted a larger percentage of the metropolitan electorate. In 1964 Goldwater had drawn 76 percent of the black-belt vote; four years later, Nixon polled 6 percent. Individuals voting in both elections were more consistent in their attitudes than the drop in 70 percentage points might suggest. In 1964 the black-belt electorate was an overwhelmingly white electorate; by 1968 it was 40 percent Negro. In 1964 Goldwater was perceived as the friend of segregation. In 1968 Wallace assumed this role and received solid white support. Negroes backed Humphrey. So who was left to vote for Nixon? The black-belt counties ranked highest in support for Humphrey. If the votes for both slates for Humphrey are added together, his county percentage computed from this, and the percentages ranked, all fourteen black-belt counties rank in the top-quartile counties (seventeen in all).

It is almost superfluous to ask where Wallace did best, what with his two-thirds of the vote statewide and his clear majority in sixty-two of the sixty-seven counties. An examination of the Wallace and Nixon top quartiles reveals the Nixon counties pretty much a contiguous bloc in the northern half of the state; Wallace's are more widely scattered, although he has a group of eight contiguous counties in the southeast corner of the state. Nixon was strongest in metropolitan counties; four of six were in his best quartile. Wallace's top quartile included eight wholly rural counties and eight that were less than 20 percent Negro; only one county contained a city as large as 25,000. Again, it should be recalled that we are discussing *relative* strength only; Wallace polled a majority vote in all Nixon's top-quartile counties. The precinct returns within Jefferson County reveal a simple pattern. Nixon took a majority only in the silk-stocking precincts. Wherever Humphrey had a commanding majority (usually as an Alabama Independent Democrat) the voting box turned out to be overwhelmingly Negro. Everything else went for Wallace.

Undoubtedly the best test of a party's strength is its performance on election day. However, it should be noted that the fact that both other parties conceded the state to Wallace probably increased his margin of victory. The Democratic National Committee's high command, convinced that they could not possibly carry the state, made practically no money available for campaigning in Alabama. Republican leaders claim that their public opinion polling organization exactly predicted Nixon's dismal 14 percent. Hence, they concentrated their efforts on saving their three congressmen from being unseated by Democratic nominees riding George Wallace's coattails. Their strategy was to de-emphasize the three congressmen's association with the Republican Party and with Richard Nixon. Instead, their publicity merely urged the voters to reelect congressman so-and-so. Certainly neither major party made a maximum effort to carry the state for its presidential nominee. While nothing they could have done would have denied the state to Wallace, greater effort on their part might well have pushed his percentage down to around 50 percent. Certainly it is hard to argue that Nixon's 147,000 votes is the best index of Republican strength. Perry Hooper, the GOP nominee for the United States Senate, outpolled Nixon with 201,000 votes; and in 1966, when James Martin lost to Mrs. Wallace, he polled 262,000 votes. Martin received a higher percentage of a much smaller total vote.

The strategy outlined above does not explain why all three Republican congressmen coasted to easy victories. None of them had a close race. Alabamians apparently know how to split a ticket. Democratic congressional nominees ran on the regular (Wallace) Democratic ticket, and these three congressional districts went overwhelmingly for Wallace. A partial explanation is that the Democratic nominees were not ideal candidates. While undoubtedly upright citizens, they were political unknowns, lacking the qualities associated with an attractive candidate. Democratic leaders made prodigious efforts to persuade well-known persons with political appeal to enter these contests, but even phone calls from the White House were to no avail. Some observers hold that able citizens are reluctant to enter a primary in which the key to victory is professing great admiration for George Wallace. The GOP incumbents, no political novices, had done an exceptionally good job of keeping in touch with their districts through newsletters and newspaper columns and by other methods. Wallace did little to help the Democratic candidates. Absent from the state and pushing his presidential candidacy, he did not urge all Alabamians to vote a straight Democratic ticket.

The National Democratic Party made a respectable showing for a brand-new party. It ran candidates for Congress in all eight districts. In three of these it managed to poll around 10 percent of the vote. Its banner district was the Fifth, where its nominee, William Branch, outpolled the Republican nominee, won a majority in two counties in the district, and finished second with 23 percent of the total vote. In Sumter County the NDPA elected the coroner and two members of the county board of education. The party also picked up justices of the peace in several counties.

The Rising Tide of Participation and Alienation

In the 1946 gubernatorial primary, 365,513 Alabamians trooped to the polls—a record number. This outpouring can be attributed to no mere population increase, because the 22 percent of the voting-age population that it represented was also a record. In November, 1968, 1,044,362 ballots were cast—a new high, representing 51 percent of the population of voting age. The rate of increase has been steady throughout the period. Although greater participation by Negroes has been important to the expanded totals, more whites than blacks have been added to the electorate over these twenty-two years. There is no simple way to demonstrate what has been or will be the effect on public policy of this great expansion of the electorate. The most plausible hypothesis is that in the fullness of time politicians will become responsive to the interests of a greater number and variety of persons.

The performance of the Republican Party in the immediate past has been unimpressive. The party's banner years were 1962 and 1964, when it was able to capitalize on segregationist resentment and to picture Democrats as soft on segregation. Republican successes in the marginal South have depended largely on economic factors. In the absence of race as the overriding issue, men may begin to

divide along economic lines. Even in Alabama in all presidential
elections save 1964, the GOP drew its strongest support from the
prosperous. Yet race is the issue that really stirs the Alabama voter.
Since Wallace has a copyright on this issue, the GOP in the state
seems unlikely in the near future to enjoy the success it has had
in the peripheral South.

However, there is peril in carrying this analysis too far. Carried
to its logical extreme, it holds: you can't lick them if you can't
"out-seg" them. The analysis certainly does not explain the three
Republican congressmen. They rode Goldwater's coattails into office the first time, but their party membership was no handicap to
reelection, possibly because they did not stress their partisanship.
In fact, de-emphasizing the party may offer Republicans their best
chance to increase representation in the state legislature. If the GOP
does not contest the governorship and thus evoke Democratic Party
loyalty and straight-ticket voting in November, voters may be willing to split their tickets and vote for Republican state legislators.
Alabamians are accustomed to a high rate of turnover in the legislature; the incumbent does not enjoy the advantage of his congressional counterpart. In nonmetropolitan counties voters may be well
acquainted with candidates and their reputations. Thus, if the abler
and more upright candidate happens to be a Republican, the voters
may ignore party lines and support him. In GOP headquarters one
hears undocumented charges of rascality in the legislature and the
argument that many members would be vulnerable to capable and
aggressive opponents. Since 1966 three Republicans have run in
special elections for vacancies in the state legislature; one candidate
was elected, and the other two ran respectable races. (The comments
about rascality do not apply here.) These results lend plausibility
to the argument.

If elections with little emphasis on party are good ones for Republicans to contest, municipal elections, which are run on a nonpartisan basis in Alabama, should be ideal for them. Two Republicans were elected to the city commission of Mobile in the 1960's.
George E. McNally, the first to be elected, described his campaign

felicitously: "I did not unfurl the banner of Republicanism in this race . . . ." [17] Possibly some Republican workers recognized McNally without his banner. George Seibels won a seat on the Birmingham City Council in April, 1963; in November, 1967, he was elected mayor of Birmingham. The elections are legally nonpartisan, and Seibels made no reference to his Republican affiliation.

The relationship of Negroes to the Republican Party should be noted briefly. When one raises this question with Negro leaders, a characteristic reaction is, "Well, I can think of only two Negro Republicans in this country. There is Reverend Smith and then there is . . . ." Or one might note that in April, 1963, George Seibels was elected to the Birmingham City Council on a nonpartisan slate of racial moderates, most of whom were Democrats. Negroes backed the moderate slate. In 1966 probably as many blacks voted for James Martin as voted for Mrs. Wallace. While there are instances on record, Negro support for Republican nominees is not an important aspect of Alabama politics.

A party's strength is relative to that of the opposition. In evaluating the Republicans' chances in anything but the very short run, we must note that they are not facing a united and disciplined opposition. The charismatic leadership of George Wallace may have made the Democrats look more formidable. He may be their chief asset. A decline in his political fortunes might create an entirely different situation.

Passage of the Voting Rights Act of 1965 marked the end of an era. Negroes may be still inhibited from reaching their full political potential by economic pressures or threats of violence, if these are not used too openly, but Negroes can no longer be denied the ballot by legal trickery. The state is not going back to the pre-1965 era. The relevant question for the present and future is: what have Negroes secured from the ballot and what can they reasonably hope to secure? That some Negroes may expect too much too soon is suggested by an incident in the city of Tuskegee. It seems that the Negro majority in the city council had been in office less than two

17 Tuscaloosa News, October 13, 1961.

months when an irate Negro voter phoned his councilman and demanded to know why the street in front of his house had not been paved yet. He continued to berate the official and concluded with the ultimate insult, "You fellows are no better than the white council." We should recall that there are localities in the South where Negroes have voted for many years but have not been able to improve their status as a result. The term *manipulated vote* is used in several studies to describe a locality where Negro voting over the years has produced no results save possibly the retirement from office of a particularly brutal sheriff. He is replaced—with black support—by an officer who pursues an indulgent policy toward gambling, drunkenness, and brawling in the ghetto. The ballot has not been used to improve the Negro's status. Negroes secure only impulse freedom; whites secure freedom from black militancy.[18]

How, then, does one measure Negro political effectiveness? One might measure it in terms of number of streets paved (or other tangible benefits), or one might count the number of Negroes elected to public office. If one had to choose, the index would have to be tangible benefits. Since Negroes are a minority in most parts of Alabama, the holding of elective office is no accurate criterion. Influence and officeholding often go together. If a Negro is elected to public office, he will be in a stronger position to bargain for or to demand benefits for the black community. A majority of Negro officeholders—Negro government—might be required to produce tangible results in some localities. However, increased registration alone may have some effects. Yarns abound of black-belt county officials who examine the most recent registration record, then hurry out and pave the parking lot of a Negro church. Not all Negro political activists believe they have to be elected to office to exert influence on community decisions. Thomas Edward Wrenn, reflecting on his unsuccessful race for the Birmingham City Council in November, 1967, felt that his effort had not been in vain. "We were able to raise the issues of open ditches and unpaved streets, and they're still

18 Alfred Clubok, John DeGrove, and Charles Farris, "The Manipulated Negro Vote: Preconditions and Consequences," *Journal of Politics*, XXVI (1964), 112–29 Holloway, *The Politics of the Southern Negro*, Chap. 6.

talking about it now," Wrenn said. "If I hadn't gotten in the race, these issues never would have been raised. People like Emory O. Jackson, editor of *The Birmingham World*, will tell you, 'he didn't win the seat, but he really won because his platform is the one they're arguing over right now in city hall.' The campaign had a heck of an effect on the city. It changed the thinking of city hall." [19]

Of course, there is a psychological significance to Negro office-holding. Historically, ethnic politics of northern cities involved recognition of a group—as when the first Hungarian-American became assistant prosecuting attorney. The number of Polish-Americans in Congress is not an insignificant matter to Americans of Polish ancestry. When the first American of Italian ancestry was elected governor of Rhode Island, it gave tremendous psychological gratification to Italian-Americans of that state. They did not necessarily expect him to produce better highways or streamline the state administration, but they took great pride in the fact that an American of Italian ancestry, like an Irishman or a Yankee, could be elected governor. One would expect a similar reaction of racial pride as Negroes are elected in Alabama.

Regardless of whether the chief benefits of officeholding are material or psychological, it should be noted that in January, 1969, Alabama had more Negro elected officials than any other southern state—a total of sixty-seven. The reader must be warned, however, that this sum is achieved by the kind of arithmetic that adds together squirrels, mice, and elephants and then arrives at a total called "number of mammals." The Alabama figure includes twenty justices of the peace, six constables, and twenty-eight members of city councils. Of the latter, sixteen are in the governing bodies of three small, all-Negro communities.[20] The most important municipal office held by a black man is membership on the Birmingham City Council. In a rather unusual arrangement Arthur Shores was appointed by the council itself to fill a vacancy caused by the death of one of its elected members. Then on November 5, 1969, Shores

19 Quoted in Julian Bond, *Black Candidates* (Atlanta: Southern Regional Council, 1969), 45.
20 "Black Elected Officials in the Southern States" (mimeograph by Voter Education Project of the Southern Regional Council, Atlanta).

was elected to the seat. In July, 1969, the state acquired six additional officeholders when six Negroes were chosen in a special election in Greene County (83 percent Negro). All had been nominees of the National Democratic Party of Alabama in November, 1968, but their names were left off the county ballot. The United States Supreme Court ruled that the candidates' names should have appeared on the ballot and ordered a new election. Four of the successful candidates won positions on the five-man county commission. The other two were elected to the five-man county board of education, which already had one Negro member.

The Greene County victories are particularly significant because they point to the area of brightest prospects for increased Negro officeholding. About ten other black-belt counties either now have or soon will have a Negro voting majority. If the full potential of the black vote can be mobilized, it will not be surprising if some time in the 1970's there are Negro governments in as many as ten counties. All-black county governments may have an understandable appeal to black-belt Negroes who have experienced only governments of and for whites. If several Negro legislators were elected from these areas, they would constitute a significant power bloc in the legislature. Yet the effectiveness of this kind of politics is limited to the small part of the state with a Negro majority. Negroes will have to develop political procedures that reflect their minority position both statewide and in most localities of the state.[21]

To maximize their influence on a state level, Negroes need to vote as a cohesive bloc. At present, their effectiveness is severely limited because of the continued split between those following the leadership of the Alabama Democratic Conference and those getting their cues from the National Democratic Party of Alabama. The two Democratic groups are affected also—or will be affected—by developments outside the state. Dr. John L. Cashin, Jr., leader of

[21] Negroes constitute almost 20 percent of the registered voters in the state. This figure is the total of all sixty-seven county registration rolls. The failure of many counties to purge their registration lists means that the names of many of the dead and of persons long removed from the county are included. Recently registered Negroes have had a shorter time to move away or die. Their strength is probably somewhat underestimated. This fact is relevant to the speculation about all-Negro governments in black-belt counties.

the NDPA, is active in the New Democratic Coalition. Democratic Conference leaders are closer to the regular party machinery. NDPA leaders offer no persuasive answers to the question of how they can work with whites to develop a winning statewide coalition. They view the present with considerable pessimism and look forward hopefully to a future wherein what are vaguely described as "fundamental changes in the power structure" will occur. Alabama Democratic Conference leaders run the risk of being dubbed "Uncle Toms" and losing their followers if they do not assume a sufficiently militant posture and vocabulary. Much more disposed to work with the white community than are the leaders of the NDPA, they are unable to secure significant concessions from the white community fast enough to assure their continued effectiveness in the black community.

In statewide politics Negroes face an even more fundamental problem—one that would be with them even if they were completely united. One cannot play balance-of-power politics unless there are two centers of power to balance. In the splintered factionalism of Alabama there are no two such centers. Negroes could be more effective in a situation of bifactionalism or two-partyism. Moving back and forth between two recognized factions, which might be difficult to engineer, would not be necessary. If there were one faction or party whose hope for victory was dependent on the support of the majority of Negroes, blacks would be in a position to demand rewards for their loyalty. The development of a strong two-party system or of Wallace and anti-Wallace factions would increase Negro political effectiveness.

The GOP scarcely exists for Negroes. They are the most loyal supporters of the Democratic Party's nominees for President and are well disposed toward the party's national image, whereas the majority of the state's white Democrats (and this means the majority of voters) are alienated from the party nationally. As recently as 1966, the Democratic State Executive Committee engaged in a heated argument before it voted to remove the slogan "White Supremacy" from atop the Democratic rooster on the November ballot. If a struggle is needed to remove so offensive a slogan, one can hardly expect congenial relations between black and white

Democrats. Awkwardness about control of the Democratic Party machinery has already arisen. Negroes correctly observe that on one ticket or another they provided more than half the support that Humphrey received, yet they have no representation on the state executive committee and very little on county committees. Since the state committee and most of the county committees are popularly elected from areas with white majorities, the difficulty cannot be speedily rectified by appointment.

Alienation of white Democrats began with a wrench when the Democrats ceased to be the party of segregation. Prosperity may also have lessened party loyalty. Poor farmers with a populist orientation regarded industry and finance as something that belonged in the Northeast—up in Yankeeland. The men who owned the country dwelt a long way off. Wall Street and the Republican Party were closely identified. In recent years Alabama has shared in the affluent society. The state still ranks low in per capita income, but the expansion of industry has spread prosperity around and has lessened the number of people who see themselves as poor farmers at odds with the industrial Northeast.

If thousands of white Democrats are alienated from their party nationally, ought they not logically to make a mass shift into the Republican Party? No. Alabamians are alienated from the nation, not merely from the Democratic Party. "Alabama Unions Found Defecting: Moderate Race Policies of State Council Blamed" was the headline of a New York *Times* article a few years ago. Some 30,000 members were lost to the state AFL-CIO when locals disaffiliated with the state organization rather than accept its support of the national AFL-CIO's racial policies. The 30,000 did not resign from their local unions; they just disaffiliated with the outside world. These unionists manifested typical Alabama resentment over "outside" attacks on cherished institutions. This spirit of separatism is incompatible with a mass shift to the Republican Party because the GOP is a large organization with branches outside the Deep South. Identifying with the Republican Party means rejoining the Union. This spirit of resentment toward the national government will continue for the immediate future, and so long as it does, the majority of the state's voters will remain alienated Democrats.

10

MISSISSIPPI
Unreconstructed and Unredeemed

CHARLES N. FORTENBERRY AND
F. GLENN ABNEY

The Primacy of Race

The story of Mississippi politics over the past two decades is in essence a story of racial agitation. No candidate, no campaign, no election, no administration has escaped the issue; most of them were dominated by it. There is nothing new about this, of course, except for the intensity of popular concern. In one way or another the bi-racial nature of the population has provided the dynamics for political action in Mississippi since 1850.

The hands of the past lie with particular heaviness on this state, shaping to a high degree its social, economic, and political characteristics. The most salient aspect of this past is the institution of slavery, and in it many of Mississippi's modern characteristics have their origin. Slaves in large numbers were brought into the territory before 1800, and during approximately one hundred years of the period of statehood Negroes have been more numerous in the population than whites. Along with its position as the state with the highest percentage of Negro population, Mississippi has the second largest proportion of rural population. Unless primary consideration is given to these two facts, no satisfactory explanation of the state's politics is possible.

Most of its political history has developed in the pattern of one-

Charles N. Fortenberry is Head, Department of Political Science, Auburn University. F. Glenn Abney is Associate Professor of Political Science and Governmental Research, University of Mississippi.

472

party politics. Although there was in the state from 1835 to 1850 an active Whig Party which elected a governor, a United States senator, and a slate of presidential electors, this group, along with the national organization with which it was affiliated, declined rapidly in the decade preceding the Civil War. The Republican Party in Mississippi, which flourished during the period of Reconstruction, disappeared for all practical purposes after 1876. Over the remainder of its history, Mississippi has been firmly under the control of one party—variously called Democratic and Mississippi Democratic, and with even more variation in its principles and programs. Within its uncertain vortex, leaders have engaged in an energetic personal politics. Factions within the party have been transient and unstable, producing no viable substitute for bipartisanship. Through the years internal conflicts over radicalism, federalism, conservatism, and the like have rocked the system, but its unity has been largely undisturbed. A state party, at times showing little relation to either of the major national parties, its chief coalescent element has been the common attitude on the race question.

A cleavage of significance over much of the state's political history can be observed in what has been designated variously as the delta versus the hills or the planters versus the rednecks. It has some geographical basis in that the delta, or the alluvial plain stretching along the Mississippi River nearly two-thirds of the state's length, is a rich agricultural area and thus historically a region of large plantations, wealthy landowners, and a high proportion of Negro population. The hills, or the remainder of the state where there is chiefly rolling terrain, are less fertile and peopled by small farmers, a high proportion of whom are white. The division is more ideological and economic than geographical, however, and has taken the form of conservatism versus radicalism, the wealthy versus the poor, large planters versus small farmers, in a number of campaigns. Some of the most celebrated political battles of the state, notably those between James K. Vardaman and LeRoy Percy and between Theodore Bilbo and Earl Brewer, have involved individuals and issues representing these divisions. There is a danger of overstating the importance of the cleavage, of course, and the conflict in ideology has been over-

Figure 1
THE SOIL REGIONS OF MISSISSIPPI

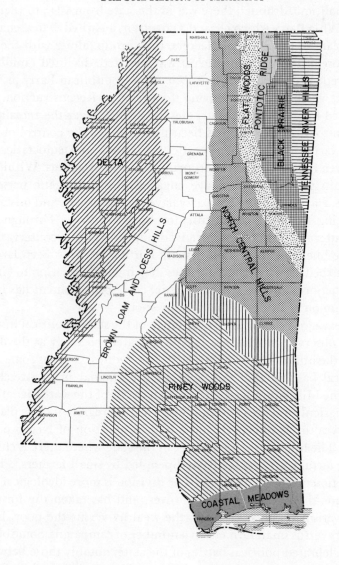

shadowed in recent years by the inordinate and near-unanimous preoccupation with the race question.

Woven into the fabric of Mississippi's political history is a strong thread of populism—southern style. Growing out of an agricultural protest movement called the Farmers' Alliance, it embraced the national Populist program of the 1890's and flourished among the small farmers under the leadership of Frank Burkitt of Chickasaw County. Although the Populist candidate attracted a considerable vote in the 1895 elections, the party declined rapidly thereafter and was never significant as a political organization. Its impact came in the influence of its principles on political figures of the next century who, though members of the Democratic Party, were really southern neopopulists. They added to the Populist program of anti-corporationism, bank regulation, income tax laws, and more government activity a strong anti-Negro harangue, thus holding out to the poor whites the double attraction of economic betterment and white supremacy. James Kimble Vardaman was perhaps the ablest of the Mississippi neopopulists, but Theodore Bilbo, Paul B. Johnson, Sr., and others used the same tactics. As has been pointed out by V. O. Key and others, Mississippi's poverty has frequently limited welfare politics associated with neopopulism to fulmination and little more. The anti-Negro theme—though expressing a view on which whites agreed—has been enduring.

The rural nature of Mississippi society looms large in the political heritage. It is an authentic influence. Mississippi ranks highest in the South and fourth highest among all the states in percentage of rural population, with 55.5 percent of its people so classified in the 1970 census.[1] Of the minority that are not rural residents, most live in small communities. There is only one city (Jackson) of more than 50,000 people, and only eight of more than 25,000. More than half the state's municipalities have less than 1,000 people. Moreover, the urban population is largely of recent origin. In 1930 only a sixth of the people lived in communities of 2,500 or more. The effects of rural residence can be seen in a lower level of education, a lower

[1] Vermont is highest, with 67.8 percent of its population rural.

Table 1

POPULATION OF MISSISSIPPI, 1800–1970

	Total Population		Race		Residence	
Year	Number	Percentage Change by Decades	White (Percent)	Nonwhite (Percent)	Urban (Percent)	Rural (Percent)
1800	8,850*	—	—	—	—	100.0
1810	40,352*	356.0	—	—	—	100.0
1820	75,448	87.0	—	—	—	100.0
1830	136,621	81.1	—	—	2.0	98.0
1840	375,651	175.0	—	—	1.0	99.0
1850	606,526	61.5	48.8	51.2	1.8	98.2
1860	791,305	30.5	44.7	55.3	2.6	97.4
1870	827,922	4.6	46.2	53.8	4.0	96.0
1880	1,131,597	36.7	42.4	57.6	3.1	96.9
1890	1,289,600	14.0	42.2	57.8	5.4	94.6
1900	1,551,270	20.3	41.3	58.7	7.7	92.3
1910	1,797,114	15.8	43.7	56.3	11.5	88.5
1920	1,790,618	−0.4	47.7	52.3	13.4	86.6
1930	2,009,821	12.2	49.7	50.3	16.9	83.1
1940	2,183,796	8.7	50.7	49.3	19.8	80.2
1950	2,178,194	−0.2	55.6	44.4	27.9	72.1
1960	2,178,141	0.0	57.7	42.3	37.7	62.3
1970	2,216,912	1.8	62.8	37.2	44.5	55.5

Sources: Figures for 1800–1940 taken from John C. Belcher and Morton B. King, *Mississippi's People* (Bureau of Public Administration, University of Mississippi, 1950), Table 1, p. 12; for 1950 from United States Department of Commerce, Bureau of the Census, "Mississippi General Characteristics," *1950 United States Census of Population* (Washington, 1952), Tables 10, 11, 12; for 1960 from *United States Census of Population, 1960, Detailed Characteristics, Mississippi* (Washington, 1962); *1970 United States Census of Population.*
* This figure represents the portion of the territorial population residing within present state boundaries.

average family income, an innate conservatism (though mixed with occasional tinges of radicalism), a suspicion of outside persons and ideas, and an excessive concern with the race question.

An agricultural economy is not necessarily poor, though the recurring economic distress of American farmers during the past century might point to that conclusion. But an agricultural economy based on one crop is particularly vulnerable to adversity. Cotton has dominated the economy of Mississippi from the early years of statehood. Until the Civil War it was produced on the plantations by slave labor, thereafter by sharecroppers. On the small farms it was produced by the owners and their families. Only the large landowners prospered in such an economy, and this prosperity was interrupted by boll weevils, bad weather, and poor markets. Still, diversification of agriculture made little headway for a long time in Mississippi. As late as the last prewar year, 1941, when the total of cash receipts from all farm marketing amounted to $200,973,000, nearly 75 percent, $147,749,000, came from cotton. The last twenty-five years have brought revolutionary changes in agriculture. The number of farms has been cut in half, the farm population has been reduced by nearly two-thirds, and mechanization has trimmed the number of persons employed on farms to one-third that of 1950. But the effects of cotton's long economic domination remain. Displaced workers from the cotton fields have not fitted into other agricultural pursuits; many of those within the productive age brackets have gone elsewhere seeking employment, sometimes leaving their families behind. This out-migration of working-age adults has left a high proportion of old people and children, with resulting increases in welfare rolls and school attendance. Thus, though cotton is less important in the economy than formerly, it significantly affects the political order. Additional money for education and welfare and efforts to expand industrial employment are among the foremost political issues in present-day campaigns.

In the center of the background is the Negro. As has been noted, for two-thirds of the state's history the Negro population has been numerically larger than the white; in all but about ten years of that history the Negroes were completely excluded from the political process. Yet they were there—the focal point of conflicts that included civil war, large-scale riots, and bitter political campaigns. They have been the foundation for the social order, the undergirding for the economic structure, the element that gave real meaning to the phrase "southern way of life." Seldom has a major part of a state's population been so politically impotent and at the same time so influential on the temper of the times.

Conflict and Consolidation

Mississippi's background cannot easily be described in a neat pattern of historical eras. One period tends to blend into another and there are frequent throwbacks that confuse the observer. But a delineation of certain stages of the past may have some meaning.

The Reconstruction period was brief but important. It is recalled chiefly by white politicians who point to the graft, corruption, and incompetence as illustrating the depths of degradation to which public officialdom may descend. The culprits, or alleged culprits, were of two kinds: (1) white Republicans who had migrated from northern states, and (2) Negro natives who also were Republicans. Objective assessment would find persons corrupt and honest, competent and incompetent, in both groups.[2] But the short span of Reconstruction government—in which Negroes won two seats in the United States Senate and one in the House of Representatives, the lieutenant governorship, and the offices of secretary of state and state superintendent of education, and in which white Republicans held the governorship and other important positions—came to symbolize bad government and to provide the most compelling argument for excluding Negroes and Republicans from political participation in the years to come.

Reconstruction ended for all practical purposes in 1876, when Adelbert Ames, the Republican governor, resigned and left the state after being impeached by a Democratic legislature that had been elected in 1875. Three other high state officials resigned along with Governor Ames. There followed a period of about twenty-five years devoted to consolidation and strengthening of Democratic control and the complete exclusion of Negroes from political life.

2 For what is generally regarded as a vindication of one of the chief offenders see Blanche Ames, *Adelbert Ames, 1835-1933* (New York: Argosy-Antiquarian, Ltd., 1964).

Employing whatever means were effective, including fraud and violence, the Democrats won the state elections of 1875 and the national election of 1876. Thereafter their control was not in danger except from federal intervention. This threat was one of the principal reasons for the constitutional convention of 1890,[3] which sought to frame a document that would legalize the methods of white Democratic control. The task was formidable. Speaking on the floor of the convention, Judge J. J. Chrisman said, "It is no secret that there has not been a full vote or a fair count in Mississippi since 1875—that we have been preserving the ascendancy of the white people by revolutionary methods . . . . We have been stuffing the ballot boxes, committing perjury, and here and there . . . carrying the election by fraud and violence until the whole machinery for the elections is about to rot down." [4]

The ingenuity of the body was equal to the occasion, and the convention (whose membership consisted of one Negro Republican, one white "National Republican," one white "Conservative," and 130 white Democrats) produced and proclaimed in effect a constitution which, particularly in its restrictions on the franchise and its unique legislative apportionment provisions, provided the authority to solidify and perpetuate white political control.[5] The job seemed done, but the clincher came twelve years later with the enactment of the mandatory, statewide, direct primary law and with exclusion of Negroes from the primary by party resolution. Thus the concern over Negro participation was ended. White rule was formalized by the 1890 constitution and made doubly secure by the white primary.

The dates from the enactment of the primary law down to World War II roughly delineate another era in Mississippi's political his-

[3] Other reasons were demands, particularly from the white counties, for democratic reforms of the judiciary, restriction of the powers of corporations, and elimination of convict leasing. See A. D. Kirwan, *The Revolt of the Rednecks* (Lexington: University of Kentucky Press, 1951), 60–64.

[4] Jackson *Daily Clarion Ledger*, September 11, 1890, quoted in Kirwan, *Revolt of the Rednecks*, 58.

[5] A subsequent decision of the Supreme Court pointed to the constitutionality of the suffrage provisions. *Williams v. Miss.*, 170 U.S. 213 (1898).

tory. This was the period of a rise in influence of the residents of the hill sections, or what A. D. Kirwan has called the "revolt of the rednecks." Prior to this time, in the struggle to establish and legalize white control, the dominant figures were conservatives—James Z. George, L. Q. C. Lamar, Anselm J. McLaurin, John M. Stone—who represented the more wealthy elements and corporate interests in the state population. Now, with the election of James K. Vardaman in 1903, there began a period when small farmers and laborers were more influential and the stalwart conservatism gave ground to neo-populist reforms: a public education program, regulation of corporations, guarantee of bank deposits, and the like. The advent of the direct primary had emphasized the need for popular appeal. The campaigns took on more color and the platforms of the candidates were more elaborate. The protagonists were, for the most part, from the hills—Vardaman, Bilbo, Lee M. Russell, Paul Johnson, Sr.— with programs and promises appealing to the small farmers and wage-earners. Interspersed among them were more conservative figures—Henry Whitfield, Mike Conner, Hugh White—but their appeal too, in large measure, lay in their advocacy of popular reforms.[6] The race question was quiescent during most of the period, not because of any change of attitude, but because the Negro was not a part of political life and thus not an issue. Although marked by scandal and rumors of scandal, by demagoguery and misrepresentation, the politics of the period generally moved the state in the direction of improvement and reform.[7] The pace was slow and the progress inconsistent.

Thus, through successive eras of Reconstruction, the structuring for white control, and the ascendancy of the rednecks, Mississippi came into the period following World War II. The state and its people were prepared—by inherited ideas and traditions, by experience with a monolithic political system, and by economic circum-

[6] The members of Congress from the state, except for Vardaman and Bilbo, were generally of a conservative cast. Among the more prominent were Senators John Sharp Williams, Pat Harrison, and Hubert Stephens, and Congressman Will Whittington.

[7] This is the thesis of Kirwan, *Revolt of the Rednecks.*

stances—to wage the memorable political battles of the fifties and sixties.

Change: Natural and Induced

New factors affected the politics of the post–World War II period. Besides the expected voicing of progressive ideas by some returning veterans, and occasional statements of tolerance of Negro voting in the wake of the *Smith v. Allwright* decision—neither of which proved very permanent or influential—there were hard elements of change at work.

The most obvious aspect of the economic system in the postwar period was that it could no longer operate by growing crops of cotton and timber. The forests were largely gone, and vast eroded areas of cutover lands and sediment-clogged streams were mute testimony to the fact. Restoration of the timber economy would take a generation or more, during which time no large need for manpower and no hope of large profits existed. More significant was the mechanization of agriculture—heralded by the improvement of tractors, the invention of the cotton picker, and the development of chemicals for weed control—that pointed to the rapid decline of the small farm and the diminishing need for unskilled farm labor. Farming henceforth instead of being a small capital–large labor operation would be a large capital–small labor enterprise. The decline in number of farms, a trend that began in the depression years of the 1930's, was accelerated after 1945. The number of farms in that year stood at 274,000. A decline each year since then brought the number down to 104,000 in 1966. The number of farm workers, family and hired, declined from 459,000 in 1950 to 159,000 in 1966.[8]

Accompanying this steep drop in the number of farms and farm workers was a marked decline in cotton as the dominant crop. Cotton acreage dropped from 2,240,000 acres in 1945 to 995,000 acres in

[8] From U.S. Department of Agriculture reports.

1966.[9] At the same time farm production has become diversified, with livestock and livestock products increasing to the level where, in 1966, they provided half the cash receipts from all farm marketing. In that year also, soybeans produced half as much cash income as cotton; the latter produced only slightly more than one-fourth the total farm income.

It is obvious from these figures that Mississippi agriculture no longer rests mainly on cotton but on a variety of crops and animals. It is equally obvious that the economy is no longer based primarily on agriculture but on manufacturing as well. Along with the significant changes in agriculture has come a similarly important growth in industrial production. This resulted in considerable part from a state-sponsored program of industrial attraction, which included public subsidies through local-government financing of plant construction along with liberal tax exemptions. Additional attractions to industry were cheap labor and abundant natural resources such as water and natural gas. Since the public effort to attract industry —designated the Balance Agriculture with Industry program—was launched in 1936, public industrial bonds in the amount of $264,-675,000 have been sold in 558 issues.[10] Mississippi has sustained substantial industrial growth, as revealed in the figures of manufacturing employment which, in 1968, stood at 165,000. Since March of 1965 manufacturing employment has exceeded agricultural employment.[11]

The changing economy has effected important changes in the population. The low level of education and training among Negroes has resulted in increasing unemployment because many of them did not meet the education and skill requirements of the industrial

9 The number of bales produced annually has remained fairly stable; thus the yield per acre has more than doubled.

10 The figure is that of the Mississippi Agricultural and Industrial Board for January 1, 1968. *Mississippi Magic*, March 1968, p. 8.

11 This information is from the Bureau of Labor Statistics, U.S. Department of Labor, and the Mississippi Employment Security Commission. The commission estimated that in 1968 there were more than 2,000 manufacturing establishments in the state.

plants.[12] The out-migration of employable Negroes was somewhat matched by immigration of whites with the result that, while the total population has remained almost static, the percentage of Negroes has declined from 49.3 percent in 1940 to 37.2 percent in 1970. (See Table 1.)

Related to the economic changes, but having more far-reaching implications, is the growth of urbanism. This process, though not rapid enough to transform swiftly the nature of the population, may eventually have an important modifying effect on its politics. Urban residents, increasing steadily, have gained political importance through the recent court decisions requiring reapportionment of the legislature on the basis of population.[13] Thus, while remaining rural-oriented the lawmaking body has recently shown increasing concern over education, legalization of alcoholic beverages, government reform, and other ideas more often associated with urban communities. The 1968 session of the newly reapportioned legislature proposed constitutional amendments lowering voter residence requirements and providing for annual legislative sessions, and passed laws increasing markedly the salaries of public school teachers.[14] There is less evidence of urbanism in other aspects of legislative behavior. Municipal pressures for more revenue finally succeeded in obtaining authorization from the legislature to levy a local 1 percent sales tax—but have not succeeded in obtaining a share of the gasoline tax for street construction and maintenance. Public officials representing mostly rural people, such as county supervisors and sheriffs, have maintained some of the most effective lobbies in the legislature. The effects of urbanism thus are not yet clear but could have a long-range significance.

[12] Many of the new industries coming into towns under the BAWI program made off-the-record agreements to give white applicants preference in employment. See B. P. Joyner and J. P. Thames, "Mississippi's Efforts at Industrialization: A Critical Analysis," *Mississippi Law Journal*, XXXVIII (1967), 433–87.

[13] *Baker v. Carr*, 386 U.S. 186 (1962) and *Reynolds v. Sims*, 377 U.S. 533 (1964). The Mississippi Legislature was reapportioned by order of a federal district court on March 2, 1967.

[14] Memphis *Commercial Appeal*, June 12, 1968.

Figure 2
URBAN POPULATION OF MISSISSIPPI, 1960

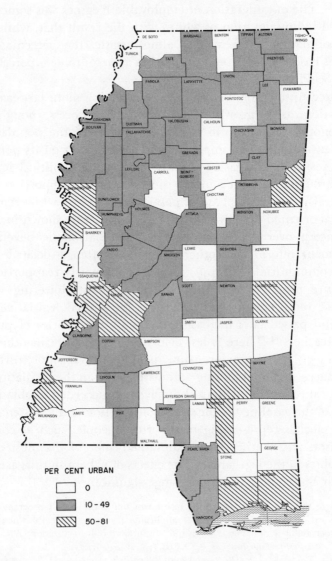

PER CENT URBAN

☐ 0

▨ 10 - 49

▨ 50 - 81

Of immediate and obvious importance as a modifying force in the state's politics is the changing status of the Negro population. Although the proportion of Negroes to whites is steadily declining, it is evident that this minority is potentially the strongest element of change in the body politic. It is not necessary to relate here the long history of events leading up to the generally free exercise of the voting privilege by Negroes at the present time. It is a sordid story of a bewildered white population deceived and misled by their own elected leaders, whipped into a rage by wild and exaggerated statements from political platform, press, and pulpit. Demagogues exploited the fears and ignorance of the electorate. Having fanned the fires of racial hatred to gain election, officials found themselves forced to advance to even more unreasonable positions to keep ahead of the flames. Elections were decided on the sole issue of which candidate was the more devout segregationist. All public decisions—political, economic, educational—were made in the light of their effect on the integration issue. A decade of sorely needed progress was sacrificed.

The legal campaign to secure further the disfranchisement of Negroes did not begin until 1954—a full decade after the white primary had been overthrown by the nation's highest court.[15] Apparently, no great concern was felt for white domination during this period and in a few communities considerable numbers of Negroes participated in the Democratic primaries.[16] In 1954, action was completed on a constitutional amendment making the ability to read and write a requirement for voting, with the provision that it not be applied to persons who were qualified before the amendment was adopted.[17] The effect of this measure was to retain illiterate white voters on the rolls but to bar illiterates, chiefly Negroes, who sought to register after 1954. There followed other constitutional changes such as the "good moral character" requirement for voting in 1960[18] and numerous statutes designed to implement con-

15 *Smith v. Allwright*, 321 U.S. 649 (1944).
16 One of these was rural Mount Carmel in Jefferson Davis County.
17 *Mississippi Constitution*, Sec. 244.
18 *Ibid.*, Sec. 241 A.

stitutional provisions and to make it more difficult for Negroes to qualify. Notable were laws increasing the control of county registrars over the registration process allowing destruction of application records, and providing for publication of applicants' names.[19]

When the maze of restrictions began to give way before the 1964 Civil Rights Act and the 1965 Voting Rights Act of the national Congress, the path finally cleared for Negro registration.[20] Federal registrars were in fourteen counties by the end of 1965 and had registered more than 20,000 persons in addition to the large numbers added to the rolls by the county registrars.[21] The number of registered Negroes increased steadily. By the time of the 1966 elections it was estimated at 163,000, a year later at 190,000;[22] in the 1971 elections it was believed to be 300,000.

The number of Negroes registered doubtless will continue to increase since a large number of the nearly 1 million Negro residents are of voting age and are unregistered.[23] The effect of Negroes on the political process is not clear. Registration of additional white persons has probably exceeded that of Negroes and, except in a few counties with heavy black-population majorities, whites may be expected to maintain numerical superiority in any contest involving racial issues. (Of the eighty-two counties, twenty-nine have a majority of Negro population, but only thirteen of this group have two-thirds or more Negro residents.) Also, the experience thus far does not indicate very active participation by the newly registered Negroes. An estimated 40,000 voted in the 1966 elections, approxi-

19 *Mississippi Code of 1942*, 1964 Supp., Secs. 3209.6–3213.
20 The constitutional provisions pertaining to an educational test, good moral character, and reading and writing sections of the Mississippi Constitution were repealed in 1965.
21 The only real difference in the requirements for registration with the county registrars and the federal authorities after passage of the Voting Rights Act was simple literacy. County clerks required persons to be able to sign the application blanks; federal registrars accepted the mark of an illiterate.
22 The number of whites and Negroes can only be estimated since registration forms do not indicate color. Some county registrars maintain unofficial tabulations.
23 The U.S. Civil Service Commission announced on March 22, 1968, that 34 federal voter registration offices were being reactivated in Mississippi. Memphis *Commercial Appeal*, March 23, 1968.

mately one-fourth of those qualified. Though the percentage of participation increased in 1967, it was not impressive. The first large turnout of Negroes came in the special congressional election of 1968 in the Third District, where Charles Evers, field director of the National Association for the Advancement of Colored People, led in the first primary over six white opponents, though he lost the runoff.[24] This campaign was significant because it was the first time Negro groups and factions united behind an acknowledged Negro leader. In the regular municipal election of 1969 Evers defeated a white opponent to be elected mayor of Fayette, a town where black voters outnumbered white. The experience here may point the way to more successful campaigns in Negro counties in the future.

Though Negroes have just recently become active participants within the political system, tangible results of their presence exist. In 1967, a predominantly black legislative district elected the state's first Negro representative to serve in Jackson since Reconstruction. In addition, twenty Negroes in the state won election to county posts in the same year. Far more significant, however, than these obvious victories was the increased deference shown the Negro by white politicians. Aware of the large potential black vote, white candidates at all levels in 1967 campaigned in a moderate fashion that sharply contrasted with the demagoguery four years earlier. Though the gubernatorial candidates in 1967 did not dare shake hands with Negro voters for fear of alienating white support, they stayed clear of the racist oratory and propaganda that had dominated the gubernatorial election in 1963. Furthermore, the new power of the Negro has had in several instances a profound impact on white leaders in the application of the criminal law.

The long view of the importance of the Negro as a voter depends largely on the federal presence in the state—a presence which has been responsible for the progress made thus far. If the Negro is allowed to continue to participate in the political system, his bloc

[24] *Ibid.*, February 29, 1968. Evers was an unsuccessful candidate for governor in 1971.

voting will eventually no longer be a necessity. However, without the federal presence the newly won power of the Negro would probably soon vanish in many counties.

While voting rights are changing racial politics in the state, a more fundamental change is taking place in the social life of whites and Negroes. The days of the paternal relationship between the two races are rapidly disappearing. Following the 1954 desegregation decision, whites could say that Negroes did not want an end to the way things are. And for the most part they were right; Mississippi abounded with Uncle Toms. Those formerly acquiescent Negroes are now registered voters who since the middle 1950's have been exposed through television to a way of life nonexistent in the state, and who have taken on a new identity from the leadership of such activists as Medgar Evers and Martin Luther King. Today many whites lament what has happened to the Negro. While blacks are showing less deference, whites are becoming less paternalistic. Both trends will strengthen the Negro ego.

Desegregation is coming slowly in the social lives of the citizens.[25] Negroes continue to be intimidated by physical and economic reprisals and thus prevented from asserting their constitutional rights. For the present the Negro must continue to rely upon the federal government to assert his rights for him. However, one should recognize the weak but significant dissent within the white population. Confined mostly to the universities and some of the religious communities, the protest is still only a feeble voice. Nevertheless, it is strongest among young people, and in time the effects of their leadership will have a greater impact.

The Abiding Political Culture

If there are factors that promise to modify the political climate of Mississippi it should be remembered that there are also stabilizing forces. Rural societies are innately conservative, but Mississippi has

25 A survey of public schools in November, 1967, revealed that 13,000 Negroes were enrolled in integrated schools. This was about 4.5 percent of the total Negro enrollment. *Ibid.*, November 20, 1967.

a special aversion to change—even an inclination to live in the past. Psychologically, this could be explained as an escape mechanism— a desire to avoid the uncomfortable present by looking to what is widely thought to be a prosperous and pleasant past. Of course, one has to look back more than a hundred years to find the ease and affluence of which Mississippians dream.[26] Whatever may explain the worshipful attitude toward the long ago, the fact remains that the pull of the past is strong, and resistance to change is stubborn. This fear of change partially accounts for the opposition of the whites to political participation by Negroes.

Though the whites have established an oligarchy to perpetuate their domination of the Negro, internally the white political culture is basically democratic. Although the state and national legislative seats were for years malapportioned and although some historians have argued that the poll tax was a weapon used by delta bourbons to disfranchise the rednecks, Mississippi whites seem no less democratically oriented than people in other states. The record of many other state legislatures on apportionment is, for example, no better. Furthermore, the white culture does pay much deference to democratic norms. Control of the government by the people is a strongly endorsed attitude. Such governmental institutions as the direct primary, election by a majority, and election of Supreme Court justices testify to the presence of this norm.[27]

In the past the relationship of whites with Negroes was largely paternalistic. The black man was supposedly unable to think for or to care for himself without the aid of his white benefactors.

[26] The idea of the prosperous society under slavery is an illusion—in terms of the general population. Less than 10 percent of Mississippi white people were slaveholders. See C. S. Sydnor, *Slavery in Mississippi* (New York: Appleton-Century, 1933), 193.

[27] When white Mississippians are compared in endorsement of democratic norms with data reported by James W. Prothro and Charles M. Grigg for samples from Ann Arbor, Michigan, and Tallahassee, Florida, they are not necessarily any less democratic in their attitudes. See F. Glenn Abney, "The Mississippi Voter: A Study of Voting Behavior in a One-Party Multifactional System" (Ph.D. dissertation, Tulane University, 1968), 58–66. See also James W. Prothro and Charles M. Grigg, "Fundamental Principles of Democracy," *Journal of Politics*, XXII (1960), 276–94.

Whites found much reinforcement for their beliefs in the behavior of the sons and daughters of former slaves, sons and daughters deprived of the educational and economic means to help themselves. However, the days of paternalism are ending. No longer is white racism cloaked in the soft raiment of the white man's burden. Today with blatant opposition from the Negroes and with growing reaction from within the white society and from outside the state, the justice of the old ways is being questioned.

Nevertheless, most of the whites apparently remain convinced of the virtues of segregation. Their desire to preserve the segregated way of life renders them unable to tolerate protest from "outside agitators" or from within the society. Punishment for the rebellious has often been swift and cruel. Phone calls in the night, bomb threats, anonymous letters, economic reprisals, and violence against the dissenters have constituted the weapons of the "true believers." Many of the more sophisticated middle class do not condone such tactics, but neither do they dare object to the activities of the rebellious. In the last ten years hundreds of white residents of Mississippi have suffered the consequences of dissent.

Though there has been protest within the white society, it has been mild and generally ineffective. The real challenge to segregation comes from the outside, in particular from the federal government. This federal intervention in the social life of the state has produced an alienation from the national political system that has significantly affected Mississippi politics. The data in Table 2, drawn from a survey of 162 white Mississippians, indicate a low level of support for national political institutions and leaders.[28] The alienation runs so deep in the Mississippi culture that instances of schoolchildren cheering upon learning of the assassination of President John F. Kennedy were not uncommon. The affection that children in the American society usually feel for political lead-

28 The survey was conducted in Mississippi counties in the summer of 1967. The respondents were chosen by selecting in a systematic fashion names from voter registration books from twelve counties. For further information on the survey, see Abney, "The Mississippi Voter," 15–18.

Table 2
OPINIONS OF MISSISSIPPI WHITES IN SUMMER, 1967,
ABOUT NATIONAL COMMUNITY, REGIME, AND GOVERNMENT
(N = 162)

Attitudes about National Political System	Agree	Don't Know or Refuse to Answer
1. Most of the Supreme Court's rulings have not been in the country's best interest.	79%	14%
2. Congress has passed more unconstitutional laws in the last five years than in any other five-year period in history.	59%	28%
3. Unless the national government stops its present course of action, we should stop obeying some of the laws.	11%	11%
4. We need a new Constitution which would preserve the rights of each state to govern itself.	46%	8%
5. Because of the actions of the government in Washington, I feel less proud of the country than ever before.	64%	4%
6. The national government has become so powerful that we are living in a dictatorship.	57%	4%
7. Because of the actions of our national government, it is more difficult to pay taxes to Washington than ever before.	66%	8%

ers contrasts sharply with attitudes manifested by these children.[29]

When the statements in Table 2 are analyzed through the use of Guttman scaling techniques, the least educated, the more elderly, the lower-status, and the authoritarian tend to be the most alienated.[30] Probably their alienation results largely from their more

[29] See Fred I. Greenstein, *Children and Politics* (New Haven: Yale University Press, 1965), 27–54.

[30] For a further statement on the effects of alienation see Abney, "The Mississippi Voter," 43–54. The seven items in Table 2 were selected from nine questions asked white residents of Mississippi in the summer of 1967. For any item to be included in this scale, it had to cross-tabulate with each other item in the scale so that less than 10 percent of the responses fell into the nonscale category. Interviewees with two or more nonscale responses or with one nonscale response and with one "no comment" were excluded from the scale analysis.

racist orientation. Though the level of alienation is indeed rather significant, Mississippians retain much affection for the political system. When the 162 persons in the survey were asked what things about the United States they were most proud of, 68 percent of them made at least one reference to the governmental and political institutions of the nation. While this percentage is smaller than that found for a national sample (85 percent) by Gabriel Almond and Sidney Verba, it is much larger than percentages reported for samples in Great Britain (46 percent), Italy (3 percent), Germany (5 percent), and Mexico (30 percent).[31] The collapse on system supports in the state comes on racial matters; Mississippians continue to be unwilling generally to support laws designed to provide for racial equality. A hundred years ago the breakdown resulted in a civil war. Such a break with the system is now, of course, out of the question.

Political Parties: Disunity in Diversity?

The domination of politics by the Mississippi Democratic Party is the most obvious aspect of the political scene. This says little, of course, since many diverse ideologies and persons have paraded under the banner of this organization. They range from loyalist Democrats to secessionist Democrats with all the shades in between. In the past they have been united by a common support of segregation, but little else, and even that foundation has begun to crack under the strain. Yet the party meanders on, held uncertainly together by the constant grouping and regrouping of political leaders who see in it a device for obtaining or retaining the public offices. No durable faction has developed within the party. The well-known divisions of the past, such as the Bilbo and anti-Bilbo combinations, were constructed for each campaign. Since the death of Bilbo other powerful political figures—Hugh White, J. P. Coleman, Paul B. Johnson, Jr., and others—have headed factions only while incumbent governors. This meant only four years, since governors can-

---

31 See Gabriel Almond and Sidney Verba, *The Civic Culture* (Boston: Little, Brown and Co., 1931), 64.

not succeed themselves. Moreover, the aphorism that Mississippi politicians "can get votes for themselves but not for anyone else" seems to be taken seriously and there is little slate-making or effort by one officeholder to campaign for another person who is a candidate for office. (One exception was the active effort of Senator James Eastland in behalf of Paul Johnson in the governor's campaign of 1963. Even this was kept as quiet as possible.) The governor in office usually is conceded control of the party's delegation to the national convention, though in recent years there has been consensus—at least on the surface—on matters pertaining to national-state party relations.

Although splinters of the Mississippi Democratic Party have shown up on almost every presidential election ballot since 1948, in the form of independent or "unpledged" slates of electors (the unpledged slate backed by Governor Ross Barnett won in 1960), they have receded into the main body following the election. Of more permanence as a state organization are the Freedom Democrats; this group had its inception in the Negro campaign for the ballot. A successor to the Student Nonviolent Coordinating Committee as the organization for carrying on the main struggle for civil rights for Negroes, it first appeared as a political movement in a 1963 mock election by some 80,000 would-be Negro voters.[32] It was formally organized in April, 1964, and sought recognition as the delegation representing Mississippi at the 1964 Democratic National Convention. It gained seats for two delegates in a compromise settlement of the dispute. Three candidates of this group sought unsuccessfully to be seated in the national House of Representatives over the regular Democratic candidates in 1965. In the 1966 Democratic congressional primaries the candidates of the party were defeated but with the aid of a federal court order appeared on the ballot as independents in the November election, attracting only a handful of votes. In 1967, candidates backed by the party sought to be placed on the ballot as independents but were ruled out by the federal

---

[32] On the background of this group see S. Carmichael and C. V. Hamilton, *Black Power* (New York: Random House, 1967), 86–97.

court on the basis of a 1966 Mississippi statute which prohibits persons defeated in a party primary from running as independents in the general election.[33] The Freedom Democrats have not been able to muster the support of the state's Negroes, most of whom have preferred to attempt to work through the regular Democratic organization. Aaron Henry, state NAACP president, was the group's first chairman but left to join forces with the Young Democrats. Its best-known present spokesmen are Lawrence Guyot of Biloxi, Ed King of Edwards, and Fannie Lou Hamer of Ruleville.

Another group seeking to supplant the regular party organization is the Mississippi chapter of Young Democrats. It appears in the role of the truly integrated party that avoids the extremes of either the Freedom Democrats (Negro) or the Mississippi Democrats (white). On college campuses it has been prominent in efforts to further integration and to promote more open discussion of political questions. Typical of the group's activities was a 1967 suit in Oxford, in which the Young Democrats joined with others in litigation to invalidate a speaker ban at the University of Mississippi, which had barred Aaron Henry from appearing to fill a campus engagement. In 1968 the Young Democrats at the university succeeded in having the administration enjoined from enforcing the campus speaker ban against Charles Evers. This organization was granted a charter over a rival, predominantly Negro group by the National Young Democratic Clubs in October, 1965. Anxious to bring the state's politics into line with the national party, this group has stated its readiness to assume the responsibilities of the state's Democratic organization by providing an integrated party giving loyal support to the national nominees and platform. Douglas Wynn and Hodding Carter III of Greenville are among its leaders.

In 1968 a loyalist coalition of Young Democrats, NAACP leaders, Freedom Democrats, and labor union officials succeeded in obtaining the credentials for the state to the National Democratic Convention. Although the regulars admitted Negroes to the state convention that chose the national delegates and included three Ne-

---

[33] *Mississippi Code of 1942*, recompiled, 1966 Suppl., Sec. 3260.

groes in the forty-four-man delegation to the national convention, the loyalists claimed Negroes were not given a fair share of delegates and refused to cooperate with the regulars. Having warned Mississippi in 1964 to send an integrated delegation in 1968, the credentials committee of the convention seated the loyalists, who had sent a racially balanced delegation to Chicago. The formation and success of the loyalist coalition represent a significant symptom of change in the partisan structure within the state.

Among white Mississippians the popularity of the national Democratic Party has declined drastically in the last two decades. The defeat of the Democratic tickets in 1960, 1964, and 1968 reflects this drop in support. Nevertheless, Mississippi politicians have not made a mass exodus to the Republican Party. They remain Mississippi Democrats even though the national Democratic Party did not recognize their party in 1968 as an affiliate.

The Republican Party, dormant for three-quarters of a century in Mississippi, has made valiant efforts to become a factor in the state's politics since 1950. In the long period following Reconstruction it existed chiefly in name, though the caretaker-like Negro leaders who controlled it exercised some influence on appointments during Republican administrations in Washington. These leaders also provided loyal delegate support for administration leaders in the national conventions. Following the landslide victory of Herbert Hoover in 1928, the new President sought to consolidate his surprising southern support in the election by adjusting the organization to the realities of the segregated society. There followed the long feud (1928–60) between the Hoover-inspired Lily-White faction and the older Negro "Black and Tan" faction. At each national convention the two contended for recognition, with the Black and Tan group winning consistently. Finally the greater numbers of the Lily-White group impressed the 1956 convention to the point that it was given a share of the seats. Mississippi gave 39 percent of its popular vote in 1952 and 27 percent in 1956 to the Republican electors. By 1960 the Black and Tan faction gave up and its few supporters joined the Lily-Whites in a united party. Despite the coalition, in the 1960 presidential campaign the Republicans led in only four counties and received only 25 percent of the state's votes. In 1963, capitalizing on the considerable opposition to Paul B. Johnson, Jr., of Hattiesburg, the Democratic gubernatorial candidate—a loser in three previous campaigns—and running able and articulate candidates for governor and lieutenant governor (Rubel Phillips of Jackson and Stanford Morse of Gulfport), the Republican state ticket polled more than 38 percent of the popular vote in the November elections.

Some of the appeal of the Republican candidates in 1963 might well have been their early identification with Senator Barry Goldwater, who had visited the state and who seemed to represent what many Mississippians wanted. Thus, when the 1964 campaign came along, the young Republican leaders were already set to send a Goldwater delegation to the convention and take the lead in piling up a popular vote for the Arizona leader in November. The unprecedented 87 percent of the popular vote the Republicans received in Mississippi that year meant little in terms of converts to the party. Yet it yielded the first GOP congressman of the century (Prentiss Walker) and spurred the party's hopes for further gains. These came in small amounts, with the election of mayors in two cities (Columbus and Hattiesburg) in 1965 and the victory of a third member of the legislature in a special election (two Republican legislators had been elected in 1963). Thus encouraged, the party went out strong in the congressional campaign of 1966, with Republican candidates in four of the five House districts,[34] and challenging the major-domo of the Democrats, Senator James Eastland. All these efforts failed and in the process the lone Republican congressional seat was lost, when Congressman Walker was defeated in a race for Eastland's Senate seat. The next year's effort in the state elections was equally discouraging, the Republican candidate for governor polling a somewhat smaller vote than in 1963, with 30 percent of the total. No legislative seats were won and the party was again in the doldrums with only a modicum of local offices to show for its strenuous efforts.

[34] The seat not contested was held by John Bell Williams, who at that time was reported to be changing his party affiliation to Republican.

In the presidential election of 1968 Richard Nixon ran third in Mississippi, receiving only 14 percent of the votes cast. The candidacy of George Wallace dealt a severe blow to Nixon's chances in the state. As a result the Republican support in 1968 was similar to that in 1960—that is, it centered among middle-class citizens in the urban areas. The state Republican leaders were so certain of Nixon's defeat in Mississippi that campaigning within the state was held to a minimum, and funds collected were diverted to the national level.

Perhaps the most discouraging aspect of recent events for the Republicans is the voting pattern for their gubernatorial candidates in state elections. While the party has made encouraging gains among upper-status groups in urban areas, support for Republicans in state elections tends to be highly correlated with support for defeated Democratic candidates in the primaries, suggesting that at least some of the votes do not necessarily represent enthusiasm for the Republican cause as much as they represent antagonism toward the Democratic nominee. For example, in 1963 the Republican nominee's vote correlated $+.76$ with the vote for J. P. Coleman, the Democratic candidate who was defeated in his party's second primary. While it can be argued that much of the Coleman vote, like the Republican vote, probably came from urban and upper-class areas, much of it did not, and that which did come from such areas cannot be linked necessarily with Republicanism. Of particular interest is the fact that the Republican candidate received his strongest support from Coleman's home county. That county, Choctaw, is less than 10 percent urban and is relatively poor in terms of family income.

An examination of individual partisan identifications does not necessarily prove any more encouraging to Republicans; however such an examination is not necessarily discouraging either. In general, white Mississippians are confused about their party affiliations. The traditional attitude that the South and Mississippi are better off in the Democratic Party no longer seems valid to them. In a statewide survey of 355 whites in the summer of 1967, the responses to an inquiry about party identification typify their disillusionment and confusion. A thirty-seven-year-old housewife responded, "Democrat—but the Democratic Party has changed so much in the last few years in regard to the race issue and its wasting of money that I might vote Republican this time." A sixty-three-year-old housewife said, "Democrat. Used to be something to be proud of. I'm not proud of what we have now. I'm not a Republican." A seventy-year-old farmer responded to the interviewer, "You kinda help me out and give me some ideas; everything has gone out of sight. Don't know what to say. Democrats have always been high; things are out of sight now." A forty-year-old wife of a farmer stated, "We have always classed ourselves as Democrats, but we have voted Republican lately. But I would classify myself as independent." [35]

When the 355 respondents were questioned in 1967 about their likes and dislikes with regard to the national parties, their image of the Republican Party was more favorable than their image of the Democratic Party.[36] The most frequently mentioned point of approval for the latter was traditional support—for example, "I've been one all my life." Though some viewed the Democratic Party as the party of the common man, no more than 4 percent of the sample expressed such an opinion. The respondents criticized it most frequently for its liberalism, its leaders, its management of government, and its relationship with Negroes. Altogether the respondents made twice as many remarks of disapproval about the party as they did comments favorable to it.

Although their images of the Democratic Party were negative, the respondents did not indicate they were Republicans. While the sample revealed twice as many negative responses about the Democrats as it did positive comments about the Republicans, the interviewees made only 20 percent more favorable comments about the Republican Party than they did about the Democratic Party.

[35] This survey was conducted prior to the first Democratic gubernatorial primary in the summer of 1967 in the same manner as that described in footnote 28. For further information about the survey see Abney, "The Mississippi Voter," 15–18.

[36] For further data about the result of this survey, see *ibid.*, 92–131.

More than two-thirds of the sample had nothing to say either in praise or in criticism of the Republicans.

While many respondents criticized the Democratic Party, most of these drew a distinction between the national Democratic Party and the Mississippi Democratic Party. When asked about the similarity of these two parties, 49 percent stated that an important difference exists, while only 34 percent thought that no important difference exists. In explaining the difference between the two parties most of the respondents cited the traits for which the national party was most frequently criticized. The significance of this distinction is that many Mississippians still feel justified in identifying as Democrats. Some respondents implied that *they* were the true Democrats and that the national leaders have betrayed the party's underlying principles. A thirty-one-year-old wife of a farmer made the point rather explicitly: "They [the state party] try to uphold the original beliefs of the Democratic Party more than the National Democrats do."

While the whites distinguish between the national and state Democratic parties, they perceive similarities rather than differences in the images of the two national parties. When the interviewees were asked if they felt that the two parties were greatly different or were about the same, 77 percent said that the parties were similar. The attitude that the two national parties do not provide a real choice for the South spurred the third-party efforts of George Wallace of Alabama, with whom many Mississippians sympathize. Comments such as the following typify the feeling that the Republicans may be no better than the Democrats. The wife of an engineer living in Jackson said in regard to the Republicans: "They'll probably be just as bad as the Democrats if they ever get in; they play up to the Negro vote." Similarly, a woman in Winston County said in criticism of the Republicans: "They are trying to emulate the National Democratic Party."

The data in Table 3, indicating the partisan identifications of white Mississippians in the summer of 1967, reveal that they are no longer solidly Democratic. But perhaps the most significant

Table 3
PARTY IDENTIFICATION OF 355 MISSISSIPPI WHITES IN SUMMER OF 1967

Partisan Identification	Total Number of Respondents	Percent of Total
Democratic	162	46
Qualified Democratic	19	5
Republican	20	6
Independent	137	39
Conservative, States' Rights	11	3
Don't know or refuse to say	6	1

feature of the data is the large number of independents—twice as large as the number of independents found in national samples— and the small number of Republicans. Of the 355 persons, 16 percent claimed to have changed their identification at one time. Of these, 90 percent said they had left the Democratic Party. And 73 percent of the changers did not adopt a new partisan label but instead identified as independents. It is not surprising then that the independents tended to have more unfavorable images of the Democratic Party than did Democratic identifiers.

In terms of political attitudes the Democratic followers tended to include persons of a wide range of views, including the most liberal and the most conservative, and the most alienated and the least alienated from the national political system. The differences within this continuum are highlighted by voting patterns in the 1964 presidential election; 63 percent of the 109 Democratic respondents who recalled how they had voted, supported Senator Barry Goldwater. The voters who supported Lyndon B. Johnson were more liberal in their political attitudes, had more favorable Democratic partisan images, were less authoritarian, and were less alienated from the national political system than were the Goldwater voters. However, the social backgrounds of the two groups were scarcely distinguishable except that the Johnson voters tended to be residents of urban areas more than did the Goldwater voters. Evidently the Republican candidate in 1964 attracted the Democrats because of his conservatism, which they felt would lead to a lessening of federal intervention in the state's racial life.

Despite the relationship between authoritarianism, alienation, and the voting of the Democrats in 1964, no variable was as significantly related to the voting patterns in that election as was intensity of partisan identification. The impact of partisan identification on voting in two-party elections is further highlighted by the difference in the voting patterns of independents and Goldwater Democrats in the 1963 general gubernatorial election. Though the partisan images of the Goldwater Democrats were not necessarily more pro-Democratic than the partisan images of the independents, 84 percent of the Goldwater Democrats remembering how they voted (N=58) cast their ballots for the Democratic nominee, as opposed to only 59 percent of the independents who remembered (N=99). Evidently, as in other parts of the United States, Mississippi partisanship is an extremely important variable in two-party elections.

The most significant data about the independents show that they tended to resemble the Republican identifiers in terms of their ecological backgrounds. That is, the independents had higher incomes, more education, and better jobs; they were more likely to come from urban areas and were younger than the Democrats. Furthermore, the independents tended to be more conservative on issues of domestic and foreign policy than Democratic and Republican identifiers. Because these respondents identifying themselves as independents tended to resemble national Republicans in their socioeconomic background and because of their negative image of the Democratic Party, they may represent future Republicans in Mississippi, especially as the stigma of being a Republican declines within the state. However, there is no rush to embrace the GOP. Though the people have become disenchanted with the national Democrats, most continue to feel that the Republicans offer no better alternative.

Despite their hesitancy to identify as Republicans, the regular Democrats may be forced to do so. The national party seems to be well on the way to denying them any benefits from identifying themselves as Democrats. If the national Republicans offer hope to the disenchanted, the number of leaders and followers identifying as Republicans is likely to change radically. The offer of the Republican leader in the House of Representatives to allow southern congressmen to change their party identification without losing their seniority may seem rather tempting. Nevertheless, Mississippians are not attracted to the Republican Party.

The Sovereign Voter: Cohesive and Incoherent

While one-party, multifactional systems tend to have no permanent organized factions, this does not mean there will be no division within the electorate. The cleavage between the hills and the delta has persisted more than a century.[37] Nevertheless, the cleavage was not as sharp as that produced by party divisions within two-party states. The coefficients of product moment correlation in Table 4 illustrate a definite relationship among the voting patterns of the elections from 1919 to 1948. These coefficients result from the similarity of the voting patterns in the state's eighty-two counties in each pair of elections during this period. If the patterns in each election had been exactly like those in other contests, then each of the coefficients would have equaled 1. Disregarding the 1943 election and the signs before the coefficients, the average value of the coefficients in the table is about .50.

This cleavage in the electorate, described by V. O. Key as between the delta and the hills, was largely social and economic as well as geographical. With the less fertile land unsuited to the type of farming operations that characterized the delta, the farms of the hill country were poor. As a result of their poverty, the white farmers of the hills responded to the politics of neopopulism. These voters supported and elected politicians favoring social-welfare measures and strong restraints upon the activities of corporations. In his affluence the delta resident was not responsive to appeals to tax his wealth or to make the state government play an economic role in the society. Joining forces with the delta resident was the business community in the urban areas.

37 Evidence of how early the cleavage was present is provided in Henry H. Moss, "Sectionalism in Mississippi, 1817–1832" (M.A. thesis, University of Mississippi, 1934).

Table 4

RELATIONSHIP BETWEEN VOTING PATTERNS FOR ELECTED MISSISSIPPI GOVERNORS, 1919–1948, AS MEASURED BY COEFFICIENTS OF CORRELATION

	Whitfield (1923)	Wright (1947)	White (1935)	Bailey (1943)	Conner (1931)	Bilbo (1927)	Johnson, Sr. (1939)	Russell (1919)
CONSERVATIVES								
Whitfield (1923)	1.00	.62	.52	.14	−.50	−.65	−.52	−.84
Wright (1947)	.62	1.00	.41	.05	−.41	−.46	−.45	−.53
White (1935)	.52	.41	1.00	−.02	−.64	−.23	−.42	−.30
Bailey (1943)	.14	.05	−.02	1.00	.01	−.27	.29	.03
NEOPOPULISTS								
Conner (1931)	−.50	−.41	−.64	.01	1.00	.23	.37	.44
Bilbo (1927)	−.65	−.46	−.23	−.27	.23	1.00	.36	.48
Johnson, Sr. (1939)	−.52	−.45	−.41	.29	.37	.36	1.00	.52
Russell (1919)	−.84	−.53	−.30	.03	.48	.43	.52	1.00

That the cleavage between the delta and the hills had an underlying economic basis is made clear by the types of candidates supported by each area. Though he was a resident of the delta, one of
the most popular candidates in the hills was the neopopulist James
K. Vardaman. And one of the most popular candidates in the delta
was Hugh White, a successful businessman in the hills. Another
candidate, Mike Conner, received support from the hills in 1931
and from the delta in 1939. In 1931 Conner ran as a friend of the
common man, but during his administration as governor from 1932
to 1936 he supported the state's first sales tax. In 1939 Conner
campaigned as an economic conservative. Thus, the sectional lines
in Mississippi prior to 1948 were evidently cleavages based largely
upon economic differences.

In addition to economic disparities between the hills and the
delta, the two areas exhibit a distinctive social difference. Possibly
as a result of the region's poverty, residents of the hills are definitely
more fundamentalist in their social mores. Legalization of liquor,
a longtime political issue in the state, has tended particularly to
divide the delta and the hills. Frequently, candidates supported
by voters in the hills have spoken out more loudly for prohibition
than have candidates supported by delta voters.

Since 1948 the nature of the division in Mississippi politics has
changed. Basically, the new cleavage results from a new direction
of the political issues of the state. In general, the conservative forces
have won the upper hand over the neopopulist elements, as a result
of the developing industrialization and urbanization and the emergence of race as the most dominant issue in Mississippi elections.

Increasing industrialization and urbanization have brought an
end to much of the farming in the hills. Many former farmers and
the wives of today's farmers now find employment in the towns and
cities which have attracted new industries, especially plants producing textiles. Often families continue to live on the farm, with members of the family combining factory and farm work. Although
these industries do not pay wages as high as they would have to pay
in the North, they have brought a new affluence to the small farmer.
As a result the hatred of corporations has disappeared. One no

longer hears criticism of big business in state politics; instead all
the candidates extol the virtues of industry. Organized labor's inability to make any significant impact on policy output in the state
is an example of the new power and prestige of the business community. Labor has failed to prevent the adoption of a "right-to-
work" amendment to the state constitution; it was approved by 67
percent of the voters. Labor's record on measures it has supported
in the state legislature has been equally dismal. Similarly, unions
have frequently failed in their campaigns to organize workers.

The 1943 election marked the beginning of the end of the old
politics in Mississippi, and the emergence of the Dixiecrats five
years later pointed the way to the new politics. In 1948 the state
bolted the national Democratic Party for the first time and cast its
votes for the Dixiecrat ticket of J. Strom Thurmond and Fielding
Wright. In his campaign for governor in 1951 the winner, Hugh
White, made a major issue of his membership in the delegation that
bolted the National Democratic Convention in 1948 and of the
failure of his opponent, Paul B. Johnson, Jr., to support the Dixiecrats. By 1951, the delayed reaction to the Supreme Court's over-
throw of the white primary had finally become evident and for the
first time in the twentieth century a sizable Negro group voted in a
gubernatorial election.[38] The whites, for the first time in a hundred
years, were concerned about Negro voters. When a Negro community, Mount Carmel in Jefferson Davis County, voted heavily
for Paul Johnson in the first primary, White charged that his opponent had Negro support—a tactic used frequently in Mississippi
politics in the postwar period. (Johnson denied the charge vehe-
mently.) The irritation of Mississippians with the policies of the
national Democratic Party and their growing fear of the federal
government and of the Negro were thus emerging as important
issues in election campaigns.

[38] The actual number of voters can only be estimated. The number of Negroes
registered, however, could be determined as late as 1955, when the law was changed,
eliminating information as to race on the registration form. A courthouse-by-court-
house count in that year revealed the names of 19,975 Negroes on the registration
books. J. Barnes, "Negro Voting in Mississippi" (M.A. thesis, University of Mississippi, 1955).

In other respects, the election of 1951 did not differ greatly from elections of the prewar period. Hugh White, a former governor and wealthy businessman who was the father of the state's program of promoting industrial development, talked of economic improvement and made no defense of prohibition. Johnson, son of a former governor whose administration had given the people free public-school textbooks, proposed new and larger programs of welfare and made a strong defense of prohibition. Nevertheless, a political concern over the Negro not present in the state since the 1800's was emerging, and decline in neopopulism was clearly evident in 1951.

If any doubt remained that the political scene in the state was changing, it was dispelled by the gubernatorial primary of 1955. The 1954 decision of the United States Supreme Court in *Brown v. Board of Education* set the tone for Mississippi politics for a decade. Each of the candidates for governor in 1955 insisted that he could insure a continuation of segregation better than his opponent could. Perhaps more significant than the race issue in that campaign was Johnson's charge that his opponent, J. P. Coleman, was receiving labor support. Less than twenty years earlier Johnson's father, in his successful campaign for the governorship, had appealed for the support of working people by proposing the creation of a department of labor. But in 1955 the neopopulist themes were no longer attractive. In fact, many Mississippians had begun to connect social-welfare policies of the national government with the increasing efforts at the national level to end segregation in the South. *Liberalism* was becoming a despised word throughout the state. An examination of the aggregate data reveals that voting patterns in this election are less correlated with the percentage of Negro population than in any gubernatorial election in the century. The low correlation reflects a decline in the cleavage between the hills and the delta, for the Negro population is concentrated in the delta.

The elections of 1959 and 1963 consolidated the changes in Mississippi politics. In these years racism was the theme. In the second primary of 1959 both candidates in many respects were alike; both were from the hills—Ross Barnett from the northern hills and Carroll Gartin from the southern hills. They had similar views: both were segregationists and both were members of the Citizens' Council. They agreed on the value of the "right-to-work" law and on the need for greater efforts to improve education and highways. The major issue in the election became the candidates' devotion to the cause of segregation. Barnett charged that Gartin, who was then lieutenant governor, would continue the moderate racial policies of the Coleman administration, which Barnett charged were integrating the state. Barnett's devotion to segregation was indicated by the following words in his campaign song, "Roll with Ross": "He's for segregation one hundred per cent. He's not a mod'rate like some other gent." [39] In reference to his merits as a defender of segregation. Gartin noted the success of the Coleman administration in blocking integration. He stated that the state had spent $65 million on a school building program to keep the Negroes happy and in their place. To one crowd Gartin remarked, "Are you satisfied with the way we've handled segregation in the state? How can we improve on perfection? We are the only southern state that doesn't have integration of some kind. My opponent has lost every race [legal] case he's been in." [40]

In 1959 the developing antilabor character of Mississippi politics continued to emerge. Barnett used the support of organized labor for Gartin to impugn the character of his opponent. He charged, "Carroll Gartin has got Jimmy Hoffa, Walter Reuther, and Dave Beck so tightly tied around his neck that he won't be able to do much more other than appease them if he ever again gets elected to public office." [41]

The voting patterns of 1959 show a marked contrast to those of the first fifty years of the century. As in 1955 the patterns do not correlate as strongly as in previous years with Negro population, but they correlate more significantly with the level of urbanization

[39] A slightly modified version of this tune was later adopted as the state's official song. See Concurrent Resolution No. 67, *General Laws of Mississippi*, 1962, pp. 1153-54.
[40] Jackson *Daily News*, August 21, 1959.
[41] *Ibid.*, August 20, 1959.

than in previous elections. The emerging pattern was a coalition between urban areas, wealthy delta counties, and prairie counties of the northeast against rural areas, especially those with Negro populations. In 1959 for the first time in the century the prairie counties voted with the delta counties. The prairie counties have a low percentage of Negro population and tend to be less racist than the other counties in the old neopopulist group. While the old neopopulist coalition was breaking up, so was the solidarity of the delta vote. If the counties in the delta are examined according to the value of the farms therein, they reflect in the second primaries of 1959 and 1963 a sharper cleavage than in any other gubernatorial election in the century. Furthermore, in 1959 the correlation $(+.47)$ between urbanization and voting patterns in the second primary is at least one and a half times higher than in any previous election in fifty years.

The 1963 election was largely a rerun of 1959. The winner, Paul B. Johnson, Jr., succeeded in portraying his opponent, J. P. Coleman, as a moderate, as pro-Negro, and as pro-Kennedy. Also, Johnson made much of the fact that he had physically opposed the admission of James Meredith to the University of Mississippi, as revealed in 1962 newspaper photographs. The major issue in the campaign was again which candidate could best defend segregation. Coleman charged that his opponents believed "uproar and turmoil are inevitable in the fight for state's rights." [42] He maintained that the battle could be won only through the use of legal and devious means. The fight could not be won, he said, "by knocking over the paramount rules of the U. S. You just have to learn how to plow around them." Learning this trick, Coleman pointed out, requires "true statesmanship founded on experience and knowledge of constitutional law." [43]

Paul Johnson countered with a much tougher approach: "We have those right here among us who believe that if we turn our back the integration problem will go away. We must face up to

[42] Jackson *Clarion Ledger*, August 1, 1963.
[43] *Ibid.*

the issues or lose." [44] He continued, "Evil days are upon the land and this has not been a happenstance. We must fight fire with fire. Every time we give an inch the opposition tries to take a mile." [45]

Since national policies had become increasingly important to the internal affairs of the state, the 1963 campaign featured much discussion of the individual candidates' positions on these policies. The debate concerned the relationship of the candidates, in particular that of J. P. Coleman, with the despised Kennedy administration. Johnson said during the campaign, "There is a candidate in this election who is sponsored by the Kennedys and while he is trying frantically to get the Kennedy albatross off his neck he is not going to succeed. This candidate, J. P. Coleman, is the original Kennedy man, who recommended Kennedy first and wined and dined him in Jackson. He even had Kennedy sleep in Senator Bilbo's bed." [46]

Coleman disavowed owing anything to the Kennedys and explained his support of John F. Kennedy in 1960 by saying, "You don't hear them calling John Stennis, Jim Eastland, George Wallace of Alabama, and Dick Russell of Georgia traitors to the South because they voted the Democratic ticket. They know, as the people of Mississippi know, that our support of the Democratic ticket was to preserve important Democratic chairmanships for the South. If our senators can't get the backing they need from Mississippi then where can they get it?" Coleman added, "I don't owe the Kennedys a thing in this world, except to fight them or anybody else who tries to bring harm to our state and the people of Mississippi." [47]

The 1967 election was different in tone, but the cleavage was very similar to that of 1959 and 1963. As a result of the national Voting Rights Act of 1965, an estimated 190,000 Negroes were registered by the time of the 1967 gubernatorial election, and neither of the two major candidates in the primaries dared praise segregation as overtly as had the candidates four and eight years earlier.

44*Ibid.*, August 2, 1963.
45 *Ibid.*
46 *Ibid.*
47 *Ibid.*

Most of the campaign oratory centered around the use of the word *conservative*. The winner, Congressman John Bell Williams, made much of his defiance of the national Democratic Party in voting for Goldwater for President and of his subsequent punishment by the congressional caucus, and his long devotion to conservatism.

Williams' second primary opponent, William Winter, proposed a number of new programs and spent much of his time discussing them. After the first primary, Winter had become aware that to win he had to speak more on the racial issue. Williams, who had previously spoken largely to the issue, remarked about Winter's switch in campaign tactics, "[Winter] has draped himself in the Confederate flag, put on a Governor [George] Wallace hat and the way he talks would make you think he's a lifetime member of the John Birch Society." [48] Williams added, "[He] began telling us what a dedicated conservative he is after he read the first primary returns. In that primary there were six conservatives and one liberal." [49]

Though the issues of the 1950's and 1960's had changed somewhat from those of the previous three decades, the 1967 election illustrates how old issues like prohibition tend to remain rather than die. For example, Williams said of his opponent, "Mr. Winter knows every bootlegger in Mississippi on a first name basis." [50] In one of his speeches Winter referred to his record of abstinence by saying, "There'll be no whiskey served and no fancy dress cocktail parties in your governor's mansion if I am elected." [51]

Although no survey research is available to document the similarity, the new cleavage that developed in the 1950's in some ways resembles the old one. The similarity rests upon a continuation of the social and economic disparities. Like the old cleavage, the more recent one has tended to set the poor man against the middle class. But the new division is greatly different, for it is based largely on attitudes about the handling of the state's racial problem, whereas

48 Memphis *Commercial Appeal*, August 24, 1967.
49 *Ibid.*
50 *Ibid.*
51 *Ibid.*, August 16, 1967.

the former division was basically economic and geographical. Survey data in Mississippi and other states suggest that persons with the least education, those in lower income levels, and those holding blue-collar jobs have tended to be more racist and to support segregationist policies more frequently. Many of these same individuals would have supported the neopopulist candidates. However, the old cleavage has come to an end. Many of the former conservatives and neopopulists apparently have realigned. Those neopopulists with less intense fear of the Negro have joined forces with middle-class urbanites and some of the more moderate delta residents to support candidates less extreme on the racial issue. In general, the members of this coalition oppose disobedience to federal court orders or the use of illegal means to maintain segregation.

The data in Table 5, which record voting decisions of the 355 respondents in the survey mentioned previously, reflect the manifestation of the new cleavage in the first primary of the 1967 gubernatorial election. At the time of the interviews many of the respondents had not yet made a voting decision in regard to the five candidates. Nevertheless, the distinctions among the five candidates are illustrative. The three candidates identified with conservative viewpoints, especially on the racial issue, received the support of lower socioeconomic groups; and the two candidates identified as racial moderates had the support of the upper-status and the least authoritarian groups. As suggested above, this cleavage is very similar to the old division in that economics is important. Today, however, the split is more of working class versus middle class than of poor farmer versus plantation owner. The politics of the neopopulists is largely forgotten. The class division in the new cleavage is largely a product of racial as well as other social attitudes likely to affect voting choices in one-party systems. That is, in Mississippi politics the personalities of the candidates are important factors in voting decisions, and probably certain types of personalities have greater appeal to one socioeconomic group than to another.[52]

While one can definitely speak of cleavage in the Mississippi

52 Abney, "The Mississippi Voter," 169–243.

Table 5

RELATIONSHIP BETWEEN SOCIAL VARIABLES AND VOTING IN
FIRST PRIMARY OF MISSISSIPPI GUBERNATORIAL ELECTION IN 1967

Social Variables	Barnett	Swan	Waller	Williams	Winter
Income					
Under $3,000	1	4	3	7	3
$3,000–$6,999	0	6	4	20	11
$7,000–$9,999	2	0	2	11	10
Above $10,000	3	1	6	12	21
Education					
Less than 12 years	3	0	4	16	8
12 years	1	8	2	16	8
More than 12 years	3	2	12	25	34
Class					
Identification chosen by respondent					
Working	5	9	8	26	16
Middle and Upper	2	1	10	29	34
Age					
20–39	2	4	4	19	14
40–59	0	5	10	25	24
60 and above	5	2	4	19	13
Occupational status					
Blue-collar	2	10	10	31	12
White-collar	4	0	8	23	35
Sex					
Male	4	9	9	26	21
Female	3	2	9	30	28
Religious affiliation					
Baptist	4	5	7	38	19
Methodist	3	2	5	14	11
Presbyterian	0	0	3	1	10
Catholic	0	1	0	6	3
Authoritarianism					
Authoritarians	4	8	9	45	29
Egalitarians	3	3	8	15	20

electorate, it must be remembered that the divisions do not possess
the permanency of electoral splits produced by bifactionalism or
by parties. Without the aid of party labels to guide their comprehension of political stimuli and with a long ballot facing them in

Democratic primaries, Mississippi voters have a difficult time in learning who the candidates are and what they stand for. Because of the difficulty, voters in Mississippi are much slower in making their voting decisions than are voters in two-party systems. For example, one-third of the electorate did not make their choices until the last two weeks of the campaign, and only 24 percent decided more than two months prior to the election. This contrasts with two-thirds of the national electorate who have made voting decisions in presidential elections by the end of the national conventions. Without a partisan label to guide them, Mississippians apparently tend to rely more on personality and group factors than do voters in two-party systems. In listing reasons for candidate selection in 1967 in the first primary of the gubernatorial election, 21 percent of a statewide sample of 162 whites cited the personalities of the candidates while 31 percent mentioned the qualifications and abilities of the candidates. Seven percent recalled group or friends-and-neighbors factors as reasons for their decisions. In voting for lesser offices, Mississippi voters rely to a much greater extent on information gained from their spouses, friends, relatives, and fellow workers about candidates' personalities. In general, voters tend to make their decisions more frequently on a friends-and-neighbors basis in these elections. Because issues become less important in selecting candidates, the cleavages evident in gubernatorial contests disappear in voting patterns for these offices.[53]

Voting patterns in presidential elections have followed the same trends as those in gubernatorial elections in that they reflect an increasing concern with race and a growing dissatisfaction with the national Democratic Party. In presidential elections, the discontent was first manifest in 1948, when the voters cast 87 percent of the popular vote for the Dixiecrats. In 1952 and 1956, the Democrats carried the state but their percentages of the votes cast were lower than in any elections in this century, except for 1948. In 1960 the voters gave a plurality of their votes to an unpledged slate which supported Senator Harry F. Byrd of Virginia. In 1964 Barry Gold-

53 *Ibid.*

water won 87 percent of the state's vote. Significantly, George Wallace did much more poorly in 1968 than Goldwater in 1964 by polling only 63 percent of the votes. Hubert Humphrey ran second with 23 percent and Richard Nixon received only 14 percent. The relatively poorer showing by Wallace reflects the larger percentage of Negro voters in the state in 1968.

The votes received by the Dixiecrats in 1948, by the unpledged tickets in 1956 and 1960, by Goldwater in 1964, and by Wallace in 1968 tended to come from the same sort of counties. These areas largely have had high Negro populations, are basically rural, and correlate (on the average .25) with lower levels of Negro voter registration before 1965. Generally, these counties are probably those in which racial prejudice is highest.

The Ascendancy of Interests

Interest groups are likely to be more numerous and more powerful when large economic stakes are involved than when they are not. It would seem to follow that the government of a state generally ranked at the bottom economically would be less subject to group pressures and that such activities would yield the groups less in the form of rewards. Even so, in Mississippi interest groups exist in great number and variety and their influence on public policy is not a matter of dispute.[54] The nature of the state's politics enhances their power. The one-party system where personal politics is the rule leaves the public official no buffer in the form of a party platform or leader, and he is more directly exposed to the appeals and sanctions of interest groups.

The focal point of group activity is the biennial legislative session,[55] to which an estimated one hundred groups send representatives to seek legislative aid in furthering their aims. The governor and lesser executive officers are not neglected, of course, and on

[54] The number of interest groups in the state varies, depending on definition as well as other things. The Mississippi Economic Council publication *Associations in Mississippi* (Jackson, 1962) lists 165 groups.

[55] Under a constitutional amendment adopted in June, 1968, annual sessions are now held.

occasion may be more cooperative than the legislature.[56] With respect to lobbying, the organizations' methods are direct. Groups seek to obtain commitments to their objectives from candidates whom they try to help elect.[57] After election, appeal is renewed, again in direct fashion. Far from objecting to this practice, public officials frequently seem to encourage it.[58] The social lobby is another tactic frequently used; groups go to great pains to entertain legislators in Jackson. By accepting this entertainment lawmakers do not commit themselves verbally but may become indirectly obligated.

The familiar categories of interest groups—business, agriculture, labor, professional, public officials and employees—are supplemented by ideological groups which have the primary aim of maintaining segregation and which, in recent years, have exercised very great influence. Among these are the Citizens' Council, the John Birch Society, various organizations of the Ku Klux Klan, the Association for the Preservation of the White Race, and Women for Constitutional Government. Except for the Citizens' Council, which publishes a periodical, the *Citizen*, and gives out some information on its program, the size and membership of these groups are secret. Their power and influence on the state and local governments appear to have diminished since 1965. Groups of the opposite ideological bent, those concerned with integration and civil rights, usually have been branches of national organizations—NAACP, CORE, and others. Their influence, although important in Washington, has been slight with the governments of Mississippi.

A significant aspect of group power is the particular influence of organizations of public officials and employees. Organizations of public school teachers, associations of local officials (county super-

---

[56] One group, the Citizens' Council, was particularly influential with Governor Barnett and his administration. It received $193,500 in public funds through the State Sovereignty Commission from 1960 to 1964. The payments were stopped by Governor Paul Johnson.

[57] See Alex B. Lacy, Jr. (ed.), *Power in American State Legislatures*, Tulane Studies in Political Science, XI (New Orleans: 1967), 98.

[58] Note Governor Barnett's oft-repeated invitation, "Come down and kick on the door an' ask for Ol' Ross."

visors, sheriffs, mayors, etc.) have tremendous power.[59] This strength reflects in part the political potency of courthouse official-dom; it also reflects the application of hard-nosed lobbying tactics. Local officials are willing and able to impose political sanctions on state officers and legislators.[60]

In a class by itself because of its prestige, as well as its forward-looking program, is the state chamber of commerce, the Mississippi Economic Council.[61] Organized in 1948 "to promote the social, civic, and economic welfare of Mississippi," it immediately became the unified voice of business interests. Soon it was to present a complete program for governmental action. Its efforts are en-hanced by a number of regular and special publications which provide information on various problems of a political and eco-nomic nature. Since the Mississippi Economic Council endorses a large number of measures, naturally it does not achieve complete success. However, its prominence and its activity produce impres-sive results. A recent illustration is the legislative enactment of the Uniform Commercial Code. The organization has failed, how-ever, after many years of effort to secure the consolidation of local road-building and maintenance districts within counties. There are several regional chambers of commerce patterned after the state organization, but they usually confine their activities to promoting the economy of the various regions. The most active of these is the Delta Council in the Mississippi Delta area.

A comprehensive study of interest groups before the legislature gives a high effectiveness rating to the Mississippi Farm Bureau, the Mississippi Manufacturers Association, and the Mississippi

---

59 Two illustrations will suffice. A constitutional amendment separating the tax-collecting function and its lucrative fees from the office of county sheriff was ap-proved by the voters in 1962; pressure from local officials blocked the legislation necessary to implement it until 1968. A proposal of the Mississippi Education As-sociation for a flat $1,000 raise for public school teachers was adopted by a lopsided vote in the 1968 legislative session.

60 A favorite method of cultivating legislators by courthouse politicians has long been the provision of generous amounts of illegal whiskey confiscated by the sheriffs. Legalization of this commodity in 1966 probably has reduced its effectiveness.

61 The MEC is financed by annual dues from about 3,000 firms and individuals.

Medical Association.[62] The Farm Bureau, which dominates the agricultural groups, is of course effective in a state where the economy was long confined to agriculture. Labor interests, represented by the AFL-CIO Labor Council, have been ineffective in this conservative, rural-oriented society. Labor leaders, notably Claude Ramsay of the AFL-CIO organization, are among the few state leaders who have actively supported civil rights for Negroes. The enlargement of the Negro vote in the state may provide an ally for labor that will enhance its power.[63]

The rising concern about industrialization may alter the influence of various interests in the future. When every community, every region, and the state as a whole devote such energies to the task, it is clear that the promise of new industrial plants is magic in promoting government action at the state and local levels.[64] Growing industrialization in the state probably will lead to declining influence for farm groups. Furthermore, though at present it is not evident, industrialization will eventually increase the importance and influence of labor.

The Policy Constraints of Single-Issue Politics

The outputs of any political system depend on what sort of demands are made upon it. In a society where the whole structure of political, economic, and social life is devoted to a single effort, there is naturally a dearth of political demands or issues. In the past two decades Mississippi's obsession with the idea of resistance to integration has served as a substitute for genuine political issues in the period. There have been no issues in a real sense; there has been only a crusade. Except for tiny pockets of objection here and there,

[62] W. T. Wilkins, "The Role of Interest Groups in the Mississippi Legislature" (M.A. thesis, University of Mississippi, 1966).

[63] The friendly attitude toward the Negro does not extend to all the local unions. Much trouble involving the racial issue has occurred. Notable was the Masonite Corporation strike at Laurel in 1967.

[64] The principal argument for reducing the income tax in 1960 was that it would attract industry. Loss of revenue from this action contributed to government financial problems later. In 1961 two constitutional amendments were proposed and quickly ratified to meet the requests of a company planning to locate a refinery in the state.

general agreement on the rightness and necessity of the resistance has prevailed, and the few dissidents have received short shrift.[65] Hence, all political disagreements have grown out of the central issue—the candidates' varying degrees of devotion to the cause, the effect of this or that proposal on the main effort, and similar small differences. Attacks on "encroaching federal power," "Communistic decisions of the Supreme Court," "unconstitutional invasions of states' rights" have camouflaged the main theme, but everyone has understood the paramount issue. Even when other issues have been brought into the forum, the primary consideration has often been their aid or hindrance to the resistance to integration. In effect, the past two decades have been a sterile period.

At times the consensus on the need for industrial promotion has appeared to affect slightly the monolithic quality of opinion on racial matters. The revelation that industrialization had slowed noticeably, in the wake of the riots and lawlessness associated with early integration efforts, may have been more effective in changing official attitudes than is generally supposed.[66]

Whatever the impact of industrialization upon the consensus on racial policy, it has had a considerable effect on policy output. The state and local governments have made every effort to attract new industry. So welcome have these industries been that within each community the old politics of the 1900–43 era has almost disappeared. The industries have brought such prosperity to the small farmers in the hills—who were finding it more and more difficult to make ends meet in the new mechanized era of farming—that these former populists have given support to anti-union attitudes as well as to public officials who promise more industrialization. By threatening to leave a community, industries insure favorable policies, for often the future prosperity of an entire county as well as

65 See James W. Silver, *The Closed Society* (New York: Harcourt, Brace and World, 1966).

66 The "Statement of Principles" of the Mississippi Economic Council of February 3, 1965, urging compliance with the Civil Rights Act was endorsed by more than fifty business organizations and law enforcement agencies throughout the state. It followed the revelation that new industrial plant construction in 1964 declined 28 percent from the previous year.

the protection of an immense investment by the county or community rests upon the continued operation of a single industry. Companies that have moved into the state within the last thirty years have made few investments of their own, and frequently their machinery is of such a nature that it can be easily moved. As a result their threats, overt and covert, have real meaning. In summary, the need for a new source of revenue and the desires of white Mississippians for a better economic way of life have produced attitudes favorable for meeting industry's demands.

Which demands are converted into outputs depends upon which groups have influence. For example, because of its economic power, the industrial community has had much success in influencing public policy. Another successful group has been the rural community. Until a federal court reapportioned the state legislature in 1967, the rural areas were significantly overrepresented in the lawmaking body. Partly because of such overrepresentation more farmers occupied seats in the legislature during the 1944–68 period than did any other occupational group.[67] As a result the voice of urban areas was insignificant. However, with reapportionment and a growing urban population, this voice is becoming increasingly important in legislative circles.

The predominant power of the legislature in converting demands has enhanced the control of rural areas over public policy. For several reasons, Mississippi governors have few means for influencing policy. First, by constitutional provision, governors are not allowed to succeed themselves. Second, other public officials in the executive branch are somewhat independent of the governor in that they are elected independently. Such important executive proposals as the budget are not under his control. The governor's patronage powers are not extensive. Finally, the chief executive exercises little influence over individual legislators. Although he is theoretically the leader of the state's Democratic Party, his partisan influence on legislators is minute with only one effective

[67] During this period 40.7 percent of the legislators were farmers, 27.5 percent were lawyers, 15.4 percent were businessmen or held business-related positions, and 4.8 percent were teachers. See Lacy, *Power in American State Legislatures*, 92.

party in the state. Partisanship has played no role in the individual legislator's election nor does it have any value in a one-party legislature. What patronage the governor has is dealt out through those individuals called "colonels" who worked in and financed his campaign for election; as a result he has little to offer legislators. The governor's most decisive weapon over the legislature is his veto power. However, between 1944 and 1966 only sixty-six bills were vetoed—an average of ten per governor. Two executives rejected only three bills each, and one vetoed twenty-seven measures. Although the veto has received limited use, it has proved an effective weapon; during this twenty-two-year period, no veto was overridden by the necessary two-thirds' vote.[68] Nevertheless, there is still truth in the observation that the governor of Mississippi is more of a chief observer than a chief executive.

Despite their weakness in terms of influence, governors have tried to guide legislative output. Whatever success each has achieved in leading the legislature has resulted from the prestige attached to the highest office in the state, the extent of his popular support, his personal desire to lead, and the help of legislative leaders. Unless the legislative leaders cooperate, however, especially in the House of Representatives, a governor's chances of success are limited.

The center of decision-making in the Mississippi government is the legislature. Moreover, power in the legislature is centered in the hands of a few leaders. Such centralization is especially evident in the House of Representatives, where the rules give the Speaker powers resembling those which, in the early 1900's, produced powerful Speakers in the national House of Representatives. The Speaker's main source of influence lies in his power to appoint committee members. A high rate of turnover in the state legislature enhances the centralization of power. In the period 1944–68, an average of 35 percent of the members of each new House and 24 percent of the members of each new Senate were incumbents. Those experienced in the rules of operation inevitably lead the newcomers. Unity has not always prevailed among the old members, especially

68 *Ibid.*, 110.

in the House, where the office of Speaker carries so much power. But it is clear to the individual representative that it is important to be on the winning side in the selection of a Speaker.

Mississippi Politics: The More It Changes ...

A reference earlier in these pages to a "new" Mississippi politics could be attacked as an unwarranted prediction, either on the record of past performance or the facts of the present situation. Attitudes and habits are deeply ingrained and any new politics may well be exposed as a slightly revised model of the old.

There is reason, however, to predict a different—if not a new—politics because of the obvious difficulties of the present system. The pundits' reference to the "bankruptcy" of Mississippi politics is not without substance. The state has not supported a winning candidate for the presidency in the last six campaigns. In only two of those campaigns did Mississippi support the candidates of the party with which its political leaders are nominally affiliated. In three of them the state leaders supported independent or third-party candidates without chance of election—Thurmond in 1948, Byrd in 1960, and Wallace in 1968. One campaign found the leadership, in a mood of resentment and pique, marshaling an unprecedented landslide for the Republican nominee. The nadir of Democratic relations was reached in 1968, when the delegates of the regular Mississippi organization were excluded from the national convention. The futile presidential politics of the past quarter-century has thus reduced the national influence of the regular Mississippi Democrats to that wielded by members of the congressional delegation through their positions as chairmen of important standing committees.[69] Their positions are threatened at times when the seniority by which they hold chairmanships has been interpreted as requiring loyalty to presidential candidates of the national Democratic Party. The tightrope between Democratic

---

[69] Senator Eastland is chairman of the Judiciary Committee; Senator Stennis is chairman of the Armed Services Committee; Congressman Colmer is chairman of the Rules Committee.

loyalty in Congress and popular favor in Mississippi is difficult to walk and has produced at least one casualty—John Bell Williams, who was stripped of his seniority by the congressional Democratic caucus in 1965 for supporting Goldwater in the campaign of 1964. Obviously, he was a "casualty" only in Washington and something of a hero in Mississippi. This punishment by the caucus doubtless made it possible for him to be elected governor in 1967.

The 1971 elections furnish evidence of change in state politics. They indicate that the racial question may be diminishing in importance and that politics may return to a pattern of division based on economics. This would appear to be hastened by the inability of state and local governments to block effectively public school integration, and a grudging acceptance of this fact, as well as by the increasing importance of black voters and politicians. In the 1971 elections the gubernatorial candidates sounding the segregationist trumpets of the sixties suffered defeat in the Democratic first primary. In the runoff primary the candidates, Charles Sullivan and William Waller, attacked "busing" but had little more to say about the racial issue. Voting patterns in the second primary showed signs of a return to the economic and social cleavages prevalent before 1950. Some of this doubtless was due to the fact that Sullivan was a delta resident and Waller came from the hills. Nevertheless, Waller campaigned as a populist, proclaiming his identification with the working man, while Sullivan presented himself as a statesman and a conservative. Waller's victory, whatever his populist identification, is not likely to produce much change. Political power still remains in the legislature, especially in the conservative House of Representatives.

In the November election Charles Evers, independent candidate for governor, headed a ticket of 309 black candidates challenging white Democratic nominees for state and local offices. In terms of positions won, the blacks did not succeed, since only 50 of these candidates were elected, bringing the total of elected black officials in Mississippi to 117. Evers received 22 percent of the votes cast, though about 27 percent of the registered voters were black. The most significant aspect of the black participation in the elections of 1971 was the attention they gained from white candidates who, at all levels of government, covertly and sometimes overtly sought the black vote.

Three possible courses appear open to the members and leaders of the Mississippi Democratic Party in their present dilemma. They may transfer to the Republican Party in the manner of Senator Strom Thurmond and Congressman Albert Watson of South Carolina, and after the more recent example of several state Democratic leaders in Georgia.[70] The attractions of this course appear to be enhanced by the presidency of Richard Nixon and the possibilities of national patronage. A second course would be a reconciliation with the national organization and leadership of the Democratic Party. This alternative would involve accepting several Negro leaders into their midst and cooperating in a genuine effort to eliminate all opposition to Negro candidates and voters. Obviously, this course might be more acceptable to the leaders than to the body of white voters. Or, as a third possibility, the leaders may continue as an independent state Democratic Party of white people, tolerating Negro members only when it is unavoidable, and participating in national elections through the support of third-party candidates.

The first course might appear a logical choice in view of the high degree of alienation of the voters from the Democratic Party. But, as indicated in Table 3, there is also a high degree of alienation from the Republican Party. The second course might seem more logical, in consideration of the large Negro population and its increasing involvement in the political process. If this appears a likely choice, however, it should be remembered that racial attitudes among large portions of the white population still approach irrationality. The third course appears least logical and least apt to produce a viable brand of politics. Nevertheless, it is the most likely

---

70 Several minor political figures in Mississippi, including members of the legislature, also have recently made this switch.

course of action for the present leaders at the present time. Eventually, one of the other choices probably will be forced upon them, inaugurating a changed variety of politics. Different from the present system it may be, but it will also be different from the politics of any other state.[71]

71 A considerable step in the direction of no-party politics was taken by the legislature in 1970 with the abolition of party primary elections and the substitution of a nonpartisan preliminary to the general elections. H.B. 363, *Mississippi Legislature*, Reg. Sess., 1970. A federal court, however, held that the law could not be implemented because it did not have the approval of the United States attorney general, as required by the national Voting Rights Act. Consequently, the 1971 primaries and election were held as usual. See New York *Times*, April 29, 1971.

11

LOUISIANA
Resistance and Change

PERRY H. HOWARD

Although Louisiana shares with the other states of the South a history of participation in the rise of Jacksonian democracy, secession, the Civil War, Reconstruction, and post-Reconstruction one-partyism, the state differs substantially in its economic and social makeup from other southern states, including those of the Deep South. These unique features have made a major impact on the development of Louisiana's politics. From the beginning, Louisiana experienced more than the usual ethnic and religious divisions; unlike the other colonial units, the territory was originally French and predominantly Catholic, and the early period of statehood was characterized by electoral splits between French-Catholic sections and Anglo-Saxon Protestant areas. To some extent it is possible to discern the effects of this conflict throughout the state's political history. Economically, the distinguishing characteristics have resulted from abundant water resources, the subtropical climate, large areas of alluvial soil, and an enormous wealth of natural resources, such as oil, timber, natural gas, sulphur, and salt. In the antebellum period, Louisiana probably had the highest proportion of large plantations of all the states in the South because of the suitability of the land and climate for this type of economy. It also had, outside the plantation belts, a fairly substantial population of late-arrival Anglo-Saxons, who lived at a subsistence level in the hill areas of the upper central part of the state and in the

Perry H. Howard is Chairman, Department of Sociology, Louisiana State University.

middle southwestern section. Later, natural resources were to exert a strong influence on the development of trade and industry, so that Louisiana began to display its urban-industrial potential earlier than most of the southern states, especially its sister states along the Gulf coast.

Electoral Evolution

The conditions just described have produced a contemporary electorate still largely divided into rural and urban types. The rural population may in turn be said to include planters, farmers, tenants, and sharecroppers, as well as the rural parish-seat elite, who usually align with the planters. The urban population is generally divided according to manual and nonmanual occupations. In time the Negro urban category may divide, as the white has, into upper-income and labor, but up to now the black vote has remained homogeneous as this group has moved to extend its rights through the ballot.[1]

The voting behavior of the twentieth-century electorate, however, has responded to the processes of "modernization," so that some of the categories indicated above have greatly increased their electoral influence, while others have been diminished. If the percentage of males in nonagricultural employment is taken as an indicator,[2] Louisiana's industrial development reached a take-off stage in the first two decades of this century, when nonagricultural employment rose from 36 percent to 57 percent. By contrast, the rest of the nation outside the South had begun to industrialize fully thirty years earlier, increasing nonagricultural employment from 43 percent in 1870 to 55 percent by 1890. No doubt the rapid spread of lumbering in the state after 1900, as well as the discovery of oil and gas deposits, contributed to the relatively large jump in the proportion of males employed outside agriculture. Huey P. Long, elected governor in 1928, found a frustrated electorate still

[1] For statistical evidence see Perry H. Howard and Joseph L. Brent III, "Social Change, Urbanization, and Types of Society," *Journal of Social Issues*, XXII (1966), 73–84.

[2] Daniel Lerner, *The Passing of Traditional Society* (Glencoe, Ill., 1958), 46.

linked to an agrarian tradition, but by 1930 the figures were 75 percent for the nation and 60 percent for the state. The impact of World War II not only narrowed the gap but allowed the state to surge ahead, with 90 percent of its adult males in nonagricultural work, as compared to the national average of 85 percent. Using the white-collar category as indicator, the degree of complexity and of bureaucracy remained greater in the nation.[3] With 56 percent in 1960, Louisiana's manual employment rate was 7 percent higher than the national average, whereas the nation, with 45 percent white-collar employment, led the state by 7 percentage points.

The relative increase of white labor within the electorate was associated with the growth of what have been called the urban-industrial parishes. Three of these are in North Louisiana (Caddo, Ouachita, and Rapides). One of them, East Baton Rouge, is among the "Florida parishes" (the area between the Pearl and Mississippi rivers in the southeastern part of the state, so called because these parishes were originally part of West Florida). Two urban-industrial parishes are located in southwestern Louisiana (Lafayette and Calcasieu) and two more in South Louisiana (Jefferson and Orleans). Altogether these eight parishes contain approximately one-half the state population. Still, a great deal of Louisiana's economic development has been associated with primary industry and hence the labor force is spread rather widely throughout the parishes.[4] Moreover, although white labor became the most important electoral unit in terms of numbers, the relative lack of unionization makes labor's vote undisciplined.

A step in identifying the components of the Louisiana electorate may be taken by summarizing the most recent registration data and presidential election results (Table 1). Almost three-quarters of the state's potential voters had registered in 1968 (81 percent of the eligible white population and 52 percent of the Negro voting-age population) and some 55 percent of Louisianians twenty-one years of age and over had voted in the presidential election (the highest turnout in a presidential election since 1876).

[3] Reinhard Bendix, *Work and Authority in Industry* (New York, 1956), 244–48.
[4] Rudolf Heberle, *The Labor Force in Louisiana* (Baton Rouge, 1948).

Table I

The Louisiana Electorate in 1968

	Percentage of Registered Voters—October 5, 1968			Republican			Presidential Vote Cast—November 5, 1968		
	Total Voters	Total White	Total Negro	Total Voters	Total White	Total Negro	Humphrey	Nixon	Wallace
Eight Urban-Industrial Parishes (8)	49%	49%	48%	79%	80%	62%	53%	62%	42%
Florida Parishes (7)	7%	8%	6%	5%	4%	8%	6%	5%	9%
Southwest Louisiana (8)	10%	10%	10%	2%	2%	1%	8%	6%	10%
South Louisiana (16)	18%	18%	19%	5%	4%	13%	17%	14%	18%
North Louisiana (25)	16%	15%	17%	9%	10%	16%	16%	13%	21%
	100%	100%	100%	100%	100%	100%	100%	100%	100%
Total State Number	1,449,231	1,164,417	284,814	28,207	25,799	2,408	309,784	258,355	530,452
							(TOTAL = 1,098,591)		
Percentage of Total	100%	80.3%	19.7%	100%	91.5%	8.5%	29%	23%	48%

Source: PAR Analysis No. 154, December, 1968; Board of Registration, report ending October 5, 1968.

This large participation furnishes a good basis for analyzing the geographical distribution of the various categories of voters in the state and the tendencies that these voters display in their response to certain parties or factions, candidates, and issues. Almost one-third of the Louisiana population is Negro and it is important to note the upsurge in Negro political participation in recent years (in 1968 about one-fifth of the voter registration was Negro). Much talk that Louisiana is becoming a two-party state has been heard during the past two decades, as the electorate has deviated from the traditional Democratic affiliation, but the latest figures show only 2 percent of Louisiana voters to be registered Republicans. It is useful to note that the bulk of this Republican adherence is found in the eight urban-industrial parishes, but that North Louisiana has registered nearly twice as many Republicans as have those areas of South Louisiana which had traditionally delivered a substantially Republican vote. As Negroes have increased their registration, they have registered as Democrats rather than as members of the party of emancipation.

The urban-industrial parishes contribute nearly half the registration of the Louisiana electorate, both white and Negro.[5] After 1946 Negro registration increased in New Orleans, and by 1960 it began to rise in the other urban parishes and throughout rural South Louisiana parishes, because, as John H. Fenton and Kenneth N. Vines concluded, the French-Catholic population has a more tolerant attitude toward black political participation.[6] As a consequence of the national civil rights laws of the 1960's, however, Negro registration has spread quite evenly in all areas of the state, so that the proportions of the state totals of both white and Negro registration are fairly well balanced in most areas. Predictably, perhaps, the greatest imbalance is to be found in the Klan-ridden Florida parishes, where support for the candidacy of George Wallace was highest. As will be demonstrated below, the renewed political

[5] William C. Havard, Rudolf Heberle, and Perry H. Howard, *The Louisiana Elections of 1960* (Baton Rouge, 1963); see Appendix G for secular trends.

[6] John H. Fenton and Kenneth N. Vines, "Negro Registration in Louisiana," *American Political Science Review*, LI (1957), 704–13.

presence of Negroes in the North Louisiana parishes, enforced by federal registrars, helped to make the parish distribution of voting percentages again approximate the pattern of a Y, formed by the Mississippi and the Red rivers, where once the muted presence of slaves marked the plantation areas of the state.

If we inspect these percentages for the 1968 presidential election (Table 1 and Figure 1), we get a gross picture of within-state differences on which to base estimates of continuity and change in previous political patterns. The proportions of registered voters who actually voted in 1968 vary from a low of 67 percent in southwestern Louisiana (which has been found consistently to lag behind other sections of the state in voting participation) to a high of 84 percent in the North Louisiana parishes.

Louisiana Wallaceites had been quite close to being correct in estimating their candidate's chance in 1968 (at least 50 percent of the vote). The almost astonishing similarity of the support for Strom Thurmond twenty years earlier (49 percent) to the 48 percent for Wallace demands further comment. The Republican leaders were also most likely correct in their contention that a vote for Wallace would help the chances of Hubert H. Humphrey (29 percent) to the detriment of Richard M. Nixon (23 percent). The major difference between the results of 1948 and 1968 lay in the fact that Wallace ran ahead in all areas of the state, gaining at least a plurality of votes in the urban-industrial parishes (41 percent) and majorities in all the other units, ranging from the close 51 percent in the South Louisiana parishes, which had been voting Democratic in presidential elections at least since 1960, to the previously mentioned high of 64 percent in the Florida parishes.

Observation of the three candidates' heaviest vote distribution confirms the urban character of the Republican movement in Louisiana as in other parts of the South. Fully three-fifths of the Nixon vote came from the urban-industrial voter unit, while the remainder was divided equally among two sets of units, the Florida and southwestern parishes and those in South and North Louisiana. A growing amount of Republican support has been found in North Louisiana ever since the presidential election of 1944, in contrast to

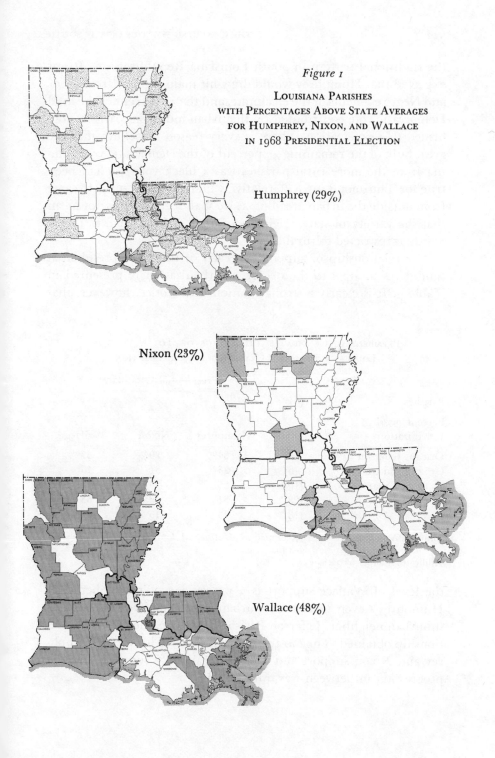

Figure 1

LOUISIANA PARISHES
WITH PERCENTAGES ABOVE STATE AVERAGES
FOR HUMPHREY, NIXON, AND WALLACE
IN 1968 PRESIDENTIAL ELECTION

Humphrey (29%)

Nixon (23%)

Wallace (48%)

the traditional pattern of South Louisiana Republicanism. It was expected that Humphrey would draw his main support from labor and Negro elements of the electorate, and the 53 percent of the total Democratic vote contributed by the urban-industrial parishes confirmed this expectation. There is every reason to believe that the great bulk of the remaining 47 percent of the Democratic vote coming from the more rural parishes was a black vote. As had been true for Thurmond in 1948, relatively more Wallace support came from outside the urban area but, as we shall see, this does not mean that the variety of states' rights sentiment in Louisiana, as in the South, is restricted to rural life.

The relationship of support for each of the three presidential candidates in 1968 to the degree of urbanization is presented in Table 2. It is clearly a strong relationship. Notice, however, that

Table 2

PRESIDENTIAL CANDIDATES' PERCENTAGE OF TOTAL VOTE IN
LOUISIANA PARISHES, CLASSIFIED BY URBANIZATION

Parishes (64)*		Presidential Candidates		
Percentage of Urbanization		Humphrey	Nixon	Wallace
Orleans-Jefferson 97%	(2)*	34%	29%	37%
Urban-Industrial 71%	(6)*	25	31	46
50–67% Urban	(10)*	26	20	54
24–49% Urban	(28)*	31	16	53
Less than 20% Urban	(18)*	23	15	62

Source: PAR Analysis No. 154; *Statistical Abstract of Louisiana, 1967*, Louisiana State University in New Orleans.
* Indicates number of parishes.

the level of Wallace support is 3 percentage points higher than Humphrey's even in the most urban area, New Orleans, and its suburban neighbor, Jefferson Parish. Otherwise, the expected relationship obtained. The most rural parishes were lowest in Humphrey and Nixon support and highest in Wallace support, and the progression in between was quite regular.

The relationship of geographical differences to the degree of urbanization in groups of parishes may be observed in Table 3. When the degree of urbanization in North and South Louisiana divisions is measured, it is found that on the high urban level there

Table 3

PRESIDENTIAL CANDIDATES' PERCENTAGE OF TOTAL VOTE IN
LOUISIANA PARISHES, CLASSIFIED BY URBANIZATION—
NORTH AND SOUTH LOUISIANA REGIONS

Percentage Urban (64)*	North Louisiana	South Louisiana	State
High—50% and above (18)*			
Humphrey	26.3%	28.0%	27.4%
Nixon	24.5%	25.0%	24.8%
Wallace	49.2%	47.0%	47.8%
	100%	100%	100%
Medium—20–49% (27)*			
Humphrey	30.6%	26.8%	32.0%
Nixon	16.1%	15.5%	15.8%
Wallace	53.2%	57.7%	52.2%
	99.9%	100%	100%
Low—Less than 20% (19)*			
Humphrey	15.8%	37.0%	23.1%
Nixon	14.4%	17.1%	15.4%
Wallace	69.8%	45.9%	61.5%
	100%	100%	100%

Source: PAR Analysis No. 154; *Statistical Abstract of Louisiana, 1967.*
* Indicates number of parishes.

is scarcely any difference in the candidates' support across the north-south division. At the other extreme, however, the percentage of support for Wallace in rural North Louisiana was at as high a level (69.8 percent) as any aggregation of parishes studied, while rural South Louisiana Wallace support was below the level found in highly urban parishes in the same area. The Humphrey support becomes curvilinear; that is, it tended to be highest among moderately urban parishes in North Louisiana and lowest among the same category of parishes in South Louisiana.

A ready explanation can be found for these variations. It may be hypothesized that to measure racial distribution using percentage of Negro registration as a scale of resistance to integration and/or change, is to show more regularity in patterns of candidate support. This is another way of saying that Humphrey support is more closely related to the degree of Negro registration than to the degree of urbanization. Indeed, the north-south distinction "washes out" when the moderately urban Humphrey support is analyzed by race (Table 4). It also can be shown that in both the north-south divi-

Table 4

1968 HUMPHREY VOTE IN NORTH AND SOUTH LOUISIANA
PARISHES, CLASSIFIED ACCORDING TO MODERATELY URBAN
AND PERCENTAGE OF NEGRO VOTER REGISTRATION

		Moderately Urban (20–49%)	
Percentage of Negro Registration (27)*		North Louisiana	South Louisiana
29.0%–45.5%	(9)*	34.5%	38.6%
20.0%–28.9%	(7)*	26.5%	28.6%
12.6%–19.9%	(5)*	14.6%	22.5%
0.1%–12.5%	(6)*	17.0%**	22.5%

Source: PAR Analysis No. 154; *Statistical Abstract of Louisiana, 1967*; Louisiana
    Board of Registration, October, 1968.
  * Indicates number of parishes.
  ** East Carroll Parish dropped, as federal Negro registration not recorded in official
    state count.

sions, the Humphrey support varies from high to low in relationship to the degree of Negro registration in each, while the reverse is true for Wallace support (Table 5). For the latter, regardless of race, the levels are higher in North than South Louisiana. The hypothesis, however, seems not to hold for Nixon support, which tended to vary irregularly. The only significant Republican regularity readily observable was that while the level of Nixon support varied positively with level of urbanization, when analyzed by race Nixon support was somewhat greater as the level of Negro registration declined. Finally an examination was made of the hypothesis that the per-

Table 5

1968 PRESIDENTIAL CANDIDATES' PERCENTAGE OF TOTAL
VOTE IN LOUISIANA PARISHES, CLASSIFIED BY PERCENTAGE OF
NEGRO VOTER REGISTRATION, IN NORTH AND SOUTH LOUISIANA

Percentage of Negro Registration (64)*	North Louisiana	South Louisiana	State
29.0%–45.5% (17)*			
Humphrey	34.0%	37.6%	35.1%
Nixon	14.2%	13.7%	13.9%
Wallace	51.8%	48.7%	51.0%
	100%	100%	100%
20.0%–28.9% (13)*			
Humphrey	24.8%	30.5%	28.3%
Nixon	16.6%	19.3%	18.3%
Wallace	58.6%	50.2%	53.4%
	100%	100%	100%
12.6%–19.9% (17)*			
Humphrey	18.5%	27.0%	24.0
Nixon	21.9%	21.2%	21.0
Wallace	59.6%	51.8%	55.0
	100%	100%	100.0%
0.1%–12.5% (17)*			
Humphrey	18.0%	21.0%	19.0%
Nixon	19.4%	19.0%	19.0%
Wallace	62.4%	60.0%	62.0%
	99.8%	100%	100%

Source: PAR Analysis No. 154; Louisiana Board of Registration, October, 1968.
* Indicates number of parishes.

centage of support for the candidates would vary in the same direction in relationship to the degree of Negro registration regardless of the degree of urbanization. Table 6, which presents these data, reveals the greater effect of race on both Humphrey and Wallace support.

Three conclusions may be drawn from these findings: (1) in the presidential election of 1968 a regional cleavage appeared between North and South Louisiana; (2) the greater the Negro registration, the greater the level of Humphrey support (the converse was true

Table 6
1968 PRESIDENTIAL CANDIDATES' VOTES IN LOUISIANA
PARISHES, CLASSIFIED BY PERCENTAGES OF URBANISM
AND NEGRO VOTER REGISTRATION

Percentage of Negro Registration (64)*	High Urban	Medium Urban	Low Urban
29.0%–45.5%　(17)*			
Humphrey	47.0%	36.4%	32.7%
Nixon	12.0%	14.2%	14.0%
Wallace	41.0%	49.4%	53.3%
	100%	100%	100%
20.0%–28.9%　(13)*			
Humphrey	32.5%	28.0%	21.0%
Nixon	26.0%	15.0%	15.0%
Wallace	41.5%	57.0%	64.0%
	100%	100%	100%
12.6%–19.9%　(17)*			
Humphrey	27.5%	20.0%	18.0%
Nixon	24.5%	19.2%	19.0%
Wallace	48.0%	60.8%	63.0%
	100%	100%	100.0%
0.1%–12.5%　(17)*			
Humphrey	17.2%	23.3%	16.1%
Nixon	27.0%	16.6%	15.3%
Wallace	55.8%	60.1%	68.6%
	100%	100%	100%

Source: PAR Analysis No. 154; *Statistical Abstract of Louisiana, 1967*; Board of
　　　Registration, October, 1968.
* Indicates number of parishes.

for Wallace and to some extent for Nixon); and (3) an urban tilt
seemed to separate Humphrey and Nixon supporters from Wallaceites. It remains to be determined, however, which elements of
the electorate were responsible for the relatively high Wallace support, even in the most urban areas.

There is every reason to believe that the Wallace vote was a farmer's vote: in the most rural parishes levels of support for the American Party candidate reached as high as 80 percent. Yet at least

two-fifths of the voters in the urban-industrial parishes favored Wallace. Which elements of the electorate were involved in this conservative tendency? Based upon previous analysis of the urban vote in Louisiana,[7] we could offer the hypothesis that on the precinct level Wallace would carry white labor areas with a majority, Nixon would carry upper-income white areas by a plurality with Wallace a close second, and Humphrey would get heavy support in Negro precincts. Table 7 presents Baton Rouge data for the past six presi-

Table 7
1948–1968 DEMOCRATIC PRESIDENTIAL PERCENTAGES OF TOTAL VOTE
IN BATON ROUGE PRECINCTS, BY SOCIOECONOMIC CATEGORIES

Year	Negro	Upper White	White Labor
1948	—	28%	50%
1952	93	26	61
1956	29	25	40
1960	56	36	47
1964	99	32	41
1968	96	18	12

Source: Howard, *Political Tendencies in Louisiana* (rev. ed.; Baton Rouge, 1971); Baton Rouge *Morning Advocate*, November 6, 1968.

dential elections, which show dramatically the reason for a dim view of Democratic chances for white labor support. It was estimated that Baton Rouge white labor gave as much as half its total support to Strom Thurmond's States' Rights Party in 1948.[8] With widespread support for Adlai Stevenson by state Democratic leaders led by the Long faction in 1952, labor appeared to follow its "rational" interest in voting Democratic.[9] Yet as the political virus of revolt spread through the South after the Supreme Court school desegregation decision in 1954, white labor, despite the announced Demo-

[7] Havard, Heberle, and Howard, *Louisiana Elections.*

[8] Perry H. Howard, "An Analysis of Voting Behavior in Baton Rouge," *Proceedings of Louisiana Academy of Sciences*, XV (1952), 84–100.

[9] Rudolf Heberle and Perry H. Howard, "An Ecological Analysis of Political Tendencies in Louisiana: The Presidential Election of 1952," *Social Forces*, XXXII (1954), 344–50.

cratic preference of the leaders of organized labor in Louisiana, showed an increasingly anti-Democratic leaning.

Upper-income white precincts, on the other hand, contained an electorate with a distinct willingness to embrace the Republican Party in presidential elections, although more than a quarter of such voters remained loyal Democrats. In state and local elections upper-income white areas manifested a pluralistic tendency to accept differences and joined Negro areas in support of moderate candidates, in what has been labeled the "Atlanta solution." [10] As blacks regained the suffrage, they have voted as a bloc in support of Democratic presidential candidates and for racial moderates on state and local levels. Louisiana Negro leaders had urged in 1956 that black voters should "give the Republicans a chance" on civil rights, and three-quarters of Baton Rouge Negro voters seemed willing. (However in 1960 the Catholicism of the Democratic candidate apparently inhibited many of the predominantly Protestant Negroes.)[11]

There was no surprise, therefore, at the high level of Democratic support in Negro precincts in November, 1968. What was startling was the extent of the confirmation of the hypothesis regarding white labor Wallace support (Table 8). Democratic defection had reached the point where support of the Republican candidate exceeded that given his Democratic opponent, while Wallace received 70 percent of the vote of this element. Less surprising was the convincing 54 percent majority Nixon received in upper-income white precincts,

Table 8
1968 PRESIDENTIAL CANDIDATES' PERCENTAGE OF TOTAL VOTE
IN BATON ROUGE PRECINCTS, BY SOCIOECONOMIC CATEGORIES

Candidate	Negro	Upper White	White Labor
Humphrey	96%	18%	12%
Nixon	1	54	18
Wallace	3	28	70

Source: Baton Rouge *Morning Advocate*, November 6, 1968.

[10] Howard and Brent, "Social Change"; Alvin Boskoff and Harmon Zeigler, *Voting Patterns in a Local Election* (Philadelphia, 1964).
[11] Howard and Brent, "Social Change."

where clear evidence of "real" Republican tendencies had been detected in recent years.

Aggregating the votes of the two categories of white precincts, it is possible to estimate roughly that a majority of these urban whites supported Wallace (54 percent), one-third favored Nixon (33 percent), and a scant 13 percent supported Humphrey. This is a long way from the situation twenty years previously, when the white vote in Baton Rouge is estimated to have split into three more equal proportions, with Thurmond receiving 38 percent, Thomas E. Dewey 23 percent, and Harry S. Truman 39 percent. If it is true that white labor and white farmers turned out in large numbers to vote for Wallace, then, depending upon the degree of their turnout, the Humphrey vote in Louisiana was a Negro vote, at anywhere downward from a level of 80 percent. It seems certain that the 1968 presidential election in Louisiana represented a culmination, or better still, a continuance of an almost quarter-century-old trend of Democratic defection similar to that in the South as a whole. The most astonishing discovery, however, is that 1968, in terms of aggregate data analysis, was nothing so much as a repeat of 1948.

Similarity in parish distributions of Thurmond and Wallace percentages are found when a simple (but as it turned out, significant) cross-tabulation is made, dividing the two arrays at a cutting point of below or above 50 percent. The resulting figures are shown in Table 9. Two-thirds of Louisiana's sixty-four parishes were in

Table 9
RELATIONSHIP BETWEEN WALLACE AND THURMOND
PERCENTAGES IN LOUISIANA PARISHES

		Number of Parishes	
		Wallace	
		Low (Below 50%)	High (Above 50%)
Thurmond	Low	12	9
	High	14	29

Source: Howard, *Political Tendencies*; PAR Analysis No. 154.

either the lows or the highs in percentage support for both states'
rights candidates in presidential elections twenty years apart. But
that is not all. Plotting the parishes located in these four low and
high categories on a parish map (Figure 2) reveals a distinctive
ecological distribution reminiscent of the traditional alluvial Y
pattern.

Figure 2

CROSS-TABULATION OF WALLACE (1968) AND
THURMOND (1948) VOTES IN LOUISIANA

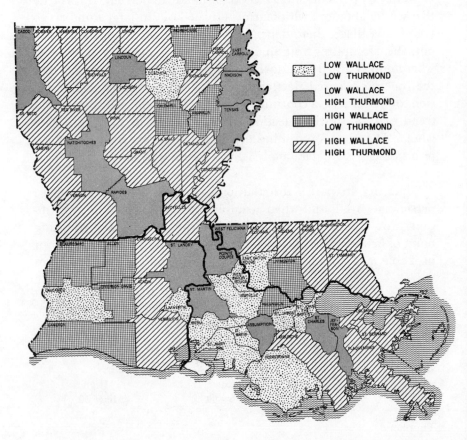

Nine Types of Voters

The parish clusters shown in Figure 3 separate the southern half of the state into five sets, while the parishes of North Louisiana can be divided into four subclusters to make sharper distinctions between delta and hills. When this is done, nine Louisiana "voter type" units may be identified. Percentage arrays of these distinctive

Figure 3
LOUISIANA VOTER TYPE AREAS

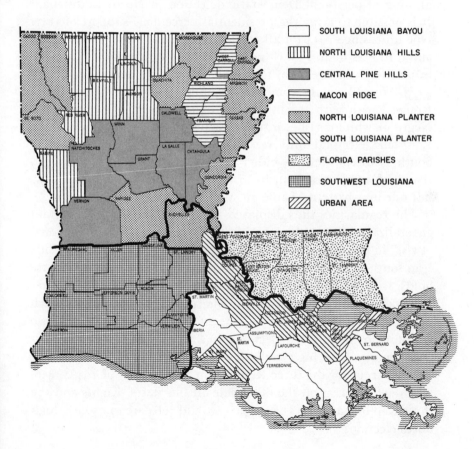

SOUTH LOUISIANA BAYOU

NORTH LOUISIANA HILLS

CENTRAL PINE HILLS

MACON RIDGE

NORTH LOUISIANA PLANTER

SOUTH LOUISIANA PLANTER

FLORIDA PARISHES

SOUTHWEST LOUISIANA

URBAN AREA

ecological clusterings for a number of presidential elections may be rank-ordered and it then appears that something more than party loyalty is being measured, most likely similarity in patterns of support of the various voter types in response to historical circumstances.[12]

Earlier analysis had discovered that in each of the elections in question the vote percentages were distributed on a distinctly north-south division. The 1944 election was found to have been a watershed of Louisiana presidential politics for it marks the beginning of persistent Democratic defection in North Louisiana.[13] It is possible to array the presidential percentage support of voter type units since 1944 for all parties, with ranks 1 to 4 taken as low and 6 to 9 as high. It was found that the Florida parishes ranked in position 5 in twelve of the eighteen cases (its average rank was 4.33). Most likely, the combination of urban-industrial East Baton Rouge Parish with the other planter or farmer, urban or rural, Negro or white parishes in the unit produces a fair sample of the Louisiana electoral universe. Placing voter types in North and South Louisiana sets on either side of the Florida parishes unit, the eighteen elections can be arranged so that the highs and lows fall out in a pattern. Table 10 summarizes these findings.

The regularities thus displayed suggest at least three important generalizations. In the first place, there is a distinct regional "twist" in the two sets of rows: eight elections on the lefthand side lean south high and north low, while on the right side the reverse holds, with south low and north high. Secondly, the 1952 figures (Democratic and Republican) and the 1948 Democratic figures each evenly divide between the regions and serve to separate the two sets of regionally distinct elections. In the third place, it can be seen that almost all the high south–low north elections are Democratic arrays, except for the three Republican election sets of 1948, 1956, and 1968, whereas on the other side all the States' Rights and the three Republican arrays of 1944, 1960, and 1964 are low south–high north elections.

---

12 Howard, *Political Tendencies in Louisiana* (rev. ed.; Baton Rouge, 1971).
13 Havard, Heberle, and Howard, *Louisiana Elections*; Howard, *Political Tendencies.*

Table 10

HIGH AND LOW RANK-ORDER IN PRESIDENTIAL SUPPORT,
BY LOUISIANA VOTER TYPE PARISH CLUSTERS

	Dem. 1944	Rep. 1948	Dem. 1960	Dem. 1964	Dem. 1968	Dem. 1956	Rep. 1956	Rep. 1968	Dem. 1948	Dem. 1952	Rep. 1952	S. R. 1960	S. R. 1948	S. R. 1968	Rep. 1960	Rep. 1944	Rep. 1964	S. R. 1956
North La. Hills	L	L	L	L	L	L	L	L	L	L	H	L	H	H	H	H	H	H
North La. Planter	L	L	L	L			L	H	L	L	H	H	H	L	H	H	H	H
Pine Hills	L	L	L	L	L	L	L	L	H	H	L		H	H	H	H	H	H
Macon Ridge	L	L	L	L	L	L	L	L	H	H	L	H	L	H	H	H	H	H
Florida Parishes			L			H	L			H			H		L			
Bayou	H	H	H	H	H		H	H	L	L	H	L	H	H	L	L	L	L
Urban Area	H	H	H	H	H	H	H	H	L	L	H	H	L	L		L	L	L
South La. Planter	H	H	H	H	H	H	H	L	H	H	L	L	L	L	L	L	L	L
Southwest La.	H	H	H	H	H	H		H	H	H	L	L	L	L	L	L	L	L
North La. Highs	0	0	0	0	0	0	0	1	2	2	2	2	3	3	4	4	4	4
South La. Highs	4	4	4	4	4	3	3	3	2	2	2	1	1	1	0	0	0	0

Source: Howard, *Political Tendencies*; PAR Analysis No. 154.

These findings can be summarized by a slightly different tabulation (Table 11), with the last seven presidential elections listed in sequence and the *high* support of North and South Louisiana voter type units indicated. Displayed this way, the figures show clearly that, although the Democratic Party was traditionally at home in North Louisiana, since 1944 Democratic fortunes have waxed greater in South Louisiana, while in North Louisiana support has been

Table 11

RANK-ORDERED DEMOCRATIC PRESIDENTIAL PERCENTAGES OF
VOTER TYPE AREAS IN NORTH AND SOUTH LOUISIANA

Party	1944	1948	1952	1956	1960	1964	1968
States' Rights	–	N	–	N	N	--	N
Republican	N	S	even	S	N	N	S
Democratic	S	even	even	S	S	S	S

Source: Howard, *Political Tendencies*; PAR Analysis No. 154.

divided between Republican and States' Rights candidates. A brief account of events may help to explain this set of circumstances.[14]

The New Deal and the Heritage of Longism

As Franklin D. Roosevelt's New Deal had stimulated turnout and Democratic support in the nation, so the reforms of the strong executive Huey P. Long and his free-wheeling destruction of bourbon rule led to a surge of voters for Longism at the ballot box. The assassination of the "Kingfish" and the excesses of his successors led to the "Louisiana scandals" and the so-called reform administration of Lake Charles lawyer Sam H. Jones (1940) and hillbilly singer Jimmie H. Davis (1944). Like the national Republican Party a decade later, the anti-Long forces chose not to turn back the clock but to preside over the more efficient administration of agencies and services established through the reform impulse of the opposition. The Longs' welfare system provided hundreds of appointive jobs and anti-Long politicians learned to live with this source of patronage.

In the four New Deal elections Louisiana led the nation and the South in level of support; only two parishes had Democratic percentages below 60 percent in the entire period. In 1928, when Democratic support in North Louisiana dropped from 82 to 72 percent, it had increased in South Louisiana, in support of the Roman Catholic candidate, Alfred E. Smith, by 4 percent. Afterward North Louisiana again led with high Democratic majorities, though in the 1940 election the regional differences flattened out and by 1944 North Louisiana had fallen below South Louisiana once more. The presidential election of 1944 thus anticipated the great hiatus in Democratic support which occurred in 1948 in the state.

Louisiana, like her sister southern states, could not remain unaffected by the continued ascendancy of the New Deal, which drew its chief support from a coalition depending more and more on the backing of organized labor and urban minorities. The war emer-

14 Details in Havard, Heberle, and Howard, *Louisiana Elections*, and Howard, *Political Tendencies*.

gency had allowed even more federal control to be exercised by Washington, and the ceiling prices upon tobacco and cotton became unpopular with southern farmers. The whole array of wartime discontent had included insistent Negro demands for elimination of discrimination and thus reinforced strains of southern conservatism. Governor Sam H. Jones had declared in 1943 that the Democratic support known as the Solid South was a political booby trap and that the region had gotten better treatment from the Republicans. A cry for rejection of the New Deal was echoed a year later by the Shreveport *Times,* which declared that for the first twelve years President Roosevelt never once referred to the Democratic Party, but either the "New Deal" or "we." The *Times* encouraged the election of Dewey to preserve the constitutional republic.[15]

The Louisiana reaction in 1944 produced the lowest Democratic support since 1928 and in North Louisiana, all but four of the twenty-eight parishes exceeded the statewide Republican average of 19.3 percent. The factor which hastened the defection of this most solid state appeared in the hassle which developed in the Democratic State Central Committee over the issue of having presidential electors pledge support for the Roosevelt-Truman ticket. It led to the replacement of three electors who refused to pledge and prompted the Shreveport *Times* to lead the protest in North Louisiana, which culminated in the relatively high Republican vote in the November election. This result should be taken as an indicator of protest rather than as a harbinger of any two-party tendency.

In the face of impending change, the state party organization increased in importance as an arena for political maneuvers. The sensitive relationships of party organization at the local, sta*‍*, and national levels may remain dormant only to become important, as in 1944, when the seeds of revolt are cast. With characteristic initiative, conservative Democrats saw in the central committee the means of blocking federal moves to modernity. The local party became an important aspect of the state's function in the presidential electoral process.

[15] George B. Tindall, *The Emergence of the New South, 1913–1945* (Baton Rouge, 1967), 724; Shreveport *Times,* November 8, 1944.

1948—Two Directions at Once

The election of 1948 took on a double importance in the history of recent Louisiana politics, for that year marked the end of presidential solidarity at the same time that it provided a continuation of the tendencies of Longism. (See Table 12.) In 1948 Earl Long achieved an astounding personal victory by gaining 66 percent of the total vote cast in turning back the second-term bid of Sam Jones. Long had lost to Jones in 1940 after the scandals (although he received 48 percent of the vote). Now Earl Long carried all but

Table 12

NUMBER OF LOUISIANA PARISHES SUPPORTING LONG CANDIDATES
IN THE LONG ERA, 1928–1956

		Below 50%	Above 50%
1928	North	12	16
Long	South	14	22
1932	North	6	22
Long	South	14	22
1936	North	0	28
Long	South	2	34
1940	North	14	14
	South	27	9
1944	North	17	11
	South	27	9
1948	North	0	28
Long	South	2	34
1952	North	21	7
	South	32	4
1956	North	6	22
Long	South	7	29
Eight-election ⎫	North	10	18
Average ⎰	South	16	20

six of the sixty-four parishes at a level of more than 60 percent, with majorities in all but two parishes.

The seeming paradox of the Louisiana voter going in opposite directions in state and presidential elections in 1948 deserves comment, although the general explanation can be quickly stated. The rise of Longism had broken the bourbon rule of state politics as Huey Long injected realism into the political context by stressing political, social, and economic changes. For the first time in Louisiana history the farmer class had managed to support a gubernatorial winner concerned with their interests.[16] The impetus which Huey Long started was enough to structure Louisiana's electoral response for at least three decades. But at the same time, change within national politics had led state party leaders to search for a vehicle of electoral resistance in presidential elections, and sizable numbers representing the conservative bourbon classes joined the new movement.

If the maintenance of states' rights (and white supremacy) could no longer be accomplished through support of the Democratic Party, then the conservatives would look elsewhere. The radical swing of all but five Louisiana parishes out of the majority Democratic percentage intervals in 1948 was indicative of that search. Yet, until a surprise move by the central committee on September 10 which joined Louisiana with Mississippi, Alabama, and South Carolina in making the Dixiecrat ticket the official one, it had been expected that the Democrats would carry the state. The welfare liberal Earl Long had just won back the governorship, increased spending, and raised taxes. But Governor Long remained neutral on the Dixiecrat movement, according to Allan P. Sindler, because he wished to avoid any controversy which might hurt the chances of his nephew and Huey's son Russell in winning the Senate seat being contested by Judge Robert Kennon.[17]

Sam Jones, Leander Perez, and other conservative leaders representing the new economic forces of oil and gas interests (rather than

[16] Allan P. Sindler, *Huey Long's Louisiana* (Baltimore, 1956).
[17] *Ibid.*, 220.

the old cotton-rice-sugar complex) managed to engineer a coup which would have denied President Truman a place on the Louisiana ballot. Only the action of Governor Long, who called a special session of the legislature, enabled the Truman-Barkley ticket to appear on the ballot at all. Even then, the Democratic symbol, the rooster, which according to political folklore is worth many thousands of votes, remained above the Dixiecrat nominees. Ironically, maybe in retaliation to the conservatives, Long used the occasion to persuade the legislature to abolish the state civil service created in the administration of Sam Jones.

Despite such dramatic maneuvers, interest and turnout for the presidential election lagged. Although registration in 1948 had reached an all-time high of nearly 925,000 and a turnout of 71 percent of these potential voters occurred in the gubernatorial contest that year, only 45 percent voted in the presidential election, the lowest since 1924. The rapid turn of events in Louisiana which suddenly gave voters opportunity to participate in the Dixiecrat revolt provided the electorate with four options: (1) stamp the Democrat rooster for States' Rights (49.1 percent); (2) vote for the Truman-Barkley ticket (32.7 percent); (3) vote Republican (17.5 percent); (4) stay home.[18] The Progressive Party candidacy of Henry A. Wallace, who received 0.7 percent, hardly counted.

The Dixiecrats found no widespread consensus for the wisdom of their revolt from the national Democrats. Thurmond asserted at a Shreveport rally in late October that his party would claim 142 electoral votes, but in the end it got only the 38 electoral votes from the heart of Dixie—Alabama, Louisiana, Mississippi, and South Carolina—all of which had entered the Dixiecrat candidates as the Democratic nominees. If the time-honored device of southern conservatives of spanning economic class cleavages by appeals to racist anxieties was effective in 1948 in Louisiana, this factor was difficult to discern in the distribution of the vote. North Louisiana parishes, for example, highest in state Republican support in 1944, might be

18 L. Vaughn Howard and David R. Deener, "Louisiana," in Paul T. David, Malcolm Moos, and Ralph M. Goldman (eds.), *Presidential Nominating Politics in 1952*, Vol. III of *The South* (Baltimore, 1954).

expected to be solidly States' Rights in 1948. Yet such was not the case. In fact, the 1948 presidential election in Louisiana is difficult to explain in terms of previous parish voter patterns, except for the emergent north-south division. Although the areas of Republican support shifted from north to south in 1948, the continuance of protest is found in the northern support of the Dixiecrats in an equally large number of parishes (twenty-three). But at the same time, nearly two-thirds of South Louisiana parishes likewise supported the Dixiecrats. In both north and south a number of parishes, some of them high in level of Long support, remained loyal to the national Democrats.

The conservatives in Louisiana were in rebellion not only against the liberalism of the national Democratic Party; they opposed the local radicalism of the Longs as well. Now an opportunity presented itself to see how far they could go while the Longs were bemused with other matters. It could be argued that the results of the 1948 presidential election turned significantly on the question of leadership and that conservatives had made the most of the failure or the inability of the Longs to take a stand on the presidential election consistent with Longism.

Comeback for Presidential Democrats

With the Longs taking sides again in 1952, thirty-nine parishes swung back to the majority columns and the Democratic candidate won a comfortable statewide majority of 53 percent. The election results have been called a triumph for the principle of party loyalty.[19] A heated floor fight at the Democratic convention between the forces of Governor Robert F. Kennon and moderates led by National Committeeman Frank Ellis and Senator Russell Long had resulted in a breach among the Democrats; afterwards the conservatives came out as Democrats for Eisenhower. In an attempt to build a two-party system in the state, John Minor Wisdom spent

[19] L. Vaughn Howard and David R. Deener, *Presidential Politics in Louisiana, 1952* (New Orleans, 1954), 97.

much effort persuading Democrats that they could vote Republican without having their grandfathers turn over in the grave.

Legally barred from succeeding himself in a second consecutive term of office, Earl Long had tried several tactics, threatening to resign and run again, and finally backing the hand-picked candidacy of Judge Carlos Spaht from Baton Rouge. Russell Long had opposed his uncle by supporting the candidacy of Congressman Hale Boggs of New Orleans. The disunited Longs lost to Judge Kennon from Minden in the January runoff primary. Then, however, liberals of all persuasions joined Longites in campaigning vigorously for Adlai E. Stevenson, and their efforts paid off handsomely at the polls.

While race was not yet an open issue, it was implicit in the distaste expressed for the Fair Employment Practice Commission of President Truman. Louisiana's interest in the tidelands oil settlement likewise became part of the attraction of Eisenhower. Yet in the outcome the Louisiana Democratic Party seemed to have recovered from the panic of 1948 to become, on the surface, more "liberal" than ever. The support of the Democratic candidate followed the classic pattern of Longism, as predominantly rural parishes, which formed the core of Longism, supported Stevenson with few exceptions. Table 13 depicts the consequence of support of Stevenson by elements of Longism, matching presidential voting behavior among the majority and minority Long parishes in the gubernatorial runoff in 1952. Three comments may be made on

Table 13

NUMBER OF PARISHES BELOW AND ABOVE 50 PERCENT FOR
PRESIDENTIAL DEMOCRATIC AND LONG CANDIDATE, 1952,
NORTH AND SOUTH LOUISIANA

| | | Democratic Candidate | | | |
| | | Below 50% | | Above 50% | |
		North	South	North	South
Long	Below 50%	6	6	15	26
Candidate	Above 50%	1	1	6	3

Source: Howard, *Political Tendencies.*

these figures: (1) the majority Republican parishes are found almost wholly in the area of low Long support; (2) while the Longs had been routed by Kennon in all but eleven parishes, the degree of support for the Long candidate had not fallen below the 40–49 percentage interval in twenty-nine parishes and in all of these the Democrats gained a majority; and (3) continued evidence of the bridging of North and South Louisiana is seen in 1952.

Yet the crucial point in the 1952 presidential election was in the cities, where support of the two presidential candidates tended to break even and the Negro vote (over 100,000 strong) proved the deciding factor in giving the Democrats a majority in Louisiana. Negroes had increased their electoral participation in the election of 1952, and as registration continued to increase in the urban areas and the rural French parishes, blacks once more became an important factor in political fortune. For the Longs, Negro registration was fortuitous as a balance to the contraction of the traditional Long support in rural areas. Using Baton Rouge precincts as indicative, Negro support for Long candidates was found in the ratio of three to one.

Earl K. Long attempted another comeback in 1956 and gained a majority of 51 percent in the first primary, marking the fifth time in the eight elections since 1928 a Long candidate had won, the third time it was done in the first primary. Thus despite scandal, crudeness, and counterappeals on behalf of respectability, the electorate returned the Longs to power. Negro registration in the amount of over 161,000 could be counted as the margin of victory. "Uncle Earl" accomplished this result without using the new-fangled television; instead he took to the stump in the kind of grass-roots campaigning in which he had no peers. In Orleans Parish, Long trailed deLesseps S. "Chep" Morrison, the young reform mayor of New Orleans, and his Crescent City Democratic Organization (with which Morrison had beaten the Old Regulars since 1946) by a scant 2,017 votes.

The traditional bridge to South Louisiana is evident in the figures in Table 14. If the pattern of Longism was a combination of farmer and worker, Negro and white, Protestant and Catholic, and

Table 14
NUMBER OF PARISHES LOW AND HIGH IN CATHOLIC AND NEGRO
REGISTRATION, LOW AND HIGH IN LONG CANDIDATE SUPPORT AND CATHOLIC,
IN NORTH AND SOUTH LOUISIANA, 1956

	North	South		North	South
Low Catholic			High Long		
Low Negro Registration	20	4	Low Catholic	22	5
High Catholic			High Long		
High Negro Registration	1	20	High Catholic	1	23

Source: Howard, *Political Tendencies.*

North and South Louisiana voter categories, then the distribution of parishes high in Long support would divide both high and low on the incidence of such variables as percentage Catholic or percentage Negro registration. This hypothesis is confirmed in cross-tabulation of the two variables against the highs and lows of Long support in North and South Louisiana. Although a cleavage is found in the regional distribution of heavily Catholic and heavily Negro registration, when high percentages for Long are compared with high percentages of Catholics in this manner, a quite different outcome is obtained. Catholic and non-Catholic parishes join in support of the Long candidate.

The rather complete balance between North and South Louisiana is considered important in subsequent elections, for if either race or religion should reenter Louisiana politics, the north-south bridge of the Longs would be broken. North Louisiana would separate from South in the race-religion cleavage pattern last seen in the gubernatorial election of 1924 when the issue of the Ku Klux Klan was raised, or as it has emerged in presidential elections since 1944. This division was exactly what happened in the 1960 elections.[20]

When Adlai Stevenson, as titular head of the party after the Democrats' defeat in 1952, succeeded in establishing a national advisory committee to chart the future of the party, one action had

[20] Havard, Heberle, and Howard, *Louisiana Elections.*

been to start harmony moves, including overtures to the southern branch.[21] In Louisiana this move reinforced the degree of unity which had prevailed in the presidential campaign. At the August, 1954, meeting of the Democratic State Central Committee, Governor Kennon received a shattering blow when Camille Gravel was elected to the post of national committeeman vacated by Frank Ellis, instead of the governor's choice, Robert A. Ainsworth. Some observers detected Earl Long's hand in this action, as Gravel was a Long supporter.

The Republican Hour and the Resistance

In the summer of 1956, then, the stage was set for a rerun of the 1952 Stevenson-Eisenhower contest. Gravel exuded confidence that Stevenson would double his previous Louisiana margin, since this time he would receive the support of all Democratic factions, including Earl Long, Russell Long, deLesseps Morrison, Allen Ellender, Frank Ellis, and all but one of Louisiana's congressmen. John Minor Wisdom did not share Gravel's confidence and countered that Eisenhower would get a strong silent vote to overcome the efforts of Louisiana's political machine in the hands of professional Democratic politicians. The Republican leader proved correct. The spokesman of a newly established States' Rights Party with local headquarters in North Louisiana, Robert G. Chandler, was equally optimistic and pointed to the consternation over the effects of the 1954 Supreme Court school ruling. Already politicians were plotting resistance such as the effort by the Louisiana Legislature to outlaw the state organization of the National Association for the Advancement of Colored People, a move led by Willie Rainach, North Louisiana chairman of the legislature's Un-American Activities Committee and one of the architects of the Citizens' Council movement within the state.

The outcome of the election on November 6 was a victory for Eisenhower, with a majority of 40,550 votes (329,047 Republican, 243,977 Democratic, and 44,520 States' Rights). Eisenhower gained

21 Howard and Deener, *Presidential Politics*, 104–105.

53 percent of the total vote cast. Wisdom hailed the victory as marking the realization of a two-party system in the state. The Republican leader speculated (prematurely) that Republican registration would go up in the state. Gravel, more realistically, found three reasons why the predicted Democratic victory eluded him: (1) the personal popularity of the President; (2) the defection of Negro voters to Eisenhower; and (3) the heavy burden of state issues.[22] While a majority of voters rejected the Democrats, they also handed Earl K. Long one of the worst defeats he had suffered by turning down his call for a constitutional convention by almost four to one (247,000 to 73,000). It was reported that many feared the governor was attempting another power grab; in the past legislative session "Uncle Earl" had roamed the aisles seeking votes to pass his tax bills. Long had been frustrated by the preceding Kennon administration, which thrust an influence far into the future in sponsoring and passing a constitutional amendment requiring a two-thirds' vote in each house of the legislature to increase existing taxes or levy new ones.

The leading tendency in the 1956 presidential election was the reemergence of the regional split found in 1944 and 1948.[23] This time, however, North Louisiana leaned heavily toward States' Rights as an alternative to the Democrats, while South Louisiana favored Democrats or Republicans (three-fourths of the southern parishes maintained Democratic support above the state average of 40 percent, even though thirteen parishes had Republican percentages above the state average of 53 percent, as well). For the first time the urban-industrial parishes carried a majority for the Republican candidate (56 percent); this support had been swelled by Negro voters. In New Orleans, for example, Negroes backed the Democratic candidate at a level of only 43 percent—some 37 percent below the level of support in the 1952 election.

In 1952, the pattern of Longism, even in defeat, related closely with the pattern of Democratic victory. But in 1956 this association washed out. Although Longism still bridged the northern and

22 Baton Rouge *Morning Advocate*, November 4, 1956.
23 Howard, *Political Tendencies*.

southern parishes, in the presidential election that year North Louisiana went anti-Democratic for good. This development can be
seen in the cross-tabulation of gubernatorial and presidential support by parishes as presented in Table 15. In all, fifty parishes had

Table 15
NUMBER OF PARISHES ABOVE AND BELOW 50 PERCENT FOR LONG CANDIDATE
AND PRESIDENTIAL DEMOCRAT, 1956, IN NORTH AND SOUTH LOUISIANA

		Long Candidate			
		Below 50%		Above 50%	
		North	South	North	South
Democrat	Below 50%	6	6	22	15
	Above 50%	0	2	0	13

Source: Howard, *Political Tendencies.*

Long majorities in the gubernatorial election and these were distributed quite evenly, north and south (twenty-two and twenty-
eight). On the other hand, it is readily apparent that no such
bridging effect obtained for the presidential election results: all
twenty-eight North Louisiana parishes voted anti-Democratic.

Resistance to federal encroachment upon the southern way of
life was not left entirely to the electorate. A new turn commenced
after 1954 with wide acceptance and support of the Citizens' Council movement, which had volunteered to help local and state officials to stiffen resistance. The legislature, most of whose members
had campaigned as staunch segregationists, began to fashion a blueprint of resistance to desegregation independent of Governor Long's
leadership; one important part of the design was to "purge" the
voter registration lists. The consequences of this move were at least
twofold: (1) between 1956 and 1958 more than 31,000 Negro names
were dropped from registration rolls, more than half of them from
North Louisiana parishes, over 5,000 from Ouachita Parish alone
(which to this day has failed to come halfway back to the 1956 level);
and (2) racism was brought back into Louisiana politics, weakening
the foundation of the Long faction.[24]

24 *Ibid.*

The final collapse of moderation before the growing forces of segregation could be seen in the action of the central committee on October 8, 1958, when it managed to oust Camille Gravel from his post as national committeeman.[25] Gravel had championed a mild civil rights plank at the Democratic convention in 1956 and had claimed the segregation issue was morally wrong and legally settled. Governor Long managed to forestall committee action for over a year. However when Gravel backed a candidate for Congress against one supported by Long in September, 1958—and defeated Long's candidate—the governor interposed no longer and the segregationists' desire to get rid of Gravel prevailed, despite the national Democratic committee's action to uphold him in his position. It has been argued that by failing to protect Gravel from the central committee, Governor Long gave up his opportunity to act as a broker between the national and state organizations, "a brokerage which enabled him to secure both groups in the interest of moderation." The subsequent widely publicized events in the last year of Earl Long's administration (1959–60) tended to jeopardize the entire structure of the Long organization, "thereby further weakening its capacity to stave off extremist racial policies." [26]

"Uncle Earl" experienced a series of personal catastrophes in 1959 which brought unfavorable national and statewide press coverage. It has been claimed that these events occurred in conjunction with or even partly as a consequence of the outburst of racially oriented politics.[27] Governor Long had finally collapsed on the floor of the legislature while arguing for the passage of a bill to forestall a purge of voting rolls by the segregationists. The tide of Longism ebbed to its lowest point since the scandals twenty years before. For the first time since 1924 the issue of being "soft on race" appeared, and for the first time since 1896 the Negro per se became an issue in Louisiana politics. In 1896 the concern had been the potential of

25 William C. Havard and Robert F. Steamer, "Louisiana Secedes: Collapse of a Compromise," *Massachusetts Review*, I (1959), 134–46.
26 *Ibid.*, 143.
27 Havard, Heberle, and Howard, *Louisiana Elections*; A. J. Liebling, *The Earl of Louisiana* (New York, 1961).

a Negro-Populist fusion; sixty-four years later the rhetoric focused on the Negro bloc vote and its affinity to the candidacy of such alleged liberals as New Orleans Mayor Chep Morrison.

The details of the 1960 elections in Louisiana have been presented elsewhere[28] and only a summary account will be given here. Many people had expected former Governor Jimmie H. Davis, offering "peace and harmony," and Chep Morrison to face off in the second primary. However the candidacy of Willie Rainach inhibited any forthright prediction. Moreover it remained to be seen how the shattered forces of Longism would fare. James A. Noe (running with Earl Long for lieutenant governor), a Long stalwart from the 1930's, sought to redeem the name of Long. A fifth contender in the 1960 gubernatorial election was the perennial candidate William J. Dodd, previously estranged but never wholly alienated from the Longs.

Three issues had dominated the first primary, all of which threatened to destroy the electoral foundations of Longism as each candidate sought to fill the vacuum created by the weakness of the Long organization: (1) the liberalism represented by Morrison, which promised a basis of support beyond New Orleans in other urban-industrial areas; (2) the urban-religious question posed by Morrison's Catholic-Gallic, South Louisiana urbanism so antipathetic to the fundamentalist Protestant, Anglo-Saxon, populist ideology of the piney hills, whatever the affinity of their respective outlooks on economic matters; and (3) race, on which Rainach posed as premier guardian of the southern way of life, claiming that Noe, Dodd, and Morrison were soft on the issue and that Davis would be ineffectual. The outcome of the balloting in the first primary told its own story about the way these factors affected the traditional pattern of Longism and held portents for the results of the runoff.

The rank-orders of candidate support in North and South Louisiana are presented in Table 16. For the first time since 1924 a Long candidate failed to win outright or gain a spot in the runoff primary;

28 Havard, Heberle, and Howard, *Louisiana Elections.*

Table 16
RANK-ORDER OF CANDIDATE SUPPORT IN GUBERNATORIAL FIRST PRIMARY,
1959, IN NORTH AND SOUTH LOUISIANA

	Total		North	South
			Rank-Order	
Morrison	278,956	(34%)	4	1
Davis	213,551	(25%)	2	2
Rainach	143,095	(17%)	1	3
Noe	97,654	(13%)	3	5
Dodd	85,436	(11%)	5	4

Source: Howard, *Political Tendencies.*

the Longs had slipped badly. Since there was no runoff in 1956 by which to judge, the big question was whether Morrison had reached his maximum potential vote, which remained decidedly regional. Jimmie Davis, well known as a former governor, showed a nearly equal drawing power in both regions of the state. While Rainach received his highest percentage in the North Louisiana parishes, the extent of segregation sentiment is perhaps measured in the fact that his total vote was divided almost equally between north and south. Among the urban electorate, Morrison led in upper-income white and Negro precincts (the pattern of his New Orleans success). However Davis was runner-up in the upper-income white precincts, and it was plain that he had the ultimate advantage, for he drew the greatest support among the most numerous voter category, white labor.

Jimmie Davis won his second term as governor in 1960, receiving 54 percent of the 901,791 total votes cast with a solid 76 percent of the North Louisiana vote coupled with 46 percent support in the rest of the state, and breaking even in the urban-industrial parishes (50.8 percent). Morrison had gained 60 percent of the Orleans vote and 55 percent of the Jefferson Parish vote, but in the periphery of the industrial strip (and areas likewise less heavily Catholic) such as Baton Rouge and Lake Charles, he slipped badly. A frequency distribution of the Davis vote by parish revealed, predictably, that as Davis support increased, the percentage of Catholic and of Negro registration by parishes decreased. At the same time this regularity tends to blur when the Davis vote is compared with the percentage of urban voters.

If comparing the degree of urbanization and the Davis vote does not produce meaningful variation, then it may be surmised that including an index of race would reveal a significant relationship. However, comparing Davis support with the level of Negro registration in parishes both low and high in percentage of urbanization, the hypothesis must be rejected. The race factor produced more variation in the Davis support than the urban factor.

The 1959–60 gubernatorial primary elections, then, were disruptive. Their outcome was to substitute for Longism a pattern which pitted north against south, Protestant against Catholic, and rendered race the primary issue in place of economic realities. Gubernatorial voting behavior had come to parallel that of recent presidential elections. The revival of racism and the intrusion of religious and cultural xenophobia carried over to the 1960 presidential election.

Racism and Xenophobia

The Democrats were optimistic again with the nomination of John F. Kennedy, a Roman Catholic, as the standard-bearer. The Republicans' confidence was shadowed by the entrance of the States' Rights Party again, for many foresaw that if the conservative vote was split, a candidate as attractive to South Louisiana as Senator Kennedy might win Louisiana's ten electoral votes by a plurality. Actually the Democratic Party got a majority (50.4 percent of the record 807,891 presidential votes cast), while the Republicans ran second, with 28.5 percent, and the States' Righters got the rest, 21.1 percent. The north-south division was apparent: all but one North Louisiana parish (Natchitoches, whose population was 30 percent Catholic) gave Kennedy less than 40 percent of their vote, while Kennedy carried South Louisiana, with twenty-one parishes voting Democratic by more than 60 percent.

The intriguing (but difficult-to-answer) question is, why did

Kennedy win and Morrison lose, given the similarity between the two candidates? Although the average percentage of support for the two candidates by voter type areas arrayed in almost identical order, the mean averages for Morrison in North and South Louisiana were 21 and 53 percent, respectively, whereas the mean averages for Kennedy were 27 and 59 percent. Morrison received only 35 percent of the vote in Baton Rouge white labor precincts, but Kennedy gained 51 percent; given the large proportion of this category among the total electorate, the Kennedy advantage is obvious. Yet their state averages were quite close (47 and 50 percent), and in New Orleans white labor precincts support was almost identical for the two candidates.

Whatever the impact of the increment of white labor votes in the Kennedy support (labor leaders endorsed Kennedy but not Morrison), race and religion proved to be the key variables in determining the direction of the presidential vote in Louisiana, just as in the gubernatorial elections. As for the religious factor, Bernard Cosman found that Democratic percentages in 1960 followed the rise in each level of Catholicism, while the inverse was true for the Republican vote. In 1956, however, no such variation could be found. As for the racial factor, Cosman found that whereas voting behavior in the least Catholic parishes varied with the size of the Negro-white population, the presence or absence of Negroes in the Catholic parishes did not seem to have been important in determination of voting tendencies. Religion seemed related to racial tolerance as measured by the greater percentages of Negroes registered to vote in the Catholic parishes.[29]

The Davis administration almost immediately (fall, 1960) faced the state's first experience with court-ordered desegregation of public schools. Segregationists urged the governor to call a special session of the legislature in which an attempt would be made to build a bulwark against the inevitable. This episode has been the subject of an able case study by Edward L. Pinney and Robert Friedman,

[29] Bernard Cosman, "Religion and Race in Louisiana Presidential Politics, 1960," *Southwestern Social Science Quarterly*, XLIII (1962), 237.

who made the point that in Louisiana, where the office of the governor is such a strong one, it seemed out of place for Governor Davis to acquiesce to the demands of the legislature.[30] Yet on this explosive issue it could be argued the governor led by indirection, granting concessions in the form of packages of segregation legislation but avoiding dramatic shows of resistance such as occurred in Arkansas, Mississippi, and Alabama. The Davis administration, it can be seen in retrospect, managed to contain the issue; nearly all the groups who might have exploited these issues tactically were held in check.

The disruptive trends introduced into Louisiana politics in the elections of 1960 were affirmed in the 1963–64 elections.[31] This appeared to be true despite the eventual election as governor of an ostensible Long candidate, for the racial issue remained heated and the candidates vying for position did not campaign on the traditional issues. Rather than the charges and countercharges of excessive spending, patronage, and graft against the Longs or the "do-nothingism" and favoritism toward vested interests of the opposition, the candidates attacked or defended the Kennedy administration, the Supreme Court, and federal authority in general. All these are easily perceived as issues related to race.

Top position in the first primary was conceded to Chep Morrison, making the run for the third straight time, something of a record in Louisiana politics. His opponents' strategy became one of finding issues and getting support of enough voters to capture the number two spot and thus become the candidate to defeat Morrison in the runoff. The entries included two with backing of different remnants of the Long forces, John J. McKeithen and Gillis Long. The former enjoyed the active support of Mrs. Blanche Long, wife of the late "Uncle Earl." As Long's floor leader, McKeithen

---

[30] Edward L. Pinney and Robert S. Friedman, *Political Leadership and the School Desegregation Crisis in Louisiana*, Eagleton Institute Cases in Practical Politics (New York, 1963).

[31] Charles W. Tapp, "The Gubernatorial Election of 1964: An Affirmation of Political Trends," *Proceedings of Louisiana Academy of Sciences*, XXVII (1964), 74–87.

had participated in the now-famous tax-raising legislative session of
1948, before he had won a position as public service commissioner
from North Louisiana (the springboard of Huey Long and Jimmie
Davis, as well). Gillis Long, a young lawyer with a private practice
in Washington, D.C., and experienced as counsel for a congressional
committee, had won the seat for Louisiana's Eighth Congressional
District in 1962. A distant cousin of Senator Russell Long, Gillis
got his wholehearted support after Russell decided not to run himself, partly due, no doubt, to the legislature's failure to endorse a
constitutional amendment in 1962 which would have allowed a
governor to succeed himself with another four-year term.

A familiar figure on the anti-Long side was former Governor
Kennon, who enjoyed the backing of business and industrial interests and whose known views on race and states' rights meant that
at least some of the segregationists would back him. The fifth of the
major candidates, State Superintendent of Education Shelby Jackson, was the other staunch segregationist, who counted his strength
among teachers and professional educators to give him a base from
which to expand his support.

The assassination of President Kennedy two weeks before the
date of the primary election produced an unknown effect on the outcome, although its immediate effect was to require several of the
candidates to alter their campaign tactics. Kennon, Jackson, and
McKeithen had been running hard against the "feds" in general
and the Kennedys in particular. McKeithen had claimed that Long
and Morrison, at that time serving as Kennedy's ambassador to the
Organization of American States, were the candidates of Washington. Hence Morrison and to a lesser degree Long could expect to
gain whatever benefits might accrue from the tragedy.

In the results of the first primary Morrison gained an identical
percentage point support in the lead as the previous time (33 percent). His closest rival was McKeithen, with 17 percent of the total
vote cast, much less than Davis had received in 1959. Gillis Long
(15 percent) missed gaining the runoff by fewer than 20,000 votes,
while only 10,000 behind Long was Kennon (14 percent). The

"soaring eagle," Shelby Jackson, landed fifth, with 12 percent of the vote.

A comparison of the Morrison support in both 1959 and 1963 reveals that the presence of this candidate served to crystallize electoral forces on something other than the traditional pattern structured by thirty years of Longism. In both first primaries, Morrison got 66 percent of his total parish support among the sixteen of his top quarter parishes (all in South Louisiana), and the pattern was identical except that in 1963 Morrison lost two parishes but gained two others in their place. Morrison lost only 1.1 percent in his North Louisiana total average and 1.5 percent in South Louisiana over the two elections. McKeithen and Long competed for second place in South Louisiana, while in North Louisiana the candidacies of Kennon, Jackson, and McKeithen were a dead heat. McKeithen's northern parish support seems to confirm his affinity to Longism, but in reality his top quarter was a composite of the parishes to be found in the Davis and Noe top support in 1963. Gillis Long, accumulating less of his total vote in his top quarter than the other candidates, drew votes rather equally from among South Louisiana parishes, where traditional Long support had been found. Long cut into Morrison's strength and in fact was runner-up to Morrison in fourteen parishes. Gillis Long seemed to attract backers among a new element in Louisiana politics, a rising class of young business and professional men, a potential new base for Long-style liberalism. Had Long's appeal not competed with the Morrison style and lost its chance as the Negro vote was drawn to solid backing of Morrison, quite likely Gillis Long would have entered the runoff.

The two conservative candidates, Kennon and Jackson, tended to split the vote between themselves in North Louisiana, where their upper quarter parishes were located. Quite obviously had the conservative and segregationist votes been united behind one candidate, *he* could have made the runoff. It seemed apparent to many that McKeithen would easily receive the bulk of the Kennon and Jackson votes in a showdown with Morrison and in point of fact,

McKeithen won the Democratic nomination for governor in 1964 by getting 52.2 percent of the 944,066 votes cast, carrying forty-four parishes compared to the forty-one that Davis carried four years previously. The distribution of the McKeithen vote was almost a carbon copy of the 1960 Davis vote.

John J. McKeithen accomplished this feat through the display of remarkable political talent in melding together three seemingly contradictory images and using them to advantage. After having floundered for position in August and September, McKeithen shortly began to put together an impressive campaign presenting himself as reformer, progressive Longite, and segregationist. He established himself as the real opponent to the incumbent Davis administration by branding himself an "uncontrolled" candidate, thus reflecting a reform image in a state where such candidates had enjoyed political success. He combined this image with that of Long progressive, acknowledging his "guilt" in voting for tax increases as Long floor leader in 1948, but pointing out all the programs these taxes had financed, such as free school lunches, old age pensions, and veteran bonuses.

McKeithen needed one more image, that of the segregationist. The Longs, of course, had been race moderates and had in fact come under attack for "allowing" too many Negroes to register to vote. McKeithen had been part of this administration, but while admitting to being a "one-hundred per cent segregationist" and an opponent of federal intervention, he carefully stressed he was not a "hater." These three images—reformer, Longite, and segregationist—coalesced in such a way to reduce their contradictory nature; flexibility was the hallmark of his campaign. McKeithen proved to be a great political counterpuncher. Once in the second primary, he could strategically play up any one, any two, or all three of his images.

The Republicans had mounted a statewide challenge in the general election of 1964, supporting Charlton Lyons, a Shreveport businessman. Modern-day Republicanism in Louisiana had been extended from the single concern with presidential patronage politics beginning around 1952 and, particularly in the Shreveport area, efforts had been made to build a grass-roots party organization. Lyons not only had money (and sources of money) required to make the campaign, he also had fire in his eyes. As an enthusiastic supporter of Senator Goldwater, he had found the Democrats in 1960 following a blueprint for socialism; as a thoroughgoing conservative, he appeared able to pick up support from among traditional anti-Long voters. He likewise stood to gain from disheartened Morrison supporters, who might cross over in the gubernatorial election. Contrary to the advice of many political pundits who counseled that to take Lyons seriously was to give him unnecessary publicity, McKeithen went all out and in so doing proved his intuitive political skill.

After winning the runoff, McKeithen hastened to heal Democratic wounds by a number of well-chosen appointments. In late February, 1964, he announced some provisional appointments which included Morrison as director of a crash program for new industry and Shelby Jackson as head of a program on Americanism. McKeithen also managed to shelve a fight by the Democratic State Central Committee between segregationists and "loyal" Democrats over a so-called free presidential elector plan. Perhaps the only exception to McKeithen's unity moves turned on the support he gave another distant Long relative, Speedy O. Long, who won the congressional seat in the Eighth District later that summer and thus removed a political base from Gillis Long.

In the March general election John McKeithen beat back the strongest Republican challenge in almost a century by gaining 61 percent of the more than 725,000 votes cast, only 200,000 short of the record total in the Democrats' heated second primary. Lyons gained far more than the 83,000 polled by Francis Grevemburg in 1960 against Governor Davis and, as expected, scored his heaviest gains in the urban areas. Both candidates had professed to be segregationists, but in the parishes where Willie Rainach had found his greatest support, the affinity with the Republican candidate proved greater. A positive association was found between Morrison's urban South Louisiana vote and the vote for Lyons. Factors in this association included the following: (1) traditional anti-Long urban voters; (2) newly emerged urban Republican supporters; (3) moderates alienated by McKeithen's use of the race issue and his attack on the national administration; and (4) Morrison supporters bitter that their candidate—seemingly incapable of losing just weeks before —had experienced his third and perhaps last defeat.[32]

Many asserted again that the day of two-party politics had come to Louisiana, when in November, 1964, Senator Barry Goldwater, the Republican candidate, swept the state and won its ten electoral votes. But with nominal Democrats such as the incumbent secretary of state, Wade O. Martin, and the lieutenant governor, C. C. "Taddy" Aycock, backing the Republicans (Governor McKeithen sat out the election but later claimed he was one southern leader who had not backed President Johnson), and with Louisiana one of only five southern states which joined Arizona in supporting Goldwater, an answer to the question of what the vote meant was in order.

As racial tensions increased in the early sixties and as disaffection with Presidents Kennedy and Johnson set in over their advocacy of civil rights legislation, the segregation issue was easily exploited in local and state elections. With a candidate who declared himself a champion of southern states' rights, the issue was more susceptible to exploitation on the presidential level. The white electorate voted for the man they perceived as the candidate of the southern white man.[33] This vote was the continuation of a protest—a compulsion, almost, to support whatever held most promise of perpetuating the identity of the traditional South, manifest since the forties.[34]

President Johnson, the Democratic candidate for reelection, got only 43 percent of the 896,293 total votes cast in the 1964 Louisiana presidential race, which provided the highest percentage turnout of registered voters (73 percent) since 1868. Louisiana joined her sister states of the old Confederacy in providing 62 percent of the counties of the United States carried by Goldwater. Their dis-

32 Tapp, "Election of 1964," 85.
33 Bernard Cosman, *Five States for Goldwater* (University, Ala., 1966), 62.
34 See the version of this in Howard and Brent, "Social Change."

tribution was pronounced, as Goldwater swept North Louisiana with the same solidarity Republicans and States' Rights had enjoyed in 1960, while Johnson carried 22 parishes in South Louisiana. A quite remarkable stability in the pattern of voting behavior since 1960 could be seen in the parish distribution of the Johnson vote in comparison with that of his counterpart Kennedy in the previous presidential election (Table 17). The number of parishes

Table 17

NUMBER OF PARISHES IN KENNEDY AND JOHNSON PERCENTAGE
INTERVALS IN NORTH AND SOUTH LOUISIANA

		0–39%	40–49%	50–59%	60–100%
North Louisiana	Kennedy	27	1	0	0
	Johnson	27	1	0	0
South Louisiana	Kennedy	4	8	3	21
	Johnson	6	8	13	9

Source: Howard, *Political Tendencies.*

in each percentage interval remained the same for both candidates in North Louisiana, while in South Louisiana the number of majority parishes for Johnson decreased by two. Also observed is a tendency for parishes to move from highest into the 50–59 percentage interval.

Governor McKeithen began to build a consensus, Louisiana style, which was a function of a number of features of his administration, dependent upon chance but equally as much upon his political acumen. In the summer of 1964 McKeithen found himself without major opposition as Gillis Long lost his seat in Congress and Morrison lost his life in an airplane crash. In this political vacuum, talk of a two-term amendment was renewed and groundwork laid for its eventual passage by the legislature and referral to the electorate in the November, 1966, general election.

The issue of gubernatorial succession was tied by the governor himself to the issue of the great powers of the governor's office. The succession issue must follow a reduction in the powers and to that end Governor McKeithen resorted to a favorite stratagem—he appointed a study committee, this one headed by former Governor Sam H. Jones. Several Jones Committee recommendations were submitted to the people along with the two-term amendment, all "sweetened" by an amendment to provide a domed stadium in New Orleans. The Jones amendments included reduction of the vast appointive powers of the governor and provision for "veto sessions" of the legislature.

The only major objection to the two-term amendment had been raised by Gillis Long, who cogently argued that given the great power of the Louisiana governor (regardless of passage of Jones amendments), it would be impossible to marshal support and find the financial backing needed effectively to oppose the candidacy of an incumbent. Long's arguments fell on deaf ears as many charged sour grapes and still more advanced the quaint and rather undemocratic position that to defeat the two-term amendment would guarantee another nonsuccessive term for the now unpopular Jimmie Davis (how, if Davis was so unpopular, was not explained).[35] The McKeithen consensus expanded as the electorate endorsed a second term for the governor by a sizable 70 percent of the total vote cast, a percentage found quite uniformly throughout all the voter type areas in an election McKeithen had said would be a vote of confidence in his administration.

Racial unrest erupting in the paper-mill city of Bogalusa in 1964 tested the governor, and McKeithen made it clear he intended to use the power of his office to maintain law and order. He authorized a Biracial Committee and staffed it with a permanent counsel. In making the announcement Governor McKeithen said in effect, We all are going to learn to get along with each other. Compared to the rhetoric of many other southern politicians, this was the voice of moderation. In the hot summer of 1967 as the prevailing calm was threatened, McKeithen repeated his position in words sure to im-

---

[35] Gillis Long was no doubt chagrined at this turn of events since if the amendment had been defeated then *he* would have been in a strong position to offer his candidacy again.

press his listeners; he said violence would not be tolerated and if it occurred a lot of people would be shot.[36]

The use of citizens' committees to work on the solution of critical statewide problems proved quite effective, and has worked, up to now, for the thorny problem of labor-management racketeering, allegedly widespread in the capital-city area. The whole question became clouded in 1967 when *Life* magazine charged mobster influence in the McKeithen administration. This article gave the governor's major opponent in his second-term election, Florida parishes Congressman John R. Rarick, his most potent issue. Despite the large Klan support Rarick had received in ousting twenty-four-year veteran Jimmie Morrison from his House seat and the seeming potency of the rackets charge, the McKeithen consensus held. It became a phenomenon as the governor won his second term in November, 1967, with an unprecedented Democratic primary support of 80.6 percent of the record-breaking 1,037,102 total votes cast. The prediction of Gillis Long was confirmed as the McKeithen umbrella covered the state. Although he received a majority in every parish, McKeithen's strongest support had come from South Louisiana—a reversal of the 1964 results, an indication that the governor's executive actions had pleased the more moderate electorate of this part of the state.

Shortly thereafter (December, 1967), rumblings came from the state central committee. The loyalist chairman, Edward Carmouche, of Lake Charles, was ousted and replaced by backers of Alabama's George Wallace with the staunchly conservative Arthur C. Watson of Natchitoches. The vote of the 117-man committee, with 3 members absent, clearly followed the pattern of north-south cleavage (Table 18). Despite the popularity of Governor McKeithen, the actions of the central committee were considered significant.[37] Where there has been such upheaval in the state committee, it has been found that the voters react exactly the same way and have swung to the Republican or States' Rights parties.

36 Baton Rouge *Morning Advocate*, April 9, 1968.
37 *Ibid.*

Table 18

NUMBER OF PARISHES FOR OR AGAINST ARTHUR WATSON AS CHAIRMAN OF THE
DEMOCRATIC CENTRAL COMMITTEE, 1967, NORTH AND SOUTH LOUISIANA

	North	South
For Watson	35	30
Against Watson	3	46

Source: Howard, *Political Tendencies.*

The Vice-Presidential Hopeful

With the governor firmly in charge of political affairs in the state,
a McKeithen–for–Vice President boomlet enhanced his position
in the spring of 1968. Although it may appear improbable that the
eventual Democratic presidential candidate, Hubert Humphrey,
would have chosen McKeithen as his running mate, yet as the presidential year progressed, good reasons existed for considering Mc-
Keithen a potential choice. At the annual AFL-CIO convention in
April, at which Vice President Humphrey was a featured speaker,
McKeithen's stock rose when Humphrey reportedly indicated that
the governor was one of those being considered for the post. At the
Democratic convention in Chicago, Humphrey called McKeithen
one of the nation's greatest, most articulate, and most progressive
chief executives.[38]

The hard political strategy in June, as McKeithen forces were
negotiating with Democratic leaders, made it appear plausible that
as the vice-presidential candidate, McKeithen was the only man
who could partially offset the big Wallace vote in prospect for
Dixie. Had 1968 been in any way a normal presidential year, the
traditional insurance of southern Democratic votes from a regionally balanced ticket may have seemed desirable. Although the
flirtation continued after the governor led the Louisiana delegation to Chicago as a favorite son, McKeithen made it clear he did
not expect realistically to be named, for Humphrey had apparently

[38] The following discussion of political activities in 1968 is based primarily on
reports in the Baton Rouge *Morning Advocate.*

written off the South after Spiro Agnew was selected as Nixon's running mate.

McKeithen took a careful position and claimed he was in Chicago to do what he could for Louisiana regarding tidelands and law and order. The governor shrewdly explained he had lost his chance for nomination to the second spot on the ticket with the death of Robert F. Kennedy, for if Kennedy and Humphrey forces had found themselves deadlocked in the convention, as Humphrey sought southern support the South could have driven a bargain and McKeithen would have had a chance.

As a final touch, typical of the public relations flair of the governor's forces, it was revealed that had the lightning actually struck in Chicago, McKeithen's longtime supporter Judge Edmund Reggie of Crowley was to have made the nomination speech, and Louisiana's first Negro representative since Reconstruction may have seconded the nomination.

While McKeithen kept his name in the headlines of the state's newspapers as a result of the vice-presidential flirtation, the fact remained that the governor was serving the first year of his "lame-duck" administration. Increased revenues were going to be necessary to maintain and expand state services in economically booming Louisiana and the governor announced that tax increases would be requested at the June legislative session, the first to assemble legislators elected since the body was reapportioned according to federal court order. McKeithen, pointing to his own role in enacting the 1948 taxes on the basis of which the state was still operating, asserted that political promotion lay ahead for lawmakers who supported new taxes when they are needed and that he would ask his agency heads to make a case for them.

The legislature, apparently not convinced by the governor's words, dragged its feet so much that before the session was half over McKeithen gave up pushing his tax program. Due to the inhibition thrown up by the Kennon administration in 1952—the two-thirds' vote requirement—no major tax increases had been established since the two-cent sales tax imposed in 1948. The McKeithen administration had asked for $61 million in new revenue to add to an equal amount of growth revenues for state operations. The major portion would go to a long-promised teacher pay raise, a $100-per-month old-age pension, and $13 million for Louisiana State University and state colleges. The main revenues would have come from a one-cent hike in state gasoline taxes, removal of exemptions from state income tax, and a weight tax on autos.

The 1968 legislature adjourned after producing meager results. While rejecting McKeithen's tax program, it seemingly feathered its own nest by greatly increasing state employment retirement benefits and increasing per-diem pay for interim committees from $30 to $50. One veteran political observer declared so many committees had been created that it seemed half the legislature would be on hand every day of the year. These included a tax study committee to provide a program for consideration at a special session later in the year, as well as the legislative committee to study workmen's compensation measures.

Drawing conclusions from a study published by the business-sustained Public Affairs Research Council, the Louisiana Municipal Association published during the summer a position paper which said that "the powers of the legislative branch are so much under control and domination by the executive that it no longer deserves to be called a branch. It comes closer to being a twig and a badly bent one at that." The paper went on to point out that no legislature could be held responsible for the present imbalance but that "the current legislature does have an opportunity to improve their relative status." One can surmise that the legislature's rejection of the McKeithen tax program in the special session November 18–December 17 was in part a response to that challenge.

The governor claimed he could have forced taxes through at the regular session but that he preferred not to follow that route. Although fresh from his unprecedented victory in his bid for a second term, perhaps McKeithen at that time did not want to take action which might reduce his political options, for he had hinted he might not serve out his term, meaning that besides his vice-presidential ambitions he had looked more than once at the Senate seat of Russell Long (at stake in summer, 1968). By the time of

the special session in November, however, the governor showed
no additional concern beyond achieving sufficient progress in state
affairs to memorialize his administration. But the citizens of Louisiana were treated to high drama as the legislature buried the
McKeithen tax measures.

Carefully avoiding the option of getting revenue by an executive order to equalize property tax assessments—an alternative Mc-
Keithen had already rejected in his first term when a study committee had recommended that move—the governor prepared a tax
package for the special session keyed to a one-cent increase in the
sales tax. Publicly the governor exuded confidence but twelve days
into the session it was clear the legislature had not changed its mind
since June. In an unprecedented "secret" meeting with the House
which lasted two hours, McKeithen, "barely veiling his rancor,"
emerged and declared that a vote behind closed doors showed the
sales tax could not possibly pass. The extent of the impasse was
shown by the vote, 58–41 (with 70 votes needed for two-thirds).

The session adjourned after passage of only one McKeithen proposal, the one-cent hike in the gasoline tax. This measure raised the
tax to eight cents a gallon, bringing $14 million revenue to float a
$300 million bond issue for highways. This was little more than
10 percent of the taxes asked for by the governor. It was said openly
that McKeithen was more interested in the gas tax, which would
provide a bond issue, than in funds for current operations and that
he twisted arms to get it. Even so, an agreement to give New Orleans all federal funds earmarked for urban areas in the coming
year in exchange for the needed votes drew opposition from smaller
urban areas such as Lake Charles. The only appropriation bill to
reach the governor's desk was the measure to pay the expenses of
the session.

The session also produced 142 frustrated and angry legislators.
Their actions perhaps reflected the views of Leander Perez, who
had claimed the session had not been needed, that the state had
ample revenues to provide services if properly administered. Perez
had said in October that the governor's position was worse then than
it had been in June and predicted that the only legislation Mc-

Keithen could hope to get passed was that concerning workmen's compensation. Indeed, the major accomplishment of the special session was the reenactment of the workmen's compensation measures previously vetoed by the governor, for McKeithen accepted the bills sponsored by labor rather than those recommended by his own committee, in hopes, no doubt, of gaining enough support for his tax measures.

Roosters, Donkeys, and Elephants

That Louisiana Democrats continued to be divided between loyalists (national Democrats) and conservatives (leaning to Wallace) could be seen in the squabble about who should represent Louisiana as delegates to the national convention, the eventual ouster of National Committeeman Marshall Brown, and the struggle in the central committee to see which candidate (if any) was to have benefit of running on the ballot under the rooster.

Such an unlikely subject as the zoology of Louisiana politics sheds light on its folklore and tradition, and to discuss this issue first may help to explain the cleavage in the state's Democratic Party. The loyalists, whose choice for chairman of the central committee had been ousted in December, 1967, by a vote of 65–49, lost their bid to settle the question of who should get the rooster emblem in a vote of 59–51 in June to delay that decision. The conservative chairman, Arthur Watson, had agreed that the issue was premature since Governor McKeithen had not yet chosen a committee to select the delegates for Chicago. At this time the loyalists had some confidence that eventually the Democratic nominee would be listed under the rooster since the central committee had called off a planned presidential primary for August which, it was expected, would have designated George Wallace as the Louisiana Democratic nominee.

According to political folklore, the rooster is worth up to 100,000 votes for the candidate listed under it, for it is a sign to the voters that the state Democratic Party backs him. Estimates of the bird's worth fluctuated as the summer of 1968 progressed. Chairman Watson deflated its value to 10 votes in June but by September, when the question of who was to run under the emblem was taken to court for a decision, the astute Leander Perez admitted its worth at 75,000 votes—an important consideration in an election which might turn out to be close.

In September, the central committee named the ten Louisiana presidential electors pledged to Humphrey and specified that the Democratic nominee should run under the emblem of the national Democratic Party. Lawrence O'Brien of the national committee had been consulted and favoring votes over tradition, had ignored the donkey and agreed the rooster should stand above Humphrey's name. At this turn of events Wallace supporters obtained a court order restraining the secretary of state from placing Democratic presidential electors under the Louisiana Democratic Party rooster. When Judge Luther Cole invited testimony from the respective factions, a distinct contribution to Louisiana political history was made as the traditions concerning party behavior were thoroughly aired.

Leander Perez pointed out to the court generations of South Louisianians of French descent had been taught, *tapez le coq* ("stamp the rooster"); he suggested that they do so without ever looking to see whose names appeared under the emblem. Loyalist State Senator J. D. DeBlieux charged that Louisiana Wallaceites wanted Humphrey off the ballot, but that their next best strategy was to deny him the rooster. Judge Cole, submitting eleven reasoned pages summarizing the history of the rooster, ruled in favor of the loyalists. The judge found that under a 1954 state law the state central committee was responsible for designating the emblem, since the party was controlled by its actions. The national party existed in Louisiana only through the state organization and was subject to laws of this state; therefore an election to choose national officers is a "state election" and the phrase "national party emblem"—which the September resolution of the central committee used—meant "national party emblem in Louisiana." Therefore the rooster must go to Humphrey.

The fight was taken to the Louisiana Supreme Court, which in

October denied the rooster to Humphrey's electors by a vote of six to one. Justice Mack Barham in his dissent claimed the law clearly says the central committee selects the emblem, but now the issue was settled and the secretary of state proceeded with the printing of the ballots. Five columns appeared in alphabetical order on the ballot: one for Wallace (his party contested no local offices) and two each for the Democrats and Republicans—congressional, state, and local contests in one column, and presidential electors in the other. Wallace's American Party received the favored position on the lefthand side. The rooster emblem appeared over state and local Democratic candidates, the donkey over Democratic presidential electors, and the elephant over both Republican columns.

Although the result of the legal maneuvering did not mean necessarily that conservatives controlled the central committee, their power was nonetheless great as was demonstrated after the Democratic convention when they took away the seat of National Committeeman Marshall Brown, a New Orleans businessman and one of the early supporters of Governor McKeithen. Apparently the move was in the making at the convention, for before leaving Chicago Governor McKeithen had asked the Louisiana delegation not to go home and "meanmouth" Marshall Brown. Almost at once the central committee did oust Brown by a vote of 62 to 43, charging that Brown had shuffled delegates to the convention after an original list had been certified. This much was correct; Brown and the governor had juggled the list to make room for more Negro delegates and to avert a possible challenge in Chicago. Neither would disclose the changes to Watson. The committee action was questionable, however, from the standpoint of legality, even though the loyalist strategy had been to accept the removal action and then take the fight to the national committee. Camille Gravel sided with Brown and reminded the committee that a similar move to get rid of him had been unsuccessful because it was ruled that only the national committee could remove a national committeeman. To this the conservative answer was that we needed a national committee closer to the true feelings of the people of the state. The conservatives proceeded to choose a former state senator, William

Cleveland, as committeeman. If dissatisfaction with events surrounding the convention and the selection of delegates had irked the conservative faction (many of whom were Wallaceites anyhow and had decided to stay home), they had now remedied matters.

That the ouster of Committeeman Brown was a power play can be seen from an examination of the sequence of events leading to the announcement of the final list of delegates representing Louisiana at the Chicago convention. Although there was much uncertainty surrounding the selection process, the actions of Marshall Brown, with the blessings of Governor McKeithen, were within the limits set by the central committee, for at the May meeting a compromise plan had allowed the governor and a committee of his selection to pick the convention delegates (fifty delegates and thirty-four alternates). Choice by congressional district as in 1952 was avoided because loyalists claimed this would be an attempt by Chairman Watson to control the delegation. In July, Governor McKeithen made known the composition of his selection committee, which proved to have impeccable credentials: the governor, Chairman Arthur Watson, Marshall Brown, Mrs. Blanche Long, and Baton Rouge Assessor Jesse Webb, secretary of the central committee and a long-time faithful Democrat. The original list of delegates was announced on July 23 by Chairman Watson, who at that time declared "everyone wanted to go," although earlier he had said it would prove difficult to get delegates. That prediction was more accurate, as in the end only Hale Boggs and Russell Long of the congressional officers, who traditionally served as delegates, went to Chicago. The most noteworthy aspect was that a half-dozen Negroes were included in the list; this was the first time Louisiana had sent an integrated delegation to the Democratic convention.

The disinclination of many of Louisiana's top Democrats to attend the convention made it quickly apparent that some shifting of delegates would be necessary. Yet the headlines made it appear that the major factor in the question about delegates which remained unanswered until after the convention opened was that Louisiana Negro leaders complained they did not have enough representation on the delegation. With 20 percent of the voter registration the blacks argued they should have 7¼ votes rather than the 3½ on the original delegation list. Despite conservative unhappiness Governor McKeithen proceeded to add more Negro names to the list and in this action Chairman Watson demurred. Yet the convention was but a week away, with the list of delegates still a mystery. With the shuffling taking place, Chairman Watson began to blame Marshall Brown, Watson taking offense that he was not being consulted about the changes. A continuation of the loyalist and conservative fight seemed evident as loyalists shuffled delegates in order to be in control and to make sure there would be no protest from Negroes over seating the delegation.

As the vanguard of the Louisiana delegation arrived in Chicago on August 24 the question of final authorization was still unanswered, although familiar Democratic stalwarts appeared, including former Governor James A. Noe of Monroe and Colonel Frank Odum from Baton Rouge, who had attended every convention since 1932. It was discovered that Chairman Watson had canceled his hotel reservation. On August 27 the final list of delegates was announced and the labor leader Victor Bussie praised McKeithen for representing all segments on the delegation. Governor McKeithen had managed to appoint eleven Negroes, two with full votes and nine with half votes, for a total of six and one-half votes. The eleven-man Negro delegation constituted a good 20 percent of the total number of fifty-two delegates. Of the Louisiana delegation of forty-seven (plus five at large), almost two-thirds came from the New Orleans area and Baton Rouge, with an average of three each from the remaining five congressional districts. Sixty percent of both the original and final lists of delegates came from the New Orleans area and Baton Rouge. For all the fuss, only eight of the original appointments had dropped out and been replaced, but five of these additions had been Negroes.

The Louisiana delegation acted with near-unanimity on the major issues on which votes were required. Informed sources had said the labor representatives on the delegation had plans of voting for the nomination of Vice President Humphrey whether or not

McKeithen decided to run as a favorite son. At a caucus on Wednesday morning, however, Governor McKeithen said he would abandon his plans to be nominated as all the other southern governors had done, to go all-out to nominate Humphrey on the first ballot. Louisiana voted 33½ to 2½ against the minority Vietnam plank and Dr. Bertrand Tyson of Plaquemine reported that the "black caucus" had been under no pressures and felt free to vote as they wished. That night Senator Long cast 35 Louisiana votes for Hubert Humphrey and the following night (Thursday) Marshall Brown cast 36 votes for Senator Edmund Muskie for vice-presidential nominee. In a final gesture the delegation voted to approve a motion commending Mayor Richard Daley and the Chicago police. Consistent with his previous hard line, Governor McKeithen said, "I can tell you if we have disturbances in Louisiana like that while I am Governor, I can tell you I'll use force and lots of it to put it down."

Back home again in Louisiana, when Governor McKeithen made known that he would not campaign for Hubert Humphrey both factions of the Democrats agreed Humphrey had an uphill fight in the state. Leander Perez had sent a letter of congratulations to the governor saying, "Stick to it." The following reactions to McKeithen's decision were recorded:

Judge Leander Perez:	McKeithen in effect said to Humphrey I'll marry you tomorrow for a honeymoon tonight, but the honeymoon did not work out, so there's no marriage.
Former Democratic National Committeeman Camille Gravel:	I just don't know why he did it, unless he felt his own political fortunes would be bettered if he stayed out of the campaign.
Negro State Representative Ernest Morial:	The Governor may have felt he would jeopardize his position in the special tax session. The state party should have more control of membership and power to oust those not loyal to the national Democratic nominee.

Chairman   The Governor's stand did not surprise
Arthur Watson: him. It certainly is going to hurt Hum-
                           phrey, though he had such a dabble of
                           votes anyway.

The judge from Plaquemines Parish claimed that a McKeithen poll had shown Wallace with 70 percent of the vote in late August in Louisiana. This estimate shrank considerably in the next month; by the end of September McKeithen's private poll estimated that Wallace had at least 50 percent of the vote, Nixon sentiment was increasing, and Humphrey was running a poor third. A gauge of how the campaign would go was the national convention of the American Legion held in New Orleans in early September. State politicians greeted Wallace with enthusiasm, while Humphrey was almost snubbed. Sitting with Wallace on the platform were Wade O. Martin, secretary of state; Dave Pearce, commissioner of agriculture; and former Governor Jimmie Davis. Hubert Humphrey was greeted in New Orleans by Mayor Victor Schiro and a few supporters. Governor McKeithen was conspicuous by his absence. A portent of what might be expected from the new Negro political force in Louisiana could be drawn from the response of Representative Morial to this absence. He said that people who call themselves Democrats but cannot support the Democratic nominee—particularly state officials—should be ridden out of the party. He added that a coalition of Negroes and whites had been formed to back Humphrey and that looking ahead, it would work for a more loyal party in the next four years.

Organized labor in Louisiana endorsed the Democratic nominees and gave a straightforward ideological reason for doing so: Wallace and Nixon were not in sympathy with the interests of the working man. Yet all three Louisiana campaign heads could agree by mid-October that a Wallace victory was assured. The Wallace forces were headed by C. H. (Sammy) Downs of Alexandria, McKeithen's executive counsel, who estimated that Wallace would carry Louisiana with more than 50 percent and would win overwhelming support from the farmers. Thurmond's anticipated swing through the state would help Nixon very little; after all, Senator Thurmond's views and Nixon's actions did not jibe. Wallace would be strong in both north and south, Humphrey's strength would come from the New Orleans area, and Nixon would score heavily in Lafayette.

State Senator Michael O'Keefe of New Orleans, who decided to take on the task of state campaign manager for the Democrats, had no illusions about Humphrey's chances. He admitted that the loyalist-conservative split, together with McKeithen's refusal to campaign, had hurt Humphrey. O'Keefe was sanguine, saying elections seemed always to be that way, that you don't even know who is a Democrat until two months before the election. You have to organize them and with major state officials supporting Wallace or Nixon, it was a difficult task. Democratic chances rested on a base of organized labor and the registered Negro vote. In October O'Keefe estimated Humphrey would carry Louisiana with a plurality of 36 percent. Humphrey would get the middle-class and poor people's vote while Nixon would get the well-to-do vote. The only trouble with this prediction was that it left out Wallace.

The GOP chairman was Charles de Gravelles of Lafayette, who could count the aid of such notables as Charlton Lyons, three former governors (Sam Jones, Robert Kennon, and James Noe), and McKeithen's administrative assistant, Carlos Spaht. The bandwagon tactic of using tape recordings from the Goldwater campaign was employed by the Republicans and their slogan (and strategy) was that a vote for Wallace would help Humphrey (so therefore vote Nixon to begin with).

Major state newspapers such as the Baton Rouge *Morning Advocate* and Shreveport *Times* openly endorsed the candidacy of Richard Nixon, but the New Orleans *Times-Picayune* commended the Democratic candidate to the voters' consideration. In a state where politics takes on the proportions of a major spectator sport, bumper stickers are always everywhere in evidence. Humphrey-Muskie stickers were virtually nonexistent, however, while Wallace bumper stickers were seen everywhere, flanking Confederate decals on vehicles ranging from pickups to Cadillacs. Wallace campaign buttons and literature were even on sale at the state capitol. At the end, Humphrey and Nixon backers were claiming Wallace was losing strength. Because of the state's traditional voting patterns and the expectation that he would get the Negro vote almost in its entirety, Humphrey was seen as gaining. Advocates of the "new Louisiana," Democrats such as Sam Jones and Bob Kennon, who had been chafing against liberal control of the party for twenty years, were expected to persuade many Democrats to add their votes to those of white-collar and "organization men" in the urban-industrial areas for the GOP. Farmers in North and South Louisiana and the labor rank and file were expected to provide Wallace with his lead in the state.

The presidential election of 1968 continued the conservative swing of Louisiana voters which had begun two decades before, a move of protest which has become an important tendency among the new electorate in the South.[39] Significant portions of the old electorate, including farmers and workers, whose vote had helped fashion the pattern of Longism, have become increasingly less open and have joined upper-income white anti-Longs in opposition to the national Democrats at the polls. Louisiana—like other parts of the South—shows a pluralistic tendency in Negro and upper-income white voting patterns. The South Louisiana French population, for instance, showed an unprecedented openness in its tolerance of increasing Negro registration. Nevertheless the present broad support of George Wallace indicates a more conservative trend. If the phrase "new electorate" is taken to refer to the expectation of a more moderate, competitive politics, following upon the recent enfranchisement of large numbers of Negroes, at the same time objectivity requires that we take cognizance of and try to measure the tendency in the opposite direction. The upper south Republican and lower south Wallace support in November seemed to reflect the mood.

39 Perry H. Howard, "The New Electorate in the South," paper read at Symposium on Southern Politics, Louisiana State University in New Orleans, February 18, 1967 (lithograph).

From Thurmond to Wallace and Beyond

We want to find out now what happens when the percentage arrays for the conservative candidates in the two elections (Thurmond and Wallace) are cross-tabulated in highs and lows as was done in Figure 2, above. This time, however, we shall separate four regional parish clusters (Table 19).

We can observe the association of four categories of support (low Wallace–low Thurmond, low Wallace–high Thurmond, high Wallace–low Thurmond, and high Wallace–high Thurmond) in the four subareas of the state. Continuity in preference between the 1948 and 1968 elections shows clearly at the extremes. The most apparent exceptions seem to be Plaquemines and St. Bernard parishes, but when the reader is reminded that here the remarkable control of Judge Leander Perez continued to prevail, the difficulty is explained. The Florida parishes join North Louisiana in conservativism, while the southwest, likewise conservative, remained closer to South Louisiana parishes on the low side. What must be done is to explain the location of a number of parishes such as the seven northern and five southern parishes which are low Wallace–high Thurmond, as well as the location of parishes which cluster in cells of high Wallace–low Thurmond support. Figure 4 presents levels of incidence of selected variables in each of the sixteen cells of Table 19.

What is obvious here is not only a regional tilt but also a shift from urban to rural as the level of the Wallace vote passes above 50 percent. Every one of the urban-industrial parishes in Table 19 (identified by a solid line drawn beneath its name), regardless of region, falls in the low Wallace range. It can be seen also that the same Wallace leaning is associated with the percentage of labor force in agriculture. If race is an indicator of white supremacy, to control for Negro percentage of total population would produce differences in these cells, but what we find is not conclusive. North Louisiana and Florida parishes tip high Negro–high Wallace, while the southern and southwestern parishes tend to be high Negro–low Wallace. A regional influence seems to be present.

Table 19

NUMBER OF LOUISIANA PARISHES LOW AND HIGH IN SUPPORT OF WALLACE AND THURMOND, BY VOTER TYPE AREAS

	Low Wallace (43%) Low Thurmond (39%)	Low Wallace (46%) High Thurmond (57%)	High Wallace (61%) Low Thurmond (40%)	High Wallace (71%) High Thurmond (71%)
North La. (28)	Ouachita (1)	Caddo, East Carroll, Lincoln, Madison, Natchitoches, Rapides, Tensas (7)	Caldwell, Franklin, Morehouse (3)	Bienville, Bossier, Catahoula, Claiborne, Concordia, DeSoto, Grant, Jackson, LaSalle, Red River, Richland, Sabine, Union, Vernon, Webster, W. Carroll, Winn (17)
Florida Parishes (8)	East Baton Rouge (1)	West Feliciana (1)	Livingston (1)	East Feliciana, St. Helena, St. Tammany, Tangipahoa, Washington (5)
Southwest La. (10)	Calcasieu, Lafayette (2)	St. Landry (1)	Allen, Beauregard, Cameron, Jeff. Davis (4)	Acadia, Evangeline, Vermilion (3)
South La. (18)	Iberia, Iberville, Orleans, St. James, St. John, St. Mary, Terrebonne, West Baton Rouge (8)	Assumption, Jefferson, Pointe Coupée, St. Charles, St. Martin (5)	Ascension (1)	Avoyelles, LaFourche, Plaquemines, St. Bernard (4)

Source: PAR Analysis No. 154; Howard, *Political Tendencies*.
Note: Each urban-industrial parish is identified by a solid line under the name.

Figure 4

RELATIONSHIP BETWEEN LOUISIANA VOTER TYPE PARISH AREAS, CLASSIFIED BY LOW AND HIGH WALLACE AND THURMOND SUPPORT AND LEVEL OF INCIDENCE OF SELECTED VARIABLES

	Per Cent Wallace (State 48%)						Per Cent Humphrey (State 29%)						Per Cent Nixon (State 23%)			
	LL	LH	HL	HH			LL	LH	HL	HH			LL	LH	HL	HH
No. La.	49	40	63	65		No. La.	18	34	17	20		No. La.	33	21	16	16
Fla.	45	40	81	61		Fla.	28	49	11	25		Fla.	28	11	8	15
SW.	43	49	59	58		SW.	29	36	24	24		SW.	29	15	16	18
So. La.	43	48	53	67		So. La.	37	32	35	17		So. La.	20	20	12	15

	Per Cent Urban (State 53%)						Per Cent Negro (State 32%)						Per Cent Negro Regst. (State 20%)			
	LL	LH	HL	HH			LL	LH	HL	HH			LL	LH	HL	HH
No. La.	72	44	31	21		No. La.	32	50	38	40		No. La.	7	28	11	17
Fla.	85	0	22	21		Fla.	32	66	15	45		Fla.	20	29	9	22
SW.	65	35	34	43		SW.	22	43	19	20		SW.	16	35	14	16
So. La.	51	35	33	42		So. La.	40	37	31	21		So. La.	28	26	23	8

	Per Cent in Agric. (State 6.5%)						Worker Ratio (State 3.2)						Organized Labor Union Members (State 138 thousands)			
	LL	LH	HL	HH			LL	LH	HL	HH			LL	LH	HL	HH
No. La.	3	7	21	11		No. La.	2.8	2.5	5.3	4.2		No. La.	3.7	18.1	2.2	6
Fla.	1	23	8	12		Fla.	2.8	4.6	2.0	4.5		Fla.	22.7	0.1	0.9	3.7
SW.	5	24	11	21		SW.	2.9	3.3	6.4	3.6		SW.	23.4	0.5	0.5	0.2
So. La.	2	6	8	11		So. La.	3.3	3.2	5.1	4.1		So. La.	55.5	8.5	0.4	1.6

Source: PAR Analysis No. 154, December, 1968; Howard, *Political Tendencies*; *Statistical Abstract of Louisiana, 1967*, Louisiana State University in New Orleans.
LL=Low Wallace–low Thurmond; LH=low Wallace–high Thurmond; HL=high Wallace–low Thurmond; HH=high Wallace–high Thurmond.

When the percentage of Negro registration is used as a variable (which we have suggested is a measure of both French-Catholicism and openness to change) the general expectation is confirmed that the greater the Negro voter registration, the lower the Wallace vote. And this also helps to explain "exception" cells, such as the North Louisiana parishes—low Wallace but high Thurmond. Although this cell measures the highest level of percentage Negro population, and thus scores high in Thurmond support, federal action in the ensuing years resulted in a relatively high level of Negro registration of voters—enough, together with an increasing Republican sentiment, to keep the Wallace proportion of the vote below 50 percent. The same process worked for the single-parish cases of West Feliciana and St. Landry. In the high Wallace–low Thurmond parishes of southwestern Louisiana it is difficult to find an explanation for the "exceptions" with the use of these variables; however while the Negro population is relatively low in these parishes, Negro registration of total voters is even lower. A more confident guess can be made for the three North Louisiana farm parishes of Caldwell, Franklin, and Morehouse, which had held out against Thurmond but went to the Wallace majority columns in 1968. For here, Negro population is relatively great (38 percent compared to the state average of 32 percent) but these parishes have held out against the registration of Negroes (11 percent compared to the state average of 20 percent).

We have seen that the degree of rurality, agricultural labor, and Negro population associates highly with Wallace and Thurmond support. Some association may also be demonstrated between level of industrial development and the vote. A "worker ratio" was computed which indicates the number of craftsmen and operators in the labor force for every one representative of the category that includes managers, officials, and proprietors. This indicator can tell us two things: where the relative incidence of management (and thus industrialization) is higher and where the relative number of workingmen is greater. Thus, as expected, we find that where the percentage in agriculture is lowest, industrial development is greatest. But in the farm areas the worker ratios are higher, which measure a large proportion of the labor force working in secondary industry such as lumber and paper mills. We find, then, that the higher the worker ratio in every region, the higher the Wallace vote.

A complex relationship exists between the incidence of industrial workers on the one hand and its unionization on the other. Quite clearly the relatively low level of union membership in Louisiana (28 percent of national labor force, but only 12.6 percent of the state's) occurs in the more urban (and industrial) parishes. The higher the worker ratio (but the lower the incidence of organized labor), the higher the Wallace support. Organized labor's elected leaders have regularly endorsed the candidates of the Democrats, but precinct data have shown rank-and-file labor increasingly less inclined to go along. In Louisiana, in 1968, white labor (at least) leaned heavily to the conservative side.

If resistance to change is behind the voters' alienation from the Democratic Party in Louisiana, then this circumstance may contradict the assumption that liberal attitudes follow inevitably from modernization. Practicing politicians of course have always used the electoral material available. Demagogues mobilized an apathetic electorate in the twenties and more recently segregationists have done so again, finding that the old dynamic of white supremacy "works more easily than any still emerging." [40] The rise in voter turnout in Louisiana coincides with increasing industry and urban residence—but it has taken federal civil rights laws to make it effective. While it may be considered political suicide to take a stand which helps to open the door to new options, Negro and white leaders have been doing so in New Orleans and as a result this city has been carried by the Democrats in three successive presidential elections, with the aid of increasing numbers of black voters. The crucial question is what direction white labor will take—whether many of these voters will return to the Democratic Party or will continue to shift to the GOP and turn Louisiana into solid Republican territory.

[40] Thomas Ktsanes, "Introduction," *Journal of Social Issues*, XXII (1966), 3.

12

SOUTH CAROLINA
Partisan Prelude

CHESTER W. BAIN

For a state approaching its tricentennial celebration, twenty years is a very short span of time. But the significance of changes is much more important than the length of time during which they occurred. This is true for many aspects of the political history of South Carolina, for in the period from 1948 through 1968, and especially in the last few of these years, South Carolina began to break up a political pattern that had dominated its politics since Reconstruction and to move toward the type of partisanship identified strongly with American political theory and with actual political practice in many other states of the Union.

This chapter tells a portion of the story of that change. It is not a complete story, for the period is still too near, too many facts are not available, and the interrelationships of the many elements involved are still tangled and blurred. But a new phase in South Carolina politics has commenced and partial accounting is not difficult to justify. Furthermore, the analysis which follows does not attempt to provide a comprehensive political history of the period. Rather, emphasis is placed primarily on the changes that took place in the election process between 1948 and 1968 and on how these changes relate to the earlier conditions described by V. O. Key.[1] The evidence leads to the inescapable conclusion that a new phase

Chester W. Bain is Olin D. Johnston Professor of Political Science, University of South Carolina.

1 V. O. Key, Jr., *Southern Politics in State and Nation* (New York: Knopf, 1949).

has commenced in South Carolina politics and that many traditional patterns have been drastically and irrevocably altered. That
new phase represents the early stages of partisanism in the election
process.

The Order Changeth

South Carolina in 1968 was both similar to and different from what
it was twenty years earlier. Because many of the changes embody
factors generally regarded as relevant to political activity, a brief
account of some of them is in order. There are several gaps in the
presentation, however, for much of the pertinent data will not be
available until the results of the 1970 census are published. A reliable indication can nevertheless be given of the major changes in
the state's total population, its general redistributions, its racial
composition, and the types of employment opportunities. Also pertinent to this analysis is a brief review of the major geographic divisions of the state.

The total population of South Carolina increased 12.5 percent
between 1950 and 1960 and has continued to grow since that time,
although at a rate of growth estimated to be slightly lower than the
national average. Statistically, South Carolina is still not urban
when compared with the national average of 69.9 percent urban
dwellers, even though the state increased from 36.7 percent in 1950
to 41.2 percent in 1960. Moreover, during this census period the
state had no cities with more than a hundred thousand inhabitants,
only three with more than fifty thousand, three with twenty-five to
fifty thousand, and nine with ten to twenty-five thousand.

These statistics may be somewhat misleading for political analysis, however, for by 1968 South Carolina had within its boundaries
three Standard Metropolitan Statistical Areas (SMSAs)—Charleston
(with Charleston and Berkeley counties), Columbia (Richland and
Lexington counties), and Greenville (Greenville and Pickens
counties)—and Aiken was a part of the Augusta, Georgia–South
Carolina SMSA. One of the major urban centers was in the low
country, a second was in the up-country (or Piedmont) section, and

an urban corridor of three counties extended from the center of the state westward to the Georgia state line. This distribution in the small state put all the population except that in the extreme eastern section in close proximity to a rapidly changing urban center and made most of the people subject to the influences generated by changes in these centers.

As has been true in other states, many areas of South Carolina have grown rapidly while others have declined. Between 1950 and 1960 twenty-one of the state's forty-six counties lost population, two of them by over 10 percent and ten of them by 5 to 10 percent. The counties losing population included fourteen of the twenty-one that had over 50 percent nonwhite populations in 1950. Twenty-five counties gained population—two of them by more than 50 percent and six of them by 25 to 50 percent. Some of the greatest gains are explained by the enlargement of military installations. As has also been true in other states, the urban fringes in South Carolina have grown at a faster rate than the central cities. Between 1950 and 1960 the urbanized areas increased 88.9 percent and the central city 46.1 percent, while the urban fringes increased 165.6 percent. The impression generally prevails that these trends have substantially continued since the 1960 census was taken.

The proportion of Negroes in the state's total population has steadily declined for a number of decades. In 1950, the early part of the period covered by this study, 38.8 percent of the state's population was nonwhite, and this level declined four percentage points by 1960. The ratios in the counties ranged from a low of 10.1 percent in Pickens to a high of 68.3 percent in Clarendon. Fifteen counties had populations over 50 percent Negro and fourteen had under 30 percent. These counties are identified in Figure 1.

An important fact for this study is that the proportion of Negro population dropped in every county except Fairfield, which had an increase of less than one percentage point. Even the counties with large population increases had substantial drops in the proportion of Negroes. This fact and other information make it clear that the urban areas generally were absorbing groups other than Negroes leaving surrounding counties in search of better economic oppor-

Figure 1

DISTRIBUTION OF NONWHITES IN SOUTH CAROLINA COUNTIES

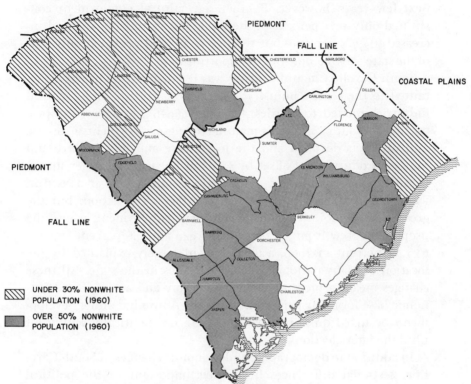

UNDER 30% NONWHITE
POPULATION (1960)

OVER 50% NONWHITE
POPULATION (1960)

tunities. All these trends continued after 1960, but exact figures are not yet available.

Another politically significant change in 1948–68 concerned employment opportunities.[2] Throughout much of its history South Carolina was primarily oriented to agriculture. As late as 1940 agriculture, forestry, and fisheries accounted for 39.6 percent of the state's employment, and manufacturing for 22.8 percent. In 1950

2 The statistical information on employment was taken from Charles E. Edwards, "Introduction—The South Carolina Economy in Perspective," in Charles E. Edwards (ed.), *The South Carolina Economy in Transition*, Essays in Economics (Columbia: Bureau of Business and Economic Research, College of Business Administration, University of South Carolina, 1967), 1–8.

these two types of employment still provided over 60 percent of South Carolina's total. The distribution changed rapidly in the next few years, however. By 1966 agricultural employment constituted only 12.5 percent of the total, and manufacturing had increased to 37.4 percent—but the two combined provided only half of the state's total employment opportunities.

South Carolina manufacturing was for many years heavily committed to the textile industry and to those apparel and chemical industries related to textiles. During 1960–65, however, the proportion of South Carolina's manufacturing employment in textile mill products declined and the losses here and in furniture and lumber products were offset by gains in apparel and other manufacturing categories. In this same period, employment increased in wholesale and retail trade and in contract construction, but the greatest change of all was in government employment, where the proportion grew from 2.6 percent in 1940 and 9.6 percent in 1950 to 14.4 percent in 1966, a development largely explained by the location of many national defense activities in the state. All these changes meant a more diversified economy and an improved economic base for many persons in the state. A number of the developments occurred quite recently and were not politically significant until the later elections.

In addition to demographic and economic changes in South Carolina, sectional differences have been important in the political process. In the past, two basic regions have been identified as useful for political analysis, and the division continues to be relevant for this study. The first is the upper-state, or Piedmont, region lying north and west of the fall line, which, as shown in Figure 1, traverses the state on a southwestern-northeastern axis. This region comprises twenty counties, two of them constituting the Greenville SMSA. Generally speaking, the counties in this grouping have relatively low percentages of Negro population, large numbers of textile rather than agricultural workers, and higher median family incomes than much of the remainder of the state. Only three counties in this region had over 50 percent nonwhite populations in 1960, and eleven of the fourteen counties with under 30 percent nonwhites in 1960 were located here. Despite its industrial base, only three counties were over 50 percent urban, with the population in the other counties grouped in relatively small governmental units and subdivisions.

The Coastal Plains make up the second major region of the state. This region comprises twenty-six counties lying south and east of the fall line and between the Georgia state line on the west and the North Carolina line on the northeast. In contrast to the Piedmont, these counties have high percentages of Negro population and lower median family incomes. Charleston and Richland are the only counties with significant levels of urbanization, and almost half the counties are less than 25 percent urban. Twelve of the fifteen counties with over 50 percent nonwhite population in 1960 are in this region, but only three of the fourteen with under 30 percent nonwhite are included. Much of the region was devoted to agriculture and fishing during the period of this study, although many new industries and defense installations have located here in the last few years. Once again, however, these developments were so recent that so far they have had only limited effects on political activities in the Coastal Plains.

A third region of South Carolina is frequently identified. Known as the Pee Dee, it consists of those counties bordering on North Carolina at the northeast and extending south and somewhat west to the Lynches River. There are six counties in this grouping— Chesterfield, Darlington, Dillon, Marlboro, Marion, and Florence —to which some people add Horry. Chesterfield is in the Piedmont and the others are in the Coastal Plains. The Pee Dee grouping was not found significant for this study, however, and the counties therein are included in the two major geographic regions of which they are a part. All other categories used here are based on socioeconomic factors and are explained in the context of the subjects being examined. The first to be considered is the change that took place in South Carolina voter registration during the years between 1948 and 1968.

The Right to Participate

Citizen participation in the selection of public officials is a *sine qua non* of the American political system. Consequently, trends in enfranchisement are considered valid clues to political developments within a particular governmental unit. The most obvious and readily available index of enfranchisement is the number of persons registered to vote.

But registration figures are not always a satisfactory base against which to measure certain types of political activity. The principal reason is that most places have either permanent or long-term registration periods and have not yet solved the problem of keeping their voting lists current. Where the lists are not regularly reviewed, the registration figures include an undetermined number of persons who are deceased or who have moved to another location, and therefore caution must be exercised in using registration figures as a base for analyzing political participation. Despite this possible shortcoming, however, a review of the trends in voter registration can give some insight into the politics of a people.

During the twenty years covered in this study, there was a definite increase in the number of voters registered in South Carolina.[3] Table 1 gives the total registration in two-year intervals from 1948 through 1968 and relates these totals to the population twenty-one years of age and over. The figures for 1958 and 1968 are perhaps the most significant, for new statewide registrations were held in those years in accordance with the state's policy of ten-year registration periods.[4] As of the 1958 registration, 43.8 percent of the voting-age population were registered to vote. The total number registered and the proportion of the voting-age population included in this total steadily increased through 1966. Although the total registration in

[3] The general qualifications for registration are United States citizenship, at least 21 years of age, one year's residence in the state, a literacy test, and none of the general disqualifications.

[4] For a description of the present procedure, see Robert H. Stoudemire, "Voter Registration in South Carolina," *South Carolina Governmental Review*, X (August, 1968).

Table 1

VOTER REGISTRATION
IN SOUTH CAROLINA, 1948–1968

Year	Voting-age Population*	Registered Voters	
		Number†	Percent of VAP
1968	1,396,000	853,014‡	61.1
1966	1,353,000	888,090	65.6
1964	1,310,000	772,572	59.0
1962	1,288,000	666,694	51.8
1960	1,266,251	595,989	47.1
1958	1,223,000	536,205‡	43.8
1956	1,199,000	761,162	63.5
1954	1,182,000	701,079	59.3
1952	1,164,000	625,000	53.7
1950	1,150,787	567,467	49.3
1948	1,069,000	506,818§	47.1

* The figures for 1950 and 1960 are from the United States census reports; those for 1948, 1952, 1956, 1964, and 1968 are from the United States Bureau of the Census, *Statistical Abstract, 1967,* p. 378; and those for 1954, 1958, 1962, and 1966 were computed by averaging the difference between the figures for the preceding and the succeeding periods. The heading is abbreviated as VAP.

† The figures for 1956–68 are from the *Supplemental Report of the Secretary of State to the General Assembly of South Carolina: Election November 5, 1968, and Primary of June 11, 1968* (Columbia: Printed Under the Direction of the State Budget and Control Board, n.d.), 59. The figures for 1948, 1950, and 1954 were furnished by the Executive Director, South Carolina State Democratic Executive Committee. The figure for 1952 is an estimate reported in the Columbia *State,* November 2, 1952, p. 12-E.

‡ New registration of all voters.

§ Designated as the "enrollment" of the Democratic Party.

1968 was lower than that of 1966, the decrease was not nearly so pronounced as had been the difference between the 1956 registration and the new registration in 1958. The sharp increase in the number of registered voters between 1958 and 1968 undoubtedly helps explain the increase in the level of voting described further below.

A most significant development in South Carolina politics between 1948 and 1968 was the increase in the number of Negroes who registered to vote. In 1947 only 13 percent of the Negroes of voting age were registered.[5] When the books closed for the new registration in 1968, thirty days before the November general election, a total of 853,014 persons had registered, of which 200,778, or 23.4 percent, were Negroes.[6] On the basis of 1960 census figures (obviously not accurate for 1968), 54.1 percent of the Negro population of voting age were registered. While this figure was still considerably below the 72.8 percent of the white population of voting age that were registered, the increase in Negro registration from 13 to 54 percent, most of which occurred in the 1960's, was a decided improvement.

Although a simple causal relationship is not suggested, it can be noted that the enfranchisement of a significant number of Negroes came after the demise of the white primary. In the one-party southern states, nomination in the Democratic primary was usually tantamount to election. By being denied a vote in the party primary, Negroes, even if they had been registered to vote, were barred from effective participation in the selection of all public officials except the presidential electors, who are chosen in the general election. When the United States Supreme Court declared the exclusion of Negroes from the primaries to be unconstitutional,[7] South Carolina responded by repealing all statutory and constitutional provisions relating to primaries.[8] The primaries were then conducted under rules prescribed by the Democratic Party, until this practice too was struck down by the United States district court in *Elmore v. Rice*.[9] The Democratic Party then sought to evade the effect of these rulings by vesting the nomination of candidates for political office in private clubs from which Negroes were barred, a practice which

[5] Donald R. Matthews and James W. Prothro, *Negroes and the New Southern Politics* (New York: Harcourt, Brace and World, 1966), 148.

[6] *Supplemental Report of the Secretary of State to the General Assembly of South Carolina: Election November 5, 1968, and Primary of June 11, 1968* (Columbia: South Carolina State Budget and Control Board, n.d.), 61.

[7] *Smith v. Allwright*, 321 U.S. 649 (1944).

[8] S.C., *Acts*, 1944, No. 810, pp. 2323–25; S.C. Constitution, Art. II, Sec. 10 (1895).

[9] 72 F. Supp. 516 (E.D.S.C. 1947); 165 F.2d 387 (4th Cir. 1947); certiorari denied, 333 U.S. 875 (1948).

was also declared to violate the United States Constitution.[10] Since then, no further general effort has been made to bar Negroes from the Democratic primaries.

Again, although causality is not meant to be implied, it is evident that the enfranchisement of a significant number of Negroes also came after the 1959 report of the United States Commission on Civil Rights. In its comments on South Carolina, the commission noted that in 1958 "nonwhites were 10.8 percent of all registered voters," and that the "number of nonwhites registered in 1958 represented 14.9 percent of the total 1950 population of voting-age nonwhites." [11] The commission further reported that "in 15 counties, nonwhites were a majority of the 1950 voting-age population. In one of these counties, no nonwhite was registered to vote in 1958. In four of the other 14 counties, the number of nonwhites registered in 1958 was fewer than 5 percent of the county's 1950 voting-age nonwhite population." [12] The contrast between these conditions and those found after the 1968 registration are little less than startling. The comparative information is given in Table 2.

The striking degree of change in the level of Negro registration from 1958 to 1968 can be further illustrated by examining the registration at the county level. After the 1958 registration the county with the *highest* percentage of nonwhites registered (Greenville) had 23.6 percent, whereas after the 1968 registration the county with the *lowest* percentage (Anderson) had 31.2 percent. No county had as many as 50 percent of its nonwhites registered in 1958. After the 1968 registration only sixteen counties had registered less than 50 percent of the nonwhite voting-age population, and three counties had registered more than 70 percent. In Beaufort and Dorchester counties the percentage of nonwhites registered was higher than the percentage of whites. Although the percentage of the white

[10] *Brown v. Baskin*, 78 F. Supp. 933 (E.D.S.C. 1948), and *Baskin v. Brown*, 174 F. 2d 391 (4th Cir. 1949).

[11] *Report of the United States Commission on Civil Rights, 1959* (Washington: Government Printing Office, 1959), 47. The nonwhites registered totaled 57,978 out of a 1950 population base of 390,024.

[12] *Ibid*. The correct number of counties is forty-six, not forty-seven.

Table 2

PROPORTION OF VOTING-AGE POPULATION REGISTERED IN SOUTH CAROLINA, BY COUNTY AND BY RACE, 1958 AND 1968

Registered Voters, 1968

County	Voting-age Population, 1960*		Number†		Percentage of VAP		Percentage of VAP Registered, 1958‡	
	White	Nonwhite	White	Negro	White	Negro	White	Nonwhite
Abbeville	8,733	3,215	5,998	1,229	68.7	38.2	60.6	3.2
Aiken	33,646	10,040	26,769	5,129	79.6	51.1	91.2	17.8
Allendale§¶	2,531	3,205	2,222	1,909	87.8	59.6	100.0	3.6
Anderson	47,542	9,598	26,186	2,996	55.1	31.2	55.6	16.3
Bamberg	4,371	3,807	3,698	2,246	84.6	59.0	72.7	8.8
Barnwell¶	5,652	3,242	5,542	2,234	98.1	68.9	100.0	11.1
Beaufort	12,098	7,247	5,850	4,359	48.4	60.1	50.1	16.9
Berkeley	10,122	7,619	11,451	6,069	88.4	79.7	86.3	23.5
Calhoun§	2,623	3,318	2,166	1,451	82.6	43.7	63.2	1.7
Charleston	77,909	35,499	51,748	18,560	66.4	52.3	55.3	21.3
Cherokee	16,037	3,360	12,037	1,817	75.1	54.1	69.3	18.0
Chester	11,172	5,664	8,068	3,052	72.2	53.9	75.1	10.0
Chesterfield	12,099	5,219	10,944	3,445	90.5	66.0	68.2	23.1
Clarendon§	5,223	7,735	5,316	4,677	98.3	60.5	67.5	3.5
Colleton§	8,203	6,180	7,220	3,550	88.0	57.4	71.7	10.9
Darlington	16,706	9,900	13,167	5,103	78.8	51.5	67.4	23.4
Dillon	8,725	5,529	6,773	2,695	77.6	48.7	58.1	12.5
Dorchester¶	7,121	5,370	9,019	4,557	79.0	84.9	89.9	7.1
Edgefield§	4,103	3,764	3,538	1,207	86.2	32.1	78.0	6.3
Fairfield§	4,975	5,536	4,163	3,627	83.7	65.5	81.0	12.6
Florence	27,047	15,951	22,910	9,549	84.7	59.9	65.3	11.2
Georgetown§	8,855	7,173	7,743	4,594	87.4	64.0	58.1	12.4

Greenville	102,365	18,605	64,793	8,884	63.3	47.8	56.7	23.6
Greenwood	19,218	6,764	14,648	2,942	76.2	43.5	60.1	12.4
Hampton§	4,711	4,052	4,223	2,391	89.6	59.0	69.5	5.4
Horry	27,518	7,429	18,869	3,822	68.6	51.4	63.3	17.6
Jasper§¶	2,689	3,333	2,131	1,610	79.2	48.3	90.6	14.9
Kershaw	11,258	5,903	10,070	2,629	89.4	44.5	91.4	15.3
Lancaster	16,213	4,762	14,097	2,669	86.9	56.0	82.9	17.5
Laurens	19,775	6,818	12,569	2,971	63.6	43.6	53.3	12.7
Lee§	4,394	5,446	4,045	2,778	92.1	51.0	91.2	11.9
Lexington	28,774	4,782	26,481	3,142	92.0	65.7	68.4	4.5
McCormick§	1,915	2,248	1,748	1,136	91.3	50.5	67.4	0.0
Marion§	8,103	7,684	5,868	3,659	72.4	47.6	65.0	11.2
Marlboro	8,230	5,932	7,146	3,105	86.8	52.3	81.9	5.3
Newberry	12,204	4,954	10,030	2,226	82.2	44.9	63.7	8.4
Oconee	19,762	2,230	12,430	1,119	62.9	50.2	41.6	22.8
Orangeburg§¶	16,381	17,355	15,121	12,212	92.3	70.4	65.6	11.6
Pickens	24,015	2,356	15,716	1,116	65.4	47.4	52.3	12.6
Richland	79,050	32,670	52,137	19,823	66.0	60.7	52.9	23.5
Saluda	5,573	2,327	4,790	1,379	86.0	59.3	75.0	7.3
Spartanburg	73,317	17,047	52,374	7,277	71.4	42.7	60.7	18.1
Sumter	22,004	15,380	12,523	7,663	56.9	49.8	52.4	18.3
Union	12,826	4,125	10,958	2,070	85.4	50.2	88.8	21.0
Williamsburg§	7,560	10,535	6,771	6,475	89.6	61.5	81.3	1.9
York	31,799	10,196	20,027	3,598	63.0	35.3	58.9	22.1
STATE	895,147	371,104	652,096	200,778	72.8	54.1	63.2	14.8

* Bureau of the Census, 1960.

† Supplemental Report of the Secretary of State to the General Assembly of South Carolina: Election November 5, 1968, and Primary of June 11, 1968 (Columbia: Printed Under the Direction of the State Budget and Control Board, n.d.), 61.

‡ Report of the United States Commission on Civil Rights, 1959 (Washington: U.S. Government Printing Office, 1959), 572–73.

§ Counties with more than 50 percent nonwhite population in 1960.

¶ Counties under the Voting Rights Act of 1965.

population of voting age who were registered was generally higher than that of the nonwhite population, the gap certainly narrowed between the 1958 and the 1968 registrations. This development is a current one and its full effects on the state's politics may not yet be evident.

It should be noted that five South Carolina counties—Allendale, Barnwell, Dorchester, Jasper, and Orangeburg—are covered by the Voting Rights Act of 1965. A comparison of the changes in these five counties with changes in the other counties, especially the ones whose 1960 total populations were more than 50 percent nonwhite, reveals very little difference. Although the degree of indirect influence was not studied, one can safely conclude that the registration of nonwhites was carried out in most South Carolina counties with about the same degree of success as that experienced in the counties under the Voting Rights Act.

The Results: Increased Voting

The number of South Carolinians participating in statewide elections steadily increased during the twenty years covered in this study. Not surprisingly, however, voter participation tended to be highest in the presidential elections and where there was partisan competition in the general elections and strong competition in the primaries.[13]

This increased political participation was most clearly reflected in the choice of the state's presidential electors. As shown in Table 3, the vote in 1948 was 142,416, whereas the 1968 vote numbered 666,- 978—an increase of 524,562, or over 400 percent. In only one presidential election in this period was the total vote less than that in the preceding election. The drop came in 1956, when 40,503 fewer votes were cast than in 1952. This decrease is somewhat surprising in that three slates of presidential electors were offered—a condition which frequently results in a higher level of voting.

The overall rise cannot be attributed exclusively to the increase

13 All South Carolina primaries between 1948 and 1968 were held by the Democratic Party. The Republican Party nominated candidates in conventions.

in the number of persons aged twenty-one and over; it clearly shows greater participation by those who were previously eligible but not actually voting. This trend can be shown by comparing the ratios of votes cast to voting-age population. The difference between the presidential vote in 1948 and 1968 was 524,562, an increase considerably larger than the 327,000 difference between the voting-age populations of those two years. Again with the exception of 1956, the ratio of votes cast to voting-age population steadily increased from a low of 13.3 percent in 1948 to a new high of 47.8 percent in 1968. Despite the sharp gains, the state's level of participation in presidential elections continues to fall below the national average. The gap is rapidly narrowing, however, as is shown in Figure 2.

A similar trend can be observed by relating the presidential vote to the number of registered voters. Here we find an increase from a low of 28.1 percent in 1948 to a high of 78.2 percent in 1968. Although this index must be used with considerable caution, as noted

Figure 2

PERCENTAGE OF VOTING-AGE POPULATION OF SOUTH CAROLINA
VOTING IN SELECTED ELECTIONS, 1948–1968

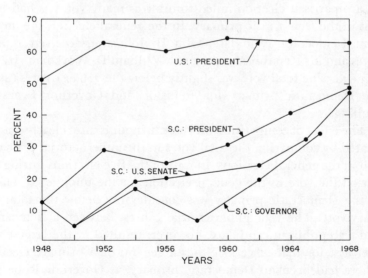

previously, the 1968 figure is especially valid because of the decennial registration in that year. In this particular election, most of those interested enough to vote took the trouble to register, and vice versa.

The total number of votes cast in South Carolina elections for United States senator and for governor also steadily increased during 1948–68. An analysis of this trend must include both the primary and general election results, however, for here we find clear evidence of the effect of competition on voter turnout. Comparative data are presented in Table 3.

After the election of 1950, in which the candidates who won the Democratic primary were unopposed, the total number of votes cast and the proportion of voting-age population who participated increased in every election except two. One exception came in 1958, when Ernest F. Hollings, the unopposed gubernatorial candidate, polled fewer votes than had been cast in the 1954 unopposed election for that office. The need for two primaries to select the Democratic candidate and the lack of elections for either the presidency or the United States Senate in that year probably account for the lower turnout. The second exception was in 1962 when, surprisingly, a bipartisan election failed to draw as many votes as had been cast in the Democratic primary. In the general election the incumbent Democratic candidate, Olin D. Johnston, received 178,712 votes and his Republican opponent, William D. Workman, Jr., got 133,930. The total vote was slightly below the 326,941 votes cast in the Democratic primary for Johnston and Governor Ernest F. Hollings.

The effect of competition on voter turnout is most clearly demonstrated by comparing the total votes in the gubernatorial primaries and in the general elections. In four of the five elections during this period the vote in the general election for the unopposed winner of the Democratic primary was considerably below the total primary vote. The 1966 gubernatorial contest between a Democratic and a Republican candidate, however, resulted in the largest vote ever cast for that office in either a general or a primary election. There had been no Democratic primary, as Governor Robert E.

Table 3
Voter Participation for President, United States Senator, and Governor in South Carolina, 1948–1968

Election Year	Voting-age Population*	President		U. S. Senator				Governor			
				Election		Primary		Election		Primary	
		Vote†	Percentage of VAP	Vote†	Percentage of VAP	Vote‡	Percentage of VAP	Vote†	Percentage of VAP	Vote‡	Percentage of VAP
1968	1,396,000	666,978	47.8	652,855	46.8	392,929	28.1				
1966	1,353,000			435,822§	32.2	323,000	23.9	439,942	32.5		
1964	1,310,000	524,779	40.1	436,252¶	32.2	299,271	22.1				
1962	1,288,000			312,647	24.3	326,941	25.4	253,720§§	19.7	328,291	25.5
1960	1,266,251	386,687	30.5	330,269§§	26.1	305,931	24.2				
1958	1,223,000							77,740§§	6.4	377,239	30.8
										335,853**	27.5
1956	1,199,000	300,583	25.1	245,371††§§	20.5						
				279,969¶	23.4						
1954	1,182,000			227,209	19.2			214,211§§	18.1	302,483	25.6
1952	1,164,000	341,086	29.3								
1950	1,150,787			50,495§§	4.4	345,084	30.0	50,642§§	4.4	346,329	30.1
1948	1,069,000	142,416	13.3	141,006§§	13.2	314,018	29.4				

For source see Table 1. Includes population twenty-one and over. Abbreviated as VAP in other columns.

† The returns are those reported in the *Supplemental Report of the Secretary of State to the General Assembly of South Carolina*. These reports are issued separately but are included in *Reports and Resolutions of South Carolina* (Columbia: Joint Committee on Printing, General Assembly of South Carolina) for the fiscal year in which the election occurred.

‡ The returns through 1962 are from Frank E. Parker, Jr., *The Primary State: A History of the Democratic Party in South Carolina, 1896–1962* (Columbia: R. L. Bryan Co., 1968). Those for 1966 and 1968 are from the *Supplemental Report of the Secretary of State to the General Assembly of South Carolina* for the years indicated and are bound as indicated in the preceding note.

§ Election for a two-year term.
¶ Election for a six-year term.
§§ Unopposed candidate.
** Second (runoff) primary.
†† Election for a four-year term.

McNair, who was completing the unexpired term of Governor Donald S. Russell, had no Democratic opposition. The bipartisan contest with the Republican nominee, Joseph G. Rogers, Jr., undoubtedly accounts for the high level of voter interest in this particular office.

Voting participation in the United States Senate elections presented another interesting pattern. Of the four regular and one special elections from 1948 to 1960, primaries were held in only two contests, in 1948 and in 1950, and the voter turnout was much greater than in the general elections, where the primary winners were unopposed. The Senate elections held during 1960–68, again consisting of four regular and one special contests, presented a quite different picture. In all five elections in this period, primaries were held to choose the nominees of the Democratic Party and two-party competition was present in four of the general elections. In three of these four partisan elections, the vote exceeded the primary vote by substantial numbers and in the proportion of the voting-age population which participated. Only in 1962 did the Democratic primary attract more voters than did the two-party race in the ensuing general election, and the difference between the totals was less than fifteen thousand.

The foregoing analysis clearly indicates that South Carolinians steadily increased their participation in the election process during 1948–68. Although the level of voting in the state continues to fall below the national average, since 1956 South Carolina has steadily moved closer to the national level. An obvious factor in this rising participation, besides the increased number of registered voters, is the unprecedented competition for votes, whether in the general elections or in the primaries. The South Carolina experience during the past twenty years adequately demonstrates that as competition increases, so does voter turnout. Should the trends evidenced in recent years continue—and there is every indication that they will— even more South Carolinians will take an active role in the selection of their government officials, and many further changes will occur in the political behavior of the state.

A Spell Is Broken

Against this background of changes in the extent of the total vote in South Carolina during 1948–68, attention may now focus on how the vote was distributed. This section examines the voting patterns in the presidential elections during this period as seen in partisan distribution of the vote and in certain geographic and socioeconomic variables.

A standard variable in studies of voting behavior is the degree of partisan competition found in the elections for public office. For a number of years, classifications of the political systems of the fifty states have identified South Carolina as a one-party state, dominated by the Democrats.[14] A familiar index of South Carolina voters' support of and identification with the Democratic Party is found in the state's vote for presidential electors.[15] Democratic slates polled overwhelming percentages of the popular vote in every election from 1900 through 1944. The details are given in Table 4. The lowest proportion received during this period was in 1944, when the Democratic electors received 87.6 percent of the popular vote. The high was 98.6 percent in 1936.

Presidential electors for the Republican Party received only token support during the same period. The greatest support came in 1900, when Republican electors received 7 percent of the popular vote. At the other end of the scale is the 1.1 percent of the popular vote the Republicans received in the 1912 election.

The highest percentage of votes won by slates of electors other than those supporting Democratic or Republican candidates came in 1944. In that election 7.5 percent of the popular vote went to the Southern Democrats and 0.4 percent went to the Prohibition electors. In three of the twelve elections in the 1900–44 period, there

[14] A recent example is found in Herbert Jacob and Kenneth N. Vines (eds.), *Politics in the American States* (Boston: Little, Brown and Company, 1965), 63–70.

[15] An excellent study of this topic, which has been used extensively in the preparation of this section, is Donald L. Fowler, *Presidential Voting in South Carolina, 1948–1964* (Columbia: Bureau of Governmental Research and Service, University of South Carolina, 1966).

Table 4

STATEWIDE VOTE FOR PRESIDENTIAL
ELECTORS IN SOUTH CAROLINA, 1900–1944

Year	Total Vote	Democratic Vote	Democratic Percentage	Republican* Vote	Republican* Percentage	Other Vote	Other Percentage
1900	50,792	47,233	93.0	3,559	7.0	—	—
1904	55,670	53,100	95.4	2,570	4.6	—	—
1908	66,397	62,290	93.8	3,963	6.0	144†	0.2
1912	50,350	48,357	96.0	536	1.1	1,457‡	2.9
1916	63,952	61,846	96.7	1,550	2.4	556§	0.9
1920	66,808	64,170	96.1	2,244	3.4	394¶	0.6
1924	50,755	49,008	96.6	1,123	2.2	624¶¶	1.2
1928	68,605	62,700	91.4	3,188	4.7	2,717**	4.0
1932	104,407	102,347	98.0	1,978	1.9	82††	0.1
1936	115,437	113,791	98.6	1,646	1.4	—	—
1940	99,838	95,470	95.6	1,864	1.9	2,496‡‡	2.5
1944	103,382	90,601	87.6	4,617	4.5	8,164§§	7.9

Source: Reproduced, with slight changes, from Donald L. Fowler, *Presidential Politics in South Carolina, 1948–1964* (Columbia: Bureau of Governmental Research and Service, University of South Carolina, 1966), 15.

* In 1936, 1940, and 1944 there were two Republican slates of electors.
† Independents 100, Socialists 44.
‡ Progressives 1,293, Socialists 164.
§ Progressive Republicans 259, Progressives 162, Socialists 135.
¶ Insurgent referendum 366, Socialists 26, Socialists (Debs Faction) 2.
¶¶ Progressives 623, Andrew Gump 1.
** Anti-Smith Democrats 2,670, Socialists 47.
†† Socialists 82.
‡‡ Jeffersonian Democrats 2,496.
§§ Southern Democrats 7,799, Prohibition 365.

were no third- or fourth-party slates. Summarizing the dominance of the Democratic Party, Donald L. Fowler notes that "not a single county in South Carolina gave a majority vote to any slate of electors other than the national Democratic party." [16]

Presidential elections since 1944 had quite different results. In the elections from 1948–1968 Democratic electors were victorious on only three occasions—in 1952, with 50.7 percent of the popular vote; in 1956, with 45.4 percent; and in 1960, with 51.2 percent. The lowest point for the Democratic Party came in 1948, when its

16 *Ibid.*, 14.

slate of electors received 24.1 percent of the vote, as compared with the 72.1 percent received by the States' Rights electors pledged to the native-son candidate J. Strom Thurmond. Democratic electors were also in the minority in 1964 and 1968, when Republican electors carried the state. Selected details of these six elections are presented in Table 5.

Table 5
STATEWIDE VOTE FOR PRESIDENTIAL
ELECTORS IN SOUTH CAROLINA, 1948–1968

Year	Total Vote	Democratic Vote	Percentage	Republican Vote	Percentage	Other* Vote	Percentage
1948	142,416	34,423	24.1	5,386	3.8	102,607	72.1
1952	341,086	172,957	50.7	9,775	2.9	158,243	46.4
1956	300,583	136,372	45.4	75,700	25.2	88,511	29.4
1960	386,687	198,129	51.2	188,558	48.8	—	—
1964	524,779	215,723	41.1	309,048	58.9	—	—
1968	666,978	197,486	29.6	254,062	38.1	215,430	32.3

Source: See Table 3[†].
* Four different slates of electors are included: 1948—the States' Rights slate pledged to J. Strom Thurmond; 1952—the Independents for Eisenhower; 1956—South Carolinians for Independent Electors, who were pledged to Senator Harry F. Byrd; and 1968—the Independent Party slate pledged to George C. Wallace. A few write-in votes were excluded.

In his impressive study of presidential voting in South Carolina during 1948–64, Fowler found several distinctive patterns of voting behavior in the forty-six counties of the state. One such pattern occurred in the group of counties in the Coastal Plains. After excluding Richland, Charleston, Aiken, and Lexington, because of their metropolitan status, Fowler found that the remaining twenty-two counties more consistently supported the Republican and independent candidates in every election than any other grouping of counties. "Eleven of these twenty-two counties ranked in the top fifty percentile of all counties in support of the Republican and independent candidates in all five of the elections under analysis. One other was in the top twenty-three in four of the five elections, and

four more in three of the five elections. Only two counties—Marlboro and Dillon—failed to rank in the top twenty-three counties in
percent of vote for the Republican and independent candidates in
any of the five." [17] Fowler summarizes the influence of the racial factor in this grouping: "In the greater number of cases the candidates
who received majorities from these counties favored racial policies
which were more congenial to the southern point of view, or at least
less hostile to it." [18] During these five presidential elections majority
support moved from Strom Thurmond, to Dwight D. Eisenhower,
to Harry F. Byrd, to Richard Nixon, to Barry Goldwater.

Another area of the state in which Fowler found a distinctive
voting pattern in the five elections was the Piedmont. These twenty
counties provided the main source of support for the Democratic
Party during this period. Only one of them, Edgefield, ranked in the
top fifty percentile of all counties in support of the Republican and
independent candidates in all five elections. The other counties
were less consistent in their support. Three counties ranked in the
top fifty percentile (twenty-three counties) in four of the five elections, three others were in this grouping in three elections, two
other counties appeared in the ranking in two elections, and eight
others were included in only one election. Four counties—Abbeville,
Anderson, Chesterfield, and Oconee—failed to rank in the top
twenty-three counties in percentage of vote for the Republican and
independent candidates in any of the five elections. The greatest
deviation from the Democratic pattern came in 1956, when fifteen
counties ranked in the top twenty-three that supported either Eisenhower (twelve counties) or Byrd (three counties). The relatively
small percentage of Negro population in these counties is interpreted as the chief reason for the lesser appeal there of candidates who
favored racial policies more congenial to voters in the Coastal Plains.
Fowler observes that the Piedmont counties "have been the most
consistent supporters of the Democratic candidates in presidential
elections, but in 1956, 1960, and 1964 in the upper-income neigh-

17 *Ibid.*, 112.
18 *Ibid.*, 113.

borhoods of the towns and cities of this area, substantial support for Eisenhower, Nixon and Goldwater was evident." [19]

The metropolitan areas of the state had distinctive voting patterns. Fowler found that since the 1952 election, the metropolitan counties of Charleston, Richland, and Greenville "have ranked in the top twenty-three in percent of vote for the Republican and independent candidates, except Richland in the 1964 election. A close investigation discloses that, while these counties were strongly opposed to the Democrats, they were not consistent in whom they supported." [20] For example, Charleston County gave heavy support to Eisenhower in 1952, to Nixon in 1960, and to Goldwater in 1964. Richland County, which includes the city of Columbia, gave sizable support to Eisenhower in 1952, to Nixon in 1960, and to Goldwater in 1964. In 1956, however, Byrd received 42.5 percent and Eisenhower 30 percent of the total vote. Greenville, unlike the other counties in the Piedmont, gave strong support to Eisenhower in 1952 and 1956, to Nixon in 1960, and to Goldwater in 1964.

The pattern of voting evidenced in the presidential elections of 1948–64 tended to follow the basic socioeconomic features dominant in each of the geographical groupings. Fowler summarizes his findings in these words:

> While the analyses . . . have produced some varying results, they all suggest the substantial importance and relevance of racial and economic factors as basic correlates of the move away from the Democratic party toward Republican and independent positions. In the coastal, rural counties the presence of high percentages of Negro population seems to have forged substantial unity among white voters, while in the Piedmont counties the smaller concentrations of Negroes apparently permitted divisions among the white voters. These divisions seem to have occurred along economic lines. One could also suggest that the whites in the coastal counties were reflecting their relatively well-to-do economic status in voting against the Democrats because the Republican and independent candidates were generally presented as more economically conservative than the Democrats. The two parties apparently have groups of

19 *Ibid.*, 100.
20 *Ibid.*, 113.

strength in both principal areas of the state, i.e., the Republicans seem to have the allegiance of the whites in the coastal counties and the allegiance of the groups living in the upper-income wards and precincts in the urban areas of the Piedmont counties. On the other hand, the Democrats apparently command the loyalty of most working class whites in the Piedmont, and the loyalty of Negroes throughout the state.[21]

The presence of three strong presidential candidates in the 1968 election greatly complicated the already highly intricate task of analyzing voting patterns. This was especially true in South Carolina, where the 1968 election blurred and confused trends that appeared to be emerging between 1948 and 1964. The following analysis concentrates primarily on fitting the results of the most recent presidential contest into the previously described patterns.

A major difference between the 1968 presidential election and the preceding ones was the shift in the source of support for the Democratic Party electors from the Piedmont to the Coastal Plains. This shift was particularly evident in the Piedmont, which was the major area of support for the Democrats during the 1948–64 period, with some exception in 1956. The slate of electors for Hubert H. Humphrey carried only three of the twenty counties in this area, whereas the electors for Lyndon B. Johnson had carried thirteen in 1964. Democratic presidential electors won fewer South Carolina counties in 1968 than in any previous contest, and the 1968 election reduced to two, Chester and Fairfield, the number of counties that have remained in the Democratic column for every election considered in this study. George C. Wallace carried the largest number of counties in the Piedmont, a total of nine, while Richard M. Nixon won eight. Most of the state's counties went to the winner by pluralities, but in the Piedmont Wallace gained majorities in four counties, Nixon in two, and Humphrey in one.

With the exception of Greenville and Pickens, which gave Nixon majorities, the Piedmont counties were the major source of support for Wallace. Of the twenty-three counties that gave Wallace larger percentages of their vote than his statewide average, seventeen were

21 *Ibid.*, 78.

located in the Piedmont. Moreover, fifteen of the twenty-three counties (half of the state's total) which gave Wallace the highest percentage of vote were in this region. But the vote in this area was not
exclusively for Wallace. Seven of the eleven counties in which
Nixon polled higher than his statewide percentage were located in
this region. Moreover, eleven of the twenty-three counties which
gave Nixon the highest percentage of their vote were also in the
Piedmont. Humphrey trailed in both of these measures; only five
counties gave him better than his state average and only three were
in his top twenty-three counties.

Because of the low percentage of Negroes in the Piedmont counties it would seem that some variable other than race caused this
continuing shift of voters from the Democratic Party to the candidates of other political parties. As suggested earlier, that variable
seems to be an economic one. Clearly, in 1968 Wallace was the first
choice, with Nixon second, for the blue-collar, industrial, white
voters who predominate in the Piedmont. Whether this vote will
return to the Democratic column in future elections or will continue to support Republican or other party slates of electors is,
of course, impossible to predict.

The Coastal Plains counties, which had been the major base of
support for Thurmond, Eisenhower, Byrd, Nixon, and Goldwater,
provided the state's major support for the Democratic ticket in
1968, thereby emphasizing the significance of the increase in Negro
registration since 1964. Of the twenty-six Coastal Plains counties,
Humphrey carried sixteen, Wallace carried three, and Nixon carried seven. Nixon won the only county in this grouping, Richland,
that gave a majority to any candidate; the others were won by pluralities. President Johnson in 1964 had not carried a single county
in this group, and only eight of the counties were in his top twenty-
three.

Only Humphrey, who received 33.7 percent in the Coastal Plains,
exceeded his statewide percentage (29.6 percent) in the total vote
of this region. When the counties were taken separately, however,
it was found that Wallace ran better in twelve of these counties than
he had statewide, while Humphrey surpassed in twenty-one and

Table 6

COMPARISON OF VOTES RECEIVED STATEWIDE AND IN SELECTED CATEGORIES IN SOUTH CAROLINA ELECTIONS FOR PRESIDENT AND UNITED STATES SENATOR, 1968

Category	Humphrey		Nixon		Wallace		Hollings		Parker	
	Percentage	Deviation*	Percentage	Deviation*	Percentage	Deviation*	Percentage	Deviation*	Percentage	Deviation*
Statewide	29.6	—	38.1	—	32.3	—	61.9	—	38.1	—
Piedmont (20 counties)	24.4	− 5.2	38.4	+ 0.3	37.2	+ 4.9	61.0	− 0.9	39.0	+ 0.9
Coastal Plains (26 counties)	33.7	+ 4.1	37.8	− 0.3	28.4	− 3.9	62.6	+ 0.7	37.4	− 0.7
Counties with 50% of Negroes Registered (10)	30.1	+ 0.5	42.4	+ 4.3	27.0	− 5.3	60.3	− 1.6	39.7	+ 1.6
15 Counties with Highest Ratio of Negro to Total Registration	42.5	+ 12.9	29.2	− 8.9	28.3	− 4.0	68.2	+ 6.3	31.8	− 6.3
15 Counties with Lowest Ratio of Negro to Total Registration	22.5	− 7.1	40.2	+ 2.1	37.3	+ 5.0	59.0	− 2.9	41.0	+ 2.9
Counties with over 50% Nonwhite Population, 1960 (15)	41.9	+ 12.3	28.9	− 9.2	29.2	− 3.1	67.7	+ 5.8	32.3	− 5.8
Counties under 1965 Voting Rights Act	39.4	+ 9.8	27.0	− 11.1	33.6	+ 1.3	68.1	+ 6.2	31.9	− 6.2
Charleston County	32.8	+ 3.2	43.5	+ 5.4	23.7	− 8.6	64.2	+ 2.3	35.8	− 2.3
Greenville County	21.6	− 8.0	52.9	+ 14.8	25.5	− 6.8	52.9	− 9.0	47.1	+ 9.0
Richland County	35.4	+ 5.8	51.0	+ 12.9	13.7	− 18.6	57.9	− 4.0	42.1	+ 4.0

* Difference between percentage statewide and for category.

Nixon in only four their state averages. As was true in the Piedmont, Nixon's vote came mostly from the more urban, industrializ-
ing counties. The counties in this region that gave the heaviest
support to Wallace were, for the most part, those which are still primarily agricultural and in which there are large concentrations of
nonwhite population.

Other evidence also illustrates that race is still a significant factor
in the pattern of presidential voting in South Carolina. The 1968
Democratic candidate did poorly in the counties which previously
had supported that party's slate of electors, but he found substantial
support in the counties with the highest percentage of Negro voters.
Humphrey carried eighteen of the twenty-three counties with the
highest percentages of Negro registration and in the top fifteen of
these ran 12.9 percentage points above his statewide average, while
Nixon and Wallace fell below their state percentages in the same
counties. In marked contrast, Humphrey did not carry a single one
of the fifteen counties with the lowest percentages of Negro registration, and he ran far behind his statewide percentage in the combined vote for these counties, whereas Nixon and Wallace both ran
somewhat better here than they did statewide. Further evidence of
the influence of the racial factor is that Humphrey carried thirteen
and Nixon carried two of the fifteen counties which, according to
the 1960 census, had populations over 50 percent nonwhite. Humphrey also ran considerably above his state average in the combined
vote for these counties, whereas Nixon and Wallace fell below their
statewide averages.

Donald Fowler recently reported an analysis of a group of 198
precincts with 50 percent or more of the Negroes registered which
further emphasizes that the Negro vote was a major source of support for the Democratic candidate in South Carolina. Humphrey
won a majority in 188 and a plurality in 9 of these precincts, and
Wallace received a plurality in 1. Of the total votes cast in all the
precincts, Humphrey received 73.1 percent, Nixon 13.6 percent,
and Wallace 13.3 percent. Fowler reports that "the intensity of
Negro support for Mr. Humphrey can further be seen by categoriz-

ing the Negro precinct by level of Negro registration." He provides a useful table:

Percentage of Negro Registration	Humphrey	Nixon	Wallace
50.0–60.0	14,897 (55.5%)	5,718 (21.3%)	6,217 (23.2%)
60.1–70.0	13,858 (66.5%)	3,492 (17.3%)	2,839 (16.2%)
70.1–80.0	14,709 (74.9%)	2,551 (12.9%)	2,460 (12.5%)
80.1–90.0	8,773 (86.2%)	697 (6.8%)	713 (7.0%)
90.1–100.0	16,147 (97.5%)	272 (1.6%)	154 (.9%)

Fowler concludes, "There is a clear correlation between the percentage of Negro registration and the percent vote received by Mr. Humphrey; for example, the higher the Negro registration the higher the percentage of the vote received by him. In those precincts with 90.1 to 100 percent Negro registration, he received almost all of the vote." [22]

A pattern of support for Republican presidential electors which emerged in 1952 continued in 1968 in the three largest counties in the state—Charleston, Greenville, and Richland. Nixon carried all three counties, with only Charleston failing to give him a majority. Wallace ran far behind his state average in all three counties, but Nixon exceeded his statewide percentage by substantial margins. Humphrey, on the other hand, won uneven support, receiving better than his state average in Charleston and Richland, a result which is probably explained by the relatively high number of Negro voters in these counties. His poorest showing of the three was in Greenville, where only 12 percent of the total registration is Negro and the nonwhite population (as of 1960) was only 17.6 percent of the county's total. All three of these counties were in the top fifty percentile of the counties voting for Nixon, and Charleston and Richland were included in the twenty-three counties which gave

22 Donald L. Fowler, "The 1968 General Election in S.C.," *University of South Carolina Governmental Review*, XI (May, 1969), 4.

the highest percentage of their vote to Humphrey, but none of the three were in the twenty-three counties which gave the highest percentage of their vote to Wallace.

It is clear that the long dominance of the Democrats in South Carolina has been shaken and that the state can no longer be counted as "safe" for the presidential candidate of the national Democratic Party. There is also strong evidence that race is still an important variable in the presidential vote, with substantial numbers of white voters having abandoned long attachments to the Democratic Party in favor of candidates of other political parties. The recent emergence of a substantial number of registered Negroes, however, presents a new factor in South Carolina politics. In 1968 the black voter clearly considered the Democratic nominee his best choice. Where this vote will go in the future is uncertain. It is abundantly evident that in 1968 the vote in counties with large Negro populations and high levels of Negro registration generally split along racial lines, with the white vote distributed between Nixon and Wallace. Whether these voters will merge in future elections or will remain divided, with some returning to the Democratic column, is also impossible to predict.

The logical interpretation of Wallace's strong showing in those counties with a lower percentage of Negro voters—counties that had previously given strong support to the Democratic slate—is that voters in these counties were responding to appeals directed to pecuniary considerations. Further industrial development and the continued weakening of agriculture as the financial base of the state almost certainly means that economic factors will begin to mitigate the past dominance of race in South Carolina's voting pattern in presidential elections.

In 1968 it also became clear that the winner must have strong appeal in the more urban counties. Just over 50 percent of the registered voters in South Carolina in that year were in ten counties. Nixon, who carried only fourteen of the state's forty-six counties, carried eight of the ten most populous counties. The influence of these ten counties on the state's total vote is clear: their combined vote gave Nixon 52.9, Humphrey 50.2, and Wallace 48.8 percent of the total vote each received in the state. As urbanization increases, as interests become more diversified, and as the racial issue is mitigated by economic factors in these areas, a strong, two-party competition in future presidential elections appears to be a distinct possibility for South Carolina.

Further Defections

Leaving the presidential race and turning to other South Carolina elections, one finds the voting patterns much less distinct and considerably less evidence of an abandonment of the Democratic Party during 1948–68. Partisan competition has been present since 1956 in the election of members of the United States Senate and has spread, later and to a lesser degree, to the election of members of the national House of Representatives and possibly to selection of the governor. Partisan competition for other offices, while present in some parts of the state, is much more uncertain and problematic. The search for voting patterns in these elections must include senatorial and gubernatorial primaries and general elections, as well as contests for offices filled by subdivisions of the state.

South Carolina is technically a two-party state insofar as the United States Senate is concerned. This status was achieved when Senator J. Strom Thurmond crossed from the Democratic to the Republican side of the aisle on September 6, 1964, as another move in his long disagreement with many policies advocated by the Democratic Party. This was a major decision for Senator Thurmond, despite the substantial showing he had made in South Carolina against the Democratic Party in the 1948 presidential election, for he had first entered the Senate wearing the Democratic label that was so strongly identified with South Carolina.

Thurmond was first elected to the Senate by an overwhelming write-in vote in 1954.[23] Senator Burnet Rhett Maybank, who had been renominated by the Democratic Party without opposition,

---

[23] This story is described in W. D. Workman, Jr., *The Bishop from Barnwell: The Political Life and Times of Senator Edgar A. Brown* (Columbia, S.C.: R. L. Bryan Co., 1963), 239–75.

died on September 1, 1954, just three days before the date set by law for party certification of nominees to be placed on the general election ballot.[24] The State Democratic Executive Committee in extraordinary session nominated State Senator Edgar A. Brown to carry the Democratic standard, a move which created so much ill feeling that it led to the successful write-in movement for Thurmond. In an unprecedented political event, Thurmond was the winner with 143,444 votes (63.4 percent) to 83,525 for Brown and 240 for Marcus A. Stone, another write-in candidate. Senator Thurmond resigned on April 4, 1956, pursuant to a 1954 campaign promise "to place the office in a primary." He had no opposition in the general election in his 1956 bid for the remaining four years of the term and for a full term in 1960, but ran against R. Beverly Herbert in the Democratic primary.

In 1966, after he had made the switch to the Republican Party, Senator Thurmond was opposed in the general election by P. Bradley Morrah, Jr., who had defeated John Bolt Culbertson in the Democratic primary. Thurmond received 62.2 percent of the popular vote and became the first and only Republican South Carolina has elected to the United States Senate in this century. Because of the strong personal factors in Senator Thurmond's case, however, it is unrealistic to regard this election as a Republican victory or to infer from the distribution of the vote that South Carolina has definitely moved from the Democratic to the Republican Party in the selection of its national senators.

Considerable partisan competition has been seen in recent years for the Senate seat now held by Senator Ernest F. Hollings. For most of the years covered in this study this seat was held by the late Senator Olin D. Johnston, who defeated "Cotton Ed" Smith in the 1944 Democratic primary. Senator Johnston was unopposed in the general election in 1950, after defeating Governor J. Strom

---

[24] Senator Maybank was first elected in November, 1941, to fill the unexpired term of James F. Byrnes, who had resigned to accept an appointment to the United States Supreme Court. He was elected to a full term in 1942 and again in 1948 without opposition in the general election but faced strong opponents in both Democratic primaries.

Thurmond in the Democratic primary. Although unopposed for the Democratic nomination in 1956, Senator Johnston faced Republican opposition in the general election and defeated L. P. Crawford by a vote of nearly five to one. In 1962 Senator Johnston defeated Governor Ernest F. Hollings in the Democratic primary and faced as his Republican opponent W. D. Workman, Jr., a Columbia newspaperman, who received 42.8 percent of the vote and carried nine counties. Except for the Republican presidential electors chosen in the same election, Workman received the highest Republican vote for public office cast in South Carolina to that date.

Senator Johnston died before the expiration of his term and was succeeded by Donald S. Russell, who resigned as governor on April 22, 1965, and was appointed to the Senate by his successor, Lieutenant Governor Robert E. McNair. Senator Russell was defeated by Ernest F. Hollings in the 1966 Democratic primary for the two years remaining in the term. The general election of that year resulted in a sharp contest between Hollings, the Democratic nominee, and the Republican candidate, Marshall E. Parker, with Hollings winning by only 11,758 votes. The narrowness of the Democratic victory in this partisan election assured that Parker would run again in 1968 when a full term was at stake. This time, however, Hollings, who had easily defeated John Bolt Culbertson in the Democratic primary, captured 61.9 percent of the vote and won by a margin of 155,280 votes.

The only other statewide election that attracts major public interest in South Carolina is the one for governor. Despite this interest, the winner of the Democratic primary was unopposed in the general elections of 1950, 1954, 1958, and 1962. The election of 1966, the most recent one in the period under discussion, had no primary, but there was a partisan contest in the general election between the Democratic nominee, Robert E. McNair, and the Republican candidate, Joseph G. Rogers, Jr. This race is included with the partisan elections for the United States Senate in the search for a pattern in the voting.

Republican candidates entered a total of six statewide elections in South Carolina in 1948–68—one gubernatorial and five senatorial contests. The election of a United States senator in 1956 arbitrarily has been excluded from the following analysis, primarily because the one-sidedness of the vote is interpreted as meaning that South

Table 7

DISTRIBUTION OF THE VOTE FOR REPUBLICAN CANDIDATES
FOR UNITED STATES SENATOR AND GOVERNOR IN SOUTH CAROLINA, 1962–1968

	Workman[*] Senate 1962	Parker[†] Senate 1966	Thurmond[‡] Senate 1966	Rogers[§] Governor 1966	Parker[¶] Senate 1968
Vote					
Total	133,930	212,032	271,297	184,088	248,780
Percentage	42.8	48.7	62.2	41.8	38.1
Counties Won					
In Piedmont (20)	3	8	19	0	0
In Coastal Plains (26)	6	7	26	4	0
With over 50% Non-whites, 1960 (15)	4	4	15	1	0
With under 30% Non-whites, 1960 (14)	3	7	14	2	0
County Vote Exceeded Statewide Percentage					
In Piedmont (20)	4	9	9	6	9
In Coastal Plains (26)	14	9	8	14	7
With over 50% Non-whites, 1960 (15)	7	4	3	8	2
With under 30% Non-whites, 1960 (14)	4	8	8	4	9
Under 40% of County Vote[¶¶]					
In Piedmont (20)	14	3	6	12	11
In Coastal Plains (26)	7	3	6	8	19
With over 50% Non-whites, 1960 (15)	4	3	7	6	13
With under 30% Non-whites, 1960 (14)	10	0	2	7	5

[*] Defeated by Olin D. Johnston.
[†] Defeated by Ernest F. Hollings for two-year term.
[‡] Defeated P. Bradley Morrah, Jr.
[§] Defeated by Robert E. McNair.
[¶] Defeated by Ernest F. Hollings.
[¶¶] For Thurmond, the bottom quartile, twelve counties, was used.

Carolina voters were not quite ready to accept two-party competition in any election except that for the presidency. The exclusion of the 1956 senatorial election from this analysis, however, is in no way intended to minimize its importance, together with that of the presidential elections of 1956 and 1960, in developing the partisan competition that has been most evident since 1962.

Senator Thurmond was the only Republican candidate to win one of the five elections. Despite his personal strength among South Carolina voters, he was unable to carry either Parker or Rogers to victory with him in 1966. Thurmond's vigorous campaigning for Nixon in 1968 did not prevent Parker from losing every county in the state to Hollings. These facts are interpreted to mean that a distinction must be kept in mind between Senator Thurmond's personal appeal to voters and the existence of a basic Republican vote.

Republican strength has ranged from a low of 133,930 for Workman in 1962 to a high of 271,297 for Thurmond in 1966. As shown in Table 7, Parker and Rogers received more votes than Workman had four years earlier, but both fell considerably behind Thurmond in the same election. Parker in 1968 received the second highest number of votes cast for any of the Republican candidates in the five elections studied. His portion of the total vote cast, however, was considerably lower than that of the Republican candidates in the other elections, indicating that the increased voter turnout in the 1968 election went primarily to the Democratic candidate. When the Thurmond vote is excluded, however, the Republican vote has ranged from around 38 to 49 percent, sizable enough to encourage continued efforts by party leaders.

Because Parker did not carry a single county in 1968, no county gave a victory to the Republican candidates in all five elections. Only Aiken County has been carried by a Republican in four elections, but six counties—Barnwell, Clarendon, Edgefield, Greenville, Lexington, and Pickens—gave the lead to Republican candidates in three elections. Three of these counties were in the Piedmont, two had nonwhite populations of over 50 percent (as of 1960), two had nonwhite populations of under 30 percent (as of 1960), and three were included in SMSAs. There appears to be no discernible pattern here. It can be noted, however, that with the exception of Marshall Parker in 1968, three Republican candidates carried more counties in the Coastal Plains than in the Piedmont, the area most strongly identified with Democratic presidential elections before 1968.

An analysis was made of the counties that gave each Republican candidate a higher percentage of the vote than his statewide average. This analysis reveals that Workman and Rogers had many more such counties in the Coastal Plains than in the Piedmont, whereas strong support for Parker and for Thurmond was about evenly spread between these two regions. This finding was reinforced by a tabulation of the counties that gave Republican candidates less than 40 percent of the county's vote; in Thurmond's case the bottom quartile, twelve counties, was used. Although the total number of counties for each candidate ranged from a low of six to a high of thirty (both extremes were for Parker), again there was a distinctive geographical distribution. Rogers and Workman had many more counties in this category in the Piedmont than in the Coastal Plains, whereas support for Parker and for Thurmond was evenly distributed in 1966. In 1968 Parker had nineteen Coastal Plains counties which gave him under 40 percent of their total vote; included among them were ten of the twelve counties in this region that had over 50 percent nonwhite populations in 1960. These distributions appear to mean that generally more Republican support was found in the Coastal Plains than in the Piedmont—a conclusion that would hardly have been challenged between 1948 and 1968.

Of the state's three largest counties, Greenville was the strongest supporter of the Republican candidates. It gave majorities to Workman in 1962 and to Parker and Thurmond in 1966, and awarded all five candidates larger percentages of the vote than their statewide averages. Charleston County gave majorities to Workman and Thurmond and gave Rogers better than his state percentage, but failed to support Parker as strongly against Hollings, a native son (Parker won 47.9 percent in 1966 and 35.8 percent in 1968).

Richland County delivered a majority to Thurmond (but less than his statewide percentage), 49.9 percent to Workman, and votes higher than their state percentages to Rogers and Parker in 1966 and 1968.

An analysis was also made of the vote given the Republican candidates in the fourteen counties with less than 30 percent and the fifteen counties with over 50 percent nonwhite populations (according to the 1960 census). With the exception of two counties in each group, these lists also contained the counties with the lowest and the highest ratios of Negroes to total county registration in 1968. Workman and Thurmond each carried one more county with low Negro populations than they did in the other category, whereas Parker and Rogers reversed this pattern in 1966. Workman and Rogers collected more counties with high Negro populations than with low Negro populations of all counties giving them a higher percentage of the vote than their statewide average. On the other hand, Parker (in both 1966 and 1968) and Thurmond attracted the greatest support in the group with under 30 percent nonwhite populations. Of the counties that gave the Republican candidate below 40 percent of their vote, Workman ran best in the group with low Negro populations, Parker and Thurmond ran best in those with high Negro populations, and Rogers ran almost equally well in both groups. The pattern is mixed here and may be better explained by considering the home county of the candidates than by any clearly defined Republican vote in either grouping.

The number of cases is too small and the elections too recent to assume that any patterns observed in them are more than temporary or unique. Only the 1968 Parker candidacy came after a significant number of Negroes had registered to vote in South Carolina, a factor that was quite important that year and is certain to influence future elections. In 1968 Parker had about the same total vote as Nixon and also did best in the counties in which Nixon was strongest, with the exception of Charleston, Hollings' home county. The total vote in the Piedmont and in the Coastal Plains counties was within one percentage point of each candidate's statewide average. As shown in Table 6, Parker ran three percentage points above his state average in the total vote of the fifteen counties with the lowest ratio of Negroes to total county registration, while Hollings ran six points above his state average in the fifteen counties with over 50 percent nonwhite populations (as of 1960) and in the five counties under the 1965 Voting Rights Act. These computations provide clear evidence that a large portion of the 1968 Negro vote went to Hollings. Moreover, the Hollings vote was about equal to the combined vote of Humphrey and Wallace, clearly providing a basis for the contention that the Wallace voters also supported Hollings rather than Parker. How these two categories of voters will combine in future elections is purely speculative for the present.

Friends and Neighbors No More

For many years in South Carolina the word *election* was synonymous with *primary*, and *primary* meant *Democratic primary*. Winning the Democratic primary was tantamount to election, and the general election was only a formality to legitimatize the decision. Under these conditions all political competition for elective public office was concentrated in the primary and partisanism, although it was an underlying assumption, had little direct influence on the formation of voters' attitudes from contest to contest.

The absence of partisanism did not mean that there was no factionalism in the one-party states, however; the factionalism simply took a different form in those states. V. O. Key maintained that the absence of two strong parties gave rise to a system in which there was a multiplicity of candidates and a pattern of friends-and-neighbors voting in which the vote received by a candidate roughly varied with the proximity of the voting place to the candidate's home. "In a factional system organized around friends-and-neighbors nuclei, it is but a short step to larger groupings of voters formed along sectional lines by the addition of nearby counties to local followings." [25]

25 Key, *Southern Politics*, 135–36.

Key applied his generalizations to South Carolina in these words:

> By now it has become clear that in the absence of well-organized politics, localism will play a powerful role in the orientation of voters' attitudes in state-wide politics. South Carolina is without a well-organized factional system. In its gubernatorial politics, localism provides the electoral nucleus to which candidates hope to add a sufficient number of votes to carry the day. South Carolina localism, however, has peculiarities unto itself. In so small a state with so few counties it is a short step from localism to sectionalism. When a few counties are annexed to a local friends-and-neighbors following, a candidate has organized about himself, for the moment at least, a sectional faction.[26]

Key added that despite the absence of "whatever circumstances might force political leaders and voters into two camps, South Carolina gubernatorial races start out as a free-for-all among three or four principal contenders," many of whose "candidacies are not regarded seriously by either the candidates or the electorate." [27] Although "the many-sided first-primary contest reveals the multiplicity of personal and local followings," he observed, "in the second primary, . . . the voters are compelled to line up with one or the other of two candidates. In South Carolina this dual division often shapes up along low-country–upcountry lines, though voter consciousness of such differences is not sharp." [28] Key believed that the "recurrence of the cleavage between Plain and Piedmont makes it clear that a basis exists for a bipartisanism, which, however, cannot develop because of racism." [29] The obvious question is how well Key's generalizations fit the statewide primaries in the twenty years that followed his study.

From 1948 through 1968 South Carolina held twelve statewide primary contests to choose candidates for the United States Senate and for the governorship. All were conducted by the Democratic Party.[30] The choice of a gubernatorial candidate was at issue in five

---

26 *Ibid.*, 132.
27 *Ibid.*, 134.
28 *Ibid.*, 136.
29 *Ibid.*, 142.
30 Much useful information on the Democratic primaries is found in Frank E.

of these contests, but one was a second, or runoff, primary in 1958. The winners of four of these contests were unopposed in the general elections. There was no gubernatorial primary in 1966; Governor Robert E. McNair, who was completing the unexpired term of Donald S. Russell, was not opposed in the Democratic Party, and Joseph G. Rogers, Jr., was nominated by the Republican convention.

Although more than two candidates ran in three of the primaries, one candidate received strong majorities in each of four contests. The type of voting pattern Key described was present to only a very limited degree, as was clearly evident in the 1950 primary, which had four candidates: James F. Byrnes, Lester L. Bates, Thomas H. Pope, and Marcus A. Stone. Byrnes received an overwhelming 71.6 percent of the vote and carried every county in the state except Newberry, the home county of Pope. Only two candidates entered the 1954 primary, and George Bell Timmerman, with 61.3 percent of the vote, defeated Lester L. Bates. Bates carried only five counties, two of them adjacent in the Piedmont and three of them side by side in the Coastal Plains. Sectional factionalism and localism were not sufficiently present in either of these primaries, however, to generate a strong political contest.

The Democratic Party needed two primaries to select a gubernatorial candidate in 1958. The first primary involved Ernest F. Hollings, William C. Johnston, and Donald S. Russell. Hollings led in twenty-nine counties and received 41.9 percent of the vote, which was short of the necessary majority. Only four counties in the Coastal Plains failed to give him the lead, but the other two candidates, both from the Piedmont, led in thirteen of the twenty counties in that region. Russell was second with 35 percent of the vote and led in nine Piedmont counties and four Coastal Plains counties. Johnston trailed the field with the lead in only four counties in the Piedmont and with 23.1 percent of the vote. Each candidate carried his home county and adjoining counties, thereby following

Jordan, Jr., *The Primary State: A History of the Democratic Party in South Carolina, 1896–1962* (Columbia, S.C.: R. L. Bryan Co., 1968).

Key's friends-and-neighbors concept, but Russell, from Spartan-burg, and Johnston, from nearby Anderson, divided many mutual "neighbors." In the second primary, Hollings received 56.8 per-cent of the vote and lost only seven counties. His total included the four counties that Johnston had won and four that Russell had won in the first race, but he lost Lee (by nineteen votes), which he had carried by a substantial margin in the first primary. Russell carried five counties in the Piedmont, all "neighbors" of his home county, and Richland and Lee in the Coastal Plains. In both primaries there was some evidence to support Key's generalization. Localism and friends and neighbors were sufficient to force a runoff primary, but "the cleavage between Plain and Piedmont" was not sufficient to provide a close contest between representatives from each of these two major regions of the state.

The 1962 gubernatorial primary had a greater number of candi-dates than any other during 1948–68. The field included Donald S. Russell, Burnet R. Maybank, Jr., A. W. "Red" Bethea, Dero Cook, and Milton Dukes, but only Russell and Maybank were regarded seriously by the electorate. Russell overcame his 1958 defeat and won 60.8 percent of the vote. He lost only three counties—two to Maybank, and Bethea's home county. Once again the electorate was sufficiently united to give one candidate a substantial majority, and the "many-sided first-primary contest" failed to produce "the multiplicity of personal and local followings" that lead to sectional factions and runoffs.

In addition to the gubernatorial primaries, seven statewide pri-maries to choose candidates for the United States Senate were examined for evidence of sectional factionalism. There were no runoffs in these contests, and only one of them had more than two candidates. The winner of the primary was unopposed in the gen-eral election in 1948, 1950, and 1960. Although there was no sena-torial primary in 1954 or 1956, competition developed in the gen-eral elections, as has been observed.

The senatorial, like the gubernatorial, primary of 1948 attracted a large number of entrants. Incumbent Senator Burnet R. May-bank—who was opposed by William Jennings Bryan Dorn, Neville

Bennett, Alan Johnston, and Marcus A. Stone—received 51.5 percent of the vote, more than the majority required to avoid a second primary. Maybank lost the lead in only six counties—five to Dorn and one to Bennett. Localism and friends and neighbors operated to a limited extent for Dorn, but Maybank's strength was sufficient to overcome this sectional faction.

The 1950 Senate primary between incumbent Senator Olin D. Johnston and Governor J. Strom Thurmond was a clear example of Key's argument that when there are two candidates a sectional controversy emerges between the Piedmont and the Coastal Plains. Johnston won 53.9 percent of the vote and twenty-five of the forty-six counties. He carried every county in the Piedmont except Laurens, while Thurmond took the lead in twenty of the twenty-six counties in the Coastal Plains. This election was the clearest example of the cleavage between these two regions that occurred during 1948–68.

Ten years passed before there was another senatorial primary. In 1954 Senator Maybank was unopposed but died before the general election, which Strom Thurmond won by a write-in vote. Senator Johnston was also unopposed for the Democratic nomination but ran against L. P. Crawford in the general election. The next primary came in 1960, when Senator Thurmond opposed R. Beverly Herbert, who entered the primary at the last moment. Thurmond received an overwhelming 89.4 percent of the vote and did not lose a single county.

In each of the four senatorial primaries since 1960 (three regular elections and one election to fill a two-year term occasioned by the death of Senator Olin D. Johnston), with the exception of one race in 1966, there have been only two candidates, and every winner received a substantial majority. Senator Johnston defeated Governor Ernest F. Hollings in 1962 with 65.7 percent of the vote and with the lead in every county except Calhoun, which he lost by thirty-four votes. Hollings did not even carry his home county, Charleston, against Johnston, but came back in 1966 to defeat Donald S. Russell for the two years remaining in the term to which Senator Johnston had been elected, and in 1968 to defeat John Bolt Culbertson for a full term. Hollings received 60.8 percent of the vote in 1966 and 78.4 percent in 1968. Russell carried only seven counties, four of which were in the Piedmont. He failed to carry his home county, Spartanburg, and won only one county, Jasper, that he had carried against Hollings in the 1958 primaries. Culbertson did not carry a single county.

Another senatorial primary was held in 1966 to choose a candidate to oppose Thurmond in his first bid for election to the Senate as a Republican candidate. The candidates were P. Bradley Morrah, Jr., of Greenville, and John Bolt Culbertson, of Spartanburg. This primary was the only close contest since the Johnston-Thurmond primary of 1950. Morrah received 55.9 percent of the vote and carried thirty-one counties, including fifteen of twenty in the Piedmont. The contest was fairly close in most counties, however, and neither location nor sectionalism played any appreciable role in influencing voter attitudes. Although there were two senatorial primaries in 1966, only one county, Williamsburg, was carried by both losers.

Other statewide primaries were held in South Carolina in 1948–68, but those discussed here were the contests that generated the most public interest and, therefore, were most representative of the role of factionalism in organizing voter attitudes from primary to primary. Although there was some evidence of Key's friends-and-neighbors nuclei of voting and of the cleavage between the Piedmont and Coastal Plains sections of the state, the 1948–68 primaries generally followed a different pattern. Only three races had more than two candidates and in only one of these did the multiplicity of candidates result in a second primary. The large majority the winner received in all except three of these contests must mean that the personal popularity of the winner was so broadly based that it effectively overcame any friends-and-neighbors nuclei of voting strength. Moreover, in only one primary was there evidence that differing interests in the Piedmont and Coastal Plains provided a basis for factionalism and strong competition when only two candidates were involved. The evidence is suggestive rather than conclusive, but there is certainly basis for an argument that during

1948–68 South Carolina began to make the shift from nonpartisan to partisan politics, that this new development began to alter the pattern of primary politics, and that it will eventually lead to a different function or role for primaries in the political activities of the state.

A Faltering Advance

Only limited partisan competition appeared in South Carolina between 1948 and 1968 in the election of members of the United States House of Representatives and of the General Assembly of South Carolina, and most of the change occurred at the very close of the period. In the case of the national House of Representatives the first major development took place in the Second Congressional District, where Congressman Albert W. Watson switched from the Democratic to the Republican Party. Watson was first elected to the House in 1962 as a Democrat, defeating his Republican opponent, Floyd D. Spence, and was reelected in 1964 as a Democrat. After being stripped of his seniority by the Eighty-ninth Congress, he resigned on February 1, 1965. He ran as a Republican in a special election on June 15, 1965, and won, thereby becoming the first Republican elected to the House of Representatives from South Carolina since Reconstruction. Congressman Watson was reelected as a Republican in 1966 and 1968 by substantial margins over his Democratic opponents.

Republican candidates entered three congressional elections in 1966. In the Second District Watson, the incumbent, received 64.3 percent of the vote to defeat his Democratic opponent, Fred Le-Clercq, and to win his second election as a Republican. Congressman William Jennings Bryan Dorn, the Democratic incumbent in the Third District, won 57.8 percent of the vote in his contest with the Republican nominee, John K. Grisso. In the Sixth District John L. McMillan, the incumbent, received 61.7 percent of the vote in defeating Archie C. Odom.

The election of 1968 produced the largest number of partisan congressional contests in the history of South Carolina. The First

District, which is represented by Congressman Mendel Rivers, was the only one without partisan competition, and in the Third, Fifth, and Sixth districts there were three candidates. All incumbents won handily, however, rolling up substantial margins of votes. Congressman Watson won his third victory as a Republican when he received 57.6 percent of the vote in his contest with Frank K. Sloan. In the Third District, Congressman Dorn defeated John K. Grisso, a Republican, for the second time and J. Harold Morton, the nominee of the Independent Party. Dorn received 66.1 percent of the vote. Congressman Tom S. Gettys of the Fifth District gained 74.7 percent of the vote, which put him far ahead of his two opponents, Hugh J. Boyd, the Republican, and Bert Sumner, the Independent. In the Sixth District the incumbent, John L. McMillan, received 58.3 percent of the vote and defeated the Republican candidate, Ray Harris, for the second time, as well as the nominee of the Independent Party, Claude E. Harris.

The only race in which there was not an incumbent running was the Fourth District, where Robert T. Ashmore had decided not to seek reelection. Contrary to many predictions, the Democratic candidate, James R. Mann, received 61.2 percent of the vote against his Republican opponent, Charles Bradshaw.

Despite what might have been expected, all the congressional contests were won by substantial margins, with each winner carrying every county in his district. The presence of third-party candidates in three contests had no influence on the outcomes, as the Independent candidates received only 2.2 percent of the vote in the Third District, 3.5 percent in the Fifth, and 1.8 percent in the Sixth. It is too early to be certain, but there is every indication that the interest generated by the partisan competition in 1968 will assure at least two candidates in most South Carolina congressional districts in the next general election. Should that happen, then the small start made in 1962 will have become the forerunner of a series of events that contributed to the emergence of partisan politics in South Carolina.

Limited partisanship also appeared toward the end of 1948–68 in the election of members of the General Assembly of South Carolina. The first dent in a long dominance of the Democratic Party came when Charles E. Boineau, Jr., was elected to the House of Representatives from Richland County on August 8, 1961, to complete an unexpired term. He was the first Republican to serve in the General Assembly since John W. Bolts of Georgetown County was elected in 1898 and 1900 and served through the session which ended February 16, 1901.[31] Boineau was not reelected, and it was 1964 before another Republican won a seat, this time from Charleston County.

Republican candidates had their greatest success to date in 1966, when seventeen won seats in the House and six were elected to the Senate, where they were joined by one Independent Democrat. Most of the members were chosen from the urban counties, where the greatest amount of Republican interest has been generated. In the House four members were from Aiken, seven from Greenville, three from Lexington, and one from Charleston. Orangeburg, which elected two Republicans, is considerably less urban than the other counties, but the long and vigorous campaigns to gain the civil rights of the Negro residents has generated much partisan political interest. In the Senate three Republicans were from Charleston and one each from Aiken, Lexington, and Newberry (the least urban of the group). The Independent Democrat was from Greenville. As was true of the House, the Republican members were elected by the counties undergoing the greatest socioeconomic, and presumably political, changes. Primarily because of their small number in the total membership of each chamber (124 in the House and 50 in the Senate),[32] the Republican members had only minor partisan, as distinguished from personal, influence on

31 George B. Tindall, *South Carolina Negroes, 1877-1900* (Columbia: University of South Carolina Press, 1952), 51, and Francis B. Simkins and Robert H. Woody, *South Carolina During Reconstruction* (Chapel Hill: University of North Carolina Press, 1932), 551.

32 The size of the Senate was increased from forty-six to fifty members for 1966-68 "solely as an interim measure" after it was ruled to be malapportioned in *O'Shields v. McNair*, 254 F. Supp. 708 (D.C.S.C. 1966). On March 27, 1967, the South Carolina Supreme Court ruled that under the state's constitution the Senate was limited to forty-six members. *State* ex rel. *McLeod v. West*, 249 S.C. 243 (1967).

the processes and outputs of the chambers in which they served.

The Republican successes in 1966 encouraged a much larger number of candidates in 1968, and the party offered eighteen nominees for the Senate and seventy-three for the House. The results were discouraging for those interested in seeing partisanism develop in the state legislative process, for only five Republicans were elected to the House and three to the Senate. Three members from Greenville were returned to the House, where they were joined by one newcomer from Aiken and another from Williamsburg. In the Senate the 1966 Independent Democrat from Greenville was elected as a Republican, one Republican was returned by Lexington, and a new member was chosen in Aiken. As in 1966, the victories occurred primarily in urban counties; Williamsburg was the only exception. Partisan influence on the legislative process was even less significant in the 1969 General Assembly than in 1967 and 1968, but the corner was turned and it is reasonable to argue that partisanism, however limited at first, will continue to be a feature in the choice of legislators.

Thoughts on the Beginnings

The political developments and changes discussed in this chapter mark the emergence of a new phase in South Carolina politics. Here, as in most sections of the world, more people are becoming involved in their governance, and that involvement is resulting in a higher level of participation in the most direct form of political activity, the election process. The increased levels of voting and voter registration in South Carolina during 1948–68 are an index of this development.

The most significant change in South Carolina during the past twenty years undoubtedly was the increased participation of Negroes in the state's election process. A major development was the sharp rise in the proportion of Negroes of voting age who registered to vote in 1968—an increase from 14.8 percent after the 1958 registration to 54.1 percent after the new registration ten years later. It is very important to note that this development was not confined to a few isolated areas, a distribution which would have biased the state average, but extended to all the state's counties. Although there is still room for improvement, 1968 clearly marks a new level in this phase of the political process.

The involvement of Negroes was not restricted to voter registration but also appeared in the 1968 presidential election, in which 78.2 percent of the state's registered voters took part. Perhaps the most meaningful evidence of Negro participation is that in the fifteen counties in which blacks constitute more than half the population, the proportion of registered voters who voted was below the state average in only five counties. The largest deviation was 6.7 percentage points, but it is not known how many of the 2,717 registered voters who did not vote were Negroes. This obviously high level of Negro participation is a new phenomenon in South Carolina politics, but since it appeared only in the last year included in this study, its impact on political decision-makers has not yet been demonstrated.

Another distinction between the elections of 1948–68 and those of earlier years was the emergence of sectional, or regional, differences in the voting patterns of presidential elections and their decrease in other statewide elections and primaries. Before 1948 South Carolina was solidly Democratic in its presidential vote. From that year through 1968, however, a cleavage between the Piedmont and the Coastal Plains was evident in every presidential election, although to a somewhat lesser extent in 1956. The partisan trends of the two regions switched in the 1968 election, with the new support for the Democratic electors in the Coastal Plains coming mainly from the Negro voters. The presence of three candidates in this election makes it impossible to determine whether the reversed positions of the two regions was unique for 1968 or whether earlier differences are disappearing in the face of urban growth and of the increased importance of economic factors in forming political attitudes. One may speculate that newly emerging factors will continue to fractionalize sectional interests which were fairly homogeneous and that partisanship will emerge to aggregate and channel those interests for the political process.

The earlier pattern of regional factionalism and friends-and-neighbors nuclei of voting strength operated to a limited extent during 1948–68. In only one primary was there a sharp difference between voting patterns in the Piedmont and those in the Coastal Plains which could be explained by the identification of regional interests with the candidates from those regions. Furthermore, friends and neighbors and sectional nuclei of votes were sufficient in only one instance to force a second primary because of the presence of more than two candidates. In all other contests these factors were clearly much less significant than other variables, not all of which may have been identified. However, it is clear that at least one of these new factors was the presence since 1962 of partisan competition in the general elections for United States senators.

A condition that obviously altered the previous patterns of sectional and regional factionalism was the continued growth of urban centers in four areas of the state. The counties in these centers were the most partisan and deviated to the greatest degree from the one-party pattern that had prevailed in the elections prior to 1948. This change was true in presidential elections and in senatorial and gubernatorial elections and primaries as well. It is evident that the emergence of competing interests in these urban centers is contributing to the beginning of partisanism in their political activities.

This development is certain to lead to a different pattern of election results in the next few years. In 1968 just over half of the state's registered voters lived in ten counties; five of the ten were counties within SMSAs and three others adjoined one or more of these five. Only four of the ten had Negro populations higher than 30 percent, and only one, Orangeburg County, was over half Negro. These ten counties gave the presidential candidates of 1968 half or more of the total vote received by each, and all ten gave sizable support to the Republican candidates in the various statewide elections studied here. As these counties continue to grow in population and voting strength and become more partisan, it is assumed that interests within these areas will have to join with interests elsewhere in the state in order to provide a winning majority. It is further assumed that this development will quickly extend partisan considerations to the surrounding areas and will contribute to the general development of statewide partisanism in South Carolina.

Clearly, the function of the Democratic primary began to change during the later years of 1948–68. Although there were still many occasions in which winning the Democratic primary was tantamount to election, the certainty of this outcome began to weaken. Many winners of the primary went on to face strong competition in the general election, and the winner of one 1966 primary was defeated by his Republican opponent. Furthermore, the level of voting in the primaries and the general elections reversed the earlier pattern in which the larger vote was cast in the primary; this reversal indicates that for at least some elections political competition is being transferred to the general election. As this trend continues and extends to other offices, as it surely must, the basic function or role of the primary will become that of choosing a partisan candidate and not the filling of a public office. Many South Carolinians will have to adjust their thinking to this new status and modify the widely heralded "best man rule," under which, it is alleged, the voter can choose the best man without partisan influence or consideration.

As observed earlier, the presence of Republicans in the General Assembly has had little partisan, as distinguished from personal, influence on the legislative output. Rather, policy leadership came largely from the executive branch and especially from the governors who served during the past twenty years. The changing conditions have created a situation in which executive leadership could thrive and have caused the decline, but certainly not the demise, of the "Barnwell Ring" controlled by House Speaker Solomon Blatt and State Senator Edgar A. Brown, once the primary architects of South Carolina's governmental policy. The appearance of effective partisanism in the state legislature is certain to enhance even further the role of the governor as policy leader, although the reverse might not necessarily be true.

The major conclusion of this study is that the political developments of the past twenty years, and especially those since 1962, marked the beginning of partisanism in South Carolina politics.

Probably the state's politics in the near future will be characterized by sharply different election patterns and the emerging factional and partisan combinations will defy the neat categorizations of bipartisan politics. For a time at least, South Carolina voters are likely to continue the present practice of distinguishing sharply between elections in which the candidates are the nominees of national party groups and those in which the candidates are chosen by and from South Carolina and therefore considered more representative of the state's political ideology. In time, however, partisan considerations are certain to spread from the presidential and United States senatorial elections to those for the congressional seats, the governorship, and the legislature. Moreover, in the short run there may be some truth to the current claim of a few people that the South Carolina Democratic Party is primarily the party of the Negro voter, but this distinction too will fade, for the developments during 1948–68 make it quite clear that many new factors are now bringing about the partisanship that could not develop earlier because of racism.

The critical question for the transitional period, however, is whether the currently emerging bipartisanism will be based on economic or urban factors or on the polarizing effect of the racial issue. It is quite possible that in the immediate future the division may not continue primarily along economic or urban lines but may produce a predominantly black Democratic Party and a white man's Republican Party, with even the urban working class being drawn into the latter on racial ideological grounds. The racial protest vote which has been characteristic of the Deep South since 1948 may turn in the direction of the Republican Party because of past and future Democratic defections (a factor which may well have kept South Carolina from going for Wallace in 1968) and produce a bipartisanism deeply imbued with racial discontent.

Whatever happens in the next few years, a strong argument can be made that partisanism appeared in South Carolina politics between 1948 and 1968 and that the state's political practices in the future will be markedly different from what they were before 1960.

13

REVOLT IN WASHINGTON
The South in Congress

W. WAYNE SHANNON

As V. O. Key clearly saw in the 1940's, any thorough analysis of
southern politics set in the broader context of American politics
must somehow attempt to come to grips with that southernmost
of our national institutions, the Congress of the United States.
There, and only there, in recent years has the South been able to
fashion a really efficient lever of power and influence on national
policy. In retrospect, it now seems clear that the major dimensions
of the American policy struggle have remained essentially unchanged since the emergence of the mature Roosevelt electoral
coalition in 1936. In this struggle the southern Democrats in Congress have played a crucially important role. No sooner, it seems,
had the party realignment of the thirties taken place than the
southerners began to feel restive among their newfound allies—
northern labor, the ethnic groups of the great cities, and, most important of all, Negroes. By 1937 the beginnings of one durable
southern response to this dilemma had become apparent. Although
the South would not for some years actually begin to reject the
Democratic Party as its historical vehicle for national influence, on
certain types of issues significant numbers of southerners began to
defect from the Democratic ranks in Congress. On these issues the
southern bloc joined forces with congressional Republicans to create
what we have come to call (somewhat oversimply) the "conservative coalition."

W. Wayne Shannon is Associate Professor of Political Science, University of
Connecticut.

Since 1937, only two really important changes have occurred. First, the sizable contingent of *northern* Democratic congressional conservatives that plagued President Franklin D. Roosevelt in the late thirties and early forties has all but disappeared.[1] Second, the disaffection of the southern Democrats with the policy stands of their northern brethren has increased immensely. In recent years southern dissidence has taken on the dimensions of a full-scale revolt. And throughout this entire period the southerners on Capitol Hill have enjoyed a critically important kind of leverage on national policy formation. In many respects they have been able to operate as a kind of third party force, largely invisible to the American public but potent, nevertheless, in the outcomes of a wide variety of important policy disputes. Under both Democratic and Republican Presidents they have proceeded to exact their largely clandestine concessions. It is today most apparent that their subtle handiwork on Capitol Hill has been infinitely more telling on national policy than the more colorful convention walkouts, third party presidential bids, and flamboyant gubernatorial antics that have received so much attention in the national news media.

Thus, a proper description of the South's role in Congress must be a key element of any attempt to explain American politics since the New Deal. So important, in fact, has the influence of the southern delegations been during the last thirty years that one need exaggerate very little to portray the present congressional system in William S. White's apt phrase as "the South's unending revenge upon the North for Gettysburg."[2] White spoke only of the influences of the southerners in the Senate, but an even more impressive case may be made today for their role in the House of Representatives. To be sure, such southern men of power in the House as Jamie L. Whitten and William M. Colmer of Mississippi are much less well known than their Senate counterparts ranging from

[1] On the opposition of northern Democrats to some major aspects of the New Deal, see especially James T. Patterson, *Congressional Conservatism and the New Deal* (Lexington: University of Kentucky Press, 1967).

[2] William S. White, *Citadel* (New York: Harper, 1957), 68.

Theodore Bilbo to James O. Eastland. (Probably fewer than 5 percent of American voters know anything at all of these men and their work.) But their influence on various aspects of American public policy is no less pervasive. At midcentury, it is to such gray eminences of the American political system as these, even more than the southern senators, that the task has fallen to render the programs of modern Presidents and of their cohorts "the bureaucrats" palatable to the South and to conservative small-town and rural America generally. While evaluation of this state of affairs depends very largely on one's politics, recognition of it as fact requires no more than an ability to perceive the obvious.[3]

It is the purpose of this chapter to analyze the behavior of southern Democrats in Congress from 1951 to 1967. The choice of this particular time span is an obvious one; it takes up conveniently close to where V. O. Key left off,[4] and it spans a period roughly comparable to that covered in his work. Since Key's analysis of four sessions in the thirties and forties remains the most systematic and inclusive attempt to deal with southern Democratic behavior in Congress, his classic study serves as a point of departure here. While certain portions of this investigation differ substantially from Key's, the general aim is to extend his analysis to the fifties and sixties. By laying new data alongside Key's, one may trace certain aspects of southern behavior from the early thirties to the present. Chronological perspective of this sort is all too rare in studies of party behavior in Congress, and in this case the results

[3] I do not mean to imply that I am a "value neutral" observer of Congress. As the reader will no doubt perceive, my preferences for an open, competitive, egalitarian, and majoritarian brand of national politics lead me to be critical of some aspects of congressional organization and procedure. I do maintain that factual description and evaluation ought to be considered as logically distinct components of political analysis. It seems to me inescapable that two or more observers of "the facts" about Congress will produce evaluations that are conditioned by differences in ultimate values and by judgments linking factual conditions to the attainment of those values. There is, then, no single demonstrably correct way to evaluate the operation of Congress, or for that matter any other political institution.

[4] See V. O. Key, Jr., *Southern Politics in State and Nation* (New York: Vintage, 1949), Chaps. 16 and 17.

are rewarding.[5] Over these years the differences in southern behavior are striking—so striking, in fact, that most of Key's conclusions must be substantially modified for the years after 1950.

Although it would be ideal to analyze both the Senate and the House of Representatives, for two reasons the focus here is exclusively on the House. First, the collection of data for a study of this kind continues to pose formidable problems for political scientists. Given the time and resources available in this case, concentration on one House of Congress amounts to a reluctant compromise with reality.[6] Second, the House of Representatives recommends itself over the Senate because its small and relatively homogeneous districts permit a type of analysis that statewide Senate constituencies foreclose. For example, consideration of the social and political correlates of southern conservatism is facilitated by the size of House districts. Such analysis, given the nature of Senate districts, is less likely to yield clear results.

In order to analyze southern behavior in the fifties and sixties, several closely related questions have been posed. So that the general scope of the study may be grasped at the outset, it will be helpful to array these here in the order in which they are treated in the pages that follow. First, there is the matter of establishing continuity with Key's treatment of the House in *Southern Politics*. Here I have simply asked whether or not southern behavior in the last two decades has continued to manifest roughly the same patterns that Key described in 1949. To facilitate comparison I have mainly taken his analytic scheme as a given and sought to collect data to "fill in the cells," so to speak, for the later period. Replication of this sort is surely not the most exciting or creative aspect of political analysis, but it does, as the present case reveals, help to

5 I have discussed the general problem of historical perspective in congressional behavior studies in *Party, Constituency, and Congressional Voting* (Baton Rouge: Louisiana State University Press, 1968), Chap. 2 *passim*.

6 As frequently as these data are used, one would suppose we would have gotten around to collecting them in a standard data archive. Such a project is now underway under the auspices of the Inter-University Consortium for Political Research. When the roll call data for this study were collected it was still necessary to transcribe raw data manually from the *Congressional Quarterly Almanacs*.

clarify phenomena that change with the passage of time. Second, I have tried to place the rise of the "conservative coalition" in the House in historical perspective by asking whether data from *Southern Politics* and other studies of earlier periods might be juxtaposed to those of the present study so that a trend, or at least certain significant time periods, might be revealed. Third, I have tried to gauge what may be called the "policy dimensions" of the southern revolt against the House Democracy in recent years. Since a number of recent studies have established that congressional voting behavior varies significantly along several such dimensions, this exercise should not only facilitate accurate description but might also provide clues to the causes of southern congressional behavior since the 1930's.[7] Fourth, I have asked how one of the major institutional arrangements of the House—the seniority system—relates to southern influence on national policy formation. Here two major questions arise: does the seniority system operate in such a manner that the South enjoys greater influence on national policy than its share of the American population justifies, and does the system amplify the importance of southern dissidence by promoting to positions of power men whose policy views are substantially different from those of northern Democrats? Fifth, I have sought to relate southern voting behavior to several constituency characteristics in order to make some rough judgments on the reasons for southern conservatism in recent years. Sixth, I have attempted to assess certain changes in southern congressional politics which may suggest that the South's traditional attachment to the Democratic Party has eroded so massively that a full-scale party realignment will ultimately occur. Finally, I have tried to state some of the most important consequences of the southern congressional revolt for the people of the South and the nation as a whole. Admittedly, these are large questions, many of which can by no means be settled here. But the perspective in which they are all set—the politics of the

[7] See especially Duncan MacRae, Jr., *Dimensions of Congressional Voting* (Berkeley: University of California Press, 1958), and Shannon, *Party, Constituency, and Congressional Voting.* Several other studies lending support to this generalization are cited in Shannon, Chaps. 1 and 2.

South in its national context—is too large to admit any narrower confinement.

Southern Voting in the House: The "Key Years" and After

Has southern voting behavior in the House changed appreciably since Key studied four evenly spaced sessions from 1933 to 1945? The most direct and effective way to answer this question is to make a parallel analysis of a more recent period. Accordingly, new data are presented here for five evenly spaced sessions from 1951 to 1967.[8] In order to ensure comparability with the earlier sessions, House roll calls have been selected for analysis on the same criteria that Key employed. All roll calls for each selected session have been analyzed, with the exception of those on House organizational matters and those on which the minority consisted of less than 10 percent of the majority. The latter votes are excluded on the ground that they reflect near-unanimity on the part of the House, and cannot reveal much of importance about the differences among various congressional groups.[9]

What are the results when southern behavior during these two roughly equal periods of time is compared? Table 1 presents data on the first important question posed by Key: How often do majorities of southern Democrats in the House oppose majorities of Republicans? If coalition between southern Democrats and Republicans were as common as is sometimes supposed, he reasoned, majorities of the southerners would hardly be found opposing Republicans on a large percentage of House roll calls. But such was not the case, Key found. Indeed, during the sessions he analyzed, majorities of southern Democrats opposed majorities of Republicans on 70.5 percent of all roll calls studied. However, when the data for the more recent sessions are laid alongside those collected by Key, a sharp drop is immediately apparent in southern Demo-

[8] Collecting data for only one of every four sessions is again a necessary compromise. The starting point is, of course, arbitrary. And one must always wonder just how much analysis of other evenly spaced sessions or all sessions would influence the findings presented here.

[9] Key, *Southern Politics*, 369.

Table 1

HOUSE ROLL CALLS ON WHICH A MAJORITY OF SOUTHERN DEMOCRATS
OPPOSED A MAJORITY OF REPUBLICANS,
BY SESSIONS, 1933–1967

Congress, Session, Year	Total Roll Calls	Roll Calls with Majority in Disagreement	
		Number	Percentage
73:1 (1933)	56	47	83.9
75:1 (1937)	77	50	64.9
77:1 (1941)	67	50	74.6
79:1 (1945)	75	47	62.7
TOTALS	275	194	70.5
82:1 (1951)	79	40	50.6
84:1 (1955)	56	27	48.2
86:1 (1959)	75	50	66.7
88:1 (1963)	89	48	53.9
90:1 (1967)	159	55	34.6
TOTALS	458	220	48.0

Source: Data for the first four sessions are from V. O. Key, Jr., *Southern Politics*
(New York: Vintage Books, 1949), 371.
Note: Near-unanimous roll calls have been omitted for all sessions.

cratic opposition to Republican majorities. As the table clearly
reveals, the average percentage of roll calls pitting southern Democratic against Republican majorities has fallen a full 22.5 points
to 48 for the sessions after 1950. Moreover, the table indicates a
rather interesting trend over the years since the beginning of the
New Deal in 1933. By 1937 a marked decline was apparent in southern Democratic–Republican opposition on House roll calls. Although there is some fluctuation, it appears that a kind of plateau
was reached by that time which extended through the 1945 session.
The data for the fifties and sixties with the exception of those for
the Eighty-sixth Congress suggest that a yet lower plateau had been
reached by the beginning of the Eighty-second Congress in 1951.
Finally, the extreme drop in southern Democratic–Republican opposition in the Ninetieth Congress suggests the possibility that a

Table 2

HOUSE ISSUES OF HIGH SOUTHERN DEMOCRATIC COHESION (90 PERCENT OR
MORE) IN OPPOSITION TO REPUBLICAN MAJORITIES,
BY SESSIONS, 1933–1967

| Congress, Session, Year | Total Roll Calls | Roll Calls of High Southern Democratic Cohesion | | Number on Which Southern Democratic Majority | |
		Number	Percentage	Agreed with Nonsouthern Democratic Majority	Dis-agreed
73:1 (1933)	56	28	50.0	28	0
75:1 (1937)	77	25	32.5	20	5
77:1 (1941)	67	35	52.2	32	3
79:1 (1945)	75	24	32.0	21	3
TOTALS	275	112	40.7	101	11
82:1 (1951)	79	13	16.5	11	2
84:1 (1955)	56	9	16.1	9	0
86:1 (1959)	75	18	24.0	18	0
88:1 (1963)	89	8	9.0	8	0
90:1 (1967)	159	8	5.0	8	0
TOTALS	458	56	12.2	54	2

Source: Data for the first four sessions are from Key, *Southern Politics*, 372.
Note: Near-unanimous roll calls have been omitted in all sessions.

new low may again have been reached by the late sixties. At any
rate, by 1967, majorities of southern Democrats were opposing Republican majorities much less than half as often as they had during
the first year of the New Deal.

A slightly different approach to the question of southern
Democratic–Republican opposition is taken in Table 2. Here the
concern is with the ability of southern Democrats to maintain high
cohesion on House roll calls, and with their tendency to support
either their northern Democratic colleagues or the Republican
"opposition" on high-cohesion roll calls.[10] The table demonstrates

10 Group cohesion, or ability to maintain relative degrees of unity on roll calls, is
discussed here in terms of the familiar Index of Cohesion, first used by Stuart A. Rice.
It is calculated by dividing the votes cast by the majority of a group by the total of

that the southerners continue, as during the sessions Key analyzed, to support the northern Democrats, not the Republicans, when they maintained very high cohesion; but it also establishes beyond question the relatively greater difficulty the southerners have had in maintaining cohesion in recent sessions. They attained an Index of Cohesion of 80 or higher (90 percent unity or more) on nearly 41 percent of the roll calls Key analyzed, but they did so on only approximately 12 percent in the more recent sessions. The table testifies to nothing less than a striking change in the cohesion of the southern Democracy since the years Key studied. Then, they were capable of maintaining something very close to complete unity on half the roll calls studied in some sessions. In the later years they have never been able to do so on more than a quarter of the total, and even this level of southern unity has been quite atypical. During the Kennedy and Johnson administrations the southerners have been unable to maintain 90 percent unity on even a tenth of the roll calls studied.

Table 3 takes up another question posed by Key—the relative solidarity of northern and southern Democrats when majorities of both groups oppose a majority of Republicans in the House. The results of his analysis are plainly apparent in the table. When both Democratic groups opposed the Republicans, the southerners were more cohesive in the great majority of cases; on 125 of 164 such votes the southern Democratic group maintained higher cohesion than their northern colleagues. The data for the later sessions again present a strikingly different picture. During the five sessions of the fifties and sixties, when both Democratic groups opposed Republican majorities, it was the northerners who maintained greater unity in a vast majority of cases. Of 182 roll calls of this variety the northern Democrats were able to close their ranks more effectively on 145. In the later sessions the table reveals that the southern Democrats not only voted more often with Republicans against

---

group members voting, multiplying by 100 to get the percentage in the majority and converting the percentage from a 50–100 scale to a 0–100 scale by subtracting 50 from the percentage and multiplying by two.

Table 3

RELATIVE SOLIDARITY OF HOUSE SOUTHERN AND NORTHERN DEMOCRATS
WHEN MAJORITIES OF BOTH GROUPS OPPOSED A
MAJORITY OF REPUBLICANS, 1933–1967

Congress, Session, Year	Total Roll Calls	Southern and Northern Democrats Against Republicans		
		Number	Higher Southern Democrat Cohesion	Higher Nonsouthern Democrat Cohesion
73:1 (1933)	56	44	38	6
75:1 (1937)	77	41	27	14
77:1 (1941)	67	39	36	3
79:1 (1945)	75	40	24	16
TOTALS	275	164	125	39
82:1 (1951)	79	37	5	31
84:1 (1955)	56	23	7	16
86:1 (1959)	75	40	13	25
88:1 (1963)	89	43	4	38
90:1 (1967)	159	39	4	35
TOTALS	458	182	33	145

Source: Data for the first four sessions are from Key, *Southern Politics*, 377.
Note: Near-unanimous roll calls have been omitted in all sessions.

northern Democrats; when they did join the Democratic group, they were less unified in their opposition to Republican positions on a large majority of roll calls. Interestingly, the data for the more recent sessions establish findings that are precisely the opposite of those Key presented in *Southern Politics*.

What, then, of the "conservative coalition"? How often have actual majorities of southern Democrats joined with Republican majorities to oppose positions taken by northern Democratic majorities over the last four decades? Given the data presented in the foregoing tables, a substantial increase in coalition voting should appear in recent sessions. As Table 4 demonstrates, this is indeed the case. The roll call analysis in *Southern Politics* reveals that the

Table 4

CONSERVATIVE COALITION VOTES: HOUSE ROLL CALLS ON WHICH
MAJORITIES OF SOUTHERN DEMOCRATS AND REPUBLICANS
OPPOSED A MAJORITY OF NORTHERN DEMOCRATS,
BY SESSIONS, 1933–1967

Congress, Session, Year	Total Roll Calls	Number	Percentage
73:1 (1933)	56	0	0.0
75:1 (1937)	77	7	9.1
77:1 (1941)	67	9	13.4
79:1 (1945)	75	12	16.0
TOTALS	275	28	10.2
82:1 (1951)	79	22	27.8
84:1 (1955)	56	8	14.3
86:1 (1959)	75	11	14.7
88:1 (1963)	89	15	16.9
90:1 (1967)	159	57	35.8
TOTALS	458	113	24.7

Source: Data from the first four sessions are from Key, *Southern Politics*, 375.
Note: Near-unanimous roll calls have been omitted in all sessions.

coalition formed on only approximately one-tenth of the House
votes that excited more than a minimal level of controversy. On
the basis of this analysis Key concluded that the importance of the
conservative coalition had been highly overrated by the pundits of
his time.[11] Now, the picture is quite different. Table 4 demonstrates
that conservative coalition voting since 1950 has been on the average approximately two and one-half times as great as during the
earlier sessions. Since the Eighty-second Congress (1951), the coalition has appeared on nearly a quarter of those roll calls in the House
that have occasioned more than minimal controversy. Again, the
more recent data necessitate substantial revision of Key's conclusions. While various observers will differ on the amount of con-

11 Key, *Southern Politics*, 374.

servative coalition voting they regard as acceptable or tolerable,[12] there can be little doubt that a biparty coalition that pits southern Democrats against their northern fellow partisans on a quarter of all reasonably controversial recorded votes is a fundamentally important phenomenon in the politics of the House. There is simply no possibility of dismissing the conservative coalition as a highly overrated phenomenon in the fifties and sixties.

The data in Table 4 again suggest a long-term trend toward increased southern disaffection with northern policy positions over the years since 1933. Clearly, in the early years of the New Deal the southerners were seldom tempted to kick over the traces of party and join Republican majorities in opposing Democratic policies. By 1937, this situation had changed. Although the data indicate that there have been substantial fluctuations in southern movement toward Republican positions since 1937, they do suggest that a kind of plateau had been reached by 1940. Throughout most of the sessions since that time southern Democratic dissidence has remained substantial and reasonably uniform. Again, it appears that the late sixties may mark the beginning of a still higher rate of southern alienation from the Democratic congressional party. The first session of the Ninetieth Congress was marked by nothing less than a general southern Democratic revolt. On nearly 36 percent of all roll calls analyzed, southern majorities joined ranks with Republican majorities to oppose the policy positions staked out by majorities of their fellow partisans.

The magnetic attraction of Republican policy positions for southern Democrats in recent years may be still more clearly demonstrated by a somewhat different approach. The data in Tables 5 and 6 are the result of an inquiry based on the following question: On

---

12 This is part of a common problem in the social sciences. Two or more observers see the same "facts" and conclude different kinds of things about their importance or desirability. Thus, it is common that observers of Congress see the same data on such a matter as party unity and come to different conclusions on what they imply in both empirical and normative terms about the congressional party system. At what level does something like conservative coalition voting become important? The answer is, I suppose, that each observer must decide for himself.

Table 5

SOUTHERN DEMOCRATIC "REPUBLICANISM": NUMBER AND PERCENTAGE
OF HOUSE ROLL CALLS ON WHICH SOUTHERN DEMOCRATS WERE MORE
LIKE REPUBLICANS THAN LIKE NORTHERN DEMOCRATS,
BY SESSIONS, 1951–1967

Congress, Session, Year	Total Roll Calls	Number	Percentage
82:1 (1951)	79	32	40.5
84:1 (1955)	56	23	41.1
86:1 (1959)	75	31	41.3
88:1 (1963)	89	32	36.0
90:1 (1967)	159	102	64.2
TOTALS	458	220	48.0

Note: Near-unanimous roll calls have been omitted in all sessions.

Table 6

SOUTHERN DEMOCRATIC "REPUBLICANISM": NUMBER AND PERCENTAGE
OF "MAJORITY OPPOSITION" HOUSE ROLL CALLS ON WHICH SOUTHERN
DEMOCRATS WERE MORE LIKE REPUBLICANS THAN LIKE NORTHERN
DEMOCRATS, BY SESSIONS, 1951–1967

Congress, Session, Year	Total Roll Calls	Number	Percentage
82:1 (1951)	54	17	31.5
84:1 (1955)	30	9	30.0
86:1 (1959)	47	11	23.4
88:1 (1963)	55	15	27.3
90:1 (1967)	88	51	58.0
TOTALS	274	103	37.6

Note: Near-unanimous roll calls have been omitted in all sessions.

what percentage of roll calls during the five sessions since 1950 have
the southern Democrats been more like the Republicans than like
their northern Democratic counterparts in the House? Stuart
Rice's traditional Index of Likeness permits a direct and effective

response to this question.[13] In Table 5 the question of "likeness" is raised for all of the 458 roll calls in the analysis set for the later sessions. The results are remarkable indeed. On nearly half of these roll calls the southern Democrats voted more like Republicans than like their northern fellow Democrats. And, amazingly, in the first session of the Ninetieth Congress (1967), they more closely resembled the Republicans on nearly two-thirds of the roll calls. In Table 6 the same question is raised but treated in the context of the 274 roll calls on which majorities of Democrats opposed majorities of Republicans. The affinity of the southern Democratic with Republican positions is again striking. On nearly 40 percent of these party opposition roll calls since 1950, the southerners have more closely resembled the Republicans than the northern Democrats. Again, the first session of the Ninetieth Congress marks the high point of the southern rebellion; when the southerners had the opportunity to take Republican or northern Democratic positions in 1967, they gravitated to a more Republican-oriented stance on a full 58 percent of the 88 roll calls analyzed for the session.

The answer to the original question posed above—Has southern voting behavior changed appreciably since the publication of *Southern Politics* in 1949?—is most assuredly yes. Since 1950 the Dixie Democrats in the House have opposed Republican positions less often and manifested much greater internal disunity. When they *have* joined their northern fellow partisans to oppose Republican positions, they have done so with much less solidarity than the northern group. Moreover, they have engaged in a great deal more conservative coalition voting in recent years. In short, everything has changed. Professor Key's conclusions, accurate enough for the sessions he analyzed, no longer fit southern behavior in the fifties and sixties. Finally, although there are no comparable data for the Key sessions, employment of the Index of Likeness has established the presence of a staggering amount of

[13] The Index of Likeness is a simple arithmetical device which may be used to compare the voting behavior of any two legislative groups. It is calculated by subtracting the percentage of yea votes cast by one group from the percentage of such votes cast by the other and subtracting the resulting figure from 100.

what might be called "southern Democratic Republicanism" since 1950. In recent years, the evidence suggests, southern Democrats in the House have staged nothing less than an open revolt against the national Democratic Party.

Southern Democratic Dissidence: Toward Historical Perspective

All of the foregoing data on southern congressional behavior over the last four decades suggest the necessity of taking a long-term perspective on the development of southern Democratic dissidence since the 1930's. Most clearly, it is not a "time-free" phenomenon. Although the data presented above have already established this point, it will be helpful to go a bit farther. What is needed is some indicator of southern dissidence that is reasonably stable over long periods of time. Although the literature of congressional voting behavior leaves much to be desired in this area, it is possible by trimming and compromising a bit to find such an indicator in Julius Turner's Index of Loyalty and *Congressional Quarterly*'s Party Unity Scores.[14] A piecing together of these measures provides a general picture on a number of sessions since 1921. Such an exercise is not without problems. First, there are slight differences in the definition of "the South" in the various studies employing these concepts to gather data. In this analysis as well as in an earlier work, I have followed Key in defining the South as the eleven former Confederate states.[15] Turner has added Oklahoma to the list.[16] The *Congressional Quarterly* defines the section as the eleven former Confederate states plus Oklahoma and Kentucky. Second, a problem is posed by slightly different means of calculating what amounts to the same index, although it is variously called both the Index of Party Loyalty and the *CQ* Party Unity Score. Although each gauges the average percentage of times that individual mem-

---

[14] Essentially, these measurements get at the same thing—the number of times a member supports majorities of his party on roll calls pitting majorities of each party against one another.

[15] Shannon, *Party, Constituency, and Congressional Voting*, 65.

[16] Julius Turner, *Party and Constituency: Pressures on Congress* (Baltimore: Johns Hopkins Press, 1951), 131.

bers supported majorities of their party when Democratic and
Republican majorities opposed one another, the *Congressional
Quarterly* since 1955 has treated absences as failures to support
party positions, thus somewhat depressing individual scores. In
order to get on with the job of creating the long-term picture which
is needed, the existing data must be employed despite these difficulties. The differences in sectional definition will have to be
glossed over on the ground that they are not substantial enough
to produce great variations in the data. The absence factor in the
CQ index will simply have to be kept in mind. Fortunately, it does
not prevent us from measuring the relative loyalty of northern and
southern Democrats in any given session. It only poses a problem
as one attempts to gauge the absolute decline of southern support
for Democratic Party positions over the various sessions for which
data are available.

What, then, can we learn from taking a long-term view of southern Democratic behavior? Table 7, if cautiously interpreted, helps

Table 7

RELATIVE PARTY LOYALTY OF NORTHERN AND SOUTHERN DEMOCRATS,
HOUSE OF REPRESENTATIVES, 1921–1944

Year	Number of Representatives		Average Index of Loyalty	
	North	South	North	South
1921	32	98	81.2	88.9
1930–31	61	99	83.8	92.9
1937	217	105	82.8	79.3
1944	106	108	88.5	70.5

Source: Julius Turner, *Party and Constituency: Pressures on Congress* (Baltimore:
Johns Hopkins Press, 1951), 135.

to throw some light on the problem. It makes clear that in the
1920's and early 1930's, the southern Democrats were on the average
the more loyal supporters of the House Democratic Party on party
opposition votes. It must be understood that during these years
the southerners constituted the bulk of the House party, and a
unified stand by a sizable part of their numbers would have been

necessary to produce a party opposition vote in the first place. Yet, we may reason that the northerners had the opportunity to go along on these votes. Their low numbers do not determine their loyalty scores. The evidence suggests that most did go along most of the time, but their average loyalty score is somewhat lower than that of the southerners. By 1937, the table suggests, the situation in the House Democratic Party had changed somewhat. Now the northerners made up the great bulk of the party, and they showed somewhat higher unity scores than their southern allies. By 1944 the condition that most modern observers of party voting in the House have come to expect was present; the southerners were, on the average, significantly less supportive of Democratic majorities on party opposition roll calls. As all the data presented here suggest, something very important had happened to the House Democrats between 1937 and 1944. Substantial southern dissidence had begun to appear.

These average loyalty scores cannot, however, indicate as much as we need to known about the general distribution of loyalty (unity) scores in the two geographic sectors of the Democratic Party.

Figure 1

RELATIVE PARTY LOYALTY OF NORTHERN AND SOUTHERN DEMOCRATS,
HOUSE OF REPRESENTATIVES, 1930–1931

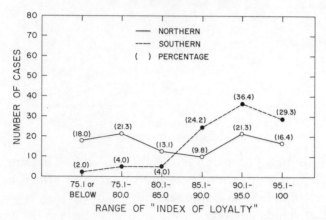

Figure 2

RELATIVE PARTY LOYALTY OF NORTHERN AND SOUTHERN DEMOCRATS,
HOUSE OF REPRESENTATIVES, 1944

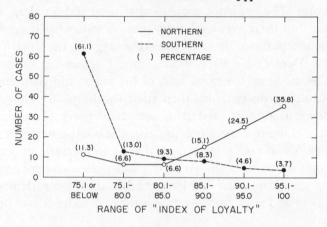

Figure 3

RELATIVE PARTY LOYALTY OF NORTHERN AND SOUTHERN DEMOCRATS,
HOUSE OF REPRESENTATIVES, 1959

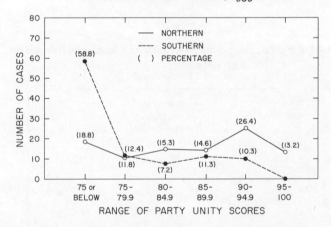

Figures 1 through 4 provide additional perspective. They are based
on full frequency distributions of individual scores which happen
to be available for four House sessions—1930–31, 1944, 1959, and
1961. What stands out very clearly in these figures is the general

Figure 4

RELATIVE PARTY LOYALTY OF NORTHERN AND SOUTHERN DEMOCRATS,
HOUSE OF REPRESENTATIVES, 1961

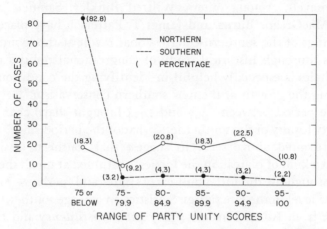

reversal of relative loyalties of the two sectional groups that occurred somewhere between the early thirties and 1944. While the
great bulk of the southerners are to be found in the highest ranges
of loyalty in the first figure, they fall into the lowest ranges in each
of the others. Again, it is plainly apparent that very substantial
sectional cleavage had emerged among the House Democrats by
1944—cleavage that has endured, we must assume, in much the
same form throughout the forties, fifties, and sixties. In each of
the last three figures, presenting data for the 1944, 1959, and 1961
sessions, an absolute majority of the southerners fall into the least
loyal category—below 75 percent. In none of these three sessions
do more than a fifth of the northern Democrats rate such low
scores. In Figures 3 and 4 it should also be noted that the northern
group contains all of the border state Democrats. Other studies
would suggest that these "northern Democrats" constitute a large
proportion of the northern group in the lowest range of loyalty.

Between 1937 and 1944, then, very substantial southern Democratic dissidence evolved. Not surprisingly, this period has been
identified by several commentators as an important watershed in

national politics, marking the origin of the conservative coalition in Congress or the beginning of major southern disenchantment with some of the major policies of the administration of Franklin D. Roosevelt. Among others, Wilfred Binkley, Samuel Lubell, James MacGregor Burns, and James T. Patterson have placed the beginnings of the southern congressional revolt at this point. Patterson's thorough historical study of congressional politics in the late thirties is especially helpful in identifying the conditions surrounding the growth of the new southern conservatism.

If the period between 1937 and 1944 brought sharp changes in the party loyalty of the southerners, what of the period since? Other data presented above seem to suggest that southern dissidence reached a kind of plateau in the forties, continued at much the same level throughout the fifties and early sixties and, perhaps, jumped to a new level in the late sixties. Statistics on average southern party support from Julius Turner's *Party and Constituency* and from a recent article by Joseph Cooper and Gary Bombardier help to throw additional light on this question.[17] Figure 5 presents a time series

Figure 5

DECLINE OF SOUTHERN DEMOCRATIC PARTY LOYALTY,
HOUSE OF REPRESENTATIVES, 1937–1966

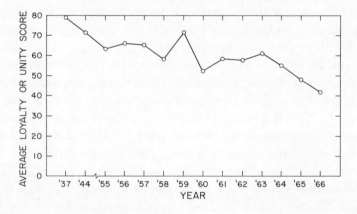

17 Joseph Cooper and Gary Bombardier, "Presidential Leadership and Party Success," *Journal of Politics*, XXX (1968), 1012–27.

of southern Party Loyalty (Unity) Scores from 1937 through 1966. Viewed in this form, these data suggest a definite long-term trend toward increasing southern dissidence. Just how much of the drop between 1944 through 1955 is the result of the "absence effect" noted above is not easy to judge. It would seem reasonable to be cautious on this point and say that there is no great drop between 1944 and 1955, where the *CQ* data begin. From that point, at which the following figures become absolutely comparable, it seems clear that there is a gradual decline of loyalty from the fifties until about 1963. At this point, the rate of decline becomes appreciably sharper. Whether these data are interpreted as a single trend or as two trends makes little difference in the long run. The decline in southern willingness to back Democratic majorities in the House since 1944 is all too clear. A drop of at least 25 points in the average Unity Scores occurred between the middle forties and the late sixties.

That the trend toward greater southern Democratic dissidence to which all our data have pointed is real and that it continues to increase is confirmed by yet another approach. In a recent study entitled "Voting in the House" the Democratic Study Group demonstrated that the number of Democratic members voting *against* as often or more often than *with* Democratic majorities on party opposition roll calls has continued to increase steadily in each House session since the early fifties. As late as the Eighty-third Congress in 1953–54, not a single Democrat voted as often or more often with Republican than with Democratic majorities. Since that time, the percentage of the House Democracy engaging in this extreme form of dissidence has increased as follows:

1955–56	2%
1957–58	5%
1959–60	6%
1961–62	9%
1963–64	11%
1965–66	16%
1967–68	21%

No less than fifty-three House Democrats voted as often or more often with the Republicans on party opposition roll calls during the Ninetieth Congress. Of these men, only one, Walter S. Baring of Nevada, represented a district outside the southern and border states. The extreme dissidents included the entire Democratic delegations of North Carolina, South Carolina, and Mississippi; 90 percent of the Alabama and Virginia delegations; and 60 percent of those from Florida, Georgia, Louisiana, and Missouri.[18] By the late sixties, then, a very large segment of the southerners had gone as far as they could go to protest Democratic policies without formally calling themselves Republicans. Since in politics, as elsewhere, actions speak louder than words, their nominal Democracy meant little aside from its ability to qualify many of them for important committee and subcommittee posts under the seniority system. As we shall see, this feature of nominal Democracy is not without huge importance for the southerners and for the American political system.

Policy Dimensions of the Southern Congressional Revolt

Reference has been made to a "new southern conservatism" that began to develop in Congress about 1937, but nothing more precise has been stated about the policy dimensions of North–South disagreement in the House Democratic Party since that time. Now this question must be directly faced. What are the policies that have occasioned the southern revolt and produced on many occasions since 1937 coalitions of southern Democrats and northern Republicans?

In order to answer this question, some groundwork must be laid. First, it now seems quite likely on the basis of several studies of congressional voting that the major outlines or dimensions of the policy struggle in Congress and in the nation have not changed substantially since the late 1930's.[19] It also appears very likely that these

18 I am indebted to Congressman James G. O'Hara (D.—Mich.) for a copy of "Voting in the House," released by the Democratic Study Group early in 1969.
19 See generally the works by MacRae and Shannon cited above. See also David B.

dimensions, as well as those of previous time periods, are largely fixed by national party realignments. There are no doubt minor modifications that come about as a product of the forces leading up to such realignments, but it is the cataclysmic realignment itself that fixes the broad outlines of national policy for relatively long periods of time.

Second, the congressional voting studies suggest that several broad policy dimensions have been apparent in congressional voting since 1937. One seems to include domestic economic and social policies, cutting broadly across such areas as social welfare, economic regulation, housing, labor, and education. These and similar issues form the basis for the kind of Guttman scale that Duncan MacRae, Jr., labeled the Fair Deal Scale in his study of the Eighty-first Congress.[20] It seems apparent that there is a great deal of overlap in the issues incorporated into these scales and those that the *Congressional Quarterly* selects each year to gauge individual and party stands on issues that may be termed Larger Federal Role.[21] This dimension is obviously at the heart of the major liberal–conservative interparty and intraparty divisions that appear in all the congressional voting studies cited above. Since 1937, the bulk of House Democrats have taken relatively liberal positions on this dimension, while the greater proportion of the Republicans have taken relatively conservative positions. Another dimension has consistently appeared on matters related to the civil rights of Negroes. Here the evidence seems to be that the bulk of Democrats have been consistently more liberal than the Republicans, although there has been quite marked movement on the part of the latter group toward more liberal positions over the years since 1937. A

Truman, *The Congressional Party* (New York: John Wiley and Sons, 1959), and David R. Mayhew, *Party Loyalty Among Congressmen* (Cambridge: Harvard University Press, 1966).

20 MacRae, *Dimensions of Congressional Voting*, 223–26.

21 The staff of the *Congressional Quarterly* selects each year a number of roll calls that seem to bear generally on the question of federal expansion. Quite pronounced party differences are usually apparent on these votes. Most of the issues seem to be of a domestic social and economic nature like those in MacRae's Fair Deal Scale for the Eighty-first Congress.

third broad dimension has consistently appeared on matters of foreign policy. This dimension is probably best labeled interna- tionalism. Here again it has been the Democrats who on the average have taken liberal positions more consistently; the Republicans have somewhat softened their conservative position in the years after World War II. Still another major dimension may exist on matters that have to do with civil liberties, although there is some question about the extent to which the civil liberties dimension is really independent from the domestic economic and social dimen- sion.[22] For our purposes here, it will be most helpful to treat the two separately. Viewed in this light, the civil liberties dimension, like the other ones, has clear partisan overtones. The Democrats have been far more liberal than the Republicans on these matters in recent years.

If these have been some of the most important policy dimen- sions in national politics since 1937, where have the southern Demo- crats stood? The evidence is overwhelming that they have been much more conservative than their northern Democratic confreres on not one but on all of these dimensions. Several studies employ- ing one or another variant of Guttman scale analysis provide a parsimonious and comparable expression of a great variety of data that might be brought to bear on this question. Scale analyses of sessions after World War II testify to sharp differences between northern and southern Democrats on all dimensions save agricul- ture.[23] Three of the four dimensions cited above may be seen in Table 8, which summarizes individual scores of northern and southern House Democrats on civil rights, foreign policy, and social welfare scales constructed from roll call votes taken in the second session of the Eighty-fifth Congress in 1958.[24] Clear dif-

22 On this point see MacRae, *Dimensions of Congressional Voting,* 226–27.

23 See *ibid.*, 215–55, and Shannon, *Party, Constituency, and Congressional Voting,* 81–94. See also the scales by Warren E. Miller and Donald E. Stokes reported below, and Jack VanDerSlik, "Southern Democrats in the House of Representatives: Varia- tions in Roll Call Voting," *Public Affairs Bulletin,* Public Affairs Research Bureau, Southern Illinois University, I, No. 3 (May–June, 1968).

24 I am grateful to Professors Warren E. Miller and Donald E. Stokes and to the Inter-University Consortium for Political Research for the use of these data.

Table 8

CUMULATIVE SCALE SCORES OF HOUSE SOUTHERN AND NORTHERN DEMOCRATS IN THREE ISSUE AREAS, 1958

Issue Area	Scale Types										
	0	1	2	3	4	5	6	7	8	9	10
Civil Rights											
Northern	10	0	2	7	4	8	115				
Southern	76	4	9	3	1	0	0				
Foreign Policy											
Northern	5	9	6	21	61	44					
Southern	33	22	8	14	13	3					
Social Welfare											
Northern	0	1	0	2	3	0	6	8	11	51	64
Southern	24	8	10	5	8	7	10	5	5	7	4

Source: Survey Research Center, University of Michigan, 1958. The South, as defined here, consists of the former Confederate states with the exception of Tennessee. The North includes all other states.

ferences between northern and southern Democrats are apparent
in each case. In each of these issue areas, the northern Democrats
cluster at the liberal end of the scale and the southerners at the
conservative end. The difference between the two sectional groups
is most clear, as we would expect, in the case of civil rights, but it is
unmistakable in the other two scales as well. On each of the scales
the great majority of northerners are to be found at the liberal end.
In each case extreme Democratic dissidence is overwhelmingly
southern. House roll calls on civil liberties issues are far less common than those in the areas just examined, but a scale in this area
is available for the Eighty-sixth Congress.[25] The distribution of
northern and southern Democrats on the scale is the same as in
the case of the civil rights, foreign policy, and welfare scales—
northerners at the liberal end and southerners at the conservative
end.

The southern revolt, then, is very clearly not a limited disagreement on one or even a few specific policy questions. It is general,
cutting across the most important policy dimensions that have
characterized American national politics over the last thirty years.
On three of these dimensions, domestic welfare and regulation,
foreign policy, and civil liberties, many of the southerners have
deviated sharply toward conservative positions that they have
shared with a large group of House Republicans. On the other,
civil rights, they have in recent years maintained their traditional
conservative stance alone, deserted on roll call votes by all but a
handful of their former Republican allies. In this area they have
become a truly isolated sectional minority.

That civil rights questions have often divided northern and
southern Democrats since 1937 is not at all surprising. More interesting are the other kinds of issues that have created Democratic
cleavages and occasioned alliances with northern Republicans.
Surely, these issues should be most clearly revealed in roll calls
on which southern dissidence has been sufficiently strong to prompt
actual majorities of southerners to desert their party and align
themselves with Republican majorities against the northern Democrats. Since a grand total of 113 such conservative coalition votes

25 Shannon, *Party, Constituency, and Congressional Voting*, 93.

took place in the five sessions selected for analysis since 1950, it will not be feasible to attempt to describe all of them. Rather, the focus here will be on the most recent of the sessions, the first session of the Ninetieth Congress (1967). Even so, it will not be possible to describe each vote, but it will be helpful to provide a brief overview of the kinds of issues that most frequently brought the southerners and the Republicans together. Examination of the 57 conservative coalition roll calls (nearly 36 percent) in this coalition-prone session leaves little doubt about the common concerns underlying the southern Democratic–Republican liaison in recent years.

Over half of the coalition votes in this session involved domestic social and economic legislation of the sort that has been at the center of the New Frontier and Great Society programs. In this general area, several themes are apparent in the votes—hostility to urban social and welfare programs, opposition to increased spending and growth of federal activities, and concern for state control of various programs. Specific coalition efforts were made, for example, to block rat control legislation, to cut funds for Model Cities, to prevent greater local autonomy in the District of Columbia, to cut rent supplements appropriations, to replace categorical grants with block grants to states in crime control and education programs, to reduce the federal share of expenses in the food stamp program, and to block establishment of a public broadcasting corporation. Also very clear in these conservative coalition votes is the common cause of majorities of Republicans and southern Democrats in the area of civil liberties. In this session the coalition formed to oppose attempts by northern Democratic majorities to authorize hearings on funds for the House Committee on Un-American Activities and to prevent the passage of legislation extending the life of the expiring Subversive Activities Control Board. Closely related, it would seem, was a coalition effort to block the conference report on legislation creating a federal judicial center. A third area—foreign aid—also brought the coalition together on several occasions. Here the biparty alliance acted most often to reduce authorizations or cut appropriations. On one occasion the coalition formed to attempt to abolish presidential authority for military trade transactions with nations doing business with North Vietnam and to withdraw "most favored nation" status from Poland unless no additional Polish supplies were sent to North Vietnam. In still another area, the coalition formed to delete the twenty-one–day rule[26] from the rules of the Ninetieth Congress and to attempt to block funds for members' telephone expenses in their districts. Finally, the coalition appeared on five roll calls concerning the fate of Adam Clayton Powell. The Powell affair, cutting as it did across several of the issues that have excited southern passions in recent years—the Negro, "wasteful spending," the cities, and "law and order"—produced extremely high southern cohesion. On a series of five roll calls (on all the southern delegation was virtually unanimous) the coalition defeated the Democratic leadership's attempt to seat Powell and appoint an investigating committee to consider charges against him, blocked Powell's seating with a $40,000 fine and removal of his seniority, and finally adopted a substitute measure excluding Powell from the Ninetieth Congress.

Both scale analysis and examination of conservative coalition votes provide much the same perspective on the policy dimensions of southern dissidence in recent years. Clearly, the southerners have been agitated by a wide range of specific policy disagreements with the northern wing of the Democratic Party. These disagreements go far beyond the matter of civil rights. The evidence presented here suggests the development of a general revolt against the most basic policies of the northern party in recent years. A proper appreciation of this situation raises a most important question—can it continue? We may take for granted that the major parties have often papered over differences on one or a few specific policy questions. American political history is rife with examples of intraparty cleavages tolerated for relatively long periods of time in the interest of unity on other important questions. To be sure, no major American party has ever evidenced agreement on all matters of policy. It is something else again, however, to imagine that a party completely divided along sectional lines on all or nearly all of the great policy

[26] The twenty-one-day rule, designed to curb Rules Committee blockage of liberal legislation cleared by other standing committees, was first adopted in 1949. It was repealed on a conservative coalition vote in 1951. It had been reinstated in slightly modified form in 1965.

disputes of an era can long survive. If, as the data presented here suggest, the alienation of large blocs of southern Democrats in Congress has hardened into a state of general revolt, we may reasonably begin to wonder if the national Democratic Party can continue to exist in the form it has taken since the middle thirties. We may begin to doubt that the most alienated of the southerners will care to maintain even their nominal Democracy much longer. More important, perhaps, is the other side of the question—whether the northern party will continue to witness the wayward behavior of the southerners and still reward them with the sweet fruits of committee seniority. These questions will be raised again below.

Southern Democrats and the Committee System

The foregoing analysis has established beyond any reasonable doubt the increasing estrangement of southern Democrats from northern Democratic positions in the House over the last two decades. The House of Representatives, however, is most assuredly not an aggregation of individuals possessed of equal status and influence on matters of policy. On the contrary, it is a highly structured legislative body characterized by many deeply encrusted traditional practices which serve to enhance the influence of some individuals and render others relative lightweights. All this is too well known among students of Congress to require explanation. At this point, however, it will be useful to consider two of the House's traditional practices—the committee and seniority systems—in the context of our larger concern with the southern Democratic congressional revolt.

The committee structure of the House has been ably discussed in a great many places since Woodrow Wilson noted its crucial importance in *Congressional Government* in 1885. Here we need only note briefly that most students of Congress agree that the lines of committee jurisdiction are firmer today and the powers of committee chairmen even more important than they were in Wilson's time. The benefits of chairmanship are many and impressive. We need not run through the familiar list to make the point that these positions confer upon incumbents a tremendous influence on the conduct of business in the House. Although the committee chairmen are formally elected by the entire House of Representatives, in practice since the early years of this century they have been, overwhelmingly, the members of the majority party who enjoy the longest unbroken service on each committee. This practice is, of course, the familiar seniority system, which is too well known to

Table 9

SOUTHERN DEMOCRATS IN THE COMMITTEE PROCESS,
HOUSE OF REPRESENTATIVES, EIGHTY-SECOND CONGRESS (1951–1952)

Committee	Chairman, State
Agriculture	Harold Cooley, North Carolina
Appropriations	Clarence Cannon, Missouri
Banking and Currency	Brent Spence, Kentucky
District of Columbia	John L. McMillan, South Carolina
Education and Labor	Graham Barden, North Carolina
Executive Expenditures (Government Operations)	William L. Dawson, Illinois
Foreign Affairs	James P. Richards, South Carolina
House Administration	Thomas B. Stanley, Virginia
Interior and Insular Affairs	John W. Murdock, Arizona
Interstate and Foreign Commerce	Robert Crosser, Ohio
Judiciary	Emanuel Celler, New York
Merchant Marine and Fisheries	Edward J. Hart, New Jersey
Post Office and Civil Service	Tom Murray, Tennessee
Public Works	Charles A. Buckley, New York
Rules	Adolph Sabath, Illinois
Un-American Activities	John S. Wood, Georgia
Veterans' Affairs	John E. Rankin, Mississippi
Ways and Means	Robert L. Doughton, North Carolina

Percentage of Southern Chairmen	Percentage of House Democrats from South	Percentage of House Members from South
52.6	44.6	24.1

Average Party Unity All House Democrats	Average Party Unity Nonsouthern Chairmen	Average Party Unity Southern Democratic Chairmen
78	96	49

Source: All Party Unity Scores have been taken from the *Congressional Quarterly Almanac*, 1952.

require elaboration here. Two questions, though, do need to be discussed. First, what does the South get out of the seniority system in the House as it has operated since the 1930's? Second, does the system have any important amplifying effect on the southern revolt? The answers to both questions are quite clear. They are also central to an understanding of contemporary national politics.

Table 10

SOUTHERN DEMOCRATS IN THE COMMITTEE PROCESS,
HOUSE OF REPRESENTATIVES, EIGHTY-FOURTH CONGRESS (1955–1956)

Committee	Chairman, State
Agriculture	Harold Cooley, North Carolina
Appropriations	Clarence Cannon, Missouri
Armed Services	Carl Vinson, Georgia
Banking and Currency	Brent Spence, Kentucky
District of Columbia	John L. McMillan, South Carolina
Education and Labor	Graham Barden, North Carolina
Foreign Affairs	James P. Richards, South Carolina
Government Operations	William L. Dawson, Illinois
House Administration	Omar Burleson, Texas
Interior and Insular Affairs	Clair Engle, California
Interstate and Foreign Commerce	J. Percy Priest, Tennessee
Judiciary	Emanuel Celler, New York
Merchant Marine and Fisheries	Herbert Bonner, North Carolina
Post Office and Civil Service	Tom Murray, Tennessee
Public Works	Charles A. Buckley, New York
Rules	Howard W. Smith, Virginia
Un-American Activities	Francis Walter, Pennsylvania
Veterans' Affairs	Olin E. Teague, Texas
Ways and Means	Jere Cooper, Tennessee

Percentage of Southern Chairmen	Percentage of House Democrats from South	Percentage of House Members from South
63.2	42.9	24.4

Average Party Unity All House Democrats	Average Party Unity Nonsouthern Chairmen	Average Party Unity Southern Democratic Chairmen
71	69	62

Source: All Party Unity Scores have been taken from the *Congressional Quarterly Almanac*, 1956.

Table 11

SOUTHERN DEMOCRATS IN THE COMMITTEE PROCESS,
HOUSE OF REPRESENTATIVES, EIGHTY-SIXTH CONGRESS (1959–1960)

Committee	Chairman, State
Agriculture	Harold Cooley, North Carolina
Appropriations	Clarence Cannon, Missouri
Armed Services	Carl Vinson, Georgia
Banking and Currency	Brent Spence, Kentucky
District of Columbia	John L. McMillan, South Carolina
Education and Labor	Graham Barden, North Carolina
Foreign Affairs	Thomas F. Morgan, Pennsylvania
Government Operations	William L. Dawson, Illinois
House Administration	Omar Burleson, Texas
Interior and Insular Affairs	Wayne N. Aspinall, Colorado
Interstate and Foreign Commerce	Oren Harris, Arkansas
Judiciary	Emanuel Celler, New York
Merchant Marine and Fisheries	Herbert Bonner, North Carolina
Post Office and Civil Service	Tom Murray, Tennessee
Public Works	Charles A. Buckley, New York
Rules	Howard W. Smith, Virginia
Science and Astronautics	Overton Brooks, Louisiana
Un-American Activities	Francis Walter, Pennsylvania
Veterans' Affairs	Olin E. Teague, Texas
Ways and Means	Wilbur D. Mills, Arkansas

Percentage of Southern Chairmen	Percentage of House Democrats from South	Percentage of House Members from South
60.0	35.0	24.3

Average Party Unity All House Democrats	Average Party Unity Nonsouthern Democratic Chairmen	Average Party Unity Southern Democratic Chairmen
72	68	52

Average Larger Federal Role, All Democrats	Average Larger Federal Role, Nonsouthern Democratic Chairmen	Average Larger Federal Role, Southern Democratic Chairmen
74	82	40

Source: All Party Unity and Larger Federal Role Scores have been taken from the *Congressional Quarterly Almanac*, 1960.

Table 12

SOUTHERN DEMOCRATS IN THE COMMITTEE PROCESS,
HOUSE OF REPRESENTATIVES, EIGHTY-EIGHTH CONGRESS (1963–1964)

Committee	Chairman, State
Agriculture	Harold Cooley, North Carolina
Appropriations	Clarence Cannon, Missouri
Armed Services	Carl Vinson, Georgia
Banking and Currency	Wright Patman, Texas
District of Columbia	John L. McMillan, South Carolina
Education and Labor	Adam Clayton Powell, New York
Foreign Affairs	Thomas E. Morgan, Pennsylvania
Government Operations	William L. Dawson, Illinois
House Administration	Omar Burleson, Texas
Interior and Insular Affairs	Wayne N. Aspinall, Colorado
Interstate and Foreign Commerce	Oren Harris, Arkansas
Judiciary	Emanuel Celler, New York
Merchant Marine and Fisheries	Herbert Bonner, North Carolina
Post Office and Civil Service	Tom Murray, Tennessee
Public Works	Charles A. Buckley, New York
Rules	Howard W. Smith, Virginia
Science and Astronautics	George P. Miller, California
Un-American Activities	Francis Walter, Pennsylvania
Veterans' Affairs	Olin E. Teague, Texas
Ways and Means	Wilbur D. Mills, Arkansas

Percentage of Southern Chairmen	Percentage of House Democrats from South	Percentage of House Members from South
55.0	30.2	24.4

Average Party Unity All House Democrats	Average Party Unity Nonsouthern Democratic Chairmen	Average Party Unity Southern Democratic Chairmen
71	71	61

Average Larger Federal Role, All Democrats	Average Larger Federal Role, Nonsouthern Democratic Chairmen	Average Larger Federal Role, Southern Democratic Chairmen
74	83	50

Source: All Party Unity and Larger Federal Role Scores have been taken from the *Congressional Quarterly Almanac*, 1964.

Table 13

SOUTHERN DEMOCRATS IN THE COMMITTEE PROCESS,
HOUSE OF REPRESENTATIVES, NINETIETH CONGRESS (1967–1968)

Committee	Chairman, State
Agriculture	W. R. Poage, Texas
Appropriations	George H. Mahon, Texas
Armed Services	L. Mendel Rivers, South Carolina
Banking and Currency	Wright Patman, Texas
District of Columbia	John L. McMillan, South Carolina
Education and Labor	Carl D. Perkins, Kentucky
Foreign Affairs	Thomas E. Morgan, Pennsylvania
Government Operations	William L. Dawson, Illinois
House Administration	Omar Burleson, Texas
Interior and Insular Affairs	Wayne N. Aspinall, Colorado
Interstate and Foreign Commerce	Harley O. Staggers, West Virginia
Judiciary	Emanuel Celler, New York
Merchant Marine and Fisheries	Edward A. Garmatz, Maryland
Post Office and Civil Service	Thaddeus J. Dulski, New York
Public Works	George H. Fallon, Maryland
Rules	William M. Colmer, Mississippi
Science and Astronautics	George P. Miller, California
Un-American Activities	Edwin E. Willis, Louisiana
Veterans' Affairs	Olin E. Teague, Texas
Ways and Means	Wilbur D. Mills, Arkansas

Percentage of Southern Chairmen	Percentage of House Democrats from South	Percentage of House Members from South
50.0	33.2	24.4

Average Party Unity All House Democrats	Average Party Unity Nonsouthern Democratic Chairmen	Average Party Unity Southern Democratic Chairmen
63	74	40

Average Larger Federal Role, All Democrats	Average Larger Federal Role, Nonsouthern Democratic Chairmen	Average Larger Federal Role, Southern Democratic Chairmen
71	83	37

Source: All Party Unity and Larger Federal Role Scores are taken from *Congressional Quarterly Weekly Reports*, October 25, 1968, and November 15, 1968.

Just how much the committee–seniority system in the House means to the South may be seen in Tables 9 through 13, which present data on this question for five evenly spaced congresses since 1950. It will be immediately apparent that in none of these congresses have less than a majority of House standing committee chairmanships been held by men from the eleven former Confederate states. This fact, in and of itself, is an important demonstration of the South's hold on Congress, given what we know of the extraordinary influence of committee chairmen in congressional politics. Even if the southerners were reasonably typical of the Democratic Party nationally, one would be entitled to wonder about the logic of an institution that so disproportionately rewards the spokesmen for a single section of the nation. However this situation is viewed, the South is vastly advantaged in the House under the present system of awarding chairmanships. The tables clearly reveal that the eleven former Confederate states, collectively embracing no more than a quarter of the American population, have controlled from half to nearly two-thirds of the standing committee chairmanships since 1950. Even if it is assumed that the proportion of southern committee chairmen might fairly be permitted to correspond roughly to the percentage of southern Democrats in the House Democratic delegation, they are still impressively overrepresented. This has been the case in each session examined since 1950, but has become especially apparent since 1960. Since that time approximately a third of the House Democratic delegation has represented districts in the eleven southern states. This same third of the delegation, as the tables make clear, has controlled from 50 to 60 percent of the standing committee chairmanships.

Some may argue, however, that spokesmanship for southern districts has little to do with performance in committee chairmanships—that sectional imbalance in allocating chairmanships is thus less important than it might seem at first glance.[27] The evidence is

[27] This is the kind of conclusion that many people are likely to take away from one article that has been widely quoted by textbook writers. See George Goodwin, Jr., "The Seniority System in Congress," *American Political Science Review*, LIII (1959), 412–36. Actually Goodwin does not ask this question precisely, but concerns himself

to the contrary. Two sources of information on this question suggest strongly that southern chairmen have on the average mirrored the dissidence of their rank-and-file sectional brethren in recent years. First, average *CQ* Party Unity Scores and Larger Federal Role Scores (where available) may be compared for all House Democrats, northern chairmen and southern chairmen. Tables 9 through 13 present such data. Although substantial fluctuations are apparent in the comparative scores, they leave little doubt that there are significant differences in the party loyalty of northern and southern chairmen. The Larger Federal Role Scores, available for the sessions after 1959, are particularly revealing. As noted above, the issues on which these scores are based cut across some of the most controversial liberal–conservative domestic social and economic questions of recent years. In each of the three congresses examined since 1959, the cleavage between southern and northern chairmen and between the southerners and the rank and file of House Democrats is much too clear to occasion any dispute.

Another useful source of information on the recent behavior of southern chairmen confirms this picture. The DSG study "Voting in the House," cited above, concludes that current opposition to party positions by Democratic committee chairmen appears to be "far greater than is generally thought." [28] Interestingly, the study found that over half of the House Democrats who voted more often with Republicans than with Democrats on thirty key liberal–conservative issues in the Ninetieth Congress were committee and subcommittee chairmen. These forty-two men include the present chairmen of eight of the twenty-one standing committees—William M. Colmer of Rules, Wilbur D. Mills of Ways and Means, Richard H.

---

with voting differences between seniority leaders and party members (both Republicans and Democrats) during the Eightieth to the Eighty-fifth Congresses. He does conclude that voting differences between seniority leaders and rank-and-file members of their parties are most often exaggerated. A similar argument runs throughout Barbara Hinckley, *The Seniority System in Congress* (Bloomington: Indiana University Press, 1971), a major treatment of the seniority system that appeared long after my contribution to this volume had been completed. As readers of this chapter will be able to see, I have multiple and rather basic disagreements with Mrs. Hinckley's interpretation of the seniority system and the South.

28 Democratic Study Group, "Voting in the House," 6.

Ichord of Internal Security (formerly Un-American Activities), L. Mendel Rivers of Armed Services, John L. McMillan of District of Columbia, W. R. Poage of Agriculture, George H. Mahon of Appropriations, and Olin E. Teague of Veterans' Affairs. Seven of these eight men are from the South, as were all but a handful (mainly representing border states) of the entire forty-two.[29]

Data from the DSG study may be used to provide an even more startling perspective on the dissidence of the bulk of southern committee and subcommittee chairmen. During the Ninetieth Congress a total of forty-one southern Democrats held one or more committee chairmanships. Of these men, no less than thirty-four evidenced equal or higher opposition to Democratic stands on the thirty key votes selected by the DSG than did the average Republican.[30]

The answers to the two questions raised at the beginning of this section are clear. Attachment to one-party politics until relatively recent times has given the South a tremendous advantage in the allocation of House committee chairmanships since 1950. The seniority system has worked miracles for the region under these conditions. There can be no doubt at all that the committee-seniority system greatly amplifies the effects of southern Democratic dissidence. Given the powers and prerogatives of committee chairmen, the crucial placement of such men as Colmer of Mississippi, Mills of Arkansas, Rivers of South Carolina, and Poage of Texas can mean nothing less than a vastly disproportionate southern voice in many areas of national policy formation.

The Causes of the Southern Congressional Revolt

If, as we have seen, the southern Democrats have altered their voting behavior substantially since the Key years—if they have become sharply more conservative on the average than their northern Democratic colleagues on a wide range of policy questions, and if their dissidence (as our evidence suggests) has continued to harden over the years—we must now attempt to come to grips with the reasons behind the southern congressional revolt. How can we explain

29 *Ibid.*, 7–8.
30 *Ibid.*, 7.

these events that have come to have such an important effect on national politics? Unfortunately, the kinds of data that would be
necessary to treat this question fully are not available. Ideally, we
need a wide range of information on such phenomena as the policy
preferences of voters in southern congressional districts, the perceptions of congressmen of these preferences, the personal preferences
of the congressmen, and their voting behavior on several distinct
policy dimensions over fairly long periods of time. However, such
data are for the most part simply not available. Yet the changes in
southern behavior are of sufficient importance that we must grope
along with what we have. Several sorts of information can be
brought to bear on this question. They will not settle it beyond dispute, but they do offer important clues.

A first step may be taken by relating southern Democratic loyalty
to several aggregative characteristics of House districts. A look at
southern behavior in any recent House session will immediately reveal that not *all* southern Democrats have been equally deviant.
Rather wide variations in individual behavior are apparent. Key
took notice of such variations in the sessions he analyzed and reported that they seemed to be more closely related to southern
urbanism than to any other factor.[31] After examining the propensity of various southerners for conservative coalition voting, he concluded that those who represented rural districts were on the average more likely to kick over the traces of party and vote with the
Republicans—that their conservatism seemed to be based on "anti-
pathy toward urban people and perhaps a common lack of understanding of the problems of an urban industrial society."

Other constituency factors may provide additional clues to variations in southern Democratic voting behavior. One that comes to
mind readily is the percentage of nonwhite population in various
districts. Given the importance of this variable in several of Key's
state chapters, it seems likely that congressional districts with relatively large black populations may produce more conservative
representatives. Another important variable might well be the occupational composition of various southern districts. Here, it seems

31 Key, *Southern Politics*, 378–80.

reasonable to suppose that the more heavily working-class districts (as compared with relatively heavy farm and middle-class districts) may produce Democrats who are more loyal. In addition, it seems possible that the loyalty of southern Democratic congressmen may vary with the electoral support of recent Democratic presidential nominees—that those areas manifesting substantial alienation from the Democratic Party in presidential voting would also produce more dissident Democratic congressmen.

In order to test these suppositions, indicators of these four aggregate district characteristics—urbanism, nonwhite population, blue-collar occupations, and electoral identification with the national Democratic Party (as reflected in percentage of vote for John F. Kennedy in 1960) have been related to two measures of southern dissidence—Party Unity Scores and Larger Federal Role Scores—for the Eighty-eighth Congress. The results are presented in Tables 14 through 16.[32] A matrix of simple product-moment coefficients for these variables may be found in Table 14.

Table 14

SOUTHERN DEMOCRATIC VOTING BEHAVIOR AND
FOUR RELATED VARIABLES: EIGHTY-EIGHTH CONGRESS (1963–1964);
MATRIX OF CORRELATION COEFFICIENTS (PRODUCT-MOMENT)

	LFR	PUS	% U+S	% NW	JFK '60
				(n=85)	
LFR					
PUS	.831				
% U+S	.313	.382			
% NW	−.235	−.355	−.149		
JFK, '60	.416	.291	−.191	.034	
% BC	.142	.068	.034	−.111	.124

LFR = Larger Federal Role, calculated from *CQ* scores
PUS = *CQ* Party Unity Score
% U+S = Percentage of urban and suburban population
% NW = Percentage of nonwhite population
JFK '60 = Percentage of vote in district for John F. Kennedy, 1960
% BC = Percentage of blue-collar labor

32 U.S. Bureau of the Census, *Congressional District Data Book (Districts of the 88th Congress)*, Statistical Abstract Supplement (Washington: Government Printing Office, 1963), and the *Congressional Quarterly Almanac, 1964*.

It will easily be seen that there is some relationship, in the direction expected, between both measures of southern loyalty and each of the other variables except blue-collar population. The Party Unity Scores and Larger Federal Role Scores are closely linked, and both rise with increases in urban population and increased Kennedy support and with *decreases* in nonwhite population. When the relationship of each one of the four district variables is related to the two loyalty measures (with the three other variables held constant), a clearer picture emerges. Table 15 accomplishes this result by pre-

Table 15

SOUTHERN DEMOCRATIC VOTING BEHAVIOR AND
FOUR RELATED VARIABLES: EIGHTY-EIGHTH CONGRESS (1963–1964);
PARTIAL CORRELATION COEFFICIENTS

	Larger Federal Role	Party Unity Score
% U+S	.419	.450
% NW	−.230	−.360
JFK, '60	.514	.427
% BC	.059	−.035

% U+S = Percentage of urban and suburban population
% NW = Percentage of nonwhite population
JFK '60 = Percentage of vote in district for John F. Kennedy, 1960
% BC = Percentage of blue-collar labor
n = 85

senting partial correlations for each of the four district variables. Moderately high association between urbanism and southern Democratic liberalism is apparent. Independent of that, moderately strong association with electoral support for Kennedy is also clear. Independent of both, there is a somewhat less impressive relationship between nonwhite population and liberalism. The multiple correlation coefficients presented in Table 16 suggest that urbanism, Kennedy support, and nonwhite population, collectively, may be considered to "account" for roughly 37 or 38 percent of the variance in southern voting behavior.

The major difficulty, of course, with aggregate constituency data

Table 16
SOUTHERN DEMOCRATIC VOTING BEHAVIOR AND
FOUR RELATED VARIABLES: EIGHTY-EIGHTH CONGRESS (1963–1964);
MULTIPLE CORRELATION COEFFICIENTS

	Larger Federal Role	Party Unity Score
R	.610	.613
R^2	.372	.376

Note: The four variables in the multiple correlation equation are urban and suburban population, nonwhite population, presidential vote for John F. Kennedy in
1960, and blue-collar population.

is that they cannot by their very nature reveal much about the actual linkages and causal mechanisms operative in the representative
process. They provide only a very crude *indication* of other things
that we should like to know about. Given this limitation, it is not
really very surprising that they account for such a small portion of
the variations in southern Democratic voting behavior. Moreover,
several other factors have obviously worked to produce southern
Democratic congressional deviance in recent years.

Southern congressional conservatism may be more pronounced
in rural districts, those with high black populations, and those evi-
dencing relatively low Democratic presidential voting—but it is
clearly apparent in many other kinds of districts as well. How may
this be explained? First, it seems that few southern congressional
districts of any kind are likely to produce the kind of politics common to most northern Democratic districts in recent years. Whatever the makeup of southern districts, there is simply no social base
for the kind of labor-Catholic-ethnic or "amateur Democratic"
politics that sustains most of the Democrats who represent northern metropolitan areas. Not only are southern Democratic electoral
coalitions different, but it is likely that southern districts, lacking
strong party organizations and the kinds of groups that are affiliated with them in the North, produce different kinds of congressmen than northern Democratic districts. In northern districts either
liberal, labor-oriented candidates or "amateur" liberal Democrats

are most likely to be recruited. In southern one-party (or predominantly one-party) districts, a much broader range of individuals is likely to use the Democratic Party as a springboard to Congress.

Second, as Key and others have pointed out, political participation in the South generally is heavily weighted in favor of those groups holding more conservative political opinions.[33] In all but a few southern districts, persons most likely to vote or engage in other sorts of political action are those who hold the most conservative positions. While many of these individuals maintain Democratic "party identifications" their policy preferences would put them in the Republican camp in any American political environment other than the South.

Finally, it is obvious that southern districts generally have reflected strong dissatisfaction with the civil rights positions of the national Democratic Party since the 1940's. As recent Democratic stands in this area have become more and more offensive to the region, southern concern has given rise to a new era of "race politics." However much liberal sentiment there may be in the South on other kinds of policy questions (e.g., domestic economic issues), in recent years racial questions have either taken precedence over them or have cast them in a very unfavorable light.

Each of these factors has undoubtedly influenced the development of the southern congressional revolt. Most important of all, however, is that white southerners, generally, have come to feel more and more "out of place" in recent years in a Democratic Party that will not and cannot serve their contemporary purposes. Although existing data cannot establish much about the precise causal mechanisms at work, it seems clear that it is the reaction of a broad range of southerners to national Democratic policies that lies at the root of the southern congressional revolt. These policies emerge

33 On this point see V. O. Key, Jr., *Public Opinion and American Democracy* (New York: Knopf, 1961), 105. For an alternative explanation of southern congressional conservatism, which I do not find convincing, see George Robert Boynton, "Southern Conservatism, Constituency Opinion and Congressional Voting," *Public Opinion Quarterly*, XXIX (1965). 259-69.

naturally enough out of the politics of northern Democratic districts, but many of them seem quite "foreign" in the South.

In retrospect, it seems clear what has happened. The South soon found itself in a new and strange party after the Roosevelt revolution. The realignment of the thirties had barely taken place when this became apparent. As James T. Patterson has shown, the divisions that arose among congressional Democrats after 1937 involved a number of issues such as civil rights, labor practices, and housing, that would rather permanently pit many southern congressmen against their northern Democratic colleagues in years to come. As the race issue became more important in national Democratic politics and as the party responded more and more in the development of national policies to its northern urban base, the southern resistance hardened appreciably. By the late sixties it encompassed most of the policy positions of the party. Since 1938, then, the deepening of sectional cleavages among House Democrats has rather closely paralleled other manifestations of southern discontent. The beginnings of the conservative coalition in the late thirties, the revolt of the "Texas Regulars" in 1944, the Dixiecratic breakaway in 1948, increasing southern Republicanism in presidential and congressional voting, and the George Wallace movement are surely all manifestations of a single underlying process. By the late sixties, the South's traditional attachment to the national Democraic Party had become tenuous indeed. The revolt in Congress continued to harden, and only one southern state could sufficiently tolerate Hubert Humphrey to award him its electoral votes in 1968. Clearly the South was groping for some serviceable alternative to its traditional Democratic politics. Just where this process will ultimately take southern Democratic congressmen is a subject to which we must now turn.

The South in Congress: What Will the Future Bring?

Whether the many signs of southern disaffection with the national Democratic Party that have been so apparent in recent years amount to a party realignment in progress or a process of "convergence" that will ultimately bring southern politics into line with politics in the rest of the nation remains a matter of some doubt.[34] In either case, it is now clear that the traditional attachment of the South to the Democratic Party has severely eroded in recent years. In Congress, as we have seen, this erosion has been especially severe. While the southern Democrats have maintained for the most part a formal attachment to the party, they have openly revolted against Democratic policy positions on a wide variety of matters. Now we must ask what the future of southern congressional politics holds. Is it likely that this situation can continue?

First, it is quite clear that the forces producing southern congressional conservatism are not going to be reversed in the near future. It seems a foregone conclusion that the policy stands of the northern Democratic majorities in Congress and of future Democratic presidential candidates will continue to evoke little enthusiasm on the part of white southerners. All the evidence on southern voting behavior in the House suggests that southern resistance has hardened appreciably in recent years. There is no reason at all to suppose that it will not continue on at least the same level in the near future, and it may very well grow more pronounced. Since barely a chemical trace of support can now be found among white voters in many southern districts for a wide variety of liberal Democratic programs, it seems most unlikely that many Democratic congressmen from these areas will risk electoral displeasure by defending such programs.

Second, it seems apparent that southern Republicans will continue in the next few years to make substantial gains in congressional elections. If the Republicans are not quite what the majority of white southerners would prefer in the area of civil rights, the Democrats will surely continue to be perceived as still less attractive. The same might be said for a wide variety of other policy areas. If the

[34] This problem is raised and discussed by Philip E. Converse in "On the Possibility of Major Political Realignment in the South," Chap. 12 of Angus Campbell, Philip E. Converse, Warren E. Miller, and Donald E. Stokes, *Elections and the Political Order* (New York: Wiley, 1966).

Republicans are not as conservative as a great many southerners would like, they will surely continue to appear more sensible and sound to many white southerners than the Democratic "wild men in Washington" who have so enraged them in recent years. Tables 17 and 18 testify to impressive Republican congressional gains in recent times. Especially if southern voters continue to practice the fine art of ticket-splitting in the future as in the past, these gains can be expected to encourage Republicans to contest more and more congressional elections in the South.

Table 17

SOUTHERN CONGRESSIONAL SEATS HELD BY REPUBLICANS, 1950–1966

State	1950	1952	1954	1956	1958	1960	1962	1964	1966
Alabama	—	—	—	—	—	—	—	4	3
Arkansas	—	—	—	—	—	—	—	—	1
Florida	—	—	1	1	1	1	2	2	3
Georgia	—	—	—	—	—	—	—	1	2
Louisiana	—	—	—	—	—	—	—	—	—
Mississippi	—	—	—	—	—	—	—	1	—
North Carolina	—	1	1	1	1	1	2	2	3
South Carolina	—	—	—	—	—	—	—	—	1
Tennessee	2	2	2	2	2	2	3	3	4
Texas	—	—	1	1	1	1	1	—	2
Virginia	—	3	2	2	2	2	2	2	4
TOTALS	2	6	7	7	7	7	10	15	23

Table 18

INCREASING COMPETITION FOR SOUTHERN CONGRESSIONAL SEATS, 1950–1966

Years	Total Seats	Number Contested	Percentage Contested
1950	105	29	27.6
1952	105	31	29.5
1954	105	36	34.3
1956	105	41	39.0
1958	105	21	20.0
1960	105	41	39.0
1962	105	53	50.5
1964	105	68	64.8
1966	105	58	55.2

Where does this leave the southern Democrats? Despite their desire to maintain the status quo, gather the benefits of nominal Democracy, and reap the rewards of seniority, more and more of them are likely to find themselves in trouble on two counts. First, enterprising Republicans will challenge them on their home ground. Given the depth of southern alienation from national Democratic policies, even nominal Democracy will become more and more difficult to defend in many districts. But one suspects that this will not be the southern Democratic congressmen's greatest problem. If they continue to be as dissident as in the recent past— and almost surely they will have to be, to remain alive politically in their districts—it is likely that they will reap the wrath of their northern colleagues. Here, the cases of such men as Albert Watson, John Bell Williams, and John Rarick are instructive. All were stripped of their committee seniority by the party caucus for their failure to support Democratic presidential nominees. The stage may soon be set for a more serious assault on other extreme dissidents or on the seniority system itself. The DSG study "Voting in the House" is at least an interesting straw in the wind, indicating support among some liberal Democrats in the House for movement in this direction. As the liberals experience the frustrations of opposition and as they continue to lose close votes on cherished programs to coalitions of Republicans and southern Democrats, it will be surprising if they do not turn on the most dissident southerners.[35] Unless something unforeseen happens that will permit a reversal of the southern congressional revolt, there will almost certainly be more Watsons, Williamses, and Raricks.

In such an event, many of the victims may follow Watson's prece-

[35] The final revision of this chapter was completed in June, 1969. Since that time the movement of events in the House of Representatives has been very much in line with my earlier speculation. At a House Democratic caucus on February 18, 1970, during which one southern Democrat had to be restrained from throwing a punch at a northern liberal, the leaders of the DSG sought to pass a resolution calling for a thorough study of the seniority system. Only the unsuccessful attempt of a minority of the liberals to pass a motion of "no confidence" in Speaker John W. McCormack at this session prevented the seniority resolution from being adopted, as the southerners, led by Congressman Joe D. Waggoner of Louisiana, took to dilatory tactics. At the

dent and join the Republicans in name as well as behavior. If the seniority benefits of nominal Democracy are altered or abolished, the most alienated of the southern Democrats will have no reason to remain in a party that poses so many electoral risks. Surely some would then choose to be honest and open Republicans. While all of this is highly conjectural, it is not in any sense utopian. It is actually very much in line with a "convergence" interpretation of developments in southern politics. That is, some of the southern Democrats represent districts that have no reason at all, save empty tradition, to prefer Democratic representation. And even in the American South, tradition is not likely to resist forever the strong forces of change. The alignment of these areas with the Republican Party would do no more than sanctify an already existing union. Other southern districts would, no doubt, continue to elect Democrats. The South, after all, is a heterogeneous region. The probable changes should produce a political process that reflects differences of class, locale, ethnicity, and race that have too long been imprisoned in the mold of one-party politics.

The Consequences of Southern Democratic Dissidence

In retrospect, the development of the southern congressional revolt seems reasonably clear. After 1937, the southern Democrats in Congress found themselves in a strange new party along with a number of social groups for whom neither they nor their constituents had much appreciation. The alignment of the thirties had revolutionized their traditional vehicle for national influence by attracting northern city dwellers, Catholics, a wide assortment of ethnic groups, and, most important of all, Negroes. As the major outlines of the New Deal became apparent, and new policies were developed

---

next meeting of the caucus a compromise resolution passed easily with the support of Majority Leader Carl Albert of Oklahoma. Thus, the stage appeared to be set for the first serious challenge in modern history to the seniority system. During the opening weeks of the Ninety-second Congress in 1971, the challenge was mounted, resulting in a more formalized mechanism for challenging chairmen. Although the future of this issue remains a matter of great doubt, I see no reason to revise my speculation of over two years ago that the sectional cleavages in the Democratic congressional party portend long-run change in the operation of the seniority system.

to meet the needs of this new Democratic constituency, southern dissidence began to appear—first in Congress, then in the form of convention walkouts and electoral protest. As we have seen, both forms of dissidence have continued to harden in recent years.

By 1937 one durable solution to the dilemma of the South had become apparent. The region would stake out a major line of opposition in Congress. Through advantages derived from the seniority system and through coalition with northern Republicans, many of the more repugnant programs of the New Deal might be blocked or at least watered down. The record of southern accomplishment to date is not unimpressive. Since the late thirties southerners have enjoyed tremendous influence in Congress. From the struggle over the Fair Labor Standards Act, through the creation of the House Committee on Un-American Activities and the enactment of the Taft-Hartley law in the forties, to more recent controversies over civil rights, hunger, poverty, welfare, and a wide range of urban problems, the work of southern congressmen is everywhere apparent. Democratic defeats in the Ninetieth Congress on the twenty-one–day rule, funds for the Office of Economic Opportunity, gun control, foreign aid, consumer protection, and other matters testify to the continuing efficacy of their strategy. In sum, the South has found in Congress an efficient replacement for the influence it has lost since 1936 in Democratic presidential politics.

Southern congressional dissidence since 1937 in many areas of the South has served as a kind of substitute for a formal party realignment. Through this mechanism the Democrats could formally organize Congress (in all but two congresses since the beginning of the southern revolt they have done so), but the forces loyal to national Democratic programs have seldom enjoyed a working majority. Franklin Roosevelt was deprived of his legislative majority by 1938. Harry S. Truman never enjoyed Democratic congressional majorities loyal to a national party program. The same may be said for John F. Kennedy. Only Lyndon B. Johnson, for two brief years during the Eighty-ninth Congress, enjoyed the support of a Democratic congressional party for the kinds of programs for which the Democratic Party has stood, nationally, since the thirties. And it has now become quite clear that the South had little to do with the changes that took place in Congress during this period.[36] Despite a great deal of talk about the President's uncanny powers of persuasion and of increased southern loyalty, the crucial factor in the new congressional situation seems to have been nothing more than an influx of loyal national Democrats produced by the Goldwater debacle in 1964. When a great many of these congressmen, most of whom represented marginal northern districts, were defeated in 1966, the situation reverted to its "normal" state. Again conservative coalition politics began to prevail on a wide range of important issues.

Most obviously, all of this—the development of the southern revolt in Congress, and its operation as a kind of substitute for partisan realignment—must be evaluated by each observer in light of his own blend of values and empirical judgments. For many years, such commentators as James MacGregor Burns and James Burnham have vigorously attacked or defended these practices.[37] This old argument cannot be settled here. In any case there is scant evidence that such criticisms and apologetics influence either the general public or the elites who possess the ability to modify the system. If, as this chapter has suggested, the system has now been undermined to the point of collapse, the processes underlying this situation have as much to do with the arguments of professors and pundits as those underlying its creation since the late thirties—little or nothing at all.

If an end does come at last to one-party politics in the South and conservative coalition politics in Congress, most political scientists will nevertheless surely agree that broad majorities of southerners and Americans stand to benefit. This statement does not at all imply that the white southerner must forfeit his right to articulate honest conservative views and to receive a fair hearing in national politics. Nor does it rely on some subtle argument to the effect that the South's "real interests" will be best served by policies that run count-

[36] See Cooper and Bombardier, "Presidential Leadership and Party Success."

[37] See especially James MacGregor Burns, *The Deadlock of Democracy* (Englewood Cliffs, N.J.: Prentice-Hall, 1963), and James Burnham, *Congress and the American Tradition* (Chicago: Regnery, 1959).

er to southern public opinion. It rests only on what political scientists have known for some time about the consequences of southern one-partyism and national conservative coalition politics.

First, these practices have suppressed political competition. The South is today a very heterogeneous area—so much so that the varied interests of its people cannot possibly be successfully articulated through a one-party system. If party competition does flourish again in the region as it did in the generation before the Civil War, it will surely enable the southerner to connect his preferences with the political order far more efficiently than he could in the chaotic multifactional competition to which one-partyism has most typically given rise. Southern one-partyism has effectively enough preserved white unity on the racial question, but it has grotesquely distorted popular opinion on many other matters. That differences of race, religion, education, and occupation—and all the varieties of opinion that flow therefrom—should be confined within a single regional party is an absurd anachronism. Southern politics will make more sense to everyone if the bounds of one-partyism can at last be broken.

Second, the South's overrepresentation in Congress under the committee–seniority system as it has worked since the party realignment of the thirties is simply unfair. It stands today, despite a great deal of pseudoscientific rationalization of its latent desirable functions by congressional scholars of the fifties and sixties, as a blatant flaw in our political institutions, lacking justification in any sensible theory of democracy. Its passing will surely contribute to a more equitable national politics.

Third, and perhaps most important, the practice of coalition politics in Congress in the extreme form it assumed in the fifties and sixties has rendered some of the most important aspects of our national policy processes all but incomprehensible to citizens who are less well equipped than scholars and pundits to fathom their complexities. It seems clear that a mode of politics so resistant to popular understanding ill serves a broad majority of the American people. It is hard to see how anyone devoted to popular control of those who govern could genuinely mourn the demise of such an arrangement.

To be sure, such changes will not in any sense revolutionize the conduct of politics in the South or the nation. They will, if they come to pass, move us a bit closer to realizing the kind of open, equitable, and popular politics that we preach but too often fail to practice.

14

FROM PAST TO FUTURE
An Overview of Southern Politics

WILLIAM C. HAVARD

Then and Now

When V. O. Key published *Southern Politics* in 1949, he pointed out that there was no end to the books about the South, and that this would remain the case as long as the South continued to be the region of the United States with the most distinctive character and tradition. He also noted the extreme complexity of southern politics, especially when the type of competition that existed within the framework of the section's one-party arrangement was compared with the organized two-party competition broadly characteristic of the national political system. In the twenty-odd years since the appearance of *Southern Politics*, the eleven states of the old Confederacy have continued (with some important deviations) to constitute the most distinctive region of the country; and the politics of the South has, in the interval, become considerably more complex than it was when Key examined its workings. But the complexity is of a different order than that discerned by Key and his associates.

The massive changes in southern politics since the Second World War occurred for the most part in the 1950's and 1960's rather than in the '40's, and even the factors that were most influential in precipitating these changes were only dimly discernible by the late 1940's. Although Key provided analytical chapters on each of the eleven states, he indicated that he had concentrated more on the similarities among the different units of what still seemed to be a

cohesive political environment than on individual digressions. Even
though the Dixiecratic movement had manifested itself in the later
stages of research and writing of *Southern Politics*, the South could
still be regarded as "solid" in most of its major political attributes.
It was a one-party region, despite the fact that the adherence to the
national Democratic Party, whose title was still proudly claimed by
southerners, was beginning to loosen perceptibly. Three Republican types were identifiable in 1949—presidential Republicans,
mountain Republicans, and Negro Republicans—but their individual and collective influence was decidedly weak because their
memberships were small, their efforts were sporadic, their distribution did not place them in a strategic position, and in the case of
the Negro Republicans, little could be done to affect state and local
politics because of exclusion of Negroes from the ballot. Republican
leadership was still a holding action through which patronage could
be channeled when the Republicans were in power nationally and
delegates could be sent to the party's national convention. Only in
North Carolina, Virginia, and Tennessee did the Republicans approximate the reality of a political party. And in Congress, by contrast with the signs of disaffection in the Deep South afforded by the
presidential election of 1948, the loyalty of the southern delegations
to Democratic programs, both foreign and domestic, was barely beginning to crack.

   The forms of competition within the states did vary widely, although competition remained everywhere within the protective
cover of the local Democratic Party. The main variations in this respect depended on the extent to which intraparty factionalism had
developed from state to state. Most of the southern states were multifactional, with highly personalized leadership patterns which drew
for electoral support on a sectionally based friends-and-neighbors
following. In one or two instances, discussed in more detail below,
statewide political machines were sufficiently dominant to maintain
single factional control over the politics of a state generally; and
in one or two other cases competitiveness took the form of a bifactionalism that could be compared (at least limitedly) with the two-
party system elsewhere.

The situation today is not only different in degree, it is different in kind. In national elections southern solidarity has not merely been broken; in many respects the South's internally splintered opposition to the national Democratic Party has become one of the major regional sources of anti-Democratic political action in the country as a whole, as is attested by the simultaneous rise of the Wallace phenomenon and the development of a Republican southern strategy. Southern delegations to Congress have reversed their roles of support for the party in both foreign and domestic legislation by becoming fixed congressional centers of opposition to national Democratic Party leadership. The nature of this defection on the part of the southern electorate and southern congressmen is so diversified that it is no longer feasible to take an overview of southern politics from the perspective of the *similarities* of the southern states; it is rather the *dissimilarities* that form the primary focus of attention in this book. The taxonomy of southern politics cannot now be reduced to a single major classification of the eleven states of the South, with subspecies being identified in categories of factional competitiveness. We have indicated at least three major categories—the evolving states, the wavering states, and the protest states. And the individual variations within these three groups are sufficient to justify our suggesting that all eleven states deserve separate categorization.

Measured by the standard of two-party competitiveness, we might suggest that the Republican Party today not only approximates reality in North Carolina, Virginia, Tennessee, Florida, Texas, Arkansas, Georgia, and in a more deviant sense, even South Carolina, but is an organized and functioning entity in most of these states, and is operative to a less effective degree in Alabama, Mississippi, and Louisiana. In fact, in the rim or peripheral states of Virginia, Tennessee, Florida, and North Carolina, the Republicans are probably a more cohesive centrally organized party than the Democrats, mainly because in these areas the Democrats are still united only by a remote identity with the party name and are almost hopelessly divided over the issue of the national as opposed to the local version of the party. But this does not mean that the Re-

publicans are about to supplant the Democrats as a means of stabilizing the chaotic flux that seems to continue in election after election.
Traditional Republicanism in the South has barely survived, if indeed it shows signs of life at all. Presidential Republicans abound,
but they are different from the presidential Republicans of the past
inasmuch as they are not primarily voters who have accommodated
themselves to the local Democratic monopoly and express their
identification with the national party only in presidential elections,
but are mainly Democratic defectors who vote Republican in presidential elections when they have no alternative in the form of a
Dixiecratic candidate. Mountain Republicans are now deeply divided because their economic identifications frequently do not permit
them to vote for the national candidates of the party that they ad-
hered to originally in protest against southern secession. Black Republicanism has been overwhelmed by the massive movement of
Negroes from the Republican Party to the Democratic Party over
the past thirty-five years; the old Black and Tan Republican leadership which provided the holding action for the Negro Republicans
in the South is but a vestige of its former self. The new basis of Republican strength of a potentially permanent nature in the South is
in the rapidly developing urban-suburban metropolitan areas. And
this social and economic underpinning of Republicanism in the
South is itself still emerging rather than mature.

With the Republican Party increasingly competitive in the evolving and wavering South, with the defection from the Democratic
Party fluctuating wildly in the Deep South, and with the general
decimation of state Democratic organizations throughout much of
the region, it would be hard to categorize the politics of the South
as anything but a "no-party" system if we were compelled to bring
the region under a single rubric. The structures of the factional systems of the various states have been greatly affected by the disintegration of the Democratic Party structures and the tentative rise of
Republican organizations. Strong statewide organizations based on
rural versions of urban machine politics have all but disappeared;
the friends-and-neighbors tendency still prevails to some extent in
several states, but is less clearly identifiable than it once was; and

bifactionalism seems to have gone by the board, except possibly in Texas, and even here the growth of Republicanism has confused the lines of this form of intraparty competitiveness.

Before examining the implications of these conditions from the perspective of the South as a whole, it seems appropriate to look at the individual states briefly to determine the main alterations that have occurred over the past quarter of a century. This can be done within the framework of our broad classification of evolving states, wavering states, and protest states.

Key described Virginia as a political museum piece. At the time that he wrote, the state was governed by a single faction—the Byrd machine—which maintained its power through low voter participation and tight central control over the counties. The result was gentlemanly, honest government of an extremely conservative variety, with minimal public expenditure and low levels of public service. Blacks were not entirely excluded from Virginia politics, but they were limited to a form of outsider participation through the machine. The Byrd organization was considerably weaker in the urban areas than in the rural ones, a little mountain Republicanism existed, and such competition as occurred was, more often than not, based on the willingness of the organization to allow two of its members to compete against each other for nomination in the primary.

Today, although the state of Virginia is still conservative in its political culture, the Byrd machine is largely vestigial, a Republican occupies the governorship, Republicans control six of the ten seats in the United States House of Representatives, and the competition is at least as strong along party lines as among personalized factions. After a brief period of resistance to the civil rights movement, Virginia has accommodated itself to black political participation, the electorate has been greatly expanded, and reapportionment has brought the urban voter into a position of prominence, amounting at times to potential dominance. Much of this alteration has occurred as a result of social and economic change: the northeastern section of Virginia has become a part of the eastern urban corridor, the state has rapidly become urban and industrial, and it seems to have achieved about as much political stability within the framework of two-party competitiveness as any state under consideration. By and large, the Republicanism of the state is of a moderate variety, some possibility of a Democratic coalition along the lines of the national party organization seems possible, and elements of the Byrd faction survive in attenuated form. The feature of continuity in the state's politics is well illustrated by the fact that Senator Harry F. Byrd, Jr., was reelected to the United States Senate as an independent in 1970 over a fair showing by a liberal Democratic opponent, and a far from impressive attainment by a youthful and moderately progressive Republican candidate.

In 1949 the state of Florida had the most atomized one-party politics of any state in the South. Key characterized the situation as "every man for himself." Competition was multifactional, leadership was dispersed, and the friends-and-neighbors pattern prevailed to an unusual degree, with concentration of support in statewide elections centered around the geographical locations of the various candidates. The sectional conflict between north (mostly rural) Florida and the peninsula had not developed as fully as it was to do in the 1950's, but was present in muted form as a result of the overwhelming rural control of the legislature prior to reapportionment.

Demographic changes in Florida have swept away virtually all of these characteristics. The population has increased approximately two and one-half times since 1950, the extent of urbanism equals or exceeds the national pattern, and per capita income approaches the national level. Although the Republican Party has become strongly competitive in Florida and has produced some counterorganizational movements within the Democratic Party, the service occupational basis of the economic growth of the state and the extraordinary mixture of the population growth has not resulted in as much stabilization of competitiveness as is exhibited by Virginia. Florida may no longer be southern, but its nonsouthernness appears to approximate California more than it does the politically stable states outside the South.

In 1948, Tennessee politics was largely divided into three parts. The western area of the state was an extension of the lower Mississippi Valley's slave Democracy, since the Mississippi Delta, it was said, extended from Catfish Row in Vicksburg, Mississippi, to the lobby of the Peabody Hotel in Memphis, Tennessee. The eastern area of the state contained the largest mountain Republican segment of any place in the South, and middle Tennessee was largely moderately Democratic. Boss Ed Crump still controlled Memphis, and through an extension of this control (again maintained by patronage and a contrived low turnout in elections) his organization dominated the State Central Democratic Committee. Machine control was far from absolute on a statewide basis; its centralized organization evoked at least a partially unified oppositional movement, a tendency which was, of course, capitalized on by Senator Estes Kefauver. Tennessee, in Key's description, contained two one-party systems, Republican in East Tennessee and Democratic in the rest of the state, with limited factional diversity in the two sectors that were Democratic.

Tennessee's transition to the beginnings of two-party competitiveness has been relatively tranquil. The Crump machine had not totally excluded Negroes from participation in politics; in fact, the proportion of Negro voting in Tennessee has always been considerably higher than in most of the rest of the South. Today the tripartite division of the state still has to be considered, but variations have occurred here, too. The western area remains strongly southern, although Memphis exhibits some signs of cosmopolitanism in its political practices. Eastern Republicanism has spread, particularly into the urban areas of the other parts of the state, but has also proved to be somewhat aberrant in its original sector by virtue of the difference between rural mountain Republicanism and the national Republicanism of Eisenhower and Nixon. Statewide organizations of both the Republican and Democratic parties remain weaker than the corresponding county political organizations, so Tennessee continues to appear somewhat typically southern by reason of its attachment to county-seat politics. In a purely formal sense, and taking appropriate account of the sectional divisions of the state and the fact that it has changed less than Florida and Virginia in the social sense, Tennessee has become about as competitive along party lines as any state in the former Confederacy. The appropriate nonsouthern area of comparison with Tennessee in the national political spectrum is certainly that of the border states.

In many respects Texas has changed less politically since 1948 than any of the states under consideration. Texas has always had as much or more identification with the West as with the South, and the changes that it has undergone in the past twenty to twenty-five years were more clearly perceptible in an earlier period than was the case in the other southern states. A liberal tradition existed in Texas as far back as the latter part of the nineteenth century, and the state had managed to achieve a rough bifactional system along liberal-conservative economic lines by the time Key wrote. Today that economic-interest bifactionalism cuts across the pattern of Republican insurgency in the state, and leaves the Republicans in a more anomalous position than they would be if they were the only moderate-to-conservative party or faction in the state. At the same time, the ethnic diversity of the Texas population, the admission of a proportionately rather small black population to effective political participation, and the great growth and variation in the economy of the state have tended to bring its politics somewhat closer to the national pattern than was the case twenty years ago, even while it maintains rather more of the old practices with respect to party and factional divisions than most of the other rim states in the South.

The states that we have classified as wavering exhibit as much diversity among themselves as the evolving states. In 1948, Key found no statewide factional organization possessing either cohesion or continuity in Arkansas. He perceived a one-party system in its most undefiled and undiluted form. Few divisive factors seemed to exist, voting participation was low, social and economic issues were largely ignored in the quest for good government, and racism did not seem to be as prevalent as in most of the other southern states. The usual approach to electoral competition was to build up systems of alliances around particular candidates in each campaign, with no single candidate managing to elevate himself into even semipermanent leadership of the Democratic Party or any faction thereof.

In the late 1950's this amorphous politics underwent a sudden and drastic change. Arkansas reverted for a time to stereotypical southernness. Governor Orville Faubus managed to inject segregation into politics in such a way as to make himself for a time the leader of a statewide faction that was unprecedented in Arkansas. Gradually, however, Faubus' strength eroded in the face of the success of the civil rights movement and the gradual increase in urbanism in the state. Arkansas is now in a position of ambivalence in its two-party possibilities. Although it has twice elected a Republican governor, it is still the only southern state not to have gone Republican in a presidential election at least once since the Reconstruction period. And in evidence that it has not altogether thrown off the influence of the Faubus years, the state went with the Deep South for George Wallace in the presidential election of 1968, after having avoided previous Dixiecratic deviations; but it did so in a race that was closely divided on a three-way basis. The older pattern of organizational weakness still manifests itself in both the Republican and Democratic parties, and the change in this pattern may very well be the principal clue to the potential development of a more clear-cut competitive situation in the politics of Arkansas.

In the immediate post–World War II period, Georgia was found by V. O. Key to fall between the extremes of Florida and Virginia with respect to its factional arrangement. Eugene Talmadge had introduced some stability and form, but fell far short of exercising the comprehensive control that Byrd had managed to achieve in Virginia. This stability was achieved, however, largely at the expense of repressing the potential urban-rural cleavage through the use of the county-unit system, a system which was crucial to the maintenance of a pattern of a one-party, rural-dominated, conservative politics of the southern variety.

With the demise of the county-unit system, reapportionment, urban expansiveness, and the increase in the black vote and black officeholding, Georgia showed definite signs of moving into two-party competitiveness in the 1960's. However, the rise of Lester Maddox tended to bring back an ambience of Old South politics that had been fading as a result of Herman Talmadge's ability to accommodate himself to the metropolitan trends in the state. Thus Georgia remains ambivalent, with a cosmopolitanism in and around Atlanta that is comparable to, but more graceful than, its metropolitan counterparts in the East, while at the same time it exhibits a tendency to factionalize along the lines of personality and among friends and neighbors of the rustic variety. Even so, Georgia can no longer be considered Deep South, both by reason of Republican advances and the fuller incorporation of blacks into the larger political system of the metropolitan areas.

Many persons, including V. O. Key, have discerned in North Carolina a model for the southern transition away from race-based politics and toward a moderate politics of economic interests. Key found that North Carolina was fairer than most of the states of the South in dealing with Negroes, and that it contained a virile and balanced economy. These findings were reflected in the election of a series of governors who represented a financial and business elite but were willing to make public expenditures for education and other social purposes. His over-optimism on both of these accounts may have been the result of using the rest of the South as the only basis for comparison with North Carolina. The state passed through a period of considerable racial turmoil in the 1950's and the 1960's which left its record more open to doubts than is the case with the states of the evolving South. Furthermore, North Carolina has, somewhat paradoxically, remained rather more rural than most of the other southern states despite its emphasis on industrial growth and its more favorable starting point with respect to the proportion of persons engaged in manufactures. North Carolina has an old record of biparty competition in national elections, and has managed to translate this into some effectiveness in Republican organization and electoral strength. It has considerable capacity for economic growth without the generation of excessive metropolitan size and its attendant problems. But for the moment, it remains less changed than one might have anticipated on the evidence presented by Key.

Among the states that we have classified as protest states, the comparison of the political situation in the late 1940's with the pres-

ent indicates a movement from fairly stable modes of operation to
ferment, without any highly visible signs to indicate how the systems might eventually restabilize. In the earlier period, Key noted
that Alabama displayed a strong tendency to resist oligarchy by
maintaining factions organized along populist lines to offset the "big
mules" of Birmingham and Mobile and the planters of the black
belt. The factions were ordinarily localized (a friends-and-neighbors
effect was at work here, too), although the local bases of voting support of the various factions did merge into some sectionalism in
which northern and southeastern Alabama were aligned against the
middle (the black belt and Birmingham area). However, no faction
ever managed to emerge as a long-range, issue-oriented entity.

Today, a personal oligarchical control has been instituted by
Governor George Wallace. Ironically, Wallace began his career as
a typical populist resister against plantation and industrial oligarchs,
but he managed to consolidate his hold on the state only through
reversion to the racial issue. He has also capitalized recently on the
alienation of white voters in Alabama from the national Democratic Party, and their deeply ingrained spirit of frontier independence and rural individualism, by attacking another giant—a
national government dominated by eastern liberal intellectuals, regardless of which party is in power in Washington. Wallace has
mobilized a considerable majority which cuts across all former lines
of economic and social division (except for the Negroes). The Republican Party has not been able to counter this unity very effectively, except on those occasions when its candidates have become
the medium through which voter protest can be expressed; the national Democratic Party in Alabama is largely black and isolated
in its effect on elections, and other forces of potential opposition
seem to dissipate almost as quickly as they appear.

In 1949 Key indicated that the Negro fixed the tone of Mississippi politics relative to the areas outside the state, despite his exclusion
from politics. Prior to 1940 the proportion of black population in
Mississippi exceeded the white and even in 1940, 49.2 percent of the
state's population was black. Mississippi was by far the most rural
and poverty-stricken state of the South. The successful repression

after Reconstruction of what the overwhelming proportion of Mississippi whites regarded as the "Negro threat" did leave an opening for some political competition along social and economic interest lines. This was described as the "delta versus the hills" or the "planters versus the rednecks." Even so, the factional organizations were weak, with the delta planters acting cohesively despite the absence of a formal organization, and with the potential populism of the hills seemingly dependent for its mobilization on demagogues like Bilbo, whose apparently liberal attitudes on economic questions tended to dissolve into inaction under the thick haze of his verbal race-baiting.

Mississippi remains the most rural of the southern states, with the highest proportion of black population and the heaviest burden of poverty. Race is still capable of diverting the whites from all other issues, and it is a more viable issue today in the face of the civil rights movement than it was between 1877 and the 1950's. Mississippi shares with Alabama the strongest tendency in the South to mobilize its white population—regardless of other differences— around the candidate who most effectively symbolizes the perpetuation of segregation. Once again, the black population constitutes whatever basis still exists for a national Democratic Party; and the whites vote overwhelmingly for a Wallace, a Goldwater, and for whatever local counterparts of these regional and national figures manage to survive the primaries by being more vocal than their opponents on race.

In the late 1940's, even though Huey Long had been dead for well over a decade, Louisiana still displayed the most effectively organized bifactional competitive system of any state in the South. Just as the old oligarchy based on an alliance between the New Orleans urban machine and the upstate planters had been one of the tightest in the South, so had the populist-based faction that Long put together in opposition become what Key called a virtual dictatorship. Both major factions exhibited a high degree of cohesion and continuity; and the tendency to provide comprehensive tickets or slates in the primaries differentiated Louisiana's bifactionalism from that of any other southern state. The Long faction managed to survive Huey's death and the scandals of 1939, and was back in power as a result of Earl Long's election as governor in 1948.

At the present time, although factional identifications may still exist in the minds of individual voters, the bifactionalism which prevailed in Louisiana for thirty-five years or more has virtually disappeared. Earl Long's style of leadership had depended much less on tight-knit organizational control than had his brother Huey's. With Earl's death in 1960, the factional lines became increasingly blurred. Furthermore, the dormant issues of race and religion began forcibly to intrude themselves into the economic-based competitive structure of Louisiana politics. Partly because of the French Catholic ethnic influence in South Louisiana, that section of the state had never been as militant on the race question as had the neighboring states of Mississippi and Alabama. What is more, the Longs had not used the race issue as a diversionary tactic; they stuck instead to their populist economic and social reform programs, and so built their following on the basis of economic interests rather than on the racial, ethnic, and sectional divisions present in the state. As a result, although Louisiana has joined the other states of the Deep South in a strong expression of protest in national elections—having supported the Dixiecrats in 1948, Goldwater in 1964, and Wallace in 1968—its internal politics has not been as unsettled as either Mississippi's or Alabama's. Since 1964 John McKeithen has occupied the governor's office, and he has followed a pattern of fence-straddling that has succeeded in securing cumulative support from virtually all segments of society. At times placatory, and at other times militant on race, McKeithen looks like an interregnum leader, but he is still young enough to have further political ambitions. The state has maintained somewhat more internal calm than the rest of the Deep South, even while it joined its sister states in repudiating the national Democratic Party. But the ingredients for explosion are all there.

Key found the race question more central in South Carolina politics than in any state other than Mississippi. South Carolina had the highest ratio of Negroes except for Mississippi; no section of the state was free of this intrusive issue, and its effect was to stifle political conflict through concentration on it. Organizationally, the state exhibited a loose multifactionalism, with a high degree of localism of the friends-and-neighbors type. Earlier, some radical agrarianism had manifested itself, but leaders of this movement such as Ben Tillman, Cole Blease, and Olin Johnston had reverted to conservatism in a manner typical of this variety of politicians.

At present, one might tend to classify South Carolina as wavering, if not evolving, on the basis of an examination of the purely formal aspects of interparty competition. The friends-and-neighbors pattern seems to be out as a result of more statewide competition, and a broadly based sectionalism seems to have supplanted an almost pure localism. By and large, extremism has not prevailed in gubernatorial elections in recent years. But the nature of the state Republican leadership still prevents categorization of South Carolina as other than Deep South: Strom Thurmond was, of course, the Dixiecratic presidential candidate in 1948, and thus one of the early southern defectors from the national Democratic Party. The causes for his shift into the Republican ranks appear to be much more local than national, as is indeed the case with Albert Watson, who followed him in this move. Up to this point their rewards for defection have been sufficient to keep them cooperative with the national Republican Party; whether they can make the full transition without the residue of race as a central issue is the fundamental question.

The South in Loyalty and Stability

Though not always directly expressed, the perennial question which has nagged students of southern politics for upwards of forty years is, "How soon and under what conditions may the South's politics evolve or be brought into conformity with the national pattern?" [1] Hovering in the background of this implicit question are some ex-

[1] For a set of examples collected within one cover, see the specifically political essays by Robert J. Steamer, Donald S. Strong, and Philip E. Converse in Allan P. Sindler (ed.), *Change in the Contemporary South* (Durham, N.C.: Duke University Press, 1963), 150–222.

plicit notions about the nature of American politics and the aberrant features of southern political practices.

In much of the recent literature on the subject, national politics is perceived in its ideal type as a two-party system in which diversity within the respective parties and competition between them provide an appropriate balance between conflict and accommodation. The issues around which the competition develops are primarily economic and the patterns of voter support for the parties, as well as many of the party responses to particular problems, may be accounted for by the socioeconomic factors which delineate various social strata or classes in the American society. Ideological divisions, although present by reason of religious, ethnic, and class differences, are politically muted by the effectiveness with which the system responds to public needs (again primarily economic), its openness to broad (and expanding) popular participation, and the social mobility inherent in such a responsive democratic order. The historical adjustments of the party system, particularly the comparatively dominant position of one or the other parties over a long period of time, are conceived to be indicative of responsiveness to salient issues, a stabilizing element within the turbulence of intense political competition, and a source for the nationalization of American politics in the face of influences favoring parochialism.[2]

A corollary scholarly view of southern politics holds that practice in that section contravenes every operative principle of the national system. Since the Civil War the South has functioned politically as a one-party section, in which competition has been repressed through pressures toward conformity; the ideological issue of race (and to a lesser extent religion) has continually diverted candidates and voters from their natural tendency to divide over economic

[2] This is a composite of what seem to me to be the underlying assumptions about American party politics in the most influential writings on the subject over the past few decades. See, e.g., V. O. Key, Jr., *Politics, Parties, and Pressure Groups* (5th ed.; New York: Crowell, 1964), E. E. Schattschneider, *Party Government* (New York: Rinehart, 1942), and Angus Campbell and others, *The American Voter* (abridged ed.; New York: Wiley, 1964). The historical phasing of the party system has been best handled in broad perspective in Samuel Lubell, *The Future of American Politics* (New York: Harper, 1951).

issues; both popular participation and response to emerging problems have been systematically restricted through legal and extralegal institutions and customs; and social mobility has been minimized by a racial caste system governing the relations between blacks and whites and by an apparently inflexible class structure among the whites. Historically, southern politics has resisted change of any sort and in its lack of resilience has fostered sporadic outbursts of radical protest on the occasions when it has not been able to suppress potentially effective competition.

This view is implied, in terms somewhat less analytically categorical, in the following statement from W. J. Cash, whose interpretation still furnishes the main regulative ideas behind most of the critical commentaries on southern politics:

> The world knows the story of the Democratic Party in the South; how, once violence had opened the way to political action, this party became the institutionalized incarnation of the will to White Supremacy. How, indeed, it ceased to be a party *in* the South and became the party *of* the South. . . . The destruction of the normal party system signalizes the completion of the divorce from what I have called a part of the proper business of politics—that is, the resolution of the inevitable conflict of interest between the classes, and the securing of a reasonable degree of social equity—and the arrival of the final stage of that irresponsibility which had belonged to the politics of the Old South.[3]

Despite the plausibility of this interpretation and its obvious utility in the partisan battles currently being fought out in the Democratic Party, its generalizations require qualification in more than one respect. Perhaps most importantly, this view of the nature of party politics in the South fails to take account of the place that the South occupied in the national Democratic Party from the end of Reconstruction to some time in the early or perhaps even the mid-1940's. And, although of somewhat less importance, the usual

---

[3] W. J. Cash, *The Mind of the South* (New York: Doubleday Anchor Books, 1954), 137–38. Again, it seems to me that two other seminal works on southern politics suggest the characterization and expectations that are outlined here: Paul Lewinson, *Race, Class, and Party* (New York: Grosset and Dunlap, 1965), and V. O. Key, Jr., *Southern Politics* (New York: Vintage Books, 1949).

interpretation gives almost no credence either to the diversity of forms taken by one-party politics in the South or to the extent to which political competition in the region helped to produce an atmosphere of perpetual dissent.

In the old sectional politics which prevailed prior to the formation of the uneasy Roosevelt electoral coalition of the South with the ethnic and labor groups in the northern cities, the South clearly constituted the geographic electoral base for the Democrats while that party was in a national minority status. What has often been overlooked, however, is the fact that the South also provided strong bases of support in Congress and in the executive branch for the Democratic Party when it was in power, particularly during the Wilson administration and the first two terms of the Roosevelt administration.[4] Few would doubt the influence of the South in terms of sheer numbers: half of Wilson's cabinet were southerners, more than half of the Democratic congressional majority during his administration consisted of southerners, and all but two committee chairmanships in each of the two houses were held by southern Democrats. Though the active involvement of southerners in the New Deal may have been slightly less impressive than Wilson's southern support in absolute figures, from a perspective of more than thirty years it is easy to overlook the extent to which Franklin Roosevelt relied on southerners, both in the cabinet and in the leadership of the Congress, to get his programs underway.

Revisionism sometimes gives the impression that the southern Democrats in Congress (and even in the cabinet or in other executive and administrative positions) have constituted a continuous force for reaction ever since Calhoun. But such an interpretation does not take into account the indebtedness of Wilsonian progressivism to radical agrarian forces in Congress. On such congressional issues as the tariff, the regulation of finance and industrial capitalism, increase in income taxation, and in the many acts respecting easy credit and agricultural improvement, the southerners not only

4 The following discussion relies heavily on the excellent analysis in George Brown Tindall, *The Emergence of the New South* (Baton Rouge: Louisiana State University Press, 1967), Chaps. 1 and 18.

provided a considerable portion of the votes for the Wilsonian measures, but the leadership in developing and implementing such programs as well. The record with respect to labor and the efforts to regulate wages and hours is much less impressive, but even here it is not entirely negative. It may be argued with plausibility that if Woodrow Wilson's New Freedom was a forerunner of the New Deal, it was in many respects a rural populist prelude rather than an effort to come to grips with the emerging urban-industrial society that even the New Deal failed to cope with adequately. But if we think of the changing patterns of government that grew out of the party politics of the Wilson era, it is hard not to think of it in terms of the growth of positive, active government in which presidential leadership of both the party and the government was emerging as a dominant force.

The trend continued and was in some ways accelerated in the early days of the New Deal. If today we remember the beginnings of Democatic Party deviation by way of such figures as Harry Byrd, Carter Glass, Josiah Bailey, and later Walter George, Cotton Ed Smith, and others, that memory, too, often obscures a proper focus on such presidential stalwarts in Congress as Joseph T. Robinson, Pat Harrison, Alben Barkley, Sam Rayburn, William B. Bankhead, and the mavericks who were considerably to the left of the New Deal, including the redoubtable Huey P. Long. It may very well be that southerners, both in the electorate and in Congress, remained in the nineteenth-century agrarian mold of the Democratic Party after that party had become a majority on the basis of its real or presumed capacity to handle the problems of an urban-industrial majority brought to maturity and the brink of economic disaster by the formerly dominant Republican Party. But if the South did lag behind the rest of the country in industrial development and in responses to economic programs designed to make that development conform both to more humane and more democratic ends, it was the radical rather than the reactionary agrarian tendencies of the South that manifested themselves most clearly in elections and in congressional behavior during the period under consideration; and in the areas of government finance, taxation, social security, easy credit, provision for employment, and public regulation—as well as in agricultural innovation—the radical agrarianism of the South (a heritage of the nineteenth century) coincided with and even promoted general programs that inaugurated the changed relation among the public, party, and government that characterized postcapitalist developments from the 1930's onward.

The ready assumption of a monolithic South similarly overlooks the extent to which opposition has been an almost continual aspect of southern politics, as well as the degree to which competition has varied from state to state in the South.[5] It is certainly true that this competition has been muted, especially where race or religion had been mobilized to assimilate all potentially divisive controversy over social and economic problems into a unified response. Although the point has often been made, it bears repeating that competition within the framework of a one-party system hardly provides a substitute for the sort of organized political opposition that is possible under a two-party system. Nevertheless, it should be remembered that the Populist movement may well have exercised a more lasting influence on the South and especially on factional forms of opposition in the South than it did in the Midwest, where it was more widely noticed in its early stages.

Populism, which provided a rough organizational base for sporadic agrarian protest, manifested itself in varying ways in virtually all of the southern states, and its manifestations continued in altered forms until quite recently. In a sizable number of cases the efforts of Populist leaders to generate an opposition to the political power of eastern capitalism and its offshoots in the hinterlands were diverted into racial politics when their appeals were not sufficient to mobilize a competitive electoral base. As indicated earlier, the prototype of the frustrated southern Populist, Tom Watson of Georgia, has been reproduced most recently in Orval Faubus of Arkansas and George Wallace of Alabama. Perhaps the most successful example of a populist-based movement in the twentieth

---

5 For a more extensive treatment of this problem, see T. Harry Williams, *Romance and Realism in Southern Politics* (Athens, Ga.: University of Georgia Press, 1961); and Dewey W. Grantham, *The Democratic South* (New York: Norton, 1965).

century was the Long dynasty in Louisiana, which not only maintained a factional majority in the state's Democratic Party for more than thirty years, but was never diverted into racism and managed to institute programs that placed Louisiana at the top of the list of southern states in proportion of income spent on public purposes, especially in such areas as welfare and education. Some heirs of Populism, such as Big Jim Folsom of Alabama, still received their support on a friends-and-neighbors rather than a statewide organizational basis, and the achievements by way of social legislation and avoidance of racial extremes were noteworthy. And even in the case of the Crump machine which, more than any other except for the Byrd machine in Virginia, relied on keeping the total voter turnout low as part of its system of maintaining power, certain concessions to the support of public programs and moderate race relations were made which reflected Crump's liberal rural origins.[6]

The stress on the South's support of the national Democratic Party down to the 1940's and on the manifestations of political opposition within the states remains, however, only a partial corrective to the grosser misinterpretations of southern politics. The South was never able to build permanent oppositional forces strong enough to challenge county-seat Whig and bourbon elitism on a continuing basis or to prevent the diversion of economic issue-oriented politics into racially oriented politics. Thus, although the South was a sustaining force in the Democratic Party as a minority party, and even managed to assist in raising it to majority position in national politics, the practice of one-party Democratic politics in the South was not capable of maintaining southern congressmen in substantial numbers who could continue to cooperate with the national party in the new directions that it had to take in order to achieve a semipermanent majority status nationally. Consequently, the story of the southern Democratic Party over the past twenty-odd years is one of defection from the national Democratic Party, both in electoral support for the national ticket and in congressional support for the party's program.

6 William D. Miller, *Mr. Crump of Memphis* (Baton Rouge: Louisiana State University Press, 1964), *passim*.

The southern defection from the Democratic Party has been characterized by what might be termed an accelerating reciprocal action. This action is in two cycles: one is the countermovement of the southern and northern Democrats in Congress, and the other is the response of the southern voters to the diminishing force of the South in national party politics.

It is all but impossible to date the precise time at which the defection actually began. Some commentators talk about the southern conservative–Republican coalition as though it developed immediately out of the Roosevelt victory in 1932. Perhaps a more plausible case could be made for its origin in 1936. In January of that year a "Grass Roots Convention" was held in Macon, Georgia, to counteract the influence of the New Deal in the southern and border states and to promote the presidential aspirations of Governor Eugene Talmadge.[7] Although the convention fell a long way short of success, the term "grass roots" was to crop up again and again prior to 1948, when the States' Rights or Dixiecratic third-party movement emerged to challenge the Democratic Party in the South in the national election. Many of the ingredients of southern conservative protest were present at this attenuated "convention," such as extreme parochialism, pronouncements on white supremacy, and financial and ideological support from industrial and economic interests opposed to governmental activism in the form of government credit, income taxation, and the regulation of labor relations.

In the summer of the same year the Democratic National Convention removed the southern delegations' long-standing power of veto over presidential nominations by repealing the requirement of a two-thirds' majority of delegate votes to nominate the party's presidential candidate. In another move fraught with ethnic and racial symbolism and thus with potent signs for party disunity in the near future, the 1936 convention seated some Negro delegates.

The following year produced the great fight over the Supreme Court. A sizable number of southern liberals enthusiastically made

[7] Tindall, *Emergence of the New South*, 617 ff.

the President's battle with the court a part of their own platforms (including a young candidate for Congress named Lyndon Johnson, who was running in a special election in Texas). Furthermore, the southern congressional leadership and a majority of southern senators supported the President's bill with greater or lesser enthusiasm. But the issue did provide a platform from which the conservatives among the southern congressional delegation could attack the President and his supporters in the high name of constitutionalism, and to a large majority of southerners, in office and out, the memory of John C. Calhoun's arguments for checks and balances and concurrent majorities was potent.

In the fall of 1937, a combination of southern conservative Democrats and Republicans issued a "conservative manifesto" in what may have been the real preview of the frequently cited conservative coalition of southern Democrats and Republicans. Moves and countermoves followed in a profusion too complex to admit of detailed discussion. One might list, without claim to exhaustiveness, such events as President Roosevelt's abortive effort to remove some southern congressional incumbents from office in the 1938 elections, the attack on the poll tax, the efforts to pass antilynch legislation, the federal government's growing support of civil rights through the creation of a civil liberties unit in the Department of Justice in 1939, the establishment of the Fair Employment Practices Commission in 1941, the issuance during World War II of executive orders banning racial discrimination in the armed services and on projects under federal government contract, and the report of President Truman's Committee on Civil Rights in 1947.

In brief, the solidification of the Democratic Party majority in the country and in Congress, culminating as it did in programmatic and ideological commitments that went far beyond the South's ideological tolerance of social change, resulted in a weakening of the dependence of the party on the South, brought the party into a direct conflict with the region on a number of issues (particularly those involving race), and stimulated a revival of conservative political leadership and popular reaction against these developments. The sequence of events reached a climax in 1948 when, despite rising southern resistance, the Democratic convention still managed to secure a moderately strong plank on civil rights. In response, the Mississippi delegation and half the Alabama delegation walked out, and Richard B. Russell drew all the votes of the southern delegates to the convention, except for thirteen of the thirty-two North Carolina votes, which went to President Truman. Since many southern leaders and southern voters obviously felt that the party had moved away from them rather than they from the party, 1948 marks the beginning of overt and general southern protest and a countermovement away from the national Democratic Party which, in the case of the states of the Deep South, has taken the form of outright revolt.

The South as Defector

The consequences of southern defection have been extensive and the end result is hardly yet clear. In the effort to order our observations a little more effectively, we may take a brief look, first, at the defection from the Democratic Party on the part of the voters, then review the way in which southern congressmen have affected or been affected by this defection, and finally survey the party and factional directions taken by the defectors, with special emphasis on the possibility of developing two-party competition in the region.

It now seems clear that the South has been in the act of abandoning national Democratic one-partyism for the past twenty-odd years, at least. To look at the matter in gross terms, from 1876 to 1944 the Republican Party received the electoral votes of southern states in only 9 instances out of a possible total of 198, 5 of the 9 cases occurring in the 1928 election. From 1948 through 1968, the Democratic Party lost the electoral votes of 41½ of the possible 66 state votes that it might have received. Since 1948 no fewer than four of the eleven former Confederate states have cast their electoral ballots for a party other than the Democrats in any given election, and in 1968 only one of the eleven southern states—Texas—remained in the Democratic Party column. (See Table 1.)

Table 1

NUMBER OF TIMES THE SOUTHERN STATES HAVE GONE REPUBLICAN
OR DIXIECRAT IN PRESIDENTIAL ELECTIONS, 1876–1968

States

Year	Ala.	Ark.	Fla.	Ga.	La.	Miss.	N.C.	S.C.	Tenn.	Texas	Va.	Total
1876			X		X			X				3
1880												0
1884												0
1888												0
1892												0
1896												0
1900												0
1904												0
1908												0
1912												0
1916												0
1920									X			1
1924												0
1928			X				X		X	X	X	5
1932												0
1936												0
1940												0
1944												0
1948	XXX				XXX	XXX		XXX	*			4
1952			X						X	X	X	4
1956	†		X		X				X	X	X	5
1960	+‡		X			+§			X		X	4½
1964	X			X	X	X		X				5
1968	XX	XX	X	XX	XX	XX	X	X	X		X	10
TOTALS	3½	1	6	2	5	4	2	4	6	3	5	41½

XXX States' Rights Democratic; XX American Independent;
+Unpledged (½ or more).

Source: U.S. Bureau of the Census, *Historical Statistics of the United States, Colonial Times to 1957* (Washington, 1960), Y 32–39; and *Statistical Abstract of the United States, 1966* (87th ed.; Washington, 1966), 369–71.

* One Tennessee elector voted States' Rights.
† One Alabama elector voted for Walter Jones.
‡ Six unpledged electors voted for Senator Harry Byrd; the other five electors were pledged to and voted for the national Democratic ticket.
§ All eight unpledged electors voted for Senator Harry Byrd.

And the defection is not simply a matter of protesting against a particular candidate or set of issues affecting a single campaign or even a cited series of campaigns. A psychological withdrawal from habitual adherence to the Democratic Party has been in process. Despite the loose structure of American parties, recent voting studies have uniformly indicated that traditional party identification by the voters is a major factor in the outcome of elections over a period of time, that an overwhelming proportion of voters do not abandon their party affiliation lightly or for transient reasons, and that major party realignments resulting from shifts in party adherence are comparatively rare phenomena. Despite these tendencies to cling to party lines, public opinion polls in recent years indicate a major disaffection with the Democratic Party on the part of southern voters. The following report of a recent Gallup Poll[8] is only one of many such results:

Percentage of Party Identification Among Southerners

	Republican	Democrat	Independent
Latest	19	47	34
1968	17	52	31
1960	22	59	19

As was indicated in the chapter on Mississippi, in 1967 it was found that the proportion of persons who identified themselves as Democrats had already dropped to 46 percent, the number of independents had increased to 39 percent, and Republican identification was at a level of only 6 percent.[9] When we add to this evidence the increase in the registration and participation of black voters and the increasingly preponderant identification of the latter with the Democratic Party, both the massiveness of white dissociation from the party on a regional basis and the retarded pace of Republican gains in voter identification are dramatized.

Southern voter defection from the Democratic Party in presi-

8 Reported in New York *Times*, July 20, 1969, p. 25.
9 See Chap. 10, *supra*.

dential elections has combined with the growing support of the party in the urban areas of the Northeast to produce what may be regarded as an incipient new sectionalism in Democratic Party politics in this country. Table 2 indicates in the broadest sense the changing basis of support for the Democratic Party by regions from 1960 to 1968.

Table 2

DEMOCRATIC PERCENTAGE OF TOTAL POPULAR PRESIDENTIAL VOTE, BY SECTION, 1960–1968

		1960	1964	1968
9	Northeast	53	68	61
	New England, New York,			
	New Jersey, Pennsylvania			
11	Midwest	48	61	44
	Ohio, Indiana, Illinois,			
	Michigan, Wisconsin, Minnesota,			
	Iowa, North Dakota, South Dakota,			
	Nebraska, Kansas			
13	West	48	60	44
	Mountain, Pacific, Alaska, Hawaii			
6	Border	49	64	42
	Delaware, Maryland,			
	West Virginia, Kentucky,			
	Missouri, Oklahoma			
11	South	49	51	31
	Confederacy			
39	All Non-South	50	65	46

The figures in the table demonstrate that for the past three presidential elections the Democratic Party had had by far its strongest basis of support in the Northeast. This is the first time in the history of American politics that this had been the case. At the same time, it should be noted that through 1956, the South regularly provided the strongest basis of support for the Democratic Party in presidential elections of any region of the country. The region dropped below the Northeast in this respect for the first time in 1960, although remaining (along with the border states) one percentage point above the Midwest and the West in proportion of support for the Democratic Party. In 1964 the South gave less support to the Democratic Party candidate than any other section of the country and in 1968 the downward trend was still more precipitous. In 1964, southern support for the Democratic Party was 14 percent less than that given the party by voters in all the other regions combined. This gap increased to 15 percent in 1968. The latter proportional figure is much less dramatic than it might otherwise be, however, because of the decline in non-southern Democratic electoral support during the same interval from 65 to 46 percent.

Interestingly enough, the regional opposition between the South and Northeast has persisted through all historical changes in party adherence. Prior to the Civil War the opposition was, of course, the agrarian South against the commercial Northeast. In the era of Republican dominance, the South opposed the Northeast as a representative of exploitative big business operating through the governmental negativism of the Republican Party. Today, in addition to the race question, southern opposition seems based as much on objections to the postindustrial, centralized, welfare-oriented, intellectualist, bureaucratically organized political culture of the Northeast as anything else. Both Goldwater and Wallace —the former something of a throwback to the classical liberalism of the American industrial revolution and the latter something of a "spoiled" populist—attacked the news media, "soft-headed" intellectuals, and the life-styles of the urban East at least as much as they did their political opponents.

The southern congressional delegation has certainly kept abreast of the southern voters in the degree to which their support of the national Democratic Party has dropped in votes on legislative issues. In a study of votes in the United States House of Representatives, distributed over congressional sessions from 1933 to 1945, V. O. Key found that majorities of southern Democrats opposed majorities of Republicans on 70.5 percent of all roll calls studied.[10]

10 Key, *Southern Politics*, Chap. 17.

As the preceding chapter demonstrates, in congressional sessions from 1951 through 1967, the percentage of disagreement with the Republican majority on the part of southern Democrats averaged 48.0 percent.[11] Furthermore, in 1967 disagreement with the Republicans occurred in only 34.6 percent of the roll calls, compared with the low in the years studied by Key of 62.7 percent in 1945. Key also found that during the years he included in his analysis, the actual incidence of votes which would indicate the existence of a southern Democratic–Republican conservative coalition had been exaggerated by those who had perceived such an alliance. He found that only in slightly over 10 percent of the roll calls in which the House was substantially divided were majorities of southern Democrats and Republicans opposed to a majority of northern Democrats. On the other hand, during the period of his study, Shannon found that 24.7 percent of such roll calls resulted in a coalition of majorities of southern Democrats and Republicans in opposition to a majority of northern Democrats. Again, the high point was 1967 with 35.8 percent coalition votes as compared to the 16.0 percent found by Key in 1945. Students of congressional voting behavior have taken roll calls through a tortuous series of tests designed to indicate party cohesion, and all of them indicate a striking decline in southern adherence to Democratic Party regularity in the Congress when that regularity is measured in terms either of opposing the Republicans or voting with a majority of non-southern Democrats.[12]

Just as we can perceive some reciprocity between the growth of the Democratic strength in the Northeast and the decline of presi-

[11] See Chap. 13, *supra.*

[12] Among these analyses, the reports published at regular intervals by the Congressional Quarterly Service might be cited as particularly useful for their continuity and ease of comprehension. The extent of southern change in attitude on issues is reflected in the fact that even in the area of foreign policy the South has moved from the strongest position of support for the Democratic position to one of greatest opposition. The exhaustive examination of the polls in Alfred O. Hero, Jr., *The Southerner and World Affairs* (Baton Rouge: Louisiana State University Press, 1965) documents this change among voters. Charles O. Lerche, Jr., *The Uncertain South* (Chicago: Quandrangle Books, 1964) provides extensive evidence of the related change in patterns of congressional voting.

dential Democracy in the South, so, too, is there a reciprocity in the changes in geographical origins of Democratic majorities in the Congress and in the response that these changed majorities have produced in conjunction with southern congressional defections from the Democratic Party. In 1955, when Lyndon Johnson became majority leader of the Senate, there were 18 northern Democrats in that body and 31 Democrats from southern and border states. By 1970 the northern Democratic number had risen to 35 and the southern and border Democratic figure had declined to 19. In the House in 1955 the southern and border Democrats numbered 130, while the northern Democrats numbered 102. By 1970 the number of northern Democrats had risen to 157, and the number of southern and border Democrats had declined to 98. The change in regional alignment is expressed in Table 3.

Table 3

PROPORTIONS OF SECTIONAL DELEGATIONS ELECTED BY THE
DEMOCRATS TO THE HOUSE

	1960	1970	
Northeast	49	58	+ 9
Midwest	35	43	+ 8
West	56	56	—
Border	85	70	− 15
South	93	75	− 18

Note: Expressed as percentages of Democratic seats won. In 1966 and 1968, for the first time in American history, the 9 states of the Northeast elected a higher proportion of Democratic congressmen than was the case in the country as a whole. In 1970 the proportions were approximately the same in the Northeast as for the country as a whole.

It is almost impossible to assign precise causes to changes in structural relations within political parties, but it is difficult not to see a connection between the rising numbers and increased cohesion of nonsouthern Democrats, the falling away from party regularity on the part of southern Democratic congressional delegations, and an increasing tendency toward developing Democratic congressional organizations and strategies without an effort to placate southern dissidence. Long after the Democratic Party became the majority party in the nation, congressional Democrats continued to use a "bridging" strategy in choosing their leaders, a fact which not only reflected the effort to hold together the southern geographic–northern class-based coalition, but also the tendency of American parties in general to practice a broadly conceived policy of accommodating diverse groups as opposed to organizing party politics along ideological lines. The tendency in the past has been to promote loyal southerners, moderates from the border states, or the more unobtrusive types from the North or the West to positions of congressional leadership. In the Senate this tendency has been marked: Robinson, Barkley, Lucas, McFarland, Johnson, and Mansfield, with an occasional concession in one of the leadership posts to an acceptable party liberal such as Hubert Humphrey.

The successful challenge of Senator Russell Long of Louisiana by Senator Edward Kennedy of Massachusetts in 1969 for the position of party whip in the Senate may very well represent a major departure from the former practice. Not only was the challenge to the incumbent leadership unusual (the Republicans have been far more active in this respect than the Democrats in recent years) but the relative ease with which the victory was achieved indicates the changed nature of Democratic strength and the changing nature of party outlook. Kennedy won 31–26. Long's solid core of support from the South was reduced to a total of fourteen votes; four of the twenty-two southern senators were Republicans; and Gore, Yarborough, Fulbright, and Spong went with the majority, with the result that only twelve nonsoutherners continued to follow the bridging strategy, and we are aware that certain persons among these Long supporters based their votes more on personal than on party considerations. Kennedy's election as whip and his subsequent use of the position (as well as the actions of his northern liberal Democratic supporters) indicate a move in the direction of a "modal" strategy as a replacement for the bridging one. That is, it now looks as though policy aims of a consistent and cohesive nature will be defined by the party leadership and pressed on the party on a largely ideological basis. Since the southerners had always predicated their own concessions on the idea that these could be compensated by concessions to southern ideological stances, particularly on race, the new liberal cohesion may have decimated what has sometimes been referred to as the last outpost of the Confederacy: the leadership of the United States Senate.

In the House of Representatives, the changes which followed the development of a majority of Democrats from outside the South were largely a product of the Democratic Study Group.[13] This group, actually organized in 1959, grew out of earlier discussions among liberals in both the House and the Senate about the need for more effective means for controlling the procedure of the House in order to achieve legislative ends in which they were interested. Since the election of 1964, the Democratic Study Group has been in a tacitly predominant position in the House Democratic caucus. Among other things, the group's pressures for more effective caucus control of the committee system resulted in the stripping of John Bell Williams of Mississippi and Albert Watson of South Carolina of their seniority in 1965 because of their open support of Goldwater in the 1964 presidential election. This action was repeated in the case of Congressman John Rarick of Louisiana at the beginning of the Ninety-first Congress in 1969. The outcome of these purges was interesting: Watson, who was a freshman representative at the time the action was taken against him, followed Senator Strom Thurmond's lead and became a Republican; Williams, with eighteen years of seniority at the time of his chastisement, later left the Congress to become governor of Mississippi; and Rarick, still a short-termer, apparently remains an undeviating and unrepentant *southern* Democrat. Possibly because Rayburn (and McCormack and Boggs) did not attempt to block the Democratic Study Group—and in some ways even furnished it moderate support and encouragement—the leaders of the group did not see fit to challenge the House Democratic leadership of John McCormack, Carl Albert, and Hale Boggs.

With electoral support of the southern voters for the national

13 For a summary report on the DSG see Roger H. Davidson, David M. Kovenock, and Michael K. O'Leary, *Congress in Crisis: Politics and Congressional Reform* (Belmont, Calif.: Wadsworth, 1966), 129–42.

Democratic Party diminishing and the congressional strength of the nonsouthern Democrats growing at the expense of the southern delegation, how much longer can the southern Democrats in Congress be expected to hold a *pro forma* membership in a party which a sizable number of them no longer serve and which no longer serves them? This is one of the questions on which may turn the possibility of shifting the personal and organizational resources which keep southern Democrats in Congress to the support of a southern Republican opposition. Defection, which has proved quite successful for Thurmond and Watson up to this point, may well prove attractive to other southern conservative congressmen and senators in the near future.

The South, Present and Future: Redirection or Drift?

If the basis of southern support for the national Democratic Party has eroded to the extent indicated, and the southern congressional delegation's influence in, and adherence to, the national party leadership has rapidly diminished, to what extent has the Republican Party exploited this development to create an effective base of opposition in the South? Again, if we look simply at the gross figures it may be observed that the Republican gains have been quite impressive. Since 1952, the Republican percentage of the two-party presidential vote has hovered very near the 50 percent mark, and on two occasions (1956 and 1968) has risen above it. (See Figure 1.) Three states (Florida, Tennessee, and Virginia) have gone Republican in presidential elections in four of the five elections since 1952, and only Arkansas has failed to give its vote to the Republican Party on at least one occasion since 1952.

A closer look, however, at the presidential voting patterns will give us pause to raise the question whether the southern reaction might not be one of transitional confusion and protest rather than one that is headed directly toward Republican competitiveness. Certainly the pattern varies sufficiently in different parts of the South to suggest that that region is far from monolithic in its presidential electoral behavior. If, for example, we take the proportions

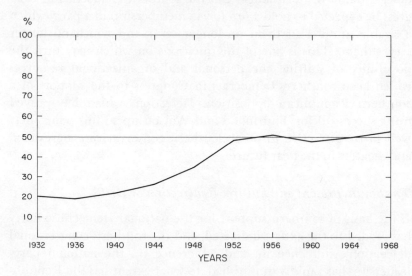

Figure 1
REPUBLICAN PERCENTAGE OF THE TWO-PARTY VOTE,
SOUTHERN STATES, 1932–1968

of the Republican vote in relation to all *three* parties contesting the 1968 presidential election rather than the portion of the two-party vote, every southern state shows a substantial decline in the percentage of its Republican vote from 1960 to 1968.

Table 4
REPUBLICAN PERCENTAGE OF PRESIDENTIAL VOTE IN THE SOUTH, 1960–1968

	1960	1964	1968
Alabama	42.1	69.5	14.1
Arkansas	46.3	43.4	31.0
Florida	51.5	48.9	40.5
Georgia	37.4	54.1	30.4
Louisiana	28.6	56.8	23.5
Mississippi	40.5	87.1	13.5
North Carolina	47.9	43.8	39.5
South Carolina	48.8	58.9	38.1
Tennessee	53.6	44.5	37.8
Texas	48.5	36.5	39.9
Virginia	52.4	46.2	43.4

Although the Republican Party carried five of the eleven former Confederate states in each of the last two presidential elections, only South Carolina showed up in the GOP column in both 1964 and 1968. This peculiar configuration of voting patterns suggests at least two things: (1) a sizable protest vote (in contrast to a vote representing a real shift in party adherence) still exists even in those parts of the South which may now be considered presidential Republican states, and this protest vote reaches majority proportions in the states of the Deep South; (2) the Goldwater election was aberrant in the region, as it was in most of the country, since a substantial portion of his support in the South showed a closer relation to the Dixiecratic vote of 1948 and the Wallace vote in 1968 than it did to the traditional and growing sources of permanent Republican strength in the South, a condition to which we will have occasion to revert later.

When we add to these sources of perplexity the results of public opinion polls indicating that, despite substantial withdrawal among white voters from Democratic Party identification, no remarkable increase has occurred in Republican Party identification among southern voters, it may be assumed that the Republican Party has a considerable way to go before it converts a sufficient portion of the southern population to become competitive throughout the South.

Presidential Republicanism, even where it may have gone beyond the point of mere protest against the national Democratic Party, is no final indication that the South has abandoned its one-partyism in favor of organized oppositional politics. Twenty years ago V. O. Key could indicate that in the South, only in North Carolina, Virginia, and Tennessee were the Republicans able to approximate the reality of a political party.[14] We have already noted that Republicanism now extends to the other rim states of Texas and Florida, and that Arkansas, Georgia, and even South Carolina show limited signs of potential oppositional Republicanism, while the states of the Deep South (including South Carolina, even with

14 Key, *Southern Politics*, 277.

its two "Republican" congressmen) are in a state of rebellion against the national Democratic Party, and use the Republican Party mainly as an agency of protest—especially when Republican candidates are closer to the Dixiecratic type than to the "modern" Republican one (e.g., South Carolina in recent elections and all of the Deep South in the case of the Goldwater candidacy).

In statewide elections Republican opposition has become commonplace in most of the peripheral southern states, if not yet in the states of the Deep South. In seven of the eleven states, Republican gubernatorial candidates received 40 percent or more of the vote in recent general elections prior to 1970.[15] In recent gubernatorial elections in five states, Republicans received a larger number of votes than their Democratic opponents, although only four were elected (in Arkansas [1966 and 1968], Florida [1968], Tennessee [1970], and Virginia [1969]) because in Georgia (1966) the lack of a majority in a three-way race forced the election into the General Assembly, where Lester Maddox achieved victory. In the 1970 gubernatorial elections both Arkansas and Florida returned to the Democratic fold, leaving Republican governors in only two southern states, Virginia and Tennessee. In the most recent elections for the United States Senate prior to 1970, six of the southern states delivered 40 percent or more of their votes to Republican candidates.[16] In four of the six southern Senate races in 1970 Republican candidates received over 40 percent of the votes; in Virginia the Republican vote fell to only 15.4 percent in 1970, when Senator Harry Byrd turned Independent and won with 53.5 percent of the vote to the Democratic candidate's 31.1 percent. Only in Tennessee, however, did the Republican candidate win a southern senatorial election in 1970. As Table 5 indicates, Republicans have succeeded in raising their total number of seats in the United States House of Representatives to twenty-seven, with major gains

15 Arkansas (1968), Florida (1970), Georgia (1970), North Carolina (1968), South Carolina (1970), Texas (1970), and Virginia (1969).
16 Arkansas, Florida, North Carolina, Tennessee, Texas, and Virginia. In addition, of course, South Carolina has, along with Florida, Tennessee, and Texas, a Republican senator, although returned in an earlier election (see Table 5).

coming in each of three elections preceding 1970. A large proportion of these victories, especially those in the peripheral South, may represent real incursions because they occurred in those urban constituencies which have displayed a growing expansion of Republican tendencies in recent years.

As one moves to electoral units of lesser size than congressional districts, the results are more sporadic. In 1955, for example, Republicans held only 45 (3.4 percent) of 1,321 seats in the lower houses of southern state legislatures and only 10 (2 percent) of 441 seats in the upper houses. Most of these seats were concentrated in traditional Republican areas in Tennessee and Virginia, with some signs of Republican life in local elections in North Carolina and Florida. By 1970 Republicans held 177 of 1,340 lower house seats (13 percent) and 57 of 465 seats in the upper houses (12.3 percent).[17] Only in Florida and Tennessee have the Republicans reached the point of competitiveness at which the seats they hold in each of the two houses approach 50 percent of the total number held by Democrats, although in North Carolina, Virginia, and Georgia enough Republicans have been elected to reinforce each other against the feeling of complete isolation and futility.

The pattern of Republican development in what might be called "lesser" positions is also sporadic. To the extent that a pattern shows, it seems to illustrate once again the growing differences between the states of what we have called the rim or peripheral South and the Deep South. Florida, Virginia, Tennessee, and North Carolina show fairly impressive results. In the urban areas of South Florida the effectiveness of one of the few well-organized statewide Republican parties in the South (together with the desuetude of the Democratic organization) has enabled the Republicans to move rapidly into a competitive (and in a number of cases, dominant) position in county commissions and municipal governments. Tennessee, with a large area of traditional Republicanism in the eastern part of the state, has also been able to expand locally. Virginia

17 Compiled for 1970 from *Congressional Quarterly Weekly Report*, XVIII, No. 50 (December 4, 1970), 2921.

Table 5

REPUBLICAN SOUTHERN CONGRESSIONAL GAINS

(House Southerners a Constant Total 106, Senate 22)

Congress	Year	GOP Representatives	GOP Senators
80	1947–48	2	0
81	1949–50	2	0
82	1951–52	2	0
83	1953–54	6	0
84	1955–56	7	0
85	1957–58	7	0
86	1959–60	7	0
87	1961–62	7	1
88	1963–64	11	1 (Tower)
89	1965–66	17	2 (Tower, Thurmond)
90	1967–68	23	3 (Tower, Thurmond, Baker)
91	1969–70	26*	4 (Tower, Thurmond, Baker, Gurney)
92	1971–72	27	5 (Tower, Thurmond, Baker, Gurney, Brock)

Note: A number of the gains may be attributed, in part, to *Wesberry v. Sanders*, the leading Supreme Court decision requiring reapportionment of congressional seats: e.g., Scott (Virginia), Frey (Florida), Thompson and Blackburn (Georgia), Kay Kendall (Tennessee), Bush (Houston), Collins (Dallas), and possibly others. It is not surprising that Senator Baker is one of the most effective and vocal defenders in the United States Senate of Supreme Court districting actions. In 1970 Virginia elected a majority of Republicans to its congressional delegation.

* Most of these are *urban*: e.g., Arlington, Norfolk, Charlotte, Atlanta, St. Petersburg, Orlando, Miami, Fort Lauderdale, Mobile, Birmingham, Chattanooga, Knoxville, Memphis, Dallas, Houston.

has now lifted its proportion of Republicans in office in all levels of state government to an estimated 25 percent; and North Carolina Republicans control the county commissions in twenty-four counties, hold seats in a number of additional counties, and are making inroads into municipal government in a comparable fashion. Of all the rim states Texas has been slowest to develop a modified two-party system on a local basis. Only about forty local offices are held by Republicans in that state, although Republicans do hold mayoralties in some other cities (including two of the largest) where elections are legally "nonpartisan." In Georgia and South Carolina competitiveness is increasing throughout the state, apparently largely as a result of better organization and, in South Carolina, of the capacity of Thurmond, and perhaps Watson, to transfer personal support to support for changed party affiliations. In the remaining states the Republican gains have been negligible and, in some instances, elections of Republicans to local offices obviously were only short-term outlets for the sense of disaffection which prevails among the voters.

In making an effort to assess the basis for further Republican expansion in the South, we might revert again to V. O. Key's identification of southern Republicanism: presidential Republicans, mountain Republicans, and Negro Republicans. None of these furnished a satisfactory base for expanding the party. Presidential Republicanism was a result of a few genuine Republicans and a number of local Democrats who protested every four years against the directions of the national Democratic Party; mountain Republicanism was traditionally based, but had ties to populism that ran counter to the general direction of the Republican Party; and Negro Republicanism was not sufficiently strong to make any inroads into the one-party structure dominated by the Democratic primaries. More recent studies have taken note of the development of urban Republicanism as a base from which to build an effective party. Donald Strong, in fact, has found a persisting urban Republicanism which is traceable well back into the thirties;[18] and the late Bernard Cosman, in dividing the South into four areas, has indicated the actual and potential growth of Republicanism in "the metropolitan South." [19] It is in the latter areas that moderate to conservative Republicanism might develop into the base for the sort of sun-belt state strategy that Kevin P. Phillips relies on in

[18] See Donald Strong, *Urban Republicanism in the South* (University, Ala.: University of Alabama Bureau of Public Administration, 1960).

[19] Bernard Cosman, *Five States for Goldwater* (University, Ala.: University of Alabama Press, 1966). Cosman's analysis uses the following geographical analysis: traditional Republican areas, the metropolitan South, the black-belt South, and the nonmetropolitan South. The 1968 presidential election, including as it did George Wallace, extends the validity of many of Cosman's findings about the changing responses in these different areas and their indications of the separation between the rim South with its "New South" flavor and the "Old South" which is largely Deep South (black belt, nonmetropolitan).

projecting the coming Republican national majority.[20] In recent years great emphasis has been placed in the South on industrial development as part of its long-time efforts to bring the "New South" abreast of the rest of the country in capital investment, income, and job opportunities. The South may be ripe for a belated urban-based McKinleyism in which a fairly broad support can be mobilized for an uninhibited industrial capitalism. Evidences already exist of this trend, particularly in Virginia, Florida, and Texas, which have all had large influxes of population and capital from outside the region. It is interesting that these states, which most consistently supported the Republican Party in presidential elections in 1952, 1956, 1960, and 1968, also seem to have repudiated enough of the southern use of race as a diversionary issue to have been able to avoid the Dixiecrat, Goldwater, and Wallace phenomena of 1948, 1964, and 1968 respectively.

But what if the Republicans should manage to establish some sort of organization and party order leading to a steady enlargement of its control of governments in the South? Will this be likely to evoke any effective Democratic opposition along national Democratic lines and thus result in the establishment of a two-party system in the South via a sort of reverse stimulus to the organization of a "real" Democratic Party? At one time a considerable number of observers of the southern scene thought that the Democratic Party might be made over in the national image only if Whig and bourbon elements could somehow be forced or induced to move into the Republican Party. And indeed some such hopes may be viable in scattered areas throughout the South, again especially in the rim area where the race issue has already begun to display a

20 Although his analysis relies on the most optimistic possible view of the distribution of future Republican votes, and his appraisal of temporal changes in party dominance nationally is not very plausible, Phillips' view of a conservative southern Republican majority which leaves the Negro as the major force in the southern Democratic Party is more realistic than the more liberally oriented view of the Ripon Society groups' expectation that *both* the urban Republican conservative vote and the Negro vote may move into the Republican column in large numbers. See Kevin P. Phillips, *The Emerging Republican Majority* (New Rochelle, N.Y.: Arlington House, 1969), especially Chap. 1; and John C. Topping, Jr., John R. Lazarek, and William H. Linder, *Southern Republicanism and The New South* (Cambridge, Mass.: n.p., 1966).

receding effect on the members of labor organizations and other cohesive groups who belong naturally to the Democratic coalition. Texas, for example, has long had its factional divisions within the Democratic Party split along liberal-conservative lines, roughly comparable to the national party divisions, which may well be one of the reasons the Republican Party has not developed more comprehensively in that state. In Florida, Miami shows signs of a cosmopolitan development (including organized labor and ethnic groups) that resembles northern urban patterns more than southern ones. And the spill-over into northern metropolitan Virginia from Washington has produced suburban areas in that state which resemble some of the suburban areas of the Northeast in their liberal-intellectualist, Democratic proclivities. The extent to which the Democratic organization has fallen into disuse from lack of competition may be the greatest impediment to a revitalized Democratic Party in the rim South.

But in the Deep South the prospects are considerably less sanguine. In those areas labor has been slow to organize, possibly because a good portion of the new labor force is no more than a generation removed from the rural areas of the Deep South, with all that this portends in the way of resistance to impersonal organization and other effective means of collective action. Furthermore, this population group is still highly susceptible to political appeals based on race. With the rapid development and continuing massive efforts to urbanize and industrialize the South, the old support for factional organizations based on radical agrarianism has disappeared, except where it still manifests itself in the struggles for civil rights and against poverty among effectively organized groups concerned primarily with the Negro. To the extent that any Democratic factions in the Deep South now extend beyond shifting, personal followings, they take the form of a reversion to the anachronistic New South appeals of Henry W. Grady (*vide* John McKeithen's ostensible takeover of the remnants of the Long organization in Louisiana) or a retreat into the racist sanctuary which the frustrated Populist so frequently utilized in the past. The old aspiration of a southern liberalism combining the blacks, as the only southern surrogate for the ethnic politics of the North, with the white workers and small farmers still appears to be out of the immediate grasp of those who have long held out for it.

If the white southerner is in the process of repudiating his old party and factional affiliations, the black southerner has already made his transition in no uncertain terms. Ever since 1936, the black population has been predominantly Democratic and has had a substantial influence on the outcome of elections in the northern metropolitan areas. The recent enfranchisement of the southern blacks has effected changes which have only begun to be felt in that region. The attachment of the black voter to the national Democratic Party has been as steady as the rise in his voting strength. In the course of this upward movement, the only period at which the blacks wavered in their support of the national Democratic Party was in 1956 when a substantial portion of the black vote in the South went to Eisenhower, largely as a protest against the type of Democratic candidates who were running for Congress and for state offices in the South. With predominantly Negro precincts delivering upwards of 90 percent of their votes to the national Democratic candidate in recent elections, and with more than three million black registered voters, it is not too much perhaps to say that the national Democratic Party is predominantly black insofar as it still exists in the deep southern states.

However, although the states of the Deep South contain the highest proportion of blacks among the southern states, blacks remain in a minority in all of those states, and their numbers are often heavily concentrated in a relatively few areas of the state, thus confining their political effectiveness.[21] If we measure the success of the Negro in southern politics on the basis of his increased participation in recent years, or even on the basis of the growth of public officeholding by blacks in the South, the result has been phenomenal by comparison with the virtual exclusion of blacks from political effectiveness only a short while ago.[22] But

[21] Only in Mississippi and South Carolina do the number of counties with Negro majorities approach 33 percent.

[22] See Chap. 1, *supra*, for the figures on gains in Negro registration and black officeholding in the South.

with respect to the outcome for the possible growth and development of the Democratic Party in the South, these results have had a polarizing effect rather than an accommodative one.[23] The concentration of blacks in support of the national Democratic Party at a time when the white southerners are breaking with their traditional pattern of support, the focusing of black voters on issues and local candidates who have an overwhelming concern for problems of blacks, and the persisting tendency of working-class and farm whites in the Deep South to react politically to racial more than any other appeals have all exacerbated the tendencies of the deep southern states to express their electoral opinions more as protest than as constructive support for a clearly organized, economic issue–oriented politics.

Thus, while the peripheral South may be moving into a new political alignment in which increasing Republicanism, and possibly even Republican dominance, may evoke organized opposition along the lines of two-party politics, the Deep South may very well continue in its patterns of radical alienation from the national system by way of efforts to establish a white Republican or (more likely) some other form of single-party politics, set over against a permanent black minority Democratic Party. Even in this case, though, it is difficult to envisage the national Republican Party making enough concessions on race to this shrinking core of the Deep South to encourage it to stay within the national framework. Although the Confederacy may have shrunk in size to only four or five states (with Mississippi and Alabama as the hard core) by virtue of the loyalist developments in the peripheral areas, those states that persist seem destined to remain for an indeterminate time closer to the model of post-Reconstruction politics than to what is generally perceived as the national model.

23 The sources indicated in footnote 22 also tell of a rising white registration, some part of which is obviously a response to voter registration drives among Negroes. This increase in registration and the accompanying marked increase in voting participation among those eligible to vote (although still substantially below national figures) is unquestionably a mark of increasing competitiveness in the South generally. But in the Deep South this increased competitiveness is still, as we have previously noted, a black-white polarizing, rather than an "incorporating," phenomenon.

Bibliographic Essay

WILLIAM C. HAVARD

The literature on southern politics and its background is so vast and is growing so steadily that any bibliography or bibliographic commentary offered must be highly selective. The following choice of basic sources has been narrowed even further than usual by excluding virtually all items pertaining to single states, by keeping individual articles in periodicals to a minimum, and by avoiding mention of public documents and unpublished materials, even though items drawn from the latter types contain information that is invaluable in analyzing the politics of the contemporary South. The footnotes to the various chapters in this book and references to sources from which tabular materials and figures are drawn cover some of the excluded items; references to excluded sources abound in the literature cited below.

Three books on, or directly related to, central issues of southern politics are of such critical importance that they merit exclusive bibliographic entry: V. O. Key, Jr., *Southern Politics in State and Nation* (New York, 1949), which has been cited, quoted, and commented on so often in this book that no further statement on its central importance is required; W. J. Cash, *The Mind of the South* (New York, 1941), which has served scholars, as well as interested laymen, for more than thirty years as the most comprehensive realistic overview of the southern culture and its psychic foundations; and Gunnar Myrdal, *An American Dilemma: The Negro Problem*

and Modern Democracy (2 vols.; New York, 1944), which remains
the seminal study of race relations in America.

On the historical background of the South, the broadest coverage
is provided in the monumental project *A History of the South*,
published jointly by the Littlefield Fund for Southern History and
the Louisiana State University Press. Nine of the planned ten
volumes of this series have now been published, and Volumes IX
and X are of most immediate importance for understanding how
the South's politics came to be what it is today. These are C. Vann
Woodward, *Origins of the New South, 1877–1913* (Baton Rouge,
1951) and George B. Tindall, *The Emergence of the New South,
1913–1945* (Baton Rouge, 1967). Some of the more specialized historical studies that reveal various aspects of southern distinctiveness include John Richard Alden, *The First South* (Baton Rouge,
1961); Dewey W. Grantham, *The Democratic South* (Athens, Ga.,
1963); Fletcher M. Green, *Constitutional Development in the South
Atlantic States* (Chapel Hill, 1930); Rollin G. Osterweis, *Romanticism and Nationalism in the Old South* (New Haven, 1949); Ul-
rich B. Phillips, *Life and Labor in the Old South* (Boston, 1929);
Dewey W. Grantham, *Hoke Smith and the Politics of the New
South* (Baton Rouge, 1958); Clement Eaton, *A History of the
Southern Confederacy* (New York, 1954); Frank Lawrence Owsley,
Plain Folk of the Old South (Baton Rouge, 1949); William Darrel
Overdyke, *The Know-Nothing Party in the South* (Baton Rouge,
1950); Katherine M. Jones, *The Plantation South* (Indianapolis,
1957); Avery O. Craven, *The Growth of Southern Nationalism,
1848–1861* (Baton Rouge, 1953); David Donald, *The Politics of
Reconstruction* (Baton Rouge, 1965); Frank B. Freidel, *F.D.R.
and the South* (Baton Rouge, 1965); and Thomas D. Clark, *The
Emerging South* (New York, 1961).

Two books by Clement Eaton do a sound analytical job on the
early development of the southern mind-set: *Freedom of Thought
in the Old South* (Durham, N.C., 1940) and *The Mind of the Old
South* (Baton Rouge, 1964). Among the most penetrating analyses
of the ambiguities, contradictions, and paradoxes that characterize
the southern outlook on social and political questions, two collec-

tions of essays by distinguished southern historians stand out. The first of these is C. Vann Woodward, *The Burden of Southern History* (Baton Rouge, 1960), and the second is David M. Potter, *The South and the Sectional Conflict* (Baton Rouge, 1968). Both books range widely over southern history, the authors are sensitive to the nuances of that history, and the results are profoundly revealing about the nature of the South and the character of its inhabitants. Several other books provide useful insights into related problems. Charles Grier Sellers, Jr. (ed.), *The Southerner as American* (Chapel Hill, 1960) contains a number of perceptive essays on the unifying and divisive factors in the South's and the southerner's relation to the nation. Hodding Carter, *The Angry Scar* (Garden City, N.Y., 1959) examines the persisting influence of the myth and reality of the Reconstruction on the social and political attitudes of the South. Robert Penn Warren's brilliant essay *The Legacy of the Civil War* (New York, 1961) provides a good introduction to the abiding effects of the Civil War itself on both North and South, and extends some sound moral advice on how we can use that historical experience for unity rather than divisiveness. T. Harry Williams, *Romance and Realism in Southern Politics* (Athens, Ga., 1961) is a brief and eclectic corrective to the general view that the South's politics is always unrealistic in its focus on extraneous or diversionary issues; and Virginius Dabney, *Liberalism in the South* (Chapel Hill, 1932) is an early example among a number of books that focus on the liberal rather than the reactionary elements in southern thought and action. In a brief collection of interpretative essays by Francis Butler Simkins, *The Everlasting South* (Baton Rouge, 1963), a serious effort is made to identify those broad features of the southern culture—its class and caste structure, its commitment to religion and, above all, its desire to remain distinctive—that have made and will continue to make the South different from the remainder of the United States. Henry Savage, *Seeds of Time: The Background of Southern Thinking* (New York, 1959) and William Peters, *The Southern Temper* (Garden City, N.Y., 1959) attempt to account for features characteristically identified with southern attitudes.

A host of memoirs, journalistic explorations, and extended essays examine the South in an imaginative and frequently introspective way. Such books vary from historically informed conservative or liberal statements to defensive polemics. Such efforts at personal and regional self-identification came increasingly into vogue in the 1930's and 1940's and continue to appear throughout the period with which this book is concerned. Of the somewhat older variety, the following are certainly worthy of note: Twelve Southerners, *I'll Take My Stand: The South and the Agrarian Tradition* (New York, 1930); William Alexander Percy, *Lanterns on the Levee* (New York, 1940); Clarence Cason, *90° in the Shade* (Chapel Hill, 1935); and Stetson Kennedy, *Southern Exposure* (Garden City, N.Y., 1946). Some notable examples of the liberal tendency which were published within the time span covered by this book include Hodding Carter, *Southern Legacy* (Baton Rouge, 1950); James McBride Dabbs, *The Southern Heritage* (New York, 1958); Ralph E. McGill, *The South and the Southerner* (Boston, 1963); Charles L. Weltner, *Southerner* (Philadelphia, 1966); LeRoy Collins, *The South and the Nation* (Atlanta, 1960), James McBride Dabbs, *Who Speaks for the South?* (New York, 1965); and Frank E. Smith, *Look Away from Dixie* (Baton Rouge, 1963). On the conservative side, the following represent a random collection: James Jackson Kilpatrick, *The Sovereign States: Notes of a Citizen of Virginia* (Chicago, 1957); Peter Molyneaux, *The South's Political Plight* (Dallas, 1948); Frank E. Westmoreland, *The South: Last Bulwark of America* (New York, 1958); and William D. Workman, *The Case for the South* (New York, 1960).

In the area of broad-based social, economic, and political analysis, using the tools of the social sciences to a greater or lesser degree, a number of books are available. One that covers a wide spectrum of the elements of social change—in demography, culture, politics, race relations, and economics—is Allan P. Sindler (ed.), *Change in the Contemporary South* (Durham, N. C., 1963). A volume concentrating more heavily on economic change is John C. McKinney (ed.), *The South in Continuity and Change* (Durham, N.C., 1965). Robert B. Highsaw (ed.), *The Deep South in Transformation: A*

Symposium (University, Ala., 1964) grew out of a conference entitled "The Social Sciences and the Development of the Deep South" and concentrates on the past and potential contributions of the social sciences to the solution of southern problems. A general sociological analysis is presented in John M. Maclachlan and Joe B. Floyd, *This Changing South* (Gainesville, Fla., 1956). Other works assessing recent or current general developments in the South include Robert W. Howard, *This Is the South* (Chicago, 1959); Keith F. McKean, *Cross Currents in the South* (Denver, 1960); Willie Morris (ed.), *The South Today, One Hundred Years After Appomattox* (New York, 1965), originally appearing as a special supplement to *Harper's Magazine,* April, 1965; and William H. Nicholls, *Southern Tradition and Regional Progress* (Chapel Hill, 1960).

Scholars who have worked on southern social and political problems in recent years have been able to build on some solid foundations of earlier scholarship. One of the foremost stimulators of social research was Howard W. Odum, whose *Southern Regions of the United States* (Chapel Hill, 1936) was a landmark. A few years earlier Professor Odum's colleague at the University of North Carolina, Rupert B. Vance, published *Human Geography of the South* (Chapel Hill, 1932), and he followed this early analysis some years later, in collaboration with Nadia Danilevsky, with *All These People: The Nation's Human Resources in the South* (Chapel Hill, 1945). A pioneering study of the southern suffrage and voting problems is Paul Lewinson's *Race, Class, and Party: A History of Negro Suffrage and White Politics in the South* (New York, 1932). Another volume of broad import was Allison Davis, Burleigh B. Gardner, and Mary R. Gardner, *Deep South: A Social Anthropological Study of Caste and Class* (Chicago, 1942).

The tradition of social analysis and commentary built up through such efforts as those just listed continues to flourish. Several special studies provide useful social and cultural backgrounds for any study of the politics of the South. Among these, James G. Maddox and others, *The Advancing South: Manpower Prospects and Problems* (New York, 1967) covers a broad spectrum of southern economic problems and possibilities within its analysis of the use and abuse of the South's occupational resources. F. Ray Marshall's *Labor in the South* (Cambridge, Mass., 1967) is a thorough analysis of the labor force of the South, including a good social analysis of the reasons behind the South's lag in unionization. On the cultural side Kenneth Bailey has written a fine analysis of the South's religious commitment and its social effects in his *Southern White Protestantism in the Twentieth Century* (New York, 1964). And, among several studies of the literary prominence of the South, we may call attention to John M. Bradbury, *Renaissance in the South: A Critical History of the Literature, 1920–1960* (Chapel Hill, 1963) and Louis D. Rubin, Jr., *A Bibliographical Guide to the Study of Southern Literature* (Baton Rouge, 1969).

Although Key's *Southern Politics* is the landmark against which all forays into the hazy territory of southern politics are measured, a number of general works have appeared, both before and after his definitive explorations. One of my favorites, because of its felicity of style (despite a tendency to overquote Henry Adams) and its caustic dissection of county-seat politics, is Jasper B. Shannon, *Toward a New Politics in the South* (Knoxville, 1949). Alexander Heard, who was Key's principal associate in the work on *Southern Politics,* followed up with an able inquiry into the prospects of interparty electoral competitiveness with his *A Two-Party South?* (Chapel Hill, 1952). Heard also joined Donald S. Strong, another of Key's associates, to compile extensive data, with accompanying commentary, on *Southern Primaries and Elections, 1920–1949* (University, Ala., 1950). Cortez A. M. Ewing joined the trend toward quantification with the production of an analysis of the nature of electoral competition in the South in *Primary Elections in the South: A Study in Uniparty Politics* (Norman, Okla., 1953). In 1948, and again on the occasion of its silver anniversary in 1964, the *Journal of Politics,* a quarterly journal sponsored by the Southern Political Science Association, published special issues on southern politics, both of which also came out in separate editions, the first entitled *The Southern Political Scene, 1938–1948,* ed. Taylor Cole and John H. Hallowell (Gainesville, Fla., 1948) and the second, *The American South in the 1960's,* ed. Avery Leiserson, (New York,

1964). Although both volumes are excellent in their own ways, the contrast in topical coverage, tone, and methods employed by the contributors is in itself an interesting insight into the way in which social change impinges on research and writing and vice versa.

The revived interest in southern politics in the last quarter-century and the improved availability of research opportunities led to a spate of specialized studies involving the constituent units of southern politics, both state and local, which we do not have space to pursue here. But it also led to some topically specialized studies covering larger areas of the South which are worthy of special attention. Emile B. Ader, for example, produced a succinct commentary on the 1948 presidential election antics of the Deep South in *The Dixiecrat Movement, Its Role in Third Party Politics* (Washington, 1955). Bernard Cosman was later to select another example of deep southern revolt for careful examination in his *Five States for Goldwater: Continuity and Change in Southern Voting Patterns, 1920–1964* (University, Ala., 1966). In two fine monographs published by the University of Alabama Bureau of Public Administration, Donald S. Strong explored the population and electoral changes that represented the beginnings of the Republican phenomenon in the South: *The 1952 Presidential Election in the South* (University, Ala., 1955), and *Urban Republicanism in the South* (University, Ala., 1960). Somewhat earlier Coleman B. Ransone, Jr., had published, through the same medium, a general overview of southern chief executives, *The Office of Governor in the South* (University, Ala., 1951).

Another carefully researched volume on a special aspect of state politics is Malcolm E. Jewell's *Legislative Representation in the Contemporary South* (Durham, N.C., 1967). Somewhat earlier, Jewell had edited a volume, *The Politics of Reapportionment* (New York, 1962), which prefigured some of the major changes in the representative structure that were to result from court decisions on legislative apportionment. On the southern shift from being the main regional support for active American intervention in foreign affairs to a posture of opposition to the foreign policies being pursued on a supposedly bipartisan basis in Washington, two major works were published within a short span of time. The first of these, which is based primarily on the analysis of congressional voting patterns, is Charles O. Lerche, *The Uncertain South: Its Changing Patterns of Politics in Foreign Policy* (Chicago, 1964); and the second, which exhaustively examines the changes in public attitudes toward foreign policy among southerners, is Alfred O. Hero, *The Southerner and World Affairs* (Baton Rouge, 1965).

Three publications of recent vintage, representing various degrees of partisan bias, assess the extent to which the Republicans might become a majority party in the South. The first of these was an effort on the part of three young members of the Ripon Society to examine voting patterns in the South and to present a program for building a moderately liberal Republican coalition on the basis of both black and white voter participation: John C. Topping, Jr., John R. Lazarek, and William H. Linder, *Southern Republicanism and the New South* (Cambridge, Mass., 1966). The second was produced by a young Nixon campaign aide, and represents a clear, if overly sanguine, statement of the way southern strategy might be applied to effect a national Republican majority: Kevin P. Phillips, *The Emerging Republican Majority* (New Rochelle, N.Y., 1969). The third volume, countering the southern strategy's implicit anti-Negro elements, is based on an optimistic examination of the extent to which whites and blacks coalesced in support of certain Democratic candidates in the 1970 elections: Reg Murphy and Hal Gulliver, *The Southern Strategy* (New York, 1971).

So much of the writing on southern politics during the past two decades has concentrated on the various ways in which the revival of the racial issue has influenced political change in the South that it is impossible to refer to more than a fraction of this literature. Included among many books on the southern reaction to civil rights are the following: Thomas Jackson Woofter, *Southern Race Progress, The Wavering Line* (Washington, 1957); John Bartlow Martin, *The Deep South Says "Never"* (New York, 1957); Dan Wakefield, *Revolt in the South* (New York, 1960); Lewis Wade Jones, *Cold Rebellion: The South's Oligarchy in Revolt* (London, 1962); James Graham Cook, *The Segregationists* (New York, 1962); and

James Wilfred Vander Zanden, *Race Relations in Transition: The Segregation Crisis in the South* (New York, 1965).

Two books by I. A. Newby provide interesting insights into the relations between the ideas which support racial inequality and actual discrimination on grounds of race. The first, *Jim Crow's Defense: Anti-Negro Thought in America, 1900–1930* (Baton Rouge, 1965), appraises the grounds for the partly overt, and otherwise tacit, acceptance of racial inequality throughout the country in the earlier years of this century. The second, *Challenge to the Court: Social Scientists and the Defense of Segregation, 1954–1966* (Baton Rouge, 1967), illuminates the mode of segregationist persuasion, particularly before the courts, during the period in which civil rights for Negroes were promoted most effectively through litigation. C. Vann Woodward's *The Strange Career of Jim Crow* (New York, 1957) is, of course, a classic on the development of legal segregation. In my opinion, the best brief survey of the various phases of the Negro drive for equality is Lewis M. Killian, *The Impossible Revolution: Black Power and the American Dream* (New York, 1968).

On the broad question of the extent and meaning of the changes that have recently occurred in Negro political participation in the South, one book stands out for its analytical detail and comprehensiveness. This is Donald R. Matthews and James W. Prothro, *Negroes and the New Southern Politics* (New York, 1966). Several books address the problem of securing the vote and then using it, on the part of Negroes. An earlier example, and something of a plea for action, is Henry Lee Moon, *Balance of Power: The Negro Vote* (Garden City, N.Y., 1948). Margaret W. Price, *The Negro and the Ballot in the South* (Atlanta, 1959) is a much-used source coming out of the Southern Regional Council, which has, both in its own right and as the progenitor of the Voter Education Project, done as much to promote the use of the ballot among southern Negroes as any organization extant. A compelling account of the effort by southern Negroes to participate in the politics of their region is Pat Watters and Reese Cleghorn, *Climbing Jacob's Ladder: The Arrival of Negroes in Southern Politics* (New York, 1967). William

Keech, *The Impact of Negro Voting: The Role of the Vote in the Quest for Equality* (Chicago, 1968) briefly examines the actual and potential use of the ballot by Negroes to achieve their collective purposes.

Some of the general studies of Negroes in American politics at large are: James Q. Wilson, *Negro Politics: The Search for Leadership* (Glencoe, Ill., 1960); Harry A. Bailey, Jr. (ed.), *Negro Politics in America* (Columbus, Ohio, 1967); Daniel C. Thompson, *The Negro Leadership Class* (Englewood Cliffs, N.J., 1963); and Hanes Walton, Jr., *The Negro in Third Party Politics* (Philadelphia, 1969). For a sample of some of the more intensely committed statements on black politics, the following are suggested: Stokely Carmichael and Charles V. Hamilton, *Black Power: The Politics of Liberation in America* (New York, 1967); Kenneth B. Clark, Julian Bond, and Richard H. Hatcher, *The Black Man in American Politics: Three Views* (New York, 1969); and Chuck Stone, *Black Political Power in America* (Indianapolis, 1968). Studies that are more confined to the southern experience are also readily available. Although limited largely to the experience in Florida, Hugh Douglas Price's *The Negro and Southern Politics* (New York, 1957) was one of the earlier examples, and it remains one of the better statements about the strength and weaknesses of the Negro position in the politics of the South. Everett C. Ladd, Jr., *Negro Political Leadership in the South* (Ithaca, N.Y., 1966) is also geographically confined in its sources of data, but contains a basis nonetheless for some broader conclusions. Harry Holloway, *The Politics of the Southern Negro: From Exclusion to Big City Organization* (New York, 1969) assays a more sweeping analysis on the basis of the social changes underlying the increased participation of Negroes in the public life of the South. As a means of keeping up with current developments in Negro political participation and related matters, the monthly digest published by the Southern Regional Council, *South Today,* as well as the Voter Education Project *News* bulletin and other occasional publications of the council on such matters as Negro voter registration and black officeholders, are highly recommended.

Index of Persons

741

Subject Index